PURSUIT

Other books by John Calder

THE PHILOSOPHY OF SAMUEL BECKETT
THE GARDEN OF EROS
A SAMUEL BECKETT READER (Edited)
A WILLIAM BURROUGHS READER (Edited)
A HENRY MILLER READER (Edited)
A NOUVEAU ROMAN READER (Edited with John Fletcher)
WHAT'S WRONG, WHAT'S RIGHT (Poems)

PURSUIT

The Uncensored Memoirs
of
John Calder

CALDER PUBLICATIONS
LONDON

First published in 2001 by Calder Publications UK Ltd.
51 The Cut, London SE1 8LF

ISBN Hardcover 0 7145 4313 6
ISBN Paperback 0 7145 4323 3

British Library Cataloguing in Publication Data is available

Typeset and Printed by Newton Printing Ltd, London, United Kingdom   www.newtonprinting.com

Follow a shadow, it still pursues you.
Seem to fly, it will pursue.
Ben Jonson

Slow in pursuit, but matched in mouth like bells.
Shakespeare. *The Tempest*

Faint, yet pursuing...
Judges (8:4)

...aspires
Beyond thus high, insatiated to pursue
Vain war with heaven
Milton, *Paradise Lost* (Book II)

DEDICATION

This autobiography is dedicated to three people described in it, three people who in different ways I know I have let down and to whom I feel a deep guilt that no apology can mitigate. They are first of all my great-uncle Jim (Sir James Calder), who did so much for me and was so generous, both to my father and myself. I lost what he left me, but I remain grateful. Secondly I still feel responsible for the unhappy death of Lisel Field, which I could have prevented. Thirdly I apologise to Reginald Attewell whose loyalty and long service deserved better recognition than was possible at a time when I was myself in deep trouble.

CONTENTS

PREFACE

My pursuits have always varied here and there:
to do well, and please and show success at times.
At others: what to do and to go where
impulse and need demanded. Now what primes
these memories of the many lives I've led
is to record what happened, who was what,
put right the lies that other books have fed
the reading public, and above all to not
add to those lies. My motivation's been
to add a little to the world, to stop the rot,
the greed and corruption that makes Man mean,
where good is bad and all ideals insane
to those who cannot think ahead and choose
destruction's path. I see ahead much pain:
both good and bad have everything to lose.
But to the end for a better world I'll sue.
The chances are not good, but there's no choice;
once young, now old, I only can pursue
what I believe in with my weakening voice.

Chapter 1

Beginnings

I inherited genes that, once in my body, rebelled against those of my forebears and somehow became twisted out of all recognition of their sources. Both sides of my family, going two generations back, contained patriarchs and staunch conservatives, unthinking in their political views, (which were those that stood to their greatest advantage), and in their religious ones, (which consisted of a Roman Catholicism of total orthodoxy). My two grandfathers were members of an establishment that they wanted to penetrate ever deeper; both had absolute faith in the power of money and property and believed in a God who was a patriarch, like them, and who would reward them in the next world as well or better than in this. They were not unkind to those who served them, provided of course that they knew their place and were properly respectful of their betters. From an early age my instincts were very different, but this did not become obvious until my maturity, to which they undoubtedly gave another, less flattering, name.

My great-grandfather, James Calder, came from Buchan in the North East of Scotland, a member of a crofting family, of which I have never had the time to find out more. As a young man he had moved to Alloa in central Scotland, married a Mackenzie, the daughter of a local brewer. The name, Mackenzie, which is also my middle name, always had a mystical quality in family conversation, a name to be proud of. In due course he took over the brewery and changed its name to Calder's. He also acquired about twenty-thousand acres of land covering the two sides and the middle of the Ochil Hills between Perth and Kinross, bridging a wild and beautiful area of Perthshire and Kinross-shire, to which I constantly return in my dreams. He built, or more likely extended, a large house near Forgandenny called Ardargie, which had formal gardens as well as a home farm and a large walled vegetable garden. It included a stretch of river, a tributary of the May, which boasted a waterfall and a bridge called the Hummel Bummel, so rickety that one crossed it at one's peril. To prove my hardiness as a child I often bathed in the icy pool below the waterfall. In addition, Ardargie had many farms, and a large grouse moor over the higher ground and mountains, from the top of which one could see the Pentlands, south of Edinburgh, and far into the Highlands to the north. It also had a splendid view of Loch Leven with its castle on an island where Mary Queen of Scots had spent miserable years in captivity. Behind the loch rise the majestic Lomond Hills, a notable landmark to the east. Westward the mountains stretched beyond the northern reaches of Stirling, and were known as the Highland Line.

James Calder's son, my grandfather, was John Joseph Calder. In each generation down to my own there have been at least two Calder boys, the first named after his grandfather and the second after his father. My father was therefore James, being the eldest and his younger brother was John, although called Ian, its Gaelic form, and the reverse applied to myself and my younger brother. J.J. as he was often called was a patriarch like his father and he produced two sons and six daughters, which strangely enough constituted exactly the same make-up as the family on my mother's side, except that in the latter's case the two boys died as teenagers, while the six girls survived.

John Joseph inherited his father's house Ardargie and the northern part of the estate, while his younger brother James took the southern part and a second house, Ledlanet, which had been converted into a shooting lodge and extended by his father. Ledlanet will play a large part in this narrative. It was a pleasant stone-built house in the Scottish baronial style, with the usual public rooms, three of them, aside from the dining room and a small outer and large inner hall, and with nine bedrooms and three servants' rooms behind a green baize door. It contrasted in every way with Ardargie which was a large rambling house, set low down between the higher ground north and south, near a river and overlooking a small trout loch. The Ledlanet Loch was much larger, but a good ten minute walk away. Ledlanet was set high on a hill with a splendid view from the first floor over the Kinross valley and Loch Leven. Tall trees blocked the view on the ground floor. The best farmland was my grandfather's, the best grouse moor and wild mountain scenery my great-uncle's. The two brothers divided the family business interests between them: my grandfather took over the Alloa brewery, his younger brother a whisky distillery at Stronachie that happened to be on his own land and beside the winding road leading through the hills. In addition he took up a timber business, mainly dealing in home-grown softwoods and hardwood. This latter had grown of necessity because there was much forest on the Calder estates, not just in the Scottish central belt, but further up north, where more land had been bought in Ross-shire. It was my great-uncle who developed the timber business into an international concern, importing from Canada, the Baltic states and Russia, and eventually buying up timber yards at many British ports. He became Timber Controller in both the first and second world wars and received as recompense a knighthood in 1921, further to an earlier CBE. He allowed his distillery to be merged into The Distillers Company, the creation of Harry Ross, a magnate who persuaded many Scottish distilling families to pool their interests into a giant corporation powerful enough to establish Scotch whisky as an international drink.

Sir James became Chairman of the management committee of Distillers Company, at the time his most important business interest, and between the wars travelled on behalf of whisky promotion. The far-Eastern travels were commemorated in Chinese and Japanese artefacts that adorned Ledlanet. Among the many photographs later discovered in the house were those of Joseph Kennedy, a business associate, and his sons, including John

Kennedy, later to become U.S. President. The whole Kennedy family were frequent visitors. Joe Kennedy was American Ambassador to Britain in the thirties and his boys learned to shoot grouse on the moors at Ledlanet. The connection of course was whisky, which Joe Kennedy imported into the U.S. during Prohibition.

My other grandfather was Canadian, a self-made man called Marcellin Wilson. Although he was a French Canadian, the Wilson name came from an ancestor, a soldier in Wellington's Peninsular army, who, when wounded, had been left behind in Portugal and eventually emigrated from there to Canada. My grandfather grew up on Ile Bézard on the St. Lawrence river near Montreal. He was a farm boy, who by dint of will power acquired land and made successful speculations out of which he was able to found a bank, the Banque Canadienne Nationale. As a small boy I would be given $20 notes with his portrait on them. Foolishly I never kept one. He became a successful Canadian industrialist with a finger in many pies and undoubtedly made a fortune out of prohibition in the United States during its thirteen years duration, from 1920 to 1933. He was heavily involved in Canadian distilling and also imported whisky and gin from Scotland. It was this connection that brought my parents together in the twenties. My grandfather was also a politician who became a senator and treasurer of the Liberal Party, which in those days was the ruling party of Canada. He was a close associate of Mackenzie King, Canadian prime minister for virtually the entire period from 1921 to 1948.

A little should be said of my two grandmothers. The Scottish one was really English, born in Liverpool and from a Lancashire merchant family called Broadbent. Strict and stern, it was often said of her that she would have preferred to have been a nun. As a boy I spent many holidays, especially the long summer ones, at Ardargie, and although I was naturally quiet and obedient, a bookworm in fact, I was always aware of her disapproval of something. I realise now that my mother and her very different background were held against me. Consequently, I always went in trepidation of her. My grandfather had a library of leather-bound nineteenth century classics and I read my way through much of it. Occasionally she would retrieve a book from me, dismissing it as unsuitable and return it to the shelf, where I could always easily find it again once alone.

The other grandmother was a housewife from an old French-Canadian family, the Geffrions, who had certainly brought a dowry with her. She overprotected her grandchildren when they came into her orbit as she had overprotected her children. Occasionally, when I was a child, living with my mother in Montreal, in a house just a few doors away; she would see me passing and a message would be sent out to the effect that I was not wearing a hat or overshoes (in winter) or suitable clothing. In her house my hands were constantly inspected, which inevitably led to a trip to the bathroom to wash them, followed by a painful cleaning of fingernails. I doubt very much if she ever had a non-domestic thought; her phobias were dirt and untidiness. At the end of her life she went into a coma for several years, artificially fed, only occasionally emerging to murmur the name of one of her daughters.

My father was a victim of his own early celebrity. Brought up at Ardargie, he went to a Catholic public school.[1] at Fort Augustus near Inverness, where he was educated by Benedictine monks. I never heard him comment much on it and I have no idea whether he was happy there. In those days it was not an issue: children did what their parents intended for them, especially if they came from a class which was aware of its superior position and was upwardly mobile. He joined the army in 1914, and was, so I was brought up to believe, under age when he did so. As his birth certificate tells me that he was born in 1895 I do not see how this is possible, sixteen being the military age then. He started in the Scottish Horse as a Second Lieutenant. I was told that he was a Captain at sixteen, but this too does not accord with the dates. However, his military career was much honoured in the family:he was promoted to Captain, mentioned in despatches and awarded the Military Cross. He went through the trenches, was badly gassed, took Hill 60, which was his major moment of glory, and ended up in the Lovat Scouts and as an observer on a reconnaissance 'plane. My reference books tell me that Hill 60, a military observation point in Belgium, was taken on April 17, 1915 by two regiments, one of them Scottish, but lost again in May. Family pride, and no doubt commercial considerations, led to my grandfather acquiring 'the Hill' after the war and building a hostelry there. My father related this to me with disgust when I was about seven.

After the war my father showed little inclination to go to university – New College, Oxford, had at one point been on the cards – nor did he want to work for his tyrannical father in the brewery, although I believe he did so for a short time. He eventually started a pig farm, but that enterprise ended in disaster: his entire stock was wiped out by swine fever before any of the piglets were old enough to go to market. There may have been other unsuccessful business ventures. No one ever went to the trouble to tell me about my father's early days, and those who could have are all now gone. He had a romance with an Irish girl, which somehow did not please his family, presumably because she was not of their class, and they disentangled him from that love affair. He then went to Canada with introductions from his uncle to his whisky contacts in Montreal. One of these was to Senator Marcellin Wilson, and that is how he met my mother, the youngest of the six Wilson girls. Her eldest sister, Juliette, was already married to another Scot, Colonel Rupert Dawson, son of the whisky distiller Peter Dawson, whose

---

[1] Public School in the British sense (i.e. privileged private education in a strictly disciplined environment).

estate was not far from the Calder's, at Braco in Perthshire. But I do not believe there was any direct contact there before my father went to Canada.

My mother was not only the youngest of the family, but the most spoiled. She had once been taken to a day school at a Montreal Convent, and cried until brought home and in the end was educated privately – and poorly – in her parents' house. She later learned English, but must have had some lessons as a child. The Canadian-French spoken in the family must have been supplemented by Parisian as her father was a cosmopolitan by nature who often visited France, and whose philanthropic pursuits included setting up a residence for Canadian students in Paris in the Cité Universitaire district. He would have insisted that the family could speak proper French as well as the local patois. He was to become a Commandeur of the Légion d'honneur as a result of his philanthropy in France.

My mother's character was a strange one, and I shall return to it later. The spoiled baby of the family, a *nouveau riche* and indulgent one, whose cultural aspirations tended to be showy and superficial, she was accustomed all her life to having anything she wanted, rather like Galsworthy's Fleur Forsyth. Her elder sisters all married, three of them to Canadians of similar backgrounds, one to Rupert Dawson and one, the fourth, to an Englishman, Henry Winkworth. My father, who was a good-looking man with his military bearing, fashionable moustache and good manners, having no doubt a little French from wartime service in France, must have appealed to her strongly.

They were married in Montreal and my Scottish grandparents went over for the wedding. My grandmother told me many years later of her memories of that day, especially of their disgust at the 'waste' at the wedding lunch. This was large and long with many courses, each accompanied by a different wine. Most of the guests drank a little from each glass and left it when the next arrived, so that at the end of the feast the table was covered with half-full wine glasses. The sumptuousness of my Canadian grandfather's ostentatious hospitality was very upsetting to the frugal sensibilities of his Scottish guests.

At some time in the twenties my father went with his new wife to start a business at Hudson's Bay, The Calder Trading Company, which apparently did quite well, the only really successful business venture of his entire life. I doubt if my mother ever spent much time there, but in any case she could not stand the climate of a lonely and bleak outpost of northern Canada, and she made him sell it. She had earlier visited Ardargie with my father, her only visit to Scotland until the second world war broke out, and she hated every minute. The discomforts of a Scottish country house without central heating, the indifference of its inhabitants to the temperature and the climate, and the iron discipline and simple food, did not appeal to her. Worse was my grandmother's disdain of a little colonial girl who could not speak English properly and expected to be pampered and the centre of attention all the time. From then on it was either London, where she felt at home among the flappers, or frequent visits by steamer, first-class to Canada, always accompanied by a lady's maid and a large number of wardrobe trunks. Her father had made arrangements for her to have a considerable income and a house in Montreal only a few doors away from his own.

I was born in that city on 25th January 1927. My mother had preferred to return to the bosom of her family, and especially her mother and Canadian doctors, to have me. The same happened with the birth of her two other children, my sister Betty (Elizabeth Thérèse) three and a half years later, and my brother James Wilson, five years after me. We were all born in Montreal and in the care of a Dr. Goldbloom, a paediatrician at the hospital on the mountain that overlooks the city. I was born at home in a house on Pine Avenue just under the heavily forested Mount Royal itself. It must have been some time after that that my Wilson grandfather, who had a palatial house with a large garden on Ontario Avenue (now called the Rue du Musée) bought my mother's house, referred to above, as a gift, which was only a few doors higher up the hill than his own, and planted directly opposite the house of one of his elder daughters, and the Brodeur family. I was to spend much time there as I grew up, and later during the war. I still remember the address: 3525 Ontario Avenue. Today it is the Polish Embassy.

My birthday is also Robert Burns' birthday, and this was greeted as a happy omen in Scotland. Robert Burns, the national poet, has his birthday celebrated, usually in a highly ritualised manner, on or around that day, not just in Scotland, but among the Scottish diaspora all over the world. I later discovered that it was also the birthday of W. Somerset Maugham, whose novels I was so much to admire when a teenager, and of Virginia Woolf, who became a favourite author in adulthood. My Scottish grandfather, delighted to know that his family name and bloodstock would continue, immediately made arrangements to entail his house and estate on me after his death, and he put my name down for Britain's best-known public school for Catholics, Ampleforth in Yorkshire, which is run by Benedictine monks, as was my father's school at Fort Augustus. Such is the pressure to enter Britain's top schools, it is customary to put boys' names down at birth for the year at which they are expected to start. In my case it was at age eight at Gilling Castle, the preparatory school for Ampleforth.

There is little I remember about those first eight years. I was often in Scotland, at least once a year in Montreal, and spent some summers at American and Canadian resorts (I remember Spring Lake in New Jersey and the New Brunswick coast) and on at least two occasions I stayed at Palm Beach in Florida where my Canadian grandfather wintered, always dapper in white trousers, lightweight dark jacket, white shoes, panama hat, and cane. On one occasion when my father was at Palm Beach he took me to a film with Gary Cooper about the Bengal Lancers. I didn't get to see the end, dog was kept in the kennels, and almost immediately afterwards I was sent to boarding school, and thereafter spent little time at Skendelby since my summers were normally at Ardargie, I saw little of the dog and I have no idea of what happened to it after we moved out in 1939.

At Skendelby Hall there was a permanent staff of a butler, a French chef called Figue, a governess for my sister and younger brother, the latter being kept in isolation so that I hardly ever saw him, other kitchen staff and probably two housemaids. My mother had her lady's maid, who travelled to London with her. She was in any case very rarely in the country, to which she was unaccustomed and which bored her. Meal times were variable. I usually ate on my own, sometimes had tea with my father on weekends, but there were no family meals that I remember at Skendelby Hall. My younger sister and brother were fed separately and at different times. Ardargie was different. There I ate at least breakfast, lunch and tea with my grandparents, Gaffer and Gran, perhaps at times dinner as well. I was expected to speak when spoken to and to absorb the stream of anecdotes and commonplace wisdom and instruction issuing from my grandfather and receive without comment the barely-concealed criticism of my father's failure to be like them and their aversion towards my mother, whom they no doubt considered flighty and ill-mannered. My father's shortcomings (as a bad businessman and an undisciplined son) were often compared to his more promising younger brother, Ian, who died at about the time I went to school, of leukaemia. I do not remember him at all and only have a vague recollection of his photo. I occasionally met some of my cousins who lived locally in the Tay valley and around Perthshire, in particular Bunty Manners, a girl of roughly my own age. The Calders were doubly related to the Manners. Maisie, my eldest aunt, had married a Colonel Manners, while my great-uncle, Sir James, was married to another, Mildred Manners, who died just before the war of diabetes. The latter was the only member of the family who had liked music and could play the piano; she was a friend of Dame Clara Butt, the well-known Lieder and concert singer. Music among the Calders was something you heard in church on Sundays. My grandfather and his brother each said that the other could not tell the difference between *God Save the King* and *Rule Britannia*. Various aunts occasionally turned up at Ardargie, sometimes with their own children, and were civil to me, sometimes taking me out to tea. My father did not get on with his own father and stayed away, although he sometimes went to his uncle at Ledlanet to shoot grouse.

On my Canadian visits I met my cousins and their families on their side of the water, but was never particularly intimate with any of them as there was usually too big an age difference, two to ten years older or more. They were all French-speaking, but they would speak English to me, although I had some French; but I had been brought up on the English side of the great Montreal divide, not unlike the sectarianism of Protestant and

Catholic Ireland. My Canadian grandfather was important enough to be above all that, but the Catholic French-Canadians were nearly always treated as inferior citizens by the English (largely Scottish) minority, overwhelmingly Protestant, who lived in the more affluent districts and usually spoke no French. The Ostiguys, Brodeurs and Raymonds all lived near the Wilson patriarchy in large houses which had been bought for them by Senator Wilson. Three of the daughters had married British husbands, all Catholics; the English one, Henry Winkworth, lived in London. Of the six daughters, five had families, varying from one to seven children. This was to become a bone of some contention when it was realised that the will and estate of my Canadian grandfather was partially divided by family and partly by individual grandchild, the mother in each case having the income for life, with the capital to be divided among the grandchildren when the mothers died. There were nineteen grandchildren after eliminating those who died before adulthood, and coming from a family of three I was placed to receive the average, a third of a sixth one way and a nineteenth the other.

The things that were to play a large part in my adult life, literature, music, the theatre, and intellectual interests in general, were sadly missing in my home-life as a child. It was to get books that I had the biggest problem, especially challenging ones, and I had a mind that welcomed challenge or I would not have persevered with the Smollets, Thackerays, Macauleys and even heavier, mainly Scottish, writers in the Ardargie library as I did. Music consisted, other than hymns and whatever I heard on the odd visit to the music hall or panto, of my father's collection of Harry Lauder records, but that was only after 1940 and in Canada. As for theatre, that started in boarding school with Latin and Greek plays in the classroom.

The sequence of events during and after the first eight years of my life is unclear, a jumble of unconnected memories. My world changed when, frightened and trying not to show it, I took a taxi with my mother from York to Gilling Castle to start school (on the date for which my grandfather had put my name down within my first months of life). Gilling was the prep school for Ampleforth.

Chapter 2

Education

I only remember seeing the headmaster of my prep school on two occasions, once on my arrival when he welcomed me, and reassured my mother before she left me trembling in his hands, and on a later occasion when my grandfather paid a visit to see how I was getting on, which must have been after a term or two. On that occasion Gaffer was told that my nickname was 'the gangster', obviously because of my North American connection. All that was newsworthy out of America at that time were the activities of Al Capone and the gangsters who had taken advantage of prohibition to become powerful and dangerous. Both sides of my family had derived enormous advantages from the Volstead Act – stipulating the banning of alcohol, and so devastating the social fabric of American society: they had a seller's market, were perfectly inside the law themselves and the riches they derived from prohibition helped them to become even bigger pillars of society and upholders of the status quo and the moral order it implied. I of course knew nothing of this, and I do not remember the nickname except for that one occasion.

Nearly all the masters were monks. I only remember one lay teacher, a member of Mosley's British Union of Fascists, who taught arithmetic and was constantly saying in class that Britain's natural enemy was France and natural friend Germany. I believe he was interned at the outbreak of war.

Gilling was an old Norman Castle, built of thick heavy stone and very cold in winter. We ate at long refectory tables. There was hot tea at every meal, but because of my initial shyness I never asked for milk to put in it, and it was always at the far end of the table. I did not like black tea much, but went on as I had started, drinking black tea most of the time, and I think, unsweetened. I became a wolf cub -- a junior boy scout -- and we all wore a uniform in which we engaged in various hunts and chases in the woods, which pursuits I enjoyed as it fed my imagination. There was cricket in summer and rugger in winter and some track sports. On one occasion I put my hand through the window of the cricket pavilion – I can't remember how or why, but there was some mischief involved – and gave myself a nasty cut above the left thumb which needed five stitches. I was always aware of both indoor and outdoor cold, but became used to it.

At least once a term there was a retreat, when we became trappists for the day. We ate in silence while bible stories were read out to us by one of the monks. There were three church services that day and no classes, although we sat in the classroom reading prescribed religious texts, lives of the saints and that sort of thing. In class I was always best at English and History, enjoyed writing essays and was frequently complimented on them by Father Henry, the English master. I am not sure who taught me History, or even what History we studied: it was either Father Henry or Father Anthony and I presume we were learning the History of England, but religion played its part and I remember that martyrs were quite prominent. Latin took priority over every other subject and I think we had a daily class. I was soon reading Virgil, whom I enjoyed more than other Latin poets, and still remember many phrases, but I was certainly not one of the brighter boys at Latin. The endless hours of mastering declensions and learning the grammar were tedious compared to reading texts, construing and translating. I had a good memory that enabled me to learn whole passages of both a Latin text and its translation, those most likely to be used in examinations and tests, which I found easier than the labour of construing in the normal way. I was not good at arithmetic, geometry or algebra, but managed to pass. I remember a few rudimentary classes in the lab, but it was clear that science was not my *forte* and making stink bombs was the summit of my achievement in chemistry. We were encouraged to cultivate a small patch of garden, but all I remember growing was watercress, which incidentally I liked to eat. Classes went on all day and there was prep in the evening after supper, an hour in a silent classroom under a master's supervision.

The humorist among the masters was Father Anthony who, when putting out the lights in the dormitory, would regale us with funny stories and send us into gales of laughter with a simulated slip on a banana skin, which however became less funny with too frequent repetition. We all had the same pocket money, sent by our parents, but doled out by the school, eightpence a week, half on Wednesday and half on Saturday, which could be spent in the tuck shop, open for an hour on those days. This was enough to buy two chocolate or toffee bars and some boiled sweets on each occasion. I would ensconce myself in the window seat of a long room, which served both for recreation and a place to keep clothes and personal things, on half holidays and Saturday afternoons with my legs up, and get through a Magowan toffee bar, a Milky Way (one penny) and then suck sweets, all the time reading a book from the library. For the first time in my life I had enough to read. My mother on one occasion sent me a book, one I had read two years earlier, and it was far too juvenile for me. There is a letter I wrote in reply,[2] in better handwriting than I have now, that opens the first of the files of my publishing archives, now in the possession of the Lillie Library at the University of Indiana in Bloomington. The letter, at age nine, thanked my mother for the book and points out that ten shillings would be much more useful next time. As we were not allowed to have money other than the weekly pocket money, I am not quite sure how this could have been accomplished, but I do remember being tipped five shillings by my grandfather on his visit.

---

[2] The letter must have been found and put among my personal papers by Berry Bloomfield, my secretary (about whom more later) and somehow it become part of the files bought by the Lillie Library in 1975.

Summer was the best time at Gilling. When the weather was warm we could ramble through the woodland and rolling hills surrounding the Castle, a few miles from Ampleforth, the main school, and not far from Fountain's Abbey, which we would sometimes visit by bus to picnic. There were more frequent half-holidays in summer and a few religious feast days, such as Corpus Christi in July, when parents and relatives were invited to attend and a lavish tea was served to everyone present. On one such occasion I was visited, I think by my father, but it may have been another relative such as an aunt. I made myself quite sick by eating too many cakes, which may have triggered the appendicitis to which I shall come in a minute.

There was early mass every day, High Mass on Sundays. We slept about twenty to a dormitory, and I had the bed nearest to the door. Outside it was a long room where we all had lockers and drawers in a kind of recreation area. It was here that I would sit and read when I could. The bed was icy in winter when I got into it, and I waited to get warmer under the blankets before sleep. On being woken by bells we went downstairs to wash, then to the chapel for the daily Low Mass, then breakfast, and then the academic day began. One was expected to go to communion at least twice a week and one confessed one's sins to a priest, who would be one of the masters, on Saturdays. As one had to be in a state of grace before taking communion, nothing was to be swallowed between bedtime the night before (for adults it is midnight) and swallowing the communion wafer. On one occasion, unthinking and thirsty, I drank a little water while washing and then had communion. Realising too late what I had done, I was in misery for days. I had committed a mortal sin and must expect eternal damnation. When I finally confessed it the priest laughed and absolved me. It was not deliberate.

I learned to serve mass, carrying the vessels used in the mass around the altar, giving the correct responses in Latin, most of which were 'et cum spiritu tuo' to the priest's various injunctions and blessings. In 1962, at my grandfather's funeral in his own chapel at Ardargie I was able to remember it well enough to go through the motions with my great-uncle, then ninety-four, as the other 'altar boy', although I had long left the church.

As a bookish boy who took religion naturally and was hardly aware that any other religions existed, I thought at one point that I might have a vocation to be a priest. The monks, of course, were always on the lookout for someone who might grow up to join them. They were not all priests, about half of them were brothers, some of whom might be preparing for ordination. By the time I left Gilling Castle I had given up that vocational impulse.

The extreme prudery of the school must seem incomprehensible to a modern reader. None of us had ever heard the word 'sex' and everything to do with procreation was not only never thought about but never mentioned either. Twice a week we had baths, carefully supervised by the school matron or a master, and no boy ever saw another in the bath. We saw each other in the shower after games, but that too was always under the eye of a master. Showers were rapid affairs and you were soon dry and clothed again. Another anomaly will seem strange to the reader. I could not tell the time until I was thirteen, possibly fourteen, because no one had ever taught me. At Skendelby Hall I was called in to meals, or if out of earshot my stomach would tell me it was time for lunch or tea. At school, bells rang to bring you into class or tell you it was finished, and for every other activity you followed what the other boys did. I did not learn to read a clock until at school in Canada at the end of 1940 or possibly even later. Boys did not own watches in those days either.

There was one shameful incident that I still blush to remember. Charles Osborne used to say, years later, that I was the greatest procrastinator he had ever met. The following anecdote demonstrates that I started young.

One day at Gilling I had terrible diarrhoea and was unable to get to the lavatory in time. I somehow removed my underpants, heavy with liquid faeces, and put them in the drawer of my locker outside the dormitory where I slept. I intended, at a quiet moment, to take them downstairs to wash them, but somehow never did. They sat in the drawer for weeks and were eventually discovered. My shame, which the whole school knew about, remains with me to this day.

My early holidays were back at Skendelby Hall. As a public-school boy now, even though only on the prep school level, I was allowed to spend more time in my father's company and would sit with him when he listened to the six o'clock news, and tell him about the school. He was working at Boston-on-the-Wash at the pole and sleeper yard, where these heavy soft-wood timbers were cut and shaped and then creosoted. I am fairly certain however that he spent more time imbibing pink gins at the local hotel bar than doing whatever he was meant to be doing in the timber yard. Years later I was to work there myself and met some who remembered him, but only in the hotel bar. Summer holidays were spent mainly at Ardargie where my grandfather carefully questioned me about every aspect of the school. As a Scottish Catholic from a family that had never converted during the Reformation, he knew he belonged to a beleaguered minority and he was proud of it. He would on occasion write to *The Scotsman*, putting the case for the 'old religion', which Scotland should never have abandoned, and also attacking the 'grave error' of James VI (James I of England) in recognising the Tudors' Church of England in order to gain the English crown, as well as denigrating the Act of Union a century later in 1707, which created a united Protestantism, whereas otherwise a Stuart King could at least have remained a Catholic in Scotland. The Act of Union he blamed, not only for the decline of Catholicism, which was the true religion of the Stewart and Stuart monarchs, and it being persecuted by Protestantism and not once again becoming the proper faith of the northern part of the island, and eventually perhaps of the whole of it, but also being the main cause of Scotland's subservience to England. He was especially proud of belonging to a club, limited to twenty, which met and dined together once or twice a year, consisting of prominent Catholics, and also of the fact that he was the only commoner in an assembly of peers headed by the Duke of Norfolk.

He had a certain concealed bitterness at not having received a peerage himself. The whisky families, and in particular his nearest neighbours the Dewars who had acquired two peerages, had nearly all bought these during Lloyd George's time as prime minister, when they were sold fairly openly to raise funds for the Liberal Party. He had expected to receive one without payment, purely because he deserved it on merit. Had he paid the going price, and I am sure that he later regretted not having done so, I should eventually have acquired a barony.

There were occasions during the shorter holidays, when there was no one who could take me – my mother being in Canada and my father out of the country, (and it was not practicable to go to Ardargie for some reason) – when I had to stay at school. There was one such Easter holiday, not too bad as I remember, when I had the run of the school and was looked after by the matron and treated as a member of the community by the monks, and another at Christmas, when I had measles and remember being confined to a small bedroom in the school infirmary with plenty to read and, wonder of wonders, a fire going all the time in the grate, so I was comfortable and warm. Another holiday that I remember was part of a summer at Skegness, where we had a bungalow on the beach. I was recovering from whooping cough, quite the most unpleasant of childhood diseases, which I had contracted at Boston-on-the-Wash at the time of a fun-fair there, the first I had ever seen, with looping the loops, dodgem cars and shooting galleries. My mother turned up occasionally, otherwise I was at Skegness with a young lady who was I think a registered nurse, and great fun to be with. I paddled in the sea, built sand-castles and went to my first musical theatrical performance: *The Mikado*.

Then one day at school, in July 1937, shortly after the *Corpus Christi* garden party mentioned above, I developed a terrible stomach ache. It was only after a day or two that the school doctor visited and diagnosed appendicitis; I was taken to the York Infirmary where I began to feel better. The reason was that my appendicitis had burst and I was developing peritonitis. While the school said prayers for my life, the hospital was trying to find one of my parents to get a signature authorising the surgeon to operate. My mother was in Canada and my father could not be found for some days. Eventually he telephoned, said he was on his way, and to operate at once. They did, apparently at the last minute. The surgeon was a Doctor Lister, a descendant of the famous Doctor Joseph Lister, who had discovered antiseptics. For two months I stayed in the Infirmary with a tube, or rather two tubes, sticking out of my wounds, and I was syringed out several times a day. The bells of York Minister, only a few yards away, sounded throughout the night every hour, making sleep difficult. It was very hot that summer and as I began to recuperate I was forbidden ice-cream because my mother, who visited me after returning from Canada, told them that it always made me sick, which had been true on only one greedy occasion. Eventually I was able occasionally to go out for an hour or two, and on one occasion to a Shirley Temple film. I was ten at the time.

My memories of Gilling Castle are patchy. My best friend was called Nicholas Ghika, a Rumanian prince, but I never saw him again. The only boy I was to see in later years was Richard Huggett, who I remember my father, on one holiday occasion, taking to tea with me at Gunther's, a famous tea shop off Park Lane in what later became the Playboy Club, which I only once ever visited as a guest of Larry Adler in the sixties, when he was performing there. Richard, who became an actor and the author of theatrical books, was later to live in Soho, not far from my office there in the sixties and seventies. He was still a devout Catholic. I remember cold winters and hot summers, especially the long evenings on the cricket field, and a performance of Aristophanes' *The Birds,* performed in Greek by the oldest class in front of the cricket pavilion. I was just starting Greek when I left the school in 1940 because of the war.

My father was for a time, in the middle thirties, given the post of a military attaché at the British embassy in Vienna, but I have no idea how this came about. He was there at the time of the *Anschluss.* I remember visits to Austria and learning to ski at Kitzbühel at Christmas, but am not sure of the year, either 1936 or 1937. I loved skiing and eventually was to become quite good at it. On one occasion my father took me, without the rest of the family, to a hostel on a mountain top, where we spent the night. I found an English book there, a murder mystery, started to read it, and next morning was told I could keep it. Returning to Kitzbühel and the hotel where the rest of the family were staying, I continued to read it after bedtime, but my mother confiscated it and I never found out who the murderer was in *The Case of the Cobra Candlestick*. I was proud of my father in later years when I learned that the Nazis had made him *persona non grata* for creating a fuss over the vandalisation of a tea-shop owned by a Jewish woman, which he frequented.

I particularly remember the summer holiday of 1939. I was at Skendelby Hall and my father was listening avidly to the news through the time of the Munich crisis, hoping to be able once again to 'fight the Hun', but the gassing of the first war had weakened his lungs and he knew he would never be accepted for the army again as a combatant. He did eventually join the Home Guard and spent many cold and lonely nights during the first years of the war guarding bridges and looking out for parachuting German invaders, when he was known as Lance-Corporal Captain Calder. I was not sent back to Gilling that Autumn although rural

Yorkshire should have been safe enough: the whole family, my father excepted, moved to Orchil, the Dawson house near Braco in Perthshire, where my Aunt Juliette was our hostess. My mother would never have gone to Ardargie, even if invited. I got to know my Dawson cousins, Peter and Marcel, boys older than myself and engaged in such domestic blood sports as hunting bats with tennis rackets in barns and attics, and rats with golf clubs and dogs. There was a younger brother, Rupert, who was autistic and had been taken several times to Lourdes in the hope of a miracle cure, but he was soon to die. There were also three girl cousins, all much older, with the eldest shortly to be married to a Glasgow stockbroker, Sandy Buchanan, who was considered by the Dawsons to be socially inferior. The two younger girls, Luce and Dorothy, were very pretty, but inseparable and they never married. They both would have received substantial dowries from their rich father, and not surprisingly they were much invited out by young men from the local lairdocracy, but Dorothy would not go out without Luce and vice-versa. My grandfather would later remark that if my Uncle Rupert had put his foot down there would have been two Lords in the family instead of two spinsters.

We were not at Orchil very long, mainly because my mother did not like living in other people's houses, and we moved to Pitlochry, where we stayed over Christmas and New Year 1939 at the very grand Atholl Palace Hotel. When my father joined us, largely I imagine for reasons of economy, we moved to the more modest Fisher's Hotel, next to the station. For a short time I went to the village school and at one point had a tutor. I cannot remember what he taught me, but I do remember bicycling with him all over the surrounding countryside and climbing the local mountains, especially Ben y Vrackie. There was little awareness of the country being at war from what I remember of the atmosphere around us. There was talk of rationing, but I cannot remember anything being in short supply at the time. I was eventually sent back to Gilling, where I had now fallen behind my classmates and stayed there until the end of the summer term of 1940. I remember suggesting to my classmates that Britain might lose the war – it must have been about the time of Dunkirk – and I was sent to Coventry as a result. It had never occurred to anyone else in the school that there was any such possibility and that we might find ourselves under German occupation, a fate about to fall on the French.

One incident during my time at Pitlochry was to be useful later in 1970 (See Chapter 6). On the day that Italy came into the war I was still in Pitlochry and went one day to the village shop to buy my boy's weekly paper and an ice-cream cone, only to find the place smashed up. The owner had an Italian name and local vandals had used that as a pretext to do their worst and ruin his livelihood. It was perhaps my first encounter with violent prejudice.

I spent a few days in London during the blitz. I think my mother was trying to arrange a passage to Canada. Many children were being evacuated, but it was dangerous. I know that we were booked at one point to sail on the *Lusitania*, but at the last moment my mother changed her mind, presumably because she didn't want to leave my father. The boat was torpedoed and sank. We did however sail a little later, somewhere near the end of 1940, on a Cunard boat in a convoy. Margot Buchanan, the eldest of the Dawson girls, whose stockbroker husband was now in the army, came with us, as well as my mother's elder sister Marcelle Winkworth and her son Peter. We at any rate knew many of the people on the boat and from our point of view the crossing was uneventful on a very crowded vessel.

We had not been long in Montreal when my Canadian grandfather, Senator Marcellin Wilson, died. He had been ill for some time, confined to bed, and I am still not sure what the lingering malady was, because it was never discussed in front of children and I had been brought up not to ask questions, or at least not to expect to have them answered if they did not concern my everyday existence. His was a public funeral, with a long procession of mourners following the coffin, led by a large number of his relatives. Three small boys, myself and two cousins of about the same age, came first, followed by other descendants, his daughters and their husbands, and the multitude that followed stretched back for a mile, wending its way to the Cathedral of St. Jacques, with many onlookers watching from the pavement.

I was then sent to a Church of England school near Sherbrooke, some hundred miles away, because it was an English-speaking boarding school, and I was one of several refugees from Britain who would otherwise have been at public school in their own country. We mostly gradually developed Canadian accents, which we lost again as adults. Although I was old enough to go into the third form, I was put for another year in the prep school of Bishop's College School, where I redid classes I had already taken, being years ahead in Latin, although, with boredom, I soon relapsed to the level of the others. From there I went through the school to the end, detesting it heartily. I had been much happier in Yorkshire.

Although I did not realise it at the time, as one of the few Catholic boys, I was in a kind of ghetto, lumped together with a similar group of Jewish boys, some also from Britain, like Leo de Rothschild of the banking family and George Hurst, who was already a young musician. Religion in the Province of Quebec was, as in Ireland, a matter of great importance, socially and culturally. Although I was very like the Protestant boys in class and general outlook, I had to go to a separate church on Sundays, whereas the others, including I think the Jewish boys, went to the chapel at Bishop's College, the nearby university to which the school was attached. The village barber, who came to give haircuts at the school, had the additional responsibility of keeping an eye on the Catholic boys, about seven of us, who went to a church in Lennoxville, a mile or so from the school where the mass was long and deadly, conducted of course in Latin, with much Gregorian chant from the choir and an interminable sermon in French. The priest was fiercely anti-English and anti-war and he went on for at least half an hour. A constant theme was that women should stay at home with their families and not take part in war-work in a war which did not in any way concern French-Canadians. As the years passed I was not the only Catholic boy to evade the barber's watchful eye and skip church to go to the local ice-cream parlour instead.

The school was modelled on Dr. Arnold's Rugby. The pecking order among the boys went from the prefects, who had the right to cane all the others, down through the senior class to the third-formers, who were picked on by everyone; everywhere the stronger bullied the weaker. Third formers were not allowed to use the front entrance to the school, had to stand to attention in line against a wall before the bell rang for meals, and various pretexts were used to make you get out of line, which meant a caning. At the end of my first term as a third former (I had of course moved up from the prep school by then), I was summoned to the Head Master's office – he was a stern immigrant from Scotland called Dr. Grier, who also taught history to the senior boys – and told that I had been caned more than any other boy that term. Nearly all those canings had been the result, not of deliberate misdemeanours, but either of ignorance of some arcane and sadistic rule, or of mischief on the part of boys in my class or senior to me. Dr. Grier, having scolded me, then caned me again, presumably to set an example. If later, and throughout my life, I sided with the rebels and the underdogs against the establishment, the foundations of my attitudes were laid down in that school. In my last and senior year I plucked up the courage, whenever another school came to play Bishop's, to cheer for the other side, and was willing to suffer the consequences afterwards.

Except for one year, I think in the sixth form when I had a mathematics master who was able to make algebra and calculus interesting, I was always at the bottom of the class where numbers where concerned, but that year I was top or very nearly. I always did well in English and History, but had become very bored with Latin, was pretty bad at French grammar, although I had no trouble reading the language and was soon to speak it fluently, only because a certain Herbert Hall was the most boring master I can ever remember, although a nice man. I was good at Spanish and matriculated in it. A Mr Evans taught me English. In my final year for university entrance we were studying the Romantic poets with him, Byron, Shelley, Keats, Wordsworth and Tennyson, but that did not stop me from reading all the others, including the poetry of my birthday-mate, Robert Burns, much of which I knew by heart.

I had had a poem published in the Montreal Gazette, probably at about seven or eight, and I continued to write poetry myself, most now lost, usually in the strict verse forms I knew from my models. I won the school poetry prize in 1945, a prize named after Kenneth Hugessen, a schoolboy poet at Bishop's, who had only recently been killed in the war. He had been two years ahead of me, and I was the first winner of the prize, which had been established in his memory by his parents. I also, during my last two years, edited the school magazine under the guidance of the Spanish master, who rather turned me into his favourite pupil. I was often in his study and noticed that he took a quick nip of whisky between classes. It was obvious from his breath, but few of the boys or the other masters seemed to notice. I think his name was De Castellis, but his nickname was Fifi; he wore a reddish wig, was smartly dressed in an old-fashioned style as if for the boardwalk at Monte Carlo with a dapper white waistcoat, and much fun was made of him behind his back. But he was a good teacher.

One of the older boys who had an influence on me was George Hurst, another refugee from Britain, later to become the conductor of the Birmingham Symphony Orchestra, among others. He had been something of a child prodigy, had worked with the Edwin Fischer Orchestra in London and had even, while still a small boy, conducted it at rehearsals. He obviously came from a musical family, was a good pianist, and had a collection of twelve inch records which he would play on the gramophone in the school library. I would go there to listen to them.

I have mentioned that as a child I never had any contact with real music. I think it was in the short period between my arrival in Canada and going to Bishop's that on a certain Sunday afternoon I was taken to a concert by a friend of my mother's, a Madame Éledi Taschereau, who for some reason we called Aunt Plum-Plum. My mother obviously wanted me out of the way that day, which became my personal Damascus Road revelation. I only remember finding myself in a daze of glorious sound and coming out with instruments and voices ringing in my ears. The work was Elgar's *Dream of Gerontius*, and my love of music was born. From then on, money that did not go on books went on records. From George Hurst I learned much about music and composers and received tips about what I should listen to, and I read all the books in the library – there were not many – that dealt with music. There was a sprinkling of other British boys, but we were at different ages and in different forms and we did not stick together much except when there were special interests in common. Robin Brackenbury, who was in my class, later became mayor of Nottingham. I came to know Leopold de Rothschild much better later in England, because we were both interested in music. Peter Winkworth, my first cousin, eventually followed me at Bishop's, but in a lower class, as did my brother the year after I left the school. George Hurst was my mentor in music, but he was a class or two ahead of me and left when I was in the fourth form. Such was his prowess at sport that he became known as 'the tank', due to his unstoppability in Canadian football, a cross between English rugby and American football; he also held the school's record for the hundred yard dash.

I had of course by now learned to tell the time. I also learned about sex, the subject of much discussion, most of it misinformed, among the boys, who in the main were regular masturbaters. Until about the age of fourteen I had thought that babies came from under women's breasts and that that was where penetration took place. Little by little I became better informed. Holidays were in Montreal in the house on Ontario Avenue. My father, who had come out to Canada in 1943, was already a very ill man (sitting up all night guarding bridges cannot have helped his condition). His lungs, already weakened by gassing in the first world war, became worse, and aggravated by too much drinking developed into the tuberculosis that eventually killed him in 1944. His closest friend in Montreal was a Canadian ex-officer of Scottish origin, Gordon Sherris, who lived in the house next door, and they both whiled away the time at the United Services Club on Sherbrooke Street, a place to which I was occasionally taken, as I had on occasion been taken to the Caledonian Club in St. James' Square in London in the past. I impressed the club members and won a bet for my father by being able to consumer several dozen oysters at a sitting. As a friend of my father I would sometimes ask Gordon Sherris' advice on matters I could not discuss with my mother after 1944, matters that needed male experience.

In school sports I was best at anything that involved endurance, such as the Marathon or very long distance races, and in winter at cross-country skiing. I got by at football, being shorter in height than most boys of my age, a genetic defect from my mother who was tiny, and played cricket indifferently: BCS was one of the very few Canadian schools where cricket was available. I certainly felt no loyalty to the school and played sports in the same spirit as I went to classes. The advantage of running and skiing was that I was on my own, not part of a team. There was no female companionship at Bishop's. A nearby school called Compton came over to us or we went there once or twice a year for a dance, but I have absolutely no memory of such occasions. One or two of the more adventurous boys managed on occasion to date girls from the village and would meet them secretly at night or on weekends, which was of course strictly forbidden. I managed this myself, on two occasions, but nothing went beyond cuddling and kissing. I did once come across one boy, whom I particularly disliked as a big bully, actually copulating with a girl in the woods. I cannot be sure at this distance in time whether he was raping her or whether she was willing, but rape was what my companions and I assumed and we shouted at them until they fled.

The woods behind the school were extensive and we used them in various ways. One year three of us pooled our money to buy axes and other tools to build a log cabin where we could picnic and huddle over a stove in winter. This was eventually abandoned and a different group and I acquired another hut, built of clapboards and known as Drag Inn, where we went to smoke. I had started smoking, partly as a protest against school rules at the age of fifteen. There were certain hiding places where one went for a furtive puff, like the boiler room and a tunnel with several bends that ran underground from the school to the infirmary. I continued smoking until the age of twenty-two when I managed to give it up with considerable difficulty.

I took university entrance exams a few months after my father died, but failed to pass in enough subjects. The history exam in which I should have done best I messed up through too much knowledge and too little discipline. One of my options that year had been the *History of Serbia* and I had read the book so closely that when I started to write, as my second question, on Serbia, I was so carried away by remembered detail and my own arguments that, when the two hour examination ended, I was still on the second question on the examination paper, having filled many pages and forgotten to look at the time. The examiner made allowances and gave me a bare pass, which was not enough to bring up my general level on all subjects and compensate for the worst ones. As a result, I repeated the year in a special class at McGill University in Montreal, designed for people like me, that gave the benefit of first year university together with the opportunity to take again the examinations in which I had failed. It worked and I passed.

The war was now nearing its end and I expected to join the army. The school, BCS, had a cadet corps, and I had done all the basic training to enable me to be a qualified sergeant. Two of my school friends had enlisted quickly and were as quickly killed, but I was now at McGill, so the year passed and the war in Europe ended. I went on a troopship, as a passenger, to see my grandparents in Scotland. We were crammed six into a cabin normally designed for two, but it was better than steerage, sleeping in hammocks. The Gaffer's main concern was that I should enter the Alloa brewery as quickly as possible. He had changed little, was now well into his eighties, still running a chain of hotels as well as the brewery where his principal fellow-director, soon to be managing-director, was Sir John Gilmour, a baronet who was also the Conservative M.P. for East Fife. During my fortnight at Ardargie I came down to breakfast one morning, followed a minute later by my grandfather. 'Was that you who left the light on in the red bathroom?' he asked.

'Yes, Gaffer,' I said. 'I suppose it was. I'll go back and turn it off.'

'I've done that,' he said, and, after a pause, 'If I'd left the light on my father would have told me the first time. The second time he would have disinherited me.'

I returned to Canada, and with the Hiroshima bomb, the war ended. I registered at Sir George Williams College in Montreal where I took both day and night courses, largely in the social sciences, and came out with very high marks, thanks partly to some extra tuition from a lecturer there called

Joseph Zweig. The year at McGill had been interesting because for the first time in my life I was mixing with people from very different backgrounds to mine, Canadians from different Montreal communities, many from immigrant groups and some from the Jewish district of East Montreal whose ideas, ranging from the two-tone jackets that a BCS boy would not be seen dead in, to what constituted a good time, were all very different from my own limited and class-ridden experience. I learned quickly and adapted to this new society, developing a reputation as a humorist because of my way with both written and spoken words. I composed humorous addresses to be read in public, which amused my classmates and discovered a facility for making up jokes on the spot and for puns. 'It's raining cats and dogs,' a classmate said. 'Be careful not to step in a poodle,' I countered. At BCS I had been much bullied in the third form and grew more remote from my peers as I progressed through the school, staying out of the schoolboy limelight, having only two or three close friends. I was never made a prefect, never took advantage of my seniority over the junior boys, and became, in the sixth form, school librarian, sharing this office with Philippe Stern, the son of a Parisian banker who had moved to New York before the German occupation. We used the library as the centre of a black market in cigarettes and other unobtainables at a time when the school was in quarantine because of an epidemic. I never had the popularity that belonged to the sports stars and although I had a few friends, I became more and more of a loner at Bishop's. Now, in a very different environment, I became more of an extrovert, even in some ways, a show-off.

Montreal had very cold winters and hot summers. I would ski at weekends in the Laurentians at Ste. Agathe and Mont Saveur, swim at summer resorts in lakes in the vicinity of the city and walk a lot. When still at school and during a holiday, a group of us went one night to a brothel, where some kind of sex show was put on for us during which two girls made love to each other, but we were too nervous to do anything ourselves, perhaps because of the fear of the diseases about which we had been warned at school. I lost my virginity with a cousin, the same Margot Buchanan who had come over to Canada with us, the only Dawson girl who ever married. Her husband, Sandy, had been killed in the war. One summer evening at Estorel, a resort in the Laurentians, where she had taken a chalet, it happened. I was staying with her, as was a very attractive lady called Maxine in her late twenties: we all got drunk together and I hoped that I had an opportunity with the latter. But she preferred another man in the party that night, and so 'faute de mieux' I got in bed with Margot. We had been drinking sloe gin and my hangover the next morning was a tremendous one. My memory of the occasion is otherwise vague. I have never touched sloe gin since.

Before returning to the subject of sex, I should recount my religious unconversion. At Gilling Castle religion was central to life, and at Ardargie there was even a chapel inside the house, seldom used but consecrated, and always there for personal prayers. The boys at Bishop's College School were nearly all Protestant and subjected to Church of England rituals and services. The Catholic and Jewish boys only attended the annual Christmas carol service at Bishop's College, the nearby small university, but otherwise the Catholic boys went to mass in the village and the Jewish boys to Montreal for the Jewish high holidays, usually claiming that they had to go to town for a dental appointment. At Lennoxville in the village church Catholic boys from an English-speaking school were seen as spies from an alien culture. The group of us, varying from three or four to a maximum of seven, depending on the year, would sit together on the back row, bored stiff, waiting for it to end. In Montreal, during the holidays I would go to confession at the cathedral, where it was heard in both languages, rather than when at Lennoxville, but any devoutness I may have had before going to Canada was fast ebbing. My reading was more widespread and adult, furnishing me with new ideas and many doubts. An Irish lady in Montreal, Honor McIntyre, who was certainly in love with my father and had taken an interest in me since my arrival in Canada, and whom my mother despised as 'an old maid' brought me books that were considered daring about which I would probably not have otherwise heard until years later. I began to explore modern literature through authors like Aldous Huxley, which more than any peer pressure was leading me towards independent thinking.

I had increasing difficulty in understanding the dogma that I had been fed since childhood and I now began to question it, often in the confession box. The answer was always the same: great minds had thought about such things and come up with the answers which were now the dogmas we had to believe. Asking by what arguments and thought processes the great minds (Thomas Aquinas in particular was often cited) had come up with the answers we had to believe got me nowhere. An exasperated priest sent me to a Monseigneur, who in no way satisfied me better, and finally at the age of fifteen I was sent to see a Jesuit bishop at the cathedral of St. Jacques in Montreal. I was ushered into a large room and told to sit in a chair at one end of it. At the other, seated behind a large desk, was the Bishop, signing letters. After a few minutes he looked up, beckoned for me to come forward, and I stood in front of him while he looked me up and down.

'Why are you here?' he asked.

'I think Monseigneur Mitchell has written to you,' I said. 'He thinks you might be able to answer some problems that puzzle me.'

He found a letter on his desk, read it quickly, asked me a few brief questions about myself, and said, very nonchalantly, 'Some people have to leave the church and you're one of them. Good morning!'

I was stunned, and went out into the sunlight not believing my ears. I had been expelled from the Roman Catholic church. For a few days it worried me, then I forgot about it. I kept this incident to myself for many years, went through the rituals of attending mass when the family required it, especially in Scotland, and on only one occasion, as an adult and at a moment of extreme grief, did I ever seek comfort in religion, and that only for a few hours.

* * * * * *

At twelve years old, during my stay at the Atholl Palace Hotel in Pitlochry, I was very struck by the appearance of a very pretty blonde girl of about my own age, but never even spoke to her. My feelings were no doubt the same as those of Dante when he saw Beatrice on the bridge in Florence. During my teens I admired and was attracted to different women with whom I came into contact, usually in their twenties, but could only fantasise about a physical relationship. I went out with a few girls in Montreal and eventually developed a chaste but fairly passionate relationship with a girl called Lorraine Morgan, the daughter of friends of my mother, but not close friends. She came from the French-Canadian community, and was totally bilingual. We spoke English, except occasionally when with other people. I took her to films, the theatre, (for which Montreal was not particularly well served), to restaurants of course, and we began going to dances, especially on Saturday nights, to the Victoria Palace where the black jazz pianist Oscar Petersen played with a dance band. There were professional hockey matches, wrestling and boxing matches at the Montreal forum to which everyone went as a matter of course, but by fifteen I was thoroughly bored with all spectator sports. My interest in music was now very great and I went to such concerts as there were and to my first two operas, *Hansel and Gretel* and *Fidelio*. I knew more about music in theory than in practice, and was reading as many books about the subject as possible. Ernest Newman's *Beethoven the Creator*, devoted mainly to three works written in 1806 told me all about *Fidelio*, so that when I finally had the chance to see the opera I was fully prepared. I could not understand why the emotions I expected to feel at the key moments were not there. The performance, by a touring company, may have been a poor one, but I remember my disappointment, similar to Proust's when he sees, after much anticipation, La Berma's *Phèdre*, only to suffer a similar let-down.

During 1946 and early 1947 Lorraine was my steady girl-friend, but we did not progress beyond kissing. It was understood we were in love, that the relationship was permanent and one day, when married, we would enjoy all the pleasures of sex. That day never came. It was now more or less settled that I would go to Oxford after my concentrated year at Sir George Williams College, where the day and evening lectures were now giving me an expanded outlook on many branches of knowledge. I was visiting Britain every year and I passed responses (entrance exams) at Oxford, where my tutor would probably have been Lord David Cecil, then a Don at New College. I spent an afternoon in his study and was asked to write, on the spot, an essay on a writer of my choice. I sat down and wrote a long analytical appreciation of the novels of W. Somerset Maugham, which he found interesting. I was in principle accepted for New College, which might not have overly pleased my grandfather with his bias against higher education, but it would have been acceptable because of the prestige of the college and for at least being in Britain. But it was not to be.

A new influence had entered my life and not a particularly good one. A returning Canadian solder, John Barnard, had started to woo my mother, newly widowed. What interested him was my mother's very considerable income and the life of ease it offered. He began an affair with her of which my sister and I, living in the same house, soon became aware. Realising the importance of not antagonising us, he paid considerable court to all three children and on one occasion took me to New York to show me the sights and introduce me to the nightlife. There were drinks at the Plaza Hotel bar, dinners in Longchamps restaurants (a mid-priced rather gaudily-decorated chain, now long gone), visits to night clubs and the theatre. I remember Kurt Weill's *Street Scene* in its first production, *Oklahoma* and *Carousel* and some plays, but certainly not all on the one visit. It was only later that I discovered the Metropolitan Opera. I was rather flattered, I suppose, by being treated as a young man about town by John Barnard, who not long after that married my mother.

John Barnard was in some ways not unlike my father, but much more motivated. He was the same height, had a similar moustache, and what he wanted was an easy life and to be successful at something without too much effort. Marriage to a rich widow offered him that or at least the opportunity to start some enterprise of his own. I never positively disliked him, but it was transparent enough what he was and wanted, and I had to humour him, which was not difficult.

In Montreal there were a number of debutante balls to which I mostly escorted Lorraine Morgan, dressed in full evening attire, and a group formed of her friends and their escorts rather than of mine, who seemed to have melted away. I saw very few of the boys I had known at Bishops'. I had shared a room in my last year there with Philippe Stern, who was now in New York, and with Edward Bromfman of the Seagram's distilling family who had now moved into his own enclave of rich Montreal Jews, which mixed little with either the affluent French-Canadian community to which I properly belonged in Canada, or the Protestant one of the suburbs who lived around the mountain, English-speaking and anxious to maintain their ascendancy. My two best friends had been Hugh Evans, a very good-looking Welsh boy, a refugee who came out to Canada rather later than I, whose father was a judge in British-ruled Palestine, and Brigham Day, a Montrealer whose family had been connected with the Canadian Pacific Railway, in which my own Canadian grandfather had had a stake. Hugh had returned to Britain and was in the army. I was invited to sherry parties by Mrs. Day, a tall, angular widow who had a very fat man called Fred as a permanent fixture in her sitting room, but I gradually lost touch. I was seeing more of my Montreal cousins, the Ostiguys and Brodeurs, and speaking more French.

I had developed the ability to move in different circles and be accepted in all of them, and I must have had a fairly generous allowance because escorting Lorraine to balls and such fashionable meeting places as the Ritz Café, which had a glamorous cabaret of star entertainers, and to plays at His Majesty's Theatre and concerts at Plateau Hall must have cost a fair amount. Lorraine did not attend concerts as much as the purely social events. I was often taken by cousins who had subscription tickets and I remember the very conservative tastes of the audiences, who considered Richard Strauss to be almost unbearably modern and discordant. The repertory consisted mainly of Tchaikowsky, Beethoven, Brahms and the better known works of a few other nineteenth century German composers with a smattering of French works. Mozart was a rarity, except for his masses in Catholic churches, where they competed with Palestrina. I still went to church out of politeness on Sundays. Mass was usually followed by a big lunch, often at the Ostiguys, who had taken over the Wilson tradition of big family gatherings. Particularly lavish was the *réveillon* after midnight mass at Christmas, a party that went on until five or later in the morning.

One play that I saw at His Majesty's at this time was Ibsen's *Ghosts*. The cast consisted of Hollywood stars on tour, trying to do some real acting for a change, and it included Sybil Thorndike and George Zukov as well as a strikingly attractive Regina, whose name did not register on me at the time. She was to play a major part in my life in the not too distant future.

By now, John Barnard had decided to plan the lives of my mother's three children, since she certainly had little idea of her own what to do with us, although Ardargie was quite plain about my own future, which was to join the brewery as soon as possible. My sister Betty had been to Compton and earlier to a finishing school called Miss Edgar's, but had never been encouraged in any way to think of education as anything other than preparation for marriage, and higher education never seemed to have come into anybody's thoughts. It would often make her bitter in later years when she attempted to take courses to make up the gaps. Barnard read an article in *Fortune* magazine, an American publication for businessmen, about Zürich, which was becoming the financial centre of Europe in the emerging post-war world of reconstruction. He suggested that I should go to the university in Zürich and study economics. My visit to Oxford had not overly impressed me. Post-war Britain was a joyless place with its restrictions, shortages, uninteresting rationed food and landscapes of destroyed buildings. And being resident in an Oxford college seemed too much like boarding school. I did not feel inclined just yet to become a kind of apprentice in the Alloa brewery and to live at Ardargie in daily contact with

Gaffer and Gran, which was their plan for me. My father had often told me what a tyrant his father was, that the period during which he'd worked for him after the first world war had been an ordeal more excruciating than the trenches, and it was one lesson I learned from him that I believed. Zürich, untouched by the war, seemed an attractive option, and I assented. My brother, five years younger, was told that he would be going to a boarding school in Switzerland. My new step-father had decided he wanted to spend much of the year and much of my mother's income in Europe. He was also probably finding that Montreal was not an entirely comfortable place to be. He had had a pre-war affair with a married lady called Rita Lemay, which had scandalised the section of the city's society to which my mother belonged. Scandal was, perhaps, always her biggest interest in life, in a voyeuristic way, and having the former lover of a well-known local beauty in her power undoubtedly appealed to her. In Montreal he was known only as an adventurer and a rake, and he certainly felt that he could cut a more acceptable figure in Europe.

My excellent marks and reports from Sir George Williams College, where I had done two years in one, impressed the University of Zürich favourably enough – they were in any case interested in attracting foreign students and foreign money – and I was accepted for the autumn of 1946. I had studied German privately with an old German-Jewish woman, a Miss Goldstein, for some months. She was a good teacher, very fat and unhealthy-looking who drank glass after glass of water, causing her to belch constantly during our sessions. But she gave me a good grounding in grammar and pronunciation, so that I had workable German when I arrived in Zürich in June.

I had been booked into the grandest hotel in Zürich for the first two weeks, the Dolder Grand Hotel, high on the Dolder mountain overlooking the lake and the town. I remember that the restaurant had the most delicious strawberries, soaked in lemon juice and sugar, and that a piano trio constantly played operatic airs and melodies from the classics, interspersed with the popular tunes of the day, like *La Vie en rose*. The triumphal march from *Aïda* came up every hour. I went to the university and registered for my courses in *Nationalökonomie*, noting that there were interesting courses in literature that I might be able to attend. I had tea on the Bahnhofstrasse, about which James Joyce, (buried in the local cemetery), had written one of his most poignant poems, and also in a café called *Der Grüne Heinrich*. The menu was full of quotations by Gottfried Keller. On enquiring from the waitress, I was told that the café was named after the greatest novel of the Swiss national poet. I went out to buy the book, which was the first long novel I read in German in Zürich. Years later I was to publish the first, and so far the only, English translation.

One fine June afternoon I walked past the opera house and saw people going in. I followed them and found that Wagner's *Götterdämmerung* was about to begin. I knew that my newly acquired student card allowed me a considerable discount from all ticket prices and bought a good seat in the *Orchester* (stalls) for a very reasonable price, no more than a very ordinary meal would cost. I thought I was in heaven! I had read the story of Wagner's *Ring* in an operatic reference book that I had acquired long ago in New York, but knew nothing of the music. The singers included Kirsten Flagstad, Max Lorenz, Ludwig Weber, Elsa Cavelti and Andreas Böhm, the conductor was Hans Knappertsbusch. You could have found no better cast anywhere in the world at that time and the performance was glorious. During the interval the lady next to me, a distinguished-looking woman of about fifty with a dapper and equally distinguished-looking gentleman, started to talk to me, asking how I liked the performance. I admitted my ignorance of, but by now enormous admiration for the music, and it was evident that my primitive but adequate German amused her, as well as my overflowing enthusiasm. After the second interval they asked if I would like to join them for supper after the performance and I accepted with alacrity. They took me to the restaurant of the Schauspielhaus, the city's repertory theatre, and discussed the performance. They much admired Lorenz' masculine Siegfried and I was naturally bowled over by Flagstad's Brünhilde, which thereafter I never missed an opportunity to hear again. My host was Dr. Dembitzer, but I cannot remember the name of his robust mistress. Both were widely cultured, discussing the theatre and literature as well as music, bringing me into the conversation and showing much interest in my background, my forthcoming studies and expanding cultural interests, and in my admission that I wrote poetry. The opera had started at about four in the afternoon, and it must have been about midnight when we finished dinner.

They then announced they were to move on to a late soirée thrown by Madame Flagstad in her suite at the Dolder Grand Hotel. Would I care to join them? I could not believe my luck in being seated next to them at the Stadtsoper. We took a taxi up the hill to the hotel and joined about forty people drinking champagne in Flagstad's suite. After a while Kirsten Flagstad herself emerged from her bedroom – the suite had several interconnecting drawing rooms and we were by no means crowded – wearing a long loose flowing gown. She was very tall, broad and buxom, shaped as dramatic sopranos nearly all were in those days, but I would describe her as statuesque rather than fat. She moved around the rooms, alternately drinking glasses of beer and champagne, chatting to everyone, including briefly to me after I had been introduced. I did not dare admit that it was my first Wagner opera, but I certainly expressed my enormous admiration for what I had heard that evening. Her voice, powerful and perfectly tuned, had cut through the heavy sound of Knappertbusch's orchestra like an arrow of focused tone, eclipsing everything else going on under the stage or on it. Even more than half a century later I can still hear it in my head and in my inner ear. It was probably, up until that moment, the most exciting night of my life.

The June night sped by and dawn could be glimpsed coming up on the horizon. Flagstad had drunk a phenomenal amount. How many litres of beer and bottles of Champagne could only be guessed at, but from the moment she entered the room there was always a glass in her hand and someone was always refilling it, or rather both, the beer glass and the Champagne. Then, the room already quite bright, the lights switched off from the chandelier and table lamps, she sat down at the grand piano, the dawn behind her, and very softly, perfectly audibly, and to my ear perfectly, with supreme beauty, began to sing. The Dembitzers whispered to me that it was Grieg. For half an hour she sang, accompanying herself on the piano, then suddenly stood up and asked us to leave, thanking us for coming. At about eight o'clock I went to bed feeling like the dying rose in Berlioz's *Nuits d'Été* on the morning after the ball.

The following week I went to hear Flagstad again, in *Die Walküre* and a second performance of *Götterdämmerung*. I also went, during that June Festival, to Stravinsky's *Persephone* and Hindemith's *Nobilissima Visione*, an opera-ballet double bill, and soon started to attend performances of plays by Goethe, Schiller, Kaiser and Shakespeare at the Schauspielhaus. The art gallery also became familiar to me, and I went to films in various languages at the town's cinemas, always for very little entrance fee thanks to my student card. I was now living in a boarding house where no one spoke anything but German, so my conversational use of the language was improving daily. I had a two-language dictionary, which I still possess, in which I underlined every unknown word I had just come across. The second time I would put a cross against it. When it had three crosses I transferred the word to a list which I wrote out weekly on a sheet of paper and studied every morning while shaving or sitting on the lavatory, so that my confident German vocabulary increased by at least twenty new words every week, a system I recommend to others.

I was reading in three languages -- English language paperbacks of classics and standard works, largely from Swedish publishers; poetry; sometimes plays I had seen, such as Shakespeare which I already knew well from teenage reading, but which came over differently in German performance where the hammered rhymes made him sound very like Schiller; and of course erotic literature, published in English in Stockholm or Paris: Henry Miller, D. H. Lawrence and some others without any literary pretensions. I made new friends, one of them an Israeli called Willi Sichel, who introduced me to a Jewish group who were as German, as compared to Swiss-German, in their tastes and behaviour as any Germans I have ever come across. I went to some Friday night ceremonial dinners where word games were played. I learned a great deal from them, especially Willi, and I had a fling, a chaste one, with one of the more passionate girls, who nevertheless clung firmly to her virginity. Willi was soon to return home to Palestine: he was a Sabra, born there and full of liberal feelings of brotherhood towards the Arabs he had grown up with, but I was fairly certain that he was about to join one of the Jewish nationalist groups who were starting to fight the British. I met many people in my first year in Zürich, but there was so much coming and going that friendships tended to be transient. I nearly started an affair with an Argentine girl whom I first met during my first fortnight at the Dolder Grand. She declared that she loved me passionately but when we were in bed together, at the crucial moment she suddenly announced, 'But, of course we will get married right away.' My ardour suddenly cooled and the affair remained unconsummated. She was, I gather, a very eligible heiress, so I am sure her parents would have appreciated my reticence.

What about my Canadian fiancée, if I can call her that? I wrote, at first almost daily, to Lorraine Morgan and she replied very frequently, but with time the correspondence diminished and one day I received a letter telling me she had been going out with another young man called O'Keefe, who wanted to marry her, and he eventually did. Long absence is not conducive to maintaining love, and I was in any case far too young to get permanently involved. I have never seen or heard of her since.

My courses started in September and I was registered to study both theoretic and practical economics, international law, economic geography, statistics and sociology. John Barnard had thought of me becoming a banker, which was the last thing on my mind. My interests were still in literature and the arts, but economics, which I thought of as a social science, seemed a reasonable compromise. Economic geography and statistics were not only deadly boring, but those courses started early in the morning, eight o'clock in the winter months and seven in the summer. International law had special difficulties as Professor Giacometti, who was related to the sculptor, had a thick Italian accent in German that no one could understand. We students would compare notes afterwards and try to work out what he had said. My favourite Professor and the most interesting was René König, who taught sociology. He assigned different books to each student for individual study in addition to the standard texts, and mine was Karl Popper's *The Open Society and Its Enemies* which I was able to read in English and which greatly influenced my political thinking, although I did not agree with all of it. König was the only Professor who treated his students as individual human beings, and he gave seminar dinners, which were very enjoyable. One led to a dramatic incident which I shall relate below.

The core of the course was of course the economic lectures. I had Professor Büchner for theoretical economics and I was recommended to read the text book of his colleague from Geneva, Wilhelm Röpke, *Die Lehre von der Wirtschaft* (The Study of Economics) as the best short introduction to the subject. I still have it. The other Professor was a white Russian, Saitzev, who taught us the workings of the stock market, company practices and how international financial dealings encourage growth and new wealth. From him I learned how holding companies are set up and function, which years later I was to put into practical application with disastrous consequences. Büchner was humdrum but straightforward, not unfriendly to his students. Saitzev was remote, a Russian aristocrat of the old school, who expected military levels of obedience from his class. Questions were not encouraged and he seldom repeated himself. There were no particular text books for his course: you had to listen, take notes and absorb his ideas well enough to be able to analyse them, write about them and in due course pass examinations. He was a director of many of the biggest Swiss companies, especially in chocolate and engineering, and of the Swiss Railways, and he sat on many public committees. His investments had apparently made him very rich. He would regularly visit night clubs in the evening and sit there with his attractive wife and less attractive mistress – the three were a *ménage à trois* – but woe betide any student of his classes if his eye fell on them there. He could refuse to put his signature on the *Testatheft* which every student presented to each Professor at the end of each semester. The signature was the student's necessary proof that he had taken the course.

Lectures started first thing in the morning and could go on until seven at night. There were days when I had an early lecture, a late morning one and perhaps one or two in the afternoon, often separated by several hours; the problem was how and where to spend the intervening time. The most obvious answer was the library where I not only went over my lecture notes and read the required texts, but found recreational reading as well. Another answer was to go to lectures for which I was not registered but which interested me, often more than my own studies. There was a world authority at the university on the novels of Thomas Hardy and I went to hear him. I attended lectures on German literature and sometimes French. Carl Jung was lecturing at the Polytechnik, about two hundred yards away, and I attended his sessions fairly often, sometimes at the expense of my own subjects.

I took no part in other student activities or sports other than going to drinking places with classmates on occasion. There was often some form of challenge, usually to prove you could still do something difficult after so many glasses of wine or beer. I found these stupid. There was a bar in the old town run by a motherly lady called Mary, although I am sure that was not her real name. The bar was called Mary's Old Timer's Bar, and I became an habitué, making drinking friends there. One in particular was a French Swiss, Paul Pettivel, also a student of *Nationalökonomie*, but he had largely dropped out and seldom went to the university, knowing that the day of reckoning would soon come when his family would stop supporting him. I met them when he invited me for a weekend to his home in Neuchatel: I was well looked after, even pampered with breakfast in bed, and taken to a new wine festival, which gave me a severe stomach upset.

American G.I.s on leave from Germany were frequently in Zürich, and many found the Old Timer's Bar and would confide their troubles and homesickness to Mary. Another bar, much more cosmopolitan, was the Huguenin on the Bahnhofstrasse. I met Dr. Dembitzer on a few occasions there, but the clientele was very varied, some very smart men with well-dressed and worldly-looking ladies, diplomats and business men, and a great variety of languages. There I met a man one day of indeterminate nationality who handed me his card which said 'American Secret Service'. But among the many mythomanes and phoneys in post-war Zürich there were real spies, American, British, French and others from the Soviet bloc, and one became aware of them in various ways. They were also among the student body. Onc, a German who had spent the war in America, told me late one night that he had been ordered to return to East Germany by his controller and he was afraid to do so. He did not know what might have been reported about him and if he might have been a scapegoat for someone else's mistake or report. He was a genuine communist with a materialist flair – he had made some money in Switzerland by importing and selling second-hand American clothes – and he wanted to lead a normal life and not be in constant fear.

All this came out over a bottle of Pflümliwasser, the local plum brandy. For some reasons I have all my life received confidences from people who trusted me not to betray them and I think I have been able to justify those confidences.

I found some interesting ways of supplementing the considerable allowance that I received from my mother, and this enabled me to live more confortably, have the odd good meal in one of Zürich's many good restaurants, pay for skiing holidays, and buy books and tickets to performances of music and theatre. I met a painter who had a profitable sideline importing art works from Germany. German families under four-power occupation, often in considerable difficulty because of their Nazi pasts, would sell valuable paintings and other possessions for very little to get foreign currency, and my friend would sell these quite illegal imports to individuals, often professional or business men, living in or visiting Switzerland. He recruited me to make contacts, especially as he spoke little English. I would go to the bars of the leading hotels, especially the Dolder, the Baur au Lac and the Savoy, sit at the bar with my patron's money and talk to lawyers and business men, most of them American, eventually confiding that I knew where they could buy old masters and work by the most celebrated early twentieth century painters for much less than the going market-price. Although they had been smuggled out of Germany the owners had signed away any entitlement and they could be legally acquired from the present owner, who was an adept at acquiring export licences if they were to leave Switzerland.

There were several Vermeers among the paintings I negotiated. As this was the period when Van Megeeren, the expert Vermeer forger, was at work, it is possible that some of them were forgeries, but I have no idea of the outcome, which would not have emerged until years later. The other source of a little extra money was the Neue Zürcher Zeitung, the very serious local paper. I met one of the financial editors in a bar, who asked if I would be willing to read through for him every week the British and American financial newspapers and do a summary of the most interesting information. I did this for a few weeks, gutting the Economist, the Wall Street Journal, Time Magazine, the Times and Financial Times, and giving him a two or three page resumé. Then he gave me my own column in the paper, but not under my name, which would have given me some kudos at the university. I produced the same summary as before in my best German, sometimes with a little help from a friend. It was a nice little source of revenue and took up only two or three hours a week.

One of the earlier boarding houses I stayed in, near the lake and the Stadtsoper, had a member of the chorus living in the room next to mine; she was strikingly beautiful and her name was Lisa della Casa. She had a considerable number of male visitors and at night I would go wild with jealousy at the sound of their love-making. Soon she had become a principal singer at the opera house, and she moved to her own apartment. Thereafter she became an international opera star, whom I would later hear at Covent Garden, the Met in New York and elsewhere. Later, for a considerable time, I was at a boarding house run by the headmaster of a local school, half way up the Dolderberg. On my first night there I met another British student, Dick Soukup, an ex-RAF and Battle of Britain pilot, who was studying at the Polytechnik. We had a party in his room on my first night there and I remember Dr. Kleinert, our not very genial host, coming in and looking at his new arrival accusingly: 'Herr Calder,' he said to me in German, 'I had expected better of you.'

Dick and I soon became good friends. There was also a German-Swiss staying there called Henrich Sandmeier, about to finish his studies, of whom I was to see more later. He was a very serious student, very Germanic, and did not mix in with the antics of others like Dick and I, who saw no reason not to make our student days as enjoyable as possible.

Dick started to have an affair with Su Kleinert, the headmaster's daughter, living in the same house and engaged to a Count, an Austrian aristocrat, a match much encouraged by her parents. She was soon mad for him and trouble loomed ahead. It was Christmas-time and Dick was returning home to Sidcup, outside London, for the holidays – it must have been the end of 1947 – and he, Su and I went to the station together to see him onto his train. He wanted to break off the affair because Dr. Kleinert would soon learn of what had happened and he did not want to be tied down to marriage. I had been charged to take Su to dinner, explain that he was not really serious, and she should think about marrying the Count. We drank a great deal and, resenting the dirty task that had been foisted on me, and swayed by the passionate insistence of my companion that she and Dick were madly in love and ideally suited to each other, ended up saying the exact opposite of what I'd been asked to. I told her that I was sure that everything would work out, that the English were never very demonstrative in love, and that Dick's recent coolness towards her meant nothing. As a result of telling her what she wanted to hear, we had a pleasant if rather drunken evening. I shall relate the consequences of this in the next chapter.

Sometime before my twenty-first birthday I moved into a small hotel, the Rigihof, not far from the university where I had a sort of flatlet with cooking facilities. Here I made a new friend, a French student with an aristocratic background called Raymond de Miribel. He had been caught by the Germans while doing work for the Résistance under the occupation and had been sent to Dachau and Buchenwald, surviving by constantly changing his name and presenting himself as a tradesman, an electrician or plumber, and therefore always in demand and getting better treatment than the other prisoners. On his arrest he had had enough wit to inform his father of what had happened to him by addressing the short and monitored postcard he was allowed to send before being sent to Germany, to Château des Déportés, rather than Château de Miribel. He had weighed less than a hundred pounds at the end of the war, but was now bordering on obesity, a shambling hulk of a man, studying like me to get his doctorate in Economics. He hardly ever seemed to leave his room, drinking cognac all day, reading and studying. We often ate, drank and talked in the evening. We celebrated the New Year at a hotel party to see in 1948 at the Rigihof and later that month I turned twenty-one and organised a similar party. On that occasion the hotel manager tried to seduce me when I was drunk, but I managed to dissuade him by a hard kick.

I spent a few pleasant days with Raymond at his family chateau near Grenoble. I well remember the first evening when the two of us sat up late drinking a bottle, perhaps two, of Chartreuse. The next day, after having breakfast brought to me in bed, I met his father the Comte and the family, was given a tour of the grounds and lunch with many guests, which I did not enjoy as it started with black pudding, continued with tripe, not foods I like and ended when the cook, who told me with pride that she had spent some time in England and had specially made an 'eengleesh pouding' for me (I have always detested all milk puddings), stood over me to watch me eat the large portion of this pudding she had deposited on my plate, which I got through with the utmost loathing, trying to smile. I drank a lot of red wine at that meal.

My mother and John Barnard would occasionally show up in Zürich and stay at the Dolder Grand. I would go for dinner and be questioned about my studies, but I had more to say about the theatre, the opera and the wonderful concerts. In addition to such great singers as Flagstad, who returned to sing Wagner every summer, there were leading singers from Germany and Italy, and all the great instrumentalists. I heard Gigli and Tebaldi in *Aïda*, not at the opera house, but in the *Tonhalle* (concert hall) where the stage had been adapted with a proscenium for the occasion. Franz Lechleitner was the local Heldentenor, very popular with local audiences and among those performers I particularly enjoyed were Andreas Böhm, a wonderful Boris Godunov as well as a great Wagnerian bass, Maria Reining in *Der Rosenkavalier* and a long roster of international singers, including of course Lisa della Casa, whose amorous pleasures had once excited me, now developing into a major prima donna. At the Dolder, when my mother and John Barnard were there, I met a lawyer from Washington D.C., Jim Mann, who having worked for the U.S. government blocking suspect bank accounts of European investors in the States, and of Americans in Switzerland who were avoiding tax, was now in private practice doing the opposite, trying to unblock the same accounts. One of his clients was Baron Thyssen, the elderly German steel magnate, who having been released by the Allies, was living in Switzerland in a large house, having succeeded in getting most of his money out before the war ended. His much younger and elegant wife was a princess and she was having an affair with Jim Mann. He used me as a reluctant go-between to carry messages, because his wife was frequently around, as was Thyssen. It was Jim Mann who first excited my interest in the Alger Hiss case, because the Hiss scandal broke at that time. Jim was a good friend of Hiss's and could not believe the accusations being made against him by Whittaker Chambers, a Time Magazine editor, whose claim was that he and Hiss had both belonged to a Communist cell before the war, and that they had regularly passed information over to the Russians. I followed the events of the scandal and the two trials which were to lead to Hiss' conviction and imprisonment by reading all the newspapers, which I had in any case to scan for the Neue Zürcher Zeitung. Later, when I became a publisher, I was to take both a personal and a professional interest in Hiss, and publish his book. Talking of politics, I also remember the night in November 1947, when Harry S. Truman, the U. S. President, was, against all expectations, reelected. I listened all night to the radio, hearing the numbers add up in Truman's favour while commentators kept insisting that Dewey had already won and what we were hearing could not be true. They must have had red faces the next morning, like the editors whose newspapers, printed too early, gave Dewey the victory which he had decisively lost.

In March 1948 during the Easter holiday I went skiing at Zermatt, the highest station in Europe, where great snowfields lie under the shadow of the Matterhorn, a mountain of awesome splendour. I stayed at the

Zermatterhof, one of the best hotels, and skied from the first-light to dark. There I met a man who was to become one of my closest friends, Jacques Chaix. We had both spotted a lady on the slopes worth pursuing, and at one point, all skiing too close together, we collided and ended up in a heap together, which served as an introduction. She was a nurse at the local hospital, Jacques was in the same hotel as I, and we agreed to have dinner there together. During the following week we all skied together, but Jacques won Heidi, which I accepted with good will, even going so far as to facilitate her entry into the hotel late at night by opening a window at the back. Our last day in Zermatt was a Friday the thirteenth, and on that day every member of the group of half a dozen of us who had become friendly enough to ski together had an accident, except me. Most of them were minor, a broken ski at the end of the day in Heidi's case, but Jacques Chaix had a bad fall that would trouble his back all his life. It was late in the afternoon and the sun was setting when the remaining members of the party still able to ski passed through a long descent on a narrow trail through a wood with many corners. Heidi, who was very fast, was first, then came Jacques, with myself at the rear. Turning a corner, my eyes on the narrow piste, I thought I saw, out of the corner of one of them, something moving in the snow. Stopping with some difficulty a hundred yards or so further down, I herring-boned my way back up the hill. I had not been mistaken. A pair of skis were waving in the air above a large snowdrift. I unburied Jacques, who had gone in upside-down, was unable to move and nearly unconscious. We descended slowly, found Heidi at the bottom, who had broken her ski at the end of the run against a tree, and we spent our last evening together. Friday the thirteenth has never been unlucky for me, but it certainly was for all the others that day.

The next morning Jacques and I took the train to Brig, from whose junction different trains took us off to Paris and Zürich. We had exhausted our last funds, but by now were good enough friends to evenly divide up the few coins we still had, hardly enough for a sandwich. I promised to look Jacques up in Paris and a few months later did so. Many of my evenings there were at the opera – I saw most of the French repertoire at the Palais Garnier and Opéra Comique, then and on subsequent visits, with singers like Nadine Renaux, Denise Duval, Mady Mesplé, Raoul Jobin and René Bianco – and Jacques introduced me to the night-clubs of Montmartre and Pigalle, when it became only natural to end up in bed with someone I had met or picked up there: it all seemed very innocent in Paris. There was an evening at the Moulin Rouge where we dined with two of Jacques' girl-friends, an old flame that he was trying to pass on to me and a new one he was cultivating. The evening did not work out as planned. Both girls were only interested in Jacques, loathed each other, and bristled throughout an evening whose end I cannot recall. Over a period of time I came to know them both quite well: the first was to take her own life some years later, not as far as I know because of Jacques, and the other, then a young concert singer, was later to become a friend and remain one more than fifty years later. But I learned then how insensitive this new friend of mine could be where women were concerned, although his nature was generous and he was intelligent enough to realise the pain he inflicted by playing the rôle of the stolidly dominant male who did everything to suit his own convenience. He never married, and juggled many women, usually simultaneously, throughout his life: most of them were genuinely in love with him, but on only one occasion did he ever admit to me any guilt, and that was regarding the first of the two ladies mentioned above, and several years later.

As Jacques Chaix was to be a close friend until his death in 1989, a short portrait is necessary. He came from a family of small industrialists who had land and vineyards in the Vaucluse as well as a factory just outside Paris, making washers and small metal objects for motor cars and industry generally. He had spent the war with the Maquis in the area where his father's family originated and by 1942 was commander of the whole guerrilla army in the region of south-east France, with many thousands of men under his leadership. He harried the German garrisons, blew up trains and bridges, and exerted whatever force, and where necessary terror, over the local population to ensure the procurement of provisions, tactical information and loyalty. When necessary he was ruthless and collaborators did not live long. It was Jacques who met the British commando force that invaded the south of France in one of Churchill's less successful adventures and it was he who had to do the interpreting. His English was so rudimentary that I cannot imagine how he managed and it is incredible that a British commando leading the invasion had no one able to speak French. Jacques was an effective Maquis commander and he became an effective administrator when he took over his father's business in the late fifties. But his objective in life was always his personal convenience and pleasure. Business lunches and dinners were not part of his professional life. He only liked to eat with people he liked. Being good-looking, healthy and fond of physical sports, he had as many women as he wanted and spent as much time as possible on holiday, which never seemed to injure his business, where his sister was also in the administration. Over many years I was to ski with him in late February and early March, and after 1963 he would come shooting with me in Scotland; I would go to stay with him at his villa at Cap Ferrat and meet him in different parts of the world. We had nothing in common except for a liking for the opposite sex, skiing and tennis, and a male bonding based on mutual respect and loyalty. He considered me his most eccentric friend, whose motivations could not be understood, but had to be respected. Politically he was on the right and I was on the left, but we never argued. He had no more belief in religion than I. Jaques was no intellectual, but certainly no fool, and in no way anti-intellectual, counting artists and actors among his friends. He had a great tolerance for other people, for life styles different from his own, and was no snob in any of the categories where snobbism applies, but at the same time he had his intolerances, usually towards any group, culture or phenomenon that could in some way affect him adversely. He was politically right because not to be would threaten his economic freedom and thereby reduce his capacity to live for his own pleasure, and he considered that whatever applied as being in his own interest also led to the well-being of France. He perfectly understood France's colonies desire for freedom, but was against giving it to them. He would always side with the police against any radical demonstration.

It is to Jacques that I largely owe my knowledge of Paris and of a vernacular French, very different from the polite French of refined society. Jacques was a man of the people, his friends came from every background and class, and their conversations tended to be colourful with argot expressions I might otherwise never have learned. On visits during my remaining student days I came to know the Paris of Parisians increasingly well and Jacques, affluent in his own country, was always a good and generous friend.

I sampled the French theatre and boulevard fare in the company of Jacques or a lady friend, and more serious theatre and the opera on my own. Raoul Jobin, who particularly impressed me, was one of the most versatile lyric tenors I have ever encountered. He had a voice of great beauty that I heard in *Carmen*, *Romeo et Julette*, *Werther* and Wagner's *Lohengrin*, but also in new works where he could act the clown and have the audience in stitches, like Henri Rabaut's *Mârouf, Sauvetier de Caire*. He was the greatest of all the French tenors I have ever heard and one of the best actors. Unfortunately he was soon to give up his career to manage his wife's, a French-Canadian singer like himself, and to open a singing school in Montreal.

At the university I continued my studies with reasonable application but little enthusiasm, although a few of the lecturers did attract my attention. René König, lecturer in sociology, was by far the most interesting. At a seminar dinner that he gave before Christmas, I believe in 1947, we all drank a fair amount of wine and a German student, resentful of the presence of someone who represented the powers that had defeated Germany, decided to provoke a quarrel. Insult was followed by counter-insult, and then a glass of wine was thrown in my face, to which the only reply was a slap in the face. He then formally challenged me to a duel. Duels were illegal at Swiss universities but they frequently took place. Not long before Heini Sandmeier had taken me to a dinner of his *Studentenverband*, where part of the ritual was to create circumstances that would provoke a duel. In this way students proved their courage and often sported, unless things went drastically wrong, a proudly worn scar on the cheek. Even at that age the stupidity of the whole thing was apparent to me. A student at such an evening would wait until his large stein of beer was nearly empty, then shout to his proposed victim, 'Ein grossen Vor' (a large before) to which his opponent had to respond by first emptying his glass (a moment would have been picked when it was full) within a given time span, perhaps a minute, but certainly less than two. If he could do it, he would then reply 'Ein grossen Nach' (a large afterward) and wait for the opportunity to do the same back. Everyone got totally drunk and many such evenings terminated in challenges to duels. These were held in the woods early in the morning, and it was rumoured that the Rector was often the referee, and there would always be a doctor present.

When I was challenged I accepted, but being a foreigner and without training, I was given two months to take a sabre course. The rules were complex. You were not allowed to move your feet, the left being in front of the right; your shoulders were protected by a heavy harness of leather and steel, you wore a helmet that covered your head and nose, you had goggles for the eyes, and the breastplate also had a rising section that protected your throat and chin. The purpose was to slash at the cheeks. You moved your wrists to slash, but your elbow had to remain within the levels of your wrist and shoulder. In brief, it was wrist action that mattered. Dick Soukup and Heini Sandmeier agreed to be my seconds and they negotiated with the seconds of the other man. I began to take lessons and soon learned I was quite dexterous with a sabre, and that being shorter than the other man I had a considerable advantage: I could slash up and might get under his nose, which was only protected from the top, whereas he, slashing down, could only hit my protected parts unless he slashed my cheek. My instructor, a professional fencing-master, was pleased with me and assured me I would come off best.

Two days before the appointed day the seconds had a meeting. It became obvious that the challenger wanted to get out of it, but had to find the right formula for an apology, while I had to be willing to accept it. Dick and Heini took me out for a drink. 'Look, old boy,' said Dick, 'we Brits shouldn't get involved in these outdated customs. He wants to call it off, so don't be difficult.' I was frankly disappointed, since after so many lessons, and sure of my new skill, I was almost looking forward to this new experience, but reason prevailed. I accepted the apology, we shook hands, and the duel never happened.

I had many difficult texts to read and master, but the hardest of them all were the writings of the English economist David Ricardo, which I had to read in German because there were no English texts available at the university. Like my white-Russian Professor Saitzev, Ricardo had turned his theories to practical account, made a fortune for himself and then written important tracts on value theory and the promotion of growth, and he was the very devil to read and understand. Mentioning my difficulty to John Barnard gave him the idea of inviting Heini Sandmeier for a month to the Engadin valley where, with my mother's money he had rented a castle for the summer. Heini would tutor me through these difficult texts and also give some tutoring to my younger brother who was now at a school at Zuoz, quite near by. For a month in Crap da Sass, a gloomy castle sunk in a valley between ponderous mountains, isolated and about two miles away from the nearest village, I slaved over Ricardo and others, occasionally taking a walk with Heini to the village for a beer and on one occasion climbing a fairly high mountain. I forget the name of it, but well remember the last two hours returning downhill, bone-weary and then having to spend two days in bed with mountain fever.

Some time early in 1948 I was given the degree of Licentiate, probably the equivalent of a B.A. This was earned largely by a thesis that I wrote on the theories of Thomas Malthus, whose ideas on population control made much sense to me and still do. He is out of fashion today but his observations still seem evident to me when you look at the world. If mankind does not find a way of controlling its numbers, said Malthus, nature will do it, through war, pestilence, or natural disasters, and these will affect the overcrowded regions most. I read Malthus in French without difficulty and my long essay, written in German, was well received. I decided that for my doctoral thesis I would make an analysis and comparison of the basic ideas and theories of John Maynard Keynes and Karl Marx and had already read much of both. They both still interest me at the time of writing and I am pleased to see that Keynes is finally making a come-back.

I was writing poetry at this time, inspired principally by T.S. Eliot, although Ezra Pound also interested me, and I was beginning to get to know the Auden generation. But most of my reading was in other languages, classics for the most part, but modern novels, plays and poetry as well. I sent poems off to British magazines and had occasional acceptances, one in *Horizon* and one in *Poetry Review* and some in other little magazines of the time which have long since been forgotten. It was rather dry, free verse for the most part, conversational in tone, rather like Eliot's *Prufrock*. But I knew that although derivative, it was getting better and that in time I would find my own voice. But it was music that enthralled me most. I went, nearly always on my own, two or three times a week to concerts and opera. High points were hearing Artur Schnabel playing the entire Beethoven piano works, sonatas, concerti and variations, over a single month, the Griller and other string quartets, which introduced me to the principal works in that form of Mozart, Haydn, Beethoven and Schubert, whilst I was also discovering Bartok, Hindemith and upcoming Swiss and other European composers. I made friends with a few musicians, professional players who were not particularly well-known and eagerly discussed music with them. One of them, a pianist who played concerts in schools and around the smaller towns, used to pick up Zürich prostitutes and having had his pleasure would send them to my room as a present. Nice Swiss girls were not very accessible, although I had a few pleasant nights with some girls from the university, not all Swiss. Sex with so-called 'nice' girls was always difficult to get. There were a few, not many, who simply enjoyed sex in the same way as men, and they were in high demand and therefore difficult to win. Prostitutes were easy to find, but often did not call themselves that: there was a certain *delicatesse* when it came to the pretence of mutual pleasure, and it may not always have been pretence. I also received a surprising number of homosexual invitations and had to find a way of turning these down without giving offence. I knew a few male students who would accept such advances for a payment and no doubt some of the girl students did too.

One night during the summer of 1948 I won a large sum of money at poker. Poker games were fairly frequent among foreign students and the equivalent of about £50 or £200 might change hands, but this time it was different. There were about eight of us, of many nationalities and I had an extraordinary run of luck. At the end, two of us, a Swede and I, had cleaned out all the others and we were playing the last hand. I had three of a kind, Jacks or Queens I think, and I was fairly certain my opponent had something similar. We eyed each other, looking for signs of a bluff: it was important not to seem too confident because then your opponent would cease to bet and to raise you, while nervousness would indicate you might easily lose what you had on the table if your hand was weaker than your playing suggested. We went all the way until one of us could no longer raise the ante, and I won. It was something like £1000 and it was now broad daylight. We all went to have breakfast at the Bahnhof Buffet, open all night, for which I paid. I then decided to have a really good holiday on the Côte d'Azur and at the end of August went by train to Cannes where I stayed at the best hotel, spending all day on the beach, slowly acquiring a fashionable tan, and lunching at the hotel's beach bar. In the evening I usually went to the casino where I played roulette. Overall I won a little, so my evenings paid for themselves. August turned to September, so the worst of the summer heat was over, and the weather warm and idealistic. I made a few holiday friends, but never saw any of them again. I did however have a very nice little affair with an Austrian lady who owned a factory making rubber contraceptives, condoms in particular, of which she always had a handy supply with her. During my second week in Cannes I was usually sneaking out of her room (in another hotel) at about five in the morning to return to my own to sleep a little before returning to the beach, where I discovered one day from a man next to me that I was not the only one to have enjoyed the lady's favours.

When I left Cannes I had used all my money and didn't even have enough to buy a snack and a glass of beer at a bistro opposite the station before catching my sleeper back. The barman, seeing my distress as I rummaged through my pockets, told me not to worry. I could pay if I ever came back. Perhaps it was his generosity that inspired my own that night. The train was packed and there was an elderly lady in the corridor outside my *couchette*. I let her have it and spent the night in the corridor.

Nineteen forty-nine was my last year at the university and as the year advanced I prepared for my final examinations, both written and oral. I had much reason to be nervous because on my *Testatheft*, which documented my studies, there were one or two missing signatures. It had to have the verifying signature of the professor or lecturer, both at the beginning of the course and at the end. If you missed the end-signature for whatever reason you had to try to catch the relevant signer in a good mood later on, and persuade him to sign; otherwise you were obliged to take the course again, or at least pay for it and obtain the two signatures at the appropriate times. The most difficult signature to get was of course Saitzev's. I had about five written exams ahead of me and a thesis to finish. After that there were two oral examinations during which I would be cross-questioned to make sure I had the knowledge I was supposed to have.

I holed up in the Dolder again, where by now I had the privilege of a cheap room and began to reread – and in some cases read for the first time – the set books. I was occupied in this way on a Sunday afternoon when there came a knock on the door: it was the room maid. The lady in the room next door was giving her problems and the maid couldn't understand her: the lady could only speak English, and not in a very pleasant manner. It seemed there had been many complaints about her and I was asked to speak to her and find out what it was she really wanted.

I knocked on the door and heard an American voice issuing from the bathroom, 'Who is it?' I explained my presence, standing in the open doorway.

'I'm in the bath,' said the voice. 'I'll come to see you when I'm out of it.'

After nearly an hour an apparition in pink appeared in my room. Long reddish hair that was really a light red-blonde surrounded a carefully made-up face and large grey-green eyes. She was in a kind of pink playsuit, decolleté and doing very little to disguise a beautifully rounded young body in its early twenties. Having overcome my astonishment, I found out what the problem was: she was accusing the room-maid of having taken some jewellery, although it was not clear whether her complaint was against an individual or the hotel, and I was soon to doubt the whole thing. She certainly wasn't going to contact the police and her general vagueness about the whole matter should have sent me a warning signal. But I was already too smitten. On one occasion at Cannes, I had played tennis for a few minutes with Rita Hayworth, a similar-looking beauty, to fill the time until the Ali Khan came to join her, and of course I had seen and even slept with one or two beautiful women, but I had never seen or been so close to anyone like this, and I was in a state of shock. My memory of the next week is limited to the next two paragraphs.

I took her to the hotel dining room for dinner that night, which attracted a good deal of attention, although the Dolder was quite accustomed to unusual scenes among its customers and rarely blinked. During my first visit there I had become accustomed to seeing a Baron Rothschild sitting every night at his table, opposite a life-sized blown-up rubber doll, dressed in a high-couture Parisian evening gown and covered with large jewels of every description. Other diners and the staff had been careful never to stare. But they did stare at us. I took her to a concert in the town on one of the next two nights and was very nearly late because she had no concept of time. In spite of frequently knocking on her door, she took, to my growing annoyance, forever to make-up, get dressed and be ready to leave. It mattered to her not at all whether she went to the concert, was on time or my concern to get there: she was only interested in how she looked and how much attention I was paying to her. Somewhere towards the end of the first week I managed to get into her bed. It was of course wonderful and my lust seemed inexhaustible. If I did any studying I cannot remember it.

I was given her account of why she was in Zürich. She had diverted there because London hotels were all full, so ran her explanation, but as I was soon to learn it was almost impossible to distinguish the truth from whatever fanciful version of events it suited her to tell at the time. She was a Hollywood star, so she said (starlet would have been a more accurate description), who had had to leave Hollywood because Louis B. Mayer, head of MGM studios, had taken out a contract on her life, the reason being that her mother had tried to blackmail him. It gradually emerged that she had been his mistress, had gone away for a weekend with him, and been slightly injured on the way back in a car crash. Most Hollywood hopefuls in those days had to endure a sexual initiation from agents, producers or studio heads in order to get their start. Friends had helped her to leave Hollywood so she was now in hiding, but with letters of introduction to film producers in London. She had with her a considerable wardrobe, three mink coats and a sable one, and some jewellery, but it was probably fake. Sense, reason, and the ability to think clearly had all deserted me.

What happened next is that we took a train to Lausanne, spent two days there, mostly making love, then went on to Paris, where after some difficulty we finally found a room at the very old-fashioned Hotel de Quai d'Orsay, now a museum, but then the station hotel of the Gare d'Orsay, serving the suburbs. The room was enormous with high ceilings and ornate turn-of-the-century furniture. Hotel service, other than a restaurant was almost non-existent, but the room had a big bed and a bathroom, which was all I needed. But Christya wasn't happy. She wanted to be in whatever was the most expensive and fashionable hotel, to be looked at and admired. Her name – it has taken me a while to come to that – was Christya Myling, which was in fact a stage name. Her real name was Mary-Ann Simmonds and gradually I learned her history. She was born in Brooklyn, the illegitimate daughter of a local woman whose father, or it may have been grandfather, had been a Jewish cantor. Her father, who would not publicly admit anything or recognise her as his daughter, had nevertheless helped her mother financially. He was a lawyer called Fabricant of Swedish origin, which accounted for her very northern looks. The father was apparently dependent on and under the thumb of his own, very strict, mother who was the overriding influence in her son's arms-length stand-off-ishness. Christya was the girl I had seen playing Regina in Ibsen's *Ghosts* in Montreal. She had a book of press cuttings, mainly from Hollywood gossip columnists, because she had never actually made a film, although she had been under contract at different times to several studios, one of the army of good-looking hopefuls who passed through producers' beds. The only cuttings that had anything to do with actual performances were photographs and brief reviews of the touring *Ghosts* production.

As a teenager she had been able to get a job in New York in one of the womens' clothing boutiques of the Waldorf-Astoria Hotel, where the woman owner found that male customers would buy clothes she modelled and then take her out, giving her the clothes. One such was Billy Rose, a cabaret showman and producer of musicals, and he hired her to join his chorus line. She took dancing lessons and became a 'Billy Rose Showgirl'. Then she met Red Skelton, a Hollywood comic actor, who took her to the west coast and introduced her to producers, and she had a contract with Selznick before MGM. Her big opportunity came from Charles Chaplin who wanted her to play the lead rôle in his film *Limelight*. Her stories were always a blend of truth and make-believe, so I learned never to wholly believe what she told me, but that story seemed to have some credence. Chaplin was under fire at the time for his leftist sympathies, and she was told very strongly that if she worked with Chaplin she would never work again in Hollywood, so she turned him down and Claire Bloom got the part. The truth may of course have been very different and I was never wholly convinced either that her life had really been under threat from Louis B. Mayer. However she had earned money in Hollywood, been under contract, made screen tests, and toured with a starry cast in *Ghosts*. One of her letters of introduction was to a certain Bob Wolf of RKO Pictures.

John Barnard and my mother were in Paris and eventually, almost certainly because I needed money, I went to see them and introduced them to Christya. That changed things very quickly. I was given enough to get me back to Zürich and with a one-way train ticket and a sleeper was seen off at the station by the two of them, Christya having gone back to the hotel. I disembarked at the first station stop, which was Troyes, had a long cold wait, and took a train back some hours later, arriving at dawn. I then spent another two or three days in Paris, caring about nothing other than my passion, and was quite ready to end my young life for the sake of a few more days or hours of sexual bliss. Then she set off for London and I went back to Zürich and took my exams, which I somehow managed to pass.

Then I took a train to London. I remember sitting up all night in a railway carriage, reading Joyce's *Ulysses* for the first time. Christya was staying at the Savoy Hotel and for two days I moved into her room. She was now seeing Bob Wolf, who had become very interested in her. He was a typical American film producer, I think about fifty, but I did not meet him until some weeks later. I then moved into what was basically a maid's room, high up under the roof of the Savoy, but overlooking the river. I wrote some of my best poems there, one of which, *Swedish Rose*, at least survives, because it appeared later in a little magazine called *The Glass*. She was certainly seeing Bob Wolf at this time, who was probably paying for her room, but whether she was sharing her sexual favours with him or not I never found out. She was wily enough to know that it was better to keep him waiting. I bothered her endlessly to marry me and I think she was in love herself, but she was always confused, knowing well her powers of attraction, but full of insecurities. She certainly enjoyed our sex, and was capable of having multiple orgasms, and our sessions, several a day, went on for hours. Eventually I obtained a special licence, and took her to the Westminster Registry Office where I married her, going back to Zürich the next day to take my oral examinations.

She followed me ten days later. She told me that Bob Wolf had proposed to her and that she wanted to get a quick divorce in order to marry him and continue her career, but that whatever happened she would still see me because she loved me. Within twenty-four hours I had talked her out of that and then made preparations to leave Zürich. I had all my things sent to London and we went on honeymoon to Italy, spending a few days at the Villa d'Este at Como. It was idyllic, lovely weather, with a beautiful lake to swim in and wonderful local white wine to drink, so light that it could not travel. I seem to remember getting through three bottles on my own, since Christya was unused to alcohol, without succumbing to sleep or the diminishing of sexual desire. The days in Como were undoubtedly expensive, but when in London I had been able to procure some money from my father's estate, which was held for me by lawyers, and this had enabled me to pay most of my way until now, although Christya was also using her own money. From Italy, we moved to Cannes. There was no time on the beach now: what I remember best is always being sent on errands to get things for her, from the chemist or for special food shops or odd items of clothing. She was very dependent on sleeping pills, stimulants and sedatives. She was also very faddy about foods and almost lived on yoghurt. I had swum in Como and no doubt I did so occasionally in the Mediterranean, and I may have read a little, but other than fetching and carrying, the end of the honeymoon is an ill-remembered blur. I then saw my mother and John Barnard who had arrived on the Côte and they had to accept that I had crossed the Rubicon, but took it with an ill will. There would be little more help from that source.

I had seen little of my siblings during my years in Zürich. My sister was still a teenager, mainly at school in Canada (John Barnard had sent her off to Compton as a boarder about the time he married my mother) and my brother James was at Zuoz in the Engadin, which I gathered is where all the Nazis had sent their sons and daughters. He was to become in his outlook very Nazified himself and eventually to marry a German girl from the same school, but only some years later, and after a spell at the Polytechnik in Zürich, followed by M.I.T. in Boston, where he was to qualify as an engineer. I was now on my own and had to earn a living. My formal education was over and I went with Christya to London to start a new life.

Chapter 3

London

I was twenty-two years old, in London, and married. I was in love and the poet who had always been present in me emerged as I found my own voice, expressing my feelings and interests, having escaped the influences of the favourite poets of my teenage and university years. I was prolific now and the lines poured daily out of me. A growing pile of poems was building up and I would send two or three at a time to *Poetry Review*, *Poetry Quarterly*, *Horizon* (then in its last year), *Poetry Manchester* and a number of others, sometimes quite new little magazines, usually only producing a few issues before closing. One I particularly remember fondly was *The Glass*, set by hand and printed on a hand-press by its eccentric editor, Anthony Borrow, who was by profession a chemist, but had a real enthusiasm for new literature, a penchant for the arcane, the occult and the mythical, and who also wrote verse plays. He liked my poems and published at least two; I cannot remember how many appeared elsewhere: there may have been one or two dozen. Sex, love and poetry went hand in hand and fed each other. Christya, both source and subject of many of the poems, was flattered, but did not quite know what to make of it all. Her preoccupation was with money, getting and spending it, with fame and frequenting the places where the richest and most important people were.

On coming to London, the first thing was to find a place to live. Philip Frere, an eminent solicitor, whom I went to because of the investigations of John Barnard, began to handle my affairs in terms of unlocking my father's money (not a large amount) and obtaining the income from a trust which had been set up by my Scottish grandfather with the money left by my Uncle Ian, my father's younger brother who had died intestate as a bachelor at the age of thirty-six shortly before the war; my father's three children were the beneficiaries. There was enough to live on modestly. Philip Frere, himself tall, handsome, urbane, with the bearing of a self-confident English aristocrat, owned and invested in properties all over London. He would not normally have wasted any time on someone like me, but he was intrigued by the flamboyant Christya and he found me a temporary flat in Lowndes Street until I finally rented another, only a few yards away at 6 Lowndes Street, a circular corner building, christened 'the gasometre' by residents and taxi drivers. I was on the eighth floor if I remember rightly, which had a view over much of south London with the twin towers of Battersea Power Station prominent on the horizon. The flat was let to me by a man called Eric Turrell, who had recently been fired from the publishing company Hutchinson. Walter Hutchinson, it seemed, had a habit of inspecting his employees' desks when they were out at lunch and if he did not like what he saw he left a note to leave the firm immediately. Eric was one such victim, who now filled in time working for a friend in property, whose profitable specialisation consisted of splitting up large flats into smaller ones and letting them on a rising market.

'June 1949 was a very fine month'. With these words I was later to begin a theatrical chronicle in 1989 of forty years in publishing and again in 1999 of fifty. It was a warm and sunny June, and London was just coming back into its own after the war's aftermath. A few visual memories are stuck in my mind from that busy time. I remember an open Sunbeam-Talbot, a very fashionable sports car of the time, flashing past me in Belgrave Square, with a young man and his girl, her long blonde locks streaming in the air behind her in brilliant sunshine. This iconic image seemed to epitomise the post-war return of a *jeunesse dorée* without care. I remember The Antelope, a well-known pub near Sloane Square, where Sir John Squire, last of the Georgian poets, would hold court every Sunday morning from opening time, surrounded by young admiring acolytes, talking of village cricket and his detestation of 'that charlatan' T. S. Eliot, who had recently won the Nobel Prize for Literature. I kept my mouth shut, bought and presented for signature the *Collected Poems* of J. C. Squire, which I found worthy but dull, and listened to the conversation, stereotypical of the English university-educated middle-class. I met a sub-editor of the *Daily Express* there who introduced me to his newspaper and it gave me occasional employment as a part-time junior reporter, and for about three months that autumn I was sent to report on fires and minor crimes, like burglaries, which were common.

I saw my grandfather occasionally. He took the news of my marriage better than my parents had. When he first met Christya he had evaluated her hips for their child-bearing propensities and apparently concluded that he would soon have good-looking grandchildren to carry on his name. He had a house in Cadogan Square, where my unmarried Aunt Muriel now lived, and he stayed there when in town, still going quite frequently to the Ind Coope and Allsop offices in Southhampton Place. He had insisted that we get remarried in the Catholic church in Cadogan Gardens, and I seem to remember that Christya was telling him she would be happy to become a Catholic. If it had been to her advantage to become a Sufi she would as easily have done so. Of course it never went beyond words.

He turned up at the Lowndes Street flat late one Sunday morning without warning and was very incensed that I was still in bed and had not gone to mass. He of course knew nothing of my rejection of the faith. I was always busy with something at that time, but do not remember exactly with what. Writing poetry and making love certainly took up much of my time. During the last months of 1949 I considered involvement in business opportunities that were offered to me, one to do with property which involved spending a couple of weeks in an office near Sloane Square, but nothing went ahead except for the one venture, in publishing, that was eventually to be my principal career in life. As the autumn advanced into winter we came to know what a real London pea-souper fog was like. I remember days and evenings when I could not see my hand in front of my face and had to grope along the railings from corner to corner. Everyone had a coal fire in those days and when they were banned eventually, the fogs, which led to many deaths, quickly stopped.

My grandfather still saw me as his heir as far as his property was concerned, but he no longer wanted me in the brewery from which he was in any case gradually retiring in favour of Sir John Gilmour. He expected me to eventually become a Scottish laird like himself, even if I opted for a different career. He gave me a sinecure, a directorship of Archibald Tower and Co., a company in Gateside, just outside Newscastle-on-Tyne, that bottled beer and mineral waters. I attended half a dozen board meetings of a company where my grandfather was chairman and indirectly the principal owner, but he was never present. The managing director, a Mr. Avison, was a bluff unimaginative old Geordie. At one such meeting he told us, the three of four directors present, that the company had been offered a contract to bottle Pepsi-Cola for the whole North of Britain, but said that he had tasted the stuff, hated it and was certain that it would never catch on in Britain. I tried to persuade him to think again: it was a world name with unlimited advertising budgets, but he had made up his mind and turned it down. Not too surprisingly the company closed its doors a few years later.

An old boy-friend of Christya suddenly showed up in London. His name was Charles Frank, and he had nothing to do with the film industry, but imported cameras and similar goods from Germany to sell in the States. He had bought much of Christya's wardrobe, including the sable coat and had helped to keep her life luxurious in Hollywood, (which he visited mainly to see her). He was perturbed by her unavailability, but made the best of it. We took him out for a day on the river in a rented boat one Sunday, and I looked him up once in New York, where he offered me a sandwich and a cup of coffee in his office. Bob Wolf had by now returned to the States.

It was a year when the new Labour government was making itself very unpopular with the middle classes. Not only was it blamed for the continuation of shortages, although rationing was ending, but the taxes, on even moderately high incomes went rapidly up the scale towards nineteen and sixpence in the pound (97.5%). This meant that no one had much spending money and the standard of living that the average middle-class family or individual had taken for granted before the war was drastically reduced. Many of the West End plays of the period were comedies about the plight of the bourgeoisie under socialism. But there was a health service for the first time ever, free education, including entry to universities for those bright enough to pass exams, and the arts were getting some government money. For many these were additional reasons for hating the government. Labour had encouraged the BBC to bring in the Third Programme, which a small minority, including myself, listened to avidly. It kept up a constant stream of serious music and interesting lectures and talk programmes. A new class was developing because of the 1947 Education Act, which filled the universities with young undergraduates from working-class backgrounds, and this was to fuel the coming art scene of a decade later. Somerset Maugham was later to sum up what he thought of this new wave of state-educated intellectuals with a single word: 'Scum'.

I went frequently to the opera and to concerts. I thrilled to Llubja Welitsch's *Salome* in a notorious Peter Brook production with sets by Dali, I heard singers I had known from Zürich like Franz Lechleitner in Wagner operas, I heard Boris Christoff as *Boris Godunov* and my first *Peter Grimes* with Richard Lewis and Joan Cross. I heard my idol, Kirsten Flagstad, again in London, both that year and later, and Elizabeth Schwarzkopf in *The Magic Flute*. I was now keeping a record of performances, and I've kept this up ever since. At the time of writing this, I have recorded over three thousand opera performances and getting on to nine hundred different operas, and with advancing years have put down much more detail and comment. I am often consulted over who sang what on certain occasions, to settle arguments or assist other memories, but perhaps the biggest benefit is that my opera records help me to date other events with some precision. In the London theatre there was a constant diet of the three mainstays, Rattigan, Coward and Maugham, but French plays by Anouilh, Sartre and André Roussin were frequently performed in English, and there were more experimental theatres like the Watergate under the arches at Charing Cross, run by Tondi Barr and her husband, the Arts Theatre near Leicester Square and the Bolton's Theatre Club in Chelsea. The Festival Hall was not yet built and most concerts were at the Albert Hall where I was soon to hear Gigli for the last time in the Verdi *Requiem*. Life was exciting with constant new experiences, but also a constant turmoil since my wife was a target for every male who came our way. She also had no notion of keeping within any budget.

One such male suitor was Eric Turrell. Having let me a flat, he would hang around a great deal, mainly hoping to seduce Christya, but thankfully there was no incentive for her to yield to him. I presume she had yielded to Bob Wolf at some point before he went back to Hollywood. Eric Turrell now started to talk me into starting a publishing company, combining his experience and my money, and I eventually decided to risk five hundred pounds, quite a tidy sum in those days; most people lived on much less in a year. We started to plan a list and to look for manuscripts, but the company itself was not registered until the following year, nor did we have an office address until then. Manuscripts began to arrive and I read them. The first one we accepted was called *A Spy Has No Friends* by Ronald Seth, who may or may not have been a real spy; I always had my doubts.

I joined my father's old club, the Caledonian, that year, but used it infrequently because it was too close to home. It had a resident barber and I went most often when I needed a haircut. My uncle Rupert Dawson was a member and frequently there when in London, but he paid me little notice until later when I was publishing books of which he could disapprove. I had spent a few days in 1945 at Orchil and noticed on one occasion a handsome set of George Bernard Shaw's plays and writings locked in behind glass. I was not allowed the key because no one was allowed to read socialist literature in his house; unfortunately the books were a present, so he could not throw them out. In the club, like many of the other members, he cut a military figure, mixing principally with generals and other senior retired officers, and I found the atmosphere too blatantly right-wing for my taste. No subject that interested me ever came up in conversation and my personal views would have gone down badly. I also joined the fashionable Les Ambassadeurs, a club that was really a restaurant with a dance band in the basement, because the film crowd went and Christya wanted to be seen there. I was beginning to realise, however, that her film career as such was probably over, and that she probably had little acting talent. What she did exude was glamour and sexiness, something very different.

We met Baron, the fashionable photographer, who specialised in royalty, ballet, theatre and opera, as well as being available to photograph the glitterati of the day. I think Christya must have contacted him to be photographed, but I am sure I never paid him anything. We were invited to one or two of his lavish parties, but not to those where apparently refined orgies took place. He was a small, rather sinister, wizened man, and I always had the impression that he was involved in some murky business, perhaps blackmail. He seemed to know everyone's secrets and had ample opportunity to reveal them publicly. As I remember it, he either died suddenly and unexpectedly or was murdered. There was certainly some mystery about it all.

I came to know Carl Foreman well, famous in particular for having made *High Noon*, the quintessential western. He was one of the many American exiles who had been chased out of Hollywood by Senator Joe McCarthy, and I soon knew many more who had had to leave Hollywood or New York. One of them was Sigmund Miller, who became a lifelong friend, dying in 1998. He had been a radio writer, mainly of series like *The Creaky Door*, of thrillers and of some Hollywood films, but was now a film doctor, rewriting other people's scripts and dialogues, presumably to make them more commercial, and usually anonymously. Sigi was a bon viveur without any money. He had a wife and two small boys in London, a wandering eye for other women, and at some point Christya had picked him up, probably at Les Ambassadeurs. An entrepreneurial maker of low-budget films, much in evidence in these American circles just then, was Hannah Weinstein. The new television industry was greedy for product and she was making film series for television, both for British and American consumption: she was good at exploiting the talents of these new London Americans and finding cheap British actors for costume series such as *Robin Hood*. Although she was not overtly attractive and certainly not young, she emitted a strong sexual odour such as I have always found intriguing: had the opportune moment occurred I certainly would have taken advantage of it. There are some women that men of my kind cannot resist, whatever their scruples, because the invitation and the need is so blatantly obvious. She nearly employed Christya, but 'nearly' was becoming my wife's trademark. I realised in the end that she was really very frightened of putting anything other than her glamour to the test.

She went for a few acting lessons, but had never had any real experience other than screen tests and the production of *Ghosts* that I had seen in Montreal. After a few classes she came back and refused to go again, saying that if the teacher knew what she was talking about she would be acting, not teaching. She was always busy plotting, not only for her own career, which she had by now almost decided to let go, but for mine, especially trying to get me back into my grandfather's good books, making me write him a stream of letters. I saw him occasionally, but he never invited us to Ardargie, which was just as well, because my uptight grandmother would hardly have been welcoming.

New Year's Eve 1949-50 is worth recording because I gave my first London party that night, in my eighth floor flat in Lowndes Street. A French lady who worked for a family on the floor above helped with the arrangements which included a large bowl of French onion soup with which to end the party at four o'clock and mitigate the impact of the hangovers. I had invited my new London friends and had costumes for Charles Wrey-Gardiner, editor of *Poetry Review* and author of autobiographical novels considered very daring, to appear as the Old Year (a Father Time Costume) and Howard Sargeant, another poetry editor, who was to wear a diaper as the New Year. Among the guests were Muriel Spark and her boyfriend Derek Stanford. Muriel in those days was thirty-one, dowdy and overweight with frowsy red hair, a recognised poet, but living in considerable squalor with Derek, also bedraggled-looking and considerably older. Derek was a literary man-of-all-work, reviewer, translator, anthologist and poet. He was to be cruelly caricatured later in Muriel's novel *A Far Cry From Kensington*. I cannot remember who else was there. New Year's day was the beginning of the Age of Aquarius and as an Aquarian myself I took an interest, even though I would see little of an age which, according to the astrologers, would continue for five hundred years.

I had several meetings with my Uncle Jim, who out of the blue offered me a job with his timber company, and I took it, because I needed the money. In the first week of January 1950 I presented myself at Surrey Docks in Rotherhithe, a long ride by underground and a ten minute walk down Plough Way to the timber yard of Calders Ltd., a few hundred yards from the docks themselves. I was put first into the softwood department and within a short time realised that there was a civil war between the two yard managers. One was an affable but solidly Tory head of softwood timbers, which were used either for building work or for railway sleepers: these last had to be sawn into shape and then creosoted under pressure in special tanks, both for British Rail, recently nationalised, and for private companies with their own rail sidings. The other manager was a very pushy red-headed East-End Jew called James Vogel, who was the current wonder-boy of the firm, bringing in big profits with what was the firm's new undertaking, imported hardwoods to be sold to the furniture trade. Brierley, the softwood manager, gave me various jobs around the yard. I spent a day with the man who ran the kilns that dried the sleepers before creosoting. 'Waht (sic) do you like to do, Jack,' he asked (I had concealed my last name which was that of the firm, and John automatically became Jack in that working-class environment).

'I like to write,' I answered unguardedly.

'Alright,' he said. 'Here's a pencil and here's a note-pad. Now write down these numbers as I call them out.' I spent the day recording steam levels and temperatures and getting nastily damp in the hot steamy kilns while doing so. I should mention that it was a very cold January, either snowing or raining most of the time, and I was mostly out of doors, which was preferable to the wet heat of the kilns.

At lunch time I went most days to the nearest pub, The Plough, with Brierley, where Pat, the fat publican kept up a stream of banter and comment while sipping neat gin all day. When Wimbledon came round, the conversation was mainly about 'gorgeous Gussie', a tennis champion who wore particularly frilly tennis shorts, much played up by the tabloid press. Every round of drinks was greeted with 'Cheers, Pat,' 'Cheers, Jack,' 'Cheers' to whoever was in the circle. Then back to more hours in the yard, cold and damp outside, cosy and warm in the office when I could get there. I tried to keep on good terms with both the softwood and hardwood sides, and was eventually, having learned something of the first, shifted to hardwood. The activity here consisted mainly of turning imported African exotic woods, imported as logs, into boards, and as spring arrived I was learning the names and qualities of these woods. It was difficult to move across the lines of the civil war. When I was in one office I was treated as an enemy by the other, and as a possible spy wherever I went. Perhaps only Vogel knew who I was and why I was really there, and he went out of his way to be affable, inviting Christya and myself to dinner at home in his flat near Regent's Park, where everything glittered with novelty. Christya, recognising another upwardly mobile pusher from a similar background to her own, made it her business to get on with Jim Vogel and his wife Sheila. Vogel was a rough diamond and Sheila definitely felt that she was a class above her husband, but she appreciated his success and drive. She took many opportunities to remind him of her superior background and previous boyfriends' prominent cachets in the London Jewish world.

Little by little I was moved to the hardwood side of the Rotherhithe yard, spending much more time outside, tallying wood off the arriving ships a few hundred yards away, or measuring the planks as they were sawn in the big bandmill. 'You married, Jack?' the overweight elderly sawyer asked me. 'Yes,' I responded. I never volunteered much information about myself.

'Ever 'ave it orf on a Sunday aftahnoon with the blinds dahn?' he probed.

'Perhaps.' In fact I seldom spent a Sunday afternoon doing anything else.

'Mine's got 'her 'ole orl worn aht,' he went on, and further indiscreet revelations followed, typical working-class talk. I would try to change onto a subject like politics. A surprising number of the men were working-class Tories: to be known as one might give a man an advantage if he could become part of the salaried staff instead of an hourly wage worker with no security. Overtime on weekends might often give the casual workers more money, but staff expected to be kept on the pay-roll whatever the situation might be. Labourers were then earning about a pound a day with overtime, but seldom took home more than £5, even with weekend work. Tax was of course heavy on everyone then; the reconstruction of Britain and the new social services had to be paid for.

The local MP was Bob Mellish, a Labour warhorse, who I was later to learn had his corrupt side, but he was well enough liked down there, and was later to become Chief Labour whip and hold other government offices. The one thing I did not hide were my Labour sympathies. Brierley's assistant was a Labour supporter and we exchanged a smile every time Brierley would go on about how much better everything had been under the Tories before the war. The man who ran the kilns regularly went to meetings organised by the Workers Educational Association, and on two or three occasions I accompanied him to listen to unpaid lecturers educating those who wanted to know something about the world of learning by teaching history, literature and cultural studies. The WEA has long disappeared, but it was a splendid hangover from the nineteenth century when many working men would spend their evenings trying to educate themselves. The open university may perform a similar function today, but without the intimacy and comradeship that I felt existed at those WEA meetings. I do not believe that there was any objection to women sharing the classes, but I never saw any.

There was only one black man, a Jamaican, at the yard, and I felt sorry for him, although to my shame I never spoke to him. He was employed to paint the metal girders. No one ever spoke to him at all, but they all joked about him as if he had just come out of the jungle. He was bewildered when it snowed. 'What's this white rain,' he was quoted as saying. He must have been lonely and miserable like so many other black immigrants at that time.

I also attended in the evenings, always on my own because such things did not interest Christya, a number of poetry readings, mostly in South London. Dulwich was one such centre for poets and on one occasion, when Stephen Spender was reading his work, Roy Campbell, a well-known South African poet and avowed fascist, who had fought for Franco in Spain and later had a career there as a bull-fighter, climbed onto the platform, hit Spender hard with his fists, and with many more blows pushed everyone else off the platform. He then launched into a diatribe about 'all you pansies' and then began to read his own poems, ignoring the shouts and boos from the seventy or so sitting in the audience. I also went several times to the Black Horse public house in Rathbone Place in Northern Soho, where poets such as John Heath-Stubbs, tweed-suited and nearly blind, would recite from memory. Dylan Thomas would often appear. Many volumes of poetry were lost in that pub when Thomas began to declaim! By the third pint he was well underway and line after line, metre after metre, would roll out from his organ voice, extemporaneous verse that flowed endlessly and effortlessly out of his mouth and throughout the pub, terminating all conversations. He could go on for hours, and to my ears it seemed like perfect and resonant poetry of great beauty. You strained to catch every word and think about it, but could not. Not a line was ever written down and remembered. It just came out of him, and the more he drank the better it sounded. I was privileged to be there, but what a terrible waste! I also met and heard him at the Wheatsheaf and other pubs where poets met. Among others I remember were George Barker and David Gascoyne, but at every such gathering there were many poets and their admirers, and of course I was drinking like everyone else, so much of it is only a blur now.

My admiration for Dylan Thomas in particular has never diminished from among the many poets I met in those days. I bought and read with love and envy his published work, and my appreciation of it has never changed. That was in 1950 and perhaps later as well, but within three years he would be dead. When, in 1953, I heard the BBC broadcast of *Under Milk Wood*, those evenings in the Black Horse came back vividly. I never met him anywhere other than in pubs, where only closing time could stop that voice that could easily have gone on for hours more, fuelled by many pints.

It was at this time that I first met T.S. Eliot. I forget who brought me to the Author's Club, just off Whitehall, but I was introduced to him there and on three occasions had long chats with him, usually at tea time. He obviously appreciated my great admiration of his poetry, which I could quote by the yard, and he was willing to give me glimmers of information about a few passages that puzzled me, but I can no longer recall exactly what they were, mostly in *The Waste Land* and the *Four Quartets* as I remember. On one occasion he invited me to lunch with him the following week and I hastily cancelled some other appointment to accept. I told him that I was a poet myself and he invited me to send some poetry to Faber, which I eventually did, as I shall relate later. Eliot was very kind. His interest in a young poet, at the time heavily influenced by him, was genuine I think, and he asked me many questions, advising me to do what he had done himself, to keep another occupation to ensure a reasonable living. The poetry will always come when it is ready, he said.

As the winter of 1950 drew to an end I was moved to the head office of Calders Ltd. on Lower Regent Street. Eros House overlooked Piccadilly Circus from the south-western side of the street and I was put to learn about the accounts under Bill Battson, the friendly and very competent company secretary, and his assistant Peggy. Here above all I practised mental arithmetic as no one could later do. I sat at a desk with big ledgers of around sixty lines to the page and added up the columns of pounds, shillings and pence. First the right hand column, coming to so many hundreds of pence, which then, divided by twelve were carried to the next column, less the left-over pence, and this column was added up and divided by twenty in the same way to find the number of pounds. There were no calculators in those days and I had to add up each column five or six times to be sure the result was right. Thus did the clerks in the offices and counting houses of Dickens' time do their work. To make this dull task more interesting I would make little bets with myself as to the eventual outcome. Next to me sat Charlie Thompson, a stout Scotsman in his sixties who had been doing this for decades as well as other clerical work. The general office had a door into my uncle's office. He frequently opened it and called to Charlie to come in to explain some shipping document or statistic, often compiled by me.

I got on well with Battson, an intelligent and genial man who well understood the complicated politics of the firm and the personality battles and feuds between the directors. Three of them considered themselves to be gentlemen and the others not to be. The deputy-chairman was called Kirkup, a Northumbrian country landowner who hunted in the winter months: we had acquired his Newcastle timber firm and he had every expectation of succeeding my uncle, then eighty-two, in the near future. The financial director was called Billington, an outside accountant whose firm was responsible for the audit. He was blind and always accompanied by a young clerk from his firm; he understood nothing about the business, was always critical of the accounts and especially of Battson who compiled them, and he too saw himself as the next chairman. The third came from the same Scottish background as my uncle: his name was Gordon Hutchison and he was a mildly alcoholic, suave and red-raced individual, much under the influence of Philip Rann, about whom more later. Hutchinson's function was to take government officials, especially those from the nationalised industries with which we had extensive dealings, out to meals and to corrupt them, which he was extremely good at doing. The roughest diamond on the board was called Ashley, who ran the profitable pole and sleeper yard at Boston-on-the-Wash, the yard where my father had worked before the war. He revered my great-uncle, kept to himself in Lincolnshire, and came to London only for board meetings, staying out of the rivalries and leaving it to Philip Rann, whose office was in Eros House, to acquire the poles and sleepers from abroad that he dressed and creosoted. He was also responsible for a smaller timber yard that dealt in home-grown timber at Brandon in Suffolk, but he interfered very little with Jack Knight, its manager. William Ashley was from the provincial lower middle-classes, self-educated, with no interests outside his own area of work and management, but with the shrewdness and ability to judge character that one finds in similar persons as described by Dickens and Balzac, and he lived a life of unvarying routine. He never drank more than half a pint of mild and bitter, was church-going and practical, having worked his way up through hard work and competence. He was to be my next mentor at work. And then there were the two tough directors, Rann and Vogel, who were in effect joint managing-directors. The principal rivalry was between them: Rann was in charge of softwood imports with a general control over the yards that treated the timbers he brought into the country; he had been with the company since the thirties, while Jim Vogel, the most recent director, was now making big profits through imported hardwoods, a new activity for Calders Ltd. They sparred around each other, each trying to get more of my uncle's attention and support for their candidacy as managing-director. Perhaps they were *de facto* managing directors in name as well, but with power only over their immediate sectors. There was one other non-working director, Harry Watson, who had been married to the daughter of another timber merchant, whose firm had been acquired after the war. Once called Grandidge in Birkenhead, it was now another Calder pole and sleeper yard; Harry Watson, a blunt Lancastrian, seemed to have come with the purchase.

There were many branches of Calders Ltd. and little by little I was to learn about them all. They were situated at Bo'ness, Port Talbot, Rotherhithe, Boston, Birkenhead, Scunthorpe and Newcastle-on-Tyne, all ports where the timber imports arrived, and in addition there were a number of small yards inland which processed home-grown timbers for pit props, fencing, building and furniture, some attached administratively to a larger yard, some on their own, such as Aviemore in the Scottish Highlands. I was cautiously wooed by Rann and Vogel, more by the latter, because the first saw me as a future threat, and Vogel badly needed an ally. My uncle had obviously intended me for rapid promotion if I showed myself worthy of it, but my heart was still in literature, and aside from my own poetry, I was now running a small publishing company with Eric Turrell, who worked partly from home and, once I had moved into my next address, partly from the basement room I rented underneath it.

It was Philip Frere, the solicitor with whom Christya and I dined occasionally at his house in Mayfair, who found me the large and imposing flat at 2 Wilton Terrace on the north-west corner of Belgrave Square. His interest was in Christya of course, but he had to tolerate my presence and he was mildly amused by it. The flat ran across the first floor of two large houses which constituted a short block and had two large drawing rooms, separated by large gilded double-doors, a large master bedroom looking onto the Terrace and Belgrave Square, as did the front drawing-room and a dressing-room which I used as a study; there were also a large dining-room and two smaller bedrooms, as well as a kitchen, two bathrooms and a considerable amount of hall space. There could not have been a greater contrast to where my grandfather suggested I should look, which was Barnet on the extreme north of the city suburbs. When he came to visit me, however, he was impressed and said nothing, and my uncle also enjoyed going there. He had himself had a socially ambitious wife, my great-aunt Mildred who enjoyed her title and had made him in the twenties acquire a house in Park Lane, as well as a country house in Norfolk. In those pre-war days Ledlanet in Scotland was only used as a shooting lodge for the grouse season. So my uncle understood all about extravagant wives and mine was flamboyant as well. Philip Frere had heavily invested in property all over London. At this point he was just retiring from Frere Cholmely, his very well-known and established old firm, where he obviously did not get on with his staider partners, in order to run a small but obviously profitable practice from his Mayfair house, where a Hungarian partner, versed in international deals, also worked. That the whole set-up was in some ways shady was soon apparent, even to my untrained eye, but Frere, tall and handsome in his sixties, was a consummately smooth English gentleman, well-educated, well-read, and with excellent taste in everything from food and wine to the decoration of his flat. He was a director of many public companies and Chairman of the Guardian Assurance Company. His wife, now estranged, had been a lady-in-waiting to Queen Mary, mother of the then present king, George VI. He could get away with anything.

I no longer remember how much rent I paid. It was considerable, but I am sure low for the place I had rented, and I managed to furnish it in suitable style. Philip Frere once invited us to a day at Ascot, which consisted of spending much of it lunching in a private dining-room, occasionally going out onto a balcony to watch a race, and general conversation. We did not go into the Royal Enclosure. It was one of only two days I ever spent at the races, but my presence at other sporting events was no more extensive.

After a spell at head office, with many days spent back at Rotherhithe where I was now usually asked to compile statistics, I was sent to Boston to learn from Ashley. This meant living in a hotel at Boston Spa and driving every day to the yard. Christya was hardly ever there and I would return to London on weekends. I learned about the treatment of telegraph poles, mainly watching the work and tallying numbers. I spent time with the assistant manager, calling on customers and meeting suppliers of machinery and other necessities, and I also spent time with a salesman called Reggie Graves with whom I got on well, but whose sales techniques I was sure I could improve upon. I noticed his extreme nervousness before each appointment, sitting still for a moment in the car to order his thoughts and screw his courage up for the coming encounter, made no easier, I am sure, by having to drag me along with him. So passed the summer of 1950.

In the autumn I was back at Eros House, but was sent out for half of the week to learn about making boxes at the factory at Peasmarch, near Guildford. There I watched the construction of beer crates, mineral water crates, ammunition boxes for the army and various other wooden containers. Most of it was done on an assembly line, but some special orders were knocked together by hand. This was part of Philip Rann's empire and he came down about once a fortnight, had a long boozy lunch with the manager, greeted me briefly if he saw me, and returned to London. Again my time was largely spent compiling statistics as I had to do something other than just watch, but I also now started writing some advertising and promotional copy. That was the winter of 1950-51, during which I was often sent out by Vogel to sell in London's East End to furniture-makers. This community was almost exclusively Jewish and as an obvious goy, there to be taken advantage of, I encountered many difficulties and had to work out ways to counter the impulse to cheat me. The buyers made constant mischievous complaints about the quality and the quantity of the hardwood that arrived, trying to get the invoice reduced, which Vogel then had to sort out. In spite of the difficulties I did reasonably well, and I was also selling to builders, mainly joists and scaffold boards. I was never quite sure whether Vogel saw his interest in discrediting me with my uncle, as Rann would have liked to do, or in binding me to him as an ally, perhaps a bit of both. He was still the only director I saw socially, except for Ashley during my time in Boston, and then not often. Ashley was certainly not a stimulating conversationalist. I remember him showing me a long-past wedding present from my uncle, a set of silver-plated cutlery in a fitted box. It was heavily tarnished and had never been used.

The publishing company, John Calder (Publishers) Ltd., was started in 1949, but only registered in July 1950. It had accepted a number of books, of which I have earlier mentioned two. One day Eric Turrell handed me a manuscript whose title I forget, about the current London scene. Reading it I realised that the author could only be Eric himself. He had given it to me saying only, 'This came in. I thought it rather good. What do you think?' Not only was the hero an amalgam of Eric himself and other recognisable members of his circle, but there was an accurate portrait of his current girl-friend, while incidents related were very close to the amorous problems of Eric's friends. There was a heavily disguised picture of myself and Christya.

'Eric,' I said the next day, 'the novel's not bad, but how would you react if I suggested publishing my own poetry? We can't start a publishing company by publishing ourselves.'

He swore that he had not written it, but very unconvincingly, and in the ensuing quarrel said that he would not stay unless he had editorial control. Just then I was seeing a little of Howard Sargeant, publisher and editor of a reputable poetry magazine and, largely at the bidding of Christya, suggested that he might like to join us. There was a board meeting with a formal agenda I had drawn up and Eric supported the idea of bringing Howard on board, but he still wanted editorial control. In the end he resigned and Howard warily declined as well. Two publishers whom I had met were then consulted. One was George Weidenfeld, then living at Eaton Place. He was mainly interested in getting my uncle to put money into some Israeli venture of his, but I could certainly make no promise there. He had recently been a secretary-advisor to Chaim Weizmann, President of Israel, and was heavily involved in Israeli politics. He had teamed up with Nigel Nicolson, an establishment figure and son of Sir Harold, the diplomat and author, and of Victoria Sackville-West: Weidenfeld and Nicolson were beginning to become known. I remember George waving his arms around in his living room as he told me he was thinking of making 'a Victorian-Edwardian marriage', by which he meant that he was hoping to marry the daughter of Marcus Sieff of Marks and Spencer with whom he had already negotiated a deal to produce popular classics for their chain stores under the imprint Contact Books. It was obviously money, not love, which was the incentive and the marriage did take place, but was eventually dissolved.

The other publisher was André Deutsch. André had been sales manager of a technical publishing house, Ernest Benn, which among other things published the trade journal of the timber trade in which I was otherwise engaged. He had started Alan Wingate Ltd. some two years earlier with a number of other directors, one of whom was the son of Sir Philip Gibb, the historian. I had a meeting with Anthony Gibb, an English gentleman of the old school and quickly came to the conclusion that he didn't like foreigners, especially Jews. André was a Hungarian Jew. As more investors were introduced into Alan Wingate, all with directorships, most of them in the same mould as Gibb, André's position in the company he had founded became ever more untenable and eventually he had to leave. Then he raised funds, largely through the agency of the publishing solicitor Stanley Rubinstein, and started André Deutsch Ltd., just at the time when Eric Turrell and I were breaking up.

We made a deal and he moved into my basement. He would have free rent in return for being the caretaker of my fledgling publishing company and we agreed to share a secretary. This was at the time when my days were spent at Eros House or at Rotherhithe. I would tear back in the late afternoon to get some letters out and deal with business matters, but André was not very co-operative. Stella, our joint secretary, was always loaded up with his work and everything she did for him was urgent, while my affairs could wait. André had also developed a crush on Christya which she did not encourage and she treated him insensitively. When, after a few months, he left, it was with more insults directed towards her than me.

He did, however, prosper. Both he and Weidenfeld, as well as some other publishers who had arrived in Britain in the thirties as refugees, were able to use their knowledge of German to get books for translation from old Nazis, which had a ready sale. Deutsch's great *coup* was in publishing the memoirs of Von Papen, Hitler's foreign minister, and selling serial rights for a large amount to a Sunday newspaper. By publishing books by prominent new German politicians he made himself well-known in Germany, so he had first refusal on potentially best-selling titles.

I then met Neville Armstrong, one of three partners in the small and very new publishing company, Peter Neville. Neville Armstrong and Peter Owen had put their first names together to form the imprint; the other partner was Malcolm Kirk, an accountant, who looked after the financial side. Armstrong and Peter Owen had recently fallen out as happens more often than not in publishing, and the former had started Neville Spearman Ltd. Neville's background was in the theatre (he had been a theatre manager and he looked very much like one) and at about this time he had rented the Bolton's Theatre Club, a small theatre in Chelsea where he was mounting a season of modern drama with Basil Ashbourne as his artistic director. I went there to see Henry James' play *Guy Domville* with that fine actor Hugh Burdon, later to play Vladimir in *Waiting for Godot*, in the cast, and this was to be followed by *Dulcinée* by André Obey. Hoping to attract some money from me to channel into his theatre, he proposed casting Christya in the main part. There were negotiations but for reasons that have escaped my memory, probably difficulties brought about by her, this never happened, although at one point she was certainly attending rehearsals. But Armstrong also made me a publishing proposal, which I considerably modified, whereby we could publish a joint list under a joint imprint, and this became Spearman and Calder, not a limited company, but a partnership of two existing companies to publish a number of books together.

It was Neville Armstrong who then brought me a number of unpublished translations from the Russian made by April FitzLyon and her husband Kyril, whose real name was Zinovieff. I met this extraordinary couple, he a white Russian aristocrat who worked at the Foreign Office, she a trained musician who had never entered the profession, but had learned Russian from his mother and spoke several other languages. I was to retain a friendly contact with them until April's death in 1999. At the time of writing he is still alive.

The first joint lists of Spearman and Calder contained the FitzLyon's joint translations of Tolstoy's first and last short novels, *Family Happiness* and

The Devil, April's translation of a collection of previously untranslated Chekhov short stories, *The Woman in the Case*, and shortly afterwards Kyril's English rendering of Dostoevsky's *Summer Impressions*, the last in a particularly elegant edition with a cover design and illustrations by Philippe Jullien. They were well reviewed by Desmond McCarthy in the Sunday Times and went through several impressions. Spearman was not involved in the last, because by then we had broken up. Among the other, rather bizarre, volumes that appeared under the joint imprint were books Armstrong had acquired, where I agreed to take my share of the risk in order to fill up the catalogue. There was a book on beer cookery and another on crocheting and needlework, both of which did fairly well. Titles that Armstrong found and thought the most commercially viable he kept to himself. We also, and this was our very first joint title, published a totally unexpurgated edition of *The Satyricon* of Petronius in English, which was both risqué and risky. Other editions had left the most erotic passages in Latin.

Armstrong took on the responsibility for distribution while I did most of the editorial work. The stock was housed with a trade distributor. My arrangement was that Armstrong would get most of the production money out first, but I would get more of the profit if the books did well, which they usually did. I forget exactly why we separated – there were many disagreements, most of them about money and the agreed division of it – but when we did I made a deal with Arco Publications, run by a rather shady East End cockney called Bernard Hannison, soon to give up publishing for property speculation, to which he was probably better suited.

I was living different and parallel lives, but I seemed to have time for everything, although somewhere in the late winter of 1950 I had a bad bout of yellow jaundice, which kept me for at least two weeks in bed. It was also during that January that I decided to give up smoking. I did it by forcing myself not to smoke during the day (in those days smoking in the office was not allowed, and it would have been dangerous in a timber yard), and in the evening I put severe restraints on the conditions under which I would smoke. For one week it was only while sitting on the side of the bath, which was boring, so the cigarette was quickly extinguished. During the second week I made myself go down into the street and smoke there. It was a cold January, so that too was short-lived. The third week I picked a spot some two hundred yards away where I would allow myself to smoke out on a cold corner and the discomfort quickly put paid to that. The fourth week I went to stay with my grandfather at Ardargie, where no one was allowed to smoke. After that the habit was gone, although for at least a year I still dreamed about smoking.

There was always time for holidays. I would go shooting at Ledlanet during the grouse season for a week. The first time, I remember a particularly hot and gruelling day, up and down steep hills in the heather – my uncle at that point only went out for the mornings and left after the picnic lunch – and by the late afternoon I was puffing badly. I overheard one of the guns say to his neighbour, 'Young Calder looks a bit tired.'

'Fucked out, poor chap,' said the other. 'What do you expect with a wife like that?' Christya was staying too and she looked very different from the other wives in the house-party, who took care not to associate with her any more than was necessary.

I managed to go skiing at Val d'Isère with Jacques Chaix, which soon became an annual ritual, and that same year, in the summer of 1950, to go to Italy, travelling around the north in a hired Topolino, which culminated in a strange week in Rapallo. There, Christya refused to stay in the small hotel we had booked and moved to the grandest, a palatial establishment overlooking the town and bay. After two days we had to move to another floor because King Farouk of Egypt had arrived with his yacht and his entourage. They took over a whole floor of the hotel and would feast all night and sleep all day. Egyptian guards with sub-machine guns patrolled the corridors. That August we also went to the Edinburgh Festival for the first time. We saw Glyndebourne perform *Ariadne auf Naxos* and *The Marriage of Figaro* at the King's Theatre. It was an unforgettable performance of the first version of *Ariadne*, conducted by Sir Thomas Beacham, where the opera was set into a shortened version of Molière's play, *Le Bourgeois Gentilhomme* with the appropriate accompanying orchestral music, and Miles Malleson in the lead. My grandfather then offered me an old Vauxhall car if I would pick it up in Alloa. Although constantly breaking down, it was useful at the festival and afterwards I drove it to London, stopping at Newcastle and Doncaster overnight on the way. It looked very out of place among the Bentleys and Sunbeam-Talbots of Belgrave Square, but it meant that I could often drive to Rotherhithe instead of taking the tube.

In 1952, or it may have been earlier, I met a man called Sinclair, who answered an advertisement I had placed looking for a partner in publishing, or it may just have been for someone to carry out certain essential services for me. I forget if money was the main reason for the advert, but I remember having several telephone conversations at the time with possible investors. Sinclair turned out to have a half interest in a printing press at 22 Cross Street in Islington, in which his principal partner was a publisher of rather fundamentalist religious books called Parry Jackman. Jackman was very Welsh, very smooth in his own way and certainly not very honest. He was an artist of sorts and employed other artists to illustrate some of his books and others which he packaged, and at some point in our negotiations he persuaded me to produce a children's book on the lives of some popular saints with coloured illustrations in the manner of a children's bible. This later appeared in 1957 under the imprint of Acorn Press, a small publisher of children's books, which I acquired somewhere in the middle fifties. Jackman was a member of the author's club where I had met T. S. Eliot, whom I occasionally saw again when Jackman brought me. Jackman used the club above all to impress Americans who published books he produced for them to sell in the bible belt. I discovered that one of his ploys was to go to religious lectures, tape them secretly, and then produce a book without notifying the lecturer that he was using his work. Such is the nature of that particular fraternity that he could usually rely, when found out, on the author's vanity having been satisfied, and would offer copies of the book in compensation. My negotiations with Sinclair involved me with the two of them, and at the end I acquired a printing press, because of my association with them -- one more activity in addition to those I was already engaged in, and soon one more worry..

I then found myself dealing with sellers of second-hand printing machinery, paper merchants and, of course, the printing unions. And I had to keep the presses busy, not just by printing for myself. In fact I printed very few books that I was publishing and mainly did work for other clients. I think it was through Baron, the photographer, that I met Richard Buckle, a ballet critic, who wrote for The Observer and edited Ballet Magazine, and I acquired the contract to print it monthly. One of its backers was the Earl of Harewood, who having started to contribute an opera column to Ballet, then started Opera Magazine as a sister publication in 1950, employing Harold Rosental as assistant editor, although in practice it was Rosenthal who did nearly all the work. He was then the archivist of the Royal Opera House. So I had to make sure that the two magazines were produced by the end of every month, and soon I also had a contract to print for the British Film Institute: this included their bulletins and the monthly magazine Sight and Sound. I found a manager, but was myself frequently in the plant which ran between Cross Street and the street immediately north of it, just off Upper Street. When there was a dispute between the machine minders and the compositors, due to one of the workers having an affair with the wife of another belonging to a different union, the compositors were not allowed by the machine minders to pass through their part of the premises to get to the lavatory. This meant that they had to go out into the street and walk about two hundred yards to go round the corner into the next street and come in by the back door to use the facility and then return the same way, a considerable loss of time, made worse in winter or wet weather by having to put on extra clothing for the trip. Eventually I sold part of the company to a young man who ended up buying me out.

But the contact with Buckle and Harewood, and also Rosenthal, had further consequences. Richard Buckle, very public school in manner and a Captain of a good regiment during the war, was very good at getting money out of backers. Extremely gay, to employ a word not in use then, he had an entourage of other gays, mostly fairly well-off, whom he exploited in many ways, some of them working for him for next to nothing, others financing his magazine and other projects. Harewood was not gay, but he too was much manipulated by Buckle. When Harewood later became Director of the

Edinburgh Festival, he commissioned Richard Buckle to mount a massive exhibition around the work and career of Diaghilev, which later transferred to Forbes House in London. Buckle then tried to get money out of me to keep Ballet going. I had been more than tolerant about his long overdue printing bills, and I knew that he still owed money to his previous printer. Harewood felt that he had already done enough for Ballet and was in any case now only interested in his own magazine. I tried to work out a business plan to put Ballet into the black, which would mean reaching an accommodation with past creditors or other backers to clean up the past mess and allow there to be a future. One problem I think, and I was not the only one to think it, was that Buckle's expensive life-style was the largest overhead item. When I finally made it clear that I could only help if past creditors could somehow be satisfied, Buckle became abusive. In his autobiography he comments acidly: 'Well, there it was: Calder would not sign an agreement with us while we owed two or three thousand pounds. I suppose it was unreasonable of me to wonder why he should not fork out this sum in cash. It appears that he had not the ready money. Rich people never have.'

I was not above doing some exploiting myself, and I talked Lord Harewood, with whom I was by then on first name terms, into becoming Chairman of a company I set up to distribute abroad what was printed in Britain, which was called British Print and Export Ltd. Its exact function, I now forget, but at any rate, it never got off the ground. I left printing and concentrated on my two main activities, timber and publishing. I became very friendly with Harold Rosenthal, the archivist of the Royal Opera House, who having earlier constantly bothered the management with questions that only an archivist could answer, ended up being given the job. I saw him frequently in connection with Opera magazine. One day I suggested to him that I would like to publish an *Opera Annual* and he enthusiastically agreed to edit it. We planned a large-format glossy album to come out every year before Christmas, something that would be both an informative book to read, carrying reviews of the opera year in different countries, with features on operatic personalities and events, and with news and opinions, that would also be a reference book with details of forthcoming seasons, premières, debuts and deaths. It was to be filled with high-quality illustrations.

The first *Opera Annual* appeared in late 1954, just after the opening of the Covent Garden season. What caused its success more than any other factor was Lord Harewood's name on the front cover. He had written a two-page introduction and that sold it. Lord Harewood was much in the news at that time. He was first cousin to the Queen and high up in the line of those who could succeed her if a series of accidents or assassinations should wipe out the monarch and her closest relatives. His mother was the Princess Royal, who had married the sixth Earl, his father. The Lascelles family have been Yorkshire aristocrats for hundreds of years, and had acquired much wealth two centuries back from the slave trade, which I think Lord Harewood does not like to talk about. His tastes were very different from those of his forbears and class in general, all interested in hunting, sport and country pursuits, not music and culture. Taken prisoner during the war (he was a Captain in the Grenadier Guards at the time), he was given VIP treatment in the prison camp and allowed to receive, having requested it from his family, a complete edition of *Grove's Dictionary of Music and Musicians*, which he read all the way through. He was married to a commoner with a musical pedigree, Marion Stein, daughter of the noted musicologist Erwin Stein, much associated with Schönberg; Marion was a concert pianist, but since her marriage she no longer performed in public. My later friend, Arthur Boyars, who had been at school with her, told me that at age thirteen or thereabouts the class had been asked to write an essay on 'My Ambition' and hers had been to marry a member of the British aristocracy. She had certainly succeeded!

Harewood had become a director of the Royal Opera House, Covent Garden, in 1951 and he joined the staff in 1953. He was a prominent member of the circle around Benjamin Britten, and suggested, during the time arrangements were being made for the coronation of Queen Elizabeth II in 1952, that an opera might be commissioned from Britten, recognised as one of the leading younger composers, although he was under a cloud for having spent the war in America. The suggestion was taken up and Britten wrote *Gloriana* for the occasion, based on the life of the first Queen Elizabeth, depicting her in an unfortunately unflattering light. The libretto was by William Plomer, based on the iconoclastic book *Elizabeth and Essex*, by Lytton Strachey, whose speciality was debunking the reputations of nationally admired heroes and heroines, and both composer and librettist should have realised that they were on dangerous ground. The Queen was certainly not pleased, and court circles, attending the opera, found it offensive and did not much like the music either, not a surprise as few members would have been opera-goers in any case. The occasion was a fiasco, mocked by the tabloid press, and Harewood was *persona non grata* for a considerable time at the Palace. He was however newsworthy and his name made the *Opera Annual* a great success.

One incident involving Harewood sticks in my memory. I went to a concert at the Royal Albert Hall and a few seats before me was the diminutive figure of Erwin Stein, Harewood's father-in-law. One obviously German-Jewish lady just behind his group commented to another, 'Da geht Herr Stein.' Her friend replied, 'Nein, Herr Königstein,' suggesting that he saw himself as the ancestor of future kings.[3]

At the turn of the century the *Opera Annual* still reads well and is useful for reference. The frontispiece of the first number, showing Mattiwilda Dobbs and Howell Glynne in *Coq d'Or* at Covent Garden which opened the

---

[3] 'There goes Herr Stein (Stone).' 'No, Herr Kingstone.'

season, brings back vivid memories, as do the other photographs, one showing the same Dobbs, a black American coloratura, in *Ariadne auf Naxos* the previous summer, but this time without the play, at Glyndebourne; with her is Dorothy Dow, Sena Juninac and a marvellous cast. I gave a party at Wilton Terrace for the publication and many of the stars of the current season at Covent Garden came, as well as conductors and senior staff. Harewood made a little speech; Sir David Webster, the administrator, was more than friendly and promised to sell the Opera Annual in the opera house. It was soon doing well in all the bookshops, which now began to treat me as a serious publisher.

I was also publishing other books on music. There was a fine June day in 1953 when I remember having to lunch at home a large group that included my old school mentor George Hurst, now an established conductor, Lord Harewood, Peter Ustinov, some actress from Hollywood, and one or two others. Peter Ustinov was not the only wit, and conversation flowed easily, but I was a little worried about time because I had tickets to Glyndebourne: it was my first visit, and I intended to drive there after lunch. It turned out to be a real rush, the roads being very slow in those years, but Christya and I arrived just in time. It was the same *Ariadne*, in the two act version, that I mentioned above.

There was a plump, gentle and very friendly gentleman sitting in the row in front of us. We were, as is obligatory at Glyndebourne, all in evening dress, and Christya always dressed to be noticed. He had taken one look at her, turned around before the opera began to get into conversation, and glued himself to us in the interval. He showed us around the garden and lily pond and kept up an animated conversation. When he heard I was a publisher, he became interested in me as well as my wife. He was Edward Lockspeiser, a musicologist specialising in French music, in Debussy in particular, about whom he was writing a two volume biography. He was also a music critic with an ambition to become a conductor, which was rather late in the day for a man of forty-eight. He drove back to London with us and became a friend who was soon putting up ideas for books on musical subjects. He suggested that I might translate Hans Redlich's pioneering book on Alban Berg, announced but not yet published by Universal Verlag in Vienna, who owned all Berg rights. The author was living in London. I met him, agreed to publish his own translation, which required some heavy revision of the author's Germanic English, and it appeared in 1957, not long after the original German edition. Through it I became a devotee of the music of Alban Berg, as of his teacher Schönberg and co-pupil Anton von Webern. It was the first book on Berg to appear in English. Edward Lockspeiser then suggested that I should commission from him an anthology of writings by French musical figures, which eventually appeared as *The Musical Clef* in 1958, the same year that I published the first book to appear in English on Francis Poulenc, which Lockspeiser translated himself, editing it heavily and dehagyographing it from the French biography of Henri Hell. Over many years, until his death in 1973, he remained a friend. His advice and contacts in those early years were a considerable help to me as I developed a list of books on music, which was in any case one of my greatest pleasures, and I learned much from Edward and from others to whom he introduced me in ways that widened my knowledge and tastes. It has been a privilege to be able to combine a hobby with a profession, and it has kept me in touch with music and musicians.

I think it was John Barnard who told me about this time that Dr Dembitzer, who was in fact a Baron, had been arrested by the FBI in New York. Apparently he was the Secretary of an international passport ring that forged British, American and Canadian passports, for those trying to leave Europe, a lucrative activity. I remembered the evening of my first *Götterdämmerung* and introduction to Flagstad. Some time later I heard that he had been released from prison because he had brokered a deal with the U.S. government, no doubt to help the CIA with some information. I heard no more of him after that, but remember him still as a man of wide culture and great charm who had once been very kind to me.

In retrospect it is a mystery how I managed to do so many things, largely unrelated to each other, and still not only keep a full-time job with Calders Ltd., but even to do well at it. Christya meddled in everything, and her fondness for intrigue – her Becky Sharp factor as I often thought of it – never made things easy and often caused me embarrassment and serious problems. Her mother suddenly showed up in London and expected to move in with us and be supported by us, that is by me. There were rows in public and in private until she moved into a hotel, keeping up a campaign of molestation from there until I had to apply for a court order to stop her, after which she returned to New York.

Once I was telephoned by Christya at the office and told that there had been a burglary at Wilton Terrace; all her jewellery was stolen. I went home and found that she had already called the insurance company and the assessor was present. She had given an exaggerated account of the jewellery she possessed, which had been listed at excessive values, and I could see that the assessor was very sceptical. Two days later, hunting around the flat, I found a cache of the missing items in the place where she had hidden them. The only thing missing was a pair of emerald earrings I had bought her once in Edinburgh during the festival. Before she knew of my find I telephoned the insurance company and told them the jewellery had been mislaid and I had found it. She was furious when she knew and the row went on for weeks, but I was not going to be party to a fraud. The emerald earrings, she finally admitted, she had given to her mother to sell in New York. I never bought her any jewellery after that.

At about this time Christya was opening various accounts with department stores, which I did my best to limit or cancel. She never had the slightest intention of paying for anything and, unsurprisingly, there were always creditors at the door or on the telephone. In the U.S. she had used her sex-appeal either to get men to pay her bills or to avoid payment, but at that time she had been more mobile than was possible living with me in London. I needed to be constantly ingenious in order to outwit her and to put a stop to the accumulation of quite unnecessary debt poisoning my life.

She became pregnant and in March 1952 produced a son. The birth was premature and Michael Hemans, the gynaecologist, performed a Caesarean operation, perhaps unnecessarily. He too was emotionally involved with her and I am sure his judgement was affected. The birth took place in a private nursing home in Marylebone and the boy was to be called James in line with family tradition. Hemans and his colleagues went off to the Saville Club to celebrate the evening immediately after delivery and the new-born, premature baby was left in the care of an inexperienced trainee nurse, who apparently left alone all night, was dressing and undressing it as if it were a doll. In the morning the boy was blue in the face and put into an incubator, but it was too late and he died after a few hours. The lungs had hardened and the baby was unable to breathe. My grief was great, but I had to overcome it and as Christya herself was in danger then, it was important to hide the news from her for some days. She could not understand why she could not see her child and I had to invent little stories to reassure her. I arranged the funeral and a few days after the birth I went alone to Golders Green Cemetery for the burial. Two hours later I was in the Harley Street Nursing home inventing stories about the baby. I think it was on the night the baby died, but it might have been the night of the funeral, that I bought a bottle of whisky, went home and drank all of it until I passed out.

I had sent my grandfather a telegram on the night of the birth and the next morning came the congratulatory reply. Whatever my past sins, they were forgiven. He was supremely happy that there was now a male Calder to carry on the name for another generation. I had been trying to persuade him to release a capital sum that was mine, but needed his agreement and signature, and for months he had delayed doing this. The telegram ended by saying that of course he would now agree to what I wanted. After the baby died I waited two or three days and then sent him a letter explaining what had happened. There was no reply to this. Within a month I wrote him again about the trust fund that he had agreed to break up so that I could have access to the capital. I received a cold reply, some considerable time later, saying that he had changed his mind.

By early 1951 I had been all over the main branches of Calders Ltd, had learned about hardwood and softwoods at Rotherhithe, been to the big pole and sleeper yard at Boston, the box factory at Peasmarsh, and learned the essentials of the home-grown sleeper trade at Brandon and Aviemore. An old sawyer at Aviemore pinned me down with a beady eye one day and said, 'So, you're another Calder. I knew your great grandfather. He always wanted to cut the wages. He said the firm was losing money. "Well, Mr. Calder," I said to him, "to my certain knowledge you've been losing money this many a year. You must have had an awful lot to start off with."' I was now ready to be given my first big responsibility, my own timber yard to manage, but not just yet. It was to be Birkenhead.

A second cousin of mine, Andy MacDonald, had been running Birkenhead for some years. Bought shortly after the war, Grandidges Ltd. had belonged to a Merseyside family of that name, and was now part of Calders Ltd. My cousin Andy had not been a successful manager. He was a Highland gentleman with a barely concealed grudge against the Calders who had taken over (robbed him of, I am sure he said in private) his family distillery, MacDonald Greenlees, which produced a famous malt, Sandy Mac. He lacked any commercial flair and had no idea of how to invest his time or money on anything other than a country estate. A great deal of capital was invested in the Birkenhead yard and it constantly lost money or barely broke even. I went to see the place, was shown around by Andy, who pointed out problems that to my mind seemed very easily soluble; they were not problems at the other yards where I had worked.

The reason I was to be given Birkenhead was obviously because the directors expected that I would do no better than my cousin and thereby blot my copybook with my uncle. To have a young man with the name of the firm learning the business obviously posed a threat to all the ambitious directors, to some more than others. Vogel, who was already isolated, needed me as an ally just then, but his long-term plans were to get Isaac Wolfson, Chairman of the rapidly expanding Great Universal Stores and a major customer, to come into the business and let him run it.

Before starting at Birkenhead, I spent two months in Bordeaux, at my uncle's instigation, in order to acquire stocks of softwood for BR, suddenly available as a result of forest fires. The point was that the trees, although charred on the outside and effectively killed as standing wood, still contained good usable timber on the inside and these were right for railway sleepers. British Rail hoped to acquire large stocks cheaply and were borrowing professionals from industrial timber firms to negotiate and inspect. My uncle appointed me to go and our biggest rival Montague Mayer Ltd. sent Harold Wilson, ex-President of the Board of trade, who after the Labour government went out of power in 1951 had been given a sinecure directorship. Questions had been previously asked why Montague Mayer seemed to have greater facility in getting timber import licences than other firms. The answer was now evident. Sending Wilson to France was a way of giving him a holiday.

I then spent two months in Bordeaux, an interesting experience that was hard on my liver because the owners of the forest also owned the vineyards. Mid-morning usually meant Chateau Yquem or similar gourmet wine, lunches were long and there were feasts in the evening. There is a restaurant called Le Chapon Fin, to which I was frequently taken, that had a wine list at least a thousand pages long. When I asked how they could sell thousands of different local wines I was told that when a wine grower came in with his guests he always ordered his own wines and therefore they had to stock them all.

My work consisted of going to a number of places in the Bordeaux and Landes districts where piles of sawn railway sleepers had been laid out for my inspection, and selecting those that came up to British Rail's minimum specification. I had to look at the quality and condition of the wood and measure the wane on the top where the iron shoes that hold the rails would be fitted. But a commercially significant fact was that anything I had to reject for British Rail could be bought by a private firm and the rejects were usually between five and ten percent. There was competition for these rejects which could be negotiated for private purchase at a variety of prices, but usually considerably higher than those which British Rail had fixed. There were attempts to influence my inspections, bribes hinted at, but I did only what I was there to do. There were several commercial British timber merchants going around, most of them not working for British Rail and they were my competition, because Calders Ltd. were interested in buying as many rejects as possible. Those who were showing me sleepers were not necessarily interested in letting me know of others that were sub-standard, precisely because someone else was interested and a price was being negotiated. Two middle-men coming from somewhere in Eastern Europe, took me around for several days and their private conversation was in German, which of course I understood, but never let on. They were always puzzled by the way I would insist on looking in corners they did not want me to see, where there would be piles of sleepers exactly right for the needs of customers who had their own sidings, other than British Rail. I would count them, confirm their ownership, and then send a series of telegrams to London so that Rann could buy them for the firm. Towards the end of my period I negotiated for several thousand sleepers to be sent directly to Birkenhead, but not to be shipped until my arrival there. I did not tell London and as prompt payment was coming through for those going to other timber yards, I was never questioned by the exporters. I suspected that Rann would starve Birkenhead, having no reason to be helpful to me there. Payment for those ordered on my own account I would worry about later.

Christya came to visit on two occasions for about a week and considerably complicated my life during those visits. She was interested in the clothes and jewellery shops and wasn't slow in extracting expensive presents from those trying to impress or please me. I did what I could to arrest her progress. On a few occasions I found myself staying at some country inn where Harold Wilson was also staying, and we played chess and discussed politics.

In the autumn of 1952 I went to Birkenhead. I had been found a comfortable hotel in the Wirral, but Christya made herself so objectionable and demanding there that I was soon asked to move and found a house in Heswall on the Mersey with a floor to let. My landlady was Dolores Allen and she was married to a travelling salesman who was seldom at home. From here I had a half hour drive every day to the timber yard on the docks at Birkenhead and I set about making the yard a success. First I had to deal with some technical problems. It was often wet and the procedure was that the men, all working out of doors (except for the small office staff), would go on working for two hours in the rain and then could go home. As the rain would constantly start and stop this meant that we were often paying for two hours work or less on a bad day. I altered this so that the men could take shelter until the rain stopped. When we were working at full stretch, I negotiated reasonable overtime payments with the union representatives on the work force. By talking to the men, which my predecessor had never done, I gradually untangled all the logistical problems. There was a machine that made incisions with small blades piercing the sleepers before creosoting which was constantly breaking down. We were paying an outside firm of engineers a considerable amount to keep one or two men constantly doing repairs on that or on other machines. I employed one of them directly to join the staff at less than half the previous cost, but at a considerable salary increase for the man concerned. The machine stopped breaking down.

One reason for the low output was that the cranes all had to cross a rail junction in the yard, and there was always one, sometimes as many as three cranes waiting to get by, sometimes for more than an hour. I asked permission to put in a loop to stop the congestion, but this was refused by London, partly because the board did not want to spend money on a yard with a bad profit record, but also probably because the directors didn't want to give me any opportunity to show that I brought about an improvement. I summed up the cost, had the work done and described the expenditure as general repairs without specification. When my uncle paid a visit he looked at the new loop, scratched his moustache, hesitated, then said nothing.

Two or three days a week, I would leave the yard early on and go out to sell, calling on old and new customers all over Lancashire, the Midlands and as far away as Leeds, which really was the territory of another yard. My sleepers arrived from Bordeaux and I had to hire extra space to store them, while selling as many as I could as fast as I could. It was not difficult because there was a shortage and much demand, but it needed time and energy that no one had been willing to put in before. I was not only selling my own products, but taking orders for other yards, but these still boosted my sales as I was entitled to a commission on them.

Calders Ltd. owned a flooring company which it had bought from a very sleepy old Lancastrian called Brookes, who still ran it. I took orders for him and he had to start working harder to fill them. I made friends with another flooring manufacturer called Douglas Mitchell, a man who read and had intellectual tastes, and spent many evenings with him and his wife Chris; they were keen golfers, but I had no time for golf, although I went out on the course with them once or twice. What I didn't know about flooring I learned from him, not Brookes, and we co-operated in various ways. He even read some proofs for me.

By the end of December I found that we had done more business in four months than in the previous two years and that was only the beginning. By the end of the financial year I had turned the previous year's loss of £20,000 into a profit of over £230,000, and in addition had taken orders from other yards of about £200,000. Having the extra sleepers was the biggest single factor, but listening to those who knew what the technical problems holding back the yard were (they had never been asked before), enabled me to find the answers and triple production. The rest of it was finding new customers and just hard selling. I had been promised a commission on sales over a certain target and on increased profits. When Battson showed the figures to my uncle he had trouble in believing them. Then he told me that he would not give me the more than £80,000 that was due to me. I said I would take half if I received a directorship, and after some argument he agreed to the directorship but only gave me a quarter of what was owed.

I saw little intellectual life outside of my work during that year from 1952 to 1953. I went occasionally to the Royal Court Theatre in Liverpool and to some other theatres and occasionally took British Rail sleeper inspectors out to the local music hall and dinner. I was lunched two or three times by Harry Watson at the Adelphi Hotel's prestigious French restaurant, but that was a waste of time. His cronies were all old Lancastrian Tories, some of whom had had their coal mines nationalised and been given jobs with the National Coal Board, which they constantly derided. The good food and wine in no way compensated for the perpetual dismal flow of reactionary conversation, and I pleaded pressure of work in response to further invitations. I did go, with Christya, to the Grand National at Harry Watson's invitation, but all I can remember of it was a long car jam in the Mersey Tunnel and on the road to Aintree, and drizzle and much drink in another private dining room overlooking the race course. Just like Ascot! During that year I saw little of Christya except when I drove to London on weekends, usually leaving after work on Friday and leaving London early on Monday morning to be back by ten o'clock. It took five hours by car on the A5, most of it the old Watling Street Roman road that went from the Edgeware Road northward, over the top of Birmingham and then north-west to Chester and the Wirral: I knew it by heart.

During the week Dolores Allen, my landlady, a plump, attractive forty-year old housewife, who was usually on her own, often came up to talk to me in the evenings. I would bring sacks of firewood from the yard, usually the cut-off tops of telegraph poles, for both her fires and my own. On the very last night of my stay we had a bit too much to drink and ended up in bed together. It was my first sexual infidelity since marrying Christya, and although I experienced some guilt, I enjoyed it immensely. After returning to London I made opportunities to see Dolores again and I also visited her when in the area.

I was now back in London and at head office, but there was no real job for me there. I was made *a* sales manager, but was not *the* sales manager and it was not clear what I was selling. I made my own job, but was hampered at every turn by the other directors (I was one now myself), anxious to deny me the opportunity to shine as I had at Birkenhead. Kirkup and Billington, both coveting the chairmanship, saw me as a bigger threat than each other, while the working managing-directors, Rann and Vogel were both fearful of my potential rivalry: they could see the day coming when my uncle might give me a senior position to theirs, given that I had proved I knew the business and could run things successfully. They jealously guarded their fiefdoms, excluding me from everything. There was a special dinner to celebrate a birthday of my great-uncle's (it may have been his eighty-fifth) at which I was asked to make a little speech. I hired a professional to help me, prepared it carefully and gave a highly-charged oration that brought tears to the eyes of some of the older employees and my uncle was, I could see, moved himself by it. That was viewed by the ambitious directors as a challenge and a declaration that I had my eye on the top of the tree.

I was now intent on acquiring shares in the company. I spent all my commission on ordinary shares and my uncle, who had put 20,000 shares aside for me if I proved worthy, now passed these on to me. I made an agreement with two Robertson sisters, whose brother had been a managing director before the war, to acquire their shares at some future date and they gave me an option on them at a fixed price. The ladies were elderly, lived in Polmont, and I paid them several visits to explain how their shares could help to keep the company in the family, an aim of which their dead brother would certainly approve. Calders Ltd, which seldom raised its dividend in line with increased profits, was run on old-fashioned lines, putting money into reserves against future hard times every year and the reserves were now considerable. It was exactly the kind of company that the new breed of speculative accountants, typified by Charles Clore, were eyeing as targets for take-overs where the reserves would more than repay the cost of the bid. If I could persuade my grandfather to free the trust that he had previously been willing to let me have on the birth of my infant son, I would be in a position to buy a considerable further block and own more of the company than all the other directors, apart from my uncle, put together.

Christya had become pregnant again and in April 1954 she produced a baby girl. I had been pacing up and down in the waiting room, and was asked to go to see her immediately after the birth, which was again by

Caesarean section. She then said, 'Listen. No one must know this is a girl. Send your grandfather a telegram right away saying it's a boy and you'll get your money.' I was very uneasy about this and thought it over. But Christya had an hypnotic influence over me in many ways and in the end I did what she said. She may even have sent a telegram herself to force my hand. I cannot exactly remember the circumstances.

The baby was called James again, which later became Jamie. The pretence was kept up for some months and then, inevitably, the deception was found out. But in the meantime everything went well, although I was now more involved in the politics of Calders Ltd. than in the work I was actually doing for the company. I certainly had more time for holidays and I remember a month at Cap Ferrat that summer, when I took the villa next door to Jacques Chaix, where I became a part of his large house party, but with my own quarters. I drove down to the south of France with everything needed for the villa, while Christya, a nanny and the baby flew down to meet me. I had several bottles of whisky in the car and was told by French customs I could only bring in one bottle duty-free. 'But I'm meeting my wife and baby in France,' I protested. 'They're going by 'plane.'

'We'll allow you a bottle for your wife,' the man said, 'but not for the baby.'

'But it's a Scottish baby,' I exclaimed, whereupon the man laughed and waved me on. Christya and the baby stayed a month at Cap Ferrat, while I had to make two trips back to Britain to deal with something or other and show my face.

During my year in Birkenhead I was also publishing books and running Skyline Press, the printing company in Islington, one of the trading companies that came under Calder and Co. (Printers) Ltd., which enabled me to cover many of my expenses and do odd deals that came my way. I often drove down to London on Friday night, spent all Saturday and Sunday morning working at publishing at Wilton Terrace and printing at Cross Street and then driving back, either late Sunday or early Monday. As I think back and try to remember those years when in my twenties I seemed to have the time and the energy to do whatever was needed, I marvel. I certainly never stopped and was working twelve hours a day or more, every day of the week, and that does not include travelling time.

Back in London I was giving more time to publishing and was now building a list without the help of anyone else. I made a few trips to New York to visit publishers there and picked up several books. Senator Joe McCarthy was now becoming active in the wake of some sensational spy trials, especially after the Alger Hiss case. This had interested me since my university days, and I was still in touch with the Washington lawyer Jim Mann, who had known Hiss well. Lord Jowett wrote a book about the case[4] which I bought and read, and it reawakened my interest. Jowett, who had

---

[4] Lord Jowett. The Strange Case of Alger Hiss. London 1953.

been Lord Chancellor in the first post-war Labour government, had come to the conclusion that a British court would never have convicted Hiss on the circumstantial and highly dubious evidence that had led to his conviction and imprisonment for perjury after a second trial; the first had been dismissed by a judge who Richard Nixon then tried to impeach. Nixon's controversial career had started with the Hiss case.

I decided to get in touch with Hiss and to commission a book from him if possible. I did so immediately after he was released from prison. He was a very sad man, broken in spirit, but courteous and dignified. He said that he did not really think he could write a book about his own case. He had been framed on false evidence, and he didn't see how he could ever prove his innocence, although he certainly wanted to try. It was still too recent and too painful. He was a proud man and just meeting him convinced me that he was also an honourable one. His time in prison must have been not only supremely humiliating, (in the way other proud men like Dreyfuss and Oscar Wilde had been humiliated), but also an experience that would depress and humble him for the rest of his life. He told me that he might be willing to write an historical book about other miscarriages of justice that were similar to his, and mentioned Dreyfuss. We kept up a correspondence, and finally he wrote to me, saying that he had decided, yes, after all, he would write a book about himself. One big incentive of course was that he needed money. I offered him £2000, a large sum then, and he signed a contract and started on the book. But he was in poor health, and it was nearly two years before he finished it.

In New York I came across several radical publishers as well as the conventional ones around Madison Avenue. Everyone in New York was welcoming then to a young British publisher looking for books and I made many contracts to publish American books in Britain, in some cases importing part of the American edition, either a small number of copies or a thousand or two in sheet form for binding under my imprint in Britain. This considerably cut down the risk, and I sold my own books to American publishers as well. I met Paul Sweezy, a philosopher who had lost his teaching job at Harvard because of his left-wing views and writings. In 1949 he had founded the radical magazine *Monthly Review* together with Leo Huberman, which by now was also publishing books. I became particularly friendly with the latter, who was having, like everyone known to be on the left at that time, considerable trouble with the various right-wing pressure groups and Congressional committees who were persecuting him. On one occasion, probably in 1954, I telephoned him on arrival at La Guardia airport. His voice answered, and when he recognised mine, he said quickly, 'Don't give your name. I recognise your voice. My telephone is tapped and I don't want you to get into any trouble. How long will it take you to get to New York?' He then suggested that I should meet him some two hours later at Liggett's Drug Store at Grand Central Station. I was to catch his eye and follow him out and not speak to him until he was sure we were not being followed. This cloak and dagger routine soon became familiar to me as I met more Americans who were being persecuted because of their past or present political allegiances. Huberman guided me on to Angus Cameron, previously senior editor at Little Brown in Boston. Angus had been fired when the company was attacked in keeping with the McCarthyite siege on publishers, following on from the persecution of Hollywood and New York writers, actors and directors. Angus had set up Cameron and Kahn as an imprint for books that frightened the more conventional publishers, all terrified of McCarthy and the House Un-American Activities Committee, cynical politicians who had found an easy way of acquiring electibility by recourse to a phoney patriotism, proving that Dr Johnson's old adage was still true.[5]

Angus Cameron and I became good friends and I acquired several books from him. One in particular brought me into conflict with the American Embassy in London. I had contracted to publish *The Judgement of Julius and Ethel Rosenberg* by John Wexley, a dispassionately written but quite terrifying description of a spy trial carried out in an atmosphere of hysteria. Much significant evidence that might have saved the Rosenbergs, an idealistic but misguided couple, was suppressed. Convicted of passing atomic secrets to the Russians, they were electrocuted in June 1953. The book gave a quite different description of the circumstances of the case and of the trial itself to the account which had been reported in the newspapers, and I considered the book an important one. When I announced publication (this was in 1956), I received a telephone call from an official at the American Embassy. The conversation went as follows:

'Mr Calder.'

'Yes.'

'Am I talking to John Calder, the publisher?'

'You are. How can I help you?'

'I understand you intend to publish a book about the Rosenberg case.'

'Yes, I am. I consider it an important book.'

'Mr. Calder, I must advise you not to publish that book. It contains serious libels.'

'Who is libelled?'

'Mr. Herbert Brownell is libelled for one. He will sue you personally if you publish that book.'

The official, whoever he was, would not give him name, and I ignored the matter at first, but then as a precaution I bought a defunct publishing company off the hook and used it to publish the Wexley book. It was the only publication to ever appear from Bookville Publishers Ltd. There was no libel case, very few sales and I cannot remember if there were any British reviews, certainly no prominent ones. But there must still be copies in the

---

[5] Patriotism is the last refuge of a scoundrel.

more important libraries and I was pleased to have published it. It may yet get republished.

I am not sure how I came to publish Paul Baran's *Political Economy of Growth*. My own grounding in economics at Zürich had given me an ongoing interest in the subject, but more from a political and academic point of view than from its application to business, which was Saitzev's speciality. I do not remember ever meeting Baran, and it was probably offered to me by Huberman, because Huberman later wrote a book about the author. But I do remember reading it and being much impressed. The author was Professor of Economics at Stanford when he completed it in 1955, then the only left-thinking academic in such a post in the United States, and I published it in London two years later. He was of course under major attack, but he was immensely popular with students, and having tenure the university found it impossible to fire him without losing face. He had been a more than impressive official during the war with the OSS, American military intelligence, and John Kenneth Galbraith in his memoirs praises him highly, saying that this Russian-born Jewish-Polish immigrant to the U.S., a slovenly soldier who never rose above the rank of technical sergeant in the American army, but had played a major role in investigating the effectiveness of Allied bombing during the war and questioning Nazi officials, 'was one of the most brilliant and, by a wide margin, the most interesting economist I have ever known.'[6] Having reacquainted myself with his book during the course of the writing of these memoirs, I think I must republish it in the not too distant future. Let me offer the reader a single Baran quote from his last paragraph:

> 'To contribute to the emergence of a society in which development will supplant stagnation, in which growth will take the place of decay, and in which culture will put an end to barbarism is the noblest, and indeed, the only true function of intellectual endeavour.'

From the mainstream commercial publisher, Putnam, soon to apply political censorship to their own list, I acquired a good novel about the witch-hunt then going on in eastern American universities. Entitled *The Searching Light*, it was written by the daughter of an American ambassador, Martha Dodd, who had been fired from her own university as a radical thinker, and I seem to remember that it also blighted her father's career. I followed this with *The Unamericans* by Alvah Bessie, who had been one of the Hollywood ten, and whose brother Michael Bessie was soon to emerge as one of the most interesting of a new generation of American publishers. I published four novels by Lars Lawrence, the pen name for an established writer, Philip Stevenson, also under a witch-hunt cloud, brought to my attention by his friend Albert Maltz, another of the Hollywood ten. Two of them had appeared in the States under the imprint of International Publishers, which was a Marxist imprint run by the colourful Alexander Trachtenberg. This

---

[6] A Life in Our Times. J.K. Galbraith. Boston 1981.

latter had established his firm in 1924 and had flourished up to the advent of McCarthyism, being one of the only publishers willing to publish black authors such as W.E.B. Dubose and histories of labour struggles in the U.S., as well as the works of Lenin, Trotsky and Bukharin. He was jailed about the time I was corresponding with him, under the Smith Act, which by implication convicted people of conspiring to overthrow the American government by force because of the contents of the books they published. I sometimes wondered in those days why publishers of crime fiction were not prosecuted for advocating murder. Lars Lawrence wrote in the tradition of John Steinbeck and his series of novels about industrial exploitation in New Mexico were intended to be published as a trilogy under the title *The Seed*, each part to consist of two large volumes. The first two I imported in sheet form, the second two were set and printed in England, (Trachtenberg being then, I now presume, incapable of publishing anything), while the third, and I here hang my head, was probably lost when we moved offices in late 1962. Our building was to be demolished in the next few days and tons of paper, including some unpublished manuscripts mixed up with submissions were lost in the rubble. The third part, to be called *The Sowing*, barring some miracle, is lost forever. Stevenson was, I believe, the writer of the film *Christ in Concrete*, but I am not sure what else he did.

We also published two novels by Albert Maltz himself. One came through Angus Cameron, *A Long Day in a Short Life*, set in a prison and exposing American racialist attitudes, the second which was about two people who manage to escape from Auschwitz at the end of the war, fall in love, but do not survive, was published only by me. Maltz would turn up periodically in London, bringing manuscripts, looking with some dismay at other authors we were publishing such as Beckett, who he did not realise was exploring much of the same vein as himself, but in a very different way.

Angus Cameron, after leaving Little, Brown, where a new President had quickly responded to pressure to get rid of him, in accordance with the McCarthyite attack on publishers, now started Cameron and Kahn with financial help from Albert Kahn, a best-selling writer of political books. This soon became Cameron Associates and eventually Cameron and Marzani. Cameron came from Indianapolis from mixed Scottish, Irish and German bloodstock, one of his ancestors having fought at Culloden, and he had been a bookseller as well as a publisher. He had a fiercely independent nature and built up a sizeable list of books that could no longer find publishers on Madison Avenue, many of which came to me. I also imported small quantities of his titles whose British sales would not exceed a hundred copies, mainly to be sold to libraries and the political bookshops. In character Angus made me think of the old Scotsman in Arthur Miller's play *The Crucible*, who being crushed to death, still will not yield. Carl Marzani, his last partner, was an old Marxist who had spent some time in prison on a treason charge, having previously worked for the State Department.

Although I became fairly friendly with him, I think Marzani considered me to be an old-fashioned liberal to be treated warily by those further to the left, and no doubt he was right. I.F. Stone, the journalist, whom I first met around this time, disliked him and distrusted him totally. I came to know many writers in New York and one was the poet Norman Rosten, a close friend of Arthur Miller's, who I subsequently met through him. On one occasion I wanted to see Sean O'Casey's play *Red Roses for Me*, but it was about to close and suddenly there were no seats. I rang Arthur Miller, who said that he had wanted to see it too, and he was able to pull strings to get two seats. Afterwards we discussed it. 'I don't know what it is about that play that appeals to me so much, that makes it different,' he said hesitantly. At that point he and similar playwrights were having to deal with political subjects through metaphor. 'Could it be that it simply says what it has to say directly without looking over its shoulder?' I ventured. He nodded his head. 'That's it. None of us dares to be direct any more.'

George Braziller was starting to publish his own list just then. He had been a packer at the Book of the Month Club and had observed how a book club operation worked. The public that was too lazy to read reviews or form their own judgement of what they wanted to read were happy to allow others, literary critics and publisher's editors to choose their reading for them, and what counted to win the trust of members of the Book Club was the prestige of the jury of choosers. Braziller noted that the choices were nearly all best-sellers and required little attention from that jury. What if a prestigious group of literati were to pick books of a higher intellectual calibre that would look well on the shelves of those who wanted to impress? This was the idea behind the Book Find Club that he started, which was brilliantly successful for a while. When it began to decline, due largely to other Book Clubs starting up, he sold out and began publishing his own trade list, largely books on art, but with some literary titles as well. He had been contacted by Maria Jolas, a forceful, determined lady whose own literary background as the patron of James Joyce and wife of the founder of Transition, the best pre-war literary journal in English in Paris, was impeccable. She convinced him to publish Nathalie Sarraute and later Claude Mauriac as well as other French writers and he had an editor called Edwin Seaver (no connection with Dick Seaver) to look after the literary part of this list. I had met Braziller at some function and made an appointment to see him in his office early one morning. I was put into his room by a secretary and Seaver came in to chat for a moment, then left just as the secretary returned to tell me that Braziller had 'phoned that he was held up, but would get there as soon as possible. Within a minute another man came in and began to talk to me. After a quarter of an hour I said, 'I wonder how long Mr. Braziller will be?'

He looked at me and the look was not friendly. 'I'm George Braziller,' he said. I apologised for not having recognised him at this second meeting, but he was very annoyed and over the subsequent years I think he always held it against me. He was very sensitive about his lack of higher education, inability to read other languages and probably to understand much of what he did publish, and always on the look-out for snubs. Most of his publishing was to consist of art books bought from other publishers where the text was less important than the visual appearance, which he could judge without having to read anything. On all our subsequent meetings he had a reserve towards me, and our dealings, mainly over authors where we had separate rights for our respective markets, were always strained.

Angus Cameron was having trouble distributing his books because booksellers became increasingly nervous of having books on their shelves that could make them vulnerable to attack. He would advertise in what was left of the left-wing press, such as PM and The National Guardian, both soon to close, and Monthly Review. He started the Liberty Book Club so that he could get subscribers and send books through the U.S. mails. But it was difficult and he eventually handed the whole thing over to Marzani and found a position, although only a junior one, with Knopf. I received books from other publishers, and one that did well was *Fräulein*, a novel about the fall of Berlin to the Russians, by James McGovern. It sold several editions, probably because of the raunchy rape scenes. I cannot exactly date it because the only copy I possess is faulty and missing the title and copyright page. We followed it with another novel by the same author *No Ruined Castles*, in 1958.

The success of the *Opera Annual* gave me the idea of publishing a similar volume to cover the theatre and I approached the drama critic I admired most, Harold Hobson, whose column appeared weekly in the Sunday Times, to edit an International Theatre Annual. Harold was another enthusiastic personality and the first annual appeared in 1957. It was followed in subsequent years by a Concert-Goers Annual, edited by Evan Senior, who also edited the monthly magazine Music and Musicians; a Film Annual, edited by William Whitebait (the pseudonym of Campbell Dixon, reviewer for the Daily Telegraph,) and an International Literary Annual, edited by John Wain (the novelist, poet and Oxford Don, not the film actor). But Hobson did more than edit my annual: he was then the most ardent advocate in London of the current French theatre and he brought new authors to my attention, the most important of them being Eugène Ionesco. I frequently met Hobson in Paris and would go to the theatre with him. Together we saw *The Chairs* and *The Lesson*, a double bill at the Théatre de la Huchette that is still running more than forty-five years later, and I tracked down the author, who was beginning to earn just enough to give up teaching, but still lived in a rather humble Paris suburb. I offered to publish him in English, but he was nervous of committing himself as he did not yet have a French publisher. It was only when Gallimard had taken him on that I was able to get a contract for English-language translation, signed with them.

Hobson's French was not very fluent. I went several times with him to see Edwige Feuillère in different plays, but mainly *La Dame aux Camélias*, one of her greatest roles. To say that he was in love with her would be an understatement; he worshipped the air around her and the earth under her feet. On two occasions he took us both to lunch at Le Grand Véfour, the fashionable restaurant near the Palais Royal, so that I could keep her in conversation while he looked and worshipped. He was later to write a book about her that I would have published had it been less of a hagiography. It was actually announced in my catalogue for 1959, and I rather regret not having published it now. I have produced worse books; it could have been salvaged with heavy editing, as Lockspeiser had done with the Henri Hell Poulenc biography, and it would have given Hobson much pleasure.

Harold Hobson was a remarkable character. As a child he had been stricken with polio, which stunted his growth, so that he was only four feet high at most and walked with great difficulty, using two sticks. He had very bright eyes, always searching, observing, and usually mischievous. His mother had belonged to the Christian Science Church and it was her faith, so he believed, that had pulled him through the polio and saved his life. He still adhered to Christian Science and was London drama critic for The Christian Science Monitor in Boston as well as for The Sunday Times. He was open-minded and perceptive as a critic, and also unusually kind, especially to new playwrights. His taste was catholic in every way: he enjoyed musicals and farces as well as Shakespeare and the great classical dramas of past and present. He had a particular love of French theatre and would go to see the Comédie Française's productions of Molière and Marivaux, and to the boulevard theatres to see Anouilh, Sartre and Feydeau, but also to the pocket theatres to see the new emerging playwrights of the avant-garde: Beckett, Ionesco, Adamov and Duras, all of whom he promoted in his Sunday Times column. The French theatre came up very often in his reviews, but so did every kind of play: he was a genuine eclectic who loved the theatre, leaning over backward to be kind and to register the best aspects of plays that were mediocre. Unlike Kenneth Tynan, soon to become theatre critic of The Observer, he never tried to show off his cleverness by recourse to cruel invective, or by satirising material whose meaning had eluded him.

Harold Hobson and I lunched often as we became both collaborators and friends: he frequented the best restaurants, provided he could get his car parked and didn't have to deal with steps to get to his table. We went regularly to the Caprice, and the Ivy and sometimes to the Ritz Restaurant overlooking Green Park. Once I was walking down Piccadilly and heard my name called. He had stopped his car across the street and was beckoning to me. When I reached the window he handed me sixpence, which on a previous occasion I must have lent him for a telephone call, with a mischievous smile. 'I won't have you saying I don't pay my debts,' he twinkled at me and drove on. *The International Theatre Annual* came out for seven years and then stopped for reasons I will explain later. Hobson also wrote an excellent history of the French Theatre, which I published in 1978 and which continued to sell slowly for many years after his death, even up to the time of writing.

I also saw Harold Rosenthal quite frequently, but never became intimate with the other editors of the annuals. John Wain I found to be rather in the mould of Sir John Squire, very English in a pub-loving, xenophobic, academically stilted way. He was pleasant enough, but like the other member of 'The Movement', which had attracted some attention in the early fifties, he was limited in his thinking and knowledge, and opposed to the avant-garde. Nevertheless he did a good job with the three issues of the *International Literary Annual* which appeared.

I was at home with Christya one Sunday afternoon when the doorbell rang and in walked my old university friend Dick Soukup. With him was Su Kleinert, whom he had once asked me to discourage. They were married now. Su kissed me and whispered in my ear that the drunken evening in Zürich, when I had disobeyed Dick's instructions, had been the real cause of her sticking to him. Now they were happily married. They stayed an hour and although we spoke once or twice on the telephone, I never saw them again. Our worlds were too different now.

It was the summer of 1956 in which Arthur Miller's *A View from the Bridge* was being produced in London. Since I knew him from New York and had kept up a correspondence with him, he invited me to the opening, asking me to telephone him at the Savoy Hotel. He had only recently married Marilyn Monroe and this put him doubly on the map. He asked me to come round for breakfast on the morning of the opening and I was shown into their suite, where Marilyn stayed in bed drinking coffee and chatting to us, while Arthur and I sat at the table over breakfast. I cannot remember the conversation, but even at that time of the morning she was stunning.

I waited in the foyer of the Theatre (I think it was the Comedy) to say Hello, but I couldn't get anywhere near them. There was a battery of photographers, blinding TV lights and film cameras, and when they entered the theatre, he in a white dinner jacket, she in a white sequinned full-length dress that looked as if it had been sewn onto her, it was as if the Gods of Olympus had arrived. I think Christya was with me and if so she must have been very jealous. But I lost touch with Miller after that, partly because from about that time I was going less frequently to New York and had so many other people to see when I did. I also fell out with his close friend Norman Rosten. We had arranged to meet in a bookshop and I was inexcusably late for which I was not forgiven. That however happened a considerable time later.

There were not that many new friends. Life was too busy, combining publishing with a job in timber which had become increasingly meaningless as the other directors ensured that I was given no further responsibilities which might enable me to show results as I had done at Birkenhead. There were plans to move me to a yard at Port Talbot in South Wales, but not in a managerial capacity, and to avoid this I feigned a stomach disorder so as to remain in London.

My uncle was now showing his years and couldn't face the constant pressures from the rival directors and it was clear that the battle for future control of the firm had started in earnest. There was a proposal to make a new share issue: this would water down the holdings I had acquired and give Wolfson an opportunity to buy up most of the new shares. Vogel was doing ever more business with Great Universal Stores and keeping Wolfson happy was important: there was the ever-present danger that Vogel might start a new company and take all his hardwood business away with him, a prospect that would not dismay Rann. My own position was especially precarious because I had used my shares as collateral to buy more shares. If the price were to fall my loans would be called in.

My Uncle Jim was no fool, but at his age, he had to believe what it was comfortable to believe and the prospect of Wolfson buying a block of shares did not seem threatening to him. When I tried to discuss the matter he would not believe that Wolfson wanted control of the company, just a stake in it, but in his heart of hearts he must have known otherwise. Old men who keep active do not necessarily lose their mental powers, but they lose the will to stand up to opposition. My uncle increasingly wanted a quiet life, and it was clear that sooner or later either Wolfson would acquire the company or else Rann would find a way of making a take-over with another backer. Either way I had no future. Aware of this I devoted ever more time to the publishing company which now had a list of some hundred and fifty titles, about half of it fiction, much of it American, but now increasingly European as I acquired French and German books that I had seen reviewed in the literary press or were recommended to me by others, usually authors already published in their own country. Political books tended to have a short life as national and international issues came and went, so I was publishing fewer of those. The music list was growing, and largely on the contacts I had made through Harold Hobson, I was also publishing plays and books on the theatre.

One day in 1955 Douglas Mitchell rang me and said he was coming to London. Could we go to the theatre together? He wanted to see *Waiting for Godot*, which I had already seen once and liked, but with a very limited understanding of what it all meant. Hobson was the only British critic who had given the play a good review, and he had returned to see it again and again, advocating it to his readers more strongly each time, while Tynan denigrated it as pointless nonsense. Tynan at this point was mainly interested in plays that showed an obvious political commitment, and was beginning to champion Brecht, still totally unknown in Britain. I went with Douglas to see *Godot*, and on this second viewing the power and beauty of

Beckett's masterpiece, in Peter Hall's first English production, hit me with all its force.

The next day I telephoned the theatre to ask where I could get the publishing rights. I was given an address in Paris, that of Editions de Minuit and I wrote to ask for English rights. But the address was wrong and the letter went unanswered. My second letter arrived some weeks later, and on the same day, but by a later post, as a similar letter from Faber and Faber. As Faber's letter had arrived first Jerôme Lindon sold the play to them. In the meantime I somehow managed to get Samuel Beckett's Paris address and had written asking if I could meet him, saying I was often in Paris. He wrote back instantly, asking me to ring him at the number he had given me when I was next over. A few days later I telephoned him from London, went to Paris and we had dinner together. We talked about many things, and walked around Montparnasse afterwards, ending up drinking beer in a café and playing chess. We ended up having breakfast near Montparnasse station and then separated. I was aware that I had had an exciting night of conversation on many subjects of common interest, literature, music, drama, politics, the state of the world and personalities who interested us, and that I had met a remarkable man. We were to remain friends until he died in 1989, but the one thing he would not discuss with me were his publishing rights. He would be very happy to have me as his publisher, but he had given all the decision-making to Lindon to deal with. When, a few days later, we both realised that Lindon had accepted an offer from Faber to publish *Waiting for Godot*, he told me not to worry. Faber would lose money on him and he did not expect the limited success of that one play to be repeated; we would enjoy a better friendship if we didn't have a business relationship. For many years he had been totally unsuccessful as a writer and he did not expect what he regarded as a flash in the pan to harbour well for the success of his other writings.

I have often been asked what we talked about all night on that first occasion when we met and on many later occasions. I simply cannot remember. We talked about life certainly, its pointlessness, the cruelty of man to man, the politics of the time, which was mainly about the Algerian war which preoccupied all of France. And we also talked about suicide, although it was later, just after the death of Hemingway by his own hand, that we spent an entire night discussing the subject, considering in particular how to accomplish such an act properly in a way which wouldn't inconvenience others. There were many paradoxes and dichotomies that came out of his conversation and I tended to be aware of these, but when challenged he would shrug off contradictions. I realised that in *Godot* he had identified one great current anxiety, one which is more applicable to the twentieth century, with its greater growth of awareness and loss of religious belief, than to previous ones: the fear of being totally anonymous, of being born, going through life and dying, leaving not a single trace of one's short existence on this planet. The idea of falling back into the nothingness from which we came both attracted and frightened him. He spoke approvingly of the Marquis de Sade's last testament where he asked to be buried in an unmarked grave in a wilderness. Sam's extreme honesty with himself, especially when looking at the unpleasant aspects of reality was like rubbing salt in the wound. But he always saw both sides. On another occasion, some years later, I had dinner with Jean-Pierre Fasquelle, publisher at Grasset, and a group that included Claude Roy, best-selling novelist and author of the macho novel *La Loi*. Roy, looking like a skeleton, almost hairless from chemiotherapy, and smoking incessantly, was dying of cancer and everyone knew it, but Roy was clinging to the hope that he would be cured. The whole table was reassuring him and acting as if it was just another literary evening of gossip and exchange of ideas. When I said to Sam at dinner the next night that I thought it a pity to witness such hypocrisy – surely Claude Roy had a right to confront reality and not be given false hopes – he turned on me: 'Another fucking moralist,' he said.

During a visit to New York I called on a publisher named Ken McCormick, of Doubleday. He told me of a new publisher whom he suggested I should contact as he was engaged in a very similar enterprise to myself. His name was Barney Rosset and his new publishing company was called Grove Press. I found him in a small office on Fifth Avenue and we had a chat. A little later, getting back to my hotel, which in those days was the Gotham, I received a 'phone call from Barney. Was I free for dinner? I was and he came around at dinner time with an attractive and very well-groomed blonde called Link, an artist and his girlfriend at the time. We had dinner at the Coq d'Or, very near my hotel, and we talked about books, places we had been and politics. He brought up the name of Beckett, who I now had contact with as a friend, but not as an author. Barney had recently signed up his pre-war novel *Murphy*, apparently on the advice of Sylvia Beach, who on a visit to New York had told him about Beckett as a pre-war friend and disciple of James Joyce, who Sylvia had done so much to help, publishing *Ulysses* and *Finnegans Wake* from her pre-war bookshop, Shakespeare and Co. on the Rue de l'Odéon. Barney had acquired world rights to *Murphy*. He also had the rights to Beckett's little book on Proust, first published in 1930. I read *Murphy*, which was new to me. I had up till then, of Beckett's novels, only read the three volumes which became known as the *Molloy* trilogy, all written in French, which I assumed would eventually appear in translation under the Faber imprint. Barney did not know them, and he was unable to read French.

During my remaining days in New York on that trip I had several more meetings with Barney, always at night and very late nights they were, dinner followed by the bars and jazz clubs of lower Manhattan. I began to learn more about this unusual and enthusiastic man. His father had been a banker in Chicago, Jewish but a Catholic convert, and his mother was first generation Irish. He told me that he disliked Jews on high holidays because in some ways they got in the way of his pleasures and the Irish on St. Patrick's Day because they fouled up the traffic with their parade. He was a rebel against all authority and could afford to be because his father had left him several fortunes, which came to him on key birthdays between the ages of eighteen and thirty-five. He had been seventeen when his father died, but by the time I met him he had already received two or three tranches of the money, each consisting of several million dollars. He was obviously spending it as fast as possible, on his personal pleasures, a luxurious property on Long Island, and on things that interested him, but he was not generous to others beyond paying for meals. The things that interested him were sex, politics and publishing, in that order.

When I returned to England I had an arrangement to import his editions of several titles that were appearing as Evergreen Books, a paperback series in what was then called an egghead format, larger than the mass market paperback. These included his *Evergreen Review*, a magazine of avant-garde writing, of which No. 2, devoted to Pataphysics, had just appeared. The twenty or so first titles that came in included *Murphy* and *Proust* and later I contracted the exclusive British rights, the first from Grove Press, the second from Beckett himself. This enabled me a year or so later to produce my own British editions, the first in 1963, the second two years later. The reason for the delay was shortage of money at that point. I sold many thousands of the Evergreen edition in the meantime.

When on my return I told Beckett that I had met Barney and would be selling two of his publications at least, he was very pleased, and it was shortly afterwards that I received a telephone call from him one day to say that Faber were not willing to publish the French novels which they considered obscene and possibly prosecutable. If I was still interested I should speak to Lindon he suggested and I immediately did. Jerôme Lindon saw no reason to let Faber hesitate any longer and offered me a contract for *Malone Meurt* and *L'Innommable*, the last two parts of the trilogy; he had sold the first novel *Molloy* to Olympia Press. Barney acquired the same rights for the U.S. and we then had to work out how to acquire *Molloy*.

Molloy, like Beckett's first post-war novel *Watt*, had been published by Olympia because of Maurice Girodias' connection with the Merlin group, and that story is well documented in my history of the literary adventurers who brought the post-war publishing scene back to life after 1950,[7] but I will briefly recount the details here.

Maurice Girodias, who was eventually to become a good friend, but not one I could trust very far where business was concerned because of his volatile and unprofessional approach to almost everything, was the son of Jack Kahane, who had left a family business in Manchester to come to France after the first world war and had started a publishing company together with a French partner, a Monsieur Person. Kahane wanted to

---

[7] The Garden of Eros. London 2002.

publish unconventional literature and also to write it, which he did under the pen-name Cecil Barr. The purpose of the enterprise was to take advantage of the extreme prudishness of British and American laws on obscenity and to publish books in English which couldn't be published in the countries of their authors. The difference between the partners was that Kahane had an eye for quality, while Person was only after profit; the latter's taste was for bodice-ripping novels describing female underwear in detail, rather like the risqué French postcards and popular paintings sold in reproductions to tourists. Kahane, having published books that included Norman Douglas' *South Wind* and Cyril Connolly's *The Rock Pool*, and the scandalous reminiscences of Frank Harris, was suddenly offered Henry Miller's *Tropic of Cancer*. He recognised its quality and originality, but it took him over two years to pluck up the courage to bring out a book that really would shake the dovecotes, and then only after Anaïs Nin, Miller's close friend and occasional lover, offered to subsidise the printing costs.

Jack Kahane died at the very beginning of the second world war and his elder son, Maurice, who had worked part-time as a teenager for his father and had designed the first cover for *Tropic of Cancer*, hoped to keep the firm going, Monsieur Person having departed some time earlier. But the German occupation, which forced Maurice to change his Jewish name to Girodias, his mother's, made a literary career impossible. During the war years Maurice Girodias survived by turning his hand to any enterprise enabling him to live without papers, always in fear of being stopped on the street and searched, and taking the metro in constant danger of being trapped, but at the liberation he started to publish art books. A series of misfortunes (he was a bad business man and easily deceived by flattery and empty promises) led to his losing everything, but he started again with a new imprint, Olympia Press, which published some later Miller novels and made many discoveries among anglophone writers whose work was too daring for London or New York, while at the same time collaborating and often sharing offices with Jean-Jacques Pauvert, who was busy publishing semi-clandestine editions of the Marquis de Sade and other erotic out-of-copyright French classics. Girodias found in Austryn Wainhouse, the literary and unconventional son of an American diplomat, a translator for Sade. At that point the French authorities were little interested in what appeared in France in English. Girodias had two imprints, Ophelia Press for straight pornography, and Olympia for erotic works with some literary quality. The latter appeared in a distinctive green cover 'Traveller's Companion' series, and sometimes in hardcover as well.

Girodias had noticed a group of English-speaking expatriates who frequented the cheaper cafés of the Boulevard St. Germain and discovered that they were all literary hopefuls, some of them putting out a magazine called Merlin. The guiding spirit was Alexander Trocchi, a Scot of Italian parentage on his father's side, a former brilliant student of Philosophy at

Glasgow University, who had received a special grant to travel and write, and was now living impecuniously in Paris, extremely ambitious and convinced that his chance to forge a big literary career for himself would come. That chance, up to a point, came when Girodias in return for subsidising Merlin, commissioned the young hopefuls to write pornographic novels for him, some of which became erotic classics of their kind and a few others major modern literary works. Trocchi was the most prolific as well as the leader of the group and he churned out a series of sado-masochistic fictions under a number of pen-names, which included Francis Lengel and Carmencita de la Lunas. Many of these were posthumously and commercially published, often in pirate editions, under his own name after his death. He also became a friend, advisor and purveyor of ideas to Girodias. Both liked good food and wine and Alex Trocchi took full advantage of his host's generous nature, Girodias invariably paying the bill.

One American in the group was Richard Seaver, who lived on the Rue de Sabot with his girlfriend, a French violinist who later became his wife, and their room, over a junk shop filled with African antiquities, became the meeting place where the Merlin editors planned successive issues of the magazine. The Rue de Sabot is just around the corner from the Rue Bernard-Palissy, where the offices of Editions de Minuit have a display window with their new publications. It was there that Seaver saw the first French copies of Samuel Beckett's novels displayed, and he went in and bought them. As a result he and Alex Trocchi read them and became enthusiastic fans of the Irish writer about whom they otherwise knew nothing. They persuaded Girodias to give them the funds to acquire English language rights to *Molloy* and to publish the second issue of Merlin, which appeared in the autumn of 1952 containing a perceptive article by Seaver on Beckett. It said that Samuel Beckett had recently published two novels, written in French, which 'defy all commentary' (*Molloy* and *Malone Dies*), but the article also gives an accurate summary of the earlier pre-war novels written in English. It is an intelligent article and probably the first to recognise not only Beckett's originality, but his importance in world literature, commenting also on the still unpublished and unperformed *Waiting for Godot*, although some extracts had been broadcast on French radio. Seaver comments that the extracts reveal 'the same illogical profundity, that same dark, terrible humor (sic) which characterise *Molloy* and *Malone*.'

Seaver managed to get to the radio recording of the parts of *Godot* that Roger Blin, then looking for the money to stage the play in Paris, had persuaded an avant-garde programme of the French radio to broadcast, and he hoped to meet the author, but the shy Beckett, very typically, did not attend. When they did meet, it was unconventional and brief. Seaver had been translating Beckett's *nouvelles* (short stories) and he was told by Jérôme Lindon that there was a manuscript of an unpublished novel in English. A letter was sent to Beckett enquiring after it, and shortly afterwards, during an editorial meeting of Merlin on a rainy afternoon on the Rue de Sabot, there was a knock on the door. Beckett was standing outside. No one recognised him, but he handed in a parcel with a brief word and left. The group started reading the contents of the parcel, the yellowing manuscript of *Watt*, aloud to each other and were soon convulsed in laughter. An extract appeared in the third issue of *Merlin* and the whole novel was published by Olympia Press in *Collection Merlin*, a series financed by Girodias in return for receiving a steady flow of pornographic manuscripts from the editorial group which put the magazine together.[8] Girodias later republished it as part of his green-backed Traveller's Companion series, not mentioning the previous editions on his copyright page. I eventually acquired the rights to both *Molloy* and *Watt* for British publication, but this was some years later.

When I did finally persuade Girodias to subcontract *Molloy* to me and to Grove Press for the United States, I was at last able to publish the trilogy of *Molloy*, *Malone Dies* and *The Unnamable* (the last two acquired from Minuit and already individually published) as a single volume, in accordance with Beckett's desires. This happened in 1959 after long negotiation: Girodias was finally persuaded when I had the idea of having three editions of the trilogy available, allowing all three novels to be published by Olympia in addition to Barney's and my own. Buyers of the Traveller's Companion edition (now quite valuable in the rare book market), must have been very puzzled to read Beckett's view of life as seen by those at the bottom of the human species, a twentieth century equivalent of Dickens' underworld, in a series intended to create sexual excitement. For some time I imported and sold the Grove Press edition of *Watt* in Britain and produced my own edition only as late as 1963. Money was short at the time, but I could make Beckett available by importing the American editions. The first Beckett publication that appeared under my own imprint was *Malone Dies* in 1959, a year that belongs to the next chapter.

My own list was filling out with American imports, sometimes sheets bound up with my own imprint and price, but part of the American printing, sometimes whole series in the American edition, stickered over with the British price. From Barney Rosset I began to import several hundred copies of each new Evergreen title, and these included the novels of Henry James and Herman Melville, both of whom had been published by Grove Press before Barney Rosset bought the company while still a student. From Hill and Wang, New York drama publishers, I imported a series of Drama Books, mainly plays from the Jacobean and classical repertoire, and I bought a large quantity of sheets of an *Encyclopaedia of the Opera*, edited by an American

---

[8] Apart from the aforementioned, the other editors of *Merlin* were Christopher Logue, the poet, John Coleman, an accountant who wanted to be a writer and was business manager; Baird Bryant, who eventually married Trocchi's girlfriend and backer, Jane Lougee, after he left his wife; and John Stevenson, among several others.

anthologist of popular books on music, David Ewen, which sold well. I had published a few children's books as well, some of them packaged by Parry Jackman. One of them, a book called *Nico*, was by André Maurois, the story of a boy who turned into a dog, and was illustrated by photographs by his son Gérard. This I translated myself in a single evening. I acquired a production manager, Lesley MacDonald, a Scots lady married to a German artist, who was teaching drawing in London. They had started their own firm, Acorn Press, and they offered it to me for nothing if I could keep their small backlist going, add a few new titles, and occasionally employ Helmut Weissenborn, the husband, to design a few covers for us. He also illustrated a few books, most notably a fine edition of the early German novel *Simplicius Simplicissimus* by Grimmelshausen, the source from which Brecht drew his inspiration and subject matter for *Mother Courage*. The two of them had translated it together. Whenever Lesley was involved in a manuscript to which she and her husband had devoted their joint talents, she made it a book of which any bibliophile collector could be proud.

When skiing at Val d'Isère with Jacques Chaix I had bought a novel from the local bookseller called *Les Gommes*, a crime novel, but rather unusually written and with many enigmas. I enjoyed it, but only partially understood it. Some time later, in the office of Jerôme Lindon, during negotiations over some other book, I noticed *Les Gommes* on the shelf behind him. I had in the meantime come across the author's name, Alain Robbe-Grillet, bandied about in the French literary papers and knew that he was associated with a new school of fiction which was attracting some attention. I discussed the book with Lindon and eventually made him an offer to publish in English. I then wrote to Barney Rosset to suggest that he might acquire the American rights. By now Dick Seaver, one of the former editors of Merlin, was back in the States and had become an editor at Grove Press: he was making suggestions to Barney for French and other books. Barney's taste did not often rise above the erotic and the political, his main obsessions, although he occasionally had an instinct for a writer such as Beckett, but he was also now becoming interested in the 'Beats', some of whom he had met in San Francisco; he liked their passion for freedom and anti-authoritarian ethos. Together with Donald Allen, who edited it, he was planning a large volume to be entitled *The New American Poetry*, which I eventually distributed in Britain. Seaver approved Robbe-Grillet, but Barney insisted that he wanted an American translator and settled on Richard Howard, a poet and an academic, who was teaching French. Then Barney decided, having had the other novels of Robbe-Grillet explained to him, that *The Voyeur*, written later, sounded sexier and he wanted to publish it first, the fact that it was also shorter being another factor in its favour. Barney had the money and therefore the whip-hand and I had to agree: we both published *The Voyeur* and followed it with Robbe-Grillet's other novels, of which the most successful became *Jealousy*, a short and very vivid picture of a man's jealous mind, obsessed with the fears he has regarding his wife's fidelity during his absence. Robbe-Grillet represented the beginning of my involvement with the French *nouveau roman* and I was eventually to publish most of its practitioners.

I had been much influenced by a dramatisation of Wyndham Lewis' trilogy of novels, *The Human Age*, on the BBC Third Programme, especially by the first part of it, *The Childermass* in which Donald Wolfitt, one of the outstanding Shakespearian actor/managers of the day gave a memorable radio characterisation as the Bailiff, who is really the Devil. This modernisation of Dante's *Divine Comedy* is set during the first world war and the two main characters are an officer and his batman who are killed in the trenches. They then go through a series of landscapes, limbo, purgatory, hell and, in the unfinished fourth novel, of which only a few pages were written, heaven. I bought the novels in the Methuen hardcover editions, illustrated by Michael Ayrton, an artist I knew, and was fascinated by the visual images, as well as by the writing, of Lewis, a painter-writer, who had once led the Vorticist Movement, the British form of expressionism, which is nearer to futurism.

Methuen, I soon learned, had lost interest in Wyndham Lewis. I probably heard this from Lewis himself, because I arranged to meet him to contract his out of print novel *Tarr* and then acquired paperback rights to *The Human Age*. Lewis was old, blind, rather grumpy, but quite friendly with me and I had tea with him on two occasions, when he reminisced a bit about the old days and painters and writers he had known. He wrote like Proust, long-hand in bed, throwing the pages with only a few lines on them in large handwriting onto the floor where his wife picked them up and typed them out. He could not read what he had written, of course, and his very late work could have seen but little revision. I had the impression that they were living on a subsistence level and that every penny he could earn was important.

He died soon afterwards in 1957. I kept in touch with his widow and later contracted his autobiographical *Blasting and Bombardiering*, a fascinating account of his life up to 1928 (first published in 1937) and of his life in Paris and London as a young artist, followed by a very personal account of the first world war. Once, in the late sixties, I saw a small Lewis landscape in an art gallery. It was under £1000 and I bargained to get the price down, or alternately to pay in installments. It would be worth much more now, but I probably would have lost it anyway for reasons that will be clear at the end of Chapter 5.

Most of my publishing up to the late fifties had been in the conventional hardcover format and there was nothing to distinguish my books from those of other publishers visually, but with a new designer, Brian Sewell, our covers began to have a modernistic look, often based on cubist, surrealist and collagist models. We began to issue our own paperbacks in the same format as our hardbacks, which made them appear similar to

Evergreen Books. The typography was the same for both editions and soon we were dividing the sheets we printed between hardback and paperback editions. The term 'egg-head' was now applied to these large format paperbacks to denote the presence of a more intellectual content than was contained in the smaller mass-market paperbacks. This was also the period when a new generation of state-educated intellectuals had arrived on the scene and were open to new ideas and serious culture: many of them were making that culture. The better bookshops accepted these books, but they were treated with considerable suspicion by the more traditionally-minded. University bookshops sometimes stocked titles that they thought would appeal to academics and the more adventurous students. The egghead paperbacks had an easier time in America because the example of Barney Rosset was soon followed by the big companies. Random House put out a series of Anchor Books aimed at the educated reader, largely non-fiction. The editor was a friend of Barney's, Jason Epstein, who soon came to be much admired in the American book trade. I met Epstein many times with Barney, both in New York and later at the Frankfurt Book Fair, but Barney's love of night-clubs and the lust industry that went with them quickly turned Epstein off. Evergreen and Anchor were soon followed by other series competing to get into the university market.

At Calders Ltd. my position was becoming ever more problematic? At head office I was more or less left to my own devices, but had little to do. I had a small room and a secretary who worked for me, called Berry Bloomfield, who occasionally came to Wilton Terrace to do some publishing work for me there. Then the inevitable happened: the deception over my son who was really a daughter was discovered. We had a nanny, who was of course in on the secret and really wanted to see it come out. One day she let my sister change the baby's diapers. Betty did not tell me she knew, but she told the whole family, starting with my grandfather, and I was disgraced. Soon the directors at Calders Ltd. knew about it as well and I was met everywhere by unfriendly, knowing smiles. Explanations were of course provided, but they did nothing to alleviate the censure, although with time things calmed down. My grandfather immediately set about disinheriting me. He decided first to leave his estate to my brother, but he didn't like him, nor had Jimmy ever had the slightest connection with Scotland, and he eventually decided to will Ardargie to a cousin of mine, who had other characteristics that had the Gaffer known about would have disqualified him as well; the rest of his property he eventually willed to a convent.

Now the battle for the future of Calders Ltd. came to a head. Vogel was arguing to enable Wolfson's Great Universal Stores to receive acquisition of a block of new shares. Rann, although he disliked and feared Vogel, felt at the time that I represented the biggest danger to his own future, and now that I was in disgrace with my relatives he saw the possibility of pushing me out, whereas up to now he had only tried to block my progress. I had used the security of all my shares to borrow money to buy more and with my options from the Robertson sisters I was, after my great-uncle, the largest shareholder. Many shares belonged to cousins of mine, mainly on my uncle's wife's side (not blood relations) and they were all up in arms against me. It was obvious that I could soon be pushed out, but now I had a heavy bank debt and the issue of more shares would bring the value of mine down. I went to see Uncle Jim at Ledlanet, explained why I had carried out the deception, which single purpose had been to get my grandfather to release funds that were mine: this had enabled me to become a major shareholder in a company in which I had already proved my ability, but where I had enemies who saw me as a threat to their future. The company was about to pass out of my uncle's hands as well as mine unless he took a decision to issue no more shares and thereby stop Wolfson coming in. The company had ample reserves, did not need more capital, but was afraid of losing business if it offended Wolfson.

Uncle Jim understood everything I said, weakly replied that he did not believe Wolfson really meant any harm, but we both knew that he really thought otherwise. An old man (he was nearly ninety) may not lose his capacity to think and understand, but he does, as I commented earlier, lose his power of resolution and the ability to stand up against hostile pressure. My uncle was thoroughly sick of the turmoil in a company that he had built up from a small family concern into a publicly-quoted national enterprise with timber yards all over Britain, a healthy balance-sheet and considerable reserves, the latter being the result of a large share of the annual profit having always been ploughed back rather than distributed in bigger dividends. He was sick of it all because he had no peace as the jackals fought over their pieces of the main body and the vultures outside swooped in, looking for an opening to take over the company. I told my uncle, of whom I was genuinely very fond, who had treated me with great kindness and who encouraged my initiative, of my dilemma and my peril. But he was now incapable of standing up to pressures from Rann and Vogel, from the scheming accountant Billington, and from the Wolf at the door who could take his profitable business away from the company if he did not get his way, thus creating a big hole in the firm's profits.

One of my functions, during those last two years at Eros House, was to occasionally entertain relatives of people who were important to Great Universal Stores. The company had the use of a shoot in Suffolk, near our timber yard at Brandon, where Weeting Hall had once stood, the pre-war house of my great-uncle, which his wife, Lady Mildred, had made him buy and where she entertained her friends. The house had been demolished and the land probably sold to local farmers, but with shooting rights retained. In the early fifties my uncle took me with him to Brandon occasionally for a weekend's shooting, usually near Christmas. We stayed at a local inn with a hearty Scottish landlord: the food was good and the inn warm, but outside on my first visit it was snowing, which was usually the case. There would be two days shooting driven pheasants in the crisp cold air. By the middle fifties I was often myself in charge of a shooting party, which meant having three or four customers of the firm and perhaps a friend of my own. On two occasions I brought my musicologist friend Edward Lockspeiser. Edward, who loved food, was overweight and on the doctor's advice was going in for various forms of exercise, such as riding in Epping Forest twice a week, was delighted to come shooting and to mix with people totally outside his usual range of acquaintanceship. On one such weekend I took Edward down with me in my car, together with a keen sportsman called Freddy Fox from somewhere in the Midlands and an older man, whose son was the manager of one of Wolfson's many furniture factories. Edward had never touched a gun before and none of the others had ever met anyone who earned his living from music. 'Thinking of sticking to it,' said the older man, scratching his head.

'I think I should after thirty-five years, don't you? Most of us stick to what we've always done,' Edward answered mildly. It was an amusing weekend and Edward's delight when he actually hit a pheasant was touching. He crowed about it for weeks.

Edward Lockspeiser's special study was Debussy and at that time he was well into his important two-volume study of the composer, for which he had presumably received a large advance from the publisher. What he brought to me were less commercial works, like the Henri Hell biography of Poulenc, the first in English, which I published in 1959, and a proposed autobiography of Galina von Meck, granddaughter of Tchaikovsky's patron.

The list had expanded considerably by the late fifties, helped by many series of American imports. Barney Rosset and I bought a series of heavily illustrated paperbacks from Editions du Seuil that we translated and named Profile Books. I was mainly interested in the series on music, composer biographies for the most part, but Barney's interest was purely in the jazz volume. When I commissioned some English titles, a *Handel* and a *Mozart* from Stanley Sadie and a book on Wagner's operas from Audrey Williamson, Barney wouldn't take part. But he was very interested in a semi-sociological series, one of whose titles was on Hollywood film stars, and he also translated several historical titles. I also took on some British series which were produced to be sold in market places and cheap stores, such as the Abbey Classics: these were published and printed by a remainder dealer who was unable to reach normal book outlets that only ordered small quantities of a single title. By 1957 there were several hundred different titles listed in our catalogue and every year the number was greater. They were not there without reason: whatever the edition, each title was a book I would have been happy to publish myself or at least read and keep on my own bookshelves.

Barney occasionally came to London and I took him around the night-clubs; he often ended up with some girl he met there. We also met in Paris, occasionally saw Beckett together, but more often separately. On one occasions Beckett, having spent the evening eating with Barney near his hotel, the Port Royal, and gone on to several bars, spent the night in Barney's room. They were both totally drunk, their situation calling to mind a scene in Beckett's novel *Mercier et Camier*. I was not present on that occasion, but heard about it the next day.

Once I spent a weekend skiing with Barney and Link at a ski resort called Hunter, in the Catskills. Barney drove us up and we spent the evening at a small comfortable hotel where, after dinner, Barney distributed manuscripts that he had brought with him among the three of us. One of these was a barely disguised homoerotic novel (it was still difficult to be frank about homosexuality in those days) by Richard Howard, the poet and translator who was at work translating Robbe-Grillet for us at that time. We each read a part and passed it on. Link and I liked it, Barney didn't, and went on to talk about his bewilderment as to how a good-looking athletic man could be homosexual (the word 'gay' had not yet come into usage).

The next day we skied and Barney was so miffed that I (much more experienced from the French Alps and elsewhere) always beat him downhill that he was grumpy until we arrived back in Manhattan on the Sunday evening.

I was occasionally approached by professors at British universities to publish anthologies from Eastern Europe, in which case the country of origin was willing to subsidise printing in their own country if I would sell the book in Britain. In this way I published *A Century of Latvian Poetry* and *The Parnassus of a Small Nation* (lyrics from Slovenia), soon followed by other similar books, which even decades later led to invitations to attend conferences in those countries as I was obviously 'seriously interested' in their literature. The cart usually came before the horse, but reading later on what I had agreed to publish, my original motive having been to increase the list and make it more international, often led to my taking such a serious interest. The amount of good literature in the world, not known outside its own national borders, is staggering.

I was always meeting new people and entering literary enclaves previously unknown to me. The small literary publisher who was in some ways most like me was John Lehmann, who in spite of his name had come mainly from a Scottish background; his family had been the founders of the Edinburgh firm of Chambers that produced the famous dictionary. His career in publishing, starting just after the war, came to an end in 1952, not for any reason that seemed very valid to me. If you have a list that sells badly, so it seemed to me, you have to diversify it so that books you might not care for personally help those that you do, and you have to learn to work hard on a shoestring. Lehmann was well connected in literary circles, much in touch with the old guard of Sitwells, Woolfs and the Bloomsbury circle, and with European literature too. When he gave up I was approached by many who had worked with or for him. One such was Norah Wydenbruck, an Austrian countess, living in genteel poverty, but always keeping up appearances. She was married to a painter, also Austrian, called Alfred or Aloyiseus Purtschner, and they had a house in the very genteel Holland Park area, looked after by a series of Austrian au-pairs, presumably sent by good families to improve their English, and not needing to be paid. Purtschner was very gentle, very elderly and very lecherous. His tall stooping white-haired presence might never have left the court of Franz-Josef. He painted richly textured portraits, while, hidden at the back of his studio, were very erotic nudes, extremely well and naturalistically painted; it was obvious that he must have had great difficulty keeping his hands off his models, if models they were: they might well have come straight from his imagination. Norah Wydenbruck called on him for support and decoration. She had written a book on Rilke, published by Lehmann, and had also translated Rilke into English. She always had some new book coming out, usually a translation. Her afternoon parties, normally on Sundays, were decorous affairs. There would be one glass of spritzer, and then a Lieder recital or piano piece from her current au-pair or a professional friend, then a few words from the hostess about her new publication, copies of which were piled up on the piano and which she had on sale or return from the publisher at the author's discount. If you were there you had to buy a copy. In such ways she made ends meet.

One day she approached me with a proposition; a Milanese lawyer, a Signor Pozzi, had had a daughter, Antonia Pozzi, who was a poet, although this was only discovered after her suicide. Her father, remorsefully, having discovered the poems in her room, decided to spend the money he might have given her for a dowry in publishing an edition, which in the event was favourably reviewed and sold well in Italy. He now wished to pay for translations to appear in other languages. Norah had translated the poems into English and we arranged to bring out a small *de luxe* edition and a larger, one thousand copy, trade edition. This came out in 1955 to a few reviews and very small sales. The disappointed Signor Pozzi, denying me the time to carry on offering the book to bookshops, insisted on taking back the books he had paid for, and they were sent to him in Italy. Nevertheless I have become very fond of these poems by a tragic, secretive girl who loved dogs and children and died very young. Her father must have been a big fascist in the thirties and probably a tyrant at home. When, years later, I put a few of the poems, (including the one very poignant one she had written before drowning herself) in a series, *New Writing and Writers* (No. 13), it was picked out by the reviewers and highly lauded. Norah Wydenbruck also brought me a biography of Titian, which she translated from the Italian and other books.

By the late fifties I was in touch with many who had belonged to the old Merlin group in Paris. Alister Kershaw wrote an elegant, if often macabre

History of the Guillotine for me, Patrick Bowles, who had translated Beckett's *Molloy*, was willing to translate anything we gave him, and I was now extending my series of European classics with Goethe, Storm, Keller, Mörike, Eichendorff, Chamisso, Droste-Hülshoff and Gotthelf from German literature, usually with covers designed by Helmut Weissenborn containing apt little drawings in the period style of the book, and with Stendhal, Zola and others from nineteenth century French literature, while some other titles came from Spain, Italy and Russia. April FitzLyon persuaded me to let her translate the *Memoirs of Princess Dashkova*, the friend and confidante who had greatly influenced Catherine the Great, and I produced an elegant edition with, rarely for us, a full-colour cover. She had earlier written a biography of Lorenzo da Ponte for me. He was a colourful character, librettist of Mozart's best operas, a revolutionary, a rascal in most of his dealings and a formidable seducer of women; the title I gave the book, *The Libertine Librettist* came to me in a dream. April did not like it, but assented. It was retitled *Lorenzo da Ponte* in subsequent editions.

Da Ponte's life was so interesting that the book received major reviews. Born a Jew in a suburb of Venice, he was converted to Catholicism, took minor orders, but was arrested by the Inquisition for sedition and revolutionary activities. Rescued by his friend Casanova, he arrived in Vienna just as the court poet, Metastasio, died, took his place and wrote opera texts for several composers in addition to Mozart. Poisoned by a jealous husband he left Vienna in a hurry, ran the Haymarket Theatre in London into bankruptcy, and then started a new career in America, becoming Columbia's first professor of Italian. I never failed, in later visits to the Columbia University bookshop, to tell this story and so get them to stock the book. It required April FitzLyon to undertake a great deal of research, and was much plagiarised by biographers in other countries, but at least it served as a useful antidote to Da Ponte's own boastful and unreliable memoirs.

Meanwhile, at Calders Ltd., things went from bad to worse. My uncle had not the will to resist an issue of new shares and I was in debt to the banks and in serious jeopardy. I went to see a firm of big city solicitors -- Clifford-Turner, where I dealt with one of the partners, a Mr. Batchelor. We decided that, as my days with the company were in any case numbered and my uncle had agreed to open the door to Wolfson, my only option was to get a good price for my shares and that meant inviting a third-party to make a take-over bid. Clifford-Turner then wrote to Montague Meyer, our principal competitor in the pole and sleeper side of the business, and they responded, finally putting up a bid at forty-five shillings a share on the understanding that they would get over thirty percent of the shares from me, which included the block on which I had an option from the two Robertson sisters in Polmont.

This caused consternation in the company and Vogel got to work. I was summoned to a meeting with Isaac Wolfson, the first really high-powered negotiation of my young life. For two weeks I went every morning to his headquarter offices overlooking Oxford Circus. Batchelor and I would sit in one office while Wolfson went round a circle of five or six connecting rooms. He had a different negotiation going on in each. In those days Great Universal Stores was rapidly expanding and buying other companies to add to the Wolfson empire. He would bargain for five or ten minutes, leave you to think about his latest proposition, then go on to another negotiation in the next room, and be back in about half an hour. He used every form of flattery, both on Batchelor and myself: his voice would sometimes threaten, sometimes cajole. I found that I had to decide what I wanted to get and accept nothing less, or I would have no chance against this master negotiator. After all, the Montague Meyer offer was on the table, but it would not stay there for long once the rival timber company realised that they were in an auction. Batchelor often seemed to be breaking down under threats to drop the whole thing which Wolfson used to browbeat us with, and I would have to wait until my lawyer and I were alone again after Wolfson had left the room, suppressing my own anxiety and steeling us both not to give way.

In the end we reached a deal, forty-seven and sixpence a share for my own block and options, which was nearly double the stock market quotation, but only slightly above the Montague Meyer offer, which was also hedged with difficult conditions. I then insisted that all the family relatives should receive the same, but finally backed down slightly to agree that he should offer them forty-five shillings, still about a pound over the market price. He laughed at the time, telling me that I might be very gallant in protecting relatives whom for the most part I hardly knew, but none of them would ever thank me. He was right.

Part of the deal was that I would retain my seat on the board and my uncle would remain the chairman. I had nothing to do for the company after that, although some of the customers I had been dealing with personally continued to ask for me, and I still went to see some of them, but unofficially. Wolfson ended with a majority of the shares and he had had to pay a high price for them. After a while, impatient because my uncle showed no sign of weakening physically, he was asked to step down and a new chairman, picked by Wolfson, was installed. He was a retired civil servant to whom Wolfson no doubt owed some favour, a self-satisfied and pompous individual who the directors all tried to flatter and kow-tow to, but he was little seen, only attending the board meetings and the annual general meeting. 'He's not my sort of man, but no doubt he'll do the job alright,' my uncle told me, and he gradually withdrew from London and stayed at Ledlanet. At the last annual general meeting I attended, with my uncle still chairman, my relatives, whose interests I had protected in my dealings with Wolfson, tried to raise a motion to have me removed from the board, but a proxy was present to vote Wolfson's shares and I was returned with a comfortable majority. I did not feel happy however! I was of course now quite well-off with a large deposit in the bank and not quite sure what to do with it. All this happened in the spring of 1955.

* * * * * *

At the time of the Calder's Ltd. take-over, Christya and I were not getting on at all well. We belonged increasingly to different worlds and our tastes were very different. I have no diary from those years, but I do have a record of the opera performances I attended (fifty-two in 1955), which serves largely as a diary would to bring events back to mind. We both knew an ex-actor called Lesley Linder, who had a background in films, had become a film agent and would, just a little later, open a very fashionable restaurant in Mayfair called The White Elephant.

One day Lesley telephoned me with a proposition. There was a need and a market just then for short films that had some of the characteristics of a feature film, to introduce the feature. Most of those being made were concerned with travel to exotic places, but some kind of a plot was desirable. One such project he knew about needed some end-financing and if I could raise the money he would see that Christya got the part of the female star. She was always reproaching me for having ruined her promising film career by marrying her, and I thought that this might be the way to give her a second (or more accurately a third or fourth chance). I could then launch her back into her own world: it was obvious we were not designed to stay long together.

The director was to be Paul Dickson, who had recently been assistant director to Anatole Litvak on the film version of Terrence Rattigan's *Deep Blue Sea*. Sometime during the next few months the following, totally illogical events occurred: the original script was scrapped as dull; it was in any case highly unsuitable as a vehicle for Christya, who was far too temperamental to play the rather bland heroine walking on some tropical island. I then acquired the film rights to an atmospheric short story by Olive Shreiner called *The Pool*, a kind of ghost story.

Then we found a well-known Canadian actor, Arthur Hill, who was soon to star in *Who's Afraid of Virginia Woolf?* in New York and London opposite Uta Hagen. Our original cameraman, whose name was Cedric Williams, left half-way through the film and was replaced by Shuschitski, Dickson's choice. Paul Dickson spent two weeks with me looking for suitable sights in Bavaria and Northern Italy, during which time we became friends, but not for long. I decided to become business manager myself to save money. I did not do the job particularly well, but I knew when to say no to unnecessary expenditure and I could deal with Christya's tantrums, which no one else could, so I at least made some savings. Initially I was meant to put up the last twenty-five percent of the money, but with all the changes, especially those demanded by the leading actress, everyone else had withdrawn and I was left with two leading actors, one or two walk-ons, an ambitious director, an artistic European cameraman who had replaced a rather straightforward English one, an intellectual young assistant, who actually handled the camera and framed the picture, a lens focus-puller and about three others, who soon included Heinrich Falk, a German who ended up doing most of the production management.

I had bought, now that I had some money in the bank, a second-hand Bentley, and I can even remember the price: £2200, from Jack Barclay in Berkeley Square. With this I toured Europe with Paul Dickson, looking at mountain locations in perpetually wet weather and we finally settled on a hill village called Castelrotto in the Dolomites, part of the old South Tyrol, where they still spoke German. Here, in continuing bad weather the film was made.

I had hired a camera in Munich from a local film studio. The adaptations that Williams made to it so upset the owner that he would only let the camera go if his own technician came with it to protect it, thus making the crew even bigger. During the ten days in Munich, deeply troubled, I escaped to the Prinzregenten and the Gärtnerplatz theatres to see operas including Pfitzner's *Palestrina*, Handel's *Julius Caesar* and other operas by Mozart, Wagner and Strauss, which somewhat relieved my tension. At the hotel I met a very attractive Austrian bombshell and took her to *Così fan tutte*. She was willing to flirt, but I was too worried about the film to think about sex just then: the crew were all in Castelrotto, where I had myself been a few days before and I had returned to pick up film stock. What we did need was an open sports car for the film and we had been unable to find one anywhere near the village. I persuaded Inge (I think that was her name) to drive south, to meet me at Castelrotto and be around while we made the film. I, in the meantime, had to return to London to settle details and buy more film stock, which I then smuggled past Italian customs in the Bentley. I remember my annoyance when, after stopping for the night at Innsbruck and arriving at the Brenner Pass border point the next morning, I found I had left my passport at the hotel. They had kept it overnight and leaving early, I had forgotten it. This meant that I had to brave possible detection and arrest twice within four hours. The reason the film had to be smuggled was because of Italian red tape, which would have held us up for weeks, especially in summer, as well as necessitating many bribes. But I was not stopped and arrived at Castelrotto in the afternoon. And there was already trouble.

Inge, if that is her right name, had arrived the day before and Williams had taken her out to dinner. He insisted on driving her car, had obviously drunk too much, and badly damaged one side of it. First I had to calm down Inge. Then I had to see what was happening with the film. It was not going well and Williams was quarrelling with the director. Christya, who ever since I had first known her, had taken sleeping pills to sleep and amphetamines to get up, had overdone it and had slept through the only two days when the weather had been suitable for filming, and had sat around with nothing to do when it rained. This was, after all in the mountains and typically it rained in late summer and early autumn. It was decided that the sports car could be used if only one side was filmed. I promised to repair the damage and if need be replace the car. We all had an acrimonious dinner that night. However, Christya wasn't with us. She was staying on her own at a different and better hotel and never mixed with the crew or, at that point in our relationship, with me.

Before dinner Inge and I got into bed together, but we were interrupted and never had proper sex. Later, it must have been about eleven, I went to bed on my own, dead tired, and fell asleep. Inge came into my room, woke me, and we made love all night. The next day, Christya, driving past us in Inge's car for her next scene, driven by Arthur Hill, saw us together in the Bentley and gave us a long cold stare. Inge left later that day and I never saw her again. She drove her battered car away, never made a claim and never got in touch again. I hope she got as much out of our one night as I did, because once awake I was much roused and she was a wonderful sex partner.

On the last day of filming, (by now Williams had long left and been replaced by Shushitski), Paul Dickson and I had a public fist fight in the main square of Castelrotto, which was witnessed by the entire village because it was the evening hour when the whole community takes its promenade before dark finally turns to night. I forget what sparked it off: tension was high, he was not popular with the crew, and when I knocked him down and almost out, I was applauded. He left on his own the next morning. We had the film in the can, more or less. It was bad, messy and uninteresting.

Back in London I told Carl Foreman the whole story and asked his advice. He laughed, said I should write my own script about the whole adventure and he would film it. I never did, so he never had a chance to keep his promise, which I think was genuine. He also advised me to see Sam Wanamaker, an American actor in London whom I knew slightly, because he was trying to break into film in England, having made *Christ in Concrete* in New York, a commercial failure, but a success for him. He was then about to stage the Brecht-Weill *Threepenny Opera* at the Royal Court Theatre in the Marc Blitzstein version, which I had already seen in New York, where it had been a big success at the Théatre de Lys.

He saw the unedited *The Pool*, was interested in using part of it and filming new scenes in London, which would go towards making it into a short feature, I went along with the idea because I saw no alternative. I assumed that Wanamaker was part of the American diaspora which had come to Europe because of McCarthy and the Un-American Activities

Committee, but no, it was personal debt that had driven him overseas, as I was later to learn. He was happy enough for certain people to think he was in London for political reasons, but not everyone. On one occasion I went to have Sunday lunch at his house in Hampstead where other guests and his wife and small daughter Zoë were present. I was carrying the New Statesman, a left-wing but in no way extreme political journal, on arrival. 'Do you mind if I take that from you,' he said and hid it in a drawer.

I sat through several rehearsals with him at the Royal Court and met Brecht who was present for a while, giving little pointers on details that had been altered in Blitzstein's jazzy adaptation. On one occasion he heard a sound and asked where it was coming from. Investigation discovered that an upstairs lavatory behind the stage-left boxes had been left open when someone flushed it. 'You must do that every time,' said Brecht, 'and at exactly that moment in the play.'

Sam took me several times to a Soho night-club where the current cabaret singer was the girl singing Jenny and rehearsing for Wanamaker's production of *The Threepenny Opera* and his current affair. My friend Jacques Chaix visited me just then and with a little help from Wanamaker had a dalliance with one of the other singers in the show. Once *Threepenny Opera* had opened, we moved into a studio and filmed new scenes for *The Pool*. We had a famous film editor in Reggie Beck, but it still didn't work. It gave Sam Wanamaker some film-directing experience, cost me more money, but never found a distributor.

* * * * * *

1955 was a good year for me in opera. I went to the first performance of the newly formed Handel Opera Society, and saw *Deidamia* at St. Pancras Town Hall with Marion Studholme, one of the most stylish and attractive soubrettes of the day, in the name role and with Iris Kells as Achilles, and heard a marvellous *Figaro* with Sena Jurinac and Elena Rizzieri at Glyndebourne, where Vittorio Gui, who was introducing Rossini to Christie's private opera house, conducted an unforgettable *Comte Ory* with Sari Barabas, Juan Oncina and Ian Wallace, a perfect cast and one of the funniest performances I have ever seen. Wallace was later to become a friend. Tebaldi, Tagliavini and Gobbi sang the best *Tosca* I have ever heard that summer at Covent Garden. I have already mentioned Munich, where I saw ten operas during that year's summer festival to help me deal with the trauma of the film. My book, documenting the operas I had seen now, recorded 188 performances of 91 operas, and the pace was soon to accelerate.

I was now living a busy double life. I was still a director of Calders Ltd., but had no responsibilities. The publishing company was growing: suitable books came my way and I published them, although there were a few unfortunate experiences. I was approached one day by Anthony Blond, whose family were clothing manufacturers supplying Marks and Spencer, with a book of memoirs by Captain Peter Baker. Baker was the son of the managing director of Ealing Studios, where the Ealing comedies were made. Having left the army, he became a member of parliament, started a publishing company called Falcon Press and set out to be a tycoon. He acquired Grey Walls Press, a good little literary publisher, from its founder Charles Wrey Gardiner, who also edited Poetry Quarterly and wrote books of personal memoirs rather like the autobiographical novels of Henry Miller. Baker had started a new political party, The Commonwealth Party, which although short-lived, made waves during the nineteen-fifties. At the time he was the youngest member of the House of Commons.

I was to witness the pattern of Peter Baker's career many times over the years. First the euphoria of early success, then the belief that he could never go wrong, and then growth built on borrowing and acquisitions. Along with the tycooning came much entertaining and alcoholism. Reality recedes as profits do not match expectation and the risk-taking grows until only crime seems to offer a way out. Baker's empire included the British Book Centre in New York, which bought smaller quantities of British books that did not find an American publisher and sold them: it grew quite rapidly, but barely paid its way and Baker had little time or patience to devote to management. Self-aggrandisement became the pattern of his life until his fall, which came with the discovery that he had forged the signatures of three prominent businessmen on bank guarantees.

I had not known that much of the material in *My Testament*, Peter Baker's *apologia per sua vita* had already appeared in another book, which recalled his wartime experiences: he had reformulated these in the new volume which was a series of justifications for his catastrophic actions, which he blamed largely on his alcoholism. The book came out in March 1955, just after he had been sent to prison for seven years. It sold fairly well to large but not flattering reviews. I went to see him in Wormwood Scrubs where he was serving his time in the library and he tried to make a deal whereby I would supply books to the library and give him a commission, which I refused. I do not think that publishing the book did me much good.

Several books from Cameron Associates came out on my list at this time including a penetrating *History of the American Labour Movement* by Boyar and Moraes and Harvey O'Connor's *Empire of Oil*, an exposé of the international machinations of the big oil companies. William Yates, a Tory MP, brought me *Violent Truce* by E.H. Hutchinson, who had been a military observer with the United Nations Truce Supervision Organisation in Israel from 1951 to 1955, which gave a very different picture of the Palestinian situation from that which the Israelis were trying to foster in Britain. I had trouble over this with Henry Jonas, my London traveller who was Jewish, and with several friends. I was also offered an important book on American civil liberties and the McCarthy witch-hunt by Corliss Lamont, a well known American philosopher and professor. I went to see Bertrand Russell, who was quite approachable, and he instantly agreed to write an introduction. My first meeting with Lord Russell was very cordial and many more were to follow. As with many of the American political books I brought out at about this time, my status as a publisher with a mission was enhanced but sales were fairly slow. These were all hardback books selling at between fifteen and twenty-five shillings. Paperbacks, other than Penguins and a few other popular series of fiction classics and light novels, were still a thing of the future, especially for serious books of non-fiction.

In January 1957 I had my thirtieth birthday and I was on a 'plane returning from New York on the night of the 25th, seated next to an English journalist working on an American scandal rag, The National Enquirer. He was returning from Hollywood and boasted of three days he had just spent in the Californian desert with a buxom starlet while I was musing on the beginnings of my thirties. I had known much success, had done many of the things I had always wanted to do, and I wondered what was still missing. I remembered my school days in Canada when I had wanted to play an instrument, but my request to learn the violin was turned down by my mother, who said I could take piano lessons if I wanted. The piano teacher at B.C.S. had hardly inspired me and I soon dropped the lessons, but now I wondered what reason there could be against another start: I decided I would learn the 'cello, an instrument that is less painful to one's neighbours than the violin. But if I did not take steps to pursue this new hobby immediately I would soon be overwhelmed by other activities. So the next morning on arrival I went to Beare's music shop in Soho, bought a 'cello, a bow, a manual and resin, and set about finding a teacher. I ended up with a very military-looking cellist, who also played the string baritone, a practising musician with various chamber groups who had a fair number of pupils, most of them professional. I have forgotten his name.

I was also having an affair which had begun the previous year. It had started at the annual Bookseller's Conference, which had taken place in Southport in Lancashire and which was as boring as these things usually are. It is the social contacts that count: the official sessions are almost the same year after year, with the same issues, the same complaints, a few new ideas or old ones, which are never taken up, because no one ever wanted to change anything. I became friendly with an academic bookseller from Manchester called Ernest Hochland, originally from Germany; we spoke German together and finding we had many common literary tastes we took long walks over the sands which stretched for an immense distance from our hotel to the sea. There was a lady with us on one occasion, who was called Lisel Field, the academic representative for an American company, MacMillan. She had been in Czechoslovakia when the Germans invaded the Sudetenland and began to arrest Jews, and she, a teenager, having lost her family, had walked all the way across Europe to England, arriving just before the war. She was lively, intellectual and rather enjoying the conference, which was a holiday to her. We sat together at the final dinner, joking about the solemnity and fatuousness of most of the speeches, had a few drinks, and as the lift stopped at her landing, I saw the signs of a definite invitation in her eye. But I had already pressed the button and I couldn't have gone down again without attracting attention. I sought her out at breakfast, asked if she would like to drive south with me to London and she accepted. On the way, after coming out of the Mersey Tunnel, I made a detour to look at my old timber yard, but didn't go in. On arrival at her flat in Maida Vale, almost opposite the old BBC studios, we went to bed and made love. She was different from the other women in my experience, dark and swarthy with a heavy body and big breasts, but very passionate and highly sexed. I came home to Christya the next morning, saying I had been delayed, but then began having trysts with Lisel frequently, sometimes staying the night. Christya was quite accustomed to my going away on business trips, so I didn't have to invent too many lies. Lisel loved music, and we played records and went to concerts and operas together; Christya no longer bothered to accompany me to such events which bored her. My days were still taken up partly with Calders Ltd., but increasingly with publishing; I was enjoying learning to play the 'cello and I was enjoying my new affair.

It was at the beginning of this year, 1957, that Hiss finished his book, *In the Court of Public Opinion*, and my trip to New York, referred to above, must have been to see him and take delivery of this manuscript, among other business. Doubleday, sometime during the previous year, had acquired the American rights, but just as they had killed off the Jowett book, they decided not to proceed, and Knopf suddenly entered the scene and signed a contract with Alger Hiss. I had just arrived from the airport at the Gotham Hotel when I found a message asking me to ring Blanche Knopf immediately I arrived. I did so and she asked me if I would come around *immediately* to her office and not to speak to anyone until I did.

I was ushered into her room and she looked at me for a long time as if I were a strange new species. It was obviously going through her mind that here was a young, unknown publisher who somehow had managed to commission a book from a man of the importance of Alger Hiss. She played with me like a cat with a mouse, asked me how I had become involved with Hiss, all the time scratching the leather top of her desk with her long red fingernails. I felt it was my face she was really scratching. She said that she had received the manuscript, that it was being edited, and that she thought it ought to be set in type in America as Hiss was there. I could print my edition from the American finished pages. I saw nothing wrong with that provided we published on the same day, because the book would attract major press attention everywhere. We fixed a tentative date later that spring. On the way out of her office I was about to get into the elevator when Angus

Cameron came out of it and we exchanged a few words. He was now working for Knopf. Blanche Knopf, seeing me off, gave me a twisted grin. 'Oh, so you know Angus? Well, I suppose you would.' I managed to have a quick word with Angus, who had never been told that I was doing the Hiss book in England. 'Look out for that lady,' he said. 'She's dangerous.'

I spent about ten days in New York and returned to London. When I arrived I found a letter, sent by seamail, posted when I was still in New York. It was from Blanche Knopf. The gist of it was that she had decided to publish right away because there had been, so she claimed, a leak in her office, and the press had managed to get hold of a set of the proofs. She was publishing the following week. She could have called me in New York, have wired me in London, but, no, she had deliberately engineered it so that her's would be the only edition to appear that spring. I never believed her story about the leak. When the Knopf edition appeared in the U.S. the whole British press reviewed it on the news pages: Alastair Cooke's long article was in the *Manchester Guardian*, the *Glasgow Herald* and other papers. It took two months to get my edition published and it was then totally ignored by the press, old hat now. Sales were very small; in fact many of the leading booksellers had brought in the American edition. It was not Alger Hiss' fault. I still saw him, both in London and New York, and he was apologetic, but not very concerned. The book did not really do much to advance his efforts to prove his innocence: it was a little too general and he could not bring himself to question the evidence against him, as a lawyer with more objectivity would have done. But he went on striving, nevertheless, to prove his innocence to the end of his life.

I was seeing the Miller family, Sigmund and his wife Phyllis, quite often in those days. I had intended to go for Christmas and New Year in 1956 to Madeira, but for some reason to do with my passport, which might have been out of date, I was unable to go with Christya and Jamie, now two years old, so they went without me. I spent Christmas day, at the Millers' insistence (I would have been perfectly happy at home with my books and some new records), with Phyllis, Sigi and their two boys. I arrived in Madeira before the New Year and went swimming in the rather chilly sea water on New Year's day, mainly out of bravado. I remember being struck by how carefully the militia – Portugal still had a fascist dictatorship then – tried to keep the tourists away from mixing with local people. Our hotel, in warm and sunny weather, was on the coast, the waves lapping its walls, and I had a sense of total isolation.

The following summer I came home late one night and began practising the 'cello. Christya had gone to bed, and it may have been around midnight when she came into the large drawing-room, said 'You and your fucking 'cello,' picked up a silver cigarette box which had once been a late wedding-present from Dick Soukup, and threw it at me. It smashed the front of the 'cello and I went berserk. We hadn't been getting on for some time, were leading largely separate lives, everything I did exasperated her, while I was constantly troubled by her frequent attempts to cheat shopkeepers, leave hotels without paying and her string of little frauds. Something snapped in my head and suddenly I was holding her head on the balcony over the railings, strangling her, on the verge of pushing her over. Suddenly I pulled her back. There was still capital punishment in those days and a voice in my head said, 'It's not worth swinging for this bitch.' I left her recovering her breath on the floor, threw a few things into a small bag and rang Sigmund. 'Sigi, could I spend the night on your sofa?' I asked.

'Yes,' he replied, 'but not yet. Doris Lessing is sitting on it now.' He was giving a party. I took a taxi over to Bayswater where he lived, sat through till the end of the party and claimed the sofa. I stayed there for three days and during that time found myself a flat at 11 Upper Wimpole Street and moved in. Christya refused to let me have my clothes or any other possessions. I could of course have moved in with Lisel, but thought it wiser not to. So after eight years of marriage I ended the relationship and my career in timber at the same time. I was still married, but in essence free.

Chapter 4

Transition

It is very possible that I have some of the dates wrong in this narrative. The years from 1952 to 1957 are rather a jumble in my memory. I was doing so many things simultaneously that my recollections tend to be parallel rather than chronological, but the events and the people are as I remember them and the key associations that guide me are where I was living, what I saw in the theatre and the opera house (the latter could be checked from the record that I started keeping from the time I arrived in London), and from what I published: the dates are, after all, on the copyright pages of the books. Certainly 1957 was a key year, even if my memory tends to stretch it backward as well as forward.

Straight from university I had tumbled into a stressful marriage and now I had tumbled out of it with the same sense of desperation. My body found its own way to test me. Within a few days of leaving Christya I went one evening on my own to Sadlers Wells Theatre. The opera was *The Pearl Fishers*. Suddenly, just before the interval, I felt my nose running and, until the next act started, my sinuses streamed, sometimes with fits of sneezing, sometimes not, and only partially stopped when the music began again. The tension within me found a novel way of breaking though my pose of continuing to act normally. It stopped almost as quickly as it had begun, and I have had recurrences of such sudden nasal flows on a few later occasions, never lasting long, and not always for a detectable emotional reason. I also have fits of sneezing.

When I walked out on Christya I no longer had access to my papers at Wilton Terrace, and that included old diaries, which would have been useful to this book, and of course my unpublished poems. T.S. Eliot had earlier told me to go to see Peter du Sautoy, who had replaced him as poetry editor at Faber. I did and left a sizeable bundle with him. When I went back some weeks later – this was probably in 1954 but might have been earlier – he had divided my poems into two groups, a minority of these he liked and a much larger pile of those he didn't. He explained that his judgement was purely subjective, as all such judgements had to be, but there it was! 'Give me more of these,' he said, 'and I'll publish a volume.' Broadly speaking he liked the shorter lyrical poems, mainly to do with love. The longer, rather mystical and often narrative poems, were, he felt too obscure and difficult. My favourite was a very long poem based loosely on Wagner's Ring cycle, entitled *Alberich*, and in style it was much influenced by Eliot, rich in allusion to everything from world events to associations derived from my reading. I think he found it boring.

When I left Wilton Terrace I naturally expected that I would be able to collect my poems. I never saw them again[9], nor did she ever say what she had done with them. I presume that she simply threw them out. Except for the occasional serious poem, inspired by an occasion or an emotion, and some comic verse to amuse friends, I was to write no more serious poetry until I was over seventy, when I suddenly found a new voice.

After a few nights on Sigi Miller's sofa I had found a top floor flat at 11 Upper Wimpole Street with a bedroom, a sitting-room, a bathroom and kitchen and I was to stay there until 1960. I bought some second-hand furniture from a large emporium near Euston. I had of course lost my 'cello with its smashed front, but one day Lisel sent me another. I never got used to it and having been dropped by my teacher at this time, I gradually stopped practising. I missed my books. It was only many months later that Christya allowed me to remove a few and I found that she had written her name in all of them, including one that was quite obviously a school prize. There was some *quid pro quo* for this, probably paying her bill at Harrods or something similar.

I was living alone now and seeing my daughter when I could, but access was limited. She had an English nanny, who came to me one day in horror with a number of stories about how Christya was treating Jamie and about the mother's behaviour in general. Amazingly I have forgotten what they were, these reported horrors, but they were alarming enough for me to go to my lawyer who then arranged a hearing at the Court of Chancery to get custody. This I was able to do with the evidence given by the nanny. While Christya launched an appeal I took Jamie and the nanny to a residential hotel in North London, just beyond the North Circular Road, returning there from the office every evening. Christya went to another judge and managed to get the judgement reversed. Eventually the judge asked to see the child and I was ordered to produce her in court. I told her that a man would ask her some questions and that she should tell him what she really wanted, whatever it was. I think this must have been in 1957 when she was three, but I cannot be sure that it was not a year later. My feeling is that she must have been four. I would not want, now that she is herself a mother in middle age, to awaken that traumatic time for her. The judge came into court after questioning her and said: 'The little girl says that she wants to live with her father, and I am not sure what to do. He has probably promised her something and spoiled her in the past.' He then ordered that she should be returned to her mother, but not immediately. A second cousin of mine, Molly Blake, a widow with a grown-up son living with her who had lost an arm in a military accident, had volunteered to foster her for three months. I did not particularly like Molly Blake who had led the family faction against me at the board meeting after the Wolfson take-over, but I had to put up with the situation, going several time a week to Molly's house

---

[9] Some later turned up at the Lillie Library in Indiana (See Chapter 9).

in Onslow Square to read my daughter stories. Christya then took up with a minor fraudster called Victor Churchill, whom she eventually married. I shall return to them later.

The publishing company had moved in 1955 into a small room in the offices in Queen's House of Francis King and Son, our auditors, who also kept our books, overlooking Leicester Square. There Berry Bloomfield, who had been my secretary at Calders Ltd., came with me and we were soon joined by Sally Belfrage. Sally was the daughter of Cedric Belfrage and Molly Castle, both well-known journalists, who had divorced a long time previously. Cedric had spent some years in America and during the McCarthy period had edited a radical left-wing newspaper called the National Guardian, one of the few vehicles where Angus Cameron, Leo Huberman and others like them could advertise their books. It had given sympathetic coverage to the Rosenberg trial and such events as the infamous incident in 1953 when an outdoor concert by Paul Robeson was turned into a riot by a demented lynch mob in New Jersey. Although he had been many years in the United States Cedric Belfrage had kept his British nationality. He was deported after his permission to stay, and I presume to work, was withdrawn, and although he tried to edit the newspaper as 'Editor-in-Exile', it did not long survive his departure. I had of course met him in New York, and it was at his instigation that Sally Belfrage came to me for a job, at first a very temporary one. There was a big book exhibition at the Royal Festival Hall organised by the Sunday Times, at which I decided to take a booth, and I engaged Sally for a week to help me run it. I shared the booth with another publisher, Christopher Johnson, who was also the Tory MP for Carlyle. There was a considerable contrast between the nature of our lists, but we got on well enough. However, when the Queen Mother came to make a tour of the exhibition, it was the Johnson side of the booth that met her eye and it featured a rather lewdly-jacketed medical book entitled *Women in Emergency* (Johnson was a medical doctor as well as an MP and the cover depicted pregnant women who could not get quickly to hospital.) The Queen Mother, who until then had been stopping to chat at every booth, hastily averted her gaze and walked on. I had been hoping she would be photographed at our stand.

The book exhibition over, I gave Sally Belfrage a temporary job at Queen's House, where she did editorial work, which she enjoyed, but also had to process orders from our reps, which she did not. One day I discovered that her desk drawer was full of orders from booksellers which she simply pushed there because routine work, however necessary, bored her. I don't think I kept her long after that.

Francis King was an accountant and our auditor. Together with his son Peter, he kept our books and gave me financial advice. We had a sales representative called Gorlinsky for a while in London, a Mr. V. J. Camp, who sent in precise reports and a stream of orders from the Midlands, West

Country and Wales, and a lady in the north, Kay Knowles, who was adept at queue-jumping in bookshops, saying to reps in line in front of her, all waiting to see the buyer, 'Please, I shall only be two seconds,' and then staying half an hour or longer. In Scotland we had a real eccentric, a Mr. MacAndrelis, who always wore the kilt, took his wife everywhere with him, and drove an antique Rolls-Royce that had once been the Edinburgh Lord Provost's official car, and now had the Lion Rampant flying from the little flag-mast on the bonnet.

After leaving Calders Ltd I frequently made sales trips myself, often covering ground I knew well from my timber-selling days, but now I stayed in much more modest little hotels and boarding houses. The usual bad British food, brown soup, boiled meat and two vegetables, followed by soggy pudding or acid Danish blue cheese and bad coffee, could now be varied by the arrival of Chinese and Indian restaurants, even cheaper and much better. I came to know the dour bookshops of Edinburgh, the cautious provincial shops where to take one copy of one book was to represent the list, the established bookshops of Northern and Midland towns, where sometimes I did well and sometimes not. One Manchester shop put a young man in charge of fiction and he tried to read every new novel that came in. If he liked a book he would recommend it to his customers and soon he was reordering much bigger quantities. If I could enthuse him about a book I was subscribing he would order twenty-five copies, but after he left it was back to half a dozen. Hardly any of these once-revered bookshop names still exist.

I also met booksellers at the annual book-sellers' conference, such as the one where I had encountered Lisel. Robert Maxwell liked to show up and have himself paged over the loudspeakers every half-hour. The Blackwells and the Heffers, university book-sellers in Oxford and Cambridge, considered themselves the aristocrats of the book trade. Publishers were there on sufferance and had to pay much of the conference costs; they were always under attack to give better terms and to contribute to bookseller training schemes. They also paid for most of the drinks.

Among the few people I have really disliked in my life, Robert Maxwell ranks at or near the top. My first dealings with him were over the Simpkin Marshall fiasco. Simpkin Marshall was an old, long-established wholesaler on London's Marylebone Road, which stocked every book in print. Small booksellers who did not want to have hundreds of accounts with different publishers and could only order small quantities, often single copies for individual customers, could get these books quickly and economically from Simpkin Marshall, and the business was invaluable to both publishers and booksellers. Some of their staff had been with them for decades and often had an encyclopaedic memory of book titles, authors' names and who the publisher was, even of highly specialised books. But Simpkin Marshall fell on hard times and Robert Maxwell made a great show of coming to their rescue and saving the old-established company for the benefit of the book trade.

The extreme crookedness of Robert Maxwell has been well-known to the general public since his death, but even in the middle-fifties he was widely distrusted. He had used his wartime position as an officer of the Allied Control Commission in Germany to acquire valuable technical copyrights for next to nothing, probably by blackmailing Nazi publishers who were willing to give anything to have their names cleared officially, and he had built up Pergamon Press, his publishing company in Oxford with these copyrights. The main asset of Simpkin Marshall was their large valuable building on Marylebone Road, and that was his target. He was allowed to acquire control cheaply on the promise of investing new capital to save the company. What he did was to keep it going long enough to sell the building at a fraction of its value to his own family company, and then to close down Simpkin Marshall, leaving enormous debts to publishers unpaid. The second calamity came when all the stock – considerable quantities of every book in print – was then offered at remaindered prices. Booksellers went to the warehouse, made a pile of the books they wanted and bargained to get them at the lowest price possible. Maxwell did not care as the money would go to the receivers. This meant that not only did publishers not get paid, but their sales to booksellers stopped until their bookseller customers had liquidated their cheap purchases. Peter Owen was the only publisher as far as I am aware who went to see Maxwell during the period when Maxwell was running and apparently 'saving' the company, who ignored Maxwell's threat that anyone who pressed for payment or sued would do no further business with Simpkin Marshall, and he issued a writ. Maxwell paid him to stop an avalanche of other writs, which would have ruined his plan to strip the assets before putting the company into bankruptcy. I, unfortunately, when I went to see him, allowed myself to be conned, and lost all of the considerable sum I was owed. It was not to be my last unpleasant encounter with this evil man of many aliases. He had changed his original name, Jan de Koch, first to Du Maurier (name of a best-selling novelist and of a fashionable brand of cigarettes) before becoming Maxwell, which had the right British sound to it. Like Dracula, he was from Translyvania.

All the old staff were of course sacked as soon as he took over. There were wonderful characters among them. The music buyer, who had been a musician in pre-war Germany, was always telling me which composers needed a new biography, and I think he read all the books on music I published. Although no one in the book trade trusted him – his nickname was the 'bouncing Czech' – Maxwell was to wreak much more damage in his life, yet he always managed to get the banks to back him, however bad his reputation and even after Sir Hartley Shawcross, who investigated some of his dealings, had said that he was not of suitable character to be a director of a public company.

The one room we occupied at Queen's House was soon too small, and I rented the top two floors of a building in Sackville Street. There were two tailors below us, one, a Mr. Black, who forever wanted to make me a suit and eventually he did. Sackville Street is really an extension of Saville Row and runs between it and Piccadilly. In those days it was mainly tailors on Sackville Street with Sotheran's, an antiquarian bookshop, at the Piccadilly end. There were mutterings at first about what things were coming to 'with publishers moving in!'

I engaged an editor, the best I was to have, Pamela Lyon, whom I had known for some time. I think Christya had met her at some dancing class and brought her home one day. She was a pretty vivacious girl from New Zealand, who had come to Britain on a scholarship to dance with the Sadlers Wells Ballet Company (later to become the Royal Ballet), but had developed TB, which had forced her to abandon that career. The milk diet she was now forced to adopt did not help much either: her legs swelled and she had put on too much weight to be able to dance again. But she was intelligent and well-read and I offered her a job once we had adequate offices in Sackville Street. I was still living at Wilton Terrace then.

. Pamela had been working for me for a few months, perhaps longer, when I received a manuscript from the Professor of Russian at Manchester University. What D. P. Costello had sent me was however a Persian translation, and I took it home over the Easter weekend of 1957. I remember reading it on the Good Friday with dusk falling just as I finished it. I turned on the light, turned back to the first page, and read it again. It was a chilling twice-told tale by an Iranian poet called Sadegh Hedayat entitled *The Blind Owl*. The atmosphere of the first part was macabre: the narrator, as if in a dream, murders and, as if it were part of a pre-arranged ritual, buries the young woman whom he has seen through a chink in his wall, looking like a Persian miniature. The second part, which also ends in a sinister murder, is more naturalistic, the story of a young boy, dominated by an obsessive sister who seduces him as he grows up.

On the Tuesday I handed the manuscript to Pamela Lyon; 'I thought this quite interesting,' I said, 'tell me what you think.' She came in the next morning. 'Did you really read it?' she asked.

'Yes, do you like it?'

'It's extraordinary. I couldn't put it down.'

'I'm glad you agree with me. We'll accept it.'

We published *The Blind Owl* in December 1957 and on the same day as Beckett's *Malone Dies*. Several newspapers reviewed them together, but not favourably. 'Mescaline might help,' said the reviewer of a Sunday newspaper, 'but don't count on it.' I think he was referring to them both. And the sales, of course, were terrible. I knew that Beckett would do better with time; he already had an international reputation and was being discussed in the universities. We were selling the imported Evergreen edition of *Murphy*, while *Waiting for Godot* had been the talking point of its year. But *The Blind Owl* was a one-off with the author dead. Once a friend of Sartre, and an opium addict, he had committed suicide in Paris in 1951 at the age of forty-eight. How could I create interest in a book in which I believed, that had fallen into the hands of insensitive reviewers. I decided to try an experiment.

I went to the library and picked a hundred names out of *Who's Who*. They were the names that caught my eye as I leafed through: some were novelists like Graham Greene and Iris Murdoch, some poets with exotic attitudes like William Empson, some important personalities that I had met like Bertrand Russell, and others included broadcasters, commentators and journalists whom I knew to be open-minded and intelligent. At this distance, I hardly remember more than a few names. But they were all people of note, and they included Isaiah Berlin, V. S. Pritchett and F. R. Leavis. I sent them all the same letter, telling them I was enclosing a copy of *The Blind Owl* as a gift, that I hoped they would read it, and if they did and liked it, that they would talk about it. If they could give me a few words of comment that I could quote, I would be even more grateful. About twenty replied, all enthusiastically, and I could now place advertisements with quotations of approval from well-known names.

It worked: little by little sales picked up and we began to get more and better reviews from newspapers which had held back. I sold the rights to Barney Rosset for the U.S., to Feltrinelli for Italy, to Bezige Bij for Holland and to Helmut Kossodo for German-speaking countries. France had already published it, as I soon discovered. A French diplomat had translated it and published it with José Corti, a surrealist publisher in Paris, but with no contract with the author's estate. Costello had given me a letter signed by the author's brother, giving him rights to publish internationally. He was a Major General in the Iranian army, but this was in the days before the Shah seized power from Mussadecq, backed by the big oil companies. Corti had assumed there was no copyright, but he was wrong, because the author had deposited a copy of his manuscript with the Indian copyright office in Bombay.

I had a series of office managers whose responsibilities included sales management, although everyone did everything to a great extent. Peter Bradley was a man who had owned a record shop in Knightsbridge, who over the years had sold me many records, and he joined the firm and sat opposite me in the offices at Sackville Street. He would go through the orders and send them to our distributors, who at this time were Central Books on the Gray's Inn Road. The reason I went to Central Books is the following.

My London sales rep, Henry Jonas, invited me to his wedding in a synagogue and to the reception afterwards, where I sat next to a Margaret Mainert. She was a director of Central Books that published mainly communist and left-wing literature and distributed for other small publishers. She was very disdainful of the religious ceremony we had just attended, and when we began talking of books she said that she would be willing to offer favourable terms to distribute my list, which she liked. So it came about that we moved our stock to Gray's Inn Road. My manager however would ration the flow of orders sent to Central Books because he believed that the packers could only handle so much at a time. When I realised why our sales had become lower than they should have been, the discovery led to another row, to his leaving, and eventually to a change of distributor. We moved to a company called Trade Counter in South Kensington, where Miss Sladden, a large, cheerful, overweight lady puffed cigarettes all day while a large Alsatian dog lay at her feet, typing thousands of invoices, without, so it seemed, ever making an error. The manager, Oliver Moxon, I had first met at the Antelope with the crowd surrounding Sir John Squire. We stayed with Trade Counter for many years.

Office managers followed each other, most of them really salesmen. One of them, a big bluff man, Michael Hicks, rather fell for a lady author who had published her own book, *Portuguese Panorama*, and now asked us to sell it for her. Heavily smitten by Iris Merle, he told me that she had had a hard life and he felt very sorry for her, and then gave more attention to her book than it really deserved. It was then, after he had left, that I made one of my biggest mistakes: I engaged Lisel Field to work for me.

Our affair had run its course and I had gradually let it run down. This was not easy. She had known several men in succession after leaving her husband, whom she had only married to have a home: he was a totally uncultured lower middle-class individual, happiest in the pub, a man with whom she had nothing in common. All the other men had dropped her once the novelty was over – married men, all of them. I was married of course, when we met, and still living with my wife, but our lives had become separate. One problem was that I had also started a new liaison with an opera singer. It happened like this.

I had two tickets for the opera and whoever I was meant to be taking that night telephoned in the afternoon to cancel. It was six o'clock before I had time to try to find someone else for the second ticket, and my third call was to Sigi Miller, not at home, but at another number that Phyllis gave me. This was the flat of Marion Wilson, an artist. Sigi was with two girls, Marion and a friend of hers from Paris, called Bettina Yonich, an opera singer. (She later, as Yugoslav names became familiar and fashionable in London, changed the spelling back to the original Jonic). It was suggested I take Bettina, but she did not care for that particular opera (I think it was Verdi's *Masked Ball*) and in the end I took Marion Wilson. I had only just enough time to pick her up and make the curtain. Afterwards we had supper and returned to her flat where Sigi and Bettina were waiting for us. They were both attractive girls and I suppose I had started to make the expected pass at Marion, but during the late night conversation I became more interested in the opera singer. I took her Paris telephone number and not long afterwards saw her there.

We first met in May 1957. That summer was of particular interest to me operatically. The two London opera houses were producing not just favourite operas, but works I had not heard before. I skipped the first night of *The Trojans* at Covent Garden, the first time it had ever been done in Britain, to get to the world première of Schönberg's *Moses and Aron* in Zürich, a memorable night with a brilliant cast conducted by Hans Rosbaud and afterwards took a group of English music critics around the old town of my university days. They included John Amis and Felix Aprahamian, and we were admitted without payment to the Café Voltaire where Tristan Tzara and his friends had presented Dadaist cabaret in 1916. Back in London I attended *The Trojans*, surely the most magnificent of epic operas after Wagner's *Ring*. Glyndebourne also had a splendid year with two Rossinis, two Mozarts, a Stravinsky and a Verdi opera,, and I managed to get to them all. In Paris I suggested to Bettina that she might like to come with me to the Edinburgh Festival, where Callas was expected to be the big sensation. She accepted with alacrity. All this time my affair with Lisel was continuing and the problem was that she was in love and expected it to be a permanent relationship, while I, liking her and enjoying her company, did not want to get emotionally involved. Lisel was still working for MacMillan, spent most weeks travelling around provincial towns and she also hoped to visit Edinburgh during the festival because that summer she was working through northern towns. I had to keep my movements as secret as possible, not just because of Lisel, but because Christya too wanted to know what I was up to.

During the week in August Bettina and I seduced each other and found we were sexually compatible, heard Maria Callas in *La Somnambula* and Eugenia Ratti in *Il Turco in Italia*, the latter replacing Callas who had been announced for both operas. The company was the Piccola Scala, which also performed *Elisir d'Amore* with a marvellous cast that included Rosanna Carteri, Giuseppe di Stefano, Giulio Fiorevanti and Fernando Corena, conducted by Sanzogno. Bettina had brought three very glamorous evening dresses, all given to her as cast-offs by a rich Parisian lady. We were staying discreetly at a small hotel on Clarindon Place, and I was able with some difficulty, to reach Lisel by telephone and put her off from coming to Edinburgh. Shortly afterwards I went to Paris again, stayed with my mother and John Barnard at the very grand apartment they had taken on Avenue Foch, where the walls had all been decorated with a special Chinese lacquer, but sneaked out at night to meet Bettina in a hotel room on the Avenue des Ternes. She was staying with people called Fliegelman just around the corner. We went to see *Così fan tutte* at the Opéra Comique, where she told me that the conductor Georges Sebastien, who had promised to engage her there to sing, had taken her one day to a *hôtel de passe* right next to the opera house, where all the walls and ceilings were mirrored. He had an unpleasant-looking liquid dripping from his penis, so she would not let him enter her, but had masturbated him instead. At that point she was quite frank about such things. The sixties, the age of permissiveness and sexual honesty, was almost upon us in contrast to the total lack of it in my adolescent years, and the continuing prudery of conventional society of the last decade, but I was hardly a member of that society. Pretences were kept up, but people I knew, even from repressive backgrounds, often maintained a hypocritical public stance very different from their private behaviour.

My visits to Paris became more frequent. Bettina was taking regular singing lessons, did series of concerts in and outside Paris for the *Jeunesse musicales* and had become a protégée of Gabriel Dussurget, director of the Festival of Aix-en-Provence, which specialised largely in Mozart operas under its principal conductor, Hans Rosbaud, who was also a foremost exponent of contemporary music. While Bettina was rehearsing or working with her teachers, I would go around the French publishers, Minuit, Gallimard, Seuil, Plon and Grasset in the main, and acquired authors and books for translation. I spent many whole nights drinking with Beckett, lunched with Ionesco, who by now was being translated by Donald Watson for British publication and performance, and took on, among others, Marguerite Duras, Nathalie Sarraute, Robert Pinget, Roland Dubillard, René de Obaldia, Raymond Queneau and Fernando Arrabal, although not all at once. The lady at Gallimard who handled foreign rights was Monique Lange, herself a novelist and living with Juan Goytisolo, a Spanish novelist. I bought the rights to her novel *Les Platanes* and later, in the summer of 1959, when I took Jamie for a holiday with me, I stayed with my mother at Monte Carlo for a week in August, and spent each day under a beach umbrella at the public beach translating Monique Lange's novel, which appeared in 1960 as *The Plane Trees*. The translation took me five days with my portable typewriter, shaded from the sun, where I could keep my eye on my daughter in the shallow children's pool. The evenings, when she was in bed, I went to Jacques Chaix's villa at Cap Ferrat.

My mother and John Barnard at this point had rented both a large flat on Avenue Foch and a series of houses or flats in Monte Carlo where my stepfather spent much time gambling away my mother's income in the casino. I had met the daughter of a friend of her's in Paris, who, as she is still alive, I will mention only by her first name, which was Jeanne. Her mother and mine had known each other in Montreal during the war. After a dinner party I took her out for another drink and we ended up in bed together. The situation became parallel to my relationship with Lisel; it was a pleasant affair with a highly-sexed lady whom I saw when I was in Paris and it predated Bettina and possibly even Lisel, although I think they took place (Lisel and Jeanne) at about the same period. Jeanne's other lover was her boss, an American who was the French head of a large American-owned enterprise, a much older man. When our affair ended, perhaps two years after it began, she inherited his considerable wealth on his death, and also his job. She will come back into this narrative a little later.

The office now consisted of Lesley MacDonald, who had become a director and was our production manager, Pamela Lyon, who shared the editorial work with me, Berry Bloomfield, my secretary, whose married name (it was years before she told me she was married) was Meredith, a series of sales managers, and a telephonist, who also did a variety of small jobs from typing to pasting up review cuttings. The sales manager sometimes wrote up the accounts as well, although the book-keeping was mainly in the hands of Francis King, our auditor, and his son Peter, who was frequently in the office. Lisel now joined us as sales manager. She was superbly well-qualified for the job and had left MacMillan. We needed someone of her experience, but the problem was the obvious one: I had told her that fond of her as I was, it was not possible to continue a physical relationship. The previous year, 1958, I had attended the Frankfurt Book Fair for the first time. Lisel was there – she had indeed stressed how important Frankfurt was and the advantages I would derive by going – and was still working for her old firm. She had assumed that we would sleep together. But I had brought Bettina, and I stayed, not in Frankfurt, but in Bad Homburg, half an hour away by train and a little longer by car. It was a pleasant spa town, which I left in my car early each morning, while Bettina followed by train later in the day. Although Lisel took every opportunity to come to my stand, the two ladies never actually met.

By 1958 the Frankfurt Book Fair had been going for twelve years and was well established. The Adenauer government had put an enormous effort into making it the symbol of a new reawakened German culture that would show the horrors of the Nazi period to be a thing of the past. It was gradually establishing the new democratic Germany as the publishing centre of the world. It had been impossible for me to go during my time at Calders Ltd, but in any case I had seen no great necessity. I had no trouble in finding books to publish and I had few rights to sell; those I did I sold mainly to American publishers from whom I also bought rights to American books. My translations, other than the French authors I had discovered in Paris, were nearly all out of copyright classics. But now I was meeting my European peers. There were Italian publishers like Giulio Einaudi and Gian-Giacomo Feltrinelli, almost all of them heavily involved in politics. Einaudi's father had been the socialist first post-war President of Italy and Feltrinelli had inherited both an industrial empire and great landed estates, but was now an ardent and active Communist. Other Italian publishers were mainly trying to live down fascist pasts, and the same was true of most German publishers, although many, like Heinrich Ledig-Rowohlt, the colourful, and the illegitimate son of one of the great avant-garde publishers of the expressionist era (1908 onward), were now firmly wedded to the new democratic Europe. I was doing some printing in Holland and I now met and became friendly with the Dutch publishers of the day, the cooperative firm Bezige Bij, Nijh and van Ditmar, and the individualist Rob van Gennep. I met other radical publishers like Klaus Wagenbach, who having been conscripted as a boy soldier into the German army during the last months of the war, ran into the woods as the Americans advanced and surrendered to the first tank he saw. Klaus was taking advantage of the German government's anxiety to keep Berlin alive under four-power Allied rule, by giving tax and fiscal advantages to those who lived and worked there. I made many new friends, acquired rights to books and sold them. From the British point of view, although all the larger publishers were there, Frankfurt was just a showcase for German publishers to sell their publications. They were not really Europeans: those that were were the refugees who had come to Britain before the war, André Deutsch, George Weidenfeld, Walter Neurath, Paul Elek, Max Reinhardt, and a few others who had little difficulty in making deals to acquire European literature and important political memoirs for their lists, while others, like Tom Maschler and Peter Owen, who had grown up in Britain and were now very English, tended to be less interested in Europe as such.

Frankfurt was still quite small then compared to later years, and it was easy to meet and know everyone in one's own interest field. The art publishers all knew each other wherever they came from, so did the technical publishers and children's publishers. Literature was a fairly small group where roughly a dozen publishers from each country met, lunched and dined, exchanging information about books and authors and gossip.

What followed, from about the time that I began to attend the annual Book Fair, was a great wave of translation. Names were traded: authors from Western Europe and Eastern Europe were invited or came on their own, the latter sometimes having difficulty in leaving their countries, although many did and found a way of getting to Frankfurt, and some managed to get contracts for international publication. This did not often result in a profit to the publisher, because foreign literature is always difficult to sell. But in spite of the future disappointments that would greet the publication of new authors from Germany, Poland or Yugoslavia, the atmosphere of excitement at making new discoveries was catching. One young Edinburgh bookseller, Jimmy Thin, sent just to see the Fair, caught the fever and acquired British rights to foreign books. When he returned home, his father paid the advances and cancelled the contracts.

In that first year, 1958, I learned my way around, took orders for my books on display from booksellers, optioned European authors I would later read, and offered my British ones to their most likely foreign publishers. I went to the opera and the theatre, took part in lunches and dinners, usually half a dozen people at the table, but never more than one from the same country. Publishers found others who were compatible with their taste and outlook.

It was some time after that that Lisel came to work for me, and the office atmosphere quickly became difficult. She was of course very good at what she did, but always wanted to be alone with me, and of course the others noticed. That was my year of the 'cello: I was taking lessons twice a week from my teacher, usually going for them to South Kensington, and I only left Wilton Terrace some time after that first Frankfurt. Then tragedy struck.

I had been to see Poulenc's opera, *Dialogues of the Carmelites*. Edward Lockspeiser had warned me that it would have an important impact on the musical scene and it was one of the factors that persuaded me to take on Henri Hell's book on the composer, just published in France. Lisel also wanted to see it and I agreed to take her, buying tickets for a second performance. But I had a 'cello lesson that night and when I tried to cancel it my teacher blew up, saying that he would not tolerate any further cancellations, so I agreed to keep the appointment and gave the tickets to Lisel, telling her to take a friend. But no, she wanted to go with me. To solve the problem I agreed to meet them both later that night at the Cheese and Grill on Leicester Square, one of a chain of new, cheap but good, restaurants that had replaced many of the old Lyons Corner Houses. When, after my lesson, I turned up, only Lisel was there. She had sent her friend home.

We had a quiet late dinner, she with little to say about an opera that must have impressed and moved her intensely. It is about sacrifice and death. Set in the French Revolution, a convent of Carmelite nuns is forced to leave and go out into a secular world of which it has no knowledge; the nuns must either renounce their faith or die as enemies of the new atheistic order of society. It ends with all of them, save one, going to the guillotine, one by one, singing *Salve Regina*, the last of them, a young aristocratic girl who had run away from her colleagues, returning during the executions to be the last to die. This overwhelmingly tragic opera, where the individual characters have to work out their own dilemmas and face their fears, must have had a devastating effect on someone as sensitive and unhappy, even desperate, as Lisel was then. We left the restaurant and took the same tube train north. She wanted me to come home with her. I said it was impossible and got out at Regent's Park. She went on to her own station near Maida Vale.

Back at home I worried about her. Should I call? I knew that if I did she would try to persuade me to take a taxi to her place or let her come to mine. I did nothing and went to bed.

The next morning I worried again, but it was a busy day. We had a publisher's party that evening; it may have been in the office or a restaurant or the Caledonian Club, where we occasionally entertained in a private room. I only remember noticing her absence – she had not come to the office at all that day – but I was too busy talking to people to do anything until late that night, when I telephoned her. There was no answer. I went to sleep with troubled dreams about her: she appeared to me with a white light behind her, looking pale and demented. At eight o'clock I telephoned again and there was still no answer. I remembered the name of her neighbour and looked her up in the telephone book, asking her then to ring the doorbell. She came back and said, 'There are three milk bottles outside the door and the dog is barking, but she doesn't answer.'

I asked her to ring the police at once and said I would be right over. I took a taxi and arrived a few minutes after the police had broken in the door. It was not unlike my dream. Lisel was lying on the bed, a white pallor on her face and dead. She had done it with sleeping pills and whisky, and I think aspirin as well. The dog was taken out and fed by the neighbour. I told the police that she had not come to work the previous day, which is why I was worried and had 'phoned the neighbour. They asked very few questions, traced the husband, who together with his sister turned up within two days. In the meantime I had arranged the funeral and cremation, choosing the Mozart *Requiem* as music, to be played by the organist. The husband, a totally nondescript working-class man in his fifties, attended the funeral, which was not religious, while his sister went through the belongings in the flat, deciding what to keep, what to sell. All the books and papers, including the partial translation of Paumgartner's book on Schubert, which at one point we had worked on together, were thrown out.

The funeral was ghastly. Berry Bloomfield came with me. 'I'm sorry, John, I know she was a friend of yours,' she said sympathetically. The three excerpts from the *Requiem* were played badly and extremely slowly, the *Lachrymose* in particular being excruciating. There was no service, no speeches, just music. Afterwards I went with the husband back to the flat where the sister, a character straight out of Céline, suspicious, shrewish and hatchet-faced, had worked out what she could get for the flat and the contents. I never saw them again, although I wrote a letter to Mr. Field, no doubt expressing sympathy, but asking after some of her papers, but he never replied. I have no idea what happened to her dog. Somewhere I heard, I am not sure from whom, that there was scandal in the air, but any anxiety I have had about unpleasant publicity was nothing to my sense of immense guilt.

The only other people at the funeral were a Russian couple, the Fenns, Lisel's only close friends and they asked me to tea the next day. They were elderly Russians, retired and living quietly near Lisel's flat in Maida Vale. They knew all about our affair and about her previous ones. They told me that at one point she had been extremely happy because of me and did not suggest that what had happened would not have happened later, even if I had responded on the night of the suicide. She had been let down by all the men in her life and I had at least tried to convert the affair into a friendship rather than running away. She and her husband gave Russian lessons, and when I said that I had always wanted to learn it, they offered to teach me. I went to buy Bondar's *Russian Primer* and for two years had two lessons a week. She found it easier (it was the wife who taught me) to teach me Russian through German, the two languages having more similarity with each other than with English. Although the wife taught me, I frequently saw the husband as well and my Russian conversation began to develop. After a year he fell ill, dying not long after, and with my life becoming busier than ever, I eventually dropped the lessons and fell out of touch. He had started to translate Furtwaengler's *Memories* for me me but died soon after starting.

On the day of the funeral I returned to my Sackville Street office late in the afternoon. I could do no work and sat looking at my desk. On an impulse, and with a dread of remaining alone with my thoughts, I rang up Sonia Orwell, whom I knew slightly. I shall give a portrait of her later in this chapter. I asked if she was free and invited her to dinner. I then unburdened myself of the whole story. She was sympathetic, invited me back to her flat in Percy Street and we got quite drunk. We played the old long-playing records of the pre-war Glyndebourne *Don Giovanni*, the famous Mildmay-Souez-Helletsgrüber-Brownlee-Baccaloni recording under Busch, until the early hours. Then she invited me to stay the night. I was too drunk to either leave or perform and too unhappy to want to, so the night was a deserved fiasco. Sonia was extremely attractive and had the kind of body that had always appealed to me and normally, even with a lot of drink, I would have been capable of making love, but not then. I left early the next morning. A few days later I heard that she had put it about that I was homosexual.

This was in February 1959, which I can date by the performances of *The Carmelites*, which I first went to in late January, and it must have been in the following fortnight that Lisel Field took her own life. Shortly afterwards I discontinued my 'cello lessons although I continued to practice on my own for a while. I never really liked the 'cello that Lisel had given me and its association with her memory must have played a part. Russian lessons replaced the music ones.

It is remembering the earlier year 1956 that has given me the greatest difficulty. I had made new friends, was moving increasingly in both literary and musical circles, and as a reader was consuming books by critics of both disciplines to expand my knowledge, which made me more open to take on or commission books that linked up with my interests. I became friendly with Felix Aprahamian, second music critic of the Sunday Times, of which the major reviewer was Ernest Newman, now nearly ninety, pre-eminent authority on Wagner, author of the four-volume biography, as well as of many books on a variety of composers and musical subjects, including a multi-volume Beethoven, some volumes of which I had read in my years in Montreal. His best-selling *Wagner Nights* and *Opera Nights* were reference books I almost knew by heart. Aprahamian and I had the idea of making a collection of Newman's Sunday Times weekly pieces on music and together we visited him at his home in Surrey, where he agreed to the project. There were many more visits, usually on Sundays to see him and his much younger wife, Vera, but more to sit at his feet and hear him talk than to consult him about the book. Ernest Newman was a pen-name, he told us. His real name was Eric Roberts, but in his younger days when he had landed a job with the Liverpool Echo, the editor said one day, 'Who is that earnest new man,' and he adopted a name that he felt was right for him.

Newman had a wide and eclectic musical knowledge, but he also had blind spots. He did not like Stravinsky or Schönberg, perhaps the two greatest innovators of the century, but he liked Carl Orff who tended to be treated as very minor by other critics. But Wagner was still his greatest love. There was a telling curlihew:

Said Ernest Newman,
Next week Schumann.
But when next week came
It was Wagner just the same.

Aprahamian spent much time in the Sunday Times' archives, and in 1956 we were able to publish the fruit of his labours, a collection entitled *From the World of Music* with a large number of short articles grouped in four sections: Critics and Criticism; Opera and Opera Singers; Composers and Their Works; and General Articles. Published as a hardcover at fifteen shillings it did very well, and we followed it with a second volume, *More Essays from the World of Music* in 1958. This included some very funny spoof articles. Felix Aprahamian was a good amateur photographer, and his photos of the old man, which graced the dust jackets of his two books, are striking. I had plans to republish some of Newman's out of print books, but somehow this never happened. I well remember those visits to 'Polperro', his Sussex house, and his ever scintillating conversation, sometimes cut short to Felix's annoyance by Vera making us listen to recordings of Orff. We often narrowly missed Elizabeth Schwartzkopf and Walter Legge, who treated Newman as their guru and a source of information about music and composers not then very well known, such as Hugo Wolf. Newman died in July 1959. I saw Vera once or twice after that, but gradually fell out of touch as one inevitably does.

I knew most of the music critics fairly well in those days and sometimes joined them for a drink or food after a performance, particularly out of London. But it was still Edward Lockspeiser whom I saw most often: he loved women, but being portly and far from young he did not have much success with them, but he never stopped trying. He introduced me to another specialist in French music, Rollo Myers, who edited for me the fascinating correspondence between Richard Strauss and the French novelist and musical writer Romain Rolland, an exchange of musical views that brought out all the differences between the different aesthetic outlooks and prejudices of their respective nationalities. Myers also compiled for me an anthology entitled *Twentieth Century Music* to explain to the expanding musical public the different schools of modern music at a time when the repertoire was expanding and interest growing. This sold well, was reprinted, and because such books go quickly out of date, I had intended to periodically update it with new articles and revisions. But with other and more urgent commitments this never happened.

I was a very frequent concert-goer as well as seeing many plays and operas, but I was also going through a period when I was much on my own. I came to know many of Lockspeiser's friends, mainly Hampstead-based, and spent evenings with musicians and others professionally engaged in the arts, film editors, actors and singers, pianists, many of them of German origin, who would discuss the technical difficulties of Beethoven sonatas, the orchestration of Richard Strauss operas or the nuances of the novels of Proust. Years later I remember the faces, the voices, the gestures, the drift of the conversations, but very few of the names. One falls into a circle of people whose interests one shares and is happy there, but in my case I was always being drawn somewhere else as well, meeting other people, falling into other milieus that also interested me, and so, gradually, I was always moving without consciously realising it out of one group and into another or several others. There comes the day when one sees, perhaps in a theatre audience, someone who one once thought one knew well and realise that the other person does not recognise you. It happens also, of course, the other way round. One is greeted, as of a long-lost brother, by someone who has disappeared entirely from the memory.

So that Hampstead circle of pianists with small careers and reputations, but much serious and scholarly knowledge, that other group who were friends and admirers of Sylvia Fisher, a wonderful Wagnerian soprano, whose stage presence was so unfortunate that she never became much of a star outside London – a circle that consisted largely of amateur singers all going to the same singing teacher – and various literary gatherings where I found myself discussing Thomas Mann or Rilke, or others again with an interest in new trends in contemporary music, where are they all now? Mainly in pockets of pleasant memory, where I cannot recall the names. Life has been rich in acquaintanceship, but so many one-time friends have dropped away because of the changing patterns of my life. An unavoidable pity!

One day Felix Aprahamian rang me up. 'You have a car, and I have two tickets to a new festival,' he said to me. I can date the month, May 1957, because of my ever invaluable opera record book, where it is listed as Performance 268. We drove to the palatial home of the Earl of Shrewsbury, Ingestre in the West Country. The Countess had ambitions to become a professional singer and had studied with Maggie Teyte. The new festival at her house was to be her launching pad. Alas, for her, John Pritchard, the conductor, would not accept her to sing Purcell's *Dido and Aeneas*, so she saved face by reciting an introductory poem written for the occasion, while Magda Lazlo sang the part with a splendid cast that included Adèle Leigh,

Monica Sinclair, Bornd Sönmerssstedt and Alexander Young. It was produced by Anthony Besch with decor by Peter Rice, so there was nothing lacking in the standard. *Dido and Aeneas* was followed by *Master Peter's Puppet Show*, Falla's mini-opera, which I was seeing for the first time and have recorded as Opera No. 121, performance 269. As part of the press we were lavishly entertained and I returned to London with a car full of music critics, all discussing the blighted ambitions of Nadine, Countess of Shrewsbury, which Maggie Teyte was encouraging for her own reasons. There was never, as far as I am aware, a second Ingestre Festival.

I have mentioned Sylvia Fisher, who sang *Turandot* at Covent Garden the same month that I went to Ingestre. It was a good year for opera. In New York I went to Cyril Richard' famous and successful production of Offenbach's *La Perichole*, saw a wonderful *Götterdämmerung* there with Martha Mödl, Ramon Vinay, Marianne Schech, Hermann Uhdc, Kurt Böhme and Blanche Thebom (singing Waltraute), magical names under the baton of Fritz Stiedry and produced by Herbert Graf, and the next night heard Mary Curtis, Jean Madeira and Leonard Warren in *Trovatore*. At Covent Garden there was *The Trojans* in June, following my trip to Zürich for *Moses and Aron*, Glyndebourne was now reviving Rossini under Vittorio Gui, Sadlers Wells gave me my first complete Puccini *Trittico* and the Handel Opera Society, of which I was an enthusiastic member, performed *Alcina* with Joan Sutherland and Monica Sinclair among a fine cast. The company, doing one or two Handel operas a year, had opened two years previously with *Deidamia* (with Marion Studholme and Iris Kells in the cast) and was kept going by the dogged persistence of Charles Farncombe, who conducted the operas, and by a splendid hard-working lady, a civil servant, who organised the Society, Gwen MacLeary. How many such individuals have given years of their unpaid time to keep such organisations alive without recognition or thanks, except in a few grateful memories like mine? I cannot help contrasting them to others who are given a variety of public honours who better deserve to be behind bars! My own involvement with Handel operas was to come later.

While I was still working for Calders Ltd at Eros House, I received, at home at Wilton Terrace, a letter asking me to advertise my books in a literary magazine called Mandrake. It had presumably chosen its name to be similar to the short-lived, but much-praised Merlin, which Alexander Trocchi and his friends were publishing in Paris. The editor, Arthur Boyars, was very insistent on meeting me, and after a telephone call or two I reluctantly gave him an early appointment at my home at eight o'clock in the morning. He was there on time and I discovered to my surprise that during the day he worked over my head on the top floor of Eros House, for a small publishing company producing popular biographies of football stars and the like in little paperback editions. He was a poet and had been at Oxford together with a group that included John Wain (later to edit my

International Literary Annual at his suggestion), Kenneth Tynan, Philip Larkin, Kingsley Amis and others who just then were beginning to build a literary reputation, while he, who had published them all in the university magazine which he had then edited, was now doing this strange editorial job, while putting out *Mandrake* on his own and doing some reviewing for the Daily Telegraph, often of European literature, so that inevitably he was then or later receiving many of my own publications. I came to like Arthur, whose rather didactic approach to literature I found rather appealing. He was also a great party-goer and through him I extended further my involvement in the many groups that made up London's artistic sub-culture. There were bottle parties (you brought your own) at people's flats in Chelsea, Kensington, Soho and elsewhere. I met many more poets, painters, literary agents, critics and reviewers. A few names come back to me at random: Arthur Waley, Victor Passmore, Gwenda Davids, David Sylvester, Michael Horowitz, William Empson, but there were dozens of figures in the arts, all struggling to get known.

Arthur Boyars had a girl friend called Valerie Desmore. She was a painter who had studied with Oskar Kokoschka; she had an English father, a Cape-coloured mother and both she and her sister had been born in South Africa, but because of the apartheid system had been brought to Britain. Valerie was now living in the World's End section of the King's Road in Chelsea. I went to many parties with Arthur and Valerie, who was sexy, talented, interested in everything and very uninhibited. During the long winter of 1958-9, I was living alone at Wimpole Street, working during the day at 17 Sackville Street in Mayfair, publishing books that on the whole were doing well, although there were many disappointments like the Alger Hiss book. I was working hard, had no permanent involvement among the different ladies I saw occasionally and many of my evenings were free, so that I spent some of them with Arthur and Valerie, eating, drinking and talking. Arthur and I would arrive with food, Valerie would cook it, and we would sit, drinking and talking, often listening to music on the radio, for we all liked serious music. Then I would leave so that the others could have sex, after which Arthur would find his way home to Hampstead. Or sometimes I would give him a lift. He was still living with his parents and it was a long way home. Sometimes I just took him to a convenient bus stop. Valerie did a painting of me that winter, showing me keeping warm at her round stove. I am in blackface and she had Don Juan in mind.

Arthur Boyars plays rather a large part in this book, and this is the best place to describe him. His father was the very orthodox Cantor of a big Hampstead synagogue, and his mother, equally orthodox, had started to have a life as a concert singer, but had abandoned it because of the immorality associated with the life, as Arthur put it. His father had made a great effort and some sacrifice to give him a good English education, and when he was admitted to Oxford it was with the expectation that this studious young man, interested in literature and serious music, would take a good degree and become an academic, someone like Isaiah Berlin perhaps. He seemed to have the right qualities, and in my opinion, as he was also very kind and cheerful by nature, he would have made an excellent university Don. But such were the many extracurricular activities in which he engaged himself at Oxford, he only received a second class honours degree, which devastated his father, who had confidently expected a first. He rent his garments and made Arthur feel he was a total failure. There was no good reason why with effort and a second class honours degree he could not have pursued an academic career, but he had, by the time I knew him, effectively given up. Life was now to be lived without ambition: pleasure and survival became his only motivations. As a poet he had written little and was not to write much more. He did have a few poems in a Penguin anthology of modern British poetry (*The New Poetry*) that came out in 1962, that was edited by Alfred Alvarez, but there was no career ahead of him as a poet.

One day I heard that the building in Upper Wimpole Street where I lived needed a janitor; a basement flat went with the job, which was the only inducement as the salary was small or non-existent. I mentioned it to Arthur who was anxious to get away from the parental home and he applied for the job. He was willing to sweep and clean, which was all the job demanded in return for the flat and so he became the janitor. From then on he frequently came up to my second floor flat to chat and have a drink. At one literary party in Chelsea, shortly afterwards, I was chatting to Gwenda David, a literary agent who liked to gossip and she said to me, pointing to Arthur, 'You see that man over there. He calls himself a poet, but he's really a janitor. If you're over thirty and you want to get anywhere, you have to give up janitoring and that sort of thing.'

Barney Rosset came to London fairly frequently in those days. We were selling his Evergreen Books, achieving good sales, but making too little on them as I had set the prices too low, perhaps necessary to get the sales. This meant that we frequently had cash problems and our payments to him were becoming slower. Not surprisingly he was interested in examining other offers and they were there, especially from George Weidenfeld, who at one point put together a deal whereby a new company would take over my sales, those of Barney, his own Weidenfeld and Nicolson books and the list of Sweet and Maxwell, law book publishers who were now thinking of branching out into trade publishing and had started a new imprint to do so. The latter was run by a man called Stevens, and it was his new venture that triggered the whole plan because the only one of us that had serious money was Sweet and Maxwell. I did not like the prospect of being buried under so many other publishers, but I had to go along or lose my important connection with Rosset. There were many meetings which involved discussion of warehousing, car-parking space in the Sweet and Maxwell building (mine had already been allocated) in Fetter Lane and how what would surely end up in a merger of all parties would work. But it all broke down in the end with Weidenfeld taking the Grove Press distribution away from me. Whereas I had sold at least several hundred copies of a title and in some cases thousands, the sales within a year had become so small that Barney changed again to distributors in Holland and thereafter Evergreen Books were rarely seen in Britain.

During all this I would take Barney out in the evenings to night-clubs, which he usually left with one of the 'hostesses' who joined men on their own. He was never interested in the theatre or other ways of spending the evening. On one particular Sunday I had my daughter Jamie with me for the day, and he came along with us to lunch and an afternoon spent at the London Planetarium, where the functioning of the universe is explained in an entertaining and educational way. Afterwards we returned to my flat, not far off. Valerie Desmore was standing on the doorstep about to ring the bell for Arthur down in the basement.

Barney took an immediate interest when I introduced them and had time for a brief chat before Arthur came to the door. Having a drink with me, Barney asked who she was, how free she was, and managed to get her telephone number from me. Then things happened very quickly. Barney telephoned her the next day from his hotel, went to see her flat and her paintings, took her out to dinner, and asked her to come to New York, saying he would organise an exhibition for her.

Valerie was a good painter, an expressionist much like her teacher Kokoschka, but she painted for pleasure and had little ambition for celebrity or recognition. She earned her living by designing clothes for Marks and Spencer, mainly for children. But she was impulsive and had a temper. She had no inhibitions about making a scene in public or at a party, and she always spoke her mind. Her appearance could be seen by different people in different ways. Her skin was dark, but not exceptionally so, and her features were more negroid than Indian, whereas her sister, who I met a few times with her, was exquisitely Indian-looking, like a temple icon, and she dressed as an Indian, usually in a sari. Valerie Desmore was warm-hearted and generous, talented and intelligent, but she could turn into a tiger when crossed and I could pity any racist who provoked her. She had been Arthur's long-term girlfriend, and although I am sure she had other sexual flings, she certainly loved and respected him. But Arthur was a member of a strictly orthodox Jewish family, who would have looked with horror on marriage to a totally secular half Cape-Coloured English girl. Were his parents dead Arthur would have married Valerie without hesitation, but he did not even dare admit to them that he was, to all intents and purposes, living with someone who was not even Jewish. And the resentment had been building up in Valerie for some time.

One night, quite late, Arthur rang me and asked if he could come up. He was quite shaken, walked up and down my carpet, and told me that

Valerie wanted to accept Barney Rosset's invitation and he didn't know what to say or do. Barney had arranged the ticket on a flight to New York. Arthur discussed his dilemma, his parents' attitude, and his worry about what would happen if Valerie left the country. Two nights later he came up again and spent the whole night pacing up and down, because Valerie was leaving the next morning. She had told him that if he promised to marry her within a month she would tear up the ticket to New York. If he did he would be disowned by his father and thrown out of their particular Jewish community. Maybe Valerie could convert to Judaism, I suggested. Yes, she could, he said, and possibly be accepted by some Jewish community, but not his, which was far too strict. Anyhow Valerie was not the kind of girl who would put herself out hypocritically to satisfy someone else's prejudice.

Neither of us went to bed. Arthur could not make up his mind, but had promised to go to the airport with Valerie. In the end I drove them there and we saw Valerie off. Three weeks or so later she came back, and Arthur and I were there at Heathrow to meet her. She breezed out of the 'plane early in the morning and said she wanted breakfast. Arthur blanched and suggested we might wait until we were back in town. 'Oh, you're worried about the cost,' she said. 'Well don't. I'll pay for it.' Barney had filled her purse with dollars and she also had a suitcase full of oil paints, a luxury which usually took up most of her British income.

Late that night Arthur came up again to see me. Valerie had told him everything. John Pizey, who was Barney's sales manager at the time, had been in London, and we had speculated as to how Barney was going to import Valerie, given that he was living with Link. What happened was this: Barney met Valerie at the airport and immediately took her onto another 'plane leaving for Los Angeles. They spent a week there, then went to San Francisco for a second week and then back to New York. She had resisted his advances up to San Francisco, then succumbed. He had taken her around all the bars and other places associated with the beat poets, who were then becoming known but were not yet legendary, and she had enjoyed all that because their life-style was natural to her. In New York he put her in a hotel, but took her to a number of parties where she was not a success. New York political correctness was hardly her scene: words like Jewess and Negress were not used, but they were by Valerie, and not appreciated. Barney was especially sensitive on political correctness, although he was in every other way a natural rebel, and she constantly embarrassed him. I think that at one point he may have felt that Valerie was his ideal spouse (he had already been married and divorced twice), but he quickly changed his mind when he had to cope with her in New York, and was only too happy to send her back to Arthur and London with enough pocket money to see her through a few weeks, and enough paint for several months. Once again Arthur paced up and down my sitting room. He would never touch Valerie again: she was soiled. But he would always look after her. I told him he was a fool, but he had taken a position and meant to stick to it.

Time passed. Valerie and Arthur were to all appearances a couple, but I knew better. They were friends, but began drifting apart. I was concentrating almost entirely on promoting my books, the list becoming increasingly literary, although some unusual titles, as had always happened, came to me by accident. In 1957 I had imported from America in sheet form, for binding under my imprint in England, a large *Book of Catholic Quotations*, ideal for priests who wanted to sprinkle their sermons with the wisdom or quips of others, which sold quite well both in general and in Catholic bookshops, and at the same time sheets of a quasi-medical book, *Variations in Sexual Behaviour*, which gave me an opening into a very different kind of bookshop. The latter reprinted endlessly and helped subsidise the serious literature, and slow-selling authors like Beckett.

In early 1958 I published an anthology entitled *Is the Monarchy Perfect?* The genesis was in a number of articles which had appeared in the August and September issues of the National and English Review the previous year, which had attracted much comment and some outrage. In particular there was an article by Lord Altrincham, who was soon to become the second peer to give up his title under a law passed in 1963, as a result of the campaign by Anthony Wedgewood-Benn who wanted to keep his seat in the Commons and not in the Lords. Benn, on inheriting his father's title, had automatically ceased to be an MP, but went on being elected in by-elections until the pressure to change the law made it happen. This also enabled Lord Altricham to become simple John Greg.

When I contacted Altrincham he agreed to help me make a book out of the material that had already appeared, supplemented by additional articles. The whole took a neutral but critical look at the British monarchy as an institution, and it included a particularly hard-hitting piece by Malcolm Muggeridge entitled *No Bicycle for Queen Elizabeth*. The gist of the whole book was that if the monarchy wanted to survive it should become more democratic as the Scandinavian and other surviving European royal houses had done. There were twelve sections in the book and one of them, pleading for the royal art collection to occasionally be open to the public, I wrote myself under a pseudonym, Mackenzie John, my two Christian names reversed. Various friends told me that the book had much annoyed Buckingham Palace and that if I had any hopes of ever receiving a public honour, I had better forget them.

Pamela Lyon left us to get married and her place was taken by Ethel de Keyser, a South African and a militant anti-apartheid campaigner. She was married to an actor, David de Keyser, but about the time she came to work for me the marriage broke up and she went to live with the Caribbean writer George Lamming, whose novel *In the Castle of My Skin*, published in 1953, had been highly successful and had won the Somerset Maugham Award for

Literature. Ethel and David were in daily touch by telephone and I often answered it myself. When a voice asked for Ethel I might say, 'Is that George?' and be told, 'No, it's David,' or the other way round. David's and George's voices sounded identical to me. David was unaccustomed to living alone and always wanted to know where something had been put, or where to take his shirts for washing. George's calls were probably more about their political concerns.

I am not sure whether it was Ethel or someone else who told me that a book was being written about the notorious treason trial that had followed the arrest of 156 persons in December 1956, all known to be opposed to the apartheid régime in South Africa, but she certainly threw her heart and soul into the matter, and I acquired the rights to publish an account of the trial[10] by Lionel Forman, a Capetown barrister and E.S. (Solly) Sachs, former head of the South African Garment Worker's Union, who had been a refugee in Britain since 1953. The book was written jointly by two people who had never met, but were totally in sympathy, and it is an account, not so much of the trial, which was still going on, but of the treatment of those arrested and the nation-wide demonstrations it provoked. The purpose of the book was to state the facts, expose the régime and loaded justice system and invoke further international protest. It succeeded in doing all three.

I saw much of Solly Sachs, an old-style trade union leader in many ways, with a limited understanding of my own circumstances as an independent publisher. He came to me one day and asked for a large sum of money. I think it was £10,000. I looked at him. 'But, Solly, we have just paid you an advance, a good one, and if the book goes well, there'll be more. We can't give you more money just now.'

'I come to ask you for money and you humiliate me like this,' he said. When I asked Oppenheimer (a well-known diamond-mine millionaire) for money he gave it to me right away.'

'He's a rich man.' I exclaimed. 'We have no money to lend. It all goes into publishing books and paying royalties.'

'You're a capitalist, aren't you?' he went on. 'Of course you have money, and I need some right now.'

I was unable to explain to him the difference between a small publisher with limited resources and a big capitalist like Oppenheimer. We separated on bad terms, although he was happy enough when the book came out, which led to many interviews in the press and other media coverage. He never knew about another matter where he might have had a right to complain.

I met him at a party with an Italian lady called Elena, who had spent much time with her English husband in South Africa; he was still there (the husband), a businessman not interested in politics. We talked, liked each other and agreed to meet the next day, a Sunday. I took her to the

---

[10] *The South African Treason Trial*, London, 1957.

Hurlingham Club where there was a swimming pool because it was a very hot summer day. We warmed to each other and she came back to my flat where we started an affair of sorts, but I did not want to get deeply involved, which she did, being by nature possessive, although married, but not very happily I gathered. She had just tried to get in touch with a previous lover whom she had met during the war in Italy. He was Richard Hoggart, whom I knew to be an important and sometimes controversial educationalist, but he was now married and had refused any new contact, which she much resented and saw as cowardice. After Lisel I was very wary of women whose needs were as blatant as Elena's, and I no longer let any brief relationship, which usually could be turned into a friendship, get too heavy. Solly never quite understood how an affair that he considered as in the bag somehow escaped him. Elena returned to South Africa that autumn and for some years kept up an occasional correspondence with me.

During that same year I published *What Man Has Made of Man* by Mortimer Adler, the distinguished American philosophical psychologist, and *God in Search of Man* by Abraham Heschel, a psychological study of post-platonism by an American rabbi, whom from his book I assumed would be liberal in his life-style. When he came to London and I invited him to lunch I found that he was extremely kosher and I had to find a suitable restaurant – not easy in London's West End – in a hurry, where he could eat.

We had many political books on the list just then. That was one reason why I was approached by Chatham House, a semi-governmental think-tank, and institute for foreign affairs to bring out a paperback trade edition of Philip Noel-Baker's important book *The Arms Race*, which won him the Nobel Prize for Peace in 1959. It became No. 21 in my Calderbook paperback series that had started with the paperback edition of Alger Hiss's ill-fated *In the Court of Public Opinion*. In the series I was also reissuing my European classics, translations from French, German and Russian for the most part, which came out alongside modern authors, literary, historical, theatrical and musical, and which even included paperback editions of the literary and theatrical annuals in a smaller format. The covers were largely designed by Brian Sewell, and on the inside of the covers we advertised other titles in the series. I have never understood why so few publishers use the blank spaces in their books to advertise others on the list.

One Saturday morning in March 1958, I went over to Paris, intending to spend nearly a week there, and my first call, that same morning, was on Jerôme Lindon, with whom I was now doing much business. In addition to the considerable number of French authors I had acquired from his Editions de Minuit, he had taken one of mine, the Irish writer Aidan Higgins, on the recommendation of Samuel Beckett, about to be translated by Edith Fournier. On this day he handed me a new publication that had already been through two rapid printings and suggested that it might interest me. It was a book about the Algerian war, the main topic in every French conversation, and the overriding French issue of the day. The author was a French journalist who had been tortured in Algeria by the army: the book was in large part an account of that torture, which was commonplace just then. I took it away, went to the Café Flore, ordered a light lunch and began to read *La Question* by Henri Alleg.

I could not leave the table until I had finished it. It was horrific, gripping and deeply moving, a total and damning condemnation of what the determination of the French government to hang onto its remaining colonies had led to. The French army was behaving as badly and sometimes worse that the German units had behaved in France fifteen years earlier. Significantly the French Foreign Legion, which has traditionally accepted any healthy recruit without any questions asked, now had a majority of Germans, largely ex-SS soldiers who had escaped from Germany and joined the Legion. They were now carrying out massacres and repressions unthinkable in any civilised country: the worst butchers of the German army and police were now showing the other legionnaires what cruelty and ruthlessness was all about.

I telephoned Editions de Minuit. Lindon was still there. He told me that I had one of the only copies. Just after I had left his office the police had arrived and seized his entire stock. He was lucky not to have been arrested as well. Over the telephone we agreed a contract. I went to my hotel and spent the afternoon going carefully over the book and making notes. The next morning I returned to London and started translating. On Monday morning I hired a temporary typist from an agency and dictated the English translation of the whole book, which was finished and corrected by noon on Tuesday just as the second post brought in an introduction by Jean-Paul Sartre, which he had written after the seizure for a clandestine edition. This was about to be published by the French Communist Party, which Lindon had posted to me. I had a printer ready and sent off the finished translation; I then translated the Sartre. On Wednesday I had proofs and everything was corrected and returned by Thursday. The presses were rolling off a first edition of 5,000 copies on Friday, ready for binding on Monday morning. But I went with Lesley MacDonald, my production manager, to the binder's premises on Saturday morning, where the two of us hand-bound about thirty copies. I then spent the afternoon and early evening visiting the newspapers that had London offices, not just the national press, but the main provincials as well. Most of them were in the vicinity of Fleet Street in those days and with a car you could get to them all within three hours, often being able to see the editor himself.

Sunday morning saw *The Question* described everywhere in the press. It was a big news story because the war in Algeria had become front page material. Some extracts were printed and the experiences of Henri Alleg created shock and horror. Many more extracts and more news coverage were in the Monday newspapers. We reprinted 10,000 more copies, and soon this smallish hardback book, selling at ten shillings and sixpence had sold twenty-five thousand copies. Then came the famous date, the treize mai (13th of May) when de Gaulle was called back to power, went to Algeria, spoke to thousands of cheering French *colons*, all afraid that they were about to lose their ascendancy and said to them, 'Je vous comprends.' He did not mean what they thought he meant: he wanted peace, the end of the war and was ready to compromise.

The biggest villain in the book was General Massu, the commander of the army in Algeria, who was only named by his initial M. Soon there was a general conviction that he was about to lead an invasion of Paris with the French army from Algeria and accomplish a *coup d'état*. I was in Paris again and was taken by John Barnard and my mother to the Tour d'Argent, the most prestigious restaurant in the city, the only time I have ever been there. Claude Terrail, the owner, went around the tables, all discussing the crisis and came to ours. My mother was quite excited by it all. M. Terrail struck a dramatic pose, presenting himself as a pillar of solidarity in a collapsing world. 'When there is a crisis,' he said, 'il faut être là!' As long as the Tour d'Argent was functioning any crisis would soon roll by, at least as far as his customers were concerned. I wondered if he was saying that in 1940.

More stories kept breaking from Algeria, but with de Gaulle back in power and leading the government, no invasion could succeed and the crisis receded. In Alleg's book we hear of the death of Audin who died in custody. He was another journalist active against the French government and Minuit published a little book about him, *L'Affaire Audin*. I used it to write a piece for the *New Statesman*, which was widely noticed. *The Question* was then published by George Braziller in America, but he omitted my preface, substituting one of his own, which was really a paraphrase. He paid for the translation, but gave me no credit as translator. My relations with George Braziller have always been spiky, perhaps because of that early meeting when I failed to recognise him.

French translations were now prominent on the list. Ionesco's early plays were out in Donald Watson's idiomatic translations and getting performed. Peter Hall produced *The Lesson* at the Arts Theatre Club in 1955 and Peter Wood *The Bald Prima Donna* in the same theatre the following year. *The Chairs* was done at the Royal Court in 1957 by Tony Richardson, and Peter Zadek produced *Amadée* in Cambridge at about the same time. Ionesco's name was known largely thanks to the advocacy of Harold Hobson's Sunday Times column and my editions were selling fairly well. *The Killer*, one of Ionesco's major plays only came to London in a small theatre in Islington, but Jack Magowran was soon to play Bérenger, who became Ionesco's alter ego in many plays from the late fifties onward, in a different production in Bristol, which is after all the city where the play is set, and not long after, in 1960, *Rhinoceros* conquered the world. It is not Ionesco's best play, but it carried a simple message about the tendency towards and the dangers of conformity in society that was easy for the public to understand. It opened in January, on my birthday, at the Odéon in Paris with Jean-Louis Barrault playing Bérenger, and in London with Laurence Olivier in the same rôle on 28th April in a production directed by Orson Welles. *Rhinoceros* started at the Royal Court and quickly transferred to Wyndham's on the Aldwych. Hundreds of copies of my edition were sold by the programme girls every night.

Beckett had urged me to see Marguerite Duras' *Le Square* in Paris, an adaptation of her novel by the same name, but as it has one setting, in a public garden in a small town, and as the novel consists only of dialogue, it was barely an adaptation. I saw it in 1956 in Paris with Kitty Albertini and R. J. Chauffard and was bowled over by its poignancy, two lonely people meeting and talking in a park. I eventually published both the novel, which Sonia Orwell and Tina Morduch, a friend of hers, translated together, and later Barbara Bray translated the dramatic version. Other Duras translations followed. Among French authors appearing on the list at this time were Robbe-Grillet, Nathalie Sarraute and Robert Pinget, and others in a more traditional mould, such as André Pieyre de Mandiargues, an erotic writer of considerable quality. I took on some books of a more psychologically political character, such as André Gorz's *The Traitor*, which had received major reviews in France, a book that looked at the long-term results of the Nazi occupation, and for which Sartre again wrote a preface, but it had little impact in Britain. I now knew most of the French literary publishers intimately and when in Paris had many lunches and dinners with them and their authors, so I was inside literary Paris in many ways, meeting many more writers than I could possibly publish.

Then Minuit offered me another book about the Algerian war: if anything it was more savage than *The Question*. Called *Gangrene*, it was a record of more French atrocities and on a wider canvas. I was uneasy now. Sitting in London, sniping at the French government for its colonial policies that were not that much different from the British refusals to recognise the aspirations of our own subjugated colonial peoples, who were now claiming their independence, was hypocritical. The British were also trading partners with some of the ugliest regimes in the world. I acquired the rights to *Gangrene* from Lindon, but I was uncomfortable and made no effort to rush publication.

My brother was to marry Jutta Lindtner, the German girl he had met at his school in Zuoz, and the wedding was to take place in Munich. Both families gathered there. I knew nothing of the Lindtners, who lived in a small German industrial town, but had a strong suspicion that they were probably all old Nazis. By 1959, Germany, which had been reconstructed under the Marshall Plan, with her destinies guided by the stern figure of Adenauer and the economic genius of Erhard, was again a rich country, and even the Eastern part under Russian control was prosperous. We all stayed at the Vierjahreszeiten (Four Seasons) Hotel. On the night I arrived there was a Carl Orff triple bill at the Prinzregenten Opera House, and I resisted the temptation to skip the reception given by the other family the night before the wedding, but with considerable regret.

The reception was for about a hundred people, mainly young Germans related to the bride. John Barnard and my mother were there of course, together with my sister and Raymond de Miribel, who John Barnard had met through me and now frequently invited around to their new flat in Paris on Avenue Foch, only a few doors away from where my other French friend, Jacques Chaix, also had a family home. A lot was eaten and drunk at a lavish buffet, but Raymond, hearing German voices again in Germany, which sounded very different from the Swiss German we had been accustomed to hearing in Zürich, was now under the influence of drink and becoming dangerously nervous. As the party broke up he wanted to go outside the hotel and I decided I had better accompany him.

He led the way into a little bar where we overheard a conversation about a *vierte Reiche* (fourth German Empire). Raymond pricked up his ears and began to swear in a loudening voice, soon expressing his hatred of all things German. The little group in the bar turned towards us and was obviously prepared for violence. I went up to them. 'Listen,' I said. 'My friend is drunk. He was in Buchenwald. You know what that means. Please leave him alone.' They grumbled, but turned back to their own conversation and I managed to get Raymond back to the hotel.

I was expected to make a little speech at the wedding reception, and in the bath the next morning I thought about it. The incident with Raymond the previous night was still on my mind, but I thought up some conventional little speech and framed the right German words to deliver it. There was a ceremony in a church and then we all returned to the hotel where a banquet began at about one o'clock. After it there was an interminable speech from an uncle of the bride, referring often to the 'knightly Jimmy' and the 'fair damsel' or whatever German equivalent he used, but with such pomposity that those who were not politely bored were having trouble in not giggling. My mother had said to me, 'Keep it short,' but as the drone with its histrionics went on, my inclination was increasingly to send him up and mimic him. I was sitting next to a very pretty Hungarian girl, not a relative of the Lindtners, whose reaction was similar to my own. 'Wake them up a bit,' she whispered to me, and when my turn to speak came, I gave her a wink and launched into, not what I had prepared in the bath, in fact nothing that I had prepared at all, but an improvised, deliberately sarcastic imitation of the uncle's tone of voice in which I picked up his words about troubadours and medieval references, but then went on to give a political speech about the war in which our nations had been engaged – which this union symbolised as being over – but went on to mention the overheard remarks in the bar the previous night, referring as well to what Raymond de Miribel had undergone in Dachau and Buchenwald, and to the Holocaust, expressing then my hopes that no one present had either taken part in or approved the evils of the Nazis. None of this was intended in advance. Raymond kept clapping his hands and shouting 'Bravo.' My German, which had been little used of late, suddenly became fluent, and I can only use the Welsh word hwyl to describe what took me over. I sat down to deafening silence except for Raymond, received a kiss on the cheek from the Hungarian girl and not a single member of the bride's family, except for the bride herself, ever said a single word to me thereafter.

That afternoon I took a 'plane to Paris, but had no onward reservation. While trying to get my name put down on the waiting list at Orly, I found myself behind a tall Englishman who looked familiar. 'Aren't you John Stonehouse?' I asked him. He managed to get his name down on the list before mine, and then we went for a drink together. He was at the time Shadow Labour Party Minister for the Colonies. He knew about the books I had published and I told him about my problem with *Gangrene*. He then revealed that he had an extraordinary document in his possession. It was a report made by a Captain Law, who had been a prison officer in the Hola camps in Kenya. The tabloid press had created a great panic about the Mau Mau, a militant group of Kikuyu tribesmen. They were few in number and reputedly led by Jomo Kenyatta, a nationalist who was working for Kenyan self-rule, but who always denied any terrorist associations. The Kikuyu had been largely driven off their ancestral lands by white settlers, who had a vested interest in creating an emergency to keep British troops active in repressing the natives. Mau Mau activities had started in 1952 and had consisted largely of threats against non-militant Kikuyu and other native Africans, but the Daily Express and much of the British press had whipped up British public opinion to believe that a general massacre of white people living in Kenya was imminent. The British army's answer was to build giant concentration camps, the Hola camps, and to intern tens of thousands of Kikuyu tribesmen on suspicion of being part of a Mau Mau conspiracy. There were over 80,000 Africans detained in the most brutal conditions, with beatings and torture. Many had died, both from deprivation and violence. Captain Law had made complaints to the authorities, which were ignored, but eventually led to his being victimised, imprisoned, dismissed from the service and sent back to Britain. His report on the camp was now with Stonehouse, who was uncertain how to bring it to public attention with the press being almost universally favourable to the army and the fears of the settlers. As a previous Secretary for the Colonies under the last Labour government and now Shadow Secretary, he also had much information on the bad behaviour of the army in Cyprus where the EOKA campaign for union with Greece was also the object of repression, and in Aden, where the conflict was not to erupt for some time yet. We sat together on the 'plane to London, and by the time we arrived the blueprint for an expanded *Gangrene* had been worked out: it would document the excesses which had been covered up by both the French and the British governments.

Peter Benenson, a barrister who had founded the organisation Justice, a pressure group of concerned liberal lawyers, wrote the long and lucid introduction. It was followed by the French texts written by various hands, largely eyewitness reports, which I had acquired from Jerôme Lindon, and then came the British material by John Stonehouse and Captain Law. We intended to publish in September 1959, but Britain was suddenly hit by a printing strike. It was not a reasonable strike: printers were very well paid compared to other trades, but the newspaper compositors and machine-minders, the aristocrats of the industry, who were the best paid, wanted to keep ahead of the other unions which then had the country by the throat. It was the period of 'I'm alright, Jack!' attitudes, which did so much to put the middle classes, together with those who did not have the power of the biggest and most militant unions behind them, into a state of boiling resentment, which a decade later was to bring in a triumphant anti-union Thatcherism. But at the time powerful unions had become accustomed to getting their way. There I was with an urgent book and no way of getting it printed. I had announced it, and the word had gone around interested government circles – Henry Brooke was Home Secretary then (who strangely enough had given Captain Law a job as a parliamentary messenger) – and suddenly I received a 'D' notice. This is a warning that the book or article one intends to publish may contain secret government information and is liable to prosecution. The offending person is liable to arrest on a variety of charges that may include treason. It is less dangerous after publication than before, because once the facts are out they cannot be withdrawn, and action by the police then becomes punitive rather than precautionary. This became bluntly clear years later with the 'Spycatcher' and similar cases where secret agents published what they knew.

There was only one thing to do if I intended to proceed and that was to get the book printed abroad. But it was autumn and the Frankfurt Book Fair was coming up. Every publisher in Europe was anxious to display his new books in Frankfurt and all the book printers of Europe were working overtime. Getting the book printed in America would create transport delays and also a greater risk of seizure by customs. In the end I found a printer in Regensburg in Bavaria, largely thanks to my musical contacts, as the Heinrich Schiele printing firm printed scores as well as books. I flew to Regenburg with the manuscript and on my first evening was taken to dinner by the two brothers who owned the press. We went to a restaurant outside the town in a sports car driven by one of them at a speed that must have been around three hundred kilometres an hour: the driver simply put his foot down to the floor when there was a straight stretch of road ahead and braked violently when we approached a turn; I cannot ever remember being so frightened in my life. We discussed music that night and from odd bits of conversation I realised that their politics were far to the right. I told them as little as possible about the book they were to set and print.

During the week I corrected the proofs as they emerged and printing was to start that weekend. I had found a photograph for the cover of a Promotheus-like figure (*Roland furieux* by Duseigneur from the collection at the Louvre). Talking to the workers I discovered that the bosses, the two brothers, had instructed the machine-minders not to hurry. Having realised that the book would embarrass a right-wing government, they had decided to hinder, not help. I persuaded the workers, who seemed to support the Social Democrats locally, to ignore the hints of the brothers and 10,000 copies were printed. I was back in England when I was told that the binding machine had broken down. I had to get the flat sheets imported on palettes by air and then managed to get them bound in Britain, the strike being over.

The British General Election was now imminent and this book could play a rôle. Stonehouse did what he could to persuade his Labour Party colleagues to make use of the book to attack the government, but Morgan Phillips, the Party Secretary, decided that any book exposing the misdeeds of the army would not win votes, and he ignored it, while I was rushing it into the bookshops. It did much better in the North than the Tory heartland of the South, and I soon sold out and reprinted in Glasgow, the strike being over.

The Conservatives won the election, but with a much-reduced majority, and the Harold MacMillan cabinet, at its first post-election meeting, discussed the book, which had attracted much press attention, and decided to wind up the Hola camps and release the suspected Mau Mau detainees. None of them had ever been charged. This was not followed by riots and massacres of whites, as had been predicted by the right-wing press. The Kikuyu made no trouble and shortly afterwards, with the nationalist movement pursuing a moderate course, independence arrived. Eleven years after the emergency Jomo Kenyatta became President and opted to keep Kenya in the Commonwealth. I had successfully ignored a 'D' notice without prosecution and had reason to be proud of *Gangrene*'s influence in righting a wrong and changing the course of history. My second and third printings brought the sales up to 20,000 copies, but with the emergency over, returns came back, in particular from the Home Counties. The original cost of printing the first edition abroad and air-freighting flat sheets could not be recovered on a paperback selling at seven and sixpence, so commercially the publication was a quixotic gesture.

Public reaction was another matter. The book was debated in the House of Lords and several peers demanded my arrest, one proposed that I be charged with High Treason; and no doubt then taken to the Tower for execution! Letters in the press all assumed that I was making money by humiliating the British army, and I received abusive telephone calls as well as ugly correspondence and even death threats.

Quixotic publishing was causing other problems, financial ones. The list consisted largely of slow-selling literary titles by authors such as Beckett, Robbe-Grillet and Duras, and some British and American authors, often receiving good reviews, which seldom translated into good sales. I made regular trips around the provinces to see booksellers and promote my books. Booksellers were nearly all a very conservative breed in those days (and they have not changed much since), and they did not like what I published very much. The odd enthusiast would support me, like John Sandoe in London, a Mr. Jackson who had a good bookshop on Albion Street in Leeds and a few more. But I was an eccentric publisher outside the accepted mould, bringing out literary books that few people could or wanted to understand, and that sold too slowly. Bookshops that ran their own circulating libraries, like the Edinburgh Bookshop on George Street, found that no-one wanted to borrow my books. The popular author of the day was Neville Shute, that is until he blotted his copybook with *On the Beach*, a novel predicting the end of the world after a nuclear war, that lost him his popularity with the novel-reading public. There was also a suspicion that my creative literature, not being written just to make money, was in some way subversive. When I called on Ainslie Thin (uncle of the bookseller of the same name at the time of writing), the principal university bookseller of Edinburgh, he said to me one day, 'Some of my customers have been asking for your dirty friend Mr. Beckett. But I'll no stock him.' It was on that same visit that I offered him Gottfried Keller's *Green Henry*, just published, the first, and so far the only, translation of the Swiss classic that I had read shortly after my first arrival in Zürich. It was a fat book of 706 pages that had been translated by A. M. Holt, Professor of German at Toronto University, and was after all an established nineteenth century German classic and the type of book of which Thin's, a well-known and highly respectable university bookshop could be expected to approve. Mr. Thin's long dour face smiled slightly. 'Yes, I know it,' he said. 'We sell it in German. It's a wee little book.'

'Not so wee, Mr. Thin,' said I, 'in fact it's rather a large book. Here it is,' and I took it out of my bag. He picked it up gingerly, looked at it, turned it over, glanced inside, and handed it back. 'No,' he pronounced, 'that's not it. It's a wee little book.'

Edinburgh bookshops were not easy territory for my list. There were other university bookshops and some general ones, but they liked books they knew, and disliked those they didn't. Resistance to anything new was almost total. Glasgow was better, but not much. There were library suppliers there who bought some books but not too many of those I offered, novelists like Beckett and Aidan Higgins, playwrights like Ionesco, or books on musical composers, or on current political and social issues, ever found themselves on the shelves of the nation's bookshops, or libraries either. A few of the less conventional bookshops, those that could sell books that were often slightly erotic, took some titles, novels like *Fräulein* and non-fiction like *Variations in*

Sexual Behaviour, and often they were the bookshops interested in radical political books as well. Political titles had a short life, and I had to push them hard when the issues they covered were still in the news. I came to know all the radical and non-prurient shops from Aberdeen to Brighton, usually on backstreets and the seedier parts of town, like Soho and Camden in London.

David Austick was the university bookseller in Leeds. Years later, when we were both Liberal Party activists and I campaigned to help him become MP, we became friendly, but in the late fifties he was quite hostile. 'Why should I sell funny books?' he asked in his strong Yorkshire accent. I pointed out that these were exactly the books that interested the lecturers at the university – Leeds after all was more open to new literature than Oxford and Cambridge – who were teaching modern languages and the literature written in them. One of my translators and authors taught in the French department, Richard Coe; he had given me some splendid renderings of the musical and travel literature of Stendhal, on whom he was writing a book, and he had also translated Robert Pinget for me. Austick would reluctantly take a little, but not much. My best Leeds customer was the aforementioned Mr. Jackson. There was a similar bookseller in Hull and another in Colchester, who having told me that his accountant had forbidden him under any circumstances to put another book on his overcrowded shelves, then took nearly everything I could offer him. The man and the shop are both long gone, but bless his memory!

We took on two new authors on the recommendation of Samuel Beckett. One was Aidan Higgins, a young Irish writer from a small town outside Dublin, who wrote about relatives of an earlier generation, decayed minor Irish gentry, where, as he described it, what was left of the money of the Langrishe family was now sunk in the house and property shared by four elderly sisters, all spinsters, eking out their last years in genteel poverty. Aidan was a brilliant word-spinner, had trained as an engineer, spent time in South Africa, was married to a New Zealander and had two small sons. He was greedy for fame and the money he expected to go with it. We published a collection of his short stories under the title *Felo de Se,* the legal term for suicide. It was a book of high style and considerable morbidity. One story, the longest, was about a depressive alcoholic, looked after by a minder (who in real life had been the author) and another, about the same four spinsters, was a dry run for the novel that followed, *Langrishe, Go Down.* This was well-reviewed and won Aidan the James Tait Black Prize, which is given annually by the Professor of English at Edinburgh University. Both books were well received by the press and had reasonable sales, and in Ireland they established Aidan Higgins as a leading new writer in the great tradition of Irish prose. He was living in Muswell Hill in North London, writing in starts and stops, drinking heavily when he had money in his pocket. His wife also worked at occasional jobs. Aidan was a talented cartoonist and he would adorn his letters to me with drawings, especially self-portraits of his goyaesque face and red beard. We were successful in getting him a number of subsidies, several grants from the Arts Council over the years, an invitation to spend a paid year in Berlin with no obligation to do anything, and some American money. He also won the Irish-American Prize, which is given annually in Dublin by the American ambassador, this latter some years later after he had returned to live in Ireland.

The other writer sent to us by Beckett was Nick Rawson from the North-West of England. Like Higgins he was eccentric, but unlike him never knew success. He was a poet who wrote poetic prose works with striking imagery, but only on the edge of the non-abstract. We published him first in a new series for experimental work, *New Writers*, the first issue of which appeared in 1961. and many years later his book-length *Shards* was published in a later series for individualistic literature called *Signature*. I kept up a correspondence with Nick for some years, during which he wrote much verse that mostly went over the line into rather crude pornography, about which I could develop no enthusiasm.

A young musician called John Carewe came to see me one day. He had noticed my publication of books on Schönberg, Berg and Webern, on Janacek and other twentieth century composers, and the Rollo Myers book that surveyed the whole spectrum of modern music. He wanted to start a society to promote new music, of which little was heard in London in the fifties, where the concert scene was firmly wedded to the big names of the eighteenth and nineteenth centuries. Carewe was a conductor. He had also recruited the young English composer Marc Wilkinson, whom I already knew slightly as he had set passages from *Waiting for Godot* in an effective short piece for voices and chamber orchestra called *Voices*. I took up the project enthusiastically and soon our committee included Lord Harewood, the composers Iain Hamilton and Susan Bradshaw, the critic, music publisher and later agent Howard Hartog, the violinists Paul Collins and John Woolf, and later Sir Robert Mayer, a music-loving financier who ran children's concerts at the Royal Festival Hall on Saturday mornings, who became our most generous donor. There was also a John Croft in attendance, I think from the Arts Council. I suggested that there was one avant-garde public for music and another for literature, both small and little aware of each other, and that it might be possible to mix them. We did this by putting a literary spot in each concert, which became my special responsibility.

We called ourselves *Music Today*. Our first concert, on February 8th, 1960, at the small recital room of the Royal Festival Hall, had a formula which worked very well: two new or modern compositions, one of them a major work unknown to the British public, would be played before the interval, after which it would be discussed (the major work) and played again. Then there would be a literary spot and a serious classic played to end the programme. The evening consisted of Schönberg's *Verklärte Nacht*, the

British première of Boulez' *Marteau sans Maître*, which was played twice, discussed by Iain Hamilton (then our Chairman), Martin Cooper of the *Daily Telegraph* and Howard Hartog, and a Brahms Trio ended the evening. The literary spot was Patrick Magee reading an extract of Beckett that I had chosen for him. The Morely Quartet and New Music Ensemble played the music. We sold out because we had the mailing list of the Festival Hall at our disposal and we were included in it, but my having publicised the Beckett certainly brought in a few more people. Listeners learned something about literature and readers learned something about music. We were happy with our formula and at the second concert, on March 14th, which also sold out, I had a reading of a short Ionesco play as the literary spot. The discussion on this occasion was chaired by Hamilton with Peter Maxwell Davies and Peter Heyworth. At the third I put in a reading of Genet. Funding for the concerts came largely from Robert Mayer and Harewood, but we did not need much.

Then we made a mistake. Because the audience was bigger than the recital room, which took less than two hundred, we moved our concerts to the Royal Court Theatre on a Sunday night. Having only our own mailing list and with some limited advertising in the press, we could not reach enough people and the audience dropped in numbers. After two more concerts we decided not to continue. But in the meantime the musical situation had changed, which was one factor in our decision to disband. The distinguished musicologist William Glock, who had been a part-time musical advisor to my firm for a short time and among other occasional jobs had been secretary of the International Music Club in Mayfair during its brief heyday,[11] was appointed Head of Music at the BBC by Sir Hugh Carleton-Greene, the new, reforming Director General. Suddenly the Third Programme, the cultural channel, was open to atonalism and dodecaphonic music, to playing the works of British composers such as Humphrey Searle, who had been struggling in the wilderness for years. And at about the same time the Third Programme began to be more interested in intellectual drama and the authors I was publishing, when P. H. Newby, Donald McWhinney, Barbara Bray and later Martin Esslin, were allowed to become more adventurous and international.

I have mentioned that we had growing financial problems. The money that I had made on leaving Calders Ltd. had gone largely into publishing and that was where I was spending my time. I had a little flirtation, if that is the appropriate word, at working for Wolfson; he seemed anxious to add me to his team, but I think he was hardly serious. He invited me to come round

---

[11] The International Music Club occupied a large, well-furnished house on South Audley Street in Mayfair and was the brainchild of a Mrs. Hubbard, a Woolworth heiress, who wanted it to be the centre of London's musical life, where all the top musicians could eat, drink, meet and use the library and luxurious facilities. The restaurant was first class but fairly expensive. I once took Richard Coe there and introduced him to Tournedos Rossini, after he had translated the Stendhal Rossini biography. Musicians were wary, rather overawed and used it little. Glock first heard of its sudden closure through the press.

to his flat early one morning, and I waited while he read the financial columns of the daily papers and checked his stock exchange prices, after which we were driven to Dagenham, and to the Collaro factory, which he had bought the previous year. We were met by Major Collaro, the managing director, a jovial man, who conducted us around the factory which made radiograms and record players. Afterwards I sat through an embarrassing session in Collaro's office where this big, hearty man was turned inside minutes into a wet rag of a grovelling employee who did not earn enough money for the group. An earlier Collaro joke about an amateur group doing the *Merchant of Venice*, but having trouble finding someone to play Shylock, went right over Wolfson's head. I doubt if he had even heard of Shakespeare. In the same way, when he discussed finding a position for me, I was not forthcoming: what I had seen did not make me want to work for him, and in any case I had my own publishing company. But I could no longer finance it out of commissions earned elsewhere and the sales were inadequate.

At one point Wolfson, perhaps to test me, had suggested that I find ways of exploiting a cordless vacuum cleaner, that one of his companies had developed, and this was a time when, on visits to Montreal, I had discussed setting up with one of my Ostiguy cousins a company to sell my books in Canada and other things as well because Canada is not a big market for books, especially not for intellectual ones. We took on the cleaners and I came across a series of convincing reproductions of well-known old master paintings produced in London by Mrs. Fiehl. They were framed prints that had been painted over with glaze to give the impression of oils. A company was set up in Montreal called Stratford Sales and it was developing quite well because my cousin was an enthusiast and gave it much effort, but his least interest was in the books and I soon realised that I was involving my time and money in another business in which I had no real interest. I sold out to my cousin, Claude Ostiguy, and he carried it on until he retired. I also was invited to take an interest in The Montrealer, a monthly magazine that set out to imitate The New Yorker, and I joined the board with an investment intending to take an editorial part in its development. But soon I was too busy in the U.K. to keep in touch. Then one day I received two 'phone calls within an hour from other Montrealer directors. They were fighting for control and made me an offer for my shares. I sold to one of them and came out with a profit. I have no idea how it fared after that. It disappeared after another year or two.

I had other serious expenses as well, including what was to become a long-running legal battle to get divorced from Christya. I was paying considerable maintenance for her and our daughter. The money was running out and I had to start to look for new capital, and the obvious way to do this was to take an advertisement in the trade magazine The Bookseller. I received a few replies, one from a Marion Lobbenberg. I invited her to lunch in a small intimate restaurant near Sloane Square. She was a *petite* dark woman, near my own age, although I never discovered what it was until her death in 1999, enthusiastic and self-assured. Her marriage was dull and to relieve her boredom she had recently taken a two-year course at the new and still experimental University of Keele. She wanted a career. She had money enough, but had no intention of taking too much risk. She had heard of some of my authors and was impressed by their names, but everything had to be looked at by her accountant.

I soon met him. His name was Roy Jones, a wheelchair-bound victim of multiple sclerosis with a beady eye, a sense of humour, an iron will that made light of his affliction, and a formidable German wife. He was also the current lover of Marion Lobbenberg, although by no means the only one. Having looked at my balance sheet, and sent his partner Montague White to inspect my offices in Sackville Street, he told her she was mad and not even to consider an investment in a firm where profit had such a low priority. But she was already interested. She knew that some of my current authors, Eugene Ionesco in particular, were in intellectual fashion, and to be in the fashionable swim was her immediate aim. Her husband, George Lobbenberg, had a successful manufacturing business in Shrewsbury that made women's undergarments and she wanted to get away from the quiet and socially snobbish county-town where she had felt cramped and intellectually starved while raising her two small girls. She took a flat near Paddington and, torn between her desire to join me and Roy Jones' caveat, tried to make up her mind.

I suggested that she should come to work without pay to see for herself what we did and how the firm operated. She could take a few months to make up her mind and nothing in the office would be closed to her. Our need was getting greater, but I saw no other way, and she accepted.

Some time later Pamela Lyon got married and left, with Ethel de Keyser replacing her. Marion took on some of the editorial work, but she mainly wanted to meet the authors and to entertain them. I took her to Paris with me, hoping that a tour of French publishing houses and meeting Beckett, Ionesco and Robbe-Grillet would finally convince her. The investment under discussion was £10,000, and I was sure at that point that subject to inevitable conditions that Roy Jones would impose, she had really make up her mind to join me. She spoke reasonable French, good German, because her father was German, and she enjoyed the Paris trip. We stayed at my usual hotel, the Michelet-Odéon, and on different floors. We went to a concert at the Théâtre de l'Odéon one night, right next to the hotel; it was the world première of Boulez's *Pli selon pli*. Afterwards we went to the Coupole in Montparnasse, the most popular meeting place in those days for artists, intellectuals and those who wanted to be around them. I suggested a drink afterwards at a night-club nearby and we went to Elle et Lui, which I had often visited with Barney Rosset. The scene was largely lesbian, something which had always fascinated Barney, and I was curious to see Marion's reactions, but I think she hardly noticed. Afterwards, back at the hotel, I detected an invitation in her eye, but I had no intention of getting involved with someone with whom I expected to have a business relationship. 'I'm not feeling well. I think I drank too much,' I mumbled. 'I think I'm going to be sick.' And I rushed up to my room on the next floor.

Arthur Boyars would frequently drop into the office, and he and Marion, both Jewish, took a hearty dislike to each other. 'You can't take that appalling women into partnership,' he said, while she, once he had left, would ask why I let him waste my time. She was not impressed by a third-string book reviewer who had written a few poems and knew a great deal about the classical music repertory, not much in vogue among her friends. My love of opera also puzzled her: it was not intellectually fashionable according to her lights.

It was about this time that I met David Tutaev, I cannot remember how or where. He was a play director from a Russian background, very agile and light-footed, with long flowing whitish hair, a long nose, bright eyes, a gesticulating, enthusiastic presence, not tall, but thin and nervous, and always casually dressed. He had been an attaché at the British Embassy during the war , and had managed to get the NKVD girl who shadowed him pregnant. He was unable to get her out of Russia after the war, so he still had a child there. I am not sure how many marriages lay behind him. I was soon to meet his previous wife, an actress called Judith, and his current one who was Caribbean, a nurse, whom he had met on a boat who had already had two children by him, although I cannot be sure if they were actually married. He was an accomplished seducer of women and always trying to con something out of men, the financing of a play or some other scheme: his fertile mind always had many projects to pursue. Aside from the theatre he was full of book projects, the most ambitious of which was to publish a Library of Russian literary classics, philosophy and thought. Although attracted by the idea, I am glad it did not proceed. It would not have worked without heavy long-term subsidy. In any case Tutaev's quicksilver mind would never have allowed him to give it much effort. I met several theatre people through him – he had directed quite a number of plays, but I am not sure I ever saw one – and I especially enjoyed meeting Dorothy Tutin with him, a favourite actress of mine, but there was never any continuity of contact among people he knew. He certainly had talent, but I think he was little trusted, which is probably why he never seemed to have any work. Certainly I lent him small sums of money, which were never returned, but it was much more disturbing when he put a Serbian girlfriend in my living room for a night and she thought she was there for good, making herself very much at home. David would visit her for sex in the afternoons. It took me perhaps a month to get her out, but worse was to follow.

I was at the Frankfurt Book Fair – it must have been the autumn of 1958 – when I received a telephone call from Berry Bloomfield in my office. 'John, I have to warn you, David's wife and children are in your flat.'

'What do you mean? How could they get in?'

'He got the key from me. You know what David's like.'

I did indeed. Every hour of his life he had a crisis and he counted on other people to get him out of it, while he incurred new ones. I did not dare reflect on the means he had used to get my keys. He was hypnotically unrefusable and Berry had a soft heart. I told her she had to get them out somehow, I phoned my flat and spoke to the unfortunate woman (I forget her name) who had put herself in perpetual insecurity because of David, and I tried to reach him: all to no avail. I returned to London and after a day or two in a hotel, moved into Voronin's Boarding House and stayed there two months. Voronin's is worth describing. It was a boarding house for concert artists visiting London. Madame Voronin was an old white Russian lady, who when she was short of rooms would sleep on a camp bed next to the boiler. Every room had a grand piano in it. There were some compensations to my distress: at breakfast I would meet great pianists and singers, there to perform that week: I had serious talks with string quartets and trios that made me late for the office; and conductors would ask me to their rooms to turn the pages while they played through scores they were studying at the piano. I was frequently given tickets by artists to their performances. One South African pianist propositioned me and was very disappointed when I politely declined. I did have a fling with a Canadian pianist (female) who was staying there for several weeks while studying with a particular teacher. I had to change my room frequently depending on who was there, sometimes to a larger room with a Steinway or a Börsendorfer, sometimes to a small unheated one. Eventually I managed to get the Tutaevs to move out and returned to Upper Wimpole Street. During all that time I not only had to pay the rent and rates, but the telephone bill as well.

The 1959-60 season was the year that Bettina spent at Kiel. She had earlier studied with Gabriel Dusurrget in Paris. Dusurrget was the director of the Aix-en-Provence festival and he gave her the part of Barberina in *The Marriage of Figaro* when the company was performing at Cannes during an Easter season in 1958, after which I spent a few days with her on the Côte d'Azur. It was then that I heard my first *Pelléas et Mélisande* at the Opéra in Nice with Huguette Rivière, Willy Clément and Michel Roux. Bettina knew Christine Gayreaud, the Geneviève, quite well. She asked Bettina if she had ever made love with another woman and when Bettina said no, told her that she would like to be the one to initiate her.

Bettina was engaged again to sing with the Aix company at the summer festival that year. She was cast as one of the three ladies in *The Magic Flute* and was understudying Papagena. I drove down to be there and remember stopping the night at Pouilly and sampling their delicious white wine. I stayed for a week, sharing Bettina's room in university accommodation. Bettina was despondent because Georg Solti, the conductor, had turned up with three female singers who were not under contract to the festival, all mistresses of his, and insisted they sing, thereby putting three contracted singers out of a job, including herself. During the week I met Francis Poulenc, about whom I was soon to publish the Henri Hell biography. I joined him with his entourage at the Deux Garçons, the main café frequented by the regulars, before lunch, where his group included the composer Henri Rabaut, whose opera *Mârouf, Sauvetier de Caire*, I had seen at the Opéra in Paris in 1949 during my student days, and Pierre Schneider, whose book on Schubert I had published in the Profile series, which I shared with Grove Press. I was suffering from a gastric condition at the time and had to be careful what I ate, but Poulenc, sitting next to me, ordered as it he were my doctor. We were eight at table at the Casino restaurant, the best in Aix, and everyone other than myself at the table was homosexual, as was the subject of most of the conversation. Rabaut had recently stayed at a chateau where La Comtesse had made him share a room 'avec une femme! Imaginez, Francis, une femme!' Poulenc laughed and advised him to always do what he did, stay in an hotel. Poulenc was of course a well recognised figure and other tables were peering over at us, wondering who this new man sitting next to the great composer was: could it be Poulenc's new young boyfriend. Every time he slapped my knee the impression was confirmed.

The student accommodation was adequate if not comfortable, but I spent little time in the room. I came to know Dusurrget, whom I had met several times previously, very well and was often asked to drive him up and down the town. He urged me to run down the tourists on the crowded streets: he was the Festival Director and could do what he liked. He was a great eccentric who knew a great deal about voices and had impeccable taste in programming and casting. He knew he had made a mistake in hiring Solti, a tyrant whose arrogance was as great as his own. He had raised Aix-en-Provence into the first rank of European summer festivals, and his reign was its golden age. It was almost the last season for one of my operatic idols, Teresa Stich-Randall, who other than in Aix sang mostly in Vienna and never had the international career that her voice deserved. I had heard her in previous years and always with the feeling that her voice was the most ravishing imaginable. She was perfect for Mozart. I had heard her in most of his rôles for dramatic soprano, Donna Anna, Countess Almaviva, Fiordiligi, Pamina, etc., as well as in many masses. It was she who had so thrilled me on my first visit to Aix with Christya some years earlier. In this festival she was singing in *Don Giovanni* and *The Magic Flute* and also Rosina in Rossini's *Barber of Seville*, a heavy vocal programme in a short festival. But, with all her success, she had become disillusioned with the tackiness of operatic life and intended to enter a convent. We had several long talks during that week, away from the main cafés, where she did not much like mixing with the other artists whose intrigues and affairs and jealousies she found repulsive. She had great dignity on stage, but off it, without make-up covering a rather pimply face, she looked plain and rather dowdy. She was only thirty-two, but had decided to abandon her career, which was then at its peak, with many offers to sing all over the world. She soon retired and thereafter any singing she did was in a convent. I came to know many of the singers in that season, spent time with the tenor Luigi Alva and the bass-baritone Franco Calabese, a man who offstage always looked unshaven and dissolute. We had a discussion in the Deux Garçons after the performance one night when each of us chose an historical character he would like to be; Franco chose Voltaire and then Jesus Christ. 'What a painful life and death!' I exclaimed. 'Ah, oui. Mais quelle vie intéressante,' he replied. His large rolling eyes looked at me as if savouring a crucifixion.

There were wonderful singers that year. They included Consuelo Rubio, Mariella Adani, Antonio Campo, Rolando Panerai, Mario Spina and Georgio Taddeo in *Don Giovanni*, Fritz Wunderlich, Walter Berry, Mimi Coertse, Ernst Wiemann and Sylvia Stahlmann in *The Magic Flute*, many of these as well as names mentioned above also singing in the Rossini. Bettina had made friends with the local *jeunesse doré* and in particular with the abandoned young wife of a local chateau owner with a large swimming pool where we disported ourselves. The chatelaine was always half drunk to help deal with her tragedy and remain a cheerful hostess. Bettina, staying in the shade, tried to keep Sylvia Stahlmann sitting by the pool in the sun and constantly talking in the hope that sunburn would ruin her voice and enable her to take over the part of Papagena. She was also chased by a fashionable young man with whom, to my annoyance, she went to a dance outside the town. Among the concerts I attended, Pierre Boulez conducted the world première of his *Marteau sans Maître*. I was impressed by the music, not by his conducting. His iron will would change that in the coming years.

Bettina joined me in London shortly after the Aix Festival, where in the end, although part of the company and paid as contracted, she never sang a note in public. We then went together to the Brussels World Fair, much hyped at the time, visited the Skylon and other new buildings in odd shapes that had been erected, but on the whole I found the occasion a great bore, the British tent perhaps the least interesting of all. I did see *Maria Golovin*, Menotti's opera which was part of the American contribution, but failed to record the cast other than Patricia Neway in the title rôle.

During that year I saw Bettina frequently in Paris and she came to know some of my authors, in particular Sam Beckett, with whom we frequently dined in Montparnasse restaurants. Then her German agent managed to get her, after a series of auditions, a year's contract at the Opera in Kiel on the German North Coast, which would include guest performances in other towns and the possibility of occasionally singing at the

Hamburg Opera. I must have met her a few times in Germany during early 1959 as I have recorded seeing a memorable *Elektra* in Hamburg there with Astrid Varnay in the title rôle as well as a lacklustre *Carmen*, but also operas in Munich, Frankfurt and Vienna. The latter occasion, in May, was the triannual meeting these of the International Publishers Association to which normally the larger publishers of Europe and America, and a few of the more adventurous smaller ones as well, go if they can afford a fairly expensive week, which in spite of an agenda of matters to discuss, is mainly social, or was in those days.

My first problem on arrival in Vienna was about the room I had booked. You had to show your passports on arrival and as Bettina's passport had a different name from mine, they would not let us share a room. Nor could I get a second room, because the hotel was full. We managed to get in somewhere in the end, although we may have had to take separate rooms. The Congress itself consisted, as far as I was concerned, in a reception given by the Burgermeister at Schönbrünn Palace and another somewhere else, to a fabulous *Don Giovanni* and *Figaro* with Schwarzkopf, Zadek, Seefried, Güden, London, Wächter, Ludwig and other luminaries in the casts, and a *Walküre* with Nilsson, Brouwenstijn, Windgassen, Hotter, Greindl and Jean Madeira. Karajan conducted the *Figaro* and *Die Walküre*. I never went to a single session of the discussion programme, and I am not sure that I even knew it existed. The *Figaro* was the official opera as far as the Congress was concerned, tickets being part of the participation in the occasion. At the Burgermeister's reception, which was in lounge suits, I ran into George Braziller who moaned that he could not go to the opera the next night because he did not have a dinner jacket, and, he went on, this was the opera he had always wanted to see. I omitted to ask why he had never tried in New York, but suggested he could easily hire a dinner suit. But no, he could not do that and was unwilling to let me help him. So, the next day I went to a rental shop, described George's height, girth and width and rented him a black tie and everything that went with it. I then went to his hotel and arranged to have it sent to his room.

When Bettina and I turned up at the opera we met George, but in a lounge suit, and he was not the only one. 'Why aren't you wearing the dinner jacket?' I asked. 'Thank you,' he said. 'It didn't fit. But I came anyway.' I had at least forced him to come and I hope he enjoyed a perfect performance of a perfect opera.

I first visited Bettina in Kiel in September. She was staying at a boarding house with a Frau Schmidt, whose daughter Helga was later to work at the opera at Covent Garden. I stayed with her there several times, and then she moved into a flat, sharing it with another singer, Maria Hall, an American, whose first husband had been an American evangelist preacher. Her career had started when she sang gospel songs at his services. He had made her kneel down on their wedding night to ask God to take away her lust, and the marriage was short-lived. She was now married to a German ballet dancer, who most of the time was on tour and worked from another opera house. The two of them performed *Carmen* together, Bettina singing the smaller part of Micäella, who has two lovely arias. Personally I do not like applause in the middle of an opera and normally save my clapping until the curtain comes down and the last note has been played, but singers want it. Micäella has no break after her arias: the music goes straight on, and the audience, which may be prepared to applaud, cannot do so without interrupting the music. I was therefore given the task, at the performances I attended, of coming in with a loud burst of clapping immediately as the last note was dying, which would halt the performance and bring in the applause of the rest of the audience. This I did quite effectively, but I do not think it made me a friend of the conductor. The other opera I heard Bettina sing in Kiel was *Boris Godunov*, which was performed in the full version. The two Polish scenes, in which Bettina sang Marina, the Catholic Princess who is urged by a Jesuit to marry the pretender Dmitri, just about to invade Russia to topple Tsar Boris Godunov, and thereby to convert Russia to the Catholic faith, are often cut, but they were given in Kiel.

One night the company was playing in a small market town, Flensburg, not too far from Kiel. As I went with them I was invited to the supper given after the performance in the Rathauskeller, which is usually under the town hall. I found myself sitting opposite the Burgermeister, our host, who on hearing that I was British tried to get me into an argument as to which country had the better writers and poets. He told me that Shakespeare was nothing compared to Goethe. I declared my admiration for both without comparison, but as it was soon clear that I had a familiarity with both, while he knew nothing of either other than their names, he hastily brought our exchange of across-table repartee to an end. In fact he seemed anxious to end the party and send us all back to Kiel. I have often come across similar Germans whose bullying pedanticism is based on cultural nationalism and near-total ignorance of what they claim to love. I was reminded of my near-duel in Zürich.

After performances in Kiel I usually went to eat with some of the cast and Bettina. One night the two of us were alone with Maria Hall, and I was of course staying in the flat. It was at that late supper that she told us all about her problems with her first husband and her relations with the absent current one, who had taught her to enjoy sodomy, but not much else. The conversation probably excited us all a little, because when we returned to the flat she suggested we might have a shared sex session, and Bettina, with some hesitation, assented.

I shall not go into the details of that night except to say that all three had pleasure, that the ex-preacher's wife, who was a large and well-built lady, was imaginative and open to everything, and that we had no regrets the next day. But a week or so later the husband turned up, was told about our

161

threesome by Maria and demanded another with Bettina included, who refused because she did not like him. It was not a matter of being faithful to me: she had already had a brief affair with a Finnish baritone, both in Kiel and in Hamburg, about which she eventually told me. Barney Rosset had met Bettina with me, either in New York or in London, and he too made a trip to Kiel to see her, and apparently proposed marriage, which she told me she had considered, deciding in the end that Barney was madder than I was and had less in terms of common interests with her.

During that summer of 1959, in spite of financial difficulties, I was busy and active and felt myself to be a free man with friends everywhere, interesting work to do and enough scope to indulge my tastes and enjoy myself at the same time. I had then a certain confidence that whatever was the trouble that came along, I could deal with it. I still had friends in the film industry, in music, in the theatre and in the literary world. One person I knew well, because she and her husband Terence, a film director who had made some of the early James Bond films, had lived in a mews opposite Wilton Terrace, was Dosia Young. She had a habit of giving cocktail parties at lunch-time on Sundays, when I first knew her, where she would stay in her bath and her guests would take turns to come in and chat, sitting on the edge. She was a tall, handsome redhead, who when her husband decamped with one of his female stars, Nadia Gray, had no trouble in finding substitutes. That summer she had moved to South Kensington and she invited me to a party. It was full of film people, mainly men, and I had a long talk with Christopher Lee, who specialised in playing monsters in horror films, and while chatting to him I noticed an attractive blonde, one of the only half dozen women in the room, surrounded by a large group of men. I wonder if I can beat them all and leave with her, I asked myself, and went over, when I had the opportunity, to join the group. I cannot remember how I managed to get her attention and chat with her alone, but I did, and I took her to dinner and then home, where she was due to be picked up later. I then dated her for the next day, when we had dinner at Otello in Soho on Dean Street, my first time there. Her name was Sally, she was a model, and inhabited a very different world to mine, that of bright young things with affluent parents and rather lighter tastes than mine.

I did not go to bed with Sally until the next date. I had to wait for her in her sitting room – she had a house in Brompton Square, and after I had waited some time, having come punctually, someone else came in, went up the stairs past the first floor sitting-room, came down and left half an hour later. It was some time after that before Sally emerged, made-up and very beautiful. We had dinner and I spent the night in her house and room. By now I knew more about her. She had been twice married before twenty-one, the first time to a peer, the second to an actor, whom she still saw occasionally and respected, but she had recently been going out with a young man who ran a mobile chemmy game (*chemin de fer*), a fashionable but quite illegal pastime at that period, played in private houses by groups of friends. She had been to Mayfield, a top girls' school for Catholics near Brighton. She obviously did not need to work but enjoyed modelling. All her friends were in their early twenties like herself, rich, upper-class, living for pleasure and spending their time in the most mindless ways possible. She said to me after we had known each other a few days, 'You know, I've never been to bed with a socialist before. I'm not sure I've ever met one.' I received some new knowledge, for instance that models who wear slacks or tight dresses never wear underwear, because it spoils the line. I took her to some concerts, but I do not think she took in much. I was invited to the Austrian Institute, an evening of string quartets. I thought she might have recognised the Austrian hymn or the German national anthem in the Haydn (Emperor) Quartet, but no. Sally was a thoroughly nice person and we developed some common ground over the period I knew her from the summer of 1959 to the autumn of the next year. She knew that I had a liaison with an opera singer in Germany but assumed it was not too serious, just as I did. She had a frankness that belonged to her generation and milieu. She compared my sexual apparatus to others she had known. I satisfied her, but she had known bigger, but would point out that size felt different on different occasions. Ours was an unlikely liaison, but somehow it worked

Then suddenly, one day, a Sunday, my doorbell rang. It was Bettina, whom I had certainly not expected. She had, she announced, just walked out on her opera house in Kiel, where she was under a fixed contract for several months more. The reason: they were going to mount *La Traviata*, a rôle she knew, and that was just right for her voice, but the management had brought in a guest artist. The reason given was that she knew it in Italian, but not in German. She protested that she could learn it in German in a week, but it did no good and she had walked out in a rage. 'Here I am,' she said, 'are you glad to see me?'

It was about five in the afternoon and while I was considering the position the telephone rang. It was Sally. She knew instantly from my guarded voice that something was wrong. 'I'll bet your German singer has just turned up,' she said, and put the 'phone down. She was right. I never saw her again except once in a restaurant where she pointedly ignored me.

Bettina simply moved in without another word and I accepted the situation. But what was she to do? After some thought, I rang Tom Hammond, the chief repetiteur at Sadlers Wells Opera, the next day. I knew him well and asked if he could arrange an audition for a friend of mine who had left her German opera house. They liked her at the auditions and contracted her for the next season which had, if I am correct in my dates, already started. Her first part was as the Composer in *Ariadne auf Naxos* which opened in January 1961.

What happened to the year 1960? Much was published in that year, as was during 1959 when our catalogue listed dozens of books we were distributing as well as those appearing under the Calder imprint. In the earlier year we had brought out Beckett's three great post-war novels, *Molloy*, *Malone Dies* and *The Unnameable* in a single volume as Sam wanted. They were henceforth to be known as *The Beckett Trilogy* and the hardcover was published at twenty-five shillings with a cover of abstract squares and triangles, designed by Brian Sewell. Arthur Adamov, Marguerite Duras, Alain Robbe-Grillet, Nathalie Sarraute and André Pieyre de Mandiargues all made their debut on the list that year: there were many new classics and books on music in addition to those which have been mentioned on earlier pages. We published April FitzLyon's fascinating biography of Pauline Viardot under the title *The Price of Genius* and announced a number of books that never appeared for a variety of different reasons. These included a second volume on the South African treason trial, which was never written, a translated *History of Magic* that was never translated, *Peter Daubeny Presents*, a book which Peter Daubeny was meant to write about all the foreign companies he had brought to London over the years (I think he started it and died),Harold Hobson's book about Edwige Feuillère, which was too embarrassing in its fulsomeness, and Evan Senior's book about the arts in Russia, which he had often visited as a critic (he was the editor of our *Concert-Goer's Annual*, and I think he too died suddenly), and very sadly, a brilliant book entitled *The Lives of the Librettists*, covering the careers of the least-known and understood partners in the creation of operas. The author, Angus Heriot, had written an earlier book, *The Castrati in Opera*, first published unsuccessfully by Secker and Warburg in 1956, which we took it over in 1960, presumably buying unbound sheets from Secker and binding them to become No. 11 in our Calderbook paperback series. The editor I dealt with at Secker generously asked nothing for rights and only asked us to pay royalties to the author. This however was agreed over the telephone. When we reprinted some years later, we were told that the old contract was still valid as we had kept the book in print, but we must sign a new contract to reprint and pay a new advance. We commissioned the second book directly from the author, who handed in his manuscript and then was killed in a car crash. The manuscript sat on a shelf until we had to move offices in a hurry in 1963 because the lease had expired and the building was being demolished. Much was left behind in the hurry to move, thousands of manuscripts, proofs, files and archival material, such as piles up with time in every publisher's offices, were lost. Among that material was the only manuscript of *The Lives of the Librettists*.

1960 saw more books from some of our usual authors, and we reannounced books that had been announced earlier but delayed, as well as new titles taken on more recently, and some that would never appear, such as Galina von Meck's incompleted autobiography and Furtwaengler's *Collected Essays*. But many titles of importance did appear and they included the first significant critical book on Beckett by Hugh Kenner and George

Bataille's *Eroticism*. As far as my personal life was concerned the year is a blur, except that my opera record shows visits to many German towns and of course to Paris, where the Paris Opera, being then in deep decline, I went far more often to the theatre.

At Sadlers Wells Bettina had landed on her feet. She had been well-trained, first in America, then in Vienna, and Rodolfo Mele, who had taught her in Vienna, having now moved to London, continued to teach her and keep a control on her voice. He had many London pupils, was autocratic with all of them, and had some influence with conductors, mainly the Italian ones, such as Alberto Erede. He occasionally mounted an opera with his pupils, and before Sadlers Wells, possibly before Kiel, she had sung, I think, one of the three ladies in *The Magic Flute*, with his company in Brighton with an ad hoc orchestra and the imposing and statuesque Mary Wells singing Pamina, who I remember fancying at the time. I gathered that she had a boyfriend who was a shoe salesman and she never lacked shoes. Bettina was best in Mozart and Richard Strauss which have very similar vocal demands, and she could be very good when she was good. But she had a problem: as a child she suffered from rickets, which had given her a concave chest. This meant that the volume of air that her body, not just the lungs and chest, but the whole abdomen could take in, in order to expel long notes that had to be pushed out as if by a bellows, was limited. A dramatic soprano, which is how she presented herself, needs all the air reserves she can muster, whereas a mezzo-soprano, who does not need to achieve the highest notes which give no opportunity to take in more air, has an easier time, can control her air-expellation more easily, and concentrate on producing pleasing tone. From early in my acquaintanceship with Bettina, knowing little of vocal technique, but understanding that she sounded best with her lower-pitched chest-tones, those which I had so much admired with Flagstad, who was also able to hit the top of her range with equal facility, I had asked her whether her career might not go better if she became a mezzo. She did eventually, but she pooh-poohed the suggestion for years.

Dusurrget had liked her but had only cast her in small, lighter rôles. She had sung the spinto (light) soprano part of Micäella and the basically mezzo rôle of Marina in *Boris Godunov* in Kiel and perhaps others I had not heard. I had enjoyed her in song and Lieder recitals, but thought she was always best in registers other than the highest, in the repertoire of Italian *arie antique* for instance. She had the advantage of knowing several languages and had a veneer of sophistication, but Bettina, not far under the surface, was still a Croatian peasant. Primal and often unpleasant characteristics came out when she was not on her guard, and she very often lacked the most elementary tact. The conductor for her *Ariadne* performances was Colin Davis, only just appointed Music Director. At that point in his career he did not know Richard Strauss' work very well and compared it to a German Puccini. He also mispronounced some German words. Bettina would correct him in front of the full company, neither wise nor tactful where a new Music Director with the power to hire or fire was concerned. She also flaunted herself as a European star rather more than was necessary, and in any case she wasn't one. All this made her few friends.

My divorce from Christya was now imminent. The *decree nisi* had gone through some months earlier after many difficulties and set-backs, and I was looking forward to the final decree. Then one day Tom Hammond telephoned me. 'Tell me, John,' he said, 'when are you and Bettina getting married.' I looked at the telephone in dismay. 'Why?' I asked.

'Because surely you realise we are only allowed to employ British artists at Sadlers Wells,' he said. 'When we engaged Bettina we naturally assumed you were getting married.'

She came back that evening from rehearsals and of course knew about the call. 'Well, why don't we get married?'

'But I haven't even got a divorce!'

'You will at any moment. I'm so excited to be singing with a company like Sadlers Wells. It doesn't have to be permanent. If we don't get on, I'll not be any trouble.'

I was to remember those words with much bitterness.

* * * * * *

The opening of *Ariadne auf Naxos* was only a few days away when we went, one brisk winter day at the end of 1960 to the Marylebone Registry Office, waited for fifteen minutes while others went in to get married, then it was our turn. The final divorce decree was not even a week old. The two witnesses were Marion Wilson and Arthur Boyars. Afterwards we went to the Mirabelle for lunch, a good expensive restaurant that I had rarely visited, and then to fill in the afternoon (my first thought to return to the office was not popular), we all went to the Tate Gallery to see a Picasso exhibition and I ran into Leo de Rothschild there. I had been to see Leo some months previously to see if there was any chance that the Rothschild Bank could help me financially; they gave me a very English lunch in the board-room as an old school acquaintance (from BCS) of Leo's, but of course I was far too small a company for their consideration. Leo was the first acquaintance to be introduced to the second Mrs. Calder.

Life went on as normal. Bettina had helped out a little in the office as a receptionist before her rehearsals started in earnest, but now she was preparing for her British début. I had invited various friends and relatives and had a dozen tickets to distribute. Then the 'flu struck and on the morning of the big day Bettina had no voice. Her understudy went on instead. I telephoned around, but no one wanted the tickets and they were unused. She also missed the second performance, but on the third, which was about a week later, her understudy fell ill, and Bettina was told, that voiceless or not, she was the better of the two invalids and had to appear. She did not do badly at all. Her pallor and shakiness was perfectly in character for the rôle of the composer, distraught that his opera had to be butchered at the whim of the rich Mr. Jourdain, to accommodate a lighter entertainment which has to take place simultaneously with it and be finished before a firework display. She sang all the other performances but of course did not get reviewed as the critics only went on the first night.

Her next rôle was Prince Orlowsky in *Die Fledermaus*, where she was a success, but did not stand out from what was, then as later, an excellent company. I think she had probably upset Colin Davis rather too often, because he did not seem keen to give her more work and she began to sing with smaller opera companies. She still had a German agent, but she received no more European engagements at the time. Walking out on an opera company that has contracted you does not inspire confidence. We began to see quite of a lot of Marion Lobbenberg and Roy Jones and his wife, Lucy. It was now fairly settled that Marion would invest, but Jones drove a hard bargain. He said £20,000 was needed, not half that sum, and that Marion would only come up with £10,000 if I could do the same. As it stood, he insisted, the company was worth nothing, and Marion for her investment would get half the company. If it failed she would get her money back before me. I had no option but to accept: Marion became a partner and director and owned half the company. Although she had her own ideas, she was happy enough for the time being to go along with my editorial programme, which at that time was increasingly involved in translating the most advanced European literature, while continuing to publish books on music, drama and the arts generally. I cannot remember how I raised the other £10,000, but I did somehow. The fact that Roy had begun to like me and that he had taken an interest in the work of the company helped to cement things and made me a little less uneasy at giving away so much for so little. One of the conditions was that Roy Jones also became a director. Thereafter we had regular board meetings in his office, the other director being Lesley MacDonald.

Much of our energy had gone into selling Barney Rosset's Evergreen paperbacks, a series that had greatly expanded. Where we had the rights to certain authors like Samuel Beckett, where we had previously sold the American edition, we now brought out our own. Beckett's little book on Proust had sold well and we now produced our own edition with other texts in the volume and his first novel *Murphy* as well. *Malone Dies* had come out in hardcover to mainly indifferent reviews, and when we published the *Trilogy*, with *Malone* republished as the middle part, the reviews were not much better, but at least more serious and longer. *Molloy* had been translated by Patrick Bowles to appear as an Olympia Press book, and Beckett had helped with the translation, but he was never happy about it and thereafter translated the other two himself and all subsequent work written in French. I had no difficulty in the end in persuading Maurice Girodias, who by contract owned the English version of *Molloy*, to let me include it, but in return he was allowed to publish the same trilogy, which never did particularly well in his edition, although in later years it was to become a collector's item. Gradually all of the Evergreen Becketts were published on our own list with the exception of the plays that were with Faber.

It was through that one play, *Godot*, that Beckett's reputation as the most discussed and disputed writer of the day had been established and the arguments went on. Cyril Connolly in The Sunday Times remained negative. He said that the time had come when he should advise his readers whether or not they should bother with this man Beckett and, on balance, he thought they should not. He was too difficult and obscure, and Connolly hinted that a charlatan might be hiding under the elegance of the prose.

But the academics, who needed a new idol to follow Joyce, who was now appreciated by a growing readership and the object of many critical studies, had begun to latch onto Beckett, and his name was current in the universities. It had of course all started with *Godot*, but the novels made it easier to understand the plays: it was all the same territory. Beckett looked at the world from the perspective of the underdog and, as Beaumarchais had once enabled the French aristocracy to realise that their servants were intelligent human beings who could mock them behind their backs, so Beckett now made readers aware that the beggars and down-and-outs they pass blindly on the street, see them too, despise them and often hate them as they rush by with their little everyday certainties and securities and homes to go to. Beckett was beginning to come into intellectual fashion and the academics were getting ready to make him their next prey.

One American, Hugh Kenner, came to see me and we published his book, simply entitled *Samuel Beckett, A Critical Study*, which Barney Rosset also took for the U.S. It was the first book on Beckett to appear and it brilliantly picked up the physical objects, preoccupations and obsessions that occur throughout Beckett's work. It was quickly followed by a flood of other books as the academics got to work on an author whose depth seemed to have no bottom, although he could be very entertaining on the surface. Kenner had already written on T.S. Eliot and over lunch he gleefully related the foibles of that author with whom he had had many interviews. I had in fact noticed one or two myself, such as his way of tapping the side of a cheese with his knife before cutting it. When Beckett was in London once, I took them both to the Hurlingham Club where Sam and I played billiards while Hugh Kenner sat in a corner and made notes while he watched us. 'This little circle should meet regularly,' he commented to me afterwards.

Kenner's book was well reviewed, sold quite well and Beckett's own press reception and sales were improving, although most of the literary establishment still remained hostile. The Irish had still not accepted him: his first book of fiction, *More Pricks than Kicks*, published in 1934, had been banned unread purely on the title, and although he still had many friends there, his name was barely known. With time Sam Beckett was to take an ever more militant stand against Irish censorship, and in his youth had written a telling poem against it.

But at the BBC Beckett had his loyal adherents. Foremost among them was Donald McWhinnie, who had produced his ground-breaking radio play *All That Fall* in which sound effects added a new dimension to a poignant text. The novel *Molloy* was read on the third programme as well. The gravelly voice of Patrick Magee was ideal for the gritty character of the itinerant Molloy, dragging his tired body, resting on a bicycle or on crutches, through town and field and forest in search of his mother and whatever comfort she could bring him. Beckett heard the broadcast on his radio in France and sat down to write a play for this interesting voice and for an actor he had never met; it became *Krapp's Last Tape*, written in English as the radio play had been. McWhinnie produced the play for the Royal Court Theatre in October 1958. Beckett went to London, met Magee, spent time talking and drinking with actor and producer and went very carefully over the text with Pat. The director of the Royal Court was George Devine, who became very taken by Beckett and said he would produce any other play in his theatre that Beckett gave him. *Fin de Parti* was already written, had been published in Paris, and the translation as *Endgame* in London by Faber. Devine very much wanted to produce it and eventually did. Gradually a little circle of professional admirers was forming around Beckett, people who believed in him absolutely, and none of them were ever shaken by the hostility that so many others felt towards his style and vision. McWhinnie had an assistant in the script department of the BBC, Barbara Bray, who became another Beckett admirer and soon an intimate friend. She apparently had an equally intimate relationship with McWhinnie and Beckett at about the same time.

Barbara Bray, a remarkable woman with intellectual tastes, was busy translating a number of French playwrights for broadcast on the Third Programme, in particular the work of Marguerite Duras and Robert Pinget, both authors of mine, and the BBC interest helped a little; at least it showed moral support and evidence that I was not the only member of the London intellectual world to show an interest in the new talent that was coming from France. Largely because of Barbara Bray and a few other kindred spirits working at the Third Programme, a new flavour of avant-garde modern drama became visible there and much of it was French. In time this would cause difficulties, because many complaints were to come in from listeners. A German journalist working in Paris, Werner Spiess, was commissioning radio plays for Suddeutsche Rundfunk, and he was approaching not only those mentioned above, but Nathalie Sarraute, Roland Dubillard, Edouardo Manet, Françoise Billetdoux and other writers to produce radio plays, and many of them ended up on my list and were broadcast in English by the BBC. Nathalie Sarraute had never written anything for the theatre, but she now produced a number of conversational dramatic pieces, which apart from broadcasts, could be staged, providing a director could put in suitable stage directions and find a context for dialogues which were intended to show up the ways in which we score points off each other or try to exercise a superiority over a neighbour or another family member. Jean-Louis Barrault, and later Simone Benmussa and Claude Roy took Sarraute's texts, semi-abstract conversations where the speakers were on the whole not identified, and gave them a stage presence. These plays were first performed in France at Barrault's studio theatre at the Odéon. In my opinion they worked brilliantly but only to the tiny number of people who came to them. I managed to get them produced at one or two small theatres in London, such as The Gate at Notting Hill, but again they attracted a very small audience. But I eventually published them, and other radio plays that were brought into existence by the commissions of Werner Spiess. Ionesco also accepted Spiess commissions which I believe were very well paid. There was a New Zealander around at the BBC whom I met often: he was enthralled and knowledgeable about the *nouveau roman* and the new French theatre, soon to be labelled 'the theatre of the absurd'. His name was Owen Leeming, but he suddenly went back to New Zealand. Years later very few of the surviving members of that group interested in new literature can remember him. Every time I pass Leeming Airport on the A1 main road in North Yorkshire I do remember, and wonder where he is. I lunched a few times with Barbara Bray to discuss these plays and she was in any case doing a few translations for us. My problem with her was her attitude, which was a rather typical BBC one. She was a vivacious, extremely attractive lady, then perhaps in her late twenties, well-read, intellectual and very self-assured. She would berate me for puffing up the reputations and especially the positive literary talents of my writers, Beckett in particular. 'You don't have to keep saying how wonderful a book is,' she would say to me, 'readers will find that out for themselves in time.'

'Perhaps,' I would counter. 'But by then I won't be publishing any more. I can't pay rent or salaries or printers from books that might be bought in ten year's time.' She couldn't understand this, because at the BBC money in those days had nothing to do with the creation of programmes. She was already involved with Sam at the time, but I had no inkling of it, either from her or him.

After Bettina moved in with me, it became obvious that I needed a bigger place. I found a large two-floor flat at the top of a building at the bottom of Wimpole Street, no. 76. Lynette Perry, whom I had known for some time as a writer of radio plays, took over my old flat. She was just becoming involved with a fairly mature student at Oxford called John Peter. He had come to Britain as a refugee from Hungary after the Russians had put down the Hungarian rising in 1956. Their affair eventually became long-term and ended in marriage. John Peter later managed to get a job as theatre critic on the Sunday Times and in a fairly short time became one of the senior drama critics, as well as one of the most serious current writers on drama with a wider knowledge of the European arts than nearly all his colleagues on other newspapers. I kept in touch with them both over the years.

My new flat was owned by a firm of solicitors who occupied the ground floor, while a rather unpleasant couple had the first, just below us. The wife frequently complained that classical music gave her a headache. Needless to say that was what came down to them from my record player and from Bettina rehearsing her rôles or doing vocal exercises at the piano, so there was some friction. This was to lead in July 1962 to a letter from the solicitors on the ground floor, Ross Elliston and co., who were also our landlords. They had been aware by that time that there was a considerable traffic of people through my flat, that I held parties and that there had been political gatherings, some of which are mentioned elsewhere in this book. The letter threatened to cancel my lease and said that remaining in the building meant rigidly adhering to the following restrictions: there were to be no political meetings, there was to be no singing, no posters exhibited from the windows, no groups were to gather there and I was to have no books on the premises. The letter went on for three pages. I had totally forgotten it until I came across it in the publishing archives that are kept at the Lillie Library at the University of Indiana while writing this book. I probably ignored it, but was more careful.

But it was a good flat for entertaining all the same, and we had a constant flow of writers, musicians, artists and politicians coming to drinks, lunch and dinner. Bettina was good at entertaining and could organise a presentable meal for several people at short notice, which often became necessary. There were two spare bedrooms on the top floor and one or both were frequently occupied by visitors during the next few years, the most frequent of whom was Samuel Beckett. Beckett was quite often in town to discuss readings on the BBC, productions of plays and to see friends, sometimes to be present at the *vernissage* of an art exhibition, especially if asked to be there in support of a friend. In those days he was not particularly welcome at rehearsals as far as producers were concerned, but he nearly always formed an instant bond with the actors, unless they were very traditional and careless West End actors who had their own ideas, had already been rehearsed to deliver their parts in a certain way and were not happy when Sam turned up late in the rehearsal period and wanted to make major changes. Among the actors he liked best were Jack Magowran and Patrick Magee. They were heavy drinkers, as was McWhinnie when he was with them, and Sam, although he was now being more careful, could also put down a considerable amount of beer or whisky. With me he more often drank wine, but that of course was largely in restaurants or at table at my flat. Actors often came to Wimpole Street to work with Sam in the sitting room.

Sam himself when he stayed spent much time at the piano, sometimes playing from music, sometimes without. He had a remarkable finger memory, in fact a remarkable memory altogether. When something set him off he could quote for several minutes favourite texts in his four main languages (not his own texts, although he memorised them as well for use at rehearsals). But his life-long interest in sport would always draw him to the television set, any sport, but cricket and tennis in particular. Otherwise he stayed in his room much of the time, occasionally working on something, although Sam usually only wrote or revised his work either in Paris or for the most part at his place in the country, which from about the time I first knew him was at Ussy-sur-Marne, about an hour's drive east of the city. On one occasion he gave me a typescript to read, which I tackled with some puzzlement. It was the first draft of *Happy Days*. I forget what comment I made. I certainly did not grasp the whole poignancy of this laying bare of a woman's deepest fears and the defences she builds against them. When Beckett stayed with me he was out most of the time, seeing actors, his agent, those concerned with his plays and friends and he very seldom made any comment on his movements and whom he had seen, except when he came back from rehearsals where his mood was usually irritation caused either by the difficulties the actors were having with his lines and stage directions or those he was having with a producer who had conceived a vision of the play rather different from his own. His stage directions became ever more precise to remove any ambiguity of what he wanted.

The marriage was working better than I had expected because Bettina was a good housekeeper and we both had busy professional lives. Perhaps for the first time in my life I was living a life of routine and habit, having problems at work to deal with that were within my competence and not the kind of shocks out of the blue that Christya had always caused me.

Bettina was getting odd concerts, and it was becoming obvious that she was not going to be employed much more by Sadlers Wells. Smaller opera companies began giving her parts. She sang at St. Pancras Town Hall in Verdi's early comic opera *Un Giorno di Regno* in March 1961, where the producer was Michael Geliot, my first meeting with him. He was again the producer in her next opera, a production of a new work, *Volpone*, by Francis Burt, which was given by the New Opera Company at Sadlers Wells the following month as part of a short season that included Dallapiccola's *Il Prigonerro*, a revival of the production I had previously seen two years earlier. I had met the composer, Luigi Dallapiccola, with Emily Hooke, one of the few singers who in the fifties was interested in and capable of singing difficult modern scores. A previous girl-friend of Lockspeiser's, she was now only a friend (but Edward maintained a nostalgic jealousy towards the diminutive Italian composer, whose reputation Emily had done much to establish in Britain). She was a good friend to us both in those days; between my marriages she had often invited Edward Lockspeiser and I around to eat, talk and discuss music in the evenings. Now I met Dallapiccola again, the foremost Schönbergian composer of his country, whose reputation has surprisingly faded since his death in 1975, usually in the company of Emily. There were several small opera companies performing both in London and the provinces then, which enabled me to increase the repertoire of operas I could see. I went to the opera forty-six times in 1961, rather less than my normal score, but I was going much to the theatre, much to concerts and spent many evenings at literary events or entertaining or being entertained. The Welsh National Opera was coming into prominence, started by an enthusiastic garage owner and based on the vocal power of a Welsh choral society. They produced several operas in Wales, which they brought to London, mainly rarely-done early Verdi works and rarities such as Boito's *Mefistofole*, which I saw in a production by George Foa. Foa had talked me, back in 1957, into publishing an operatic novel of his, *The Blood Rushed to My Pockets*, a comic work in which a tenor meets the real Lucia di Lammermoor who appears on stage alongside the soprano who is singing her rôle. My edition was illustrated by Michael Ayrton. It seemed to me to be perfect for Danny Kaye as a film and I had made every attempt to bring the novel to his attention. Perhaps he actually read it, but he never came back to me. Now at the end of his career as a producer, Foa was still doing good work, but dying of a wasting illness that made it almost impossible for him to talk, although he still somehow mounted operas on stage. Beckett had himself worked at an opera about that time. He had allowed Marcel Mihailovici, a friend, to set the French text of *Krapp's Last Tape* (*La dernière bande*), as an opera lasting a little over an hour. The composer, whom I later asked to contribute to a Festschrift for Beckett, told me that Sam had spent many hours with him looking over the score as he worked on it and had made suggestions for the music itself. He could just as easily have been a composer as a writer, said Mihailovici. I saw it after its première in Bielefeld when the German company came to Paris in July 1961, where it was paired with another short work by Winfried Zillig. Barrault enthusiastically gave his theatre, the Marigny, for the occasion, where he was mounting an international season for which the theatre was temporarily renamed the Théâtre des Nations. The American baritone William Dooley sang the part of Krapp.

I was travelling back and forward between London and Paris, sometimes going to German cities for a publishing event or an operatic or theatrical one, and moving between the worlds of publishing, theatre and music. My living room became something of a salon with many politicians also coming in and out. Bettina had begun to cultivate women politicians in the Labour Party, especially those who were militant about women's rights.

In those days I was often asked to lecture, usually as a result of the more controversial books I had published, and radio and television appearances, as well as much press publicity, were the usual result. One Sunday night, not too long after I had moved into the new flat, I was rung up by the ICA Gallery (Institute of Contemporary Arts), then on Dover Street. A lecture on Beckett was to take place at 7.30, but the lecturer was ill, and could I possibly replace him? I did, at a few minutes notice, and while I was talking my eye was constantly attracted to the very large, colourful and abstract paintings that were hanging on the walls of the room where I was talking. When, afterwards, they enquired what I would expect for a fee, I asked how much the paintings were. They started at £500, but none had been sold. All were by an Austrian painter called Hollegha. In the end I acquired one for £100 in lieu of fee and hung it on the very large wall of my living room (or salon as we called it), opposite large windows, where it became a talking point among all my visitors. The other acquisition to the flat was Bila, a poodle.

Jamie would come to me sometimes on Saturdays and Sundays. She was still living with her mother at 2 Wilton Terrace and I think that by now Victor Churchill, her new boy-friend, had moved in as well. A man came to see me with a white poodle puppy. Jamie, so I was told, wanted it for Christmas. Reluctantly I agreed to buy it, but within two days (on Christmas Day itself I think) I was asked to look after it myself: it was of course not house-trained and Christya had wanted to put it out onto a balcony in cold mid-winter weather all night. So I kept the dog to which Bettina gave the name Bila (white in Serbo-Croat) and of course a bond developed quickly. Jamie would come on weekends and we would take Bila to Regent's Park where she ran in circles at speed until exhausted. Two years later Bila was mated with the male poodle of Yvonne Ball, who was understudying Bettina, and had five puppies, two of whom where called Didi and Gogo. When Didi died we did not dare tell Sam for some months.

* * * * * *

Easter 1959 was the second, but the first really big Aldermaston March. The previous year I had gone to Cornwall with Bettina for the weekend, and back on the Easter Monday had spent the evening with Alfred Alvarez and his wife, a very attractive voluptuous young girl, whose name I cannot remember, only that she was a grand-daughter of Frieda Lawrence. I cannot remember her name and Alvarez in his autobiography pointedly never gives it, the reason being that the marriage, although there was no way I could have known it at the time, was an unhappy one. They had both just finished the first Aldermaston march, had very sore feet and were tired. I felt very guilty with my anti-nuclear convictions not to have spent that Easter weekend marching with them. We discussed the political situation, and also Barney Rosset, who had published *Lady Chatterley's Lover* in America without a contract and without paying royalties (they considered him a simple crook taking advantage of the ambiguous American copyright laws to rob her and other Lawrence heirs of the royalties). I believe he paid something in the end. There and then I resolved to march the next year. In 1959 I kept that resolve, and did the whole thing. I remember the assembly on Friday morning outside the Aldermaston weapons establishment, and then perhaps a thousand of us, marching to Reading, which took a day, where the local vicar would not allow anyone to use or even enter his church for shelter, then taking the train back to London for the night, and reassembling early the next morning for the long march on the Saturday. By now we were several thousand strong, people of every age and background, accompanied by jazz bands and steel bands and we were kept in a column about ten across by marshals. Onlookers lined the route, some friendly, some not, many just curious. The atmosphere was extraordinary. People had come from all over the country, some from abroad, bringing banners to identify themselves. Most were dressed casually, suitable for mixed and often cold and rainy weather, but some, like myself, dressed as if we were going to a reception in the city, quite deliberately in order not to give the impression that we were bohemians or drop-outs. 'Some of them may be sincere, but most of them are just commies,' I overheard. In some places we were clapped and cheered on, with many falling in to swell our ranks, but there was hostility too. The good humour of the marchers and their songs ('We shall overcome' was a popular one) did however leave a favourable impression and our numbers grew as we neared London. Every newspaper was grabbed up by the marchers to see how the march was being reported and how many we were estimated to be.

Bettina was there at the beginning, but as I remember it not all the time. By Sunday we were all getting tired and that day she stayed home. I remember late that Sunday, on the outskirts of London, walking with Alvarez, who needed a stick as he had a lame leg, when we were stopped by a marshall at a junction to let the traffic pass. 'Come on, hurry up, catch up with the others,' he urged us after three minutes of letting the cars go by. We were exhausted by stopping and then rushing to catch up as we moved through outer London towards Hammersmith. At one junction a marshall shouted at us to hurry up and then, seeing our distress, relented: 'Alright, I can see you're doing your best.' I suddenly felt old as the younger marchers ran past us to catch the rear of the column ahead. At the end of that day I found myself in a pub with a number of Scots, some of whom I knew slightly. Among them was the publisher James MacGibbon, founder of MacGibbon and Kee, which produced a wonderful literary list then and for a short number of years before it was taken over by Granada, and Colin Bell, a young journalist with whom I was to cross swords in the years ahead. The Aldermaston marches attracted a wide range of left of centre or concerned intellectuals from all over Britain as well as seasoned campaigners. Many friendships were made on the move or during the stops.

And finally on the Monday we all packed into Trafalgar Square, tens of thousands of us. On that day the march had been led by Michael Foot, Ritchie Calder, Canon Collins, Victor Gollancz and others who had lent their names, and perhaps marched part of the way, but were there to be photographed by the press for the last few hundred yards to the platform on the square. We never saw them until the end, those names from politics, media, science and show-business, which had helped get newspaper coverage to encourage the thousands to sacrifice their four days of Easter for a cause that the majority of the nation's citizens would otherwise never let enter their consciousness. The right to vote carries with it the responsibility to think and to be aware. Mass movements pushed by activists have no other real purpose but to create that awareness and thereby to force politicians to be not only aware, but to take decisions. The four days ended with the usual speeches and rituals on the plinth and then we scattered to eat, sleep, take trains or buses home, all elated by the press reports that more than 200,000 people had either marched or filled Trafalgar Square.

I had taken part in other demonstrations before Aldermaston, some in Trafalgar Square, once in Grosvenor Square and in Whitehall, and on one occasion had been painfully kicked by a police horse. There was a growing militancy in the late fifties against the Conservative governments of Churchill, Eden and MacMillan (the latter the best of the three) and against a Labour hierarchy that favoured a confrontational arms race and the nuclear deterrent. There were several incidents in the fifties that might have detonated a nuclear war, but fortunately sanity, or restraint, or perhaps just luck, prevailed. Those of my generation, and of the one that followed it, if politically conscious at all, were convinced that all life and civilisation were at great risk. The strength of the protest movements did much to restrain the government, whichever party was in power, which was more aware of our opposition than we perhaps realised. This was shown by the effect that *Gangrene* had had in ending the so-called Mau-Mau emergency.

In fact those protests ushered in and fuelled the sixties. As a publisher, but also as an individual, I was in touch with the new young university-educated intellectuals from non-middle class backgrounds who Somerset Maugham was to call 'scum'. One of my new authors was David Mercer, whose father had been an engine-driver of trains and an ardent socialist. David had succeeded in passing exams so that he could be educated at the expense of the state, and he became an articulate, politically-aware artist. First he was a painter who went to Paris to make his career, but he then switched to writing. He went to a literary agent, Rosica Colin, who failed to find him a publisher and never thought of me, although as a fellow-Rumanian to my author Ionesco, who had persuaded him to let her represent him, even though he was already contracted to me who was not only publishing his plays but had found theatres to perform them, she certainly knew of my presence. David Mercer had sent me a number of his short stories, one of which I published in my *New Writers* series. Before that I had published three of his television plays, and more were to follow. Mercer was typical of the new working-class writers who were then finding their voice, some of them clustered around George Devine at the Royal Court Theatre. I knew many of them, but my means were too limited to be able to contract more than one or two.

Marion had established herself in the office and began to assert her authority. Patrick Bowles, the translator of *Molloy*, was in London now. He was a very macho and handsome South African with a good classical education and much self-confidence, which always fell just short of arrogance. He was also a poet and seemed to have the ability to turn his hand to any literary activity: he did several translations for us, some rather carelessly. [12] But above all he was a ladies' man and Marion was one of his conquests or perhaps it was the other way round. Roy Jones and Marion remained close in their business tie, but each had gone on to other sexual partners: Valerie Desmore was for a time with Roy and Marion had the pick of male authors and translators. Roy had come to the conclusion that I was one of the great London eccentrics and cultivated my company: there were many lunches in Soho restaurants, visits to the theatre as a group, and meetings at parties. I had imitated Barney Rosset in buying myself a bubble car, a little two-seater Heinkel, which on one occasion took five people to a party in Hampstead, all writers: Colin Wilson, Arnold Wesker and two other literary luminaries of the time. The diminutive car, only about four feet high could get through any traffic and be easily parked anywhere. On one occasion I had to meet Roy, his wife Lucy, Bettina, and I think Marion as well, at a cinema near Marble Arch, and I was late because of a traffic jam. But Bettina could hear the approaching Henkel with its recognisable two-stroke engine beat. Roy laughed and laughed when he saw me driving up the pavement past the immobile deadlocked traffic. He now enthusiastically chaired board meetings and seldom disagreed with what I wanted to publish. He also imitated me in becoming a political radical and going to rallies in his wheelchair. Marion now wanted to edit manuscripts and translations, but I could hardly fail to notice that her interest was often as much in the man as his work. I cannot remember her often wanting to spend time with a female author, although she would take credit when such a book was well-reviewed. She brought in one author whom she had known since her pre-war Berlin days, Eva Tucker, at a time when we were publishing many more young British authors, not all from British backgrounds. In time she was to find new authors herself, often from the American publishers she went to visit in New York.

I had to find a way of increasing the sales of the French authors we were translating and publishing. Some like Raymond Queneau and André Pieyre de Mandiargues did not belong to any group (although Queneau in

---

[12] In a French book on Verdi's operas, *Un Giorno di Regno* was translated as *A Day of Rain*.

the past had belonged to several), but we now had a growing stable of writers to which several labels had been attached. First the new style was called the *a*roman (*a*novel as in *a*tonal), then the *anti*novel, finally the *nouveau roman* or 'new novel'. There were obvious links with the anti-theatre, as the plays of Ionesco and Beckett were sometimes described, with the new French and Italian cinema or Japanese films like *Roshomon*. A new subjectivity was abroad, where truth became what the individual mind saw as truth, not the perception of society as a whole or as a collective unity. New isms had followed each other in the plastic arts and now it was the turn of literature to find new paths. Antonioni in the cinema was depicting a world where the old certainties, both in human relationships and in social forms had disintegrated or changed beyond recognition. A new generation where the educated middle class had been invaded by working-class intellectuals needed new forms and a new way of looking at the world. The *nouveau roman* (the French label stuck where its English equivalent did not) needed to find a bigger British readership, and the time was ripe. In France Alain Robbe-Grillet, a brilliant theorist with that ability which is the hallmark of a great teacher to make complex ideas clear and sound simple to listeners, had convinced the press and all who came to hear him speak that a new literature had arrived. He pointed out that he had given the reader a chance to become part of the creative process, to take on some of the responsibility of the author, who no longer acted like God imposing his reality on the world, but gave the reader scope to interpret what he read in different ways according to his or her own inclination. In a sense this was bringing agnosticism into literature where before the novelist had demanded faith and where the reader had been expected to accept the picture of the world that the novelist described.

In order to explain all this we needed the presence of the authors themselves. I approached the French Embassy and a number of universities where we knew members of the faculty – some were doing translations for us – and arranged a three-author tour. Alain Robbe-Grillet, Marguerite Duras and Nathalie Sarraute all agreed to come for a fortnight to Britain, to tour university cities and explain their ideas and their work. I worked out a complex budget whereby the expense would be covered partly by the universities and partly by ourselves, with the French Embassy giving receptions that would involve the press and the British literary world in London, Oxford and Edinburgh, contributing indirectly to other expenses, including publicity.

The tour started late in 1960. Marguerite Duras and Nathalie Sarraute arrived by 'plane, but Robbe-Grillet, who in those days had never flown and refused to do so, came by boat and train. As I remember it they were all housed in a hotel by the French Embassy, but we may have arranged that ourselves, because just before their arrival a problem arose. The ambassador, M. Chauvel, had agreed to give a large reception at the end of the first week.

But all three writers had recently signed a manifesto (in September 1960), which had been much publicised, against the French government's attitude towards the Algerian war, and this was known as the 'Declaration of the 121' because a hundred and twenty-one well-know figures in the arts had signed it. The Quai d'Orsay, where the French Foreign Ministry is housed, had suddenly forbidden the Embassy to do anything to help my three writers. Poor M. Chauvel was in a dilemma. Not only had he enthusiastically given his support to the visit, but he was particularly anxious to talk to Marguerite Duras who was a close friend of the editor of a review which he hoped would publish some of his poems.

On the day they arrived, a Sunday, there was a small reception, given on this occasion at Marion Lobbenberg's flat near Paddington. A number of journalists with an interest in European literature were invited to meet the authors. They included John Ardagh, then the principal cultural features writer on The Observer, who already had a deep interest in everything to do with France, and a photographer with the same paper. Terence Kilmartin, Rayner Heppenstall and John Weightman were there and perhaps a dozen more. The next day we held a press conference in the restaurant of the Arts Theatre Club, the venue for many important plays of the previous decade, including *Waiting for Godot*, Ionesco's early plays and such memorable productions as Shaw's *Man and Superman*, Christopher Fry's *The Lady's Not for Burning* and a string of modern plays and classics mounted by that wonderful acting couple, John Clements and his wife Kay Hammond. The restaurant was a favourite haunt of mine and the staff were mainly Cypriots who I would keep encountering over the years, mainly in later years at Beoty's Restaurant on Saint Martin's Lane, only a few steps away. I had chosen it for its proximity to Fleet Street, where nearly all the newspapers in those days had their offices.

The press conference was well attended, not just by the serious press, which had been largely represented at Marion's the previous evening, but by the tabloids and some women's journals which, needless to say, knew hardly anything about the authors and what they represented, so the first questions put to us tended to be naïve, even idiotic, such as 'Why do you write?' But it warmed up and I had my stock of clichés and sound-bites to feed them, apart from the reasoned explanations of Robbe-Grillet, which had to be translated, and the help and comment from some of my better informed academic friends who had come to the conference. The three writers were to start the tour that afternoon at Reading, then on to Bristol the next day, accompanied by Marion, who eventually was to hand them over to me at Oxford later in the week. There were many news items about the press conference and the tour in the next day's papers and as a result I received a telephone call from Terence Watson of the Umbrella Club in Coventry, a small cultural centre to which I had often sent authors to read or talk and had appeared myself. Just minutes before, the Professor of French at

Birmingham had rung me to cancel the session he was to chair, because he did not believe there was any local interest. Watson was indignant that I had not included Coventry in the tour. Those two 'phone calls turned out to be the most significant events of the whole project, given their long-term consequences.

The writers were in the west country, I was organising things from the office, we had a good press and the French Embassy officials were trying to find a way to help without totally disobeying the instructions of Paris. The press had created a sense of excitement and Watson had picked it up. He would not listen to my explanation that I could see little point in going to a town without a university or any group that would ever have heard of the nouveau roman. 'Nonsense,' he said. 'Bring them here and I guarantee a big audience. So I gave him the Birmingham date for the following Friday, although I feared the worst. The Belgrade Theatre and Coventry Cathedral did not yet exist in Coventry and the Umbrella Club, that might get fifteen people to a serious lecture, was otherwise a lounge and bar where members played chess and put on amateur theatricals.

On Thursday I met the three writers in Oxford, collected them from the station and put them into the Randolph Hotel, while I was staying at a cheaper hotel near the station. All had gone well, although Richard Coe in Reading had become a little confused by Duras' provocative way of saying what she didn't believe, to get reactions. Donald Watson had looked after them well in Bristol and I forgot where else they had been. Our Oxford host was initially the French Club, run by students, who gave us a dinner before the public session. They all spoke reasonable French, but quickly admitted that 'no French literature after 1830 is taught in Oxford,' so they were all a bit baffled and intimidated. Robbe-Grillet, with his considerable sense of humour, took it all in his stride. If French literature after Stendhal was unknown, he could as easily introduce the students to Balzac or Flaubert as to his own work; they were his literary ancestors after all, and he brilliantly explained the line of descent of a hundred and thirty years that culminated in his own novels. He was clear and logical, convincing and humorous. The two ladies were less happy: they saw themselves being sidelined by the fluent Alain Robbe-Grillet and had to concentrate on their own hobby-horses, a strong political commitment in the case of Duras, who saw her novels as a way of changing attitudes, and a narrower vision in the case of Sarraute, whose work is based on her observations of tropisms, little marine cells that respond to light by opening and closing, which she uses as a metaphor for the ways in which we respond to each other. Human beings, she explained in careful and faultless English (she had once studied at Oxford), behave in the same way: our little tics and mannerisms give away what is really happening in our minds and emotions and underneath the mask we present to the world; and there are jealousies, rancours, frustrations and attempts to make ourselves more important, usually at the expense of others, thus creating similar or opposite reactions in those we are trying to impress or humiliate. Sarraute had invented a highly intellectualised new form of social novel.

The triple lecture, for so it proved to be, was a great success. Many Oxford dons had come out of curiosity and found themselves well rewarded. One of them had organised a party afterwards in her rooms at her college and later tried to seduce Robbe-Grillet, who was not interested, saying he missed Catherine, his wife. Baudelaire's biographer, the very eccentric Enid Starkie, was there, speaking in a very loud masculine-sounding voice, and there were many other famous academic figures. I wish I had taken notes, but I only seem to remember Isaiah Berlin talking to Nathalie Sarraute in Russian. I finally delivered them back to the Randolph and went to my own hotel by the station.

I had a strange adventure that night. It was so strange that I wrote a play about it a month later that very accurately reproduced it. But I never offered it anywhere. It may have been about eleven o'clock – it could hardly have been earlier – when I arrived at my hotel. There were about a dozen people sitting in the saloon bar, which was certainly closed to the public at that time, and I decided to have another drink, which as a resident I could legally do. All the remaining people seemed to know each other; they were locals and frequent customers, while I was the only resident. The barmaid, attractive but not young, served us all, sat with us and took part in a conversation that became increasingly bawdy and suggestive. Some went home, until only men were left and there was an obvious rivalry between two or three of them for the barmaid's favours. When everyone was out of the room for a moment I told her the number of my room. 'I know,' she said, and half an hour later she was in it. It was however the conversation, very like a late Eugene O'Neill play, that inspired my own literary effort, not how the night ended.

The next morning I picked up my three writers and we drove to Coventry. There an extraordinary phenomenon took place. Terence Watson received us at the Umbrella Club where we were given an early dinner, after which we were taken to the Town Hall, which had been rented for the occasion. It was packed. I had filled the boot of my car with books and these were piled up on tables at the back for sale by Terence's volunteers. They were what I had published by the present trio, perhaps a dozen titles with ten or more copies of each. As we walked up to the platform I looked at the audience: there were over eight hundred people there, jostling and talking and staring at the party of six of us walking up to the table on the stage. They were all young, late teens and early twenties, and I wondered how Terence had managed to get such an audience at a few days' notice. I had worked out a formula for the occasion, but with misgivings. The Umbrella Club members, perhaps a hundred of them, were buried in the crowd, thoughtful, professional people in their thirties and forties, and I was totally unprepared for so young an audience. First Terence introduced us, then I talked for a few minutes about what each of the writers did and what they had written, what their books were about, what they had in common, where they differed, above all why they were unlike other writers whose novels were intended only to entertain or reassure.

First Robbe-Grillet spoke, in French and never for more than a minute at a time. I then translated or paraphrased him. Although he claimed to know no English, he often interrupted my translation to make me get it exactly right. This went on for twenty minutes. Then Nathalie Sarraute spoke in slow, careful English, explaining her tropisms and why we behave like them. Then Marguerite Duras spoke in French, very animatedly, and Sonia Orwell, who had arrived in Coventry that evening, and was a good friend of Duras, did for her what I had done for Robbe-Grillet. The audience was attentive and we had been there for less than an hour when the chairman asked for questions. The first one came from a man in the front row, the Professor of French from Birmingham, where we should have been that evening.

'Whatever are you doing in Coventry?' he asked.

'There's obviously more interest here than in Birmingham,' I replied acidly, and he never said another word.

The questions then came slowly. 'You seem to write to make us sad,' said one youth. 'Why don't you write to make us happy?' I put the question to Robbe-Grillet, who shrugged his shoulders, so I answered it myself, telling the young man that the purpose of literature was to help him understand himself and his life, and maybe to make it better. Then came other questions, getting ever closer to sophistication, which increasingly interested the writers whose answers became fuller and more thoughtful. There was an excitement spreading through the hall as more and more hands went up, and soon there was a forest of them. I was working very hard, translating back and forth, and so was Sonia as the questions followed each other and a real dialogue with continuity began to take place in spite of the language difficulty.

Suddenly I felt a tap on the shoulder. It was the caretaker. 'Sorry, Sir,' he said, 'but it's nearly eleven o'clock. The hall was booked to ten-thirty.' We had been there for three hours and everyone wanted more. In the street outside, my three literary stars were mobbed. I went to collect the books: they had all been sold and the writers were now being asked to sign them. We were taken back to the Umbrella Club which overflowed with the crowd that had followed us and we left to drive to London well after midnight.

On the way back my mind was racing. I knew that something extraordinary and unexpected had happened in Coventry. A new public had been created almost by accident. The nouveau roman school of avant-garde writers had established a base in a working-class town without even a university!

The following day was the day of the French reception that M. Chauvel had been told must be cancelled. He had arranged that the cultural attaché would give a smaller party in his private flat and in his own name, and that he, the Ambassador, would accidentally drop by in the middle of it. But in the afternoon just before that I had arranged a radio discussion on the BBC's Third Programme. This was to be between the three writers and Rayner Heppenstall, a writer and broadcaster, and William Golding; a studio had been booked at Broadcasting House from 4.00 until 6.00 p.m. I had spent some time with Robbe-Grillet earlier in the day, having paraphrased his principal theories into paragraph-long phrases, and had rehearsed him reading them in heavily-accented English. The BBC had taken much persuasion, both because of what was believed to be the obscurity of the nouveau roman and because of the language, but I had not dared tell them that two of the three spoke no English or refused to do so. Rayner Heppenstall was confident that he could get over the difficulty and he did. He translated where necessary – there was a little French allowed – but Nathalie Sarraute was able, for the first time so far on the tour, to dominate the conversation. Besides she and Golding got on splendidly together. However the recording, with many retakes of parts of the conversation, took nearly four hours and it was after eight o'clock when we showed up at the reception, where we had been expected at six-thirty. M. Chauvel had been there nearly all that time.

But things soon warmed up. Marguerite Duras promised the Ambassador that she would recommend his poems to her editor friend and the evening ended well. The tour continued, but half-way through the second week we lost Robbe-Grillet to the considerable relief of the two ladies. He had constantly made little jokes at their expense which they did not appreciate and they had formed a solid feminist resistance to his self-confident masculinity. We ended the last week in Edinburgh. A very casual party was given there in Jim Haynes' Paperback bookshop, which was well-stocked with all my books. This is a good place for a little digression to introduce a man who will appear quite frequently in the next few chapters.

Jim Haynes was an American from Louisiana who had chosen to go to Edinburgh University under the G.I. Bill of Rights, where he studied Spanish, although he still worked for the army at a listening post that monitored European telephone calls for the C.I.A. He did not stay long at the university, but bought for £50 a hovel-like junk shop at 22 Charles Street, a short thoroughfare that linked George Square and Bristol Street in the middle of the university district, where students and staff passed in considerable numbers. The old lady who was retiring left him all the contents of her shop along with the freehold, and Jim got rid of them by putting up a sign that everything was free. Then he painted and shelved the shop and started what might well have been Britain's first paperback bookshop in 1957. I have already spoken of the extreme conservatism of

Edinburgh's bookshops. Jim, one of whose great advantages was an excellent memory for the names of authors and publishers, the titles of books and even their prices, had filled his shelves, not only with the usual Penguins, Pelicans and other British mass-market paperback series, but the larger format American 'egghead' imprints as well, and foremost among these were the Evergreen series of Barney Rosset, which I distributed and which were a model for my Calderbook paperback series, which appeared from 1960 onward. I cannot quite place my first meeting with Haynes, but I remember the shop well as I first saw it. There was no cash register, change being kept in a drawer, and Jim could easily be persuaded to lend books to those who could not buy them; they were seldom returned. He also, and this really shocked the local book-trade, offered free coffee and tea, and had soft music playing. He was only a business man in so far as he had to take enough money to live and pay publishers; his motivation was enjoyment. His casualness and easy friendliness, so unlike the other Edinburgh booksellers, went down well among all classes. Not only did university students and faculty use the bookshop to buy and order books, but it was a social centre as well, where people met, not just academics but members of the business and professional establishment as well. The Chairman of the Bank of Scotland, whose head office was close by, was a customer, so were broadcasters, actors, doctors and every variety of Edinburgh citizen who bought books.

Jim Haynes loved women. His approach to them was direct and uncomplicated. He would stare hungrily until he received a response, then he would date and proposition. There was no promise of long-term attachment in Jim's amours: an affair might last a week or a month or only a night. Attraction had to be immediate and satisfaction quickly follow. He never made promises, but his casual manner worked very well in this Calvinist city and he never had to spend a night alone. His trust in everyone was also unusual, and many took advantage of it. But Jim's transparent openness and charm made him many friends and it was a pattern that would continue into the next century. When he eventually had to retire at age sixty-five from a university in Paris, he had an address book with tens of thousands of names. Only politicians and public entertainers could meet as many people as Jim, and his character never changed.

Jim Haynes quickly became my best customer in Edinburgh, but because of him I found it easier to sell my books in other shops as well. This was because by stocking books that others would not, he created a demand for them, and they were asked for elsewhere as well. It was natural after the session at Edinburgh University, that I should bring Marguerite Duras and Nathalie Sarraute to The Paperback.

Let me now get back to the occasion itself. There were two Professors of French in Edinburgh, one in touch with modern literature, the other not. It was the latter, Professor Green, who chaired the joint lecture of the two ladies, and with them sitting on each side of him, he stood up on the platform and said: 'My introduction will be as brief as what I know about these two ladies.' He then sat down. But in spite of his dourness it went well. Jim Haynes had been selling their books and many people were carrying them. They were listened to with attention and the questions were relevant. It was the other professor, Professor Steel, who came to the party afterwards. There is a photograph of that occasion in this book.

The tour ended back in London and then everyone returned to Paris. The Sunday papers did a big coverage of the tour and of the new interest in Britain of a literature that could look at the world in a new way. Britain was just beginning to wake up to other European writers. The Germans of the Gruppe 47, the post-was school, were now being translated, especially Gunther Grass and Heinrich Böll, then others, and Brecht, first translated in America, was just about to impinge on the British consciousness. Soon a number of younger British writers would be looking to Europe for their models and influences, although the predominance of the English social novel was never even slightly threatened. My sales became significantly better, and I added Robert Pinget, Claude Mauriac, Claude Ollier, Daniel Castellain and Philippe Sollers to the names in my catalogue, although in some cases only by a single work. My main source remained largely Editions de Minuit, but authors came from other publishers too. Robbe-Grillet was now reader and advisor to Jerôme Lindon, spending a day a week in their office reading manuscripts, and he also pointed me towards new talent. Unlike most of his colleagues he was generous and helpful to other writers. His self-assurance put him above the jealousies of others and his skill at literary conferences, which his intelligence and fluency usually dominated, kept his name in the forefront of the literary press, especially in France. Although he adopted political positions and signed manifestos when he agreed with them, he took the position that a writer's commitment had to be to literature and his own writing, not to a cause. First came style and form and that, driven by the writer's own instincts, would shape the content. Ultimately form and content, for him at least, were the same thing.

Claude Simon, the only one of the nouveau roman group who was not with me at that time, was the only one ever to win the Nobel Prize, some twenty-five years later. I only started to publish him from about 1975 when Jonathan Cape, who were now beginning to imitate me in looking for intellectual French authors, lost interest and dropped him. That was the next problem with which I had to deal: imitation and competition. Other publishers had of course noticed our reviews and publicity stunts, and they assumed that our improving reviews and the amount of space given by the serious press to our authors meant good sales. But better was not all that good; certainly we were not achieving the sales, either from public libraries which in those days were a major source of revenue, or from bookshops, that conventional English-language literary fiction could command. The new German authors, Grass, Böll, Frisch and Dürrenmatt were coming from larger publishers and selling better than the French, but still not as well as English novels. What I could not afford to publish was picked up by others, especially Jonathan Cape, whose star editor was Tom Maschler, who made it his business to be trendy and had the financial backing to do what he wanted. So Claude Simon, Monique Wittig and others I would have liked to publish, were acquired by others. I had my hands more than full with Beckett and the nouveau roman authors I had picked up in the fifties, and something new was beginning to happen in Britain that I could not ignore, a new school of British fiction, which needed to be promoted as a school. In addition the music list had grown and there were six annuals coming out every year covering all the arts except ballet. I avoided ballet because there was already a successful *Ballet Annual* published by A. and C. Black.

The annuals had become a big problem. I had found different publishers for them in America and some were doing better than others. The *Opera Annual* now sold 2500 copies through an American publisher, the *International Theatre Annual 2000* and others less. The American deals were as different as the publishers. Then Ken McCormick, managing editor at Doubleday, became interested and I made a deal with him and a good one. He would buy all the annuals for the following year, 1958, and we had to make a special effort to meet the main conditions, that all had to be printed and delivered in New York by the first of September to be in good time for Christmas sales. Doubleday were buying 10,000 copies of each annual, under their imprint, to supply the American market. We agreed the production price and we were to receive an advance and royalties on each, which made it possible to pay the contributors and editors more generously than previously. Everyone made a major effort, the books were printed in England, not in Europe as in previous years, and arrived in the States on time. Our invoice was paid. Then, as the year approached the end, I began to get letters from readers in the States who had bought the annuals in the past. Where could they get this year's edition? I sent the letters to Doubleday and wrote Ken that I was surprised that the bookshops did not have the information, let alone the books. I received no reply. But as the complaining letters increased and I also had transatlantic telephone calls, I sent more letters, then cables, but there was still no reply. I was also unable to reach Ken McCormick on the telephone.

In January I went to New York and in the Doubleday Bookshop on Fifth Avenue – it was now late in the month – I found my annuals just being unpacked and put out for sale. They had arrived that day. I finally did get through to Ken. He was apologetic, but could do nothing. Something had gone wrong in the warehouse, he said. He thought it had something to do with a computer they were installing. He did not have time to see me and was obviously too embarrassed to risk a meeting. There was never any explanation as to why the annuals were not listed in the Doubleday autumn catalogue, why there had been no publicity, nor of how and why sixty thousand books that had arrived in New York during the last week of August were only published in January and then only in the small number of bookshops belonging to Doubleday. The answer was transparent enough: Ken McCormick, having done the deal, had forgotten all about it, had never advised the appropriate departments of the firm and nothing had happened until after Christmas when someone had noticed the books in the warehouse. They were remaindered in February.

I now had a terrible dilemma: what to do next year. All the editors were working on the next editions, but quite obviously, after the Doubleday fiasco, no other American publisher would touch them, and the continuity had been broken. Doubleday never admitted the truth, so it was assumed in the American book trade that they had just flopped. I produced an *Opera Annual*, an *International Theatre Annual* and one more *International Literary Annual* in 1959, and the first two only in the years after that. I reduced the format to a smaller-sized volume the first year and managed to get a small number of copies distributed in the U.S., and even found a publisher to take the Opera and Theatre books, five hundred of each, the year after. The smaller format enabled me to put out a paperback edition as well as a hardback, but they were visually less impressive and sold less well in Britain, so for the final year I went back to the old large format. But my heart was no longer in it and the editors too were discouraged. 1962 was the end.

A few more political titles appeared in the late fifties, but I was now concentrating more on the literary list and on playwrights. A few odd titles were still published because of accidental circumstances. Our sales manager now was George Allum, who would periodically make a trip around Irish towns, which he knew well, calling on county libraries as well as on bookshops. One evening I went with him to the station to the let him take the train to the north from which to catch the ferry to Dublin. We were early at the station and were chatting in the bar when a uniformed soldier came up and introduced himself, Corporal 'Red' Cushing of the North Irish Brigade. 'When I hear people having an interesting conversation,' he said, 'I always join them,' and neither George nor I could get in a word after that. They were going, Cushing and Allum, on the same train and apparently they talked all the way to Ireland. When George returned he told me that Cushing had a real book in him. He was a soldier of fortune, had been in the IRA at ten, a boy soldier at thirteen, then in the U.S. army, then in the International Brigades in the Spanish Civil War and after that in a number of British regiments. His most recent activity had been chasing the Mau Mau in Kenya. Mainly to please Allum, I agreed to commission an autobiography of this colourful character, but I was hardly surprised when it turned out that although he could talk a treat and had a good memory of his long career, he was incapable of writing a word on his own. But George knew a good ghost writer, and after we had brought them together and had a few drinks, subject and author got on well and the writer wrote the book after a series of long interviews, which cost a bit for the liquid refreshment which kept Cushing going. Our ghost writer caught the style perfectly, loquacious but racy and readable. The book did not sell as well as it might have done with a more general publisher, and Cushing's too frequent visits to the office were not much help either, but every publisher has a few anomalies on his list.

Our French writers were now doing much better and attracting more attention, Ionesco in particular receiving major British productions, even if only for short runs; Alan Schneider had produced several of the short plays, both in New York and London, and having staged an unfortunate first *Godot* in New York with Bert Lahr and other comic actors, which was billed as 'the laugh sensation of two continents', he had met Beckett, and was now directing him in the U.S. according to the author's precise instructions. Devine was doing the same in London. As related earlier Laurence Olivier played in *Rhinoceros* and the cast included Duncan Macrae, Joan Plowright, Alan Webb, Michael Bates and Miles Malleson. We published the play just in time in Volume Four of Ionesco's *Collected Plays* and sold hundreds of copies in what was a series of full houses, not surprising given the cast and the producer, who was Orson Welles. *The Square* was soon to be seen at the New End Theatre with Leonard Fenton and Angela Pleasance performing the parts that Chauffard and Albertini had played in Paris. I republished the play version in Barbara Bray's translation, but the Sonia Orwell and Tina Murdoch translation of the novel was reprinting regularly and was soon to appear in my new, smaller format, paperback series, Jupiter Books. Sonia had recently married a wealthy homosexual called Michael Pitt-Rivers, who needed a token wife after a much publicised scandal and a trial that had involved Lord Montague and a number of boy scouts, and she used her new married name until the growing popularity of George Orwell, whose royalties she was receiving as a result of having earlier married him on his death-bed, made her former name more noteworthy.

I had contracted, among other playwrights from France, Roland Dubillard and René de Obaldia. There was also Arthur Adamov, who had early in the fifties been associated with Beckett and Ionesco, although dramatically he was closer to Brecht and O'Casey. Obaldia, whose career was to see-saw back and forth between an absurdist boulevard drama and plays more inclined to appeal to an university audience, had his moment in Britain when he was much played by students and then achieved some professional performances in London and elsewhere. He came to prominence in Paris in 1960 and about three years later was being played in Britain in the translations of Donald Watson, who had earlier translated Ionesco for us. But his reputation did not last beyond the seventies for reasons I have never understood. Obaldia has a light touch and great inventiveness and cleverness, perhaps too much for a British audience. Where there was a part for a star, in his full-length play *Wind in the Branches of the Sassafras*, it was vulgarised by a commercial management in Britain, who commissioned Galton and Simpson, writers of soap opera comedy, to do a free adaptation that took all the subtlety out of a mock-western, with its stock characters; it became a heavy-handed farce. The play failed and the translation we published in the end, by an American, that was true to the author, also failed to make any impact. Dubillard did not either make headway in Britain, although his biggest French success, *Les Naïves Hirondelles*, rescued by the protests of Ionesco, Roussin and other French playwrights from the initial mediocre reviews of its first production, was perfectly suitable for a theatre such as the Royal Court. The fifties and sixties saw many British dramatists, similar to their equivalents across the channel, who had a brief vogue, being performed and then being forgotten. Only Beckett and Ionesco broke through among the foreign imports, but by the late eighties, Ionesco had also slipped from fashion. The reason was probably the amount of talent around and too small an intellectually curious audience.

Aside from the French, Dutch and German writers were also coming onto the list, and others from Yugoslavia, largely the result either of interest created at the Frankfurt Book Fair or of my visits to the latter country. I had already published Ivo Andric, who won the Nobel Prize for Literature in 1961, and included Miodrag Bulatovic, who had made himself flavour of the month one year in Frankfurt and nuisance of the week the following year when publishers were no longer interested in him, in my *New Writers* series. I met Radomir Konstantinovic in Belgrade and published his novel *Exitus*, in which Judas tells his own version of the gospel story. His wife had translated Beckett's *Molloy* into Serbo-Croat. But he was unsaleable in Britain. I met a charming Serbian novelist Jara Ribnikar, even had a fling with her, and published one novel and some stories, but with equal non-success. In those days there was always a library sale for at least a few hundred copies, so a failure was not as catastrophic as it would become later when the libraries found their book funds reduced to a pittance.

I had become very friendly with Monique Lange, several of whose novels we were to publish (and I had translated one myself). She worked at Gallimard selling foreign rights. Gallimard in those days was a strange place, run in a chaotic fashion by Claude Gallimard, whose more brilliant and literary brother Michel had been killed in a car crash while driving one of their best authors, Albert Camus, who had died with him. Claude was affable, liked his food and wine, and had an ambitious wife who also wanted to be in publishing. He had more than one mistress working in the company and he did not want his wife there as well, so he bought her another publishing house, Mercure de France to run. He told his friends that it was cheaper to buy her Mercure to keep her busy, even if it cost a great deal, than to give her the leisure to visit the fashion houses, where a dress could cost more than a series of books. I was to conclude a few contracts with Simone Gallimard at Mercure. She was a vivacious redhead and I can well believe that she had her own life; what was good for the gander was no doubt also good for the goose. One contract was for Valentine Penrose's biography of Erszbeth Bathory, which Sir Roland, her ex-husband who remained on good terms with her, suggested I should publish. I knew Penrose as head of the ICA gallery and art centre and as the biographer of his friend Picasso. I was eventually to publish his translations of Picasso's plays.

Many well-known authors had desks at Gallimard and many of them were editors or directors of series of books apart from writing their own. Raymond Queneau had his nest there. An eminent author himself, he advised what to publish and selected a few books, but he was a busy novelist, editor of the *Encyclopédie de la Pléiade*, a mathematician, a playwright, a humorist, poet and man of many parts. Many people like him worked there, probably during the hours that suited them because no one kept any kind of check on their movements. There were many like him: Jean Paulhan for instance, who was believed to have written *The Story of O*, perhaps the most discussed erotic book of the day, largely because he had contributed an introduction to it (Paulhan was one of the leading literary critics of the day), and François Erval, a Hungarian who chose and contracted books from Germany and Eastern Europe. There was Jacques Lemarchand in charge of the theatrical list, who picked those playwrights, both past and present, that he felt ought to be in print, and he was also the conservatively-minded critic of *Le Figaro*. Another was Michel Mohr, who looked like a *belle époque* aristocrat out of Feydeau, but thought he looked like an English gentleman, not without reason, and was to complain to me some years later that authors like Robbe-Grillet were taken to orgies in New York by Barney Rosset, whereas he, considered too proper, was never invited to anything like that, much to his chagrin. They were all like courtiers around the king, who at Editions Gallimard was Claude, son of Gaston Gallimard, who still occasionally made an appearance. They lived in a world of personal contacts and friendships, mutual literary interests and ever-present sex. I knew them all, more or less well. I had much in common with the affable Dionys Mascolo, ex-lover of Marguerite Duras and father of her child, a good person to meet in bars late at night. He owed his sinecure of a job to Marguerite, who like many other successful Gallimard authors, wielded considerable influence over Claude. Dionys was in charge of English language books, but read no English. Mascolo's name came up many times among those that Duras gave to her characters, mainly amalgams of the names of the men in her life. He was the author of a large tome entitled *Le Communisme*, which I read, or at least scanned through, thinking it might be suitable for translation. The content can be summed up as follows: any intellectual with a social conscience is attracted to communism and may become a member of the party. But he will then find that the party does not trust intellectuals and only requires them to use their talents to further the work and the platform of the party, and only in the way that the leadership commands. The writer is not allowed to be an individual or to have an independent voice. There is therefore a constant conflict between the creative abilities of intellectuals and the party they support, which is a great pity. Much as I liked the author I saw no reason to translate several hundred pages that could easily be summed up in a short pamphlet, and that was the problem with many other books that were coming from French intellectuals at this time. Many women I knew were attracted to Dionys, but my best memory of him is sitting drinking in late-night Paris bars, sunk in gloom, but always with something interesting to say. He was separated from Marguerite although they saw each other frequently, was still in love with her, and the other women in his life were only reluctantly endured substitutes. One of them was Monique Lange, who otherwise was the partner of Juan Goytisolo, an exiled Spanish novelist, also published by Gallimard in French. I saw much of Monique because of her full-time job handling foreign rights with Gallimard; and I concluded many contracts with her.

In 1961 I started to publish a series of anthologies of new writing, usually three or four authors to the volume, and I put a short novel by Monique Lange in the first one: called *The Cat Fish*, which was the affectionate term she gave to her homosexual acquaintances: it amusingly caught the flavour of much of Parisian life at that time, and was one of the first translations that Barbara Wright, who it was soon evident was the best translator of French of her generation, did for us. Alan Burns, soon to become a leading member of a new group of British fiction writers we were to launch in the sixties, made his debut in that same *New Writers One* volume. We would eventually publish twenty volumes in the series.

But even before *The Cat Fish* I had published another, longer, novel by Monique Lange, *Les Platanes*, which, as I later learned was based on her affair with Dionys. It came out in 1960 and I am not sure whether it was that summer or the summer of the previous year when I took Jamie for a short holiday, staying with my mother at Monte Carlo. There, on the beach, sitting under an umbrella with my typewriter in front of me, I translated *The Plane Trees* in five days, while Jamie played in the pool. In the evening when she had gone to bed I went to dine with Jacques Chaix at Cap Ferrat, only half an hour away. People looked at me with amazement, but my days of sun-worshipping were long over. I enjoyed the work, and the subject of the novel was appealing. The heroine goes to meet the man she lives in a Saint-Germain café, just before he leaves by car on his own for a holiday in the south of France. She persuades him to take her as far as the last metro station, then further into the next town, finally spending the night with him and driving on the next day. But then, just as he finally asks her to stay with him for the month she changes her mind and takes the train back. The reason is that she realises he is only interested in questioning her about his affair with her best girl-friend, his own ex-partner, and about her new relationship, with her current lover. Roger Vadim was intending to film the novel, which would have given me a best-seller, but in the end he dropped it.

On the beach I occasionally jumped into the water to cool off and I suddenly ran into Fa Delbaie. I had known her as the wife of one of Jacques Chaix's friends, Jean Delabaie, who was usually at Cap Ferrat at Jacques' Villa Soleia at that time of year. She and her husband had separated and she was working as an *au pair* with an American family, looking after small children. I had known them both for some years and I made the bad mistake one night of taking her to the villa with me. Her husband was there with his current new girl and the atmosphere was icy. I never made that mistake again.

I published *The Plane Trees* and sold one edition rapidly enough in spite of the expected film not materialising. There had been talk of Brigitte Bardot playing the heroine, but it was not a part that would have suited her. She was of course married to Vadim at the time.

The *New Writers* series enabled me to introduce new work by many who became our regular authors. They included Aidan Higgins, David Mercer, Alexander Trocchi, Alan Burns, Christine Bowler, Vivienne Welburn, Dino Buzzati, Simon Vestdijk, Robert Pinget, René de Obaldia, John Antrobus, Penelope Shuttle and Renate Rasp among many others. It also enabled us to use short work by Samuel Beckett, Ionesco and similar established names that would not fit into any other formula. I could put twenty pages of poetry into a volume that also contained a complete short novel and a group of short stories, could insert a play, experimental prose, even short philosophical or critical writing. It was like having a literary magazine and as the series progressed the number of different contributions per issue increased as well.

A few weeks after the big promotional tour of Robbe-Grillet, Duras and Sarraute, I telephoned George Harewood. He was now the Director of the Edinburgh Festival and I suggested we meet at Overton's, a fish restaurant on St. James Street near the Festival's London office. I told him about the tour, and in particular about the most extraordinary part of it, the Coventry experience. He listened with great interest and then I put my suggestion to him: why not do something similar in Edinburgh? Music and drama were not part of the real Scottish tradition, but literature was. Why not let writers talk among themselves in public to educate that public about their preoccupations, what literature could be about and was, and tell the audience what they were trying to do. The cut and thrust would create tension, break down inhibitions, and give the public an insight into what otherwise only a few critics and the authors' friends knew about.

Harewood was interested. He liked new ideas and audacity, and was about to give Edinburgh a large dose of Schönberg's music, which only a Festival Director with his royal credentials could get away with. His programme for that year and the year ahead was already full and so was his budget, but he agreed that I could go ahead with a big literary jamboree of up to a hundred writers from many countries, provided, and this was the main condition, I could find a way not to lose money. I felt confident about this and had already worked out an approximate budget. In a later article, Harewood remembered our lunch like this:

> 'He would take an envelope out of his pocket – have you noticed that people that work on the back of envelopes always have one on hand? – and improvise an answer to my question. What he wrote down involved a rough calculation of the cost of people he thought should be invited to attend (travel, hotels, fees, subsistence) which could be set against the tickets we would sell for the events. The difference between cost and box office income would be met by the sale of rights...even when the procedure was repeated at our next meeting, the figures were quite different, but the bottom line always indicated a balance.'

The logistics were such that we eventually decided to hold the Writer's Conference, as it came to be billed, in 1962 instead of 1961. I became busy, using all my experience of approaching the embassies of governments with interesting writers to see how far they would be willing to help their local literatures. I had of course, early on, intended to give a platform to my own writers, especially the French ones, but here I was totally unsuccessful. Robbe-Grillet, and the other French writers I had invited, thought it impossible that in the month of August, the sacred month for holidays, anyone, and certainly not themselves, would exchange the warm sun and sea of the Mediterranean for the cold climes of Northern Britain. I came to publish several authors as a result of the conference, but it did little good to those already on the list.

I made a list of desirable names, British, American and European, but also looked to the east. I had taken on, as an author, the distinguished Indian novelist, historian and journalist Khushwant Singh, and when I submitted the list to Harewood he spotted the name and became instantly enthusiastic: he knew him and said he would be good value. About that time Khushwant came to London and we got on famously. He told me an interesting story; on a previous visit to London he had been taken to Rules Restaurant by Richard Crossman, then a government minister. The manager had taken Crossman aside and said that on this occasion he would do nothing, but 'normally we do not serve coloured gentlemen.' Crossman went to the telephone and within minutes an official arrived from the appropriate Ministry to remove the restaurant's licence to sell wine and alcoholic beverages. The two diners, who had not ordered anything other than drinks, then moved to another restaurant. Khushwant loved wine, which he could not get, or at least be seen to drink, in India, and also western women, who he was too proper to approach. But he had a wicked sense of humour and a capacity to make mischief, which he indulged frequently in his political journalism; it would play a big part in the conference. A green-turbaned Sikh, he had published many novels, most notably *Last Train to Pakistan* and *I Shall Come to Hear the Nightingale*, which latter I had acquired from Grove Press. He was soon to become the editor of The Times of India, a long tenure, and he had a son currently at Oxford. We were to have several meetings over the next few years. When I told him that I had invited Henry Miller, who had already accepted, his eyes gleamed. 'I think I know who the Indian politician is in *Tropic of Cancer*,' he said to me, 'and I want to ask him.'

Henry Miller was one of several Americans on the list. I knew that Sonia Orwell (who had by now returned to using the name of her first brief marriage) had come to know many American writers during the time she was a commissioning editor for Weidenfeld and Nicolson, and I recruited her to help persuade such friends as Mary McCarthy and Norman Mailer to come. I spoke to the cultural attachés at London embassies, who proposed writers from their countries, whose names were often unfamiliar to me, but most of them spoke good English and turned out to be excellent value. They included Barbara Heliodora from Brazil, George Theotokas from Greece, Izhar Smilansky from Israel and many more, some becoming known to us too late to get their names into the programme. I made sure that everyone could speak at least one of the three official languages, English, French and German. The language problem applied of course not just to the delegates, but to the public as well, because much of the Festival audience was foreign. I contacted a firm of conference translators who did simultaneous translation that could be listened to through earphones. The audience was thus enabled to hear whatever language was being spoken alive or in translation, but as the earphones also boosted the sound and were much clearer, many preferred to hear everything through earphones;

Gradually the acceptances and refusals began to come in, but with some later changes of mind both ways. Soon we had about eighty acceptances and they included many well-known names. Graham Greene accepted but cancelled at the last minute, Aldous Huxley and Bertrand Russell did the same and Norman Mailer was a cliff-hanger, but came in the end. The conference programme book, which was really a lavishly produced literary magazine, partly produced on art paper, but with a central section on grey cartridge, gave two lists: a longer one with short biographies of participants and photographs of everyone who had accepted, which was prepared well in advance on white art, and a last-minute list, very different, but still incomplete, on grey. The latter section apologised for the inconsistencies and changes, but also gave a longish description of each day's topic and what was expected to happen, as well as listing the principal speakers for those days.

My list of names changed almost daily as individuals and organisations wrote or telephoned. The British Council sponsored several writers and they too always had new suggestions. I never really worried about there being too many writers coming, or after the first months of there not being enough; the problem was to make sure that at least half of the names would be in some way known to the public, although not necessarily just the Edinburgh local public which still made up the bulk of Edinburgh Festival audiences. The programme book was a big undertaking. Jim had found me an editor for it, Andrew Hook, lecturer in English at Edinburgh University and a former student and a warm admirer of F.R. Leavis. With some help from me he commissioned articles from many contributors. My introduction, preceded by a short preface of welcome from Sir Compton Mackenzie, who in the end did not attend, was followed by enlightening articles from J.G. Weightman (on the different varieties of novels being written), by Malcolm Bradbury (on the social versus the intellectual novel), by David Daiches (on the Scottish tradition), by David Craig (on modern Scottish literature), by Hugh MacDiarmid (on poetry), by Raymond Williams, Alain Robbe-Grillet and Andrew Hook (all on commitment), by Dennis Donoghue and Colin McInnes (on censorship) and by a variety of other well-known names all answering a questionnaire that asked about how they saw the future of the novel. There were also articles on some of the most eminent authors in vogue at that time. Looking back, nearly forty years later, I am amazed by how well the conference's programme, entitled *The Novel Today* still reads, how the issues laid out there are still with us and the arguments valid. It sold for five shillings.

The cost of bringing in the writers was almost entirely underwritten by embassies, the British Council, and publishers anxious to have their writers in the limelight. Only a few, and those were the biggest names, came out of my conference budget that had to be covered by ticket sales. I did do a little checking on most of the embassy suggestions, but lack of time did mean taking a few chances. There had to be a Scottish participation of course, and I took much advice here, some of it from Bill Watson, literary editor of The Scotsman, some from friends at the BBC like Finlay MacDonald, and much from Alex Neish, a well-read young literateur-about-town with whom I was friendly. Jim Haynes was also invaluable with suggestions: most Edinburgh writers frequented his bookshop and he could easily get information about others in Glasgow or other parts of Scotland. I went to see Sir Compton Mackenzie, then seventy-nine and the grand old man of Scottish literature. He agreed initially to be President or Chairman of the conference, but when the lure of the south of France became greater than his initial commitment, he wrote a one-paragraph programme greeting instead. During several visits to him that year I was always offered Grant's Standfast whisky, because he received a free supply for giving his name to its advertisements. His *Whisky Galore*, which had been a best-selling novel and a successful film, no doubt had something to do with it. I saw the famous chair, made to order, in which he could write his books with all his needs within reach, rather like a child's high chair. Years later I was to see it again in the literary collection of the library at the University of Texas in Austin.

That June my grandfather died at ninety-five. The funeral service was held in the chapel at Ardargie. I was roped in to be, alongside my great Uncle Jim, an acolyte and I managed, with only a mistake or two, to remember how to serve mass. Then a cortege of cars went to the Catholic church at Forgandenny, not far off, where my father, great-grandfather and numerous other Calders were buried, then back to Ardargie for a wake. The dogs of aunts and cousins were all roped to the railings outside the lodge until our return, and were then released and soon fighting, but not as hard or nastily as the aunts themselves. In particular, my Aunt Nancy Smith (who had come from Connecticut) and my Aunt Elsie (Lady Clifford) enclosed themselves in the morning room where their loud and angry argument over my grandfather's will could be heard by all. I, of course, inherited nothing.

The city of Edinburgh, from the time the press announced the Writers' Conference, took a big interest, but it was not all friendly. I went to speak to the Scottish PEN club, to the Saltire Society and to many groups of Scottish writers. Cliff Hanley and Joan Lingard among a few other local novelists were friendly and welcoming, but the more traditional ones like Nigel Tranter were highly suspicious. They spoke frequently to audiences and did not expect a fee, nor did their listeners expect to pay to hear them. Why should people pay to listen to writers? Harewood had asked the same question and I had assured him that they would, provided there was the right mixture of well-known names and those worthy of becoming better-known, and providing always that sufficient thought went into creating a format that would encourage interesting debate and bring out the important ideas that always underlay good literature. There was much scepticism, but it was fairly muted, because after all, this was the first time that literature would play a part in the Festival. Magnus Magnusson, the principal arts and culture feature writer for The Scotsman and Finlay MacDonald, a BBC arts producer, took me to lunch at the Doric Tavern, then the main watering hole for Edinburgh journalists and intellectuals on a limited budget, and quizzed me over my plans for the conference and my career as a publisher. What they principally wanted to know was: who was coming, what they would discuss and how much freedom would they be given to say what they wanted to say? My enthusiasm and in particular my libertarian approach got them on my side: they scented news value. Bill Watson, literary editor, and his deputy, Christopher Maclehose, also followed my progress as the year went on. A press conference was called by the Festival and I was also asked to address the Friends of The Edinburgh Festival, a large supporting body. Sonia Orwell came with me, not quite realising what was involved. When on the second occasion I asked her to say a few words she lost the point, and being rather sodden with alcohol, she was rather incomprehensible. I covered up for her as best I could, stressed that what we wanted to do was to return literature to its proper place in the Edinburgh arts, and to fertilise the Scottish scene with a big international presence Had George Thomson of the Edinburgh Review not commissioned songs from Haydn and Beethoven, articles and new work from Goethe and Stendhal and made Edinburgh a European centre when London was provincial? Bookshops flourished in Scotland when there as hardly a publisher in London and bookshops there had to subscribe a new book to its customers before it could be printed. My response was good. The newspapers, many of which had attacked Harewood the previous year for introducing challenging modern music into his programming, now aimed their guns at the Writers' Conference. How many of the writers we had invited would really come and would the public be interested? I remained positive on both questions.

After some difficult negotiations, I managed to rent the biggest available hall in Edinburgh, the McEwan Hall, which belonged to the University. It had never been let before, but the importance of the occasion and the official Festival backing finally convinced the university authorities. It seated 2300 people and had a large platform that could seat at least a hundred. But it would take a lot of filling.

I tried hard to interest the BBC in broadcasting the conference, and with considerable difficulty managed to get an appointment with Donald Baverstock, whose office was at Television Centre. Baverstock was one of the new brooms who were sweeping the cobwebs away from the old Reithian image, where each broadcasting service was aimed at a particular class and had been geared to its tastes and expectations. Baverstock was part of the revolution that followed the appointment of Carleton-Greene as Director-General, and gave the group that had been trained by Grace Wyndham Goldie, a legendary broadcasting figure, its head to innovate and experiment. I was told that he could see me for five minutes at most, that we would almost certainly be interrupted by outside calls and that I could not be too brief.

In the event, once I had started to explain what I was doing and who was coming, Donald Baverstock became extremely interested, and after half an hour he told his secretary to put through no more calls and he wanted no interruptions. He finally agreed to tape the whole conference for radio, to have television cameras present on occasion and to broadcast what was most interesting. He was as good as his word.

The Scottish, and especially the tabloid press kept airing local objections to the conference, but really as part of the general and continuing campaign against the festival as a whole. What the city needed, ran the constant refrain, were better drains or other civic improvements, not culture or the arts. But I noticed that letters to the editor attacking the festival attracted others that supported it, and I added to the correspondence by sending in bogus letters both attacking writers as responsible for spreading dangerous ideas and making people think (which was bad for them!) and other letters agreeing that literature was influential and so much the better. I invented names and addresses. The correspondence columns, which were much read in Edinburgh, was an excellent way of getting free advertising and of putting points of view one wanted to encourage or knock down. I spoke to every kind of group that invited me, to many rotary clubs, to university groups, to literary societies and to anyone that would listen. I was interviewed by radio and television as well as the press and began to become confident that the interest in my new venture was growing fast. I pointed out, to individuals and groups, that listening to the best minds explaining their ideas, especially in the presence of other good minds, and good minds were what writers had to have, was exciting for audiences and helped listeners to understand themselves. I promoted my own authors by explaining their theories; at that point I still expected many of them to appear in Edinburgh in August. Jim Haynes remained a great help. He introduced me to many people who were willing to help as volunteers to meet and look after the writers when they arrived, to accommodate many of them, and even to give parties during the conference, which would cut our expenses and keep them entertained. The five sessions would take place in the afternoons during the first week of the conference from 2.30 to 5.00, starting on Monday 20th August. We had to fill the evenings for those participating, and while I could probably get some festival tickets and there would be some civic receptions, to arrange parties where they could talk, meet local writers and exchange ideas was the obvious solution to the problem of keeping them busy and in the mood to debate their ideas in public. We now had generous hosts for those parties every night.

Sonia was invited to give talks on her own, mainly to women's groups, and she also made some radio and television appearances, one together with Elizabeth Jane Howard, which was presented as two women running festivals. She became better at it and made some effort to control her drinking. But she could be very moody and erratic. One evening in Edinburgh, at a Greek restaurant on Rose Street where Sonia, Jim and I were having dinner, some remark of mine annoyed her: she took the wine bottle on the table by the neck and hit me hard on the head with it, knocking me out. She was all remorse a minute later, but her alcoholic problem was growing. Once radiantly beautiful, she was becoming heavy, red-faced and glassy-eyed, still wanting to be seen as a brilliant intellectual, but ever more intolerant of others, short on tact and unpredictable. I needed her primarily for her literary contacts outside my own sphere. She had helped me recruit Malcolm Muggeridge, Angus Wilson, Rosamund Lehmann, L. P. Hartley, Stephen Spender, the two Americans I have mentioned above and one or two others who at the conference did little but sit and listen. The others I had approached myself or were being sent by their respective governments. David Daiches, eminent Scottish critic and academic, whose father had been Chief Rabbi of Scotland, had agreed to chair the Scottish day, the Tuesday, and we had a big line-up for that. Hugh MacDiarmid, Sidney Goodsir Smith, Naomi Mitchison, Robin Jenkins and Edwin Morgan figured large on the panel for that day. I put my new author, Alexander Trocchi onto the panel (more about him later), but I cannot remember whether or not I discussed his name with Daiches; probably not.

We made an effort to recruit Vivica, Jim Haynes' new wife, as a helper, but she was confused by the whole thing and only wanted a normal quiet life. The previous year I had arrived at the festival late on the first day, my car having broken down on the way north, and had given an impromptu party in the flat I had rented for the three weeks. Jim, normally the sunniest and most overtly cheerful of temperaments, was extremely restrained on that occasion, and in the small hours he told me why. He had made his latest conquest pregnant; she would not have an abortion and he had agreed to marry her, which was the last thing he wanted to do. The baby had arrived early in 1962 and he was trying to behave like a husband, but it was not in his nature. By the summer he was again picking up girls wherever he met them. We were soon to have a crisis because of it. Vivica rarely went out with him, was not willing to be a volunteer helper and I think that Jim found the time he was giving to the conference preparations a useful excuse for staying away from home.

As the summer progressed the details began to fall into place. In Paris I had various occasions to meet William Burroughs and I had read the three very controversial novels which Olympia Press had published. *The Naked Lunch* already had a colourful history. Extracts had been published in the review of the University of Chicago, but when the university banned the issue the editors all resigned and started a new magazine, Big Table, using the same excerpts. Burroughs was brought to Girodias by Allen Ginsberg[13] and the former enthusiastically published three of his novels. I had already invited Girodias to the conference, wanting him to take part in the censorship discussion, and early in the summer I took Burroughs to lunch and without much difficulty persuaded him to come as well. Of course there would be no sponsor for him.

That summer I had also been in Belgrade. I was already friendly with Alexandar Stefanovic, brother of Luba Stefanovic, the head of Jugoslavia Publishing House, which had done some printing for me. I liked Luba very much, although his hospitality on top of my workload was killing. I would get up at 4.30 a.m., go to his office, correct proofs and supervise the compositors who were setting books in English for me and drink innumerable cups of Turkish coffee. Then someone would be told to take me to lunch, usually consisting of kebabcici and rasnaci, smoked fish and other local delicacies with Yugoslav wines, after which, quite ready for a nap, another employee of Jugoslavia Publishing house, who were both publishers and printers, would turn up to give me a tour of war memorials and historic

---

[13] A fuller account of this appears in my book *The Garden of Eros*.

sights. And at night Luba, well-rested himself, would take me to dinner and keep me out late; after two hours sleep the day would start again. Often it was Alex Stefanovic who had charge of me during the day. He edited a literary magazine, the best of its kind in Yugoslavia as he assured me, which was of course subsidised by the state, but he was nevertheless an old royalist with no time for Communist bureaucracy. But he still did what he liked. He would stride through Belgrade's public parks with me, loudly denouncing the regime, and once took me into a government building and with a perfunctory knock on the door walked into a minister's office and introduced me to the minister himself. I forget which one, but it may well have been Foreign Affairs. The man looked with distaste at Alex, but shook my hand and said a few pleasant words. One of Alex's principal complaints was not having a car: 'How can a married man ever have an affair without his wife knowing without a car?' It was impossible to get away from neighbours' prying eyes! I invited Alex to Edinburgh and he agreed to fund his own passage. After all he had much to say, knew Yugoslav and European literature and spoke excellent English. He had translated Doctor Zhivago into Serbo-Croat and had brought the book to Feltrinelli in Italy who thereby had acquired western copyright, and was making a fortune out of it. All that Alex ever received from Feltrinelli was a lunch.

Jim Haynes had recruited both university staff and students, all customers of his bookshop, to do the dozens of small jobs that included meeting the writers as they arrived by 'plane, train and car, taking them to their accommodation, which varied from the grandest houses of Edinburgh to hotels of every description, from the Caledonian in the centre to the small Doric in Newington on the south side of the city. On Sunday, August 21st, they all poured in. Jim Haynes had only one major function that day, which was to take the folder of conference papers around to the principal addresses in Central Edinburgh. His recruits, whom I had dubbed the Charles Street Irregulars (his bookshop was on Charles Street) were covering the rest. One of Jim's calls was the Caledonian Hotel, where the official Yugoslav writer, the one who had been sent at the expense of his government and had been chosen by it, his name featuring importantly in the programme, was staying. Jim never got there. He met a girl he liked on Princes Street on the way, so Segedin never received his all-important folder, which included the conference programme, details of where to be at what times, invitations to receptions, Edinburgh maps and a time-table of events.

There was a big party on the Sunday night, given at the large flat of Mrs. McPhee, who was revelling at the prospect of meeting all the world's leading writers in her own home. It was a successful gathering where local Scottish writers dropped their suspicions and mingled happily with others from far-away countries. Everybody had a *per diem* spending allowance, but no one was getting a fee for attendance. I had asked everyone to come to McEwan Hall the next morning at 11.30. There, in one of the large rooms behind the stage, we drank coffee and worked out the day's format. Malcolm Muggeridge chaired the meeting. 'We'll just go around everyone very briefly and ask "How is the novel doing?"' he said. I had worked out a stage format where there would be a chairman, sitting on a kind of dais in the centre, and a different panel of four writers each day, selected to comment on the proceedings from time to time. They would be seated at a table with microphones, and there were two other standing microphones where individual writers, one by one, would make their statements. I wanted to mix debate and speeches, and also to make it possible for two writers to confront each other on different sides of the chairman across the stage. As the week progressed experience made it possible to change, permutate and improve these arrangements to get the best dramatic effects. The panel could interrupt, interrogate a speaker and openly discuss a point among themselves. The public would be allowed to come in from time to time and individual writers, sitting in a body above and behind the chairman, the panel and the speakers at microphones, could indicate their desire to be heard. It was all very new and untried, but in the event it worked. At that first morning meeting we decided the order of speakers, starting with Angus Wilson.

Then there was a buffet lunch with wine in another room, which also served as a conference office. At two o'clock I went to the front of the hall, leaving Muggeridge to lead people in at 2.30. Jim Haynes had organised a number of book stalls with the novels of the writers present where he had been able to obtain them, as well as a selection of books from his shop. An amazing sight greeted me. There was a long queue of people waiting to buy tickets. The festival office, which had never really believed in the event, especially as only a small number of tickets had been sold in advance, had sent only one person to man the box-office. Over a thousand were waiting with more arriving every minute. In addition I had ear-phones to let which enabled those who had them to hear simultaneous translation between the three languages, and there was also the official programme book to sell at five shillings each. I telephoned the festival to send more helpers and started to organise Jim's volunteers to desert the book tables in order to sell programmes and to let the ear-phones instead. Jim had to rush to the bank to get more money for floats for change. Gradually the hall filled up and the writers came onto the platform, watching with interest the different levels of the hall with its 2300 seats gradually becoming full. It was well after 3.00 p.m. when Malcolm Muggeridge started the proceedings. But the afternoon began well and very soon there were dramatic clashes, one between Angus Wilson and Khushwant Singh, the latter declaring that there was only one kind of love that was valid, which was heterosexual love. This drove Wilson into a frenzy and soon other homosexual writers were on the attack as well. What no one knew was that Singh had a son at Oxford who was gay, and the father was very unhappy about it.

Most of this I had to read about in the next day's papers, because I was still trying to get earphones into the hands of those who wanted them. At about four o'clock, a worried and confused-looking man came in. He had found the hall and the conference but did not know what to do; It was Šegedin. I took him to a seat on the platform. Alexander Stefanovic was talking just then, in English, about the literary situation in Yugoslavia.

I went back to the office behind the stage where Sonia Orwell was still sitting, finishing off the wine, looking more than a little under the weather. She was already exhausted. For a minute or two I listened in to the proceedings in the hall through earphones, which still worked backstage. It was becoming ever livelier as the actor that lies buried in the hearts of so many writers began to emerge, and each played to the public, who were applauding their statements and taking sides. The figures on the platform soon discovered where their constituency lay in that audience and they tried to please it. Different parties and rivalries were already forming: Khushwant Singh versus Angus Wilson, Mary McCarthy versus Rebecca West, those who wanted total literary freedom versus those who wanted tight control on copyright, writers from colonial countries against those from countries that had colonised them. The audience were following all the cut and thrust and loving it.

The first day was meant to end at 5.30, but in view of the late start and the obvious interest in continuing, Muggeridge did not end the session until 6.30. Then Šegedin walked over to Stefanovic and attacked him furiously. How dare he talk about the Yugoslav novel before he, the official delegate, had spoken. Was there a plot afoot against him? No one had met him, or told him where to go or what was happening, all in obvious contrast to the other writers present. With a curt 'Dove genia' he strode out, while Alex, waving his arms helplessly, looked worried. It was soon apparent that Šegedin was a man of importance, a diplomat as well as a novelist. He had been the Yugoslav Ambassador in Paris. Also he was a Croat, while Stefanovic was a Serb.

The evening was organised with another party, so having checked that all was going smoothly, I went to the King's Theatre, just before 7.30 to look for the Yugoslav cultural attaché, whom I knew well. The Llubjana Opera was performing Prokovieff's *Love of Three Oranges*. An official car drove up and out came the Yugoslav Ambassador to Britain with a party that included the attaché. I plucked him by the sleeve and he looked at me coldly. 'You have done something terrible,' he said, 'and there will be big trouble!' Then he went in.

I had much to do that evening and towards the end of it, began to hunt out information to find where the cultural attaché was staying: I found it at midnight. I waited until 7.00 in the morning, then went to the private flat where he was staying and rang the doorbell. He came out in a dressing gown. After abject apologies I told him exactly what had happened and in the end he believed me. It had been thought that the whole mishap was a plot by the CIA or MI5 to discredit and humiliate his country, and the Ambassador was contemplating pulling the opera, the ballet, a symphony orchestra, an art exhibition and other participating artists, including the Drolc Quartet, out of the festival. That year the festival's emphasis was on Slavic music and art. Finally he told me that he was breakfasting with the Ambassador and Šegadin at 9.30 at the Caledonian Hotel. If I turned up just after 10.00 he would see what he could do.

I was there at 10.00, had a cup of coffee with them and explained what had happened all over again. The messenger sent to the Caledonian had somehow failed to deliver the folder, which I then gave to Šegedin. That Tuesday was the Scottish day, but I arranged that Šegedin should have the platform to make a statement at the beginning. He told me his wife was a specialist in Adam architecture and I said that I would arrange a special tour of Adams buildings for him the following morning. We broke up amicably.

The morning newspapers announced a sensation. The conference was on most of the front pages, certainly on the Scottish ones, and there were long reports on inside pages, especially in The Scotsman where Magnus Magnusson had done us proud. In 1962, subjects such as sex were not discussed in public and the frankness of the exchanges was headline material. The hall had been nearly full and we were already the hit and the main talking point of the festival.

I had not expected the other writers, except for one or two, to turn up to hear Scottish literature discussed and had excused them from the morning briefing, but many came to that anyway and they all came in the afternoon. The format was different: the Scottish writers sat at a long table facing the audience and the others were on the tiered platforms behind them. David Daiches sat in the middle of the table and chaired the discussion. Around him sat Hugh MacDiarmid, Sidney Goodsir Smith, Edwin Morgan, Naomi Mitchison, and, at the very end, Alexander Trocchi. On the first day I had put jugs of water and some wine on the table where the panel sat. Jim Haynes, when I was contemplating what to put on the table, suddenly suggested, 'What about the wine of the country?' So I put jugs of water and carafes of whisky on the long table. Sidney Goodsir Smith, a good tippler, took full advantage, and by the end of the afternoon he was incoherent.

Šegedin's attitude changed that afternoon. As he said afterwards, 'I didn't know you had nationalism in Scotland. I thought it was only Yugoslavia!' Hugh MacDiarmid[14] launched an all-out attack on everything English, especially the perfidious influence of the English literary establishment on Scottish literature. There were more moderate voices, but the counter-attack came from Trocchi, an expatriate Scot from Glasgow with an Italian name, whom nobody had ever heard of. MacDiarmid was a

---

[14] The pen-name of Christopher Grieve.

communist who had been expelled from the Communist Party for nationalism and a Scottish Nationalist who had been expelled from the SNP, then a rather ineffective party of Scottish intellectuals and academics, for communism. As Scotland's best-known poet he was a natural enemy of Calvinist conformity and middle-class values, but underneath the rugged peasant exterior lurked an old-fashioned, often narrow-minded, puritan. Trocchi had lived in Paris, New York and California, advocated and belonged to the hippie life-style, and had experimented with every kind of drug. He had given himself a heroin injection just before 2.30. They attacked each other with vehemence, although underneath they were basically on the same side. 'I want no uniformity,' said MacDiarmid, defending himself. 'Neither do I,' responded Trocchi, 'not even a kilt.' MacDiarmid was wearing one.

Apart from the MacDiarmid-Trocchi exchange, there was much other discussion, but the half-hour transcript that BBC Scotland put out on the radio that evening concentrated on the fireworks, as did the next day's newspapers, which gave very full coverage to what had been said. But it was not only the Scottish writers who spoke. Many other writers on the platform felt that what was said about Scotland and its literature applied equally to their own situations, and, in particular, Erich Fried had much to say, most of it in connection with nationalism and its dangers. He had already made his mark on the Monday and would have much more to say during the coming days. He was one of the emerging stars who the public were getting to know and like. He became a friend of Mary McCarthy, who had her own little coterie which included Niccolo Tucci, an Italian writer whom she had persuaded Sonia to invite. The Scottish day became another international day as Scottish literary problems found their echoes elsewhere.

There was a big civic reception that night to which all the writers were invited, and I was put at a table where Šegedin was sitting next to the Lord Provost's secretary, a Mr. Murdoch, who seemed to know a great deal about Adam, so he got on well with the Yugoslav writer and diplomat, who was now in a very good mood. On other days I arranged little dinners for about ten writers at a time, putting together people who had a common language or common interests. So, for instance we had a pleasant dinner one night with Martin Esslin, Ledig Rowohlt, the Hamburg publisher, Harry Mulisch and one or two others who spoke German. Some of the English writers like L.P. Hartley and J.R. Ackerley had little to say. Others like Jennifer Johnson, Colin McInnes and Simon Raven intervened occasionally, but not often. Dame Rebecca West, who had produced a son out of wedlock with H. G. Wells, and written books of many different kinds, but who I personally associated largely with the Alger Hiss case because of her review of Lord Jowett's book that had led to its withdrawal, was an authoritarian figure on the political right, and she had her particular admirers in the audience. Her exchanges with Mary McCarthy bristled with mutual dislike as they scored points off each other, each seeking more applause from their supporters in the hall. Simon Raven asked what all the talk was about. Surely writers were interested in money, not principles, and that was why they wrote. Certainly it was only money that made him write. As the days passed Norman Mailer became more expansive and took a greater part; he too wanted to hear his words greeted with applause.

Malcolm Muggeridge left on the Tuesday. He and Sonia had been lodged in a large flat I had rented on Circus Place, and his motive from the start had been to get Sonia into bed. But she was not interested in Malcolm that way, so he took umbrage and left. Angus Wilson more or less took over his function as conference chairman, but at that point I was waking every morning at five o'clock with new ideas and daily changing the format, which by the third day had two panels of commentators that dialogued both between members of their own panel and across the stage to the other one. We now had two microphones on stands for single speakers and three roving ones in the audience, which remained a full one right up to the last day. Listeners increasingly found the earphones useful, not just for the translation from other languages, but to hear their own with clarity. Many never took them off.

From the third day we were giving the audience a real show. The two panels argued with each other and with the speakers who were called to the microphone. The third day was about Commitment: should a writer be serving a cause or only his own talent? The debate was heated and the third world countries came into their own, attacking the colonial powers which were still hanging onto their dominance wherever they could. Black writers from Africa and the Caribbean were especially forceful. This would surprise no-one forty years later, but it was very new then. Alan Paton had been invited but had been unable to obtain a visa to leave South Africa. His telegram of protest was read out to the hall and greeted rapturously.

On the fourth day the subject was censorship. Malcolm Muggeridge had wanted it to be the first day's subject, but I intended the debates to build up to a logical climax. Almost all the panel, naturally enough, were against censorship in general, but Rebecca West and Khushwant Singh were for it, on their own terms of course. The exchanges between Mary McCarthy and Rebecca West were the sharpest yet. I had invited Maurice Girodias, who turned up for that day only, and he pointed out how ridiculous censorship can be. Norman Mailer had a lot to say, so did Erich Fried, and nearly everyone managed to get their oar in, even if only for a sound-bite. But the climax was Henry Miller, long banned in Britain and still the subject of prosecutions in different American cities and states, all of them being fought by Barney Rosset at great cost. Barney had published *Tropic of Cancer* and *Tropic of Capricorn* the previous year and was not only fighting state prosecutions, but suing pirate editions that were appearing after nearly every victory he won in a local court.

Miller did not speak long, but he was clear, moving and direct. Why could a writer, the most harmless of human beings, not write what he wanted? No one was obliged to read him who did not like his work. Why should the public be protected from the author's point of view, his recorded experience, ideas and even fantasies? It was Authority's old need to restrict knowledge, as witness the Inquisition. He received a standing ovation from the audience, then modestly sat down. He was of course at that time still unpublished in Britain as far as his major writings were concerned. Trocchi had, naturally enough, a great deal to say, but Burroughs so far had only listened. The day was a great success with the audience, but so had been every other day.

On the Wednesday I received bad news. My great-uncle Jim had died, only a few months after my grandfather, his elder brother. He had been heavily sedated and only semi-conscious for some months. The funeral was to be on the Saturday, not in Scotland, but near Wheeting Hall, where his wife had died and been buried. There was also some ceremony in Kinross the day before. How could I get to it? There was no way I could leave the conference, my successful brain-child, which was going so well in spite of the dire predictions. The newspapers were giving us more and more space every day. I had persuaded the BBC to record the conference, and every evening an edited version of the day's proceedings was going out to the listening public. The whole country was talking about it. But anything could happen and I could not leave. I booked myself onto an early flight to London for Saturday morning, saying I would get to the burial late that morning, which would mean leaving Sonia and Jim to clear up and get the writers onto their trains and 'planes. From Heathrow I would hire a car to take me to Suffolk.

On the Thursday evening we had a party at the Circus Place flat, where Sonia was staying and now Norman Mailer as well. Mailer pinned me against a wall. 'I want to be one of the moderators tomorrow,' he said. 'Khushwant Singh can be the other.' I had had other plans, but Norman was not easy to resist and I eventually agreed. Morning briefing sessions were now no longer necessary and Mailer and I planned that last day of the conference there and then.

The subject was 'The Future of the Novel'. Different writers outlined the future as they envisaged it, but the big sensation of the day was William Burroughs. He had earlier been described by Mailer as 'possibly the only living American writer of genius.' He had become a friend of Trocchi, and they were to remain friends thereafter; Henry Miller had also been friendly to another writer who had been censored like himself (Burroughs had been at that point banned in Chicago and only recently published by Girodias), but the great womaniser did not otherwise have much in common with a totally frank and committed homosexual. At this time, in 1962, homosexual behaviour was still a crime in Britain, and the platform outspokenness of militants like the Dutch writer Het van Reve, who had been constantly on his feet to attack the homophobes like Khushwant Singh and Rebecca West, had titillated and no doubt shocked much of the audience and delighted the press, from the tabloids to the most serious, who were able to report views expressed in public that their editors would normally have suppressed.

William Burroughs had a similar voice to T. S. Eliot's, drawling and matter of fact, with something like a Harvard accent. He was always dressed in a suit and tie, neatly but not fashionably, and looked like an accountant. In a dry monotone, he described how he wrote and explained his fold-in, cut-up method of writing. He would put together very different texts, some from newspapers, some from other writers, some from his own past work, and by folding or cutting create a mixture or blend with fragments of different sentences which he could then edit and rewrite until it made some kind of sense. He might have added that this method, which has its painterly equivalent in collage and in various forms of surrealist art, was really what T. S. Eliot did in his mind in poems like *The Waste Land*, but without the deliberate use of hazard. In doing so, by freeing the words from the prison into which the original writer had put them, and letting them take on a new meaning outside the preconceptions of the writer, Burroughs believed he was a magus, creating magic. He really believed that he had once caused a 'plane to crash by constructing a text by his method, in which he had by chance put down the name of the pilot and described certain circumstances related to the accident. Most importantly, he had been cutting up and editing his text at exactly the time that the crash had occurred. 'Are you serious?' asked Singh. 'Perfectly,' replied Burroughs.

The last night's party was very eventful, and it again took place in the Circus Place flat. Everyone was jubilant at what had been, by general consent, a triumphal week. My own feeling was that I had tumbled onto a great discovery, and had justified the conclusions I had drawn from the Coventry experience. This was the way to put over new writing to the public and to create an interest in the writers: by putting their ideas and personalities in conflict with each other. Novelists work on their own, and the blank white paper is a challenge, but it is a lonely one. The chance to meet one's public and to become for a while an actor could make all the difference. This did not apply to the shy or withdrawn. L.P. Hartley, Henry Williamson and one or two others who had not said a word. But it had made stars of Fried and Singh, of the two tough ladies McCarthy and West, of Miller and Burroughs, of Trocchi, Mailer and Angus Wilson. They had found their admirers in the audience and had played up to them, relishing their applause.

At the party, which was attended by some who had been at the conference, but not as delegates, Max Hayward, translator of Doctor Zhivago and an Oxford Don, got very drunk and made a pass at Sonia Orwell who, elated like everyone else, was looking her best. Mailer decided to take umbrage at this and he half lifted Hayward by one arm over his shoulder.

'Calder,' he shouted, 'get his other arm.' When I did, he dragged the poor man, myself taking part of the weight, out onto the landing and told me to let go. When I did, he heaved Hayward over his shoulder and onto the stone stairs, whereupon he rolled down all the four or five flights to the bottom. Five minutes later he reappeared, blood flowing from several places, and quietly resumed drinking. His previous drunkenness had protected him during a descent that could easily have killed him. Burroughs witnessed some of this, but did not understand what was happening. He later told his biographers that groups of youths were roaming the streets of Edinburgh beating up bypassers.

Sonia Orwell was on as much of a high as everyone else, and for once she had not drunk too much. As the flat emptied towards four in the morning, a strange hunger took her over. She seized my arm and wanted me to go to bed with her. To be honest I had the same desire, and not only to wipe out the memory of my last humiliating experience in bed with her in London on the night of Lisel's funeral. The week that had begun with trepidation had ended in incredible success and that often goes to the gonads. But I had to catch the first 'plane at seven o'clock and first I had to go home to where I was staying, shave and change. There was just no time. I explained my situation and left.

I took the early flight, drove to Brandon where the burial had taken place an hour before I arrived. I joined my relatives at the hotel where there was a lunch and explained my late arrival. Of course my name had been much in the news, but I was treated with coldness for my lateness, especially as I was a possible heir. I drove back to London, taking my brother with me, who had flown from Germany to be both at the funeral in Scotland and the burial in Suffolk. We both stayed at a big hotel off Sloane Street, near my old Lowndes Street flat. My brother and I had never been able to get on well and I vaguely remember that our dinner together was a difficult one.

The next morning, Sunday, I flew back to Edinburgh. Nearly all the writers had departed and Sonia had also left that day. Bettina had been in Edinburgh, but being pregnant had stayed in the flat I had rented for the duration of the festival, and she seldom left it. On Monday I went to a morning concert at Freemason's Hall where the Drolc quartet played Shostakovich, and that afternoon received a message, asking me to call on Shepherd and Anderson, the Edinburgh solicitors. I went the next day and was told that I was my uncle's residual heir. He had left me Ledlanet and all his estate, other than a few legacies. I was thirty-five years old, had just pulled off the biggest event of my life so far in terms of prestige and imaginative thinking, had become a national celebrity, and was now the owner of a country house with ten thousand acres attached to it. Still dazed I went to see Lord Harewood, who beamed at me. He had been much criticised the year before for introducing so much Schönberg and difficult music into the Festival that normally was conservative in its programming, and that year for allowing me to stage a massive literary jamboree about which much doubt had been expressed. Both innovations had worked and my event had brought the festival onto the front pages of the national press and even been discussed in foreign newspapers.

'What about next year?' he asked.

'A drama conference,' I ventured.

'Good,' he said. 'Get on with it.'

Perhaps I should close this chapter with a quote from a letter that Mary McCarthy sent to her friend Hannah Arendt:

> People jumping up to confess they were homosexuals or heterosexuals; a registered heroin addict leading the young Scottish opposition to the literary tyranny of the communist Hugh MacDiarmid...an English woman describing her communications with her dead daughter,[15] a Dutch homosexual, former male nurse, now a Catholic convert, seeking someone to baptise him; a bearded Sikh with his hair down to his waist, declaring on the platform that homosexuals were incapable of love, just as (he said) hermaphrodites were incapable of orgasm (Stephen Spender, in the chair, murmured that he should have thought they could have two)...

---

[15] This was Rosamund Lehmann, who told me during the conference that she had been unable to write anything since the death of her daughter, which is strangely prefigured in her novels.

Chapter Five

Ledlanet

The years with Calders Ltd., especially those in which I had proved that I had managerial competence and sales ability, had given me self-confidence, and the sale of my shares to Wolfson had given me a temporary affluence, but it did not last long. Lawyers ate up my ready money very quickly as Christya and I confronted each other in court. There was the custody issue, which I lost. Then the question of a divorce dragged on as Christya changed her mind whether she wanted a divorce or not. The final decree came in 1960, and immediately after it I was married again, not this time out of great passion, but for reasons that have been explained earlier. And publishing eats up money very quickly as cash is turned into unsold stock. But now, in August 1962, I had reasonable affluence again and landed property as well.

I went to Ledlanet a day or so after seeing the lawyer. All the staff were still there: Reginald Attewell, the butler, had been hired in the twenties by my Great-Aunt Mildred when he was still a teenager to be a boot-boy. He had been in their house at Park Lane and at Wheeting Hall in Suffolk, and after the death of my aunt, shortly before the second world war from diabetes, when Wheeting was sold – my uncle had only kept the shooting rights – he had moved to Scotland. Attewell was to be described by an editor of Private Eye, a few years after I had inherited him, as making Jeeves look like an amateur. There will be more about Attewell later. The other staff were two gamekeepers, a gardener, a cook, a housemaid and some temporary staff which Attewell recruited in the nearby village of Milnathort when necessary. The gamekeeper who lived in the lodge at the foot of the drive doubled as chauffeur. But in practice Attewell did nearly everything himself.

I spent two days there, talking to the staff, telling them I intended as far as possible to make no changes and stayed in a room I had often occupied before, in the west wing of the house, facing south, with an alcove that was part of a tower built into the corner of the house. There was a big central hall, open to a central skylight up above, and on the first floor level, above it, a corridor running around three sides of it. Nine bedrooms lay behind this corridor, and a green baize door led to three servants' bedrooms with a bathroom in between. There was another bedroom in the tower on a higher floor on the east wing, and a total of three other bathrooms. The front façade, built of stone in the Scottish baronial style, faced due south. Behind the house was a field, and behind it a large wood and the Ochil Hills then sloped up to their highest point, overlooking two counties, Perth to the north, Kinross to the south. I was the fourth generation to own Ledlanet, allowing that my father's generation was missing, and to me the place was magical.

My uncle's cairn terrier was still in the house. She was called Wootsie and knew me from past visits. A distant cousin, Margory Manners, who had hoped to inherit herself, left the house as soon as she knew the contents of the will. She had been left a legacy in cash and also the right to take valuables from Ledlanet up to a certain value. Probate value being low, she arranged to take all the silver, many smaller pieces of furniture and other objects that were readily saleable. Attewell had his own house, some distance away, where he lived with his family; he had a wife who had previously worked in the house, two sons and a daughter. The house had belonged to my uncle, but it was left to Attewell in the will. The only person living in Ledlanet at the time was the cook.

On my first night there I found myself alone with Wootsie, and took her to my room with me, where she curled up at the foot of the bed. It was a warm night and I opened one of the windows wide, read for a bit, and fell asleep, perhaps around eleven o'clock. I suddenly woke up. The open window had banged down and the room door opened at the same time. Wootsie began barking furiously, jumped off the bed and ran out the door. I followed her onto the landing. It was a totally black night, and no light came from the large angled skylight over the middle of the hall. Across the intervening space on the other side of the well was another balcony and behind it my uncle's room, which had been locked. In spite of the blackness I could see Wootsie in a dim light sitting outside its door, tense and expectant and soon she began to whine. There was no apparent source for the light, a rather bright glow that surrounded the dog. No electric light was switched on and there was certainly no light coming from the skylight overhead. Feeling very frightened now, I put on a dressing gown and walked around the corridor to where Wootsie was sitting, gazing intently up at the door. I could no longer see any light and put on an electric switch to see my way back. My uncle's door was still firmly locked. I picked up Wootsie, returned to my room, closed the door and opened the window again. It was after midnight.

Then I was awakened again in exactly the same way. The window had slammed down, the door opened (had I locked it when I came back? I could not be sure) and a barking Wootsie ran around to my uncle's door. The same glow illuminated the door and the dog. This time, even more frightened, I turned on every electric light switch as I went to pick up Wootsie. The glow was gone, but the dog resisted being picked up. This time I locked my door and put a chair against it. It was 2.30. It took me a time to fall asleep and when I did, I slept until morning. This strange experience never occurred again.

I gradually took over the house and spent some time there, went through all the books and papers and moved more of my own things into the house, which I came to love more and more. I also had Bila, the white poodle, which had been bought for Jamie, but which now lived at my

Wimpole Street flat. But when Bila came to Ledlanet there was instant animosity between the two bitches. I finally found a lady who was about to move to Skye who wanted a dog, but not a young one, and she adopted the cairn terrier. A few months later she wrote me that Wootsie had settled down and was very happy on the island.

The Frankfurt Book Fair came round at the end of September and the first person to greet me as I was putting together my stand was Maurice Girodias. We had become very friendly although many of the projects we discussed did not come off for different reasons. This is an appropriate place to record what some of these projects were, but the order in which things happened is not strictly chronological.

Of the four incidents I have to relate, the one I did not have to regret concerned the Beckett *Trilogy*. I had contracted *Malone Dies* and *The Unnamable* from Editions de Minuit and had published the first in 1958 in a hardcover edition with a striking cover that depicted a particularly gruesome skull. This was in Beckett's own translation. *The Unnamable* came out on its own only many years later, also in the author's own translation, because in 1959 I managed to put the three into a single volume. We had a problem over *Molloy*, the first part of the trilogy. The English language rights had been acquired by Girodias on the instigation of Seaver and the Merlin group and published as an Olympia Press *Collection Merlin* book in 1955, then it was sold to Grove Press, and at first it was the Grove edition I was selling in the U.K. It had been translated by Patrick Bowles with some help from the author, who found the collaboration difficult and unpleasant. Sam himself saw the three works as a whole and wanted them published as such. This never happened in France, but I was anxious to please him. But this meant getting around Girodias who had become defensive and was not keen to have competition for his own edition, which sold badly in his own market, which was basically one for pornography.

The *Trilogy* is central to all of Beckett's work, as much so as *Waiting for Godot*. It was written during the same two year period of concentrated activity between 1947 and 1949 that produced *Godot* and the *Texts for Nothing*, all in a creative white heat. Beckett had thought that a visible tumour growing in his right cheek was cancerous and that he only had a short time to live. He knew what he wanted to say and thought time was short, the reason for the sustained activity. Fortunately the tumour turned out to be non-life-threatening, although the hollow in his cheek after it was removed was to give Sam trouble all his life.

I finally found a solution and it was a simple one. Why not bring out three editions of a one-volume trilogy, allowing Girodias to do his own, thereby acquiring two other major Beckett novels in exchange for letting me have British rights, with Grove Press doing their own. As he was getting more than he was giving, Girodias finally agreed and I was able to publish the trilogy as a hardcover in 1959. The first editions of all three volumes are now quite valuable in the rare book and first editions market.

I also had a contract with Girodias to publish *The Ginger Man* by J. P. Donleavy. Girodias had been brought the book by the author, liked it and contracted it in the normal way. Donleavy was exceptionally well treated by Girodias, who entertained him lavishly in Paris, getting him drunk on very good wines, which seemed to have sparked off some resentment. But all the time the author was negotiating with other publishers in London and was only using Girodias to get a more erotic version into print first. Girodias was treated with contempt from the beginning and with real nastiness later on, as I shall relate. Not knowing what was going on behind his back, Maurice offered *The Ginger Man* to me and I accepted it, only to find myself being sued by the author, who claimed Girodias did not have the rights to sell to me, which he contractually did. Donleavy had a secret deal with Neville Armstrong for Spearman to publish the book after Girodias had taken all the risks, while Donleavy received two advances. Caught in the middle with the threat of writs flying about, I backed out.

Then there were *The Black Diaries* of Roger Casement. These were the extremely private and indiscrete diaries of the distinguished civil servant who had done much to expose the colonial despotisms and cruelties that prevailed in the Belgian Congo under the personal rule of Leopold II and later similar atrocities in South America. Casement, although an Ulster Protestant, was an Irish patriot who took part in the 1916 rising and was caught smuggling German arms into the country for use in the rebellion. The diaries that were with him at the time of his arrest were a record of his promiscuous homosexual activities and they were circulated by the prosecution to selected journalists at the time of his trial in mimeograph to minimalise any public sympathy for him. Given his past record of distinguished and dangerous public service he would normally have been reprieved, but the Irish rising in the middle of the first world war, which was not going well at the time, made the government ruthless, and Casement was convicted and hanged. All copies were supposed to have been returned to the Home Office, but one was not. It came into the possession of Peter Singleton-Gates, a retired journalist, who brought it to Girodias. For him, a book that would excite the prurient, bring to light a historical scandal, and above all expose the hypocritical and malign behaviour of the Home Office was the ideal publication, and he produced a large and impressive volume. Singleton Gates, the journalist, explained the circumstances by which the transcribed copy had been obtained, Girodias wrote a long and excellent historical introduction that preceded the text itself, and in 1959 he published the book in France, while looking for an American and a British publisher. Barney Rosset finally did it in America, where the press totally ignored it, while I agreed to publish in Britain, where I knew I was taking a considerable risk. I then discovered to my dismay that some British bookshops were receiving the Olympia Press edition directly from Paris. Wen I protested, Maurice said that the French and European market for such a book in English was non-existent. He had to sell his edition wherever he could, but that should not stop me. With the Alger Hiss fiasco in mind, I withdrew from the contract. He then signed an agreement with Sidgewick and Jackson, then run by a very wily individual called James Knapp-Fisher. The book was published. Not a single review appeared, not a copy was seen in a bookshop. When I inquired I was told that the book had instantly sold out and gone out of print. The only possible explanation was that Knapp-Fisher had made a deal to sell the entire edition to the Home Office to prevent it getting to public notice. The Irish government was probably party to the deal, as it had no desire for one of Eire's heroes and martyrs to be seen, whatever his virtues, as a member of the banned and despised group of homosexuals, and a particularly active and unashamed one, obsessed with penis size and the number of his sexual encounters. Knapp-Fisher, however, made one little gesture of conscience: he donated a copy to the London Library, where it is not catalogued and can only be obtained for perusal, and not removed, and then only with the express permission of the Chief Librarian. Publication of *The Black Diaries* was a totally quixotic gesture on Maurice Girodias' part, an arrow aimed at an establishment he hated and despised. It should resound to his credit.

It should be said that another, much shorter version, authorised by Casement's heirs, the Parry family, appeared in 1997, in which many mistakes have been corrected, but there is still a controversy surrounding the diaries, which defenders of Sir Roger Casement, hero of anti-slavery in the Congo and on the Amazon, still say are forgeries.

But the most important and painful of all the deals with Girodias that went wrong was over Vladimir Nabokov's *Lolita*. A literary agent in Paris had approached Maurice. Denise Clarouin had long been established and had known his father well: she now wanted to introduce him as a matter of urgency to a Russian friend, Doussia Ergaz, an emigrée, who had a very special manuscript. He was told that it was written by a white Russian of good family, now teaching at an American university, a recognised author, but this particular book had to be published anonymously because of the content. Girodias at this point was living with Muffie, the estranged wife of Austryn Wainhouse, whose translations of the Marquis de Sade were one of the main items in the Olympia catalogue. Maurice and Muffie read the manuscript together and enthused over a long work about an affair between a pre-pubescent young girl and a paedophile, which was entitled *Lolita*. It fascinated them both. It was obvious to Girodias that Doussia Ergaz had been an ex-lover of the author by the care she took over the negotiations and her insistence on secrecy where the name of Nabokov was concerned.

Girodias had many difficulties. The book was a long one and he would have to publish it in two volumes, and it was not the kind of easy erotica on which he could expect to make money. But he sold the translation rights to Gallimard, having little expectation that he would sell it elsewhere, the author in any case not wanting it to appear in America. It soon became obvious to Girodias once he had started to correspond directly with Nabokov that the latter was not happy about being published by a house specialising in pornography and erotica, but he had no choice. His disdain for this publisher he never met became greater with time, but he was pleased about Gallimard. It was Raymond Queneau, brilliant author himself and one of the most influential of Claude Gallimard's advisors who brought about French publication, overruling the nervousness of his boss. Eric Kahane, Maurice's brother, did the translation. The book was attacked in France and successfully defended, but it became necessary, in order to do so, to reveal the name of the author. This created considerable difficulty for him at his university.

American publication came about in a strange way. The American publisher, Walter Minton, who had recently inherited the highly reputable firm of G. P. Putnam from his father, was having an affair with a chorus girl called Rosemary Ridgewell, who on a visit to Paris had bought *Lolita* and thought it the funniest book she had ever read. On her insistence Minton bought American rights, although, according to Girodias' memoirs, he never found the time to read it. But it became an instant best-seller and soon royalties were pouring into Olympia Press. Rosemary and Walter Minton went to Paris and Girodias invited them to lunch, a little discomfited when Rosemary insisted on going to the very expensive Tour d'Argent. He was nervously feeling in his pocket to see how much cash he had, when Rosemary insisted that Walter was paying. He saw them again that night when it became very obvious they were not getting on, and when he took them, along with Iris Owens (who wrote novels for him as Harriet Daimler) to a lesbian night club the evening ended in a fracas with Minton hitting Rosemary and walking out. The next morning she turned up at Maurice's flat with a bag of croissants, spent the day in bed with him, and returned to New York on her own the following day. Maurice's private life was always colourful and he never had difficulties with ladies.

But long before this he had offered the book to me and I had accepted it. I knew nothing about Vladimir Nabokov at that point, but it was obvious that this Russian emigré had a wonderful facility with English style and a caustic view of his adopted country. That he was also a fastidious aristocrat who resented having to go to a maverick pornographic publisher like Girodias to get his book into print I only realised later. Maurice's memoirs[16] are revealing and show much insight into the ambiguities of the author's complex personality, and my subsequent difficulties certainly had something to do with Nabokov's prejudice against him.

---

[16] Le Jardin d'Eros. Paris 1981.

I signed a contract for British rights and announced *Lolita* for publication, taking care to find influential figures who would defend it if attacked. One day I came back from lunch to find a man sitting at my desk with both feet on it, reading my correspondence.

'What the devil are you doing?' I exclaimed. He looked up, still holding some of my letters in his hand.

'Are you Calder?' he asked, and swinging his feet onto the ground, he went on. 'Well, I'm Walter Minton. I have a message for you from Vladimir Nabokov. You're not going to publish his book.' He took another look at the letters in his hand. 'Interesting,' he commented and stood up, dropping them on the desk. Then he went on to tell me, as rudely as possible, that Nabokov had checked me out, and believed from my past publishing that I was a Communist. He also disliked other writers in my catalogue, especially Beckett. As for my contract with Girodias, the author would repudiate it and go to court if necessary.

I decided to ask Barney Rosset to help. One of Barney's recent letters had mentioned meeting André Deutsch at the Harvard Club. Deutsch was also interested in *Lolita*. Barney made some efforts on my behalf, but when he was told that the objections to me were political, he gave up. Nabokov had soon made other enquiries and I learned from Barney that George Weidenfeld would be acceptable to him. I decided to compromise. I had lunch with George and suggested that we might publish the book together in partnership. At the Frankfurt Book Fair of 1957 we saw Girodias together. Before the meeting I had told George that Maurice was sensitive and wanted to be seen as a literary publisher rather than as a pornographer, but at our meeting Girodias was in a jocular mood, laughed about his ill-fame and agreed the proposition. I signed a contract with Weidenfeld whereby he acquired half the rights and agreed equally to share all risks and expenses. The book would appear under his imprint with myself as a sleeping partner.

But then the trouble started. Our partnership was secret and unknown to the author. Weidenfeld was directly in the firing line in the event of a prosecution and this created a problem for his co-director Nigel Nicolson, who was the Tory member of Parliament for Bournemouth and had already made himself unpopular with his constituents by opposing Anthony Eden's attack on Nasser during the Suez crisis, a hypocritical war which benefited only Israel and had little support in Britain except from the Tory faithful. To be seen now as the publisher of a highly controversial book about paedophilia would offend his constituents even further and he was nervous. Carter-Ruck, the most expensive libel lawyer in Britain, was consulted and he advised extreme caution. As legal and other expenses mounted, my own attitude, which was that once you had decided to publish a book you went ahead with it, was ignored, and I became seriously worried at the growing legal costs with little hope of getting any of it back for some time. Finally I accepted defeat and passed over all rights to Weidenfeld, getting ten percent of the profits, which never came to much, because a publishing profit is almost impossible to calculate when overheads are taken into account. Weidenfeld finally went ahead and published. The book was supported by prominent authors such as Graham Greene, whom I had recruited in the early days to support the book. The Bournemouth Conservative Party duly deselected Nigel Nicolson, who thereby lost his seat at the next election. Weidenfeld and Nicolson made a great deal of money on *Lolita*, but also had an option on all the other books of Nabokov, which the firm published over the next few years.

This account of my deals with Girodias, most of which came unstuck, has been a long but necessary digression, but as my association with him was in many ways as important as the one with Barney Rosset, it needed explaining. When, post-Edinburgh Writers' Conference, Girodias turned up at my stand at the Frankfurt Book Fair in 1962, he was flat-broke. 'Johnny,' he said, 'can you lend me some money. I need five thousand dollars.' As much of his revenue during the last few years had been from sales of rights to American publishers, he thought primarily in terms of dollars, which American publishers in his eyes always had in abundance. But I certainly had no spare cash. 'Sorry, Maurice, I can't help you. I have just enough to get me through this Frankfurt.'

'Well, let me share your room then. You can't let me sleep in the street.'

In the end, and very reluctantly, I let him share my room at the Frankfurterhof, which fortunately had another bed. On the first night he harangued me. A warm bed was not his only motive in turning to me. He reminded me of the Censorship Day at Edinburgh where he had been present, had spoken, and had witnessed the acclaim given to Henry Miller, in whom he had an almost obsessive personal interest. His father had first published him, but he, Maurice, had been cheated out of the rights of the two *Tropics* and other titles by Hachette after the war. He had published some later Miller in the fifties at Olympia Press, had on one occasion been to court over them, and he had been instrumental in helping Barney Rosset to obtain American rights. Now, he said, was the time for me to publish Henry Miller in Britain.

Henry Miller had replaced D. H. Lawrence as the most notorious writer still banned in Britain. The Lady Chatterly prosecution in 1960 had been a great show trial with prominent writers and academics and even a bishop appearing as witnesses for the defence. The publisher, Penguin Books, against all expectation, had won triumphantly. Henry Miller's acclaim at the Writers' Conference, said Girodias, showed where public opinion lay, and now was the time to publish him. And who should do it other than me, who had brought Henry Miller to Edinburgh? But I had a simple scruple: although I had had at the back of my mind the intention to bring some of my authors to Edinburgh to make them better known, and this had not worked out as planned, I did not feel that I could take personal advantage of the events that had been thrown up by what happened there. I had performed a public duty as an interesting experiment, and there seemed to me to be an element of corruption if I thereby acquired new authors. I do not think that I am less ethically inclined nearly forty years later as I write this than I was then, but the world was different at the time and ethical scruples were expected from civilised people of my background. But after two nights of listening to Maurice, I began to realise he was right. Many publishers had been in Edinburgh to support their authors or to fish for new ones and propositions had already been made to Henry Miller's Paris agent. So why, after all, not me? I looked up Dr. Hoffman, Miller's agent, who was in Frankfurt and broached the subject. He said he would speak to Henry.

Under pressure, I had advanced a few marks to Maurice, which I could ill afford, and he was always asking for more. Then I had a brainwave. I suggested that he should put it about that he was writing his memoirs. He was a notorious character who had been connected with many writers, a libertine publisher whose so-called pornography often included works of great literary merit, a man who had attacked censorship everywhere out of conviction and had also led an interesting life. He had made important literary discoveries, published best-sellers, made fortunes and lost them again though his follies, the biggest of which had been his restaurant and succession of night-clubs, La Grande Severine. At one point, underneath or over his publishing offices, there had been a Russian restaurant with cabaret, which earlier had been a Brazilian one, a Blues Bar under the roof, a theatre in the basement, all in the same building on the Rue St. Severin. In expanding his basement his contractor had dug into the graveyard of the nearby church, and had filled the local dustbins around the Boulevard St. Michel with human remains from the middle ages. Three of his mistresses were all working in the complex simultaneously at one point, one of them a film star. His memoirs could only be a best-seller.

He did not take me seriously at first. When could he find the time? That was not his immediate problem, I pointed out. He needed advance contracts and good advances. I would help him to sell an autobiography, of which not a word was written, by saying that I had seen extracts that were fascinating and put rumours about the fair. All he had to do was wait until he was approached, then say that he had thought it too dangerous to bring the manuscript to Frankfurt, but that he would consider offers. Five minutes later I ran into André Deutsch in one of the Fair's corridors. 'Is it true, André,' I asked him, 'that you have the book?'

'What book, John?'

'Girodias' autobiography. I heard you had bought English rights. I've seen a bit of it. It's dynamite. But if you have it, I won't waste my time.'

'Sorry, John. I'm in a hurry. See you later.' And off he went to find Girodias. I used the same ploy with Tom Maschler of Jonathan Cape and other British publishers, and then with German, French and Italian ones. I forget which Americans I spoke to, but I think I probably left it to others to get the Americans interested. To cut the story short, by the next day Maurice had signed three contracts or option agreements and had £15,000 in cash in his pockets. He took a suite at the Frankfurterhof, even gave a party in it, and I had my room to myself. The story is told in his own words, rather more amusingly, in the first of the two volumes of memoirs he was later to write, *J'Arrive*[17], which in English became *The Frog Prince*.[18].

All my dealings with Maurice landed me in problems. He was unable to make a straightforward deal and stick to it. By the very nature of most of the books he published, he was often doing business with authors who saw him as naive and took advantage of his unwillingness to write anything down or remember what he had given in cash payment for the manuscripts he accepted, and he was often dealing with publishers and booksellers who did not live in a culture of honesty and trust. His lack of guile was very transparent, which enabled many to take advantage of him: it was not too surprising that with experience he became very distrustful and often sought to cheat on a contract before he himself was cheated. I did less business with him after the early sixties, which made it easier to remain friends until his death in 1990.

* * * * * *

After Frankfurt I went to Paris and spoke seriously to Dr. Hoffman. Other British publishers had been in touch and had offered contracts, but always with a proviso allowing them an indefinite delay before they had to publish. I offered an advance of £2000, less than most of the others, but I was willing to guarantee publication within a year, and possibly within six months. Hoffman was anxious to see the book out. He agreed and Henry Miller agreed as well.

As soon as the contract was signed I heard from Barney. Not only had he been obliged to fight obscenity cases, but after winning he had to bring lawsuits against pirate paperback companies, who had brought out their own editions to take advantage of the strange American copyright law, whereby copyright was lost if more than 1500 copies of a book printed in another country were circulated in the U. S. Although there were no figures to prove it, it was obvious that more than that quantity must have been smuggled into the country since 1934 when *Tropic of Cancer* was first published by Jack Kahane's Obelisk Press. A large number had been seized by customs.

---

[17] Paris, 1977
[18] New York, 1981.

Barney saw an opportunity to recoup his losses through the British edition and suggested that he would like to become my partner and share expenses and profits. I had already had great difficulty in persuading Marion Lobbenberg to go ahead with the Henry Miller project. She had watched my Edinburgh adventure with amazement, unable to grasp my reason for getting involved in such a big and risky undertaking, but was aware that the publicity, front-page much of it, and not confined to Britain, had made me something of a celebrity, although I had kept my name and presence much in the background, as against the writers and media celebrities such as Muggeridge: it was after all their arguments and sayings that had created all the excitement. Several of the writers from abroad had found British publishers and some British writers as well as others present at the conference had attracted the attention of Ledig-Rowohlt and European publishers who had come, and in some case been themselves put on the platform during the last two days. Norman Mailer's praise of William Burroughs, hitherto an unknown name outside his immediate circle, had led to several contracts, notably with Grove Press for the U. S. But I had so far done nothing to take advantage of the success of the conference.

Marion's reactions to this were strange. She had bought half an interest in the company that still bore my name, but she found that at Frankfurt and in general she was not treated as my equal and she resented it, becoming on occasion rather strident in her assertion, repeated many times a day at Frankfurt: 'I am an equal partner. I own half the shares.' Edinburgh had unfortunately made my shadow uncomfortably large for her. Although she realised that our higher profile benefited her as well, there was a chancre growing in her mind, which was to emerge later. Now she voiced her anxiety over getting involved in a book that could lead to prosecution. It was Roy Jones, who tipped the balance. He was Marion's financial advisor, but also a board member, and by nature he was a risk-taker. At our crucial meeting after I had talked Dr. Hoffman into a contract, he finally said that if I wanted to take the risk of publishing Miller, it must be on my own. I would have to pay any expenses to defend the book. It was agreed, against this, that in consideration of the risk-taking I could keep half of the profits. Marion remained negative and frightened, but Roy persuaded her that in this way she risked nothing. We accepted Barney's offer because it reduced my own risk and would provide funds for a defence if we needed it. Barney was sent a contract that would give him a half share in the British edition of *Tropic of Cancer*.

I went skiing at Val d'Isère at the end of February in 1963. On the bus from Geneva airport, which is a long ride, I sat next to a charming French lady and we spent the time talking. She owned a clothing boutique in Paris, and although on holiday, did not intend to ski, but to enjoy the ambience and clear air of the Savoy mountains in winter. She had no hotel reservation and I persuaded her to come to my hotel, where, however, she would not share my room, so I let her have it for the night, while I shared Jacques Chaix's, because the hotel, and indeed the whole village, was booked out. The next morning Jacqueline and I became intimate enough for me to return to my own room. I spent an enjoyable five days skiing, and enjoyed the company of my regular skiing friends and of course of Jacqueline, but then a telephone call came from Dick Seaver in New York, then Barney Rosset's principal editor. Barney wanted me to come to New York right away to discuss the contract and publication details. I had intended to stay two weeks at Val d'Isère, but after an exchange of telegrams, with Barney becoming ever more insistent, I reluctantly cut short my holiday by a week. My final telegram said: OK COMING BUT MERDE and left. Jacqueline later told me that Jacques had suggested she move in with him, saying we were like brothers and shared everything, but she had declined.

I spent three days in New York, quite pointlessly, and returned to London. We had discussed the contract to which Barney did not object, but he had mislaid it and would send it back when he found it. Back in Britain we went ahead with publication. Our biggest difficulty was finding a printer. We finally found a small one willing to print a first edition of ten thousand copies, but we had to sign an indemnity taking all the risks upon ourselves, because a printer can also be prosecuted. He was a very slow printer with rather old machinery. I also looked for literary support in the event that a prosecution did take place, although on balance I felt that we were probably safe. Miller's good Edinburgh reception and favourable publicity must have registered with the D.P.P.[19] and his office was still smarting from their defeat in the Penguin trial. I was canvassing my own defence witnesses just in case.

The names to whom I wrote, who agreed, either to appear in the box if necessary, or to otherwise give support by writing letters or signing a document approving publication, included Anthony Hartley, Anthony Powell, Erich Fried, Charles Osborne, Robert Bolt, Brian Aldiss, Kenneth Alsopp, John Gray (a BBC editor in Scotland, who had edited my conference for the daily broadcast), R.D. Smith, Kenneth Tynan, V.S. Pritchett, Naomi Lewis, Professor Maurice Carstairs (that year's Reith lecturer), David Daiches, Terence Kilmartin, George Devine, G.S. Fraser, William Golding, J.B. Priestley, Sir Compton MacKenzie, Laurence Durrell, Sir Herbert Read, Colin Mackinnis, Arnold Wesker, Sam Wanamaker and others, an astonishing line-up for those days. Sam Beckett would do anything other than appear in court. His earlier experience as a witness in the Gogarty trial in the thirties in Dublin had taught him what havoc a clever barrister could wreak with his totally honest reactions. I wrote a letter to the D.P.P., telling him we intended to publish, giving him all the reasons we were doing it, and a list of names of those who supported us. We certainly did not expect him to prosecute, but would withhold publication until after the trial if he intended to do so, so that no booksellers would be involved. It was only ten

---

[19] Director of Public Prosecutions.

days before publication that we received a reply that after taking advice from counsel he did not intend to prosecute. I decided to keep this information to myself.

The contract had still not been sent back by Barney. I realised he was waiting to see if there was to be a prosecution or not. A week before hearing from the D.P.P. I sent Barney an ultimatum: either the contract arrived within seven days or we would go it alone without him. There was no reply.

On publication day, which was in April, I turned on the radio and heard the eight o'clock news. The BBC announced that long queues were already forming outside Foyle's and other London bookshops to buy *Tropic of Cancer* before it was banned. I had been right to keep the D.P.P.'s letter to myself. Every bookshop sold out that morning and the telephone kept ringing with re-orders. The book had been published at twenty-five shillings, a relatively high price. The cover design was simple, an exploding white star in a blue background, close to the original Obelisk Press edition that Maurice Girodias had designed as a teen-ager.

The problem was now the printer. He promised another ten thousand, but it took him two weeks and by the time they arrived we had orders for 40,000 copies. Eventually we found another printer who could give us 10,000 a week. As fast as each new printing arrived at the warehouse it was sent out, and we had to ration each bookseller. We were, for the first and only time, on the Sunday Times' best-seller list. A young man from Germany, Christopher von Schlotterer, had come to work for us for a few weeks to improve his English. On the first morning he turned up at our Sackville Street office, and he was there punctually at nine o'clock, only to find the door at the top of the stairs locked. He sat on the stairs and waited. At about half-past the receptionist was the first to arrive. 'Ah, you must be the German boy,' she said and led him in. His principal job for the next few weeks was dividing up the daily flow of orders for *Tropic of Cancer* into lots of 1,000 copies so that the books could go out according to the sequence of orders arriving, cutting back on larger ones. There was always a shortage and we had to ration for over two months until the printings caught up.

Not only was the press full of the book, but to have a copy of it in one's hand was both a signal that one belonged to what soon came to be called 'swinging London' and an act of solidarity with the new underground culture that was opposing the old traditions. William Rees-Mogg editorialised against the book in The Times, which should, he claimed, have been prosecuted. I had a considerable volume of abusive correspondence, some calling for me to be dragged to hell, others using language much more obscene than anything in the book, and much more violent (Henry Miller is never violent), and there were telephone calls of the same calibre. I was even threatened with assassination and there was a threat to kidnap my daughter and do unmentionable things to her. The appearance of the book seemed to have stimulated every kind of perverted crank as well as obsessive puritans, although that is hardly the right way to describe them. But the book continued to sell well, and within two months we had no overdraft, and I was able to take those yellowing manuscripts off the shelf, some of which had been accepted a long time previously, and others I wanted to publish, and put them into production.

Success breeds success. All our books began to do better. The *nouveau roman* was selling better. We published *Night*, a novel about the Korean war by Francis Pollini, which had come to us through Girodias, but we had some problems with the author, largely because of trouble at the source. Bruce Douglas-Mann, our solicitor and an MP, managed to sort that out and the book did well. Now we published Trocchi's *Cain's Book*, which Grove had brought out in New York in 1960. Alexander Trocchi has had several mentions in this book, mainly in connection with his Paris days at Merlin and his appearance at the Writers' Conference. *Cain's Book* is largely an account of what happened to him between those two events. It is a horrifying account of a drug-addict's odyssey through the hell of earning a living and trying to function while totally enslaved to heroin, although the dependence is not admitted as such in the book. The author, having moved to New York, married the daughter of a very conventional New England family, much against their will, persuaded her to become a junky herself, and they then lived in the 'beat' and 'hippie' communities of New York, California, Las Vegas and elsewhere. At one point he appeared on a national television programme, where he not only admitted to being a heroin addict, but started to give himself a fix in front of the cameras before the producer could stop him. He then ran quickly from the studio. He had always liked being outrageous and had tried everything to make himself noticed in Paris, as I have related elsewhere and as is told in Andrew Murray Scott's biography.[20] He did things on impulse and such was his over-confident arrogance, which had started at school in Glasgow, where he had found that he could pass exams with ease, he always thought that he could worm his way out of any consequences of his actions. But after the TV incident he had reason to be worried. The FBI were after him. He visited his wife Lynne's parents one Sunday and, changing trains on their way back to New York, gave himself a fix on the platform. The FBI, who must have been trailing him, ran towards him on the platform, but they just missed him as he jumped onto a moving train. But they managed to arrest Lynne who did time in jail before being picked up and put under house arrest by her parents.

Trocchi then hid for a few days in New York, staying with a second-hand bookseller, then broke into the apartment of George Plimpton, who was away. He knew Plimpton, editor of The Paris Review from the early fifties, when they were friendly rivals and frequented the same cafés and night haunts. He took Plimpton's passport and two of his suits, wearing one

---

[20] Alexander Trocchi. The Making of the Monster. Edinburgh 1991

over the other, and then caught the overnight Greyhound bus to Niagara Falls, and managed to get over the border into Canada. There he looked up Leonard Cohen, who put him up and helped him to get onto a tramp steamer to Scotland, where he disembarked at a northern port, went first to Glasgow to get help from his family, and then settled in London, where I first met him, and where he soon became a spokesman for drug addicts everywhere. *Cain's Book* chronicles his time on a Hudson River scow, where he had taken a caretaker's job, written most of the book, which was really put together from the many fragments he had written before his arrest by his wife, when they were both members of the Manhattan drug scene.

Cain's Book received long and interesting reviews of the kind that an arctic explorer might receive. Sales were good. It was published shortly before *Tropic of Cancer*, but the sales of the latter helped the former. Then came *Tropic of Capricorn*, which did well, but not nearly as well as the first book. The first was high fashion and everyone had to have it, no doubt reading the spicier parts and skipping the rest. The fashion did not extend to the second in the same way, because the novelty was gone. Dr. Hoffman came to see me. 'What about the paperback rights?' he asked. I told him that I saw no hurry. The book was selling well in hardcover. A paperback would make it easier for very young people to buy it, and that might start a new initiative of the censors. 'But,' he pointed out, 'I am bringing you an offer from a paperback company, and I expect a commission on the offer.' He was Henry Miller's agent and would receive ten percent, and for all I knew more, on all the royalties that he would receive from us. Now he wanted an additional ten percent on whatever we might get from a paperback sale to another publisher, and from that he would of course get a second commission when we accounted to him.

Hoffman had the whip hand and he knew it. I tried to put him off for the time being. Henry Miller had been reluctant to let Barney Rosset publish the *Tropics*, because he did not want a mass audience buying them 'just for the dirty bits' He had written them both in exuberance at having discovered the freedom of Paris after the restrictive climate of prohibition America, and he had never intended to write a pornographic novel. He explained in *Cancer* his philosophical view of the universe as well as chronicling the life he led in Paris, and always in a self-deprecating and humorous style. Money flowed through his fingers because he was not accustomed to having it. Lawyers and accountants in the U. S. were already robbing him. They had talked him into starting a company with his royalties, out of which they paid themselves salaries and expenses much greater than any tax that they said they were saving him. Now his agent was finding ways of getting additional money for himself to reduce Henry's future income as well as ours.

As it was obvious we would have to sell paperback rights, out of which we would keep half the royalties but see our hardcover sales stop, I approached another paperback firm, and got them to increase the offer.

Hoffman came back with an even higher one from the first company, which again I managed to get raised. Hoffman said enough was enough and agreed, but insisted that I still owed him ten percent on the highest offer he had brought. We paid it.

Now we had to deal with Barney Rosset. A week after publication he had sent back the signed contract, which I refused to accept. I had given him an ultimatum which he had ignored. He instructed Oscar Beuselinck, whom I knew from previous negotiation and who at the time was Harold Pinter's agent as well as being a solicitor, to sue me. Beuselinck wrote me and I made an appointment to see him, bringing all my correspondence. He admitted frankly that Barney had not a leg to stand on, and that he had advised him not to sue. But it was an amusing meeting. Beuselinck kept me for more than an hour, talking about books and about our shared interest in music, especially opera. The Mozart operas, so he claimed, he knew well enough to conduct, well... if not exactly to conduct, he knew at least what was coming next. He talked about his legal practice, especially his divorce work. Many husbands he told me, were unhappy in their marriages because the wives were too sexually conventional. Many a divorce came about because wives refused to be sodomised. So passed the hour. Barney was furious that he could not sue me and decided to break off all relationships: no friendship, no co-operation, no shared translations. He would not let me take on his authors or buy any of mine. So started a war that would continue for more than a decade.

We started publishing William Burroughs. André Deutsch had shown an interest after the publicity he had received in Edinburgh, where he had felt obliged to be present as so many of his authors, Norman Mailer in particular, were there. But I had talks with Bill, and he decided he would rather be with me, the man who had brought him to the festival, which had made his name known internationally. But the novels were as extreme as they could be at a time when things were loosening up, but not all that fast, and not where frankly descriptive homosexuality and sadism were concerned. Practising homosexuals could still be prosecuted under the law until 1967 when Leo Abse brought in a Sexual Discrimination Bill as one of the many social reforms that made Britain a more tolerant society during the sixties. But in 1963 the prejudices of judges and juries were if anything greater than that of the population as a whole. He was a dangerous author to publish, but after several discussions Bill and I worked out a fusion of the three novels that had been published by Olympia: *The Naked Lunch*, *The Soft Machine* and *The Ticket that Exploded*; we called the new text that emerged from taking chunks out of all three, *Dead Fingers Talk*. What was removed were the orgies, the sadistic hangings, even many heterosexual sex scenes. But the black satirical humour was still there, as was the biting portrayal of American racialist attitudes in such episodes as *The County Clerk* in the first of the three, and we included non-sexual scenes from homosexual life and the whole culture of the drug scene in America, then very different from the more enlightened and humane British one, which was soon to change for the worse. Even without the sex scenes it still made a vivid and frightening novel, bringing out all Burroughs' paranoia about dark forces, some from outside the planet, working towards control of our lives and our minds. We published it towards the end of 1963.

The circumstance that made the book sell, and which totally diminished any prospect of an obscenity case being brought against Burroughs and ourselves, both for *Dead Fingers Talk*, and for the novels that followed it during the next few years, was a long attacking review in The Times Literary Supplement. Like all TLS reviews it was anonymous, but we later learned that it had been written by John Willett, a deputy editor, and the leading British authority on Brecht. Entitled UGH it ran for a full page and was less a review of the book in question than a condemnation of all of Burroughs' work. The reviewer had taken the trouble to buy and read Girodias' 'Travellers Companion' editions of the three novels that had been digested for our carefully selected volume of extracts. He attacked the style, the syntax and the language, but above all the subject matter. Here are a few extracts:

> Struggling upstream through it (*The Naked Lunch*) is not unlike wading through the drains of a big city. The first shock effects are strong as the rash reader plunges in, then a steady nausea follows which hangs around him long after he has fought his way into the fresh air, finally boredom with the endless monotony as he tries to pick up his stinking feet and skip....On and on it flows, lapping slowly around what soon becomes a stereotyped debris; ectoplasm, jelly, errand boys, ferris wheels, used contraceptives, centipedes, old photographs, jockstraps, turnstiles, newts and pubic hairs...
>
> Such is the texture of the grey porridge in which Mr. Burroughs specialises...Three brimming books...Now the author has fished out an assortment of lumps...stirring the mixture and topping it up to make a fourth, slightly more hygienic bucketful which can be cast before us swine.
>
> Glug glug. It tastes disgusting, even without the detailed but always callous homosexual scenes and the unspeakable homosexual fantasies – pure verbal masturbation...

The review goes on and on, printing extracts to underline the reviewer's points, always expressing disgust and ends with the following comment:

> If the publishers had deliberately set out to discredit the cause of literary freedom and innovation they could hardly have done it more effectively. Let us hope that they are left to appreciate the probable impact on their own reputation, and indirectly on that of the other authors on their list, without any interfering body

turning them into martyrs. Any juryman can vomit, but only one
verdict can clear up the mess: that of the book world itself.

The review appeared on November 14. The following week the TLS printed
my reply, nearly as long. I objected to the attack on me as a publisher, but
defended the book, pointing out that Burroughs could be viewed as a
visionary and a moralist, who detested nasty things in society that we have
cause to fear, and might avoid if we knew about them. I also pointed to his
originality, humour and satirical talents. The same issue carried another
letter from Michael Moorcock, which called the review 'pompously
subjective, thoroughly distasteful and inaccurate'. He also defended
Burroughs on literary, scientific and moral grounds. Apart from his own
novels, Moorcock edited New Worlds, the most distinguished science fiction
journal of the time.

Then came the deluge. For thirteen weeks the correspondence grew in
volume. More and more pages were devoted to it every week, much of it was
reported in other newspapers, and the circulation of the TLS grew
considerably as ever more people wanted to follow the attacks,
counterattacks and arguments that were put forward. The anonymous
reviewer came back several times and he never retracted, but increasingly he
was on the defensive as Burroughs' fans and supporters came forward, both
in numbers and in the force of what they had to say. Eric Mottram, then
lecturer in American literature at King's College, emphasised Burroughs'
seriousness and importance, Kenneth Pitchford, an American, describing the
original review as 'a hysterical scream', stated that Burroughs might well be
one of the most important living writers, but even if he were not, he
deserved to be seriously reviewed, given that serious critics took him
seriously. Anthony Burgess came in late, pointed out that many things in life
are revolting and he was revolted by some of his own subject matter, as in
The Clockwork Orange, but the function of fiction was to describe the
unpleasant as well as the pleasant. He referred to William Burroughs himself
as 'that courteous, hospitable, erudite, gifted and dedicated writer'. Many
publishers wrote in, notably Victor Gollancz, Robert Lusty and Roger
Strauss. My duel with Mr. Gollancz in the course of the correspondence was
almost as extensive as my duel with John Willett (the anonymous reviewer). I
treated Gollancz with courtesy and respect, suggesting that our differences,
for we shared many causes and had taken part in the same campaigns, was a
generational one. I also assumed he had not read Burroughs. Back came Mr.
Gollancz: 'Mr. Calder, in the pride of his shining youth, must not accuse
even a palsied old man of commenting on what he hasn't read. I choked
down The Naked Lunch in America last spring, in spite of almost intolerable
nausea.'

One correspondent who had not read the book she was attacking was
Edith Sitwell. Her letter deserves to be quoted in full:

Sir - I was delighted to see, in your issue of the 14th instant, the very right-minded review of a novel by a Mr. Burroughs (whoever he may be) published by a Mr. John Calder (whoever he may be).

The public canonisation of that insignificant, dirty little book *Lady Chatterley's Lover* was a signal to persons who wish to unload the filth in their minds on the British public.

As the author of *Gold Coast Customs* I can scarcely be accused of shirking reality, but I do not wish to spend the rest of my life with my nose nailed to other people's lavatories.

I prefer Chanel Number 5.

Much of the correspondence dealt with censorship issues in general, rather than with the book under consideration, and many red herrings were also aired. On 26th December I received a surprising Christmas present from Harold Hobson in the correspondence, not about the book, but about me, as some of the letters had previously abused me in several ways. Hobson's warming tribute ended as follows: 'I have known Mr. Calder for several years; there are few among my professional acquaintances about whose character I have formed such definite opinions. Mr. Calder is a man of absolute integrity. His catholic and adventurous taste in literature has led him to publish some of the decisive books of our times. His courage is unshakeable: nothing will move him from what he thinks to be right. I would put a child in his care, and my bank account in his keeping.'

The final editorial came on 30th January 1964, and it was obviously written by the editor himself to close the correspondence. It summed up the arguments, drew no final conclusions and was moderate in tone. From my point of view, the correspondence had cleared the air, established the author's reputation in Britain and made it impossible in practical terms for any prosecution to be brought. We followed *Dead Fingers Talk* with *The Naked Lunch* later in 1964 and continued with the other novels. There was one we could not bring out in Britain, because Grove Press bought world rights and sold it to Jonathan Cape out of spite over our Henry Miller quarrel. It was *Nova Express*. Burroughs did not like this any more than I did, but there was nothing he could do.

Burroughs had by now moved from Paris to London. He found a flat in James Street, off Piccadilly, where he soon had a new entourage that included Michael Portman, Anthony Balch, Ian Sommerville and one or two others. I did not see him often, but sometimes arranged to sit down with him to clean up a manuscript before publication, a job that bored him. He was only interested in what he was writing that day, not in anything he had done in the past, even a week earlier.

* * * * * *

I have recorded briefly the Aldermaston march in which I took part in 1959. I did it again in 1960, but this time it was rather more like a planned party. Roy Jones, badly crippled, but hungry for new experience and excitement, wanted to come along, so we pushed him in a wheelchair. Bettina was along for part of the time, Reggy Smith (R. D. Smith, drama producer of BBC radio) was with us for much of it, pushing the wheelchair and chatting to Roy, and we had Reggy's wife, the novelist Olivia Manning, and others from their circle. There was always a crowd of actors, BBC personnel and young girls surrounding Reggy, a popular, effusive, clubbable personality, and a mainstay of the many pubs around the BBC in Langham Place. I ran into Michael Hemans, the surgeon who had operated on Christya to deliver my first child, who died, who was in a caravan with a young crowd, a mixture of *jeunesse dorée* and political friends. I realised for the first time that Hemans was a Communist, although a Champagne one. There was much champagne in his caravan, which operated as a slowly moving bar. I think Marion Lobbenberg was there for at least part of a day. One interesting sight was seeing Tom Maschler of Jonathan Cape driving up to the middle of the march and parking his conspicuous car behind a pub as we camped by the road with our picnic lunches at about one o'clock. A minute later he came out from behind the pub, casually dressed, walked around the groups who were eating their lunch, nodding to some, speaking to others, and then, when the march resumed, walking casually back to the pub. A few minutes later I saw his car whizzing past us on the road back to London. It was trendy to be on the march, but Tom was not one for the effort involved. It was at about this time that he wrote, together with Frederick Raphael, a book called *The Success Man*, which Cape published under a pseudonym. It was a guide to becoming a superficial success, being noticed, conning girls into bed with various techniques, and how to be a fashionable person with no need to have talent or do real work. The book was as shallow as its authors.

I cannot be absolutely sure that the march I have just mentioned took place in 1960. It may have been in 1961. By then CND, the highly successful campaign to get out of the nuclear arms race had enormous support and it was tearing the Labour Party in two. But the campaign, in the opinion of many, was too tame to be really effective and a splinter group was breaking off as Canon Collins and Bertrand Russell differed on policy. Lord Russell then formed the Committee of 100, dedicated to civil disorder along Gandhian lines. The reason to limit the campaign to one hundred celebrated people was that the authorities were always reluctant to arrest people who were well-known and would attract publicity. I joined the Committee, although I was not one of the first hundred members of it. In any case it soon became a movement of several thousand. There was to be a big rally in Trafalgar Square on September 17, and this was definitely in 1961.

One evening I received a 'phone call just as I was leaving the office. The big demonstration had just been banned by the police. The organising secretary had to get a leaflet out to all the mailing list overnight. It had to be stuffed into envelopes, addressed and posted instantly. The purpose was to urge our supporters to defy the ban, to come anyway, and risk arrest. The volunteers were ready, but they had no premises; could they come to my flat, which they had been told was big enough? I said yes, and arrived home just as they began to arrive. They brought trestle tables, chairs, boxes of leaflets which had just been printed and envelopes. The trouble was that Bettina and I had tickets to the theatre that night. Feeling guilty, I left them all – there must have been about thirty – and returned to find the flat a hive of industry. There could be no question of going to bed, so we joined the workers. Then from about three o'clock, three of us in different cars began to circulate around different London post-offices, pushing hundreds of envelopes through the letter boxes. The reason for the dispersal was to attract as little attention as possible. If tens of thousands had been delivered to the All-Night Post Office in central London on even the next day, it would have excited comment and they would have been seized because they summoned supporters to an illegal gathering.

On the big day, a Sunday, there was a lunch party at my flat with Tondi Barr, a friend who ran the catering at the Tate Gallery, Lucy and Roy Jones, Marion Boyars and perhaps one or two others. Then we walked to Trafalgar Square, which was already teeming with people. There were police vans and policemen everywhere, but they had stopped trying to prevent people entering the square. On the steps of the National Gallery, waiting to be arrested, was Lord Russell, surrounded by prominent members of the committee, mostly playwrights, artists and political figures. I was soon separated from my companions in the south-east corner, near Nelson's column, and everyone around me started to sit down and hug their knees. I did the same and a few minutes later was picked up and thrown into a police van. From there I was taken to Bow Street Police Station and pushed into a cell with about a hundred others. More kept arriving and we were all standing and crushed. Then we were taken out again and deposited in another police station in Hampstead and two hours after that, when it was too full, to yet another, somewhere near Barnet in the outer suburbs.

I finally spent the night with one companion in a small cell. He was a young Air Force man, not yet twenty, on leave, who had felt compelled to take part.

Late the next morning another police van took us to Bow Street Magistrates Court where we had a long wait before we were in front of the magistrate. I think about thirty thousand had taken part in the demonstration and some thousands had been arrested. When I finally arrived in the dock, there were about ten of us in line and I was the first. The Air Force man was next to me and beyond him were John Osborne, Robert Bolt, Arnold Wesker, John Arden and others. 'How do you plead?' I was asked.

'Guilty of necessity' I replied and went on to give my reasons. I was listened to for about a minute and then stopped. 'How do you plead?' the Air Force man was asked. 'Guilty of necessity,' he replied. The same answer was given by each of the others, and no further comment was allowed. We were each fined, I think £50, and released. The hearings went on all day in that and many other London courts simultaneously.

The ring leaders, including of course Russell, were all given several months in prison. To send a world-renowned 89-year old philosopher to prison on a matter of conscience was highly newsworthy, and liberal opinion everywhere was outraged, giving extra strength to the Committee of 100, which by now had put CND in the shade. I was remain an activist from then on.

Two of the others from the lunch party had been arrested, Bettina and Tondi Barr. They were in adjoining cells in Greenwich, where Tondi had rung every few minutes for assistance and then asked them to send out for champagne: she was dying of thirst! They both appeared in front of a magistrate in Woolwich who Tondi knew well, and no one could stop Tondi when she wanted to speak her mind. Both the police station and the court must have been pleased when they let her go.

One of the active directors of the Committee of 100 was Pat Pottle, a radical printer, who had escaped arrest, but was wanted by the police. I put him up in my flat for about three weeks. There was a false ceiling with an attic above it, and there was a ladder always ready that he could pull up after himself if the police ever came looking, but they never did. Pat found other places to hide and I had secret meetings with him during the next few months. He was to hit the headlines years later when he was charged with helping George Blake, a spy for the Russians who was probably a double agent and about whom there is still much secrecy and controversy to escape. Pat was acquitted after giving a brilliant speech in his own defence, which I only read in his obituary in 2000.

David Mercer, my author, was deeply involved in all this, and he had been commissioned to write a television play for the BBC about civil disobedience. This rather hampered his political activity because he did not dare get arrested. At a big demonstration at the RAF Wethersfield Air Base outside London, I took part in a big sit-down, blocking the entrances, which went on for all of a long day and into the night. I was sitting beside David's wife, Dilys, and on the other side of me was a ship's doctor in a duffel coat. I had gone in a warm town overcoat and proper suit, believing it a good way to give a more favourable image of the demonstration but I was cold and wet as it rained sporadically. Every half hour we could see David Mercer driving anxiously by and peering over at us. We were kicked by irritable RAF officers trying to get through, and at one point Ludovic Kennedy, then a BBC reporter, stuck a microphone under my nose and asked me why I was doing this. When I began to tell him and he heard my accent, he pulled the microphone away and asked the ship's doctor who also began to give him an articulate answer. Again he pulled away the microphone and found a young working-class boy who no doubt gave him the answer that he wanted, that it was all a bit of a lark.

David Mercer finished his play, *A Climate of Fear*, and we later published it as part of a trilogy of documentary dramas in a volume entitled *The Generations* in 1964. It was a success on television, although the BBC were much criticised by the right-wing press for commissioning and airing it. David Mercer is really the father of documentary television drama. We were to publish many more of his plays, although at one point we lost him to Methuen. He was a strange mixed-up character, full of guilt at not having stayed true to his father's vision of a socialist society with working-class values. With fame, came middle-class living standards and attitudes, and he coined the phrase 'Hampstead Man' to describe himself and others like him. Interestingly his brother became a nuclear scientist and was knighted for it.

My cell-mate, the Air Force man, had been arrested outside the court by the RAF as we came out and he was sentenced to an open prison. I corresponded with him and went to visit him once. He was quite miserable. Some time later he wrote me and asked me to send no more letters and I lost touch.

* * * * *

I cannot exactly place the date when Beckett and Burroughs first met. There were only two such occasions and I was present on both. The first was after a Frankfurt Book Fair, probably 1963, when Girodias, who must have been in reasonable funds at the time, gave a large dinner in his restaurant for about twenty people at a long refectory table, in the basement of his building where at one point he also had a theatre. At one end of the table were two *métisse* girls, both bed-partners of Maurice, sitting with him and Barney Rosset was at the same end. In between were other authors of Olympia, talking about their own interests, and at the bottom were Beckett, Burroughs and myself. The table was conversationally split in three and there was little contact between the three sections. Barney was interested in the girls – they were not the only ones there – and in their relationship to their host, scenting something kinky. I was next to Burroughs with Sam across the table.

Conversation started slowly. Then Beckett suddenly leaned across the table towards Burroughs and said, 'Tell me, Mr. Burroughs, about this cut-up method of yours. I don't think I quite understand what you do.'

'Waal, Mr. Beckett,' drawled Burroughs, in a voice that sometimes sounded southern, and at other times Harvard, 'what I do is this. I take a copy of the New York Times or some other paper and I cut a column in half, or sometimes I fold it. Then I find another text, perhaps of mine, or perhaps a page of your *Molloy* and I do the same thing.' Beckett was listening in rapt concentration. He opened his mouth to speak and then closed it again.

'Then,' continued Bill, 'I read across the lines of the two and copy out what I see, so that each new line has half of one text and half of the other. Later I edit the new version until a whole new text emerges. Then depending on how it looks, I may cut that up into a third text. And of course I add a word or two where it's necessary.'

Beckett could contain himself no longer. 'But you can't do that,' he said.

'Oh, I do, Mr. Beckett, I assure you,' said Burroughs in an even voice. Beckett was getting more excited.

'But you can't. You can't take other people's work like that.'

'Oh, I can. I've been doing it for years.'

Both were drinking red wine, a good one, because Girodias had an excellent cellar. They drank faster and faster as they argued, eating little. Both were small eaters at the best of times. The rest of the table ignored them, but I sat fascinated and never intervened. As they drank the words became wilder, Beckett protesting in an ever stronger language, Burroughs explaining that words had to be set free whoever wrote them, and once free they had an independent life and were able to create magic and change the course of human events. He too used stronger language as time passed. They reached the stage of total drunkenness at exactly the same time. We were sitting along the long refectory table, I think on bench seating. Both men were suddenly unable to keep their elbows on the table and began to slide under it and there was nothing I could do to stop them.

Then the table came to life. One waiter picked up Burroughs and others helped me to get Beckett on his feet. Taxis were called. I am not sure who took Burroughs back to his little hotel on the Rue Git-le-Coeur, but I took Beckett to the Boulevard St. Jacques, got him in the door and somehow into his flat.

* * * * * *

During 1963 I was preparing my second Edinburgh conference. At my meeting with Harewood after the first one, he had agreed Drama as a theme. Now I was thinking of mixing playwrights with other theatre professionals, with directors and actors in particular. It would be easy to get well-known names and faces and that would draw the crowd, although I now had little worry about that. The theatre itself was changing: new names were becoming known from Europe as well as Britain and America, new styles were emerging and a new intellectualism was in the air. The clash of ideas could make a drama festival riveting-listening for the public, which needed an education in modern drama as much as it needed it for the current novel.

I also told Harewood that I would like to make suggestions for his next year's drama programme. Harewood more or less gave me carte blanche for the conference and would listen carefully to my other suggestions.

I did not ask Sonia to help me again. Her growing alcoholism had often been an embarrassment and she had done little practical other than helping me to recruit some of the big names, nearly all of them people she had met during her time as fiction editor: Mary McCarthy and Norman Mailer had been a direct result of her foraging trips to New York for Weidenfeld and Nicolson. Angus Wilson and other British authors she knew largely from her days with Cyril Connolly and Stephen Spender at Horizon. On the other hand Jim Haynes had been a splendid helper. He had found big and comfortable homes for the stars, more modest ones for the lesser known, had housed Burroughs and Trocchi with Andrew Boddy, a tolerant young Edinburgh doctor who could give them their necessary prescriptions, and investigated boarding houses and small hotels for others who were not being housed by the British council or their national embassies. He had also found willing hosts to give parties every night. He had kept a bookstall going throughout the conference at McEwan Hall with relevant titles and had mounted with my help a display of 'Censored Books' for the day on that subject. This was raided by the police on a tip-off, which a year or so later I learned had come from the Lord Provost's secretary, a Mr. Murdoch. The police went away when they discovered that it was a historical display of 'Censored', not banned books, and in any case the books were not for sale. I asked Jim to be my deputy with the title of Edinburgh Organiser, and he immediately accepted.

During that year Jim became involved in a new activity in Edinburgh, in which I was also later to play a minor role. He had previously had readings in his bookshop, and this had led to him backing a kind of cabaret night-club called The Howf. This failed because the folk singer Roy Guest, who was running it, absconded with all the box office receipts just at it was beginning to do well, but undaunted, Jim persuaded a local entrepreneur, Tom Mitchell, let him use an old doss house called Kelly's Paradise on the Lawnmarket, just below the castle, for a nominal rent. This became the Traverse Theatre, so-called because the stage was between the two banks of seats that could take a maximum of 55 spectators. The theatre itself was the brainchild of its first artistic director, George Malcolm, but he left before the refurbishment was completed, being replaced by Terry Lane, whose girlfriend Rosalind was cast in every production during his time there. After it had been established for a while, which must have been the end of 1963, I was asked to join the board. This consisted of a mix of establishment figures like Lord Cameron, a judge, and Andrew Elliott, an accountant, and various local literati and art-lovers. There was a scandal on the second night when, at the end of Sartre's *No Exit*, Rosalind accidentally knifed Colette O'Neill, another actress, who just managed to get through the last minute of the play before collapsing. The members of the board present were in a panic. 'How can we hush this up?' they wailed. 'Nonsense,' I said. 'Tell the press instantly. We need the publicity!' And the publicity helped. Colette was back after missing a performance. I shall return to the Traverse Theatre later.

Early in the year I invited Harewood to lunch again to discuss progress, but above all to get his ideas on who should be the conference chairman. I had a list of names, but when I came to Kenneth Tynan, Harewood let me go no further. 'That's the man we want,' he said. He was certainly not my first choice, but Harewood was not interested in other names. When I contacted him, Tynan enthusiastically agreed, and he quickly had his own ideas on how to run the conference. To me it was a way of educating the public, who were in any case paying for the privilege. To Tynan it was a get-together of theatre people, and he was interested in having private as well as public sessions. We started to work out a list of names to supplement those I had already approached. Many on Tynan's list had little to do with the theatre, but were cronies from Hollywood or New York to whom he owed a favour, Jack Garfein, for example, a director of Hollywood 'B' films. He was however married to Carroll Baker, who had just had a success in the film *Baby Doll*; she would add decoration to the conference at least. Many British and American playwrights were on the list, and some French and German – this time I was determined to get Robbe-Grillet to come, as well as the new school of French playwrights – and leading directors and actors. Berry Bloomfield was busy sending out letters and so was Rozena Adler, Ken's secretary, a well-turned out, very self-conscious lady, rather haughtily aware of her status in working for a top drama critic who made it his business to be the trendiest figure in trendy London, wearing lilac suits and taking care to be noticed in the best restaurants and night places.

I was also now a laird at Ledlanet. I had much to do there. My uncle had, in his will, allowed all the farmers to buy their farms at a very favourable price, except for the home farm, which was let to a local farmer called James Provan and there was also another small one, some distance away, which was run by a manager. The farmers all took advantage of their opportunity, so that the estate was effectively reduced to half, but I still had shooting rights over these other farms and a first option to repurchase. I was still a large landowner.

My uncle's will was an old one. Reginald Attewell, the butler, who had been with my uncle all his life, was left enough to buy his own house. Unfortunately the bank, which administered the will, had never kept up with changes in the tax laws, and, because of their negligence, a large amount of inheritance tax had to be paid on the money. I agreed that this tax should be paid out of the estate. There were many other complications. Marjory Manners, who had acted as companion to my uncle for a number of years and was now past forty, was naturally bitter. She had ruined her marriage prospects as things were seen in those days and had not been rewarded as she expected. I had once asked my uncle about her future and he had told me that she would probably go to a nunnery. I had not deduced from this that I was to be his heir, although the possibility was always there. She cleared all the silver out of the house, so I had at least to look for cutlery and went to an auction in Perth just before Christmas in 1962, which was probably a date inconvenient to dealers, because for £100 I was able to buy a complete service of Victorian silver, probably at ten percent of its value.

I began to use the house from that autumn, dealing with estate affairs as best I could and enjoying the house, its amenities, its wonderful views, its walks through the woods and the hills and its leisure opportunities. It was a particularly fine autumn. I brought up some of my library from London, but most importantly put together for the first time a collection of all, or nearly all, the books I had published. What was previously the drawing room, unused for years, became a library and study. The room that had had the greatest use, the morning room, where my uncle had sat to read, talk or write letters, usually with Marjory present, remained what it had always been, the centre of things most of the time. A large billiard room, where the tiled floor had since the war been used for drying apples, became the new drawing room. There was already a piano here, a boudoir-grand sized Bechstein, which my great-aunt Mildred had played, which I now had tuned, and it was used again. There was a wall of books in the morning room, mainly the best-sellers of the previous twenty years, some of them gifts, and those that had been sent by various book clubs to which my uncle had subscribed. The dining room, between the morning room and the new drawing room, was a handsome oak-panelled room with two traditional Scottish academic paintings of grouse flying over the Highlands hanging over the sideboard, and the windows had a spectacular view over the valley towards the Cleish Hills. You could seat twenty around the table, which could expand with extra leaves or contract for an intimate gathering. I loved that room.

There was also a small conservatory just off the new library; all these rooms were in a line along the front of the house, with the entrance hall under a square tower in the middle: this opened into the large main hall.

On the east side, behind the library was a gun-room, which also had locked bookcases filled with older leather-bound books, and behind that lay a long corridor which gave onto the kitchen, pantries, servants' hall and a variety of different rooms where things were kept, washed or cleaned. There was a special larder to hang game and meat and to dry fish. Above this corridor was another, reached by the back stairs, off which were the seven bedrooms not on the front, while the three servants' bedrooms were all behind a green-baize door on the west-side. A staircase next to the master bedroom led up to a small room in the tower, which was over the front door. Although it was the smallest bedroom, it had the best view. I have already given some idea of the main hall around which everything was clustered. The staircase divided after a few steps and went to each side of the balconies overlooking the hall. There was much old comfortable furniture in the hall, a large fireplace, never used, and large paintings, not very good ones, of my great-uncle and great-aunt, hung among many other paintings that they had acquired. Above the large expanse of wall over the doorways on the south side of the hall was an enormous copy of a famous Velasquez, which at a much later date was to be claimed to be by the master, but this was soon disproved.

I have lived in many places, but Ledlanet, which I occupied from 1962 to 1976, was the only one I really loved. I began to spend more time there, especially on weekends, bringing editorial work with me. It was a long drive from London, 430 miles, but I drove it often in the days before motorways shortened the journey, and I also frequently took the train and flew. British European Airways (BEA) had early-morning and late-night flights for two guineas and in daytime it was not much more. Friends from Edinburgh and Glasgow came to visit me and I began to meet the locals. I was invited to dinner parties and to go shooting, and I myself had the best shooting in the district, although I was too busy to take much advantage. There was a large trout loch about five minutes walk from the house, one of my uncle's greatest pleasures, but fishing, which I could do adequately, always bored me, and I cannot remember fishing after I inherited the house except perhaps once or twice with visitors.

In addition to Attewell, I had inherited a cook and a cleaning maid, two gamekeepers (one doubling as a chauffeur), a gardener and a farm manager. One of the gamekeepers, I am sure, had taken my great-uncle's very valuable Purdy shot-gun, which disappeared after his death. I soon suspected him of other misdemeanours and a year or so later, dismissed him.

Bettina began to make changes at Ledlanet. She got rid of the large stags' heads which dominated the hall between the paintings, had some large Jacobean tables cut in half and one antique round table lowered to become a coffee-table in the drawing-room, crimes I should have prevented, and she began to direct the servants as if she had been doing it all her life. Backstairs they soon began to call her, certainly invented by Attewell, 'The Duchess'. My mother had inherited some furniture from her father's house in Montreal, and having sold her own house there, now had furniture in storage. I received, and now had room for, the Louis XVI suite of tapestried chairs and sofa from my Canadian grandfather's house, reproductions, but very impressive just the same. They added lustre to the drawing room, which soon also featured two large modern abstract paintings, one blue and one black, by Charles Pulsford, a Scottish expressionist painter who was the great guru teaching at the time at the art college in Edinburgh. I came to know Pulsford through some of his ex-students, painters who lived near me in

Fife. When he later moved to teach at Loughborough, he occasionally invited me to give lectures on modern literature to his class.

It must have been towards the end of 1962 that we had a house-party. The principal guests were Roy and Lucy Jones, the music publisher Bill Colleran, then London manager of Universal Edition of Vienna, who had been a friend for some time, and a lady who worked for Roy, but who was married to a violinist, called Rosemary Reuben. Bettina had brought an American pianist, Tom Gligoroff, who accompanied some of her recitals and was about to become repetiteur to London opera houses. The others had arrived the day before and Rosemary and I were to follow on the Saturday morning by 'plane. Rosemary came to the opera with me the night before (I think it was *Die Walküre*), which had such an effect on us that she stayed the night with me, following that experience by joining the mile-high club the next morning on the 'plane, partly from lust, but as much for the challenge.

That evening at Ledlanet, after dinner, Tom Gligoroff, after a few words of introduction, played one of the Schubert posthumous piano sonatas. He played very beautifully and his small audience, comfortable after a good dinner, was rapt with concentration; it was a half hour of pure magic. Roy Jones looked as if it were the happiest moment of his life. The whole weekend was a success. Bill tried hard to seduce Rosemary, and perhaps he did, but she certainly seduced me the next day when we went for a walk up the snowy hillside into the heather line and found a convenient hollow in the ground.

I had the whole family there at Christmas. There were some excellent wines in the cellar and much vintage port. I had begun to restock it with the help of my friend Jacques Chaix. I asked him to buy several cases for me every time he bought wines for himself or his relatives, and soon I had excellent reds and whites to lay down in the cellar. I found one bottle of 1812 Cognac there, bought at some long-past French hotel sale. I opened it on Christmas day and we all had a little. I put it away, and on New Year's Day we all had a little more. Then I put it away again to await the next Christmas. I could not have been more stupid. The following year it was vinegar. We should have drunk it all when it was opened. But I still remember the delicate fragrance of a brandy that had almost no alcoholic content left but which lay as softly as velvet on the tongue.

The Writers' Conference had made me a celebrity in Edinburgh, in spite of my backroom role, but The Scotsman, thanks largely to its key features writer Magnus Magnusson, now a friend, and its literary editor Bill Watson, even more of one, constantly featured my name. As a result, I was invited to address Rotary Clubs, Farmer's Unions and ladies' groups, all of which was good for spreading the names of the authors I was publishing, which sold books, and I hoped, for assuring audiences for the next conference. But I was also involved in a number of issues. I was still active in the Committee of 100, and for some time I had been asked to campaign for other causes. Anthony Gray, whom I knew at the time, although I cannot remember how I met him, asked me to help his work at the Albany Trust, which was pressuring the government to have homosexuality decriminalised. The law as it stood, where any homosexual activity at any age could lead to prosecution and imprisonment, was not only blatantly unjust and based on biblical and puritanical dogma and much hypocrisy, but it provided a wonderful opportunity for blackmailers. Anthony Gray ran the Homosexual Law Reform Society and the Albany Trust, which between them were trying to educate the public towards tolerance as a first step to changing the law. In the late fifties public opinion, according to the polls, was overwhelmingly against such a change, but the climate was gradually becoming more liberal as the many radical causes of the day attracted more supporters. The working-class, usually very conservative where moral matters were concerned, now had its own educated intellectuals thanks to the post-war Education Act, and they could influence others. I was persuaded to go on the Rotary circuit and soon found myself addressing Rotarians at their weekly lunches. The formula there never varied and was very strict. You met at 12.45, had a drink, sat down to lunch at 1.00, and the talk came punctually at 1.40. You had twenty minutes, and no more, to say what you had to say.

When talking on behalf of the Homosexual Law Reform Society, or for any other topic for which I was invited to speak, I would divide my twenty minutes into three parts. For the first five minutes I praised my listeners for being men of the world, pillars of the community, above petty prejudices, in short I told them they were tolerant and civilised human beings. Then for seven minutes (if homosexuality was the subject), I put them through hell while they looked at their shoes through the table. I reminded them that there must have been moments in their adolescence when some act took place with another boy or at least the temptation was there. But we all, unless nature has decided otherwise, grow out of that, I went on. In my concluding eight minutes I had to build up their self-esteem again. They were big enough to understand such things, and as leaders of the community they had an opportunity and an obligation to change public opinion. Some people were homosexual by nature and nothing could change that. What they did in private was their own concern, and no danger to others, just as what normal people did in private did not concern others either. I can remember no occasion out of the forty or so such lunches that I attended over the years when I did not get applause and congratulations 'for my courage' as they often put it, in the way I explained what was wrong with the law and in speaking out on such a delicate subject. I was, of course, only one of many speakers doing the same thing. I also campaigned against capital punishment and against censorship, as well as on many purely political subjects. It did me no harm as a publisher because I was frequently referring to books, which brought custom to booksellers and to me.

There was a little opera company called Kent Opera, run by two singing teachers, Audrey Langford and her husband Andrew Field, to whom Bettina was going for coaching. Ande Anderson, who at the time was the resident producer at Covent Garden, worked with them occasionally and I came to know the whole group, who occasionally used well-known singers in their productions. One day I had the idea, which must have come from the successful evening mentioned above, of having the group perform at Ledlanet. We planned a small festival to take place over two weekends in October that year, some weeks after the end of the Drama Conference. I think the impulse came largely from my not quite knowing what to do with Ledlanet. It cried out to be used and I always had the soul of an impresario inside me. But that first year I left the programming to Audrey Langford and Ande Anderson.

* * * * * *

The Censorship debate at Edinburgh and my various brushes with both political and moral censors in Britain and elsewhere had given me the reputation of a crusader against state interference in what people could read, know or do. I now received an urgent request from Carlos Barral to be present in Barcelona at the International Publishers Association Conference which was to take place there that May. Carlos Barral was one of the partners in Seix y Barral, a literary publisher with a list fairly similar to my own, but his main interest was in undermining the Franco dictatorship, which was heavily restrictive where civil liberties and any political opposition was concerned. It was also heavily moralistic, tolerating only the traditional family values. Barral had been the leading figure in setting up the Prix Formentor.

Formentor was a small island with luxury hotels in the Mediterranean off the Spanish coast, and Barral's initiative had been to found a literary prize to be judged and given there every year by an international jury of well-known writers, brought together and financed by their publishers. This year, 1963, had just seen the second Prix Formentor. Barral had persuaded Gallimard from France, Barney Rosset's Grove Press from America, Rowohlt from Germany, Einaudi from Italy, Weidenfeld and Nicolson from Britain, and publishers from other European countries, to become members of the ring that presented the prize. But once they had met they decided there should be two prizes, the *Prix des Editeurs*, which would go to an established writer whose international reputation was less than it should be (rather like the Nobel Prize for Literature), and the *Prix Formentor*, which would crown a manuscript from the ones submitted by the publishers in the group. In both cases it was the jury of writers that made the choice, but as those writers were all there because of the publishers who had brought them, those who paid the piper also expected to be calling the tune. It soon became evident that the writers who were best read and had dominating personalities would ultimately prevail. Each publisher brought about half a dozen writers to Formentor with him, and most of them were naturally chosen from their own stables. Alberto Moravia, brought by Einaudi, turned out to be the most forceful, chairing the jury. Grove Press brought Mary McCarthy in their group, and she argued strongly for William Burroughs, whom she had of course met a few months before at my Edinburgh conference. But the jury, unable to chose the previous year between Samuel Beckett and Jorge Luis Borges, had then finally divided the prize between them. As Borges was not published in Britain at the time, Weidenfeld had immediately bought him, but had little success when they published and eventually they resold *Ficciones*, his most important collection of short texts, to me for my paperback series, Jupiter Books. It appeared in the collection in 1965. The other prize went to Renata Rasp, a very attractive and trendy author. She too ended up on our list with her novel *Family Failure* which came out in a translation by Eva Figes in 1970 and her short novella, *The Walk to St. Heinrich*, being published in *New Writers* a few years later. The Formentor was an expensive luxury for a group of publishers who had little in common except liking a good time. One group, which included Barney Rosset, Einaudi, and of course Barral, were primarily interested in politics. Gallimard did not want to be left out of any grouping that might turn out to be important and the same could be said of Weidenfeld. Ledig Rowohlt was interested in publishing good literature, but a good party was what he liked most. There were only four Formentor meetings. But while they went on the lieutenants of the big publishers involved, busied themselves with meetings throughout the year, at Frankfurt, in Paris or New York, and I could not help but be envious until I realised what it was costing each of them. Soon Weidenfeld pulled out when he realised he was not getting saleable authors out of the prize and was paying much money for a dubious prestige.

The second Formentor Conference had taken place just before the International Publishers' meeting in Barcelona and I agreed to go to it. It would in any case increase my contacts for future literary conferences at the Edinburgh Festival, which at that point I assumed would be a permanent fixture in the future. The item on the agenda that ensured a bigger turnout than usual for such an event was a discussion on 'literature and the public powers of the state', which in essence was about censorship. The motion was that the state should be pressured to eliminate their power to control what was published.

I arrived with Bettina and we stayed at one of the better hotels where enormous steaks topped with truffles seemed to be the most popular dish, and I developed a liking for the rarer Spanish sherries. A large party was given by Carlos Barral at his luxurious villa on the beach, rather like the party in Antonioni's film *La Notte*, which was made about that time. It went on until dawn, was very uninhibited, and probably started more affairs than political discussions. At the hotel there were meetings of groups of publishers in suites and hotel rooms to discuss tactics and draft manifestos, and I was kept busy translating these between English, French and German. The waiters who came in and out with food and drink tended to linger and listen, and some were undoubtedly police spies.

The debate itself was lively and emotional with radical publishers from totalitarian countries sticking their necks out. Mr. Castro from Portugal told how he had spent twelve years in a concentration camp on a kind of Devil's Island, sent there by the Salazar regime as a dissident, and predicted that he would probably be arrested on his return for speaking out in the debate. Everyone had something to say, including myself and Robert Maxwell who, arriving in the middle of the debate, made a very hot speech in favour of the motion, and was heavily applauded, but not by me, knowing him for the hypocrite he was. The following day he was back, saying exactly the opposite to the general confusion of his listeners. He had been got at, probably by the Russians, with whom he was doing considerable business, and by others on the right of the spectrum, with whom he also had ties. But the motion was carried. At the final banquet a Minister from the government made a speech, deploring the debate and its outcome, talking of responsibilities and family values. For the first time in its history the International Commission of the International Publishers Association, representing the conference, was not allowed to call on the head of state, General Franco himself. Several people I met in Barcelona promised to come to Edinburgh in August.

That summer I was in Yugoslavia again and tried to see Miroslav Krleza, their most eminent playwright, but in spite of my contacts I was not even able to talk to him on the telephone, let alone see him. He was about seventy years old at the time and was not sure, as I was told, whether I was important enough for him to meet. His name might have become known outside Yugoslavia had he been less arrogant. On the way back I stopped in Rome for a day to see Max Frisch who had not answered any of my letters inviting him to the Drama Conference. I went to the address I had for him and was given another address. When I rang the doorbell, Frisch opened the door in casual clothes, with a paint brush in his hand. It was his first day in his new flat and with his new girlfriend Marianne, a Swiss girl who had moved in with him. He had only recently broken up with his previous partner Ingeborg Bachmann, one of the most original and sensitive German poets of the time, who was later to take her own life. She too would eventually be published in English in our *New Writing* series. But on the day I called on him Frisch was ecstatically happy and said that my calling on him on that particular day was a good omen. He had not intended to come, but now he would, but he must bring Marianne with him. I returned to the airport and took the next flight to London.

That summer a rather strange event occurred, which had an important consequence. It was Arthur Boyars' birthday and a group of us went to some other party and then back to Arthur's basement flat, which was three floors under my old one, now occupied by Lynette Perry. We were all in a good mood and in the party were Valerie Desmore, Tondi Barr, Marion Lobbenberg, the Kronhausens and myself. The Kronhausens have not yet been mentioned. They were two American psychoanalysts, who had already written a number of books about sex and they were totally absorbed by the subject. They had, a few weeks previously, shown me a pornographic film made in France by Jean Genet, based on his prison experiences, and had watched curiously to see my reactions, which were milder than they had expected and they were a little discomforted to see that my tastes ran to such, for them boring, subjects as music, drama and literature. They were exclusively interested in sex. They had recently met the famous Doctor Eustace Chesser, a gynaecologist whose liberal attitudes had occasionally led to his being called as a witness in obscenity trials. In one celebrated wartime one over his own book he had turned to the jury and asked it, 'If there is one man among you who has never masturbated, let him now stand up' and no-one did. Phyllis Kronhausen at their meeting had walked up to the eminent physician, opened his trousers and shaken his penis rather than his hand. Eberhard, her husband and co-practitioner, originally German, had had his balls crushed by the Gestapo during the war, which gave him great sexual problems, but he somehow managed to overcome them and in no way did this inhibit him. In short, Phyll and Ebe were a remarkable and notorious couple who at that point were trying to persuade me to publish their next book.

Back at Arthur's, supposedly just for a drink, the Kronhausens got to work. First they passed around joints, then began to take their clothes off and very soon, with little resistance, persuaded the rest of us to do the same, all except Marion, who watched with horrified fascination and sat on the sidelines watching what happened next. This was an orgy of everyone in the party on Arthur's double bed. At one point I found myself inside Phyllis, while Ebe was doing what he could to Tondi, but she suddenly cried out, 'No, I don't want you, I want him,' meaning me, and suddenly I was with a new partner, leaving Arthur with Phyllis. We enjoyed ourselves so much that after a little while Tondi and I disengaged ourselves from the other bodies and occupied a couch in the next room where Marion was still watching, not able to make up her mind whether to get involved or not. I eventually took Tondi home and spent the night with her, the beginning of an affair that went on for a year or two and developed into a close friendship. But that is not the point of the story.

The next day I had two tickets to Glyndebourne, and I took Arthur with me. In the car we discussed his birthday party and what the Kronhausens had turned it into. 'You know," said Arthur thoughtfully, "I think Marion rather fancies me.'

That was a surprise to me. I had assumed from what they said about each other that there was a mutual detestation between the commercially-minded Marion and the poetic Arthur. But he had been in good form during the orgy, potent and randy, and she had witnessed it. The opera was *Capriccio*, a perfect work for Glyndebourne with its eighteenth century décor, pre-revolutionary aristocratic elegance and neo-classical style, and it was the wonderful Elizabeth Söderström singing the Countess, wooed by Horst Wilhelm and Raymond Wolansky. It was also a perfect evening, the thirteenth of June, as my opera record book tells me.

I was to see *Capriccio* at Glyndebourne again in July the following year and this is perhaps a suitable place to record another incident of that same month, because on the occasion in question I had Samuel Beckett and Bettina with me and I would like here to counter the assertion made by some, who not liking opera themselves, have foisted their dislike onto Beckett. Beckett liked all serious music and went on a number of occasions to the opera with me and always enjoyed it. His problem was that he felt he should not enjoy it and there was always guilt mixed with his pleasure. He always said that he did not like Mozart, but the real reason was that music came too easily to that composer, whereas Haydn, whom he said he preferred, was a craftsman who had to make the daily effort to compose like every other craftsman. Beethoven also had to make that effort, hampered by ill health and deafness, therefore Beethoven was a favoured composer. Schubert, another favourite, found that music came easily, but against that there was his difficult and short life, and the overriding sadness of the works Sam liked best, the last song cycles and quartets. But underneath his attitude to life, which coloured his declared tastes, lay an ability to appreciate all that could be called real art, heavy or light, although he inhibited that appreciation in the same way that his character Krapp, having decided that storm and stress had to be his lot in life, accepts the melancholy and hermetic existence of a man who lives entirely in his reflective mind. Beckett had an emotional, not logical, reaction against art that depended on facile genius. It was part of his mannerist view of the world.

It was not to see *Capriccio* with Söderström again that I took Sam, but something even lighter, Rossini's *Pietra del Paragone*, on the 19th of June 1964. The day before I had suddenly remembered that almost everyone goes to Glyndebourne in a dinner jacket, and of course Sam did not have one. I suggested going to Moss Bros. to hire one, but he would not hear of it, so I telephoned Michael Geliot, working at Glyndebourne that summer to ask his advice. 'Don't worry,' he said, 'come as you are.' I warned him we would both be wearing sports jackets. On the way out of London I stopped to get petrol and exchanged some banter with a very jolly-looking plump girl in white overalls who filled me up. Sam had been watching from the car. 'You seemed to be enjoying yourself there,' he remarked as I climbed back in, his voice tinged with a definite note of envy. 'A very jolly girl,' I said, 'you should have got out with me.'

We arrived at Glyndebourne to find a welcoming committee awaiting us. There was Gunther Rennert, intendant at the time and producer of that evening's opera. With him was John Pritchard, conductor that night, and Michael Geliot. They were all wearing sports jackets and they chatted with us for a quarter of an hour, then had to go to change. As I remember, we all enjoyed the evening.

To return to the previous summer, I was busy as August approached with the arrangements for the Drama Conference, which Harewood had put into the third week of the Festival, a week that always sags because it is September by then and the excitement of the first two weeks has diminished, while the box office drops off. The previous year had been such a success that he hoped the Drama Conference would bring up that last week. There were 130 people to look after as against the 70 of the previous year, but now there was confidence that the big names were coming and that the conference would work. Advance booking by the public was excellent. Ken Tynan's secretary, Rozena Adler, sometimes seemed to be operating on her own. She was almost as high-handed as her boss and she constantly snubbed Berry, who was handling my list of names, whereas she was writing to Ken's. From the U.S. we now had Edward Albee, Harold Clurman, Alan Schneider, Lillian Hellman, Arthur Kopit, Jack Garfein and his film star wife Carroll Baker, some of the newer playwrights, and from Britain John Arden, Arnold Wesker, Harold Pinter, Wolf Mankowitz, David Frost, Bernard Levin, Martin Esslin, J. B. Priestly, Barry Record, John Mortimer and his wife Penelope, several Scots, including Robert McLellan and the actor Duncan Macrae, and from France, Eugene Ionesco, Alain Robbe-Grillet, Marguerite Duras, Roland Dubillard, Arthur Adamov, René de Obaldia and others. We had personalities who had become well-known through the satire boom, like the Saturday-night *That Was the Week That Was* (TW3), Bernard Levin and David Frost in particular and Peter Cook who had started the satire Night Club, The Establishment. Other countries sent their stars and once again the British Council helped. We had invited many members of the Berliner Ensemble, Brecht's company, as they were Tynan's great enthusiasm, but my German authors Peter Weiss and Martin Walser were also on the list, along with Max Frisch. I made a point of bringing back two people who had attracted much public attention the previous year, Erich Fried and Alexander Trocchi. I had some problems with Tynan here, but I had the final say and insisted that little as they might have to do with the theatre, they had a following in Edinburgh and would be good debaters. Several actors agreed to come, most notably Sir Laurence Olivier, Alec Guinness (who was in a play at the festival), Moultrie Kelsal, and the above-mentioned Duncan Macrae.

In July I went to an experimental play in Paris by a young American, which interested me for its new techniques and ideas, and afterwards I went backstage and talked to him. His name was Kenneth Dewey, and he called his play, which he had written and directed, 'a happening'. He told me it was an innovative form of mainly street theatre, where the audience was expected to participate, but without ever knowing in advance exactly what it might have to do; but there was always a point to the performance. It was intended to bring real life with all its unexpected hazards, into a performance context. The link with Artaud's epic 'total theatre', not yet the subject of fashionable debate, struck me forcibly. Dewey told me that the principal innovator of 'happenings' was another American called Allen Kaprow. I invited Ken Dewey to come to Edinburgh to talk about his work and I also contacted Kaprow and invited him.

I now had a new worry and it was money. I had organised the Writers' Conference on a tight budget, getting subsidies from foreign embassies, the British Council, publishers and some individuals, much of it in the form of air fares, hotel accommodation and entertainment. Big names had previously been housed with wealthy hosts. Ken Tynan would have none of that. Theatre people wanted comfortable hotels with room-service; there was no-one to pay airfares from California or New York. The only subsidies I managed to get, outside of a few individuals brought in by the British Council, were from Poland and Eastern Europe. Tynan had told me that the free-lance theatre critic, Ossia Trilling, really worked for the KGB as a cultural spy and adviser, and that if he were invited, it would be easier to get some official Russians to come. He was right: they came, they were all very official, and of no value to the conference. Not a single one had a word to say on the platform.

The Festival had given me little co-operation the first year, but now things were different. I sent bills to the Festival's treasurer and they were paid. I booked hotel rooms and hoped that the money to pay for them would also be forthcoming. Ken Tynan never thought of cost, only of glamour and having the best facilities that were available. Whenever we disagreed, he would appeal to Harewood, who always backed him against me. In two respects, which I shall come to later, this seriously hurt the conference.

I had a few censorship problems. I was asked to got to see Duncan Weatherstone, Edinburgh's newly elected Lord Provost. I turned up at eleven o'clock, my appointed time, and was ushered into his office. He looked at me uncertainly. 'Ah yes, Mr. Calder,' he said. There was a long pause. 'I'm feeling rather tired,' he continued slowly. 'I think I'll have a drink. Would you like one?'

'No, thank you, Lord Provost,' I answered. 'It's a little early for me.'

'Well, I think I'll have one anyway.' He opened a closet and poured himself a large whisky, and took a gulp. 'Now, let's see. What is it you wanted to see me about?'

'I'm not sure, Lord Provost. I think you wanted to see me.'

Another pause, then he flipped on his intercom. 'Mr Murdoch.'

'Yes, Lord Provost,' came the answering voice from the next room.

'I have Mr. Calder with me.'

'I know, Lord Provost.'

'Why is he here?'

'Could I have a word with you alone, Lord Provost.'

I then had to wait for a few minutes in the corridor, and when I returned his face was not friendly. Nor did he invite me to sit down again.

'About this man,' (he glanced down at a piece of paper), 'this Lenny Bruce. I don't want him.'

'I don't understand you, Lord Provost.'

'You'll understand me well enough. I don't want people like that at the Festival. Do you understand me?' His glass was empty and he obviously wanted to refill it, but not in my presence. Murdoch had told him enough to make him a real enemy, like many in Edinburgh who had disapproved of me in the past, but Weatherstone had the power, and he wanted me to know it.

'And I want no more talk about homosexuality and so on. If there is, I'll shut you down. And another thing. Don't go talking to the press about this. If you do, I'll cancel the Conference.'

And that was that. I cancelled our invitation to Lenny Bruce, a controversial American comedian who used strong language in his cabaret act. And just before the conference started we were told that Helene Weigel, Brecht's widow and other actors from her company in East Berlin would not be given British visas to enter the country. We made a token protest about that, as we had the previous year when we had invited Alan Paton and after the South African government had refused him a visa to leave. We had more publicity out of the Paton incident, because the entire assembly of novelists had unanimously agreed to send a telegram of sympathy, support and protest against apartheid, Alan Paton being then one of its most active opponents.

Ken Tynan and I discussed the topics for discussion from the time he became Conference Chairman, basically following the pattern of the previous year, but this time we had six days, not five, and Harewood had put us into the third week, hoping to bring the Festival excitement up again. Ken wanted the first day's topic to be: 'Who controls the modern theatre, the playwright, the director or the actor.' I protested that no two intelligent people would spend five minutes on such a question. The answer was obvious to anyone: if you had a dead author and a strong director like Peter Brook it was the director. If you had a big star who was the only real attraction, it was the actor. But he insisted, and when I appealed to Harewood, he, as usual, backed Ken.

I had promoted Jim Haynes to be my titular assistant with the title of Edinburgh Organiser, and as usual I kept a back seat, but with a few exceptions made the arrangements and the decisions. Jim had taken on a large new flat in Great King Street, and it became both an office and a dormitory. Berry Bloomfield and Rozanna Adler both stayed there for a week before the conference, but I think we later moved them elsewhere. They were supplemented by a volunteer, Sheila Colvin, recently returned from working in the U.S., an Edinburgh girl who had previously been with the BBC in London and Glasgow, and an assistant to James MacTaggart, the legendary producer of the Wednesday Play, but since had become a secretary in the commercial world, whereas her heart was in the arts. Sheila was so efficient that at the end of the conference Ken Tynan offered her a job to work with him at the National Theatre as his personal assistant. Instead she accepted an offer from me.

With many more people coming this year, there was much to do. At the start of the festival and two weeks before the conference, I moved into Jim's flat from Ledlanet, which was only thirty miles away, but the Firth of Forth, the great estuary that separates the Lothians from Fife and the north, had in those days to be crossed by a Ferry which could take hours, the alternative being a long drive to cross Kinkardine Bridge, near Stirling, an extra hour away, Harewood had again pushed Edinburgh audiences to new experiences in music: Janacek, then little known in Britain, but largely promoted in London by Raphael Kubelik and Charles Mackerras, was his main composer that Festival, with Liszt also featured, and I managed to get to some musical performances during our two weeks of office preparation. I had also given Harewood some suggestions for the drama that year, although he had a deputy director to do that. I had persuaded him to stage Martin Walser's *The Rabbit Race*, which I was publishing and Ionesco's *Exit the King*, which, because it had Alec Guinness in the cast, later transferred to the Royal Court in London. I had also suggested a Beckett/Ionesco double bill of two operas, Mihailovici's setting of *Krapp's Last Tape* (in the French version) together with Germaine Tailleferre's of Ionesco's *The Leader*. Harewood liked the idea, but it was too expensive and would be difficult for the Edinburgh audience.

On Sunday the first of September our conferencees began to arrive. I stayed by the telephone at Great King Street. Tynan met the 'plane as it brought the largest number of Americans, who having changed from one flight to another in London, arrived at Turnhouse in driving rain, being filmed on the runway by Tutte Lemkov. Others were met at the station and sent to their hotels. A Doctor John King, who had a large house in Murrayfield, west of the centre, gave an opening party, which I did not think I should leave the telephone to attend, so I deputed Sheila Colvin to be there in my place and help King to host it. Dr. King later proposed marriage to her, but was not accepted. One of Jim's volunteers brought in an early edition of the Monday Scotsman. I opened it to see a large cartoon of myself by Emilio Coia, the newspaper's resident cartoonist, looking sharp-nosed and thoughtful. Beside it was a large personality piece entitled 'Calder the Conference' by Magnus Magnusson. I barely had time to peruse it, because the telephone was now ringing steadily. Writers, directors and theatre personalities were arriving from everywhere, and wanted to know where to go and what to do. Sheila and others came back from the party in Corstorphine, which had gone well, everyone was settled into their accommodation, and the next day was well prepared. The simultaneous translators had arrived and had set up their equipment. Max Frisch was in his hotel with Marianne, but his baggage had been lost; the next day he was buying new clothes. There was trouble at the Scotia Hotel across the street from our headquarters. It had objected to a playwright bringing in someone not his wife. Two other male writers, both well-known names, were in a double room, both gay (the word had just come into use that year). 'What do you think those two are doing in there?' said the disappointed playwright to the receptionist. It may have been Arthur Kopit who protested, but I cannot exactly remember now. I will not say who the other two were, except that they were prominent British playwrights. The anecdote appeared later in an American article about the conference where it was certainly Arthur Kopit who mentioned Charles Marovitz as 'an American who lives in Britain and ought to stay there.'

The next morning we had our first briefing meeting at McEwan Hall in the same room that we had used the year before. We knew that we had a sold-out house at 2.30. There was only a flimsy programme to sell this time: we had not repeated the experience of producing a glossy volume full of articles, but it had introductory pieces by Tynan and myself, a list of delegates and a summary of each day's subject. There would be enough Festival staff to take tickets and rent earphones. I explained to the crowded committee-room that the point of the conference was to educate the public, and I told of the excitement that the novelists had aroused in those who had come to listen to them. But Ken often stopped me. Entertaining the public was fine, but the real discussions should, he thought, take place in private sessions. Our dissension soon became rather obvious. J. B. Priestley was to chair the afternoon under the overall chairmanship of Ken Tynan. Priestley was rather insular in his approach. When I told him that Erich Fried would always have a great deal to say, he replied that yes, he knew, 'typical little German pedantic bore!'

The first afternoon was a bore. With a non-topic all we could muster were little set-pieces, prepared in advance, without spontaneity, passion or conviction. The most articulate saved their fire for the next day when we would discuss Commitment. Laurence Olivier (he was Sir Laurence but not

249

yet Lord Olivier by then) came in late in the afternoon and gave us an elegant little speech, ending with a flourish and a 'Who controls the modern theatre? Why the actor of course!' But otherwise it was dull, dull, dull and by four o'clock many people were leaving. There were many empty seats during the next three days and only during the last two did it begin to fill up again, but to nothing like the extent of the 1962 Writers' Conference on the novel.

I had arranged for the BBC to record everything and to put out nightly a shortened version of the afternoon, as they had done the previous year. In addition the BBC were to bring in television cameras for the last two days. I had made two other arrangements: I had given TV facilities to Annie Leclerc of Belgian Television, who televised some of the conference (and in spite of a written agreement, we were never paid for this) and I had also arranged for Tutte Lemkov, a Swedish actor who worked in England in avant-garde theatre, but was better known as the ex-husband of Mai Zetterling, a much admired actress, to record all the proceedings on camera. But when the television lights were switched on during the first day, those on the platform, blinded by the light, shouted for them to be turned off, while the audience, being made extremely uncomfortable by the heat they engendered, also complained loudly. The discomfort was another factor in the early departures. Tynan ordered them to be turned off and from that point they were on and off at random while the filming went on.

The Tuesday newspapers gave negative reviews to the first day. At the briefing, I took over control and Tynan let me. I harangued everyone present, emphasising that we were there, not to posture, but to seriously discuss the theatre, its aims, influence on changing the world and what it might become. We wanted fireworks and plain-speaking like the previous year and I rearranged the panels to make this more likely to happen. In the hall, we then did have some fireworks, particularly from John Arden, Arnold Wesker, Wolf Mankovitz and Barry Rekord, the latter launching a fierce attack on colonialism, which, he said, the bourgeois theatre propagated. The audience began to enjoy itself, but it was a small audience now. Many seats that had been paid for were not being used. As the week progressed the interest of the discussions kept improving and Ken Tynan became less sure of himself and increasingly let me run things my way.

The subject of the second day was 'Differences of Approach', and it was chaired by Martin Esslin, then at the BBC Drama Department, and not yet an academic, and it was lively as British and foreign playwrights argued as to how to make a play work and what it should do to the audience in forming their opinions. Peter Brook chaired the Wednesday session, 'The Theatre and its Rivals', where the relationship between life, drama and cinema, television, radio and other performing arts was discussed. Then came 'Subsidy and Censorship', rather crassly chaired by Harold Clurman, who made it more about money than principles; it was not a patch on the previous year's debate, but we did hear some amusing anecdotes about the misunderstandings of the Lord Chamberlain's office. 'Nationalism in the Theatre' chaired by Hilton Edwards was the fieriest day yet, and I especially remember the contributions of Barry Rekord from the Caribbean and Wole Soyinka from Nigeria.

There was no Scottish day I can describe. Some of the participants are shown among the illustrations elsewhere and it was a distinguished list, but forty years later I look at the names and find it impossible to remember much of what was said and who said it, except for the final day, which I shall come to later.

In the meantime, life at Jim's flat was becoming complicated. It was a large flat, but all the space was occupied. A certain Austrian girl of aristocratic background, engaged to marry a Prince, also Austrian, was there in bed with several of us, but she was a virgin and had to remain one, as proof would be demanded on her wedding night. Everything was allowed other than penetration. She spent at least two nights with Ken Tynan, who viewed her virginity as childlike innocence and was fascinated by it. A lovely young French Professor, Marie Depuissé, was also part of the ménage, though mainly with Jim, but Bettina and I remained friendly with her after the Conference was over. Bettina was installed in another flat with her new baby, but was little in evidence. During the last few days, Kathleen Halton, a reporter on the Sunday Times, turned up. She was married, but having an affair with Ken, which had to be kept secret. I had known Kathleen for some time and did not like her much. She was the kind of journalist who twists everything to make a better story, and she had let me down in the past. Ken, although often sleeping in different places and with different women, was staying at the George Hotel and he took a room in the annex, because you could enter it directly from the street without passing a reception desk or concierge. Kathleen joined him there for the last days of the Conference.

But there were many other changes of partner going on. Two Dutch sisters came to the Conference, one married to Cees Nooteboom, the Dutch writer, who she then left for an Edinburgh doctor, while the other married another doctor, a friend of Jim Haynes. Various divorces came out of the Conference as well as new pairings. One morning I walked early into the office to find Rozena Adler sleeping there on a mattress with Tutte Lemkow. I backed out hastily because they were in the middle of a mutual orgasm, and the picture of Tynan's very prim and immaculately turned-out secretary in the throes indelibly imprinted itself on my mind. Sex was everywhere in the air during the Conference. There were parties, but not as many as the previous year, and the Conference participants seemed perfectly capable of looking after themselves outside of our afternoons in McEwan Hall. I had rented the Circus Place flat again, where Muggeridge, Sonia and later Norman Mailer had stayed the previous year, and two parties were given there. Marion Lobbenberg and Arthur Boyars had, during that summer, become a couple, and I had put them in a room there. At one of the parties they went to bed early. Arthur Adamov, quite drunk, and needing to pee, simply opened the bedroom door, saw the room was dark, and started to drown the carpet. 'Non, non, Monsieur Adamov, pas ici,' shouted Marion, but it was too late. On another occasion, in the same flat, Miodrag Bulatovic, a Serbian writer, locked himself into a room with one of the many girls who had attached themselves to us and tried to rape her. She began screaming 'Police, police.' It was Trocchi who forced the door open and rescued her. 'But she wanted it. She was saying "Please, please",' protested the disappointed writer.

At the Conference we worked through our topics. This year I occasionally put in a point or two of my own. Some writers like Harold Pinter only came for a single day. It became more relaxed and more interesting for the public, and I was able to give one or two little dinners to get people of similar interest together, one evening with French writers, another with German-speakers, Martin Esslin, Erich Fried, Max Frisch, Peter Weiss and Martin Walser. The great issues of the day were all aired: nuclear disarmament, the cold war, apartheid, the various freedom movements around the world of emerging nations, the censorship of the Lord Chamberlain which still hindered and emasculated the theatre, forcing some plays to be performed only in theatre clubs, like the Arts in London and the newly emerged Traverse in Edinburgh. The principal new theatres that did interesting innovative work in the sixties were still looked at with a beady eye by the Lord Chamberlain's office, which had to read every new play before it was performed, often insisting on cuts that could totally change the thrust of the play. These were, in the main, the Royal Court Theatre, the embryo National, about to move from the Old Vic to its new home on the Embankment, the Royal Shakespeare's London branch at the Aldwych and Joan Littlewood's Theatre Royal in London's Stratford East, as well as those theatres in provincial towns that occasionally performed new plays. They were all in constant trouble with the official censors, often reading double meanings into lines that were never part of the authors' intentions. There was much about this at the Conference, which called for an ending to all state theatrical censorship.

The last day's discussion, following the successful model of the previous year, was on the forms that the theatre might take in the future, and in advance I had asked a number of playwrights to let me have short examples that could be performed. Joan Littlewood, whose controversial *Oh, What a Lovely War*, was running in her East End theatre, enthusiastically agreed, but I had to restrain her. She wanted, as part of her demonstration, to bring in workmen with drills to rip up the floor of the hall. She engaged a model, who was to appear nude, although *that* she never told me. Joan had much to say in the first few days. Her cartoon, by Coia, appeared in The Scotsman, and she was fêted in a town she already knew well. But problems emerged during the week with her London production and she had to cancel her 'demonstration', returning to the Conference only on the day when it would have been performed. In the meantime Albee had agreed to write a piece and intended to use the model, but he had writer's block, as did the next candidate. It was ultimately Ken Dewey, whom I had brought from Paris, who took over Anna Kesselaar, who normally posed for art classes, to put her into his Happening. Others had also agreed to do something for the last day, among them René de Obaldia and Roland Dubillard, who worked out a sketch which they would perform themselves, in French.

The final briefing session on Saturday, before the last session of the Conference, on what was also the last day of the Edinburgh Festival, was broken into two parts. While Tynan and I discussed with more than a hundred theatre professionals the order of the day and who was to be on the panels and have priority to state their views on what they thought was coming in terms of theatrical subjects, techniques, performing spaces, acting styles and contact with audiences, those who were putting on demonstrations were rehearsing in the hall itself. I could not be in two places, so I never saw the rehearsals. All week long, Tynan and I had been disagreeing, sometimes in private, sometimes at the briefing sessions, but after the fiasco of the first day with its bad press, I had the upper hand, and Harewood was too busy with the many events under his control to be appealed to, and even if he had, I think that now he would have agreed with me. Tynan's desire for private sessions had been scrapped. The Conference was intended to be and had become both an entertainment and a tool for educating the public in the hope – my hope anyway – that the public would take a greater interest in international theatre and serious thought-provoking plays, wherever they came from and whenever they were written. The 'Angry Young Men,', the 'Theatre of the Absurd', the 'Epic Theatre', and 'Total Theatre' as imagined by Artaud, Barrault, Brecht, Piscator, Reinhardt, Reinhold, and many others, the expressionist theatre and the surrealist, the modern classics of Shaw, Ibsen, Chekhov, and just a little of the Brecht school of post-war (much of it pre-war) drama, were just then between them, taking attention away from Binky Beaumont's West End sureties, Coward, Maugham and Rattigan, and becoming known and recognisable to new audiences that were hungry for something different and relevant. The new upstarts from the red brick universities – Somerset Maugham's 'scum' – were serious playwrights and making waves, but the theatre-going traditional middle-classes, who patronised Shaftesbury Avenue, didn't like them on both class and entertainment grounds. I wanted to educate, whereas Tynan wanted a forum for his chums, and an elitist prestige for himself. The better I knew him the less I took him seriously as against Harold Hobson, eccentric and mischievous, but always right where it mattered: it was the contrast of brittle surface glitter, marred by suspect ideology, and on the other hand deep seriousness, searching for meaning, in a basically proletarian mind that was conservative by instinct.

Harold Hobson had been there all week, listening but not talking. While the Saturday briefing session was going on, he was sitting in the main hall, watching everything, in particular Ken Dewey's rehearsal. He could not be there in the afternoon because he had to write his piece for the Sunday Times that day and return to London. I myself had no idea of what was going to happen. I trusted Ken Dewey and I knew that he had roped in many participants for his demonstration.

Lord Harewood came to my last session and I asked him to join the platform, which he did. The BBC Monitor programme, whose producer was David Jones, was filming that day as it had the previous one. The hall was a little more than half full, the numbers having risen during the previous few days, but only a little from the lows of Tuesday and Wednesday. The level of debate had risen day by day, as had the press coverage, but that too was much less than the previous year. Ken Tynan was alone in chairing the final session. After a few statements on the main subject from different persons present, the demonstrations began.

Early on came the Obaldia-Dubillard piece, a very amusing dialogue between two writers at a Conference in Edinburgh, who every time they emerge from the hall, find that there is nothing to eat or drink, an experience that many festival artists have undergone. This was followed by another short sketch, and then came the Dewey, but it was unannounced.

First Charles Marovitz came to the microphone and began to give a pseudo lecture on Beckett. He was interrupted by actors placed in the audience, and he argued with them. Then a variety of things happened: strangely-clothed creatures began to crawl around the aisles of the downstairs seats toward the stage. At the top of McEwan Hall was a large dome with six side windows. These opened and Commedia del Arte figures appeared through the window apertures shouting at each other and at the audience below. Carroll Baker, dressed in a clinging leopard skin, began to climb, like a large cat, across the empty seats from the back of the hall, her eyes glued to the stage as if her prey were there, sometimes having to push members of the audience aside. The model, Anna Kesselaar, then appeared at one end of the organ gallery that ran behind the platform where the Conferencees sat. She was hanging onto a BBC lighting trolley and was wheeled around the gallery by a BBC technician, naked, but within the law, as she was not moving, but being moved. She was a buxom blonde, but the railing covered the lower part of her body, so that only her head and breasts were visible and only for perhaps thirty seconds. What was seen by the audience was also seen that night on television. Then came the wailing of the bagpipes, as a single piper walked as he played, around the back of the public gallery behind the audience. This was greeted with much laughter by the whole audience. Carroll Baker now reached the stage and climbed onto it. The audience was by then in stitches. Then suddenly – for the space underneath the organ gallery had been hidden that day by heavy velvet curtains – the curtains fell, revealing dozens of heads, hairdressers' dummies, perched on shelves. Ken Dewey, as he soon explained, called his Happening 'Big Head', a reference to much of the pretentious nonsense that had been heard during the week especially on the first day.

Then came the debate over what we had seen. Tynan was outraged. Theatre was about commitment to political change, he said. He asked for everyone on the platform who considered himself a socialist to raise his hand. Not a single Russian or artist from Eastern Europe did. Dewey was asked to explain his Happening and he did so with much applause. He was after all doing what Artaud advocated, shaking the audience's sense of reality and making them realise that the world is an uncertain place where anything can happen. That was an important function of the theatre. This infuriated Tynan even more. Allen Kaprow came in to defend Dewey, but he needed no defending, having most of the platform and virtually all of the audience with him. He had amazed them, frightened them a little, but above all had made them laugh and given them a new perspective on the possibilities of the theatre. The debate went on for some time, and was certainly the liveliest of the week. Then Kaprow announced that the audience would be involved in another happening on the way out, as they left the building. It was now six o'clock. Trying to leave, everyone found their exit impeded by mounds of second-hand tyres which had been placed around the building during the afternoon. To get out one had to climb over them. This final Happening ended the Conference. I think that the final difficulty in leaving may have annoyed some of the audience.

The press, which had been massively present that day, had taken Anna Kesselaar backstage where they photographed her in more provocative poses than the public had seen, but we knew nothing about that at the time. They had also given lurid accounts of the Happening to the Lord Provost, who had, knowing nothing at all about the Conference other than its presence in the Festival brochure, condemned it on their sensationalised report.

Sheila Colvin had been a tower of strength all through the week, doing exactly what she was asked to do with great competence and, it must be remembered, she was a volunteer, doing it for nothing. Both Tynan and I, as mentioned above, had offered her a job, post-Festival. But by the end of Saturday afternoon, she was in a state of exhaustion. I had arranged a final party for that night, not in Edinburgh but at Ledlanet, and had hired two buses to take the entire Conference there. Sheila just wanted to go to bed. I told her she couldn't. She was needed. I had some Benzedrine tablets, which I took occasionally in those days – my doctor prescribed them when I asked – but never took a whole one: when tired I had found that a nibble off the edge of a tablet kept me going for an hour or two, and I took more if needed later. I gave Sheila one, told her to nibble it, and when fatigue returned, to nibble a little more. She came on the first bus and helped dispense drinks.

Attewell, at Ledlanet, had organised a great buffet, with champagne, wine and everything else. I had invited about a hundred of the local gentry in order to combine my two lives, that of a newly arrived county laird and of an arts impresario and successful publisher. I had been prominent on the best-seller list that year with *Tropic of Cancer* and other books that had done well. It was my apogee of over-confidence. Two coaches were bringing about a hundred, perhaps more, people who had been at the Conference. In each bus I had set up a kind of mini-bar because the journey would take over an hour, going over Kincardine Bridge because the ferries did not operate so late. It was a bad night and getting worse. We arrived at Ledlanet very late; the other guests had been invited for seven o'clock, but it was over an hour later when I arrived on the first bus with fifty or so others. They were standing around in dinner jackets and evening dresses, looking embarrassed, with glasses of champagne but not yet having touched any of the buffet of whole salmon, barons of beef and many delicious other things which Attewell had temptingly laid out.

Actors, playwrights and theatre directors now mingled with the local gentry of Kinross, Fife and Perth, many of them not yet knowing me, although at this juncture I was fairly notorious, and would even be more so in a few hours. I changed quickly into a dress kilt and went around to greet everyone and encourage them to attack the buffet. The second bus arrived on which Tondi Barr had been playing barmaid on the way. By now it was black night with heavy rain, but indoors at Ledlanet chandeliers sparkled, the conversation flowed with the champagne, other wines were produced, and the food on the tables gradually disappeared. All the downstairs rooms were in use, my guests strolling from one to the other, and as the night progressed pairs of lovers found empty bedrooms upstairs, which it was obvious the next day had been much used. Bettina had been there to play hostess from the beginning, but she retired to bed at about eleven o'clock.

A telegram arrived from Lord Harewood congratulating me and everyone else on an exciting and entertaining end to the Drama Conference. I went to the top of the stairs and read it out to the crowd below. Gradually the locals left and at about midnight the first bus set off for Edinburgh. I packed Eugene Ionesco and his wife Rosica into it, trying to shelter them from the driving rain, and most of the older and more important theatrical figures were on the first bus. I was gathering up the survivors to get ready for the second when a bedraggled and soaking-wet group, led by Tondi, began to arrive on foot. The first driver had taken advantage of all the drink on offer, was drunk, and had run into a ditch in the dark. Except for a few who remained on the bus, a group of forty or so other passengers had walked some two and half miles back, including a steep climb up the half-mile drive to the house, which my great-grandfather had constructed almost vertically up the hill only because he had been told it couldn't and shouldn't be done, because horses would never be able to get it up in the winter.

The arrival of the wet newcomers reanimated the party, which started all over again. Towels and dry clothes were found, some wrapped blankets around themselves, new bottles were produced, and soon everything was again in full swing. The second bus did leave at about three o'clock and the A.A. succeeded in getting the first back on the road, and that left as dawn was breaking. There were still a few people around and they fell asleep on sofas or found beds. It was a beautiful dawn. The storm had stopped and a brilliant sun came over the horizon; the air was fresh and getting warmer. Andrew Boddy, the Edinburgh doctor who had put up William Burroughs and Alexander Trocchi the previous year and Wole Soyinka this year, went off for a walk in the woods with Joan Littlewood. When they returned, many hours later towards noon, they looked radiantly happy. Finding myself alone at about seven in the morning with Sheila Colvin in the gun-room I kissed her and the kiss was returned. Suddenly I had a pain in the ankle and found that from sheer exhaustion I had sprained it. Later on Doctor Boddy bound it up for me. I slept for about an hour and then returned to my duties, organised cars to get the stragglers back to Edinburgh and lunch before that, and I telephoned to make sure that both buses had returned their passengers to their various accommodations.

Then in the afternoon I drove Joan Littlewood, Boddy and one or two others to Edinburgh, using the ferry. The new Forth Road Bridge was under construction: from each bank of the Forth the great metal structure was emerging, but a great gap of several hundred yard lay in the middle. Standing on the deck of the ferry, Joan looked at it. 'It's a perfect sculpture,' she observed. 'They mustn't do any more. Leave it just like that.'

We arrived at the airport where the waiting room was full of the faces I had been seeing for the past week. There was some delay and someone asked why. 'They're waiting for Calder to bring a drunken pilot,' said Ken Tynan.

* * * * * *

The Sunday newspapers were full of us. The Lord Provost, Duncan Wetherstone, knowing only what he had been told by the Scottish Daily Record, a tabloid, that a nude had been produced at the Drama Conference which had shocked everyone present – in fact not only was no one shocked, but many did not even see the brief glimpse of the top half of Anna Kesselaar, being convulsed with laughter at the piper and surprise at the figures in the apertures of the dome – and he condemned the whole Conference, saying that three weeks of glorious festival had been ruined by this terrible event. The whole happening had been seen by the BBC television audience and not a single protest was received. The serious newspapers gave much discussion space, apart from their critical coverage, to the validity of the 'happenings', a word soon in common use. But the popular press made a meal of it. The Scottish Daily Express, always a pillar of ignorance, prejudice, pretended puritanism and reaction, called for the sacking of Lord Harewood as well as the organisers of the Conference, Kenneth Tynan and myself. This went on for weeks. I made many radio and television appearances, wrote letters to the press, gave more talks to Rotary Clubs and other groups who wanted to hear me, and generally was the centre of a scandal that was totally artificial.

Two friends came to stay at Ledlanet, Jacques Chaix, who had arrived on the last day of the Conference, and Alex Stefanovic, who had been present throughout it. We roamed over my grouse moor, shot some birds and ate them. I was now preparing for my own mini-festival, which I called, unpretentiously I hope, Ledlanet Nights. A Dunfermline printer produced a publicity brochure for me, designed by John Martin, an Edinburgh designer and artist, and I worked out all the logistics of a two-week event. The leaflets were scattered around hotels, art centres and restaurants over a wide area and I placed a few ads. Reginald Attewell planned most of the catering. We borrowed a big spit from the local Conservative party (about which I had a bad conscience, being no Conservative) to roast a sheep and rent a marquee to put on the lawn in front of the house. Then I went to Yorkshire for the weekend.

In order to get John Arden to come to Edinburgh, I had promised to visit his festival. This was in Kirbymoorside, not far from my old school Gilling Castle, and Ampleforth, of which it is the prep school, and now I was keeping my promise. For a month John had put on some event every night, some form of music, a play or poetry reading, or simply a discussion in his cottage. He had filmed the life of the village, interviewed on camera young people talking about their elders, old people talking about youth and what was wrong with it, plumbed the depth of local discontents, and brought out opinions, prejudices and attitudes, some of them ugly. Then he had shown the film on a small screen in his cottage. Young people crowded in, the old ignored it, although some came to look through the windows at their own faces and movements. I arrived on a sunny Saturday morning. The small Arden children, cherubic crawlers and toddlers, some able to run, were all naked, playing in the dust near a main road with no fences and fast traffic. I kept picking them up and bringing them back to the cottage, but John and Margarreta Arden were unconcerned. They let the children go where they wanted, heedless of the dangers.

I met several folk musicians and poets, some of whom had been entertaining the village for days or weeks. It had been an extraordinary month in a small village in Yorkshire where normally nothing ever happened and the young people were usually bored out of their wits except when they could go to a larger town for an evening. The Ardens had kept them talking, learning and entertained, had developed their talents for acting, singing or just discussing an issue. It was the last day of the month.

The Ardens would leave and there was no one with the organising power to keep something going in the future. I saw the last showing of the film, read something aloud out of some book and talked to some of those who had been coming every night. Then I went back to my London office, and then Ledlanet had its two weekend festival. The first weekend was a double bill of Rossini's *Serate musicale*, a group of Neopolitan-type songs with four singers and a piano accompaniment, and a short opera *Moonflowers* by Richard Arnell. The songs were cheerful, tuneful and easy on the ear and were given in the new drawing room, where we seated sixty. Ande Anderson, the producer, had Attewell dressed up as an eighteenth century major domo with a staff throughout the first piece, where the star singer was Josephine Veasey, who a month earlier had opened the Edinburgh Festival, singing in the opening concert. She was Ande's wife, but would not remain so much longer.

I imitated Glyndebourne by having the interval in the middle, but the food was not a great success on the opening night. The set menu in the rented marquee, in which everyone was too cold, started with avocado pears, which many had never seen before, filled with lumpfish roe, followed by barbecued sheep. Although the spit had been turning all day, the meat was still too red for the taste of the audience. The opera that followed was played in the hall, where we had moved the chairs into a semi-circle around the foot of the staircase, and the action of Arnell's comic work was played out on the bottom stairs and the small platform where the stairs divided and went up to the overhanging balconies. It was a light, pleasant evening, enjoyed by as big an audience as we could seat, performed three times that weekend. By the third performance we had found a way to heat the tent and cook the meat to the audience's taste.

The following weekend Bettina gave a recital on the Friday night, which I quickly realised was a mistake as it gave the impression that the whole endeavour was to promote her in a showcase. And for the Saturday and Sunday I brought in two performances of James Saunders enigmatic play, *Next Time I'll Sing to You*, from the Traverse Theatre. It was a favourite of mine, but it was not much liked by the audience. But that first short season of Ledlanet Nights made its impact. The loss was fairly heavy, but I could identify where more could be achieved with less expenditure in the future. The major Scottish newspapers gave favourable notices and my celebrity because of the Happening did not hurt at all where the theatre-going public was concerned. Ledlanet was soon followed by another Frankfurt Book Fair. My memories of the Fair are so numerous, and things that happened there so bizarre, that it is impossible not occasionally to get the years wrong. Because of the rupture with Barney Rosset in 1963 the following two anecdotes must have belonged to earlier years, but I connect them in my mind with those eventful early sixties when for a change Lady Fortune was smiling on me.

It may have been the year before that there was a dispute between Grove Press and my own firm, not a matter of great consequence, but nevertheless one involving a principle that neither one of us could afford to concede, although either result if it could be decided without our agreement was acceptable. Marion had tried at some point to negotiate and had been treated with scorn by Barney, who said he would only deal with me. In Frankfurt I always spent one or two nights with Barney in night clubs, some of them very sleazy and all filled with prostitutes, who were obsessions with him: he filled his mind with fantasies about their lives. On this occasion we found ourselves, together with Dick Seaver and I believe Jason Epstein (who either left early or was present on some similar occasion when he found Barney's sexual preoccupations unstomachable) in a small room with a stage which was part of a large night club called Die Hölle (Hell). Girls were doing some striptease act. Suddenly I said to Barney, 'I have an idea. Why don't we settle the dispute by chance, by flipping a coin.' He thought about it.

'No, I won't do that, but I'll play you the Marienbad game,' The Marienbad game we both knew from Alain Robbe-Grillet's film *Last Year in Marienbad*, which we had both published as a film scenario. It is played with three rows of matches and the point is to leave the other player with the last match. Unknown to Barney I had played it before and had wrinkled out its secret. When I had played it with Beckett, his quick mind had discovered that secret after one game, but there is a visual pattern that makes winning easy providing one is the first to play. You can usually allow a naïve opponent to win once or twice before winning every time. Hiding my real feelings, I reluctantly accepted and let Barney move first. Although he made wrong moves, and with several moves to play I did as well, I won. 'We said two out of three,' he said after a pause.

'I don't think we did,' I countered. He appealed to Seaver, who wriggled uncomfortably. 'It's only fair, two out of three,' he said. I agreed with much show of reluctance, and then let him win the second game, but looking worried about every move in order to reassure him. The last game was tense. Our three heads were poised over the matches with concentration. On the stage, the girls who had stripped, were doing erotic dances, but the other tables, about twenty of them, all with men who should have been looking at the dancers on stage, were largely looking at us. What was going on at our table? The manager came over and complained, both on behalf of the girls not being looked at, and the management which wanted its customers to be drinking and looking, and certainly not at us. I told him we would not be long. Then I won the last game. Barney exploded into a fury and we left Die Hölle. Outside a G.I. was arguing with a girl and pushing her into his car. He drove off and Barney gave chase. We raced through the streets of Frankfurt and out into the country at speed. Barney saw an American Military Police car and signalled it down. He showed his American officer's pass (years out of date) and persuaded the police to give chase, saying the girl had been kidnapped. When we stopped the G.I., the girl began to berate us all. Why were we following them? What business was it of ours? The deflated Barney returned to his hotel.

I think that it was that year that I persuaded him to take on Aidan Higgins for the States. It was probably 1962 when I sold Higgins' novel *Langrishe, Go Down* to the German literary publisher Carl Hanser Verlag, from whom at about the same time we acquired Reinhard Lettau, whose short works combined whimsical humour with a radical political stance. In 1963 the Higgins novel was coming out in German at the fair and Hanser gave a big party for it at the Savigny Hotel. Higgins had been sent his air ticket, but he mislaid his passport, then missed his flight and arrived by a later one, which was met by a fast car to rush him to the party, which had nearly broken up when he arrived. I had waited for him, but having another appointment, was obliged to leave before he finally was rushed in. Later that evening I was at dinner with other publishers in a restaurant, when Giangiacomo Feltrinelli came in, saw me and came over. 'I have just met your author Aidan Higgins,' he said. He had arrived late at the Hanser party when there was hardly anyone left and he had spoken to Aidan. 'I liked him instantly,' he went on. 'I am sure he is a good writer and I should publish him.'

'But Giangiacomo,' I said, 'you had an option for a year. I urged Foa (his editor at the time) to take it, but he never made up his mind. Now that he is an independent publisher, he is thinking about it again.'

'It's not a book for Foa. How can I read it?'

'We're both staying at the Frankfurterhof. Ask for my room key. You'll find a copy there. Take it and speak to me tomorrow.' And writing down my room number he left the restaurant.

Later that night I met Barney Rosset (which means it must have been 1962 or earlier as we were not speaking after that) and spent a white night with him around the night clubs and bars of the city. At eight we had breakfast in his hotel room and only then did he sign a contract that I had in my pocket, which he had resisted for hours while concentrating on the decadence of the Frankfurt night. Then he started packing to catch his flight to New York and I returned to my room to sleep until noon, when I had to get up to attend a German publisher's lunch to meet their young authors. When I arrived in the afternoon, more than a little tired, at the Fair, it was four o'clock. I was all alone in Frankfurt that year, and on my stand, unattended all day, so prominently in the middle that no one could miss it, was a large piece of white cardboard, obviously from a laundered shirt. It read like this:

'My Dear John
I sat up all night reading Aidan Higgins' marvellous novel. I am willing to make you an important offer for it right away.'

Below was the well-known signature of Giangiacomo Feltrinelli, one of the stellar constellations of the Fair, publisher of such literary best-sellers as *Dr. Zhivago* and *The Leopard*. While I was reading this – it had been on my stand since early morning – I had a tap on the shoulder from a Swedish publisher. 'I too would like to buy this wonderful novel,' he said. By that night I was inundated with offers and *Langrishe, Go Down* was soon sold for translation into virtually every language of Europe. His presence in Frankfurt, his photograph that week in the literary columns of German newspapers and his face on television screens, did not hurt either.

On the last night of the Book Fair a group of us that included Maurice Girodias, the female literary editor of Le Monde, my brother, who for some reason had turned up in Frankfurt, and some other, mainly French, publishers and journalists (one of them was Nigel Dempster, the British gossip columnist), after dining together went to a night club, called Elliott Elliott. Maurice performed his habitual party act, which may well have shortened his life, by biting pieces off a wine glass, then chewing and swallowing them. He and I must have been fairly drunk, although not incoherently so, but being bored with the floor show, we improvised our own, which was applauded by the other tables as well as ours, but not by the management, which made us leave. Our act featured in Le Monde's coverage of the Frankfurt Fair, which also reported my *coup* in selling Higgins to a dozen different publishers, but suggested that it was a con trick. During the sixties there were quite a few gimmicks to sell authors and some hoaxes. One was launched by Paul Flamand of Editions du Seuil: he announced he was publishing an author whose name was vaguely Slav or Hungarian or Nordic or Latin, a composite name: he received several offers. The author did not exist.

Frankfurt at the Fair was also a good place to get up petitions, especially to get support against a prosecution for obscenity or to show solidarity with a publisher being persecuted for political activity. I was later to get up my own petition which was signed by everyone I approached except two.

On the 22nd of November that year I went to the Royal Festival Hall in London to hear a concert performance of Benjamin Britten's *Gloriana*, the opera which had been so much maligned at its première celebrating Elizabeth II's coronation. The day was the composer's fiftieth birthday and the hall was full with Britten present. At the interval I ran into Sir Jack Lyons, head of the Leeds chain of clothing stores, who was also Chairman of the London Symphony Orchestra, playing that night. 'President Kennedy has just been assassinated,' he said, 'but Britten doesn't want anything to interrupt the concert.' All over London announcements were being made and theatres were closing, their audiences leaving in mid-performance in a state of shock, but not at the RFH. When the applause ended, Bettina and I walked across the footbridge to Charing Cross station where all the newspapers had brought out special early editions. It has been said that everyone knew where they were when the news of Kennedy's death became known. I was listening to *Gloriana* at the Royal Festival Hall.

At home the next day we were constantly watching events unfold on television. Oswald was arrested, taken to the police station, and shot by Jack Ruby. We saw it all on the screen, live as it happened. A few minutes later the telephone rang. It was Erich Fried, very excited. 'Do you realise, John,' he said, 'that this man Ruby is a Jew.' He seemed afraid that the shooting, which was convulsing the world, would initiate a world-wide pogrom. The mystery of 'Who Killed Kennedy' kept my interest high into the next year as the many conspiracy theories developed and competed. Nearly forty years later we are still in the dark.

Somewhere towards the end of the year I was told that a prosecution was to be brought against me. Complaints had been laid against the Happening by three persons who had been present, and the Procurator Fiscal, whose office in Edinburgh decided what prosecutions should be brought, formally charged Anna Kesselaar with performing an indecent act in public, and myself, as Conference Director, of being 'art and part' of the offence. It was soon obvious from the publicity that Moral Rearmament was behind it.

Moral Rearmament needs some explaining, because it has since gone underground for a number of years. It started as the 'Oxford Movement', which had nothing to do with the nineteenth phenomenon instigated by Cardinal Newman, although the confusion of names might have been deliberate. Its founder was a German, Frank Buchman, who launched it as a quasi-religious movement (quasi because he wanted all religions to identify themselves with it) and at one point in the thirties had praised Hitler as representing his ideals. Later he would quote Nehru, who apparently gave him some support. Moral Rearmament was a puritanical organisation that tried to identify all liberal attitudes with Communism. Buchman had even been able to get the American government to finance special flights to his Conferences around the world, presumably because they saw MRA as anti-Communist. The best book on the organisation is by Tom Driberg[21], which effectively exposed their hypocrisies and their methods, which were very dirty indeed. At this time they were very powerful in Scotland, receiving money from rich landowners and much support from the more extreme Church of Scotland sects, especially the Free and Wee Free branches. In the early sixties, Moral Rearmament was run by Buchman's successor, Peter Howard, a former sportsman, then a sport reporter and currently a frequent editorial writer on The Daily Express, a newspaper whose policy then as most of the time since, was to attack every kind of permissiveness. Howard's key words were 'Godlessness and dirt'. They were being used as a slogan against the newly-founded Traverse Theatre performing modern plays,

---

[21] The Mystery of Moral Rearmament. London 1964.

against the Edinburgh Festival on every possible occasion, against Harewood, and just then very much against me. Howard's purple prose struck me as being reminiscent of that of John Ruskin, another great puritan, who had once destroyed the priceless erotic paintings and drawings, perhaps hundreds of them, that Turner, Britain's greatest painter, had left to the nation. Ruskin, then Director of the National Gallery, had given as a reason that 'such beauty can only come from the Devil.' His prose, replete with disturbing words that recalled bodily functions and sexual associations that he never consciously realised, was very like Howard's. Ruskin, we might recall, was impotent and made his young bride kneel down with him to pray to God to take away her sinful lust. I made certain deductions that might apply to Howard as well.

One weekend I invited a few people to a conference at Ledlanet to discuss setting up a new Arts Association to support and develop the arts in Scotland, including of course literature. Among those who came were Peter Hemmings (administrator of Scottish Opera), Finlay MacDonald, Duncan Millar and Magnus Magnusson. Finlay was particularly impressed by being in a home with a butler, although Attewell, a free spirit if there ever was one, had a bantering and familiar relationship to me that would have been impossible in my uncle's time. It was Bettina who put him in his place and he did not like it. At the so-called conference, which never came to anything other than an interesting exchange of ideas, lubricated by wine and whisky, my forthcoming trial was much discussed. Finlay MacDonald was especially troubled. 'You must win this, John. Otherwise it will be a disaster for all the arts in Scotland.'

I made enquiries and was told that the best criminal lawyer in Scotland was Laurence Dowdell in Glasgow. I went to see him. He had no doubt who my Counsel should be: Nicholas Fairbairn was my man. There were two successful and unconventional criminal barristers in Scotland at that time; one was Lionel Daiches, about whom more later. The other was Nikky Fairbairn, who was a peacock. He was Scotland's Oscar Wilde, flamboyant, designing his own clothes, supremely self-confident, cocky, arrogant, loving publicity and always attracting attention to himself. He was also an artist and had already cartooned all the judges in front of whom he had appeared. He believed himself capable of almost any feat, he would proposition almost every woman he met to go instantly to bed with him – and many did – and, as I learned after his death, sometimes men as well. He had a wife from the Scottish aristocracy, the Rea family (his own origins were much humbler) and he now owned a castle in Fife, called Fordell, which as David Steel was later to say, was really a tower. This description of Nikky Fairbairn is of course based on hindsight.

My legal team was now Laurence Dowdell and Nicholas Fairbairn, who quickly became a friend, but not, I now think, a very sincere one. As Kenneth Dewey was the author of the Happening, it seemed sensible to get him to court and he agreed to come at his own expense. We found other witnesses who had been present at the Happening, some eminent participants, and some members of the audience, who having read that I was to be prosecuted, volunteered to appear.

The day before the case began, I met Ken Dewey at the airport in Edinburgh and drove him to Ledlanet. I was invited to a McGonigall Dinner in Fife that night and was taking Ken with me. I prepared him by giving him a volume of McGonigall's poems to read, which soon had tears streaming down his cheeks from laughter, and he became an instant fan. The dinner, organised by a group of Fife artists, was in honour of Scotland's worst-ever poet, a man who sincerely believed in his own genius. His verse is really doggerel where every second line rhymes with the one before it, but there is no detectable metre. Lines are uneven, references to classical myths and romantic imagery abound, and the juxtapositions of high-flown sentiments and utter banality can only bring mirth. But anything so bad must have its adherents and McGonigall is much quoted, read for fun and, during the last century has rarely been out of print. The dinner, an annual event in a small Fife town was attended when possible in Victorian costume, and Ken and I managed to rustle up frock coats and top hats for the occasion. There were about fifty people present at the dinner. A brass band played sentimental or military melodies, McGonigall was read and quoted, and there were speeches, all comic except for one unsuspecting senior Royal Air Force officer, who had been asked to toast the British Empire did so in traditional style, becoming uneasy as his listeners tried to restrain their mirth. Needless to say, we all got quite drunk, and on the way back my car broke down, I think running out of petrol. Sheila Colvin was working for me then and staying at Ledlanet, and I managed to 'phone her from a farmhouse. She told me that Sigmund Miller had suddenly turned up at Ledlanet, and then came to fetch me in her own car. With Sigi, more was drunk, and we went to bed late, but somehow turned up on time at the Edinburgh Central Court the next morning at 10.00 a.m.

Bernard Levin, sitting directly behind me, wrote a wonderful piece about the trial for the New Statesman entitled *Lady MacChatterley*. It was a comic experience for an outsider. I already knew that there would be no more conferences – the Lord Provost's ignorant and intemperate statements had made that clear enough – but there were other fertile furrows to sow in Scotland, as well as in England, and because I now lived in both, I was dividing my time fairly equally. We had two elderly ladies in the box who said they had been missionaries; they were very alike, and not personages one would have thought likely to be interested in listening to an intellectual arts conference, but on behalf of the prosecution they claimed to have been deeply shocked. There was a man who said he was a journalist, but could only claim to have written one or two free-lance articles and he was vague about where they had appeared. They had obviously been put in to the conference by Moral Rearmament to describe anything to which exception could be taken in the discussions, and the Happening was an unexpected bonus. The earlier days had been disappointing for them, because such issues as sexuality had hardly been mentioned during the week, unlike the year before.

Our own witnesses were splendid. Duncan Macrae, veteran actor of stage and screen, had not been bothered even to look behind him at the model on the balcony, but he had enjoyed the whole experience in which there was nothing shocking at all. Robert McLellan, a deeply serious historical playwright, denounced Moral Rearmament and all it stood for, and later wrote a play, *The Hypocrite*, inspired by the trial, but about Calvinist puritanism, which I later published, as well as many other McLellan plays. David Jones had been the producer for the BBC monitor programme which had filmed and transmitted the conference. He had been subpoenaed by the prosecution to give evidence about the model, but his evidence helped us, the defence. The most telling witness was a housewife from Fife, an ordinary member of the public who had come to the Conference on that last day, had found it entertaining, funny and very educational. She had stayed to the end. Her straight-forward honest evidence was a wonderful contrast to the put-up, obviously planted, prosecution witnesses. Throughout Nicholas Fairbairn was brilliant. He showed up the prosecution witnesses as frauds, brought out the best in our own team, and when Ken Dewey appeared – not that Ken needed any help – handled him properly. The Procurator Fiscal glared at Dewey when we put him in the box. 'We wanted to arrest him, but he fled the country,' he declared. Ken quietly explained his credentials, what he had done in the theatre and the arts, and produced for the magistrate, who happened to be the only City Councillor not on the Festival council, a beautiful little terra-cotta statuette he had made, a female nude in the classical Greek style. The magistrate looked at it with interest, and I think with awe, and handed it back. Dewey explained what it was he wanted to get over to the public, as he had in the final debate, his gratitude to me for bringing him, a young artistic theatre director, to Edinburgh to demonstrate his ideas, and his pleasure at the favourable public reaction, totally different to what the tabloid press had described.

The Procurator Fiscal made his final speech. An exhibition like this might be alright in some places, he summed up, a Paris night club for instance, but in the McEwan Hall, at a Drama Conference, No! The last word was expelled with all his force. Fairbairn addressed the magistrate with a combination of irony, humour, reason and law. No law had been broken. Anna Kesselaar had not moved; she had been moved. The nation had seen her live on television without a single complaint. David Jones' evidence had been conclusive on that. The court's time had been wasted by three people who had been sent there to make trouble, who had no interest in drama or anything artistic or intellectual. The Procurator Fiscal had made much of the

Queen having, on some past occasion, been present at McEwan Hall, which had dignified it. The Conference and the Happening had not degraded it. One thing had nothing to do with the other. People had enjoyed the Conference and had learned from it, which was good. The magistrate took little time to throw the case, which had lasted two days, out of court, declaring Anna Kesselaar innocent, so there was no case against me. He also criticised those in high places who had launched the prosecution.

* * * * * *

I took Sheila to Glasgow to see John Arden's *Armstrong's Last Goodnight* at the Citizens' Theatre, in which I was impressed by two Scottish actors, John Cairney and Leonard Maguire. I was at the time planning a Happening for Ledlanet. It was the year of the Shakespeare Quatercentenary and I had been doing much reading and thinking about the place of Shakespeare as a mannerist renaissance figure, largely from reading Arnold Hauser's masterly book *Mannerism*,[22] which influenced me deeply and was the basis of a book I was starting to write about opera and where everything in opera comes from. Cairney had an uncanny resemblance to Robert Burns, my birthday mate, while Maguire could easily be made to look like Shakespeare. I sat down to write a play for Ledlanet, *A Happening with Robert Burns*. After all, a Happening had made me notorious and I might as well make use of that that notoriety. I had also realised that the technique of blending unfamiliar objects and ideas with the familiar in a collagist way to put over a point could heighten a drama, even in an otherwise conventionally-written play. What I then wrote, much of it dictated to Sheila Colvin, was a verbal duel in which the idealistic and romantic Burns confronts the more coldly classical and 'mannerist' figure of Shakespeare. Inside the play were set-piece extracts from the work of both, a shortened *Tam O'Shanter* in the first act, for example, which had music, mime and ballet set against the narration. In the second act there was a trial of the modern arts with the two central figures as leading counsel, Shakespeare cynically attacking them; Burns defending. Each ended with a plea to the audience which became the jury. As we were in Scotland there was no doubt what the outcome would be every night. There were mime parts, diversions and surprises, quotations and passages from different modern writers including James Joyce. At the time I was being constantly asked to give talks and lectures, to take part in university debates and to defend the positions I had taken on censorship, social reforms and the innovative arts. This meant that I was always scouring my books for support for my arguments, quoting my own authors where possible to make their names and works better known, and using my growing library, increasingly housed at Ledlanet. This library grew dramatically during the summer of 1964 when I put on an exhibition of modern literature in the

---

[22] Mannerism. Arnold Hauser. London 1965.

salon (as the drawing-room was increasingly called), heavily captioned with explanatory showcards, blown up from the explanations I had written of movements, influences and connections between the writers and schools of the early twentieth century. The books came from all the publishers of the authors concerned: they were displayed, and as no-one ever asked for their books back, I kept them. Increasingly I was turning into an auto-didactic free-lance academic, trying to popularise the arts and to push up public taste, in sharp contrast to what governments and the media were to do later. Perhaps that was what I always was at heart: a popular educator with a fire in his belly to make life more interesting for others by opening up new horizons in the arts and literature.

A Happening with Robert Burns was contrived to be a didactic entertainment that would give new ideas to audiences without them realising that what they were enjoying was also adult education. It was a considerable success and I was often asked to revive it. I asked Ande Anderson, with whom I had become friendly since that first Ledlanet season, to produce it, and he gave it a week, blocking out the moves and plotting the lighting (we had only six spotlights then). Michael Geliot then took over for most of the other rehearsals; the last days I directed myself. We had built a new removable stage in the middle of the hall with raked bench-seating on both sides, but the benches were cushioned and had backs. My two gamekeepers were kept busy as carpenters. The double staircase greatly increased the playing area as well as giving height and variety to it. The eleven rows of seating – from now on we only used the main hall for performances – could take 98 people, much more than the Traverse. In the years to come the shape of the hall, with its two banks of stairs, its high-up aperture in the middle of the first floor balcony, its outer hall, which from that autumn became the orchestra pit, and its central playing area between two banks of facing seats, would give opportunities for a great variety of theatrical effects in an intimate setting.

That summer season in 1964 also had concerts, which became a regular feature with the same string quartets, chamber groups, pianists and singers returning frequently with different programmes. Although the Burns Happening went down very well with the audience, and proved that the ideas I was developing could work, there were many problems. John Cairney's flamboyant style of acting and frequent ad-libs, which the audience loved and was in keeping with the character he was playing, much annoyed the gentle and more discreet Leonard Maguire, who told me he would never act with Cairney again. My reduction of *Tam O'Shanter* by at least a third must have been very good, because every night some members of the audience (and no narrative poem is better known in Scotland) would tell me afterwards 'He never missed a line.'

Ledlanet was three and a half miles from the nearest village, Milnathort, and we never saw a policeman. I would keep the bar open until the last member of the audience left and it became increasingly profitable.

During the first seasons the marquee, which had to be hired, erected, dismantled and returned, and the catering staff, carrying food a considerable distance from the kitchen, made it impossible not to lose money on feeding the audience, but soon we could do without the marquee, because an angel, in the theatrical sense, came into our lives. His name was Jim Fraser.

Bettina talked to Jim at the bar one night and then suggested I should pay him some attention. He had come with a party and was spending a large amount on drinks. As we became friendly he returned very frequently, more for the bar and the atmosphere than for the performance, I think, although he did enjoy music. Together with some of his friends, all in the building trade, Jim Fraser, whose company was the Fraser Construction Company of Dundee, extended the conservatory, which was next to the library (the bar during our seasons), out into the garden, so that it became a restaurant able to seat about a hundred. He also extended other wings of the house so that there were urinals and extra lavatories for men and a row of four of them at the other end of the house for women.

1964 was Harewood's last Edinburgh Festival. At that point he was deeply involved with another woman, the sister of Barry Tuckwell, perhaps the most noted French horn player after the late and much-lamented Dennis Brain, who had died in a crash after driving home to London immediately after a concert at the 1957 Edinburgh Festival. Like Marion, his wife, she was a concert pianist. Harewood's affair with Patricia Tuckwell was no secret in Edinburgh. The scandal of my conference, and in particular the never-ending attacks of the Scottish Daily Express and some other newspapers, had weakened his position. I still say that his biggest mistake was in being too democratic and allowing the town councillors to call him George rather than Lord Harewood. Had he kept his status as the Queen's first cousin and a belted Earl they would have stayed in awe of him, but he had allowed himself to be just another Festival Director and therefore was expendable. There was a scandal at the 1964 Festival when Harewood went back to see an artist after a concert and Marion, seeing Patricia Tuckwell there, slapped her face with much invective in front of everyone present. A divorce followed in which Harewood lost his London home and much else, and eventually he married Pat (Bambi) Tuckwell.

Bettina had made herself friendly with Marion Harewood, would attend meetings of musical committees at 2 Orme Square, the Harewood London townhouse and she became as much socially involved in London music as artistically. I played no part in all this, being too busy with publishing and Ledlanet. Both Harewood and Sir Robert Meyer agreed to be sponsors of Ledlanet Nights, but neither ever attended a performance. When the Harewood break-up came, Bettina was resolutely on the wife's side.

Sentiment against Harewood, who was also criticised for his highbrow programming, had grown to such an extent that he resigned after the 1964 Festival. Before that he had been targeted, not only by MRA and the local philistines, but by a sociology lecturer at Glasgow University for having bare-breasted African dancers at the Festival. Had they been white, he said, they would not have been allowed to perform. Interviewed on the BBC, Harewood told a joke about a psychiatrist who really wanted to be a sex-maniac, but failed his practical. The Glasgow lecturer sued both Harewood and the BBC, which paid damages. All this added considerably to the poor man's problems.

During the second Ledlanet Nights season in June 1964, I had scheduled a mini-Schubert festival with two concerts by the Edinburgh Quartet with whom I had become friendly, especially so with Miles Baster, its leader, and two evening of Schubert song-cycles, *Die Schöne Müllerin* and *Die Winterreise*, in which both Thomas Hemsley and his accompanist Paul Hamburger appeared in period costume, the last looking exactly like Schubert. Although the audiences were small, they were very appreciative. Geraint Evans, a major opera star then, especially in Mozart comic roles and Verdi's *Falstaff* at Covent Garden, had been persuaded to sing Cimarosa's *Maestro di Capella* in which the singer pretends to conduct the orchestra. And the other major production was the *Happening with Robert Burns*. In the autumn we had a double bill of Bernstein little opera about a marriage gone stale, *Trouble in Tahiti*, coupled with Lennox Berkeley's *A Dinner Engagement*, a very snobbish, very English comic opera, and our big production, a week later, was Handel's *Parthenope*, with orchestra, conducted by Audrey Langford and produced by Michael Geliot. The cast included the tenor, Adrian de Peyer, who had sung the first season in the Rossini song cycle, and he arrived on the stage, Tarzan-like, on a rope swinging from the gallery to much applause. Bettina was in the cast together with Judith Pierce as our main soprano, and several others. The following year we had Pierce back in a revival of *Serate Musicale*. On that occasion, which was in the autumn, there does not appear to have been a summer season. In 1955, we performed another Handel, *Agrippina*, again with Bettina in the cast, but there was an amazing American coloratura in the lead, Alice Robiczek, who said she would sing anytime for the tapestried chairs in the salon, and other good singers, some of whom would appear again at Ledlanet in the future. That was the first time we had Peter Gellhorn as conductor. He was also chorusmaster at the BBC and Glyndebourne: Ande Anderson was back as producer. Larry Adler gave his one-man-show that season and was prevailed upon to compère the Members' night, failing at the time to extract from me an extra fee for it. In his Sunday Times column the following week he commented, 'Plumb forgot I was in Scotland'. Jim Fraser frequently entertained our artists, taking them out to dinner and occasionally to play golf. When he took out Michael Geliot and Adrian de Peyer, and the latter won, it was Geliot who was upset. 'I never thought tenors had anything between the ears,' he said. 'What a humiliation to be beaten by one.'

From this point, although I was having problems finding the money to pay for productions with good singers and a sizeable chamber orchestra of about sixteen players, Ledlanet Nights had established itself as an important part of the Scottish musical scene. I began to build a supporting organisation and started a membership to raise funds: at every performance a number of audience members joined. I recruited enthusiasts willing to give time, and some local businessmen, to a committee that took on much of the necessary organisation. Soon we were giving fund-raising balls, eventually three a year, special Members' Nights, one a season, when artists taking part were asked to contribute their talents to performing one or two party pieces in a kind of cabaret, which was followed by a dinner dance. As Ledlanet Nights developed into four annual seasons and nearly a hundred performances a year, it became necessary to justify a full-time catering staff, supplemented by temporaries, and to use box-office money from advance bookings to pay current bills. Soon we had two thousand members, a committee of about twenty and myriad fund-raising initiatives. I eventually began to get funds from the Scottish Arts Council. Visits by Lord Goodman, the Chairman of the Arts Council of Great Britain, and Jenny Lee, the Arts Minister, helped to get this increased from a very low starting level. But we also received subsidies after a while from different County Councils within a fifty mile radius and even from the City of Glasgow after a number of Councillors had been to performances and felt us worthy of support.

It was a period when the publishing company was flourishing. In spite of the extra activities, many of which brought in new authors, the Scottish list especially increasing as a result of my high northern profile, I still spent most of my time in the London office. Marion Lobbenberg had taken over much of the administration, and we had more staff to do editorial work, more salesmen and full-time accountants and production managers. We had left our Sackville Street offices as the building was being demolished and had rented two floors in a building in Soho at 18 Brewer Street. We had Lina Stores, a large Italian grocer below us on the street level and our landlord, Hyman Fine, on the top floor above us. The entrance was in a small passage-way called Green's Court. After about a year, Mr. Fine moved and we took over the top floor as well. Our landlord was one of the largest land owners in central London, possessing a large part of Soho and properties elsewhere, but he did everything himself. He sent out rent demands in his own handwriting and employed no secretary. We, on the other hand, had grown considerably. We had young editors, fresh from the universities, who did the copy editing on the manuscripts that Marion and I accepted. Marion began to make frequent trips to New York, coming back with books, none of which did particularly well, but which swelled the list. We also took on Denis Williams from Africa, Paul Ritchie from Australia, Dino Buzzati and Paolo

Valponi from Italy, Radomir Konstantinovic and Jara Ribnikar from Serbia and several South Americans including Julio Cortazar. D.P. Costello, who had translated *The Blind Owl*, now sent us a nineteenth century Russian novel in his new translation. It was *Nikolai Negorev*, which had become a Soviet classic, and we published it.

Three new British novelists were taken on, two of whom became quite prominent. They were Ann Quin, Alan Burns and Eva Tucker. There was also Alan Burns' wife, Carol, whom we published, but there was a mishap there, which I shall come to. Ann Quin's first novel *Berg* was very different from the run of British fiction. Set in Brighton during the off-season, the seedy atmosphere is beautifully described and three characters, Berg, a young protagonist, his father (really a portrait of the author's father) and his mistress weave around each other in a situation where sex and violence are always present. It ends in murder and the body of the older man is washed up by the tide, prescient of what, in a short time, would happen to the author herself. But basically she was writing about her love-hate relationship to her own father, on whom she had an obvious fixation. Not long after publication, Ann Quin met the elderly, distinguished and eccentrically fascist-admiring author, Henry Williamson, in a Chelsea pub and started an affair with him, an obvious father-replacement. Williamson was able to get her favourably considered for prizes and awards. She won the D. H. Lawrence Fellowship through his influence and then the Harkness Commonwealth Fellowship, which allowed her to travel on a grant and spend two years in the United States. Before she left we had published two other novels. *Berg* came out in 1964, was followed by *Three* in 1966 and *Passages* in 1969. When she returned from America she had written little else, but had spent much time with American hippies, was drinking too much and had experimented with a number of drugs. Williamson by now had lost patience with her. I managed to get her an Arts Council grant of £2,000, but they ignored my suggestion that it should be doled out over a year. She cashed her cheque into liquid currency, went to the airport, took a plane to Dublin and spent some time in Ireland. I heard rumours that she had been sighted in a number of Dublin pubs. Then she returned to Britain, took the next 'plane that was leaving, which landed her in Amsterdam and no more was heard of her until, in mid-winter, she was rescued, half-frozen from a snow-drift in Stockholm! After lengthy hospitalisation there, she was returned to Britain, but her mental condition was precarious and she had to take daily doses of Lithium to regulate her body and mind. This made creative writing impossible. She took a job as a secretary, seemed better, but was obviously unhappy. I spent an evening at her flat with other friends of her's, and could see that she was now a manic-depressive and just moving into a manic phase. She was also trying to reduce the Lithium in order to start writing again. Shortly afterwards she went down to Brighton to stay with her mother. A fisherman saw her on the beach at twilight, taking off her clothes and entering the water naked. Her body was found, a week later, washed up further down the coast. It was a waste of a great talent and helped blight my intention to try to form a group of writers, including Ann, into a school like the *nouveau roman* in France and the *Gruppe 47* in Germany.

Alan Burns' short novel *Buster*, about his period as a national service man, appeared in our first *New Writers* volume and then his extraordinary surrealist novel, *Europe After the Rain*; the title taken from Max Ernst's famous Bosch-like painting, was published in 1965. We followed it with *Celebrations* in 1967, *Babel* in 1969 and *Dreamerika!* in 1972. I always liked the first best, *Europe* not *Buster*, because of its originality and the successful way the author has of changing the reality of his narrative shift, in the way a dream does, from page to page. There is a continuity, but not of waking life. What he was trying to do was create a reality of menace, as reality might be perceived under fascism or in a prison camp, and it was the nearest we ever came to finding a Kafka-like writer. I liked *Celebrations*, but thereafter was aware that Alan's main interest at that point was in being well-known and earning big royalties, and that his books were becoming gimmicky purely to attract attention, whereas earlier it was an artist at work. The last book *Dreamerika!*, a satiric and dadaesque look at the Kennedy family did not get as well-reviewed as his previous books, nor did it sell. By that point Alan Burns had become more interested in developing an academic career and he went to an American university to teach. But he had the energy and the organising ability to lead a movement and it is a pity it never took off. We published two books by Eva Tucker, who had as a girl been at the same school in Berlin as Marion Lobbenberg (or Asmus as she was then). *Contacts* was a picture of a marriage and the tensions inside marriage. *Drowning*, the second book, explored human relationships in a frank way that was only just becoming possible in the sixties, when people were able to talk about their intimate lives and confront homosexuality and other previously taboo subjects without prejudice. Neither did as well as they should, but in those days publishers could always count on selling at least a thousand copies to public libraries, even without reviews.

Carol Burns was Alan's wife. We published a short novel, *Infatuation*, in *New Writers 6* and *The Narcissist* in 1967. The latter was a picture of a very self-obsessed and narcissistic woman, which I really published more as a favour to Alan than because I liked it. One day I received a lawyer's letter, telling me that *The Narcissist* libelled his client, Yolanda Sonnabend. I rang up Alan who admitted it was true. Alan was a qualified barrister, who had been employed for a while as libel-reader for the Daily Express. How could he allow this to happen? He had no explanation. He could hardly have thought that Sonnabend, who had been a friend of his wife, would not notice. Obviously the novel had been written out of malice and jealousy of Yolanda Sonnabend's established career: she was a successful designer for ballet, opera and theatre, as well as a painter who sold her work well. If it went to court damages would be heavy and it became obvious to me, now that I knew the protagonist was a real person, that the libel was a serious one. A libel case could mean bankruptcy. I rang up Yolanda, who I knew slightly, invited her to lunch, and she was nicer about it all than I expected. She thought I could get the damages back from insurance, but we had never carried libel insurance. Not only is it expensive, but one must then get every book read, and we would be in endless arguments with lawyers about cuts. I told her that I would withdraw and kill the book instantly; there had been few reviews and no good ones, so few people would have seen it. I would ask booksellers and libraries to return their stock. She agreed not to take action and I said I would pay her legal fees. Her lawyer was furious, told me that it was unethical to speak directly to his client, but I took no notice and the whole thing blew over. Not too long after that the Burns marriage ended. Not only was the picture of Yolanda an ugly one, but it showed her having an incestuous affair with her brother, and she had a brother who also might have sued.

Other writers not published by me, but who moved in the same circle, included Eva Figes and B. S. Johnstone. When I arranged joint readings and sessions for the public to promote a new kind of English novel, I would sometimes include them with my own writers, especially Eva, with whom I was personally friendly. She had done a number of translations for us, and was now published by Faber. Later on I published her feminist book about drama and death rituals in primitive societies entitled *Tragedy and Social Evolution* and a monologue, which the BBC broadcast, appeared in *New Writers*. But her agent, Deborah Rogers, wanted her novels and her most successful feminist book *Patriarchal Attitudes* to go to a publisher known for larger advances than we normally paid. It is obvious, looking back, that Eva Figes was the most important of the writers outside the fictional mainstream who emerged at that time. She had had a hard time. A bad marriage, not unlike that of another Jewish refugee from the Nazis, Lisel Field, had left her with two small children to support, and she managed to do it, first by translating, then by writing her own books. Her talent was not dissimilar to Virginia Woolf's, but she never compromised or tried to write commercially. For years she lived on the minimum, sent her children to state schools, but as she lived in Hampstead they were good ones, and they both later had successful careers as adults. When the Arts Council recognised her talent and circumstances, and I played a hand in that, she was one of the recipients of state aid who never splurged or used it badly. Although I occasionally had an argument with Eva Figes, I had a great respect for her character and her courage as a woman, as well as for her talent as perhaps the best serious novelist writing in London during the sixties. Although she went socially, as we all did, to parties and gatherings, she kept a fence of privacy and discretion about herself, remaining always a little apart and her private life was very private and kept out of the sight of her children. Above all she was afraid of scandal, and pride was her dominating characteristic quality. She told me once that she had been invited to a party where the food was very generous and had concealed some in her bag to take home to her small children. But something had been stolen and everyone was made by the police to turn out their pockets and open their bags; She had never forgotten the humiliation.

B. S. Johnstone also belonged to that circle and he was very different. He was strident and militant, very ambitious and very depressive when things did not go his way. This was the period when Labour having returned to power with Harold Wilson as Premier, Jenny Lee became Arts Minister, and suddenly there was money for the arts in greater abundance than ever before, and this included literature. Eric Walter White, a writer on music, became head of the new Literature Department of the Arts council, with Charles Osborne, an Australian who had successively been an actor, a poet, and assistant editor of Alan Ross' London Magazine, as his deputy. Money was made available to help writers trying to get known who had sufficient talent, providing someone knowledgeable and considered responsible would vouch for them. Sometimes writers applied, or found sponsors to apply for them, for a grant to give them time to write or to finish a novel. Sometimes publishers applied for money to reduce the advance they normally expected to pay. Not surprisingly, the Arts Council, and this applied to their Scottish office in Edinburgh as well as to London, preferred the big established publishers to the struggling smaller ones. The latter received only very minor help, whereas when Collins applied for money to help publish B. S. Johnstone, a large matching grant was given of £15,000 to go to the author for his next three books. He probably never received much of it because he committed suicide, the reasons being apparently partly writers' block and partly depression when his wife left him. But before that he was militating against all publishers and urging other writers to join him in establishing a co-operative to publish themselves. At one such meeting I recounted the history of Gallimard, founded by a group of French writers to publish themselves, with Gaston Gallimard employed to be business manager. André Gide, chairing the reading committee, turned down Proust as not good enough, and the writers all quarrelled and criticised each other; finances were a mess: finally their business manager suggested that they stick to writing their books and let him publish them, on the best possible terms, and take over both the business and the headaches. At the time I told the story in the sixties, Gallimard was possibly the largest and most successful publisher of creative literature in the world. The collective had not lasted long!

However such arguments did not sway Johnstone, but he received little support. I was one of the publishers taking on new and experimental writers just then, British as well as foreign, but so were Jonathan Cape, Secker and Warburg, Faber, and even Collins, provided that the Arts Council reduced their risk. I published much that needed subsidy, but I was not good at going through the necessary gestures, and only received subsidy for expensive translations, such as Stuckenschmidt's massive Schönberg biography, which Humphrey Searle, the composer, translated. I receive no money towards publishing Ann Quin, but obtained a grant for her, and that was usually the basis on which I applied. Even before her suicide, knowing my authors, I had pleaded with the Arts Council to give a weekly or monthly stipend rather than a lump sum, but they said they could not be paternalistic, and that any other way of paying might attract income tax. This was nonsense. Aidan Higgins asked them to give me the money and we paid it out to him weekly; he knew his weakness. The Arts Council must be considered to be at least partly responsible for the suicides of Quin and Johnstone by doing things in the way that was bureaucratically easiest for them. Most of the time they subsidised holidays and drinking bouts, not time to write.

Aside from money given to writers there was also subsidy available for the production of literary books where the return would be low, and for difficult translations, but I did not really understand that the rules were made largely by putting in applications, and I only did it when a book could not be published otherwise. I did better in Scotland however, because I was sent an application to apply to republish out-of-print Scottish classics and I responded. Only one other publisher wrote in to express an interest in the project, a Mr. Morgan, whom I met to discuss co-operation. We agreed to start a *Scottish Library* series of both classics and modern books and each take on certain titles, giving the books a similar appearance. But it turned out that he was part of Bernie Cornfeld's empire of newly starting-up companies, financed by IOS (Investors Overseas Services, a bubble about to burst). In the fall-out Mr. Morgan disappeared, but I continued on my own. The first title appeared in 1970, an anthology entitled *Contemporary Scottish Verse*, edited by Norman MacCaig and Alexander Scott. It was a good anthology with fifty-one poets in it. Clearing the rights was a nightmare, even with the Scottish Arts Council paying most of the fees. They also paid forty percent of the production cost, but, when we sold out, would not give anything towards a reprint, which would have involved more copyright fees, so there never was one. I continued the series, not always with subsidy, with three volumes of MacLellan plays, the Poems of Sidney Goodsir Smith (some time later), several anthologies of medieval prose, short stories and other works. My relations with the Scottish Literature committee was later to sour, as I shall come to relate.

I arranged lectures, readings and debates for my little stable of London-based authors, and involved their friends who were published by others. The last school of British writing that had successfully established itself was the Bloomsbury Group. There had been interest around the Georgian Poets. There had also been the various movements launched by T.S. Eliot and Ezra Pound, by Wyndham Lewis, and of course the Thirties Poets were now linked together. After the war there had been an attempt by

Wain, Amis, Larkin and their friends to launch 'The Movement', but the name had never stuck: it was a very English and inward-looking group, disliking especially Europe and America, very Oxbridge and middle-class. My group came from the newly-educated upward-thrusting working-class or lower middle. Burns had the personality to lead a new group, but not the staying-power, nor did he know enough about, or take enough interest in, the others to get their confidence. So, as a new school, it failed.

One of my best customers in London was Tony Godwin's Better Books on Charing Cross Road. It was an intellectual bookshop with a charismatic owner who loved literature. He offered me my own Calder Corner, a space where he would leave it up to me to see that it was properly and interestingly stocked. It enabled me to push my new authors along with those who had developed a following, rearrange the books as I wished and add promotional material, so that my corner resembled a display as much as a section of shelving. Then he acquired some more space in the shop next door and asked me to organise events in it. I put considerable effort into a weekly event, I think it was on Thursdays. There were debates between different writers and critics, and there were readings of my authors and of others. There was a 'Happening' organised there by Jeff Nuttall, an actor, director and art teacher, who was a leading member of *The People Show*, with his group. It was a messy affair with pieces of raw organ meat thrown around the room, but the point, which I have forgotten, was well-put-over and led to a lively discussion afterwards. I persuaded the BBC to record the Better Books events in the hope that some of it might be interesting to put on the air, but none ever was.

The problem came when other publishers began to be jealous of the considerable success of these evenings. We were filling every seat and usually having to turn people away, and the press was giving us a considerable amount of attention, which was free publicity that attracted many people to the bookshop. When Tony Godwin put it to me that other publishers would like to have a turn at organising an evening. I said 'Fine, let them,' and we gave three Thursdays during the following months to other publishers, the first being Jonathan Cape. The trouble was that Tom Maschler, who had been the loudest complainant, handed the job over to some girl in his office, who was either not interested or insufficiently competent to realise what was required, and did not know how to put on an interesting evening for what was now a faithful and alerted public. We only had sixty seats and were beginning to turn away almost as many. The Jonathan Cape evening was dull. The following week organised by another publisher, I forget which, was worse. The public dropped off and the BBC stopped recording. After three bad weeks Tony Godwin stopped the evenings or rather handed them over to his new manager, a poet of sorts, who was well known to be stealing books to sell elsewhere. Shortly after that, Tony sold out to Collins. He had just been offered a job as Fiction Editor at Penguin, so I lost my Calder Corner and was then under great pressure to sell paperback rights of authors I had nurtured during the previous several years to Penguin. I sold Tony a few, and was the only publisher to enjoy the temporary and short-lived prestige of a joint imprint with Penguin: Beckett's *Malone Dies* was the first title that appeared in this way. Then Tony went off to New York, where he became an editor at Knopf. I lunched with him occasionally on my visits there. He had split up with his wife, Fay, which no doubt was behind the move. But he did not live long in the States and died there within two or three years.

I still went skiing at Val d'Isère every year and it was probably spring 1964 when I met at Geneva Airport, on the way there, a lady who I knew and liked, who for the purpose of this book I shall call Anna. She was the daughter of a European publishing family which had moved to England before the war, but had pursued a separate career as an arts administrator. We had always flirted a little when we met, but now I was on my own, as was she, and I suggested she come to Val d'Isère with me. She hesitated, and had I had more time I think would not have resisted the temptation, but I looked her up once back in London, and after a while she succumbed to my advances. Our affair lasted some time and was mutually satisfactory, but what she enjoyed most was accompanying me to various European cities such as Amsterdam during the Holland Festival, when she met local intellectuals, and to Scotland. Bill Watson had agreed to take a series of articles for the Saturday edition of The Scotsman, for which I condensed some complex ideas of mine for a book I was planning on the main influences behind the different directions that serious modern literature was taking, and I went back to the nineteenth century impressionist movement as my starting point. These appeared on successive Saturdays and were intended to link up with four lectures that I gave on the same Saturdays for the extra-curricular department of Edinburgh University in the David Hume Tower. I remember that the first did not go as well as I had intended because I had taken an overnight boat and train from Dublin, was sleepless and tired and making the mistake of reading the lecture instead of doing what I always do best, talking of-the-cuff with the notes to refer to if necessary. Early in my relationship with Anna, I repeated these lectures in Glasgow for the Extra Mural Department where I remember that amorous dalliance with her, (and she liked to make love all night to achieve satisfaction), much reduced my preparation time. But I was becoming rather too self-confident then at my ability to lecture almost without any preparation, and whereas I usually got away with it, there were some rather lame occasions. *The Four Directions in Modern Literature* came to be repeated many times, even twenty years later, and they will eventually appear in print.

During 1964 I wrote two serious plays, apart from the more didactic entertainments for Ledlanet, both heavily influenced by Beckett. I showed Sam the first, a dialogue entitled *Tell Me Again* and his only comment was 'It's very well written.' The second I offered to The Traverse and Jim Haynes scheduled it for the end of the year as part of a double bill with Stewart Conn's play about the atom bomb, *Birds in the Wilderness*. Called *The Voice* it depicted a man caught between his wife and his mistress, but in a trance-like state as if just waking up in the morning and not yet quite awake. The wife urges him to caution, the mistress to adventure, while a voice occasionally breaks in, urging him to various courses of action, in the soothing or militant tones of radio announcements or advertising spiels. Through it I met Leonard Fenton, who became a good friend, playing my protagonist. The two actresses were Pamela Ann Davey and Helen Ryan and David de Keyser recorded the voice for me. I turned up for the late rehearsals and found to my dismay that Jack Moore, an American who Jim had met on a 'plane between Dublin and Edinburgh, who was directing it, had totally changed the sense of the play. Because he was gay, he made the man a dominant figure over the two women, reversing totally the text, which had them driving him gradually into the ground. Where the text did not suit, it had been cut, and on the opening night the principal actress cut her most important speech, which I had conceived as a set piece like an aria. Elspeth Davie, one of my Edinburgh authors, went to see it and wrote me a letter saying that she did not want to have a publisher who also wrote, although she had never written anything for the theatre.

I did other things at The Traverse, most memorably putting on an evening in which Michel Geliot, Leonard Fenton and others acted out or recited scenes from Beckett's plays and other work under my direction. It later moved to the Arts Theatre Club in London.

Sometime in the spring of 1964, Jim Haynes came to call on me in London and he, Bettina and I were sitting in my bedroom listening to a recording that had just been released of the Brecht/Weill *Happy End*. Suddenly Jim said, 'Why don't we do it in Edinburgh?' Somehow the idea took hold, probably because Bettina wanted to sing it. Traverse Festival Productions Ltd. was formed to put it on, money was raised, and Michael Geliot engaged as producer. I was a little sceptical because it would have to be done outside the official Festival, but a large hall was found, and Robin Richardson, the best-known theatrical agent in Scotland, agreed to be responsible for the management of the company.

My rôle was largely confined to raising funds and to negotiating with London managements, so the very successful production that resulted owed more to Jim Haynes' enthusiasm and Bettina's good performance than to anything for which I could claim credit. Guy Wolfendon was the conductor, much criticised as he claimed a fixer's fee from all the orchestra, Joseph Melia was the male lead, and I only remember Declan Mulholland among the other cast, because he got very sick after drinking too much at Ledlanet after the Edinburgh last night. It transferred to the Royal Court in London, a theatre too small for it to make any profit, where it had excellent reviews, and a transfer was expected and certainly would have done well. But Michael

Codron, with two shows to transfer and only one theatre available to him, decided on the other, a dance show that featured Claude Chagrin, whose brother Nicholas would soon be in a play of mine, so *Happy End* died at the Royal Court. Her success was the beginning of Bettina's next career, which was putting together an evening of German Brechtian songs, by Weill and other composers, which she continued to do for years with varying success.

* * * * * *

Until the middle nineteen sixties I remained active in the Committee of 100, but little by little extremists, who were obviously *agents provocateurs*, usually young men, would take over the meetings, never allowing such distinguished members of the Committee as Herbert Read to say anything, and always advocating violent demonstrations. I assumed that they had been put in by MI5 or MI6 to make it possible to arrest the most effective genuine activists and to keep track of the progress of what had been an effective counter-force to Government nuclear policy. One by one the distinguished personalities in the arts, science and politics, whose names had given the movement credibility, dropped out, and eventually I did too. I especially distrusted Ralph Schoenmann, an American philosophy student, who had attached himself to Bertrand Russell and who spoke in the name of the eminent leader of the movement, now too aged to appear at meetings.

One week Bertrand Russell invited me to his cottage at Penrenhydreth to discuss the campaign. He told me that he too now distrusted Schoenmann, who was in control of the finances, and who every time he saw him insisted on pursuing paths of activity that he thought would alienate supporters who were not simply anarchists trying to take over the movement, but he confessed that he now felt too weak to out-argue Schoenmann and he saw no way that he could effectively say anything in public. I told him of my own misgivings and we talked until late into the night, but got onto many topics besides politics. I was put into a bedroom in which I was surprised to find the lives of the saints and many religious books, because Russell was a well-known atheist. At breakfast with the two Russells the next morning I expressed my surprise. 'It's for my grandchildren,' he explained. 'I was brought up with religion all around me and I eventually rejected it. I brought my children up without religion, but they all took to it. One is even a missionary. So now when my grandchildren come (they may have been great-grandchildren) I let them read religious books in the hope that they will react like me.' At his great age his mind was as sharp as ever and he still worked on philosophical and mathematical problems, but as I had noticed with my great-uncle Jim, old men lose the will to fight determined opposition and give way when opposed. What the old want most is a quiet life and tranquillity. I never saw Lord Russell again after that. He died in 1970 and his will specifically dissociated himself from Schoenmann to prevent him continuing to claim that he was wearing the Russell mantel. I am not sure what happened to Schoenmann after that. He had probably been planted by the CIA, and one day we will know the truth.

One of the bravest of theatrical impresarios of my years in London publishing was Peter Daubeny. He had started as an actor just before the war, but having lost an arm when serving in the Coldstream Guards, he changed to management when he returned to the theatre in 1945. As an impresario he brought overseas companies to London, mainly at first, dance groups from Eastern and Western Europe because they presented no language difficulty, but after his big success with Edwige Feuillère in *La Dame aux Camélias*, he increasingly brought over drama companies and this developed into his annual World Theatre Season which ran from 1964 to 1973. Towards the end of this period I commissioned a book from him, *Peter Daubeny Presents*, but he died in 1975 before he could complete it.

One of the productions he brought over from Paris in the sixties was *Les Naïves Hirondelles*, by the actor and writer Roland Dubillard, which is mentioned elsewhere in this book. I was eventually to publish it as *The Swallows* and also to mount the first English production. I had seen the play in Paris, met the author, brought him to Edinburgh in 1963, and had kept in touch. I was delighted when Peter Daubeny brought the French production to the Piccadilly Theatre: the French Ambassador gave a lunch for the company and I was invited and seated next to the author. I have an egg phobia, a quite irrational one which I think goes back to a dream that I had as a child, although I cannot be absolutely sure of that. I have known several other people with exactly the same egg phobia, but at the Ambassador's lunch, I discovered that Roland Dubillard had it too, and worse than me: I could not eat an egg, but he could not look at one. Our lunch started with *oeufs sous cloches*, and Roland took one look, turned green, closed his eyes, waved it away, and throughout the whole meal nibbled at his bread roll and drank the wine in his glass as quickly as it could be refilled. I cannot remember any conversation at all, and I am sure there was none.

After lunch I went to his hotel with him because I wanted him to sign a contract for English rights which I had in my pocket. He felt too unwell to do anything, was drinking more, and asked me to ring him the next day. I had seen the play the night before and went again that night. Roland, who played the principal rôle, with his girl-friend Arlette Reinerg, who had directed the play, and was the ingenue in the four-actor cast, was obviously drunk throughout the performance. He mumbled and sometimes forgot his lines, forgot to change from his costume, a suit in the first two acts, to pyjamas in the third, and was probably keeping up his alcoholic level in the intervals. He did eventually sign the contract.

* * * * * *

Early in 1964 Marion Lobbenberg married Arthur Boyars. I cannot remember where they married, probably in a synagogue in Hampstead. I remember that Arthur's mother was very difficult and made Marion produce documentation from East Germany to prove that her mother, who had died at Auschwitz, was really Jewish, which her father, Walter Asmus, a small publisher whom I had met at the Frankfurt Book Fair, was not. I was not invited to the ceremony, but to a lunch at a Chinese restaurant in the East End, the Old Friends, which for some reason was in fashion at the time. And that evening, or it may have been the next day, I gave a reception for them at the Caledonian Club. In my congratulatory speech I made a heavily veiled allusion to a 'birthday party' which had brought them together, which they probably did not appreciate. Shortly after that Marion told me that she wanted to change the name of the company to bring in her name, and it was the new married name she wanted. At a board meeting I agreed to a change to Calder and Boyars Ltd., but stipulated that Marion must now give up her claim to getting her money back ahead of me in the event of a dissolution. Roy Jones was against this and saw no reason to change the name, but Marion got her way and lost her financial precedence. In any case, ever since *Tropic of Cancer*, we had been solvent and making profits. But I had not done as well on Miller as I should have done. It had been agreed that in return for taking the legal risk on the book that I would get a higher percentage of the profit, but Roy Jones then insisted, once the risk had passed, that this only applied to the first impression of 40,000 copies, and as he had the casting vote, I lost. The other change that happened at this time was that we had to drop Lesley MacDonald. She was more kind than business-like, instinctively tended to trust her suppliers and several took advantage of this to overcharge. She also had begun to make some quite expensive mistakes. After several overpayments due to her trust or carelessness, and unfortunately she was not good at admitting her weaknesses or errors, Marion and Roy insisted she had to go. We made her a generous settlement and she retired. We gave her back Acorn Press, but she did little with it.

We now had three notorious authors who had done well with us, Henry Miller, William Burroughs and Alexander Trocchi. The profit from Miller now came mostly from paperback royalties rather than direct sales, but we had also published and sold well the Burroughs' trilogy of novels which had formed the basis of the anthologised volume *Dead Fingers Talk*, which had started all the brouhaha in the T.L.S. These were *The Naked Lunch*, *The Soft Machine* and *The Ticket that Exploded*, works that increasingly, as they progressed through the three volumes, used his fold-in, cut-up method, which he was then to drop in favour of more romanticised and fantasy fictions that reflected his preoccupations with magic, the Wild West, gangsters, creatures from outer space, pirates, bizarre and sadistic sex rituals and the kind of space-age fantasies that were increasingly to be found in adult comic books and later in video games. Revenue from paperback companies was increasingly important to us. Aside from Penguin, who had sub-contracted some of the more serious literary authors, we were dealing mainly with Panther and Picador, both paperback companies that were owned by American publishers, and to a lesser extent with the New English Library, which had been set up by New American Library. For this latter, then being run by two highly eccentric characters, I produced a *Samuel Beckett Reader*, an anthology which I prefaced with a long explanatory introduction and much comment on the works extracted. This sold well, helped to extend the interest in Beckett, earned money for Minuit, Beckett himself, and myself as editor, and helped rather than harmed our sales of Beckett's novels and poetry that we had published.

The two eccentrics were Gareth Powell and Christopher Shaw. The former had started life as a lorry driver in Australia, but having a charismatic personality had persuaded his American principals to make him Managing Director of their British subsidiary (which in its proper context was really Sales Director), while Christopher Shaw looked after publicity and editorial content. Christopher was an ex-Etonian, married to the daughter of a Hollywood film mogul. I spent an amazing weekend with them in a large country house they had rented near Oxford. There was endless game-playing, bridge, poker, billiards, ping-pong, croquet and golf, all for money and for the highest stakes that the hosts could con their guests into agreeing. The Shaws nearly always won, and it was an obsession with them to do so. On the Sunday morning I was induced to play golf for the first time since I had left Canada as a teenager. I played no better and little worse, but had to shell out money on each hole I lost, which was nearly all of them. After lunch we went around antique shops in the area and paid a visit to Prinknash Abbey at my instigation, as we were passing it, to call on Dom Sylvester Houdouard, fairly well-known as a poet, and an eccentric Church of England monk, who had given evidence along with myself for the defence at a recent obscenity trial of a small publisher. As every game had been for money it was an expensive weekend and the hosts more than recouped whatever it had cost them.

Christopher Shaw, in his capacity as Publicity Director of NEL – he might even have been Sales Director by then – took the Royal Pavilion at Brighton during a Bookseller's Conference to give a lavish all-night party, where champagne flowed like water, lobster and caviar was on offer on the sumptuous buffet tables, there were several bands, and the *dolce vita* night passed in a daze that must have cost more than their year's sales. But Christopher, not long afterwards, was in charge of a large office in New York for the parent company, from which he eventually moved on to other adventures. He looked like an adult Billy Bunter, round and beaming, full of jokes, and even fuller of mischief at someone else's expense. His wife, who had a new baby in a cradle during my weekend with them, that she never seemed to visit, was in her way as offhandedly-eccentric as he and as uninhibited. As for Gareth Powell, he had earlier decided to publish the erotic classic, *Fanny Hill*, and so provocatively that he was prosecuted as he always wanted, but only in a magistrate's court, using the publicity to make the book a paperback best-seller. His edition was, however, so heavily expurgated that he knew he would never be brought to the Old Bailey. He then crowed about this clever exploit in The Bookseller, the trade magazine. That kind of narcissistic self-publicity normally does you little good in the book trade. Shortly afterwards, in Australia, as a stunt, he drove a lorry of his own paperbacks across the country and became stuck under a low bridge. In the humiliating publicity and aftermath he lost his job.

Panther Books bought our Henry Millers for paperback. The two editors were William Miller and John Booth. Once, when asked how he decided how much to offer for paperback rights of a potentially best-selling novel, Miller replied that he offered a thousand pounds for every erection it gave him when he read it. He was flamboyantly gay, humorous and witty, but nearly all the paperback executives in those days tended to be characters who brought colour into what had been in the past a rather staid profession, dominated by paternalistic patriarchs from old-established, often family, firms. There was for instance John Watson, a tough hard-drinking Glaswegian, the Sales Manager of Corgi. His tough exterior had impressed his American bosses, but they did not know the extent of his alcoholism: he would spend weekends holed up in a small Bloomsbury hotel just to drink. His wife Helen sadly left him and opened an employment agency. Another heavy drinking paperback editor was Frank Rudman of Four Square, which belonged to a tobacco company. He was a melancholy homosexual who inspired much affection, and respect for his literary taste and knowledge, but alcohol did for him too. It was Corgi, then run by Patrick Newman who bought the paperback rights to Burroughs' novels. He believed that I had exactly the right formula for avoiding prosecution where it might have been expected, and he slavishly copied my jacket designs, using the same blurbs. I had designed *The Naked Lunch* cover myself, taking a montage of Brion Gysin, Burroughs' artist friend, which was a photograph of Burroughs' face made up from tiny other photographs, and cutting out the eyes to put in red circles where the eyeballs would have been; this effectively demonised his face. Corgi used the same cover which became iconic.

Those were the days, the middle-sixties, when hardcover publishers published largely to get reviews and library sales, and then sold paperback rights, which became their most important source of revenue, often exceeding the money earned from all other sources. I had my own large-format series of paperbacks, Calderbooks, using the same-sheets as the hardcover, either holding them when the hardcover was printed for a year or two, or printing another edition if the hardcover sold out. This was rarely done among publishers, but not all my titles were suitable for mass market, and my Calderbooks mixed fiction and non-fiction. In 1963 I started a new series in a mass-market format, but heavier and better produced than most, on good paper and thread-sewn. These were called Jupiter Books, selling for around five shillings or a little more. The first four titles were Beckett's *Murphy* and *Watt*, a volume of three plays by Ionesco and a novel that had done well, André Pieyre de Mandiargue's *The Girl Beneath the Lion*, a fruit of our early collaboration with Grove Press. Mandiargues' novel *The Margin* would later win the 1967 Prix Goncourt and be published by us two years after that. All the Jupiter series had the author's face on the cover, which worked well for some books, but not where the face was overly grouchy or off-putting. Later we were to start other series.

Of the three notorious or scandalous authors I have mentioned, we had so far been able to avoid prosecution, and I credit this almost entirely to the public acceptance of all three at my first Edinburgh Conference and the T.L.S. correspondence over Burroughs. But trouble now loomed for Trocchi, who had made himself, through self-publicity, the best-known drug addict in Britain. In those enlightened days addictive drugs were not involved in crime. An addict would get a prescription from a doctor that would enable him to get a daily dose to feed his habit, and this was free on National Health. Many Americans staying in London took advantage of this. A little before midnight every night, the Boots the Chemist shop that used to be open twenty-four hours a day on the south side of Piccadilly Circus, would have a cluster of mainly American hippies gathering outside. At midnight they could get their next day's prescription for heroin filled. The shop assistants did not like them, treated them with barely concealed contempt and much sharpness when they were impatient, but they had to fill the prescriptions. British addicts usually had a local chemist near where they lived, and they were less in evidence at the hub of London.

Trocchi had created a niche for himself. He appeared on radio and television programmes and was interviewed by the newspapers because drugs were one of the main topics of the day. His attitude was that individuals should be free to live as they wished and dose themselves as much as they wanted. He cited Coleridge and De Quincy as evidence that drugs were useful to the creative mind. He himself, however, had ceased to be creative. We had published his most celebrated novel *Cain's Book* and republished *Young Adam*, written shortly after leaving university, published by Girodias in Paris with obscene material added to make it more suitable for the Travellers Companion series, and subsequently it was republished in London by Heinemann as originally written, but without much success. In later years, and especially after his death, his pornographic fiction, written for Olympia Press in the early fifties, would be rescued, mainly in American pirate editions, but now Trocchi had only two books in print, and his addiction made him incapable of any new sustained literary effort. He could talk, get and express creative ideas verbally, but lacked the concentration and energy to write, except briefly. We kept him going with translations: *La*

Gana by Jean Douhassot and other French novels by René de Obaldia, Valentine Penrose, Pieyre de Mandiargues, and *I Jan Cremer*, a hippie novel by a notorious Amsterdam writer, where a Dutch friend helped him. But as he could only work for an hour or two at a time, and then only when in immediate financial need, we paid him by the page. I think it was a pound a page, and we checked what he brought in against the original. He would leave with ten or twenty pounds. Burroughs was also in London now, but Bill was more retiring, willing to appear on a television programme occasionally, but not actively seeking the opportunity, like Trocchi, who saw himself as the spokesman for the British beat generation.

We heard from a bookseller in Sheffield that the police had seized much of his stock and *Cain's Book* was one of the titles taken. We could either ignore the whole matter and allow the copies in question to be destroyed, or we could go to court to defend the book. It had been well received and had sold well on publication, but now, more than a year later, sales had dropped and I decided that publicity would give it new life. I informed the police that the novel would be defended and found a number of witnesses, the most eminent of them being Kenneth Alsopp, a well-known face on television and a literary journalist, who had given the book a major review in one of the popular dailies. Among other witnesses were Kathleen Nott, a distinguished poet and critic and a very forthright and robust woman in her fifties, and there may have been some minor figures as well. Marion Boyars was there, Trocchi and myself. I was not happy about Trocchi appearing in the witness box, but having made the decision I could hardly stop him. We were defended by Bruce Douglas-Mann, a solicitor whom I had known for some time through John Stonehouse, soon himself to become an M.P., and Sheila Colvin came to take a shorthand transcript. We stayed overnight in a Sheffield hotel, and the case, in front of three magistrates called Needham, Weedham and Boddy, took place the next morning. Given the obvious conservatism of the magistrates, I think that we would have lost in any case, but we put up a good defence with sensible and persuasive witnesses. It was Trocchi who ensured we could not win. In the box he was jaunty and provocative. Asked to explain a quotation from de Sade that he had put at the front of the book, which states that literature can extend the crimes of those who commit them beyond the grave, Trocchi said he agreed with every word. When the prosecutor put it to him that the book used obscenely objectionable words such as 'motherfucker', he replied that such a word was in common usage in America. His most damning statement was that drugs were good for people and he would like to see their usage spread. He had followed me into the witness box, where I had said that books do not influence people's behaviour, only their ideas by making them analyse them. Trocchi affirmed bluntly, 'I disagree with my publisher about the effect of books. If I didn't think that they could influence behaviour I wouldn't bother to write them.'

We lost of course, and when we went to the Court of Appeal in London a month later we lost that as well. The appeal judges also brought a new concept into the law, that a detailed description of drug-taking was obscene under the Obscene Publications Act.

As I arrived at Kings Cross Station from Sheffield I was met by a man from the BBC. I had been booked to give a talk on Max Frisch on the Third Programme that night. The talk had been cancelled. I forget the excuse, but the BBC did not want to be associated with a just-convicted pornographer whose case was on the front page of the evening newspapers. As I was just coming down with a streaming cold and was losing my voice, I was not too sorry, but I had another engagement that evening, to give the same talk on Frisch at the Swiss Embassy and in front of the Ambassador. I got through that one, adrenaline brought back my voice, and I was congratulated by His Excellency. We continued selling Cain's Book, but in a very low key without advertising, and not in Sheffield.

* * * * * *

Max Frisch remained a friend and I would see him quite often when he came to London, on occasion staying with me at Wimpole Street. On one occasion Sam Beckett was also in London, but not staying, and Max was, and I introduced them. Frisch felt exactly the same way about seeing a performance of a play of his with the audience present as Sam did, and when the National Theatre mounted *The Fire Raisers* I went with Sam, while Frisch stayed in the building but would not take a seat. There was one memorable Sunday afternoon around then when I had the two of them, and also the cartoonist Victor Weiss (Vicki) and his wife or girl-friend (I forget if they were married or not) to lunch. Afterwards we decided to play chess and we played several matches against each other. Max eventually beat the three of us and I came bottom. I cannot remember whether Vicki or Sam came second, but both were good players. The conversation was superb, going from the theatre to politics, from painting to world events, and I regret that I can remember the conviviality and the brilliance, but nothing else. Everyone got on well, Sam and Max being very new friends and Vicki, the most brilliant cartoonist of the day, was meeting two men he idolised for the first time.

Shortly after that came the 1964 General Election that brought Wilson and the Labour Party to power. My mother was in London and had dropped in. Vicki had come to dinner, and we were looking at television as the election results came in. We were all, except my mother who knew nothing of politics, but would have wanted the Conservatives to win, hopeful of a Labour victory, and we toasted every announcement of a Labour gain. That was the last time I ever saw Victor. His cartoons continued to be as brilliant as ever, but he was soon so disillusioned with the Labour government that he committed suicide two years later in a deep depression. My author Howard Barker later wrote a play about him, although Vicki is not named. His hero is a Hungarian artist, like him, who survives many tyrannies and revolutions, to reach Britain in the thirties and become a war artist during the last war, where he is savagely attacked by the British wartime establishment, especially by Churchill. Barker's point was that of all artists the most dangerous to the politician and to authority is the political cartoonist.

* * * * * *

Ledlanet continued to take up much of my life. The year after *Agrippina*, Ande Anderson produced, during our September-October season, two operatic shows. First there was a double-bill of Mozart's early opera *Bastien et Bastienne*, sung by the wonderful Australian soprano Maureen London with Kevin Miller and Ian Wallace, then making his first Ledlanet appearance, and *Pierrot Lunaire*, Schönberg's eerie masterpiece, which was sung in English by Pamela Smith and effectively mimed by Alex McAvoy; it succeeded in shocking an audience who were following the words that would have been, for the most part, politely bored if it had heard it in German. My policy at Ledlanet was to do as much as possible in English, and to find ways of putting over the meaning, the emotional content and the aesthetic value of everything performed, not only to make it enjoyable, but to enable a very mixed, but largely uninformed audience go away with new appreciation and enthusiasm. I was trying to educate those who came mainly out of curiosity, or for the social cachet, which we possessed by now, and to give additional pleasure to those who normally came to such events. But our main production that season was Benjamin Britten's *Turn of the Screw*. It was a notable success, received excellent reviews, and was picked out for special mention in the report of the year by Ronald (Bingo) Mavor, who having for years been drama critic of The Scotsman, was now Director of the Scottish Arts Council. I remember driving to Ledlanet from London on a Friday night, and arriving very late with rehearsals still continuing. One advantage of performing in premises of your own, is that a producer can rehearse as late as he likes or the cast will tolerate. Ande had decided that in an intimate setting the ghosts would look too substantial, so arranged that only their voices were heard, and they were only seen as shadows. I arrived just as the shadows were seen for the first time by the cast, and it was late-night: in that setting they were frightening enough for a shiver to go through all the artists present. 'Are there any real ghosts in this house?' I was asked, and so was Attewell, who was evasive and non-committal enough to increase the general fear. This communicated itself to the audience during the eight performances we gave. Among the cast were Angela Hickey, an effective, well-sung governess, Judith Pierce as Mrs. Grose, singers who had become regulars in the other roles, but the boy Miles, played by two Edinburgh boys in alternance, attracted much attention. They were both good, but Denis Sheridan was so self-assured a ten-year-old that Jim Fraser commented that if he had had a whisky in his hand instead of a Coca-Cola in the bar afterwards, he would, given his grown-up demeanour and conversation, have seemed perfectly natural. Roderick Brydon, an excellent conductor who gave much time to the boy sopranos, pulled off the opera perfectly together with Ande. I have never seen a better or more concentrated performance, although I have seen the opera very many times.

The pattern was now that I put on the summer season at Ledlanet and used Kent Opera for the main productions in the autumn. Each season lasted two or three weeks, with a fund-raising ball to start the season or to finish it when the scaffolding had not yet been put up or had been taken down. The scaffolding was Jacques Chaix's idea; he had after all once been trained as an engineer. By putting up scaffolding in the hall we had a balcony with four rows of seats on each side of the stage and thirteen rows below, seven on one side, six on the other. We could now seat nearly two hundred. The catering was divided: the conservatory could seat over a hundred for a three course meal, the menu limited to what people liked best, like smoked salmon, steak, sweets and cheese; the salon was now a buffet during the season, with a substantial choice of food and drink at a reasonable price. From Jacques Chaix's cousin in Miribelle in the Vaucluse, I brought in quantities of an excellent red and rosé wine, on which we now had our own label. Many customers liked it so much they bought cases to take away. Our house white was a dryish Rhine wine, and we had an assortment of more expensive wines and other drinks from our main suppliers in Leith, which was usually the biggest of the end of season bills we had to pay. A staff of about a dozen did the catering under Attewell's direction.

Early in 1964 I was approached by John Watt, who worked as a salesman for the firm that did our printing in Dumferline, David Watt and Sons. Although he had the same name as the firm I think the family connection had become minor, but he was also a folk singer and a good one, who wrote many of his own songs and was well-connected in the Scottish folk song movement. He suggested putting on an evening of folk songs, and starting in the June of that year, we programmed, or rather he did, two such evenings every year. In this way I became acquainted with Ray and Archie Fisher, The Tregullion, Matt McGinn, Tommy Bonnar, Barbara Dickson, Ali Bain, Hamish Imlach, Alex Campbell and Billy Connelly, and many others, some of whom were to become stars and not just in Scotland. Our folk song nights always filled the house, were cheap to do compared to most of our other shows and brought in a new audience, much of which came back to evenings that were more demanding but just as enjoyable. Ian Wallace, an opera singer who was also a popular entertainer with his one-man evening of chat, anecdote, operatic aria, traditional song and whatever else suited his audience, was especially popular in Scotland, although known to audiences at Glyndebourne, Covent Garden and abroad, and to those who listened to a popular radio quiz called *My Music* on the BBC. He became a regular with his *An Evening with Ian Wallace*, as well as in our productions. When Scotsdisc, a Glasgow record company run by Douglas Gray, wanted to record Ian Wallace, they did it at Ledlanet and *Ian Wallace's Evening at Ledlanet* had a considerable sale in the record shops as an LP, and later on tape as well. When I was asked, in the seventies, to pick records and talk about myself in a BBC radio programme called *Man of Action*, I included among my choices of Beethoven, Mozart, Haydn, Schubert, etc., a song about a plaintive Glasgow lover with a bad cold under his beloved's window in Glasgow, which was Ian Wallace singing *West-End Perk (Park)*. He also compèred a number of members' nights. We never had an empty seat with Ian.

One of the remarkable Edinburgh characters whose career was helped by the arrival of the Traverse Theatre, which became one of the centres for non-Calvinist and pro-cultural activities in the sixties, was Richard Demarco. An artist and art teacher, he took over the Traverse dining room in its earliest days to display paintings, his own and other peoples, constantly in conflict with whoever was running the theatre itself, just underneath, where footsteps and noise would interrupt the play. Demarco much resented having to take second place to drama and once he found backers, and they included the Edinburgh designer John Martin and his friends, together with a few local grandees such as Lord Hague, son of the first war General, he moved his activities to a number of galleries, where he displayed more paintings than he sold, and behaved more like the curator of a civic museum than a commercial art dealer. In time, his interests and contacts growing with trips to America, where he found opportunities to lecture, and to Europe, especially Eastern Europe where he developed the reputation of a major arts impresario, he branched out, importing foreign artists, and as many of them, particularly from countries like Poland, were also involved in the theatre, he also began to bring in foreign theatre companies. Notable among these were Tadeusz Kantor from Krakow, and Jozef Syajna from Warsaw, and the German artist Josef Beuys, but DeMarco was soon linked with the European avant-garde everywhere. This was paid for by long-suffering backers and a little, very little, public money. He was a good talker, good at self-publicity, and able to persuade many of his listeners that everything he displayed had an element of genius. Although some saw him as a clever charlatan, others believed absolutely in his ability to spread enthusiasm and make the public art-minded. He bubbled over with energy and a non-stoppable flow of words.

In the late sixties a group of us – I cannot remember whose idea it was initially – decided to raise money for three institutions that needed it, The Traverse Theatre, Demarco Gallery and Ledlanet Nights. The designer and theatrical personality Alan Sieveright was approached, and he agreed to design a large ball to be held in the Assembly Rooms on Edinburgh's George Street, where in those days big civic functions took place and which during the Edinburgh Festival became the Festival Club because places to eat and drink after pub closing hours were very few. He made Black and White the motif of the ball and the Black and White Ball it was named, people being asked to come in appropriately imaginative costumes in line with the theme. Lord Primrose, the son of Lord and Lady Rosebery, who had largely financed the first Edinburgh Festival, joined the Ball Committee and wanted to do the lighting. A number of bands were engaged and I obtained an American blues singer from Paris, Mae Mercer, who I knew from Girodias' Blues Bar, part of his publishing/restaurant complex. Girodias, in a sudden fit of generosity, paid her fare to come and anything she was paid came from him. Mike Hart, an Edinburgh trumpeter and bandleader, who also played at Ledlanet's own fund-raising balls, was delighted to have an artist of renown. Alan Sieveright was also a great friend of Tondi Barr, who helped in various ways and came up to Edinburgh for the ball. It was well-publicised, supported by the local serious press and very well attended, becoming one of the main social events of Edinburgh that year.

I was in the Assembly Rooms office on the morning of the event when I received a 'phone call from Immigration at Heathrow. A confused official told me that this large black lady, a singer with no work permit, had arrived to work in Edinburgh and he could not admit her. A minute later I was talking to Mae. 'That you, John? Listen, you tell this man, Girodias sent me here to sing for you. I ain't getting paid; Girodias, he say, you go England, sing for John Calder and here I is.' I explained that Mae Mercer was coming for one night only to sing as a volunteer at a charity ball, that she was threatening no-one's job, and a relieved and no doubt much harassed official let her through to catch the next 'plane to Edinburgh. She was a triumph, adored by Mike Hart, all his band, and all those who listened to her. The ball went on in several large rooms with different events in each, until the early hours. Several of my current girlfriends were there and I had to be busy doing many things before I ended up at dawn in bed with one of them, not Tondi on this occasion, who was in the George Hotel. The ball was repeated the following year, but with less success. My memory of the end of one of them, probably the first, was of Lord Primrose on a stepladder unscrewing his lamp bulbs from projectors and handing them down to his wife. 'We're taking back our property,' she explained to a bewildered questioner.

In 1966 I programmed an unusual opera which I knew about from April FitzLyon's Leonardo da Ponte biography. It was Martin y Soler's *Una Cosa Rara*, with a Da Ponte libretto, which had first been given in Vienna exactly a month after the première of Mozart's *Marriage of Figaro* and with the same cast. The best-known tune in it is quoted in the supper scene of *Don Giovanni*, which was written a year later, attesting to the popularity of the Soler opera when first performed in 1787. I was told that *Una Cosa Rara*, which had not been performed for 150 years, could not be reconstructed, but we found a musicologist, Roy Jesson, who travelled all over Europe looking for the orchestral parts to fit the vocal score, and he lovingly put the whole opera together. I attended all the auditions we held to find singers. We could usually find one star singer for an opera and then audition from the large pool of available talent, at first in London, but later in Glasgow as well, for singers to fill the other parts. I forget who it was that I liked best for the soprano lead, but Ande Anderson was very keen to have a young unknown singer called Josephine Barstow and I gave way to him. I did not realise that he was having an affair with her, but after we had engaged her, it became obvious. He was at the time getting a divorce from Jo Veasey, who about that time was starring in *The Trojans*, and he soon married his new Josephine, who in a short time developed an international career that had started at Ledlanet.

Our cast was a good one with Ann Hood, Elizabeth Tippett, Beverley Bergen, Robert Bateman, Kevin Miller (a regular by now), Anthony Rafell, Michael Rippon and David Lennox. Roy Jesson conducted. It was well-reviewed, performed by Kent Opera again in London a few months later, and eventually taken up by the BBC, but with a different cast. Unfortunately, Roy Jesson died not long after, I am not sure of what.

1967 was a busy year at Ledlanet. We had introduced a spring season in March welcoming Scottish Opera's touring group, Opera for All. I was friendly with Scottish Opera, which had been founded in 1962 by Alexander Gibson and Peter Hemmings, and had attended their opening productions of *Pelléas et Mélisande* (given in recognition of Mary Garden, the Scottish singer who had sung the first Mélisande for Debussy, but was too frail to leave Aberdeen to attend a performance) and *Madama Butterfly*, and we co-operated in many ways as the only two operatic institutions active in Scotland at the time. Many singers worked with us both and conductors as well, and Peter Hemmings in particular attended most of our productions. *Opera for All* was performed in costume with piano only, and they brought *Così fan tutte* and *Cinderella* (Rossini), which in spite of poor weather attracted good audiences. Two of the singers with the company, Sheila McGrow and John Graham were to become Ledlanet regulars. I remember that Opera for All season for an incident that I record with some hesitation. The Traverse Theatre had a very attractive Scottish girl cooking for them at the time and I brought her to do the cooking for that spring season at Ledlanet. I shall call her Fiona[23], not her real name. Inevitably one night, quite late, when everyone else had gone to bed, I detained her in the back corridor, and unable to control myself, because I always had great reservations then about sleeping with anyone I employed, told her that I passionately wanted her.

---

[23] From this point in the narrative, certain persons I do not wish to identify will appear under a false name or a first name only.

She responded and for the next year we had a discreet but involved affair, sometimes at Ledlanet, sometimes at her own place, but frequently when I brought her with me to my many speaking engagements in different towns. I had other relationships at the time, but this was still under Bettina's nose, and although I knew she had her own flings, we were both on the whole discrete, especially in Scotland. It was in fact Bettina, who took over the catering of the Traverse Theatre for a while, who had first taken on Fiona as a partner to cater there. Jacques Chaix turned up and was keen to go skiing at Glenshee, because there was snow, and as Opera for All were only performing on the weekends, there were two free days. We were getting into the car, Jacques, his girlfriend from Paris and myself, when Fiona came out to see us off. Come along, I said on impulse and she did, just as she was, and spent two days with me at Glenshee, compensating for not very good skiing. We got back just as the opera singers were arriving for the night's performance. Fiona told Bettina she had had to go back to Edinburgh for two days for an emergency.

Before *Una Cosa Rara* that autumn, there was a variety of other entertainments. We gave Schumann's *Dichterliebe* in the Scottish translation of Sir Alexander Gray with three voices and dramatised it. The artists were Sheila McGrow, Sheila Laing and Daniel McCoshen. Conrad Wilson, reviewing it for The Scotsman did not approve; but the audience liked it. With it we did the Cedric Thorpe-Davie version of Burns' *Jolly Beggars* with a cast that included all of the above and Ian Wallace. The latter was very nervous because the composer was sitting in the front row. 'I was afraid that I'd get a note wrong,' he confided to me afterwards. Douglas Gray of Scotsdisk persuaded me to let him mount a ceremonial song, dance and poetry evening entitled *Harvest Home* and Mrs. Ferguson, a doctor's wife on our committee who was a genius with flowers arranged a remarkable decor for the show. But the other big production, other than the operas and song cycles, was an improvised play based on Goldoni's *Servant of Two Masters*. I transformed the original into local town names, bringing out the rivalries which I knew existed between Kinross, the county town, five miles away, and Milnathort, three and a half miles away, adding a lot of slap-stick and several songs. These I organised with John Watt, who found the music to which I put new words which he sang, but with the audience as chorus, reading from a screen which I lowered and raised and on which I projected the words. I added a dream sequence at the beginning of the second half: the stage was then covered with a map of Scotland, and one of the characters sat on the three towns of Aberdeen, Edinburgh and Glasgow, having a conversation, and then each singing a song about the town. My purpose was to make fun of all the local rivalries and have the audience laughing at them. Alex McAvoy, actor, dancer and mime, with a good singing voice as well, played the Servant, quite brilliantly and with acrobatics, juggling and performing an astounding leap onto the stage from the platform which we had built out from the first floor aperture. The cast contained established opera and folk singers as well as actors, including Dennis O'Neill, who was later to make a big operatic career, and here was a real singing actor. The audience loved it and it had a rave review from Allen Wright in The Scotsman.

In the bar after the last night, I was chatting with Alex McAvoy, who had done so much to make the production memorable, and together with others we began talking about Scottish nationalism about which, in spite of many friends in the SNP Party and the movement, I did not approve. 'If I had known that, I wouldn't have taken the part,' said McAvoy. 'I thought it was a Nationalist play.'

I have a tendency at this point to skip around perhaps too much. Memory is necessarily associative, and strict chronology would not make very interesting reading. And there are some episodes that must be told as a sequence, even if they cover a large expanse of time. Trocchi became even more of a representative of the drug culture after the Sheffield Trial, but now the climate was changing, partly because of the invasion of ever more American beat and hippie drug addicts into Britain, caused largely by the closing up of Tangiers, no longer the drug haven it had been, but also because some doctors were obviously oversubscribing and not only was this very expensive for the National Health service, but their motives in doing so were sometimes suspect. There was a Lady Frankau, a psychiatrist, who treated many addicts and became notorious and very suspect with the authorities. On some occasions I sent Alex Trocchi to my own Doctor, a Hungarian, Tibor Csato, who helped him mainly with advice, but he certainly would not oversubscribe as Alex wanted, because the latter hoped to be able to sell his surplus once it became more difficult to get drugs. The crack-down was evident by the middle sixties. There was a big event at the Royal Albert Hall, promoted by a New Zealand poet, John Esam, as a commercial venture, a large gathering of poets, where a considerable amount of box-office money disappeared, as did Esam himself. The Albert Hall was full, the air thick with cannabis smoke, and very many poets, British, American and European, read for a few minutes each from a central platform. The least popular was Allen Ginsberg, who recited an endless mantra. 'This is MacGonigall?' shouted a Scottish voice. I was not impressed by a large group of mental defectives who were in a group near me: they had been brought along by R. D. Laing, a poet, theorist and psychiatrist, very fashionable then, about whom I had enormous reservations. He was not unlike Trocchi, always keeping his name in the press and welcoming attack and controversy. Watching the twenty or so gibbering mental patients, whom he had obviously brought out of hospital to subject them to an experience that they could obviously not understand or appreciate, but that most of them found obviously distressing, could only have worsened their condition. They wandered around the area in which they had been enclosed, dribbling and making sounds, rarely looking at the stage. But Trocchi himself, acting part of the time as a Master of Ceremonies, read a little of his work, and being then applauded, took the applause as a vindication of his lifestyle and a reply to the magistrates of Sheffield. The press gave the event the coverage that might be expected, playing up the presence of drugs and describing the sillier events. The Albert Hall managers declared that never again would the hall be used for such a purpose. Properly organised, it could have been a worthwhile rather than a notorious event. I enjoyed about half of it, because there were some good poets and some good readings, but already the American hippie invasion was invoking strong reactions, and the criminalisation of drugs was becoming part of it, opening the way to professional crime.

* * * * * *

To get back to Ledlanet, Sheila had left me during 1965 to become secretary and manager of the Traverse Theatre, not an easy or an enviable task, because there was a fairly large and rancorous committee, which included me, and some of the members were very critical of either the plays, the catering, the finances, the general atmosphere or the management. Audrey Langford then imposed her daughter Ann on me to replace Sheila, and she was a real problem. She was only interested in assisting Ande Anderson, then producing *Una Cosa Rara*, and she followed him everywhere; she was not typing my letters which were sometimes about Ledlanet Estate matters, sometimes about publishing, and sometimes personal, and only in small part to do with the current season. She simply did as little as possible, and would not have done that, had her mother not told her she had to. My exasperation with her grew and finally exploded on the last night of *Una Cosa Rara*.

It was a celebratory last night of a successful production and everyone was happy, the audience mixing with the orchestra and the principals in the bar after the performance had ended. Then Audrey Langford handed me a piece of paper. It was her invoice for the production and at a glance I could see that it was greatly in excess of the budget and the quotation she had given me on which it was based. 'I'd like a cheque right now,' she said.

'Sorry,' I replied. 'I have to go over it in the morning and I'll settle it then.' She was insistent, I was firm and I moved to the kitchen. There Ann Langford followed me in and said I had been rude to her mother. The same 'hwyl' that had overtaken me at my brother's wedding happened to me again. I had been under great pressure, had had no help from the quite useless temporary secretary who had been foisted on me by Audrey, who was now screaming at me, and I let her have it back. In cold, biting words, feeling absolutely stone-cold sober in spite of several drinks a little earlier, I told her what I thought of her, the way her family was trying to cheat me, of how I intended to pay what I had agreed and not a penny more, and added other home truths for good measure.

The next morning I took out my estimates and budgets. Audrey had inflated everything and thrown in any number of unjustified extras. I worked out what was due, made some allowances in favour of Kent Opera, and gave her a cheque. She took it, but said she would sue for the balance. There were of course threats from her Chairman and her solicitors, but my obligations were clear from the correspondence, and the matter was eventually dropped. She revived *Una Cosa Rara* in London some months later with an inferior cast and a year after that performed another opera by the same composer, *L'Arbore di Diana*, to which of course I went, never having heard it. But I never used Kent Opera again, and thereafter packaged all Ledlanet productions myself.

* * * * * *

Jim Fraser had three sons, and the youngest, Stephen was the same age as my daughter Jamie. He suggested that she might like to spend a weekend at his house in Broughty Ferry near Dundee, and I drove her there from Ledlanet on the Friday, bringing with me Bill Colleran, who was staying that same weekend at Ledlanet. I dropped Bill off in Perth on the way at the Salutation Hotel, as he wanted to look around the town, and picked him up again two hours later. During that time he had discovered malt whisky and had sampled several different brands. On the way back to Ledlanet I took the picturesque Path of Condie road in order to have a look at Ardargie, my grandfather's old house, which was now a hotel. I did not enjoy the experience. The house, which had earlier possessed great charm, was now totally wrecked in my eyes and we did not stay long after walking through what had once been stately and comfortable rooms. Bill was a little wild. 'Why don't we beat the man up?' he suggested and really wanted to assault the new proprietor. I hastily took him back to Ledlanet, which we had to leave soon after, as we were going to dinner with William Mostyn-Owen, who had a house and estate at Comrie, a forty-five minute drive away. Willie was an appraiser of Italian paintings at Christie's in London and his glamorous wife, Gaia, had been much in evidence around my Drama Conference, meeting the participants and covering it for an Italian newspaper, because she was also a journalist, mostly concerned with fashion. Other guests that night, all staying with the Mostyn-Owens were Mary McCarthy and Mr West, her diplomat husband, George Weidenfeld with his daughter from his first marriage and one or two others. Jim Haynes, staying with me, was part of the foursome who had come from Ledlanet. It was a pleasant meal, ending with port. Jim, who did not drink, excused himself for a minute. Then Willie threw open the large double-doors into the drawing-room and there, in the middle of a brilliantly lighted room, were Gaia and Jim Haynes in a passionate embrace. For a second or two Mostyn-Owen looked at his wife in the arms of Jim, then closed the doors again, saying 'I think we'll have coffee in the dining-room.' Aristocratic sang-froid! The evening was not made better when Bill Colleran, who had imbibed a tremendous amount of spirits and wine that day, threw up while we were drinking our coffee, all of us saying little. We returned to Ledlanet in a chastened mood.

It may have been that summer that we all decided to visit Dugi Otok, from which Bettina's family came. She was still related to many people on this island which is off the Croatian coast near Zadar. Bettina had arranged to borrow two or three of the cottages that belonged to relatives. We left London, Bettina, Anastasia, Jamie and Anne Fletcher, a friend from Edinburgh, who had been much around the Traverse – this must have been Jim Haynes' last year there – in the car. Anne's current boyfriend, Joe Roeber, who worked on the Financial Times was to join us later. It was a long drive to Zadar and took two days through Germany, Austria, northern Italy and down the narrow Adriatic coast road which runs from the Italian border to Greece. There we formed a little colony, which included Rosemary Reuben who had found her own way to Bojava, the only little village on the island. When I arrived with several bottles of gin and whisky, she instantly began pouring for us all so that my first memories are of sitting in the glorious sunset, watching the first satellite sputniks sailing past us in the clear sky and getting quietly sloshed. Rosemary had started an affair with a German staying at the only hotel in the village who went out with his speargun to catch fish, but only managed to spear himself in the leg. The man, who was on his honeymoon, eventually left his wife on the island and departed with Rosemary. There was however one day when Rosemary and I swam around a bend and found ourselves alone in a cove. We instantly took advantage of the solitude to copulate in shallow water and had just finished when a fishing boat rounded the bend; we managed to separate and look natural without attracting attention. I have few other memories of that week or two in Bojava. While there, we recruited a young cousin of Bettina's, Dosia, to be a nanny for Anastasia. She came back with us, stayed two years, and learned English, which eventually qualified her to hold a good job in a Yugoslav hotel.

The following year I went back there with Jim Fraser, his son Stephen and Jamie, this time not driving, but taking a morning flight to Venice and after a day there catching the evening boat to Rijeca. From there we were expected to catch the bus that only left once a day and went down the coast. But the boat arrived late and the customs were slow and officious. Getting through first, I told Jim Fraser to assemble the others and our luggage on the dock and to wait on the main street next to the boat, while I raced down to where I was told the bus stop was. Sure enough, before I got there, I saw the bus coming towards me and made it stop by standing in its way. I explained to the driver in my halting Serbo-Croat that there were four people who had to catch this bus, and that the others should by now be off the boat and waiting further down the road. They were just coming off the boat as we got there, but the bus did stop and we all got on it. It was now eleven in the morning and the ferry we had to catch left at three from Zadar. I was told we would be there in time, and the bus was if anything too fast, careening down the two-lane Adriatic Highway alongside precipices that dropped down to the sea. Every time we came to a bend the conductor would lean right out to see past it, and then tell the driver the way was clear, which it seemed to me was often before he could be quite sure. When they stopped for lunch the other passengers got out to lunch as well, and the driver and conductor seemed in no hurry to get going again. As the hour for the ferry's departure got nearer it seemed to me we were still many miles away, but the conductor told me not to worry. But a lorry slowed us down and as we came onto the dockside the ferry had already cast off the ropes and pulled in the gangplank. The driver and the conductor threw our bags onto a boat that was already moving and we were pulled onto it by the sailors. Jim promptly declared that he would never travel with me again.

The highlight of that stay on Dugi Otok was the final dinner at the hotel, which had caught an enormous lobster that I was told might be a thousand years old. It fed eight people and was enough for several more, more than a yard in length. The presence of Jamie and Stephen makes me thing that the year was 1966, when they were both twelve years old, but I could be a year out either way. If so, I must have driven down earlier, left the car, and returned with Jim and the two children via Venice and the hair-raising race on the bus. On the way back we stopped in Salzburg and heard the Alban Berg Quartet, which must have been newly formed, on our one night there, and the next day we were all in Munich were we sent the two children to a children's opera while Bettina, Jim and I went to the State opera to see *Tristan and Isolde*. We got out later than anticipated and we were worried about Jamie and Stephen who had been given precise instructions how to get to a restaurant to wait for us. But the restaurant was closed and we found two frightened and shivering children standing outside it, trying to shelter from the rain that had started. I am sure they still remember it. My last memory of Munich that trip is meeting Monica von Zallinger the next morning before leaving. I knew her from the past, the very beautiful daughter of the conductor Mainhard von Zallinger, who had been a principal music director at the Munich State Opera since the thirties. Monica was a producer for both the theatrical and operatic stage, and I encountered her fairly frequently in those days and probably first met her when I was in Munich in 1955 in connection with the making of *The Pool*, when I visited her father. Jim Fraser also took a big shine to her. 'She's sending you messages, John,' he said enviously. But I'm sure she wasn't. Thinking of her brings back another occasion, sometime in the mid-sixties when, after seeing Sam Beckett shortly after he had returned from Ulm and the world première of *Play*, where he had sat in with and helped Derrick Mendel, the English producer then working in Germany, during the final rehearsals, I decided to go there myself to see the production. On that occasion Monica drove to Ulm with Bettina and I. The production was brilliant and Derrick told me many anecdotes about Sam's visit. In Ulm he had made many changes to his original play, deciding to repeat the action a second time. Derrick suggested that as the play was so short, it might be repeated more often still, indeed why not go on until the last member of the audience had left? Sam thought for a minute. 'No,' he said finally. 'This is Germany. They'll still be here at breakfast.'

Through the rest of the decade Ledlanet Nights went from strength to strength, now having four seasons a year. Opera for All was back in 1968 and there were many small but good entertainments for all tastes during the year. I mounted two operatic productions in the main autumn season, first a triple bill of Bach's only operatic work, *The Coffee Cantata*, put into a sixties context, Britten's *Abraham and Isaac*, and a one-act comic opera by Joseph Horovitz, based on one of W. S. Gilbert's *Bab Ballads*, entitled *Gentleman's Island*. This had Ian Wallace and Stuart Kale in it and was much enjoyed. It concerns two men, public school boys, stranded on a desert island who cannot talk to each other as they have not been introduced. They get over the difficulty, become friends, but not after a convict ship passes on which they recognise a mutual acquaintance: neither wants to know a convict. They end up on opposite sides of the island which has the food they most dislike. The main production was Mozart's *Il Re Pastore*, and this was the first time we sang an opera in Italian because I could not get a good translation done in time and there was no available one. Jill Gomez, who had sung some small parts at Glyndebourne, was our Aminta and Philip Langridge, whom we had had before as a member of the John Aldiss Choir, sang Philip the Great. It was a production of the greatest simplicity, which George Mully, also a regular now, produced. The climax is *L'Amero*, one of Mozart's most beautiful arias, which Jill Gomez sang on a blackened stage in a white light with perfect intonation and a voice that perfectly caught the sentiment of real love in pure affecting melody. There was not a dry eye in the house and her career, another international one, probably began with that opera, which Peter Gellhorn conducted, becoming from that year our most regular musical director.

The productions of the previous years had greatly strained our finances, especially the operatic ones, and the figures for *Re Pastore*, one of the most economic, as well as effective Ledlanet productions, has consequently stuck in my mind. We had five superb soloists, an orchestra of sixteen plus harpsichord and minimum decor, and it cost exactly £250 for each of the six performances. With Jim Fraser providing most of what we needed that a building firm could supply, persuasive negotiation with artists of real talent whose careers had not yet taken off – and Ledlanet already had the reputation of being a good launching pad – and good musicians, mainly from Edinburgh that I came to know well as individuals (the Forth Road Bridge had now been built so they could get to Ledlanet from Edinburgh in under an hour), and no overhead that was not covered by our own catering and especially by bar profits, we could do artistic wonders with very little money. More events, some of them profitable, helped bring down overheads. Spring and Christmas seasons had been added to the summer and autumn. There were imported plays and a few of our own such as I have described, many chamber concerts and recitals, and visits by groups such as Opera for All. The Arts Council rang us up and proposed artists and groups with a built-in subsidy attached. John Watt provided the popular folk nights. The catering had become very professional, with Jock Imrie, our barman and a real character, able to serve a bar with a hundred or more thirsty people in it. Sometimes Attewell's wife helped Jock.

We had the London Mozart Players in the summer of 1968 and I worked out that it was our hundredth concert, so made an event of it with an enormous cake that could feed both audience and players. The trouble was that the orchestra, which was on a northern tour, was the biggest we had ever had and it turned out to be impossible to squeeze them all onto the stage (as we did for the concerts as against operas) and also to get their conductor Harry Blech on it as well for the violin concerto, played by Georgy Pauk. Blech was a very stout man. Finally Pauk conducted the concerts from the violin and it worked out well. I used the very effective photograph of the orchestra, taken from behind the bassoons, for the 1969 motif on the front of all programmes that year.

I forget how the *Re Pastore* orchestra was recruited, but it was a brilliant one, and it included an oboeist called Jenny Paull, who later helped me to raise funds with charity concerts for the Last *Exit Case* which I have not yet come to. She was good looking, tall and blonde, very outgoing and was soon to play a small part in the subsequent history of Ledlanet. Peter Gellhorn, who had been one of the rising German conductors until the Nazis made him leave, was a martinet, strict, punctilious and an extremely good musician. He had total control over orchestra and singers. On one night when a minor singer was not well, he made her act out the part while Hazel Wood, a Ledlanet standby, sang her music from the orchestra pit. She nearly fainted on stage, but did it. Peter was not willing to consider any other compromise. During the last week of the opera (we performed on successive Wednesdays, Thursdays and Saturdays that year), I had brought with me my current extra-curricular girlfriend (Bettina rarely came to Ledlanet in those days). Our affair had gone on for some time – she was a novelist to whom I have given the name Vera for the purpose of this narrative, and she had gone to bed early. On the last night Jenny, everyone else having left or gone to bed, said she was interested in sleeping with me. Although staying in the Green Hotel in Kinross, she had spent most nights with Peter Gellhorn, whom she must have known before, because Peter had his own room at Ledlanet. As I remember it, Jenny and I made love somewhere on the premises, probably on a sofa, and I then drove her to Kinross, giving some explanation to Vera on my return. Two days later Jenny and I drove down to London together, stopping overnight at North Berwick at a hotel, which I remember as one of the most active nights of my life because she was insatiable. We stopped to renew our ardours in a graveyard off the road not far from London, and were nearly interrupted by the Vicar. When we stopped at Wimpole Street before Jenny went home, Bettina's eyes told me that she had taken in the situation, but she said nothing about it. Jenny and I kept up a pleasant and arduous relationship for a few months – I had to rent a room for us to meet, because she also had a husband – then it simmered down and we became just friends. So were things in the free-and-easy sixties. But Jenny later helped me to give fund-raising concerts, which I shall come to, and other complications lay ahead.

* * * * * *

I had met Pablo Fernandez, a Cuban poet, who was also cultural attaché at the Cuban Embassy, through the normal channels by which publishers with an international list meet such people, and he came a few times to my flat where he met Bettina. He persuaded her to look at the songs that Lorca had written, because Lorca was a composer as well as a poet. She could not make head or tail of them and showed them to me. I started to reread Lorca's poetry, and the more I did so, the more I realised that there was a strong autobiographical element that ran through his work. I read his biography and came to the conclusion that, although a recital of his songs, interspersed with readings of his poetry, was a possibility, it would be far more interesting to write a play about his life and work, using his own poems as a major part of the text. We could also use his music so that it would be a work of music theatre. Bill Colleran, a friend and music publisher, with whom I had several contracts to publish German musical books in English that were Universal Edition copyright, was consulted and he introduced me to Harrison Birtwistle, one of the composers in his stable who was just beginning to make his reputation as a member of the so-called Manchester Group of British musicians. Birtwistle's role would be to arrange Lorca's music so that it could be more effectively performed, and at that point all that was envisaged was a simple recital of the songs by Bettina. I met Harry Birtwistle, whose main activity at the time was conducting and writing music for the Pierrot Players, a chamber orchestra named after Schönberg's *Pierrot Lunaire*, now a key work in the repertoire of any small orchestra performing twentieth century music. The Pierrot Players were all virtuoso free-lance musicians, such as Alan Hacker, the well-known clarinettist. Birtwistle instantly thought of anything that he might do on the project in terms of using the Pierrot

Players, and he quickly lost interest in Lorca's music, although he was willing to collaborate with me in setting such poems as I selected. He was even more interested when I told him I had a stage work in mind.

David de Keyser, ex-husband of Ethel, who previously had worked for me as editor, was then asked by Bettina to collaborate with me. Although I saw no reason for this I agreed, and David, Bettina and I went up to Ledlanet on a Friday night to work on the project. I cannot pinpoint the date, but it must have been early in 1966, even possibly a year earlier. We discussed it at dinner, discussed it throughout the evening, and went to bed with a plan in mind. The next morning I rose early and went to the library where I started typing a prologue. This depicted Lorca in front of a firing squad and I scripted his last thoughts, which would then lead to a depiction of his life in flashback. I finished this, put another piece of paper in the typewriter and started on Act I, a fine morning in Barcelona with the boy Federico Lorca and his brother planning a play for the household. I was on page 4 when David came in.

'What are you doing?' he exclaimed in surprise.

'I just started on the play.'

'We have to talk about it first.'

'We talked about it all last evening. Now we have to write it.'

We had breakfast with David still protesting. He gave me no help for the rest of the weekend and soon dropped out. David de Keyser was a good actor, but outside of that *métier* he was a talker, not a doer. In London, my affair with Rosemary Reuben was continuing on an irregular basis. She was no longer working for Roy Jones, was divorced, and living in Hampstead's Frognal with a personable pet called Topcat, and doing freelance typing for a living. I asked her to help me produce a script quickly, because Bettina had already approached Peter Diamond, the new Edinburgh Festival Director after Harewood, and had told him she was writing a musical play about Lorca. Diamond agreed, subject to seeing the script quickly, to do it. My name could not be used because of the Happening, and Weatherstone was still Provost, although he had increasingly become a joke. His malapropisms rivalled Sam Goldwyn's, but without being as funny. For instance he had looked at a Festival exhibition of Braque's work and quipped 'It braques my heart,' and having seen a Britten opera in a festival that featured Britten and Berlioz, had confused the two and said to the press, 'The next time that Mr. Berlioz wants to write an opera, I'll give him a better libretto than that.' Being around Edinburgh frequently, I occasionally saw him and even spoke to him, but although he had probably forgotten who I was, there was no question of my doing anything in the Festival, especially as Diamond was very careful to avoid all controversy. I spent several afternoons with Rosemary, dictating much of the script and giving her what I had typed myself to retype, and by early summer it was finished, a three-act musical play. I will not pretend, Rosemary being a very sexy lady, that we did not take some time off during those afternoons, but she did a professional job for me nevertheless. The play was accepted and Birtwistle was soon writing his music, both to accompany some of the dialogue, which became a form of *Sprechgesang* or rhythmic speech and the Lorca poems. There was background music and incidental music and songs written for Bettina to sing.

Lorca emerged as a three act work and about sixty percent of the script remained in the poet's own words. In the first act I depicted the child, then the young man who loved gypsies, which gave Birtwistle scope to write a gypsy dance, and there was a ballroom scene to close the first act. The second showed a segment of *Blood Wedding* in the context of the author rehearsing it, and the whole of the lament for his male lover, Meijas, a bull-fighter killed in the ring. This was to be recited against a mimed bull-fight. In the third act I used the *Poet in New York* poems to show him in a night-club there, then moved him back to Spain during the Civil War, when Lorca and his troupe of actors were trying to come to terms with the reality of the time. There is a scene from *The House of Bernarda Alba*, put in largely for Bettina to have something dramatic to sing at that point, having given her a militant La Pasionaria-like speech earlier in the act. It ended with Lorca's capture and last night in captivity (and he did write a poem on the last night which I used), and then back to the opening scene, standing before the firing squad, and his last thoughts, interrupted by the fusillade.

It was conceived in part as a vehicle for Bettina, singing songs which would be settings of the poems and some passages of the plays. Harry Birtwistle turned out a score suitable for the Pierrot Players with vocals for one singer only, but with much incidental music to accompany mimed action and to accompany speech. As the text in places was deliberately stilted, being Lorca's own verse, sometimes lyrical, sometimes not, the rhythmic structure was very important. And some of the music was for dance.

The Edinburgh Festival accepted *Lorca* as a musical work by Bettina Jonic and Harrison Birtwistle in 1967. As Bettina and I had separate careers only a few people knew we were married, and apparently nobody to do with the Edinburgh Festival at that point did. It needed a company structure to package and finance it however and I organised all that, raising money from friends. It was sold as a package to the Festival with a minimum guarantee that would not cover all the cost, but I was confident it could come to London afterwards with a London management. To this end, I found a well-connected agent who fronted the whole thing and helped to cast it. I asked Ande Anderson to produce it, knowing his versatility and ability to work in unusual circumstances. His reputation as House Producer at Covent Garden helped us in many ways in getting the project going, and we also had Royal Opera House rehearsal rooms available to us because of him.

Tony Beckley, a minor film star who resembled Lorca, was cast in the lead, Nicholas Chagrin, a dancer and actor, who had played Puck in the first production of Britten's *Midsummer Night's Dream* played a number of parts including Meijas, whose bullfight and death he mimed against Beckley's dramatic recitation of the poem, and there were several smaller parts. We had an experienced choreographer, Gillian Lynne, to plot the movement and to direct Nicholas Chagrin. She had choreographed Chagrin as Puck at Covent Garden and obviously had a fixation on him, which became ever more evident as she danced with him in the rehearsals of the gypsy scene. Gillian Lynne was an attractive woman in her forties and she must had a flaming affair with Nick when he was still in his teens. Nicholas Chagrin was dark and leonine, thin, wiry and very Latin-looking. Beckley, who was quite openly gay, was also very attracted to him as were all the women around: he did nothing to discourage the attentions of either sex and glowed in the attention and the admiration he attracted. Rehearsals were always infused with an underrunning erotic feeling.

They started in early July and as they progressed an excitement began growing among the cast, quite different from the tension I have described above, as they all began to realise that they were taking part in a radically new form of music theatre, and it was working. Lorca's music had been totally dropped. The actors were moving and delivering their lines against Birtwistle's score and Bettina was singing it.

In Edinburgh we were performing at the Gateway, a theatre that had previously belonged to the Church of Scotland, and that in the future was to alternate as television studio and theatre again. It was managed by the formidable Sadie Aitken, a lady who claimed she always knew at rehearsals what would be a success and what not. She had strict views, but had been known to be unconventionally forthright on occasion. For instance, when an actor, forgetting his lines, inadvertantly said 'Fuck' on stage, loud enough to be heard by the audience, Sadie summoned him to her office the next morning and said, 'If you think I'm firing you because you said "Fuck" on stage, you're wrong. I'm firing you because you're a fucking awful actor.' *Lorca* was far too removed from mainstream theatre for her taste, so she predicted a flop.

Rehearsals had gone well in London with piano. Now we had a small virtuoso orchestra to play Harry's not simple score, and a theatre that left much to be desired. We had been programmed into the last week of the Festival, and we had only a Sunday to use the stage, as the previous play had finished the previous night. Ande had to use most of that precious Sunday on a technical rehearsal. Unfortunately our technical requirements were complex and there were many of them in a show that depended on back projection, several lighting and other cues, and curtain drops. When we had the final dress rehearsal on the Sunday night, the stage hands, exhausted after moving out scenery the previous night and having to move us in the next morning, refused to appear. We had the dress rehearsal without

Top Left. James Calder (great-grandfather)
Top Right. John Joseph Calder (grandfather)
Bottom Left. Sir James Calder (great-uncle)
Bottom Right. James Calder (father)

Top Left. John Calder at Bishops College School.
Top Right. Ledlanet.
Bottom. Christya (Myling) Calder with Jamie and governess.

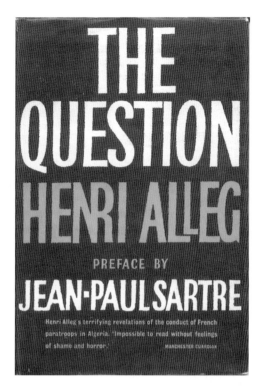

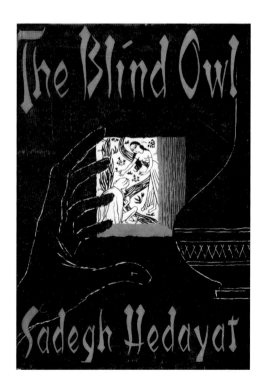

Four important fifties publications..

Top. 1964 catalogue showing 24 authors
Bottom. Creators of the French 'New Novel' with Jérôme Lindon.

Top. Programme for writer's conference.
Bottom. Double Calder/Riverrun Catalogue.

Left. Suck Magazine.
Right. Kenneth Tynan in Paris.

Top Left. The Falstaff.
Top Right. Samuel Beckett at 45.
Bottom. J C with Marguerite Duras, Jim Haynes and Natalie Sarraute in the Paperback Bookshop.

IDEALIST AS WELL AS IMPRESARIO

"Calder the Conference"

really is rather an extraordinary person: one of the restlessly busy and genuinely I use the word again?) the young men I have ever John Calder, publisher and sario of literary conferences. the Conference, one might

yet the endless busyness is apparent; the energy lers inside him. He is a short, stubby man, solidly built, his muttered, his manner dry. He but looks anything between 25 5. An organiser, but totally ted to the organisation man; an ario who does not seek to s. You expect something y effusive, or you expect a wee, tornado of a man; but with , it's all inside him.

inside him, you can be sure e is planning at least six things ce. Right now, in addition to eek's Drama Conference at the an Hall, he is planning a ed—to be specific, a hundred for children, to be written with ss honesty by major authors and

and self-discipline founded on understanding is more valuable than repressive discipline imposed on ignorance. This, I think, is the core of his philosophy, and the philosophy is at the core of all his activity.

The activity is to some extent compulsive; he has what the Germans call stoffreude—a passion for material to work on. Part of him is a born entrepreneur, a literary and cultural entrepreneur. Part of him is thoroughly opportunist, in that he cannot resist the opportunities his fertile mind envisages. But it is all subservient to the central idealism. Thus, the idea for last year's Writers' Conference sprang from an evening in Coventry when he toured a small circus of his authors—Robbe-Grillet, Natalie Sarraute, and others—and was overwhelmed by the intense response a youthful audience showed to an evening's exposure to their intellec-

year's projected Poetry Conference will be in jeopardy.

He has other ideas for the Festival, or rather for the Edinburgh of the Festival. He wants to mount an international Book Fair in Edinburgh; there is only one in the world at present, held every autumn in Frankfurt, which attracts thousands upon thousands of entries and publishers and dealers. They all loathe Frankfurt, but they cannot avoid going there. Edinburgh, thinks Calder, could take over.

Then there is an idea for making Edinburgh an international centre for art dealers.

It's the salesman in him, I suppose. After university at Zurich, he started his career as a small-time property speculator and timber salesman; a rather successful speculator and salesman, one assumes, because it was on his profits that he founded his publish-

John Calder

THE SCOTSMAN 2.9.63

NUDE SHOCKS FEST

Exit an actress . . . Carol

And Carro
scrambles (

Sunday Expre

MORE shocks at the Conference in And the biggest shock w The 2,000 audience Keseler, a 30-sec universi Hall. She was across the with her ba Then she view and at a door.

Cl
It was pa theatre " di Kenneth De way out " Angeles. Fo threw the chaos and on To a bac reorded gir from window

was crying marched in sheepl, skel platform. Then An Carroll Bak from the pla a red for c light silver she climbed ence, and nexle to a r ran out of When it w sequence Tynan, said Yugoslav oice. Scottia Macrae

at the age of 23. ally anything he magine; but what the market-place ooks, ideas in art. re the most diffi-vadays only stimu-perhaps why he likely county-set which to launch first of a series house-parties.

se £1000
erited a country Milnathort. He week-ends. The a head, a small le to enjoy music odern art and a in the compass of On September rogramme will be Nights " in the d by dinner, then rt exhibition, and opera in the hall, following week-g recital by opera Calder's wife—on two-acter by the James Saunders's g to You "—on the y. lose about £1000

James Saunders's
to You "—on the

Mixture of interests

It is this mixture of intense personal interests with acute business flair that lies behind Calder's successes as the

Dramatis Personae
by Coia

SCOTTISH SUNDAY EXPRESS 8.9.63

THE PEOPLE 8.9.63

WHAT the conference saw and gasped at . . . 20ft. above the platform, in the organ loft of the McEwan Hall in Edinburgh, 19-year-old blonde model Anna Keseler grasps an arc light before disappearing from view leaving chaos and confusion behind her.

EDINBURGH FESTIVAL DRAMA CONFERENCE

" Often wondered what they wore under yon skirts."

The opening of the International Drama Conference inspired Coia to portray three of the many distinguished people attending. They are (left to right): Erich Fried, the Austrian author; Martin Walser, who wrote "The Rabbit Race"; and John Calder, the organiser of the conference.

Cuttings from the Scotsman for Drama Conference (1963) and cartoons by Coia of Erich Fried, Martin Walser and John Calder.

THE PLAYWRIGHT'S DILEMMA

Speakers at the International Drama Conference in the McEwan Hall, Edinburgh, yesterday when the theme was "The playwright's dilemma."

RIGHT—Mr Bernard Levin addressing the conference.

BELOW — Mr Arnold Wesker (seated) discussing a point with Mr John Arden.

Wolf Mankowitz rising from his seat and Sir Alec Guinness to argue with Mr Levin.

Harold Pinter lighting a cigarette while listening to one of the speakers.

Press cuttings from The Glasgow Herald of Drama Conference with Wolf Mankowitz, Alec Guiness, Bernard Levin, David Frost, Arnold Wesker and John Arden.

1970 Election Campaign in Kinross
Top. John Calder speaking on a High Street.
Middle. With Patrick Wymark.
Bottom. Post election lunch: Alan Clark (front left), JC (next left), four ladies
(left to right) Margaret Ryder, Betty Laptew (sister), Margaret Begg, Bettina
Jonic. Front Right: Peter Roberts (agent). Richard Beith took the photo.

Ledlanet Nights.
Top Left. Dinner at the marqee.
Top Right. A happening with Robert Burns.
Bottom. Agrippina.

Top. London Mozart Players at Ledlanet (December 1969 Programme)
Bottom Left. David Mercer.
Bottom Right. Alexander Trocchi.

Top Left. Alain Robbe-Grillet.
Top Right. Marguerite Duras.
Bottom Left. Nathalie Sarraute.
Bottom Right. Claude Simon.

Top Left. Erich Fried.
Top Right. Henry Miller.
Bottom Left. Ann Quin.
Bottom Right. Robert Pinget.

Top Left. Julian Semyonov.
Top Right. His best-known novel..
Bottom. JC with Frank Delaney and Seamus Heaney in Edinburgh.

Top. John Calder and William Burroughs in London.
Bottom. Maurice Girodias and John Calder shortly before the former's death in Paris. (Both photos John Minihan)

Top. JC and Barney Rosset share a joke.
Bottom Left. JC with Eugene Ionesco in the latter's last year.
Bottom Right. JC and Jérôme Lindon in Paris 1986. (Photos John Minnihan)

Top. Jean-Louis Barrault and Madeleine Renaud in 1986.
Bottom. Maria Jolas. (Photos John Minihan)

Top Left. Jim Fraser.
Top Right. Howard Barker. (Archer Photographers)
Bottom. Samuel Beckett in the PLM. (Photo John Minihan)

Top. Three Beckett Publishers: JC, Barney Rosset, Siegfried Unseld.
Bottom. Stanley Gontarski, Barney Rosset and JC in Berlin 2000.

Theatre of Literature presentations.
Top Right. Angela Pleasance and Leonard Fenton reading Beckett.
Top Left. Rough for Theatre One woth Leonard Fenton and Raymond Segré.
Bottom. John Calder at home in Montreuil.

Left. "The Burroughs Essays"
Right. "Dougald McMillan's unfinished study" (*Beckett in the Theatre*)

SAMUEL
BECKETT

*DREAM OF
FAIR TO MIDDLING
WOMEN*

Top. JC with Auberon Waugh and Tom stoppard outside High Court.
Bottom. Beckett's 'unwanted' first novel.

Portait of john Calder by James Bown (taken in Guardian office)

scenery, or any scenery changes and with the orchestra. Although we rehearsed Monday before the opening, there was no time to do everything.

I also was dead tired, my own fault. The lady who I have mentioned before as Anna turned up at the theatre on the Sunday and came to my rehearsals. I took her back with me to Ledlanet that night, but she suddenly decided not to spend what in any case would have been a short night with me, so I had to drive her back to her hotel in Edinburgh, then return to Ledlanet again and after a short sleep get back to the theatre, arriving rather late at the rehearsal, which was remarked on, especially by Harry, who had expected me to have dinner with him the night before. Bettina was staying in Edinburgh and had already started to sleep with Nicholas Chagrin, which I had rather anticipated when I noticed her antipathy to the choreographer, Gillian's, hunger for 'that little piece' as she put it unguardedly, and with venom. I suspect that Nick had also other bed partners that week. However I was in a state of pretty total exhaustion during Monday's final rehearsals, trying to help Ande deal with the many problems that always come up when you immediately follow another production into the same theatre and the technicians are away just when you most need them.

I saw the first performance from the producer's box. The prologue went normally, but to my horror, when the lighting came up on the Lorca family drawing-room on what was meant to be a sunny morning, what the audience saw were the bricks at the back of the stage area: the scene shifters had not brought down the right flat. The stage manager then threw the stage into semi-darkness, which totally disconcerted the two boy actors playing the young Lorca and his brother, who forgot their lines. At the third scene things were running better, but the damage had been done and the reviews were mixed and far from ecstatic. At the second performance everything worked properly, but the press reviews had already appeared and audiences were not encouraged to fill the house. Ingmar Bergman, the Swedish film and stage director, who attended the third performance, liked it and wrote Bettina that he would like to stage his own production in Stockholm. I wrote him that it was felt the script needed revision, especially where the child actors were concerned, and I would come back to him. Such was the pressure on my time that year, I never did. Bettina was asked to attend the Festival's daily press conference. Birtwistle was not with her, and she had nothing much to say about the play, only about her own performance. The plans to take it to the Arts Theatre in London, hopefully preliminary to a run elsewhere, fell through, because the stage was too small for our set. Friends and acquaintances had backed the play and my depression was increased by their loss.

On the last night, which was also the last night of the Festival, there was a late-night concert in the Usher Hall where various Festival artists were asked to perform. Bettina sang an aria: I forget what it was. Afterwards she was invited to Peter Diamand's supper party, given for the artists in the concert, and as her husband I was invited. As soon as Diamand saw me arrive his face fell. He knew who I was, had often met me, but very coldly, and had not realised that I was Bettina's husband. He must soon afterwards have realised who had written the play.

I had another problem at that year's Festival. I had been much taken with a Roland Dubillard play when I saw it in Paris, *Les Naïves Hirondelles*, which Barbara Wright translated for me as *The Swallows*. On its first Paris production it had flopped with a cast that included the author as one of the two young men in the play, and with his girlfriend Arlette Reinberg playing the ingenue part and directing it. The play subtly brings out a situation where two rather indolent young men take up one mad scheme after another, subsidised for the most part by the aunt of one of them, while competing to court the older lady's young assistant, all living in the same building. It is a comedy laced with bitterness when the older woman realises that she can no longer be sexually attractive to the young man who is not her nephew, and who has lost the game to win the young woman. The play was saved in Paris by the support of other playwrights including Ionesco, Anouilh and Roussin, and thereafter had a long run and several revivals. I sold it to the Traverse in Edinburgh for the Festival period and hoped for a transfer to London. Unfortunately the director, Ronald Taylor, to whom I had entrusted the casting and the direction, had not properly understood the play, and he engaged Ewen Hooper, an established older actor, to play one of the men and a young actor for the other, so that the age imbalance, on which the play depends, was not apparent to the audience, who never saw the only too-understandable tragedy of the older woman. I had no time to go to a rehearsal or to see it at the Traverse, and was horrified when I finally did at the Arts Theatre in London.

I had intended to bring *Lorca* to the Arts Theatre from the Gateway, and as explained above could not because of the different stage size, so I put in *The Swallows* instead. I think, although at this distance I cannot be too certain, that I had raised a single pool of finance for the two productions, but in the event no one received any money back. In the theatre luck plays a bigger part than talent and even genius, and one must always be prepared for everything going wrong. There are so many unpredictables from weather, world events, illness and human nature that can defeat the most careful planning. This applies especially to a production mounted for a week in the context of a overcrowded Festival schedule, where everyone is overworked and overstretched. The same unpredictabilities can apply to publishing, but there is more time for luck to change and for new solutions to be found. In the theatre when things do not go right, it is sudden death. *The Swallows* had its run to mediocre reviews and small audiences. I have so far not been able to negotiate a revival of what I know to be a beautiful, poignant and sensitive play. But I think *Lorca* might be revived.

Bettina and I, although married and living together, and sharing most of our activities, increasingly had private lives. She developed a considerable crush during rehearsals for Nicholas Chagrin, had an affair with him which she did nothing to conceal, which I felt I had to tolerate, given my relationship with at least three other women at the time. I was however always discreet about my own amours, and I would, when necessary, tell outright lies to protect the women in my life from gossip, although in the freer and franker climate of the swinging sixties everyone was far more open, and increasingly women didn't care. Relationships changed so often, and the pill had given women such freedom from pregnancy, that the secrecy which had accompanied non-marital relationships up to then was less and less necessary or practised. My friends were frequently getting married, but few of their marriages lasted, and divorced or not, the situation in the circles in which I moved was a fluid one. I knew that I shared some of my liaisons with others, usually male friends, and women did not particularly hide their sexual lives. It was not unusual to go out to a party with one person and end up with another, or for that matter alone. There were jealousies, of course, but they seldom lasted long or had consequences. I had rather fallen for a young female journalist who worked on Harper's Bazaar, who often commissioned me to write articles on operas, concerts and plays that I saw on my European trips. One summer night in 1966 I took her to a large party that Liz Smart, an American in London, then literary editor of Cosmopolitan, gave at the Round House in Camden Town to celebrate the republication of her short novel *By Grand Central Station I Lay Down and Wept*. There were several hundred people there and if I remember right one was asked to bring one's own bottle to supplement whatever Panther, the publisher, reissuing the book, were willing to contribute to the cost of the party. The Round House had at the time been rented by Arnold Wesker, who intended to turn it into a theatre for a working-class public, and was still trying to raise the money (he never did, but it became a theatre anyway) and he let Liz Smart have it for the evening. It was an extraordinary party, with all of the London arts crowd in a still empty and undecorated building. I lost Gaia, whom I had brought with me and was confident I would seduce later that night, somewhere in the crowd, easy to do when everyone knows nearly everyone else and one is constantly stopped by friends. When I found her again she was with Giles Gordon, another publisher. A little later she kissed me on the cheek and said she was leaving with Giles. I finished the evening disconsolately drinking with Paddy Kitchen, Dulan Barber and other literary friends. A few weeks later I read in the newspaper that Gaia had been killed in a car crash on the way to Brighton.

I should put in an aside here about Liz Smart. She was an American of a certain age, perhaps fifty, living just round the corner from our Soho offices, a poet and journalist, who managed to get Cosmopolitan to give considerable space to the more forward-looking arts and especially the kind of literature I was publishing. Her reviews helped us to sell to fashionable young women, and in the sixties this was important. She was much loved in literary circles for her taste, bubbling personality and forcefulness in supporting the right causes, a good person to have on your side. She had a very sexy look-alike daughter, who I often met in the local markets, which were on either side of our office, meeting places for those who worked or lived in Soho, where the stall-holders were all personalities in their own right. My favourite restaurant, Otello on Dean Street, to which Sally had first introduced me, always had several people I knew in it, while overhead was Muriel's, a private club where you could drink all afternoon, and where Francis Bacon, the painter, who lunched two or three times a week at Wheeler's, the fish restaurant on Old Compton Street, could usually be found. The sixties are inextricably associated for me with Soho, where I spent my working days and where, a decade later I would also be living.

* * * * * *

I think it was during the winter of 1964 that I was invited by the extra curricular department of Saint Andrews University to give a lecture, and as at the time I was deeply immersed in Arnold Hauser's *Mannerism*, in which Shakespeare is presented in what to me was an interesting new light, I picked as my subject *Shakespeare and Predestination*, although I doubt if that was the actual title. My main point was that Shakespeare's villains, MacBeth, Richard III and Iago in particular, had no particular reason to fear damnation as, according to the Calvinist theory much in vogue in Shakespeare's time, they had been damned by God from the beginning and had no reason to behave other than the way they did. At the back of the hall a man in a grey suit was sitting alone, who asked no questions afterwards, and did not stay for the drink that probably followed the lecture. Some considerable time later I received an invitation to talk during the Church of Scotland's General Assembly, but only at a morning session to a youth group on the last day. I accepted, put the date in my diary and forgot about it. Then my press cuttings agency began to send me mysterious clippings from Scottish newspapers, often letters to the editor, objecting to me, depicted as a wicked corruptor of the moral fibre of the nation, having the gall to talk to Scottish youth at the General Assembly. Shortly after I received a polite letter from Edinburgh, asking, as I passed frequently through the town on my way to Ledlanet, if I would be willing to attend a meeting of the Youth Group Committee. I telephoned, fixed a date, and turned up there one afternoon. Among the six or seven grey-suited men seated round a table, I recognised the man who had come to hear me in Saint Andrews and realised that my talk, which had been inadvertently on a Calvinist theme, must have been the reason for the invitation to speak at the Assembly. I was asked what I intended to say, answered that as the date was still months away I had given it no thought as yet, but I assumed that I was expected to talk about the influence the media had on youth and I would certainly urge my listeners to be sceptical about what they read in the newspapers and other media, and to learn to analyse what was said and the reason for saying it. They discussed this for a few minutes and the chairman then summed up, 'Well, I see nothing wrong in that. We don't like these pressure groups who try to tell us what to do. The invitation stands and thank you very much for taking the time to come and see us.' The pressure group was, not surprisingly, MRA.

On the night before I was due to speak – this must have been in May 1965 – I was at Ledlanet in my library just beginning to think about the next day when at around nine o'clock, the telephone rang. It was the Daily Express. 'Are you looking at television?' I was asked. 'No, why?' I answered. I was told that the Reverend John Gray had just proposed a motion to cancel my invitation to speak the next day and it had been passed by a considerable majority. In no way troubled I absorbed the news and stopped making notes. I already knew John Gray well. He was the Minister of Dunblane Cathedral, where strangely enough Ian Fraser, the man responsible for my invitation, also lived, and I had on at least two occasions debated against him. In the sixties I was constantly debating, most often on censorship, a very popular subject then, always certain to attract a crowd, and it was seldom that I did not win. I had debated against John Gray the previous year at Aberdeen University where his arguments had been all over the place, even accusing me of Nazism in my ideas of teaching people to think for themselves. In the first part of the debate I had used some new ideas I had thought up, fairly recondite I suppose, and Gray and no doubt many of those listening, may not have understood them. I spoke first proposing the motion and then Gray spoke against it, but at the end, when we each had to close the debate in the opposite order, he launched such a blistering attack on me, that I gave him an angry and very fluent reply, knocking his simplistic argument to pieces, for which I received a tremendous ovation and his seconder said that he had no choice but to vote for me. John Gray was a proud, arrogant man, full of his own doctrines, and he had reason enough to dislike me after the Aberdeen debate. Now I suppose he felt he had his revenge.

The telephone rang again. It was The Scotsman newspaper. 'Had I heard...?' 'Yes, I had.' 'Well, then,' said the voice on the 'phone, could we print your speech?'

I explained that I never wrote out my speeches, but spoke from a few notes. I was then asked, 'Can you write it for us? We'll pay you.' I agreed and sat down at the typewriter, because the messenger would arrive in an hour to collect it. It took me over two hours, came to about four thousand words, which I had no chance to revise or correct, and I had to keep the messenger waiting, but the next morning it was in The Scotsman. It took up much of the front page and two entire inside pages. Reading it I was amazed at my own fluency, argumentation, irony and humour. If I had thought it out for a month it could not have been better. Of course, it had no connection with what I might have said to the assembled youth, but was a reasoned attack on censorship generally and in particular on the kind of attitude that had led to the refusal to have me speak, which was soon a *cause célèbre*. A few hundred people might have heard me speak for about twenty minutes (I was not the only speaker). Now tens of thousands had read me and the newspapers' initiative had made the church look extremely silly. As Ben Lassers, an American doctor, then Registrar at the Royal Infirmary in Edinburgh who occasionally fished in my loch, said to me the next day, 'Congratulations on ruining this year's General Assembly. It's just what they needed.'

But that was not the end of it. Invitations to speak poured in from all over Scotland. During the next year I spoke to dozens of youth groups on a variety of subjects, but censorship was always the most popular. The sales of my books undoubtedly benefited. I came to know a great many ministers, but also Catholic priests, and even Jewish groups invited me to speak to them. For some reason many such ministers and priests thought of me as a person to whom they could confide their deepest secret thoughts. I have always kept those confidences, but what I can say here was that many had lost their faith in God and were really agnostic but could not see their way to leaving a fairly pleasant paid occupation without too many worries, especially if they had a family to support. Many of them were basically social workers who found the church a convenient umbrella for their activities. A considerable number were homosexual, but dared not tell anyone, let alone practice, and if they did occasionally have a relationship it was fleeting, guilt-ridden and the source of much misery. Others were in love with a woman other than their own wife and did not know what to do or how to hide it. Many of those who invited me were more interested in talking about themselves and asking my advice than in hearing me speak. And what advice could I give other than general comfort, saying that they were not alone? Just meeting someone who did not judge them was in itself a relief to them most of the time.

I was to see more of Ian Fraser. Whenever I did something in Edinburgh, mount a play, do something for the Festival, which was possible again after Diamand left as Director, or be involved in a public event, he was often there in the audience. He was deeply involved in the Ecumenical Movement and ran United Churches House in Dunblane as warden and he sometimes organised conferences there to which I was invited. Most of them were on secular subjects that interested open-minded churchmen and the attendees were a mixture of academics, artists, media people and a few ministers, but never many. I enjoyed these occasions where I felt I was both teacher and pupil, and I always met interesting people.

On the day after my piece appeared in The Scotsman, Alastair Dunnett, the editor, rang me and invited me to lunch. He was full of praise, and when we met in Edinburgh two days later he was still chuckling over the things he had liked most, such as a quotation from *Tam O'Shanter* where I compared the 'warmed-up wrath' of Tam's wife to that of certain puritans. It was a good lunch with the best wine available and thereafter we remained on excellent terms. I was in the future to write his obituary. Alastair was a surprising man, much of him Scottish conservative, some of him having an impish sense of humour. He never suffered fools gladly and liked to see hypocrites exposed. He was an excellent editor and gave The Scotsman its golden era.

1967 was a particularly busy year and some of the most significant events have not yet been told. There was a great need to raise funds and Jenny Paull, the first oboe in *Il Re Pastore* at Ledlanet, with whom I now had a tempestuous but short affair, that because of the inconveniences of meeting soon turned to friendship, was the greatest help to me in bringing together musicians to play to raise funds for a cause. She knew every musician in London, and she told me she had probably slept with every wind player. When I first met her she was married to a clarinettist, who also played saxophone on occasion in night-clubs. Our situation was not unlike that of Pinter's play *Betrayal*, because until I rented a room we had trouble in finding places to meet. But the big problem came over Jim Fraser, who had taken a liking to Jenny at Ledlanet.

I saw much of Jim in those days, both in Scotland and in London. I had an old farm house called Huntley Hall only a short distance from Ledlanet, which suddenly became vacant. Jim wanted to take it over after its tenant moved out, and in recognition of the money he had spent at Ledlanet I gave it to him with about an acre of land around it. He transformed it into a sumptuous country house with an indoor swimming pool, a sauna, a music room that had both a grand piano and a harpsichord (but not the one we used at Ledlanet), a large sitting room and several bedrooms. The master bedroom had a bathroom with gold taps and steam-proof mirrors.

Jim came to know Jenny about the time he was transforming Huntley Hall. He was married, but there was no affection between him and his wife, and he obviously saw Huntley Hall, in part at least, as being a love nest. He had pursued other ladies he had met through me, most notably Lynette Perry, who told him that if he lost five stone she would consider him, but Jim was incapable of losing weight whatever the incentive, because he could not give up drink, wine, brandy and port for the most part, and he consumed large quantities of all three. Jenny was less particular and finally succumbed to his insistence. He took her off to Majorca for a holiday – by this time she had separated from her husband, and our affair had ended some time previously – but it was not a success. He was a fat man who did not want people to see him undressed, so he never went near either the beach or a pool, staying in the hotel drinking while she out to socialise and enjoy herself. He told her that he had built Huntley Hall for her, and it was obvious that he wanted to imprison her there, but Jenny was a free spirit who, whatever the generosity – and Jim could be very generous – would never allow anything like that to happen to her. As Jenny was engaged to play during the autumn season at Ledlanet the situation was becoming complicated.

I had been asked by Clive Wilson, the town clerk of Harrogate, a Spa town in Yorkshire which had a summer festival, to put on a Writers' Conference, and I organised a small one in 1968 and a larger one in 1969, when I was given a bigger budget, although not one to rival my Edinburgh Conferences, which had incidently been widely copied elsewhere by then, notably by Nicholas Nabokov, Vladimir's brother, in Berlin. The second Harrogate Conference was devoted to science fiction and my idea then was to bring together scientists, particularly those who were planning our futures in terms of innovative practices, inventions and planning, and those who were imagining possible futures in their writings. I persuaded my namesake Nigel Calder (no relation), editor of The New Scientist and a distinguished science writer, to chair it, brought novelists Alan Burns, Eva Figes, Norman Spinrad, Brian Aldiss, J. G. Ballard, Margaret Drabble, Michael Moorcock, B.S. Johnstone, and among others Erich Fried, Robert Jungk, G. W. Targett (who wrote largely for religious publications from a liberal perspective), Chris Evans, Walter Perry, D. L. Jayasuriya, Charles Marovitz, Robin Blackburn, Christopher Priest, a Mr. Jones (first name unfindable), Jeff Nuttall, a Professor Todcroft and a few others. Some of the above names may have defected and been replaced by others. I can no longer be quite sure. They were a mixture of creative writers, journalists and scientists in different disciplines, and the two-day conference was lively. From the start there was obvious hostility between science fiction writers and psychologists and psychiatrists. There was also hostility on the part of the English audience to a large group of German students who had followed Robert Jungk from Berlin and camped on the lawn of the hotel where he was staying. We were treated to several amazing descriptions of what the future might be like, for instance that future towns would be designed as long strips with a motorway running down the middle, and residential or industrial areas lying on each side, and the civic centre located in the middle of the strip with the central fast through-road running underneath it. The Mr. Jones who put this forward, a civic centre planner, later approached me to write a book, and I know we accepted something he had written, but apparently it never was published. The conference was lively and much enjoyed, but the cost was found prohibitive by the Festival Committee, who did not repeat the experience. I met Stan Barstow there, saw his play at the Festival, a new adaptation of Ibsen's *An Enemy of the People* into a modern British context, got on well with him and eventually published his play. Ian Wallace, always a major draw at Ledlanet, was part of the Festival and in an article he wrote later said that I, looking like a plain-clothes policeman, had claimed to have invented the permissive society. I'm sure I didn't, although it was a subject much discussed just then. My principal recollections is of Erich Fried walking out in a huff after I had to stop him hogging a debate, shouting, 'John Calder is a fascists'.

Jim Fraser turned up at the Conference, not because, as I had at first thought, that he wanted to support me, but to catch my ear at the final party. He wanted me to cancel Jenny Paull's engagement to play at Ledlanet. She had walked out on him and taunted him that I would never do such a thing as to cancel her. I forget how the problem was resolved: I think she finally backed out on her own.

I have mentioned Ian Wallace several times. A veteran opera singer, specialising in comic bass-baritone roles, he had often entertained me in Mozart, Rossini and the like. I had seen him at Hintlesham in Weber's *Peter Schmoll*, a small festival in Suffolk run by Tony Stokes, who had constructed a theatre in his large garden, where the stage and orchestra was covered, as were the audience, in a marquee open to the stage, but with an open space between audience and orchestra, about which more later. I had enormously enjoyed Ian's high jinks in Glyndebourne's famous production of Rossini's *Le Comte Ory* in 1954, where he had played a crusader masquerading as a nun. In fact it was so memorable that when I published the Richard Coe translation of Stendhal's *Life of Rossini*, I used a colour photograph of the production by Armstrong Jones (later Lord Snowdon) on the dust jacket with Ian in it. Wallace sang less opera now, but his one-man show, with David Money at the piano, consisting of operatic extracts, songs of every kind, including Scottish ones, and a lively patter peppered with jokes, could be immensely popular with family audiences. He appeared regularly in a BBC musical quiz programme, and this helped to make him a popular celebrity. Although Ian Wallace's political views were far to the right of mine, we became good friends. He first appeared at Ledlanet in 1966 and thereafter annually. We had his ideal audience there, as is attested by his recording, which in spite of a few technical deficiencies is very pleasurable to listen to. On one occasion when I was giving a party at the Caledonian club in London for an author and he was present (it might well have been for his own book) he was persuaded to sing a song *a capella*. Within seconds members in other rooms, hearing his well-known voice, had asked if they could come in and he was prevailed on to sing two or three more. Although most popular in Scotland, he lived in Surrey. I commissioned his autobiography, which it took him a considerable time to write, but when published, it went through three editions. He made personal appearances in Scottish department stores with book departments, doing particularly well at Jenner's in Edinburgh.

One day Ian Wallace rang to ask my advice. He had been offered the post of Principal of the Royal Scottish Academy of Music and Dramatic Art in Glasgow. I felt he should take it. He was a natural teacher and could influence the growth of the performing arts in Scotland, an inspiration to young people entering the profession, but in the end he decided not to accept. His main reasons were that he wanted to remain an active entertainer, and that a move back to Scotland would disrupt his old mother, now living near him in the south. His autobiography *Promise Me You'll Sing Mud* amusingly and very readably recounts his career, the title taken from the Flanders and Swan *Hippopotamus* song that he often gave as an encore. Ill health shortened his career after 1975, but several honours came his way, including the Rectorship of Saint Andrews University.

I have mentioned Hintlesham in connection with Ian Wallace who I heard sing there once. I paid several visits to this delightful summer festival, given by the highly eccentric Tony Stokes. He apparently had strange tastes, such as having his wife, estranged when I knew him, pull him around his garden in a dog cart, encouraged by a whip, both naked, which had earned him space in the Sunday tabloid press some years earlier. He invited me onto his executive committee, largely influenced by a musical agent, who was always urging him to mount works for Anne-Marie Satre, usually called Mimi, a personable and attractive soprano, who in my opinion ruined her chances of getting singing engagements by always trying to be present at meetings of committees, where her presence stopped her being discussed. Her agent wanted Hintlesham to mount *Norma* for her. The committee meetings were a waste of time for me, but I always enjoyed lavish hospitality at Hintlesham, which was near Ipswich. One day I took Sheila Colvin there – it was probably *Peter Schmoll* in July 1968 – and she was in considerable pain having eaten her first ever oysters the night before, and having had a bad one, but she too fell under the spell of a stage where you saw the moon rising through the open aperture at the back. The partly open-air theatre at Santa Fé has the same effect.

I must now go back to 1966. I was skiing at Val d'Isère with Jacques Chaix and the group of my French friends who normally went there in early spring when the days are lengthening and the snow usually light and powdery, and I received a parcel from London, sent to me by Marion Boyars. It was an American novel entitled *Last Exit to Brooklyn* by Hubert Selby Jr., and she had read it. She thought it risky given the considerable amount of sexual content, but there was a good sales potential. I read it and liked it instantly, seeing not so much the sexual detail, which was natural for a section of American society that knew nothing but lust for money and instant gratification, but saw it as a strong social document about what a community becomes when it is totally devoid of any contact with real education and the culture that breeds civilised values. Each chapter is centred on a character caught in the trap of his own background and values, set in a section of New York, the seediest part of Brooklyn, where there is no hope because no one knows anything different or better. The novel was set during the last war, and the local hoodlums would mug sailors on leave, often with the help of girls on the way to becoming prostitutes. All activities centred around violence, bullying and sex. The two most potent chapters pictured a trade union leader, who during his brief period of power in a strike, discovers his homosexual nature, and a narcissistic young prostitute who ends up literally on a rubbish heap after a gang rape that she brings on herself. It all rang true, and it reminded me of Zola's novels of Parisian low-life. I might also have remembered that Zola had been attacked in his own time for portraying conditions in Paris similar to those in the novel a century earlier.

I telephoned Marion and told her that of course we should take on *Last Exit*, and we published it a few months later. It received good reviews, but not extraordinary ones, and the sales were not particularly better than most of our other current fiction. Paperback publishers were not besieging us yet for the rights for a mass-market edition.

In those days we were friendly with many MPs and one of them rang me to say that a Conservative member had asked the Attorney General for a certain book to be prosecuted for obscenity. He had refused to name it as he did not want to give it publicity, but the Tory MP was passing on the title to the Director of Public Prosecutions in the hope that he would bring a case against the publisher. The book, I was told, was *Last Exit to Brooklyn*, and the Tory MP was Sir Charles Taylor. I then placed an advertisement in The Sunday Times, quoting the best of our reviews, but also quoting Sir Charles in an ironic way. He complained to the Speaker of the House that we had breached parliamentary privilege, but the House laughed at his protests and the Speaker refused to accept his arguments. Several Labour MPs wrote to the DPP, pointing out that the book had been well-reviewed and should certainly not be prosecuted. He eventually announced that he had taken advice and would carry the matter no further. The next thing we heard was that a private prosecution was to be brought against us by another Tory MP, Sir Cyril Black, Member for Wimbledon, a property developer and Baptist lay preacher. He was also Treasurer of the Billy Graham Campaign and, as we were later to learn, Billy Graham, at a recent fund-raising breakfast in London, had urged that action should be taken 'against the flood of pornographic books being published in Britain'. Largely because of Taylor's initiative, he had pounced on our book, which I certainly did not consider in any way pornographic. In fact it exposed exactly the kind of social conditions created by slum landlords like Sir Cyril.

The complaint was duly made and we received a visit from the Vice Squad, led by a certain Detective Inspector Alton, who examined our offices, looked at books in languages they could not read including Cyrillic, was obviously surprised at the conventional appearance of our rooms, which in spite of being in Soho, obviously dealt in serious books. They formally bought a copy of *Last Exit* (we always kept a small stock of our current books in the office for sale) and left. Some years later, I was to hear that Alton, who obviously took bribes from pornographic bookshops, had been convicted of corruption and imprisoned. He never dropped any hints of expected bribes to us.

The case was heard at Marlborough Street Magistrates Court by a stipendiary magistrate called Leo Gradwell. What was new in this case is that the prosecution brought witnesses, which had not happened before where a serious book was concerned, even in the Lady Chatterley case. It had always been assumed by the prosecution that the obscenity of a book was so obvious that judge or jury would automatically convict just on the presence of certain words or of any sexual description. But the Obscene Publications Act, which Roy Jenkins had managed to get passed in 1959, had for the first time allowed defence witnesses to give evidence of a book's literary merit, so that now a judgement had to be a balancing act between the amount of obscenity (which for a century had been defined as the tendency of a book to deprave or corrupt) and the amount of literary merit. The DPP had been astounded by the witnesses produced by Penguin Books in 1961, not only writers and academics, but even a Bishop, and they had convinced the jury. Until then it had been assumed that the old Anglo-Saxon word 'fuck', which almost everyone knew and which certainly had much vernacular use, was sufficient to get a conviction. Until after the Penguin trial it could not be found in any English dictionary.

The witnesses against us were the expected clutch of school teachers who saw adults as needing censorship as much as their pupils, obsessive characters such as H. Montgomery Hyde, a barrister who had written much about the Oscar Wilde trial, and who carried around with him photographs that were too obscene to be viewed by anyone other than himself, some right-wing journalists and one MP, none other than the slippery, publicity-seeking Robert Maxwell, who in addition to his other activities was now the Labour Member for Buckinghamshire, but was viewed with much suspicion by his colleagues. We knew he had not read the book, because we had heard from an employee of his Pergamon Press to whom it had been given to read, so that he could know what it was about. The man had told Maxwell he was wrong to appear in court against it, but Maxwell believed that a puritanical stance would make him more popular with his constituents. He was not a very convincing witness, but Leo Gradwell was the type of magistrate who would be against us on principle.

Our solicitor was again Bruce Douglas-Mann, but this time we had a barrister, Peter Benenson, who had written the preface to *Gangrene* for us. He floundered a little, got out of his depth and did not really cross-examine well, nor explain to the magistrate what the Obscene Publications Act really said. Our own witnesses included Kenneth Alsopp, the popular journalist, Reginald Davis-Poynter, another publisher, Elkan Allan, a broadcaster, Dr. Alex Comfort, later author of *The Joy of Sex*, Anthony Burgess the novelist, and one or two others.

We put up a reasonable case, but we did not have a good barrister. Against us was Michael Havers. He was very smooth and urbane, unlike Peter Benenson, whose heart was certainly in the right place, but who was too excitable and could not match the concentration of his opponent. We lost of course. Afterwards Havers took me aside. He said he admired our list and liked literature, and was sorry to be prosecuting us. He had a special reason for taking on this case, but he did not divulge what it was. We learned it later. When Sir Cyril Black resigned as an MP in 1970, it was Michael Havers who took over his safe Conservative seat, and thereafter occupied the top legal posts in later Conservative governments, mainly under Margaret Thatcher.

At that point I had a word with Douglas-Mann. What had happened in one London area, the jurisdiction of a particular magistrate's court, did not apply elsewhere, but Marlborough Street Court was in central London with its many bookshops, and the situation was very different from our Sheffield experience with *Cain's Book*, which we were still selling. Bruce then wrote a letter to the DPP. It was not the letter I wanted him to write, and I did not see it in advance. Instead of a conciliatory and soft-spoken letter, he sent a provocative challenge to prosecute us in a national case, saying that the book would be vigorously defended. He was soon to be a member of parliament as well as a solicitor, and he probably saw his practice becoming a famous one in the light of a show trial that would enable him to bathe in the limelight, and it would in any case be profitable to him. But Marion and I were horrified and decided we had to drop him. After much thought we went to Goodman Derrick, of which the leading partner was Lord Goodman, personal solicitor to Harold Wilson, who also represented the Labour Party. He had become Chairman of the Arts Council in 1965 and was an effective hands-on chairman who expanded its activities and its scope. He seemed the right man for us. He also represented Reginald Davis-Poynter, a good friend of mine, and it may well have been he who suggested Goodman. I would have much to do with him in the future.

At the first meeting Goodman went over the logistics of the case. The barrister he wanted was a right-wing Tory peer, Lord Hailsham (Quinton Hogg), who instinctively would be on the other side of the fence. When I pointed that out, Lord Goodman pooh-poohed me. Barristers didn't have to believe in the case they were pleading, he said, and went on to say that they were too professional for that. I disagreed. Gerald Gardiner, who had won the Lady Chatterley case, believed absolutely in the cause he was defending; he would never have adopted the tactics he did if he had felt otherwise, I argued. Goodman took umbrage. 'Well, if you won't take my advice, I shall pass you on to my partner,' he said, and so our solicitor became Mr. John Montgomerie, a big bluff man, not so different from Goodman, but more willing to listen. The barrister he picked, although a man of great intelligence, was also wrong for us, and for largely the same reason that I did not want Hailsham. His instincts were not particularly libertarian, and as a practising Catholic he believed in authority, that is in giving the jury the authoritative opinions of others, rather than in trying to make them understand the arguments for themselves. But Patrick Neill, who was selected by Monty (as he was usually called), was known for his skill in dealing with complicated financial cases, and he did his best, although I know he was never comfortable with the case.

Arthur Boyars' mother was apparently very distressed by the 'shame' of a criminal prosecution being brought against her daughter-in-law, and the relatives of George Lobbenberg, her previous husband, who died about this time, were also apparently very uncomfortable. Although I had certainly not expected things to go so far, I treated it as a crusade, or rather a worthy cause to be defended, but we were in for an expensive experience with an unknown outcome and we had to raise money. To this end I addressed several meetings, often organised by humanist organisations and the National Council for Civil Liberties whose very active Director was Tony Smythe, who, if I remember rightly, had earlier been associated with CND. He invited me to be the keynote speaker at their AGM, an event to which I brought my mother who happened to be in town that night. She found the occasion uncomfortable. Every public meeting brought in more funds and publicised our case. Other people with censorship problems were usually at these meetings, held in small halls in Bloomsbury or Holborn or Soho. A regular was Jean Straker, a photographer constantly raided by the police, and having his negatives taken from his studio. He would speak from the hall when I had finished, state his own grievances, then urge those present to contribute to the appeal. I started the Free Art Legal Fund, producing a leaflet that quoted from Zola's defence of the naturalist novel, a wonderful passage that I had come across in an anthology of international literature at Ledlanet, a volume that I am sure no one had opened before me, with an appeal form. The leaflet, distributed widely, produced many cheques. Many came forward to help, including several MPs and members of the arts and literary communities. Our meetings became fuller, our speakers more distinguished and we had to take bigger halls to contain bigger audiences. Other causes of the day were also aired. Joan Littlewood gave us her theatre for a fund-raising concert, for which Jenny Paull recruited a star orchestra that included Alan Civil, the horn player. Bettina sang in that, but so did others, and there were actors doing their bit as well. Realising then, that although our supporters were generous, they did not want to turn out just to hear speakers and give money, I started The Defence of Literature and the Arts Society with our by now substantial mailing-list, which became a properly organised society with a committee and members. We made William Hamling, Labour MP for Woolwich West, our Chairman, and the committee included several other MPs including Ben Whittaker, soon to win Hampstead for Labour, Anthony Gray, Tony Smythe and several other activists. Marion Boyars and I became joint secretaries and we ran the DLAS from our Soho offices, using our regular staff. There were frequent committee meetings as well as public meetings, and these were often now held in committee rooms of the House of Commons, courtesy of our MP members. This venue turned out to be a draw, both for supporters and for other MPs who sympathised and could just drop in to a meeting for a few minutes without having to leave the Commons. Some peers attended as well. Jeremy Isaacs came once or twice and other television and radio broadcasters as well, both out of sympathy and because we were making news. David Hockney had some trouble just then bringing in pictorial magazines that he wanted for his work, and we approached customs and got them released. We made common cause with the theatre that had its own frequent censorship problems. Actors and producers, as well as authors who had difficulty getting their plays past the Lord Chamberlain until 1968, and after that some theatre managements, offered to help. Thousands of pounds were rolling in and our eminent legal team that now included two juniors, Lord Lloyd of Hampstead and Cyril Salmon, could eventually be paid because the bulk of the costs were met through donations from the public, coming to over £70,000.

One day, returning from Ledlanet to London, I found myself following Malcolm Muggeridge onto a British Airways aeroplane at Edinburgh airport. He had been elected Rector of Edinburgh University by the students, a largely honorary post that always goes to a popular celebrity, and was returning from some meeting that goes with the ritual. I remembered a rumour that had come to my ears. I slipped into the seat beside him and he looked definitely uncomfortable. After the usual exchanges, I said to him: 'Tell me, Malcolm, if there's any truth in the rumour that you're going to give evidence for the prosecution in the *Last Exit* trial.' He wriggled and tried to avoid a straight answer. 'Because if you do,' I went on, 'there is something that my Counsel will put to you. "Do you remember one fine June afternoon in 1962 when you and John Calder were crossing George IV Bridge in Edinburgh and you said to him: "'If I were a student today, I'd fuck myself to death.'"' I paused. 'Mind you, the girls in their summer frocks were looking very attractive just then. I am of course prepared to swear on oath that you said that, as of course you did.'

'Well, of course I was asked,' he said, 'but I only thought about it.' And he changed the subject and started to look at his newspaper. As the 'plane was landing, he turned to me again. 'My dear John,' he intoned, 'of course I would never dream of giving evidence against you. You're an old friend. I wouldn't think of it.' And that was that. I had nobbled him, but fairly enough. At that point in his life he had become a professional puritan, and I knew that it was all a hypocritical pose to stay in the limelight. People like Muggeridge were always needed by the broadcasting media to give a balance at a time when fashion had shifted to the permissive left. My personal nickname for him was Hummug.

Shortly after the first trial at Marlborough Street Magistrates Court I had been asked to appear on the David Frost Show with Robert Maxwell. Most of the programme was taken up by David Susskind, talking about some current American issue, and time was short at the end of the programme. Maxwell tried to talk non-stop to prevent me getting a word in at all, but I managed to bang the table and insist on talking. In court he had been asked if he would ban *Ulysses* and had answered, 'No that's a good book.' Now I asked him, 'You said *Ulysses* was a good book. Have you read it?'

He hesitated and said, yes he had. 'Name one character in Joyce's *Ulysses*,' I challenged him and of course he couldn't.

Another encounter with Maxwell took place that year at the Annual General Meeting of the Publishers Association. During 'Any Other Business' he got up and proposed that I should be expelled from the Association as a pornographer. Maxwell had owned for some time the old Edinburgh firm of Chambers, which had recently brought out a new edition of the famous Encyclopaedia. I had bought it and realised that it was a fraud. I stood up after Maxwell with another proposition, that Maxwell should be expelled for bringing dishonour to the publishing profession, pointing out that the latest 'updated' *Chambers Encyclopaedia*, published in 1967, still said that Winston Churchill was alive, only one of hundreds of articles that had not been updated at all. There was much laughter and the Chairman, restraining his mirth, said that he though Mr. Maxwell and Mr. Calder should settle their differences outside the meeting.

In preparation for the trial we had many meetings with Patrick Neill and made up a long list of witnesses, which were gradually whittled down to a manageable number. Appearance was important and many were rejected for odd reasons. Heinrich Ledig-Rowohlt, who had already published *Last Exit* in German wanted to appear, but Patrick Neill did not want a German on the strange ground that an English jury would think all Germans were homosexual. Neill had great difficulty with the book itself. He was obviously unfamiliar with American writing, could not understand a large number of the expressions used or the events that were described. We had to explain words, colloquialisms, slang and the actions themselves, including the sex scenes. He was certainly quite shocked. But when he talked to some of our witnesses, he began to realise that there was a whole world unfamiliar to him, that people who taught literature at universities took in their stride. In the trial our witnesses would go first and would be followed by the prosecution's team. Our judge, Judge Rodgers seemed reasonable and treated us with courtesy, allowing Marion and I to sit with our lawyers and not in the box as in most criminal cases. He decided on an all-male jury, and I think we made a mistake in not objecting. The jury all came from the same part of south London, none were challenged, and most of them were middle-aged and carried The Daily Express into court. It was and still is is a right-wing philistine paper that boded us no good. There was one younger man who carried The Manchester Guardian (as it was then). We had been given permission to bring in a tape recorder, and we recorded the whole trial.

We had selected Frank Kermode as our first witness. He was Regius Professor at King's College, Cambridge, an eminent critic, who had only just returned from America with his new American girlfriend, an ex-student of his, whom he was later to marry after his current marriage had been terminated. He spent a day and a half in the witness box, explaining to the jury the function of literature, which was to describe the world we live in so that we could understand not only our own lives, but those of others, as well as the underlying motivations, often not understood by the characters created by the author, which made them do what they did because it was natural for them. The jury was taken through the book. Kermode, probed by Neill, explained how the trade union leader, Harry, a central character in the novel, was only able to realise his homosexual nature when the strike empowered him to give expression to his previously unrealised desires. The prosecuting counsel, Mr. Mathew, who was good at insinuations, handled the jury with flattery and suggestions that could appeal to their prejudices. They were obviously not regular readers. They had taken a week to get through the book, sitting in an empty court-room, often complaining the novel was too difficult, and often sending out to ask what words meant. Now they were being taken through it again, first by Frank Kermode, then by Alfred Alvarez, poet and critic, then by Eric Mottram, another academic, who admitted that he was a jazz buff, which may or may not have made him more sympathetic to the jury.

Our two junior counsel, Lord Lloyd of Hampstead and Cyril Salmon, who occasionally took over from Neill, also examined our witnesses and later cross-examined the prosecution ones. Alan Burns, our author, gave evidence for us, and fortunately his new novel *Celebrations* was well-reviewed in The Times on the day he appeared, enabling Cedric Salmon to draw attention to it. The Maudsley Hospital psychiatrist Dr. David Stafford-Clark appeared and gave evidence relative to the characters in the book, Quintin Crewe, a distinguished journalist, gave his evidence from a wheelchair, Robert Baldick, university Don and translator, praised the book as literature and Barbara Hardy from Birkbeck College, one of our few women witnesses, pointed out that the Victorian novel, which she taught, suffered from the prudishness of its time, which modern writers, having a truer sense of reality, did not. There were many more, each only kept a few minutes in the witness-box. We had Father Hester, Church of England minister from our local Soho church, St. Anne's, and his prelate the Reverend Kenneth Leach, who compared characters in the book to some of the less fortunate Soho characters who sometimes sought their help. We had two Americans, David Galloway, who taught in Germany, and whose novels we were later to publish, who gave evidence about the frankness of the current American novel, and Eric Blau, who grew up in exactly the area of Brooklyn where the novel is set. *Last Exit*, he said, was true of the actual conditions prevailing there and he had personally seen worse events than those described. I gave evidence myself, my reasons for publishing the book, and the merits I saw in it. According to the press, which daily covered the trial, at least the section of it that was sympathetic to us, I came over as sincere and committed. Marion was also in the witness box, but her testimony was mainly about reading the book and thinking it worthwhile to send it to me. We had about twenty witnesses in all and our testimony took a week.

Then we had the prosecution witnesses. Mathew was canny enough not to produce Robert Maxwell again. My team would easily have made mincemeat of him. Nor Montgomery Hyde. Their best literary witness was probably David Holloway, Deputy Literary Editor of the Daily Telegraph, and about to take the place of H. D. Ziman, the literary editor. Holloway had not wanted to speak against the book, but Ziman, not having the courage to appear himself, had made him do it. He said little other than that personally he did not like it and thought the explicit sex described was unnecessary. The other witnesses were mainly right-wing literary hacks like Robert Pitman of the Daily Express, a Professor George Catlin, an academic of the right, and a headmaster and a psychiatrist brought to neutralise our own. But there were two witnesses who undoubtedly did us harm. One was David Shepherd, now a Church of England priest, who had previously been an All-England cricketer, who would naturally attract the attention of the jury and the press. He said that he had been deeply troubled by the book, but Neill, anxious to get a popular sporting hero out of the box as quickly as possible, did not ask him how or why. It was about two years later that I learned what, as an honest man under oath, he would have replied if properly questioned, that as a student he had been a practising homosexual, that on taking up religion he had decided it was wrong, that he had married and forced himself to become heterosexual, but that on reading *Last Exit to Brooklyn* he had found the old tendencies reawakened. In other words the novel had given him self-awareness, which is exactly what good literature should do. An opportunity was missed by Patrick Neill because of his unwillingness, a part of his Roman Catholic upbringing, to encourage the jury to think for itself, rather than just being given authority. It was probably Shepherd who did us the most harm.

The other dangerous witness was Sir Basil Blackwell. He had been pushed to give evidence by his son, Richard Blackwell, who I knew from Booksellers' Conferences. I had always thought him a prig and an oaf, the conceited scion of an old established book-selling family in Oxford. He had not the courage to appear himself, but pushed his aged father to do so instead. Sir Basil, nearly eighty, was a straight-laced old Conservative unlikely to have much sympathy with modern literature of any kind or with the changes that characterised social life in the sixties with its youth culture, its reforms in capital punishment, freedom of expression, sexual permissiveness and greater equality for women. My late uncle, Sir James, and he would have agreed on all of these matters, my grandfather even more so. He was asked if he had read the book and replied that he had to read it as he had agreed to give evidence against it. He went on to say that 'my last years have been utterly vitiated by having had to read this filth.' He was not kept long in the witness box by Neill. I would have asked him why he had agreed to give evidence against a book he had not yet read, and why this judgement in advance? And why did he *have to read* a book he knew he would not like and thereby 'vitiate' his old age? But Neill just wanted such witnesses out of the witness-box as quickly as possible, trusting to the more enlightened evidence of the many professors, critics, authors and others who had appeared for us.

Mr. Mathew against us was smooth and insinuating. He played on the jury as Gardiner had done in the Penguin Lady Chatterley trial, but in reverse. Whereas Gardiner had brought out the class-bias in not wanting 'your wife or your servants' to read such a book, the prosecution's own words, Mayhew could easily flatter the jury that they were 'men of the world' who did not need 'Professors' to tell them what was what. Neill missed all that. It was not the kind of case for which he was best suited.

The judge's summing up was fair, and as far as we could make out, he seemed to be on our side. He had treated us with courtesy throughout, had explained the law, but not in all its ramifications. We did not much like the look of our jury, especially the foreman, a black-jowled, heavy-set man who probably owned a small shop, and had been heard during the evidence of one witness to mutter, 'Fiction, fiction! I thought this was about fact.' He was one of the Daily Express carriers. The court ushers in their black robes were friendly and fairly optimistic about our chances during the long wait while the jury was out.

The case had gone on a day longer than expected because the judge had reserved his last few words of the summing-up until the next morning. David Frost had intended to discuss the case and the verdict on his television programme that night, and because of the delay could not do so. He changed the discussion into a general one on pornography and censorship. That may well have influenced some members of the jury and especially their wives, who had not been in court. At any rate, after a wait of about four hours, and we thought the young man on the jury who read The Guardian might have held them up for that long, we were found guilty. Marion, very upset, looked down at her hands. I tried to show no expression.

We were given a fine of £500, probably the minimum the judge could give us. The costs ran to over £70,000, but we had been helped by the appeals we had made to the public and the funds raised by the DLAS. I instantly wanted to appeal, but Lord Lloyd in particular was dismissive.

'There's no way you can appeal against a jury decision in a case like this,' he said. I protested that other books had been banned in the past and had, if they were good books, always come back, but our team consisted of conventional barristers and such issues as literary values were of no great importance to them. I told Montgomerie however that we did intend to carry the matter further and I would find a way. Lord Goodman also took an interest. In his view the law was unworkable and what was needed was a committee of experts, rather like the witnesses we had produced in court, to decide what was worthy of publication, whatever the contents, and what was not.

Last Exit was banned, but the company went on normally, and we now had more time to devote to our other publications, which had suffered badly.

* * * * * *

Sam Beckett had stayed with me in Wimpole Street during the rehearsals of *Waiting for Godot*, which was revived at the Royal Court in 1964 (I am again returning to the past), and which was produced by Anthony Page. He would come back in the evening after rehearsal, grim-faced and unhappy because Page was not getting what he (Sam) wanted from the actors, especially from Nicol Williamson playing Vladimir. But one day he returned to the flat looking much happier. He had had a private talk with Williamson, whose previous role had been the lead in John Osborne's *Inadmissible Evidence*, and the actor had told Sam that he was using the same London accent as in the earlier play. Previously he had been at the Dundee Rep. 'But that can't be your natural accent then,' commented Beckett.

'No, normally I have a Scots accent,' said Nicolson.

'Couldn't you do that here?' asked Beckett, and Nicol did, whereupon he was asked to keep it. That was the evening Sam came back smiling. 'A touch of genius there,' he said to me. The other actors were satisfactory although not chosen by Beckett, the Estragon being Alfred Lynch. It was the first unexpurgated *Godot* given in Britain, the Lord Chamberlain having relented on what had previously been quite idiotic cuts.

Bettina and I went to the opening; Sam could not bear to sit through a performance of any of his plays with an audience present, and he returned to Paris immediately after it opened. It was an extraordinary *Godot*, different from previous productions, largely because of the anguished animality of Nicol Williamson's Vladimir. At the climax of his great speech towards the end of the second act, 'Was I sleeping while the others suffered...,' he started slowly and gathered speed, squeezing ever more feeling into his character's questioning of the events of the day. When he looked down at Estragon and reached 'Let him sleep on' his whole body became convulsed into an expression of pain. Then straightening, he released a trumpet call in all its stridency as he screamed out 'I can't go on.' A long deepening silence followed as the audience sat up in their seats, their mouths open. Then he whispered, 'What have I said.' The whole agony of the human condition was contained in that scream, one of the most vivid memories of my theatrical life. On the way out I followed a young couple. 'That was obscene, but really obscene,' said the girl to her young man. It was the first important London production of *Godot* since 1955, but now the press had accepted Beckett and the Royal Court as well, and there were good reviews and full houses. Beckett had arrived.

It was that same year, 1964, when there was an extraordinary production of *Endgame*, that was rehearsed in London, then performed in Paris, and that then moved to London, to the Royal Court, and was, later with a few changes and a different management, performed in London at the Aldwych as part of the Royal Shakespeare's season. The backers were Victor Herbert, who had recently retired from Investors Overseas Services, Berney Cornfeld's mushrooming company, and was now devoting his life to benevolent hippiedom in his palatial Paris home on the Val de Grace and to financing the theatre, together with a couple of rich Scottish acquaintances whom I had already met through Jim Fraser, and a young Frenchman, Philippe Staib, who seemed to have a finger in many pies. They had all put up the money to produce the play with Patrick Magee, Jack Magowran, Sydney Bromley and Nancy Cole in the cast. The producer was an untried young man called Michael Blake, who had already lost the confidence of the actors when Beckett turned up after the first days of rehearsals, while the decor was by Ralph Koltai. I went once only to watch a rehearsal, but Clancy Sigal had a commission from The Observer to cover them all and to write about them. His descriptions aptly catch the twelve days of the production coming together, with Blake quickly fading out and the author exerting his authority on the cast. The rehearsals were in the very desolate back room of a pub, which gave Sam opportunity enough to remember his unhappy days in pre-war London. Those rehearsals had the effect of bonding Magee and MacGowran to him, a bonding that would last for the rest of their lives. Sam did not like Koltai's set, but neutralised it with lighting.

In Paris I walked into the Studio des Champs-Elysées where *Endgame* was playing, and there was Victor Herbert sitting in the ticket office. 'Want a ticket, John?' he said, handing me a free one. The production became a legendary one, seen by many of the Parisian anglophones and it received good reviews in the French press. This shortly afterwards enabled Roger Blin, who had been trying for some time to raise the money for a French production, to do so. The English production then came to the Royal court, and some time later was revived at the Aldwych. I am aware that my memory of events is not precisely the same as in the James Knowlson biography, but I think I may well be right. *Endgame* at the Royal Court had a curtain-raiser before it, which Knowlson does not mention, which I think was the first of the two mimes that Beckett had written for the stage, and each piece was preceded by jocular versions of the British and French national anthems by John Beckett, Sam's cousin. This must have been shortly before I went skiing that year, because I met Philippe Staib's sister at Val d'Isère, and I already knew her; she was there in the company of Pierre Henri, the concrete composer, with whom I had several interesting chats. And it must have been shortly after that in Paris that at the end of an evening with Philippe and his wife, or perhaps girlfriend, it was suggested that we might have an orgy together. Bettina was game enough, but I was feeling unwell and turned it down. Shortly after I lost touch with that whole crowd of young well-heeled French people, but not with Victor Herbert, who had trouble ahead of him.

But it was Philippe Staib that I took to see Beckett's private showing of *Film*. Barney had had the idea of making movies, the inspiration, if I can call it that, coming from an experiment he had tried with an erotic Swedish film called *I Am Curious Yellow,* which he had distributed in the U. S., presumably because no one else would take the risk. He had built a small cinema next to his Houston Street building, where he both lived and had his offices, and this was to be the first of a chain of cinemas showing erotic films. The venture did not work, because in cities less cosmopolitan than New York at that time, people did not want to be seen by their neighbours queuing to see a 'dirty' film, but before that day arrived Barney had decided that if he was going into films he might as well use his prestigious authors to get scripts, and he started (and finished) with a project to make three short films by Beckett, Ionesco and Duras. Only the Beckett was made by him. Ionesco wrote an amusing short scenario, *The Future is in Eggs,* which later became a ballet, and Duras wrote a scenario for a film that she eventually made herself. Beckett wrote *Film* (*Film* is the title) for a single actor and suggested Buster Keaton to play the part. Barney then hired Alan Schneider to make it and Sam Beckett made his one and only trip to the U. S. in July 1964. The story of that trip is told in many other books.

Sam rang me one day in London to say *Film* was to be shown every night for a week in a projection room and invited me to come, mentioning that possible distributors and more formal people were coming early in the week and friends later. I arranged to come on the Saturday and asked if I could bring Philippe Staib, who Sam did not know, but had helped to finance *Endgame.* I took a 'plane and arrived to see the showing which lasted for less than an hour and we were then all told to go to the Falstaff in Montparnasse. There were about forty people there. When later in the evening I said to the *patron* that Mr. Staib and I would like to pay our share of the bill, I was told that Monsieur Beckett had paid every night all week and he was not allowed to take a penny from anyone else.

I have seldom seen Sam drink as much as that night – the session with Burroughs is perhaps the only one to rival it – and he was also very happy and jovial. We were sitting at a number of long tables, and Barbara Bray was trying hard to make him come away. She nagged him for some time until he turned on her, told her to leave him alone and to go home alone. With tight lips she left the restaurant. Pat Magee was there and he started some argument with a man at the bar that quickly turned nasty and they started to punch each other. Sam was sober enough to intervene and break it up. The party was still alive when I left at about eleven o'clock, having started about six and I took a taxi to Orly from where I had arrived. But the last 'plane had gone, the hotel there was full, and I spent an uncomfortable night on three chairs until I could catch a flight in the morning.

There are two other occasions associated with airports that I can conveniently relate here, both to do with Beckett. I cannot remember just when they happened and it does not matter. Once when I was meeting him at Heathrow, he looked both annoyed and relieved. The immigration official had looked at his passport and said, 'How long are you staying Paddy?'

'Just because you have an Irish passport, they think they can call you Paddy,' was his querulous complaint, and his annoyance lasted some time. Perhaps it was then or perhaps on another occasion that he told me that once on the 'plane a voice on the loudspeakers had announced, 'Votre Commandant Godot vous souhaite la bienvenue à bord.'[24] If the doors had not been closed, he told me, he would probably have got off again.

The other occasion was when we flew together in the opposite direction, to Paris. We had taken a taxi to the airport and he was in a strange mood. 'Let's go First Class, then we can drink free brandy on the way,' he said. It did not suit me at all to go first class, but for Sam I assented. But First Class was full, so we went Economy and paid for the two brandies each that we drank. As the 'plane was coming down, he suddenly announced, 'Suzanne is meeting us. I think we'll have dinner at the airport. Orly has quite a good restaurant.' After a pause, he went on. 'You know that Suzanne is the only French woman I've ever met who doesn't drink wine. She won't touch a drop.'

We arrived, were greeted by Suzanne and went to the restaurant. We got through our bottle of wine very quickly and Sam immediately ordered another. Suzanne put her hand on Sam's arm. 'Please don't drink so much,' she pleaded, but he was in a funny mood. 'John likes wine,' he said and the second bottle was soon succeeded by a third. But that was not all. 'Madame Ionesco telephoned me,' she said, and went on about some problem on which her advice had been sought. 'Madame Ionesco est une emmerdeuse' ('old nag' catches the meaning, but not its strength), he replied roughly, and from there on I was witnessing what must have been a daily family quarrel, wishing I could be anywhere else. I was sure that my presence would be held against me in the future by Suzanne. Strangely, although he had anticipated it, Sam needed a certain amount of drink before facing the everyday argument. On occasion, usually when the hotels were full or I had missed the last flight to London, I stayed in his spartan flat, which connected through

---

[24] 'Captain Godot welcomes you on board.'

the kitchen with Suzanne's, but I never saw her on those occasions. They lived separate lives in close proximity.

* * * * * *

After playing Vladimir, Nicol Williamson had returned to John Osborne's *Inadmissible Evidence*, which had been revived at the Garrick Theatre. It was at this time that Patrick Garland invited me to put on a Beckett evening at the Shakespeare Memorial Theatre in Stratford-on-Avon. It was to be on a Sunday night in their smaller theatre space. I asked Patrick Magee and Nicol Williamson if they would join me to read Beckett extracts and they accepted. But Nick made a condition: he would only take part if he could be coached by Sam. The *Godot* experience had made him a total devotee. Sam agreed to see us both if we would come to Ussy, so I arranged for us both to fly to Paris on a Sunday morning and return on Monday in plenty of time for Nick's performance at the Garrick. We agreed to meet for lunch on the Saturday, the day before, at Angela's Restaurant, which was very close to the Garrick Theatre, where Williamson had a 2:30 matinee that day.

Lunch was an exuberant experience. I forget what we talked about, about Sam no doubt, and about the recent *Godot* most certainly, and about the reading we had to do a week away in Stratford equally certainly, but as curtain time approached, Nick was in no mood to go to the theatre. He went to telephone his understudy to go on for him, returned to the table, ordered another bottle of wine, and went on talking until late afternoon. I then had to go home to Wimpole Street and Nick insisted on coming with me. At six, and he had not stopped talking since our meeting at lunchtime, he telephoned his understudy to play the evening performance as well, and this was Saturday night when the audience would certainly expect to see the star actor. An American professor, who was staying with Marion Boyars just then, came round to see me and stayed on for dinner with Nick and another friend of his, Peter Murphy, who worked as his dresser and had been summoned by Nick to join the party, which ended late when the other three men left together, probably for some late-night drinking place that Nicol knew. I warned him that I would be picking him up at 6:30 the next morning in a taxi. 'Don't worry, I'll be ready,' he said.

He wasn't ready and I had great difficulty in rousing him. We just made the flight to Paris, and were the last to board. By then he had taken wake-up pills, sodium something or other, and the vitality was back. He gave the other passengers an impromptu performance, putting on an American accent, prancing in high camp fashion up and down the aisle to the enormous annoyance of the stewardesses trying to serve breakfast. I was deeply embarrassed, especially as he tried to bring me into his act. On arrival we hired a car and started to drive eastward towards Ussy on the Marne, where Sam had his country cottage, stopping on the way to buy wine, fruit and cold food. Sam welcomed us at about eleven o'clock and he and Nicol got straight down to work in the garden. I had made my choice of texts to be read by the two actors, reserving a few poems for my own reading. The actors had mainly extracts from the novels. It was a hot summer day with occasional clouds and I lay down on the grass and soon fell asleep to the drone of the two voices sitting at a garden table.

Lunch was pleasant. We had brought too much of course and Sam had food of his own prepared. He introduced Nick to French cheeses he had never seen, especially Reblochon. Then they went on working until late afternoon. Sam told us we were going to have dinner at the Hayden's house at La Fierté-sur-Marne a few miles away. They had beds for us for the night. We went in two cars, Nicol in Sam's leading the way. It was a little Deux Chevaux in which I had once had a hazardous trip with Sam, not a good driver, from Paris to London, which I prefer not to remember, but a special providence always seemed to protect him in it. I could see Nick gesticulating in front of me. Apparently he wanted to stop at every bistro we passed for a drink, but Sam resisted.

Henri and Josette Hayden had hidden in the same village, Roussillon in the Vaucluse, with Sam during the war. Henri was one of the early surrealist painters, and we were given a tour of his studio, which had work from the twenties up to the present, when he had developed a flat plastic style of landscape painting and had portrayed much of the local scenery, fields and hills, in a pleasant and individual manner. He was an old man now, but the wartime comradeship had made them close friends and they were very relaxed together. It was also obvious to me that Josette, much younger than her husband, had a deep crush on Sam. Henri Hayden was of course the original for the character of Estragon in *Godot*. Originally Dutch, he had spent most of his life in France, and being Jewish, had taken refuge in Vichy France, which not being under direct German control like the north, gave a Jew a better chance to survive. Sam Beckett was there because he had had to flee the Gestapo when the Resistance network he had joined at the beginning of the war was betrayed.

There was a large friendly old English sheep-dog called Fal, that jumped all over Sam and he fondled her happily. She had been bought at the Falstaff, a favourite restaurant and late drinking-place of us all, hence the name. She bounded around the garden while we had drinks, and Nick strode around it, declaiming Shakespeare until Sam made him sit down, whereupon he continued to keep up a non-stop entertainment, even when we were at dinner, sitting at the piano to give us his imitations of several popular crooners, and never letting any general conversation get started. Also there was a language difficulty. Nick spoke no French, the Haydens no English. Henri was soon very tired of Williamson's exhibitionism and having eaten, went to bed. Sam was tired of it too.

'Can you not be serious a minute, Nick', he protested, but nothing could stop Nicol Williamson when he was on a high. Sam left immediately after dinner, driving off slowly in his old Renault, and Nicol, with an audience reduced to two, also went to bed. I talked to Josette for another hour and did the same. The next morning after breakfast we drove off. Nicol wanted to leave the house, but not the district. 'Just find a little hotel somewhere,' he said. 'I just want to be near that man. I don't even want him to know I'm here.'

'Don't be stupid. You haven't a penny of French money, and you've a performance tonight.'

'I don't care. Just leave me.'

But I drove him into Paris where I had a parcel to deliver before returning to the airport. Then I had a real problem. I was no more than two minutes delivering the parcel, but when I returned, Nicol had disappeared. For more than an hour I drove around, peering into every bar, and finally spotted him. I dragged him out with difficulty and we again just made the 'plane. At five o'clock I dropped him at his flat on Cadogan Street and went to my office where I received a 'phone call from Nicol's agent. 'Where is Nicol?'

'He should be at the theatre by now. I dropped him off at home some time ago.'

'Well, he's not. Nor is he at home. He missed two performances on Saturday. The theatre is furious.'

And he missed every performance right through the week. No one knew where he was. On Saturday morning I had asked the two actors to come to my flat. When Magee arrived at ten I explained what had happened, said we would have to do without Nicol Williamson who had disappeared, and that I had replanned the next evening to give much more for Pat to do, while I would read some of the prose extracts myself. Then the doorbell rang, and in walked Williamson. 'Where have you been all week?' I asked.

'None of your business. We're here to rehearse. Let's get on with it.' After he had read the first passage, Pat turned to me. 'That's a perfect Dublin accent,' he said to me in wonderment. Nick had perfectly mimicked Sam's voice. I wanted us all three to drive to Stratford-on-Avon together, but Nick would have none of it. 'I'm going with friends and I'll be on time,' he promised. Pat and I drove north together, quite a long way on the roads existing then and discussing what we would do if Nicol didn't appear. Pat had recently seen Sam. 'He told me he had seen Effie again,' said Magee. 'He was amazed that she had grown old like himself.' Effie is the girl in the punt in *Krapp's Last Tape*, a play written for Pat in which he excelled. I had not known that Effie existed in real life. It explained for me a little Sam's fondness for Fontane's novel *Effie Briest*.

In the theatre we were sitting at our table, facing the empty seats that in a few minutes would be filled. It was ten to eight and we were making last minute changes to the script as Nicol Williamson had not turned up. Just as the audience started to enter the smaller auditorium of the theatre, Nick came in from the wings and took his seat beside me. The reading went well, lasting an hour and a quarter and we acknowledged the applause. Then we had a surprise. Williamson strode to the front of the stage and when the applause died gave a rendering of Vladimir's great monologue, ending with a trumpet call of agony that would have awakened all the dead voices that his Vladimir discovers earlier in the play, voices that are hidden in the air. He was given rapturous applause. Patrick Magee turned to me. 'Never, but never,' he whispered, 'will I ever appear on a stage together with that man.'

* * * * * *

It was in 1964 that we published what is possibly Beckett's most difficult novel for a reader to comfortably assimilate, *How It Is*. He had translated it from the French in record time, and I decided to have a public reading to promote it. For this I recruited Patrick Magee and Jack Magowran, took the Criterion Theatre on a Sunday afternoon, the same theatre to which *Waiting for Godot* had transferred after its initial run at the Arts Theatre in 1955, and I asked Martin Esslin to chair the session. Beckett came to London to work with the actors and he stayed with me, but he would not go to the theatre. I also had a panel to discuss Samuel Beckett's work. The reading was of passages from several different works and ended with about ten minutes from *How It Is* and I taped that reading, which was by Patrick Magee. I made a ten minute L. P. recording from the tape, which I sent out with the review copies. It certainly helped the reviews. I cannot remember much about the panel discussion, but Bill Watson from Scotland, and I think Harold Hobson, took part. It went down well with an audience that filled about two-thirds of the theatre.

I was becoming ever more involved with the theatre at that time. As Ledlanet developed, so did my rôle at the Traverse. When Terry Lane had become too big for his boots, and after a row with the committee walked out, Jim Haynes was elected to be Artistic Director as well as Chairman. But he couldn't direct plays. 'Where do we find a director (producer)?' asked Jim or someone else at the meeting. 'You go into the street and whistle,' I said. In practice I rang Michael Geliot, who came up from London to take over Pinter's *The Caretaker* half-way through rehearsals. Then I brought in Charles Marovitz who directed the next play, and he soon became an Edinburgh fixture. I introduced plays by Arrabal, Ionesco, Pinget, Obaldia and Beckett to the theatre and directed a successful Beckett evening myself with extracts from different Beckett works, which included poetry and prose and the *Duthuit Dialogues* with Leonard Fenton, a fine actor, soon to become a good friend, and Michael Geliot, happy for once to be an actor.

At Ledlanet we went from one ambitious project to another with operas in the main autumn season and smaller-scale works in spring and summer. *Un Ré Pastore* in 1968 was followed the next summer by an extended musical and dramatic programme. Then in the autumn we mounted Handel's *Alcina*, which had long been my favourite of all his operas. Large scale for Ledlanet, it needs several brilliant voices and we found them. Josepthe Clément sang the title role and the excellent cast included Synna Withington, Patricia Hay, Adrian de Peyer and John Graham. But the big surprise was Lorna Brindley, a rich resonant mezzo-soprano. She also happened to be the girlfriend of Jim Colclough who was grooming her for stardom. He had come to us first as an assistant stage-manager, but was now our theatrical equivalent of Attewell, the man who could do everything. He had once been a precision worker in a Birmingham tooling factory, had lost one eye in an industrial accident, had then used his compensation money to train as a chef, and had become one in Birmingham's Midland Hotel. Next he used his salary to train as a very high tenor. He had sung Pistol in *Falstaff* at Covent Garden, had understudied at Glyndebourne, but now did odd jobs around the opera circuit waiting for an opening to come. He had in his second season with us become stage manager, but almost ran the kitchen, and was giving much of his attention to turning Lorna Brindley, not herself very motivated as a person, into a star. We were all convinced that she would shortly be one. Our conductor that year was again Peter Gellhorn and the producer George Mully. Leonard Friedman, who had been leader of several London orchestras and had recently led the Scottish National had put together our best orchestra yet, and I had on the spur of the moment named it the Scottish Baroque Ensemble, a name that stuck. Our chorus, consisting mainly of members of the Edinburgh Festival Chorus was of the same standard. Its members had worked with many of the greatest conductors of the day and its normal chorus-master was Arthur Oldham. The chorus enormously enjoyed singing at Ledlanet and some of its members were able to understudy our principals. I was proud of our rising standard and of the team we had developed.

Brian Mahoney, senior producer of Scottish Television in Glasgow, was a strong supporter of Ledlanet and took every opportunity to get us publicity. He was overwhelmed by *Alcina* and decided to take a solid chunk of it for his arts programme. We did a few things in the studio, but that could not capture the atmosphere created by a Ledlanet audience, so Scottish Television paid for one additional performance three weeks after the season had ended. The scaffolding that had been taken down had to be put up again, the cast reassembled and rehearsed, and the audience was an invited one, mainly local people and schools. All this in order to get a few shots of the audience across the stage and perhaps three minutes of music, because the big show-stopping numbers, such as the trio of female voices near the end of the opera were already in the can. Brian would have much more to do with us in the future.

* * * * * *

Our defeat in the *Last Exit* trial was always much in my thoughts. Together with Tony Smythe of the NCCL we decided on a large fund-raising scheme, having come to the conclusion that such small events as we had organised in the past in smaller theatres and public halls was too much work for too little result. Why not have a really big event? We jointly booked the Royal Festival Hall for the late autumn of 1968. And in the meantime two other things happened. The first was that Anthony Gray and I went along – this must have been early that year – to see Lord Goodman, who was keen on engineering a change in the law. As Jenny Lee had made him Chairman of the Arts Council, he had its facilities at his command, and he organised a big meeting of interested parties, a sort of Grand Committee of ninety individuals of whom twenty-one represented organisations. He then divided the committee into two, one to prepare a case for reform of the law on obscenity, and the other to put together a proposal to totally abolish all censorship laws. Frank Kermode became Chairman of the whole committee, and I think of the first sub-committee as well. I was put onto the second one. The committees began to meet regularly, the smaller ones to discuss their arguments, the large one (the separate sub-committees together) to hear witnesses with a point of view. One such witness we called was the same David Shepherd who had given evidence against Calder and Boyars at the Old Bailey. He was asked why and said that at university he had been a practising homosexual, but on taking up religion he had decided that this was wrong. He had tried to overcome his natural impulses to force himself to become a heterosexual, and to this end had married. On reading *Last Exit to Brooklyn*, which has homosexual episodes, he had realised that all the old impulses were still there and the novel had reawakened them. As I listened to his evidence, I thought back to the Old Bailey. If only Neill had asked the proper questions in the High court that he was being asked now, not only might the jury have reached a different decision, but the national debate on homosexuality, which in spite of a change in the law was still going on, might become more enlightened. It only needed a cricketing hero to come out frankly to create a greater enlightenment. But in the court he had only been asked his reasons for disliking the book, not the underlying emotional ones.

The second thing that happened earlier that year was that I had gone to see John Mortimer. I knew him from the Edinburgh Drama Conference and had become friendly with him in various ways. I asked him if he would lead an appeal. He was a barrister and a QC. His court-room experience up to that point had concentrated largely on divorce cases, but he was also a distinguished playwright and novelist who could understand what literary merit was all about. He agreed with some reluctance to take the case and do his best, but gave me no assurance at all that he expected to succeed. This meeting took place over tea at his house, not in his consulting rooms, for which his clerk would have sent me a weighty invoice.

Many of our plays were being performed by the big national companies during the sixties, and one of the most notable was Peter Weiss' unusual play about the post-Napoleonic years, linked to the fate of the Marquis de Sade, who was then writing plays in an asylum. The play had had reasonable success in Germany, and Peter Brook decided to perform it as part of his season at the Aldwych in London. It had a long title, *The Persecution and Assassination of Marat as Performed by the Inmates of the Asylum of Charenton Under the Direction of the Marquis de Sade*, which became shortened to *The Marat/Sade*. Peter Weiss turned up two days before the opening and he came to have lunch with me after a rehearsal, deeply troubled. He was not happy with all the changes that had been made in Geoffrey Skelton's translation, which we were due to publish a few days after the opening. Peter Brook had played fast and loose with the text, changed words, sentences and meanings, intruded songs with different words and sentiments from the original songs, and Weiss did not know what to do. He gave me a list of the worst things he had noticed. At the opening the next night I went backstage with Peter Weiss after the curtain and we found Peter Brook on stage. I tried to raise the author's points, but Brook rounded on us both. 'I've been perfectly faithful to the text,' he said, and he would brook no argument. I wrote him a letter detailing errors and lines that had lost their sense – it was too late to do anything else – and on repeated visits to the theatre tried to persuade Pat Magee, who was playing Sade, to get right a line about the weak tearing at the throats of the mighty (it was the mighty tearing at the throats of the weak), but Pat could not change it without Brook telling him to. Peter Brook ignored all my letters and even kept the offending line, and all the others, in the film he made after the production closed.

I was to have more to do with Brook, who was very much the producer in fashion just then. Some of my authors like René de Obaldia, whose plays were being successful in the Paris boulevard theatre, often with stars in the main parts, were very keen to have Brook produce them, but others, Beckett in particular, sensed that he would put his own interpretation on their work and ignore their stage directions, putting in his own. *The Marat/Sade* was a good example of this. It was reviewed as an astonishing production of a very mediocre play, saved by the genius of Peter Brook. As he began to take Shakespeare to pieces, and everyone began to talk about Brook's *Midsummer Night's Dream* or other classics where the author's name was barely mentioned, I began to wonder.

The Marat/Sade was in 1965. Three years later I was approached one day by Michael Kustow, an assistant to Brook, who was then about to stage an improvised play about the Vietnam War, which he had entitled *US*. Basically he had assembled his company on stage, actors, poets and musicians to jointly put together an evening that would have all the special elements that he had used in *The Marat/Sade* (and I am not denying that he made it a riveting spectacle). Kustow wanted me to publish not just the text, but also a rehearsal diary and the story of how the production was assembled and developed from that first gathering on stage up to the first performance. We had an attractive female production manager in the office at the time, who, obviously attracted to Mike Kustow, volunteered to give spare time to the book, and it appeared at the same time as the play opened. Its best moments were the simple ones, for instance when Glenda Jackson, playing a Vietnamese woman who has just lost her baby in a bombing, delivers a very moving poem by Ted Hughes about her grief. Attacked by the right-wing press for its very critical attitude to American involvement in that troubled country, it brought more attacks on the Royal Shakespeare Company, one of the bastions of sixties' radicalism, but for me it was one of Peter Brook's greatest successes. And here no author was having his work distorted. The casualness of death and killing was well caught at the end when a box of butterflies are released on the stage and fluttered all over the theatre. The last one was, in reality or in theatrical parody, set alight by a cigarette lighter. The fate of those that were freed into the auditorium cannot have been much better.

I had a project to take over a building in Soho and turn it into a theatre, restaurant and bookshop. The building was on Bateman Street. The theatre would have seated about a hundred, just right for the kind of play I had in mind, and Beckett wrote a short play for its opening[25]. The ground floor was to be a restaurant in the middle of an area that was otherwise a bookshop, the shelves lining the walls and continuing along an overhead balcony surrounding the restaurant on three sides. We had submitted architects' plans and made an offer for the building, but then things began to go wrong. I had known that there was a Soho mafia, but I had not realised how powerful it was. It did not want an important building in the centre of Soho being used for an honest and cultural purpose that would probably not be profitable, or at least sufficiently so to be able to pay protection money, and it went to work to queer the whole project. Suddenly the estate agent became uncooperative and everyone involved was got at in one way or another. Peter Brook had looked at the theatre space, given it modified approval, but warned that I would have great difficulty in getting any support from the press that loved to attack projects of this kind. It was however the Soho mafia that made the Soho Centre, on which I lavished much time and thought, unworkable, and it never opened.

Somewhere between *The Marat/Sade* and *US* I was asked by Flourish, the Royal Shakespeare Company's house magazine, for an article on a

---

[25] *Come and Go*.

theatrical subject. I had one I had written for my own theatrical magazine, Gambit, but had missed the deadline, so now I sent it to them. It was an article on Peter Brook, who had so totally changed many plays, and currently was doing bizarre productions of Shakespeare, often to critical and public applause, where it was the production and not the play that received the attention. I cited *The Marat/Sade* as an example, saying that the public were no longer sure if the playwright was good or not, but only if the production was exciting. I went on to say that the day was coming when one would question the value of Shakespeare and other classics and say how lucky we were to have a Peter Brook to interpret them for us.

At about this time Bettina and I became friendly with an attractive and very vibrant young female stage manager who was living with Peter Brook. She told us that when Peter Brook was sent proofs of my article, so that Flourish could print a reply, he smashed up all the furniture in the flat and then sat down in a hot rage to write what was really a very weak answer, the gist of which was that the theatre was in such a bad way that no one should criticise anyone else. My relations with Brook which had been cordial became frosty after that.

That was in 1968. Sometime that summer, and I remember it being a very hot day, we gave a party in our offices in Brewer Street, probably to launch a new book. A literary agent called Tanja Howarth came. I was very attracted to her and invited her to lunch a day or two later. The lunch went on rather too long and made me late for the big inaugural meeting of the Art Council's Obscenity Committee, which I have already described, and which was so named that afternoon. I arrived just as Frank Kermode was defining its role as he saw it, and I remember one telling phrase, which I paraphrase as follows: 'In the arts it is sometimes difficult to define where one stands, but in all matters relating to (high) culture, one always knows if one is near the centre or near the periphery.' I began seeing Tanja, who also had several other suitors at the time, and soon we were having an affair which would have its serious consequences.

The Royal Festival Hall booking was for the month of December that year and we began to make preparations for it. Alan Aldridge, one of the top designers of the day, agreed to do the poster for a fraction of his usual fee, and he designed a telling image that showed Adam and Eve in the coils of a serpent that had the image, winged collar and severe dress of a magistrate. We booked a number of prime sites for it in the London Underground system, delegated Anthony Blond, another publisher who was on the DLAS committee, to prepare a souvenir programme that we hoped would be stuffed with advertising – he had the contacts to get it – started to look for a producer for the evening and a variety of different artists in music and theatre willing to give their time to help Civil Liberties and our Anti-Censorship campaign.

Our appeal was due to be heard in June, just before the Law Courts closed for the summer recess. We had been nervous about John Mortimer, who reluctantly agreed to listen to the tape of the most important parts of the trial on the Sunday afternoon before the case came to the Appeal Court, and we felt at the time he was more interested in the attractive secretary he had brought with him. But in court itself he was brilliant. We were before three appeal judges, Lord Salmon, Mr. Justice Geoffrey Lane and Mr. Justice Fisher, whilst against us we had Mr. Mathew again. But he could not get away with the same populist tactics that he had used with the jury when he was arguing to three experienced appeal judges. Mortimer had several appeal points, the principal one being that Judge Rodgers had not explained to the jury sufficiently well the meaning of literary value in the Obscene Publications Act. The other points were of less importance, but we were acquitted on three of the seven. Behind me in the court were sitting Peter du Sautoy and Charles Monteith of Faber and Faber, and they leaned forward to congratulate me. It was over.

It was the end of June. Bettina and our daughter, Anastasia, were away in Dugi Otok in Yugoslavia and I took my car and drove to meet them there, leaving London together with my elder daughter Jamie, Jill Mortimer, who worked for the Publishers Association and had recently been involved in the great battle against the Office of Fair Trading to protect the Nett Book Agreement, and a journalist friend of Bettina's, called Charles Robinson. It was the longest continuous drive of my life. We stopped outside Munich in a torrential downpour under a bridge for half an hour, had a fairly long dinner somewhere in the Austrian Alps, after which I was lost for about two hours. I remember being on the right road at last with a carload of complaining overtired people, too squashed to be able to stretch out, anxious because my petrol warning light had been on for some time, when out of the mist ahead I saw a lighted ELF sign and was able to fill up. At dawn I stopped the car for a twenty minute nap, and again an hour later, and finally drove into Zadar in time to park the car at a place I had been told about and then to catch the boat to the island of Dugi Otok. There was already a community there, friends from London and they included Stuart Hood, previously Controller of BBC Television and a friend for whom I had recently tried to obtain a job as John Trevelyn's successor as Secretary of the British Board of Film Censors. I was not successful, and it is as well for both he and the Board that I was not. Stuart's wife, Renée Goddard, a TV casting director, was also there. I only stayed a week, possibly less, swimming, talking and reading. Bettina's family came from Bojava on the island and we occupied two of the several cottages that were their's. Then I had to return to London and I then spent a week with Jacques Chaix at Cap Ferrat. I remember I had a hair-raising journey to Zagreb in my car. The map showed me what looked like the shortest road, but I did not realise that it was totally unpaved, a road with large stones that peasant carts would have difficulty in manoeuvering, that was certainly not meant for cars. Once on it there was no turning back and I had to drive through the mountains in first gear for about eighty miles, steering from one large stone onto another, while night descended. Down below, beside the road I could see the wrecks of buses and lorries that had gone over, some of them falling all the way to a river at the bottom of the valley. It was nearly midnight, fortunately with a moon, when I found myself on asphalt again. I drove into Zagreb, found a hotel for a short night, left my car at the airport and flew to London. There I arranged for a reprint of *Last Exit to Brooklyn*, did the essential office things, including the correspondence, and then went down to Nice, this time taking with me a lady, whom I shall just call Patricia. I had known Pat for some time. She was Irish and an independent jeweller, making pieces for the big shops like Cartier's and she was adept at working gold, for which she had an almost religious respect as a precious metal, and silver. It was her quite extraordinary bust which had attracted me to her in the first place and I pursued her successfully, but only for a short time. She was jolly and good company, and although she had little French I was sure she would fit in at the Villa Soleia, where Jacques invited about twenty friends every August, some staying the whole time, some for a week or two.

The main adventure during my week at Cap Ferrat was going to Cannes to pick up another boat. This was a square motor-boat, able to seat about a dozen around its padded edges, a new model, but it cannot have been very successful, because I have never seen another one. About eight of us embarked on it, including its new owner, to take it back to Cap Ferrat. Out at sea, halfway back, the motor failed and we drifted. Pat was in her element. We had a bag of spirits and things to mix with them on board, and she raised ours by becoming an efficient barmaid. At about eight o'clock we drifted near enough to the coast to be heard and another boat came out to tow us in. We were then invited to dinner by our rescuers and the evening ended well. I had envisaged sinking in a storm or being blown to Algeria.

From Cap Ferrat I returned with Pat to London. In the pocket of the seat in front of me I found a boarding card in the name of Tanja Howarth; she had obviously flown to Nice on the previous flight from London that day. I put the card in my pocket as a joke. A few days later I returned to Dugi Otok, but this time took the good coast road, picked up my party and prepared to drive back to London. But more adventures were in store.

Having started to drive north from Zadar on the coast road in a car loaded with two children, Jill, Charles and Bettina, as well as everyone's luggage, we came across an enormous traffic jam. A great overnight storm had blown away a segment of the road, which is cut out of the vertical rock that descends to the Adriatic, and there was no way forward. Nor could we go back. Part of the same road, further south had also been blown away. We camped overnight and were told a ferry could eventually pick us up, but we had to wait, because of the number of cars, until the next afternoon. There were my two daughters, aged five and fourteen, and four adults, with only the car for shelter, camped on an embankment beside the sea with only a packet of biscuits. But we found some fresh water, acquired two potatoes from another car and got through the night, most of us sitting beside a fire we managed to make, while Anastasia, the youngest slept in the car. When we did get away, we took the less congested of the two roads, the one going south.

There were many rumours, some coming from the car radio. One was that the Russians, with a Czechoslovak revolt on their hands (Dubcek's Prague Spring was just behind us) and the continuing independence of Tito's Yugoslavia, had finally decided to take action. The collapse of Yugoslavia's only international and well-built roadway was not caused by a storm, some said, but by Russian dynamite. Perhaps a war was breaking out. Our journalist friend and Jill were all for the excitement. We drove through Sarajevo, the historic town that I would have liked to spend an hour in, but Bettina just wanted to drive on: any town that was not Croat could hold no interest in her view. All these other towns, Bosnian or Serb only had barbarians in them and their history did not interest her. Like all Croats, she despised her neighbours. I am not sure by what route we entered Czechoslovakia, but we did, probably via Austria, and stopped in some small town in a hotel that was full, so I spent a night on a billiard table. Eventually we arrived in Prague where we decided to stay a few days, and we were fortunate to find student accommodation near the university. The town was packed and buzzing, full of foreigners, including many journalists. We visited the castle, where new diggings were taking place, saw the vaults and an amazing art collection: it was like going to a French impressionist exhibition, except that all the names were Czech. We went to the Hotel Alcon where it was possible to make an international telephone call, among other things to arrange for Jamie to fly to meet her mother two days later. We had tea in the Alcon. I looked out over the sea of identical American young men, all with brush-cuts. 'My God,' I exclaimed, 'the place is full of CIA.' I was not wrong. In the bar American men (there were no women) were whispering in huddles, and while waiting for my telephone call to be put through, I overheard an American voice in the next cabin giving instructions for bribes to be sent to Czech officials: a bottle of whisky here, a hundred dollars there, American cigarettes somewhere else. The Russian army had left, the Dubcek government was trying to hold the country together within the Russian bloc, but with local authority ruling independently, and the CIA was being as provocative as possible. If I, without trying, was seeing and hearing what I did, what were the Russian spies and observers not seeing and hearing? It was just at that time that the American involvement in Vietnam was getting deeper, so I have often thought, since those August days in Prague, that the provocation might have been deliberate to divert the odium of the world away from America and back to the Russians.

We looked around Prague, saw the sights, ate badly but enjoyed the local beer, and I decided to leave a day earlier than planned because I had noticed that we might with luck catch *Die Götterdämmerung* in Bayreuth. On the last day I took Jamie to the airport late in the morning to catch her flight to Nice to meet her mother, and went back into the town to a meeting of the Czech Union of Writers, where we discussed the position of current Czech literature. There were no more samizdat or unpublished manuscripts of quality waiting in drawers for foreign publishers to come to pick them up, I was told. I was far too late for that. Other publishers, especially German, Italian and American, had preceded me and taken away everything of interest that was possibly publishable abroad. But the writers I spoke to were in no way complacent about the political situation. The Russian army might return at any time.

I left the meeting late in the afternoon, picked up the others, and we left Prague. The warden at the Students' hostel said he could not refund the last night's charges we had paid for and could not understand why we were leaving early. The next morning he must have thought that we had secret information. We drove past the airport where nothing seemed to be happening at about seven o'clock, stopped to have dinner at Karlovy Vary, got lost coming out of town trying to find the so-called Autobahn and crossed the frontier into Germany after midnight. We had a delay at the customs shed because we were not allowed to take out our remaining kroner: we could spend it on a Czech doll or a bottle of Russian champagne. We opted for the champagne, but were then a few pennies short, and had to change more money. This annoyed everyone in the car, but it proved that the next day's bulletins were untrue in saying that the borders had been taken and sealed before eleven o'clock.

We stopped at the first German village, found a hotel, and went to sleep. At seven I was awakened by Jill Mortimer banging on the door. 'Wake up. The Russians have invaded Prague,' she shouted.

'Go back to sleep and have another dream,' I called out, but it was true. Charles had heard it on his radio. The Russians had landed at the airport just after we had passed it. Jill wanted to be Joan of Arc and rush back across the border to save the Czechs, and she never forgave me for leaving early and missing the excitement. We also, three of us, got into *Götterdämmerung* without difficulty that night because of the international panic. 'How can you be so heartless as go to an opera on a day like this?' said Jill.

Back in London, we republished *Last Exit to Brooklyn*. It sold well, but not that well. As the jury had discovered, it was not an easy book for a British reader. Bettina found Tanja Howarth's boarding card and of course believed that she had been with me at Cap Ferrat. My affair continued with her in spite of that. It was also the year of student revolutions and unrest, starting with the spring events in Paris at the University of Nanterre, which had made Danny Le Rouge a student hero everywhere. Although I never had anything to do with the so-called student movement, and had trouble in seeing what British students, conducting sit-downs and occupations in imitation, were complaining about, I received several invitations to speak at universities, purely because of my reputation as a radical publisher. At the Frankfurt Book Fair the students were everywhere. My friend Giangiacomo Feltrinelli had been assassinated by the Italian neo-fascists, but that did not stop his German wife Inge (not his legal wife, because divorce was not accepted in Italy) running around the fair telling me and others to close our stands, saying that the police were beating up students in another hall. It may only have been a rumour, but I refused, saying that I was there to do my publishing business, and that if it were true that students were being beaten up I was prepared to go to protest at the police station at seven o'clock, provided that at least five other publishers came with me. There were no takers: at that time of day publishers preferred to be at parties, or they were having baths or making love or taking naps before another strenuous night of dining and drinking with other publishers. Ledig-Rowohl always gave a big party for his authors, and for publishers and agents with whom he did business, and the students demanded to be admitted as he was a radical publisher. They ruined his party that year, drinking up his beer and wine, eating his food, and making it impossible to move around to talk. The following year he gave two parties, one with the address announced, which was flooded by students, and another, where the address was kept secret until the last moment, for those he wanted to invite.

Among the parties that I gave at my Wimpole Street flat, two stick out in my mind. One of them was given shortly after our victory in the Appeal Court for *Last Exit to Brooklyn* and must have taken place sometime during the autumn of 1968. We invited all our witnesses and well-wishers, many members of the DLAS, and authors and friends. We also invited the whole team who had lost our case at the Old Bailey. 'What can one do with a man like you?' said Lord Lloyd of Hampstead. We tell him he hasn't a ghostly of appealing a case, he ignores us and wins. Congratulations anyway.' Michael Freyn was one of the guests and he lit up a reefer. At this point there was much debate about soft drugs and some hundreds, although not me, had signed a big whole-page advertisement in The Times, calling for a change in the laws. I asked Michael to please refrain. There could well be spies from the DPP's office present, resentful of their defeat and looking for another opportunity to get me. 'I didn't know you were like that,' said Michael. 'I don't think I want to know you.' He ground out his pot-filled cigarette on the carpet and left. I have not spoken to him since.

But the other party, which somehow I confuse a little with the above, was on a summer night, which started badly when David Mercer, ever more belligerent just then because he was drinking heavily and alcohol made him violent, picked a quarrel with Mark Patterson, a literary agent who had married David's first wife, and insulted them both so badly that they left. Then he picked a quarrel with George Lamming, a very gentle Caribbean novelist, and said, 'If you think I'm not going to hit you because you're black, you're wrong,' and then knocked him down. He then reduced his current girlfriend Kika Markham, a rising actress and a very sweet-natured girl, to tears with abuse until she too left. It was a long party that went on all night. Bettina had gone to bed early, but she called me up to the top floor to stop a disturbance. Elaine Dundy, Ken Tynan's first wife, an American novelist, then having some success, had become rather drunk and had gone up to lie down on a couch on the landing. John Stevenson, a member of the original Merlin Group in Paris, who was also a Girodias author and had done some translations for me, had been watching her and had seen her go upstairs. He picked a quarrel with his own wife, which made her leave, then went up to make love to Elaine. She resisted him, but he insisted and proceeded to rape her. I tried to pull him off, but by that time she had stopped resisting and was thrusting back, so I left them to it and returned to the party. With dawn coming up, and two or three people left who preferred to sleep on the floor or in a chair than go home, being probably incapable of doing so anyway, and the room a shamble of empty bottles and broken glasses, I turned to David Mercer, who had now sobered up and was crying. I took him downstairs and drove him home to Hampstead in my car. There he sat in the passenger seat outside his house for half an hour, crying, reproaching himself and asking me why he was such a monster. He could not control his emotions; he lived in perpetual guilt at having abandoned every principal on which his dedicated socialist father had brought him up, and he was desperately unhappy. He had many women, but could not create a stable relationship and drove them all away sooner or later. I had recently met again his earlier wife Dilys, my companion of the Weathersfield sit-down. She was a lovely person, who figured in several of his plays, but he had written her out of the script that became his most successful one, especially when filmed, *Morgan, A Suitable Case for Treatment*. She was then a social worker in Nottingham and I had met her when speaking at a Liberal Summer School where I debated against Mary Whitehouse and my friend John Trevelyn. She would not say a word against David, but I know that he had hurt her dreadfully. He could not live with his pain, but he had a deep self-honesty, which led him to portray himself frequently in his plays as the monster he was forcing himself to become. Later he was to start an affair in France with Roland Dubillard's lady, who directed a film of his there, other than one made by Alain Resnais. Then he went to Israel on a visit. I was driving to Edinburgh just before the 1979 festival when I heard on the car radio that he was dead of a heart attack. A strange and rather pitiable man. I think that even those he treated abominably still loved him in a way.

Un Re Pastore crowned the autumn season at Ledlanet. But many things kept me busy. Much of my time, and Marion's as well, was taken up with the DLAS, of which we were joint secretaries, and it was well represented on the Arts Council's Obscenity Committee. We met under the chairmanship of Will Hamling, who became a good friend in every way, espousing every Civil Rights cause. His motto was 'sans peur et sans reproche', and he was transparently committed to doing what was right without the slightest thought of whether it was good or bad for his political career. He had won his seat for Labour from the Tories and it was his personality, humour and directness that enabled him to keep it. He was respected and liked by many who would otherwise never have voted for his party. Stuart Hood's marriage broke up that autumn. He had started an affair with Jill Mortimer and would foolishly meet her in the afternoons at the Great Cumberland Hotel, right opposite his wife's offices. Renée had seen them both coming out together. As it was on Dugi Otok that they had met, the blame fell mainly on Bettina for creating the circumstances that had enabled them to meet, and on me as well; we were dropped as her friend for ruining her marriage.

Our Festival Hall booking grew nearer, the programmes were printed, but the cost of the large glossy volume was outrageously high and Anthony Blond had not been nearly as active in chasing the advertising as the articles. The evening was called 'An Evening of Depravity and Corruption'. Bill Gaskell had first agreed to produce it, but then changed his mind, and I persuaded George Mulley to take it on at short notice. The compère had a name almost exactly the same, George Melly, the jolly and outgoing jazz singer and trumpeter. I had the rights to the first performance of Beckett's *Come and Go*, originally intended for the Soho Centre, my aborted project, and I put it in as a world première, which would certainly bring much of the audience. Jenny Paull organised a classical orchestra, others organised a rock group and individual actors and performers volunteered their talents.

Then came the first set-back. The London Underground, on whose sites we had booked over a hundred spaces for the Alan Aldridge poster, refused to accept it. The stylised naked Eve, and probably the title we had given to the evening, was apparently too strong for them. I spent the night before the event fly-posting copies of it around the West End of London. Tanja volunteered to come with me and the two of us went around in my car looking for likely spots and then attaching the poster to the wall or railings or trees. We had to wait until around midnight to start when there were not too many people about. It was probably about three-thirty a.m. or later when a man complained and began following us about. I forget whether it was our activity or the contents of the poster to which he was objecting, probably the latter. Then he disappeared. A few minutes later a police van came and arrested us: the man had alerted the police. We were taken to a police station, charged and released. But it had one happy result. The Evening Standard picked up the police report, showed a picture of the poster and gave me a generous paragraph in the Londoner's Diary column entitled *Mr*

Calder takes a Civil Liberty; which probably gave better publicity to the concert than the poster would have done. As it was we packed the Royal Festival Hall. George Melly was a good compère and everything went well until the rock group started and went on far too long, playing at a volume that drove many of our supporters with tender ears out of the hall. They played so long that not everyone on a long programme was able to perform. The programme that Anthony Blond had produced unfortunately incurred a big loss, but all in all we cleared about £15,000 to be shared between the two organisations, some of which went towards our lawyer's bill and some towards the general funds of the DLAS, which was also defending other prosecutions. John Neville's magazine Oz and other publications all reaped some of the benefit. Our stage-manager friend whom I mentioned earlier in connection with Peter Brook was one of our volunteer helpers for the evening. There was a little party on stage afterwards. Bettina had left early, and the stage manager looked at Tanja and myself and speculated out loud where I was going that night. I went back with Tanya, the first time I had spent the night at her Battersea Overstrand Mansions flat, where she let rooms to another man, to an African Zulu girl and to a friend Ann Beckett, who was to remain a friend of us both. Once there I was far too tired to go out again. The concert took place on the ninth of December and from then on I was constantly seeing more of Tanja.

I did not however neglect my family and at Christmas that year went with Bettina and Anastasia to Val d'Isère, my first visit there at that time of year. I started my daughter on skis and stayed at the Hotel where I normally went, The Solaise. So ended an eventful year. Jamie was still with her mother.

The list had grown and as I became ever more involved with the expansion of Ledlanet nights, I left much of the business management of Calder and Boyars to Marion. She made all of the American trips now and many American fiction authors were added to the list, none of which did particularly well. I did occasionally have to persuade her to drop some books, which would involve us in too heavy a loss, often by sitting down with her to read aloud pages from some book she had found in New York, which was really pretentiously mediocre, and could usually persuade her to drop it, although occasionally we had to do an exchange whereby I would drop some enthusiasm of my own in exchange for Marion doing the same. She found one gigantic novel called *Miss Mackintosh, My Darling* and it took the combined persuasion of Agnes Rook, then with us as both editor and translator, and myself to talk her out of it. It was eventually published in Britain by Peter Owen, and received neither good reviews nor significant sales. It was still possible then to sell a thousand or so copies of nearly every new book to public libraries, which had expanded budgets under the enlightened government generosity to the arts in the sixties for which Jenny Lee was mainly responsible, but we were publishing far too many new books that did not pay their way and which were not up to the standards we had established in the past.

We had a series called *Open Forum* for political non-fiction and Marion took more interest in this as time went by, commissioning titles from the large network of people we knew in politics, the arts and the academic world. We started a second series for more experimental non-fiction entitled *Ideas in Progress*, and Marion found her ideal author in an ex-Jesuit Yugoslav priest called Ivan Illich, whose special gift was to deflate the traditional wisdom of almost every subject, education, medicine, transport, social life and politics. He had special appeal to the generation that had grown up in the sixties, especially students who now wanted to pick their teachers, choose the subjects they wanted to study without rules or compulsion, and who thought they were wiser than they were. In many ways the mould of society was breaking too fast, and revolt became an object by itself, needing no cause. There was a growing resentment among the middle classes and those of a more conservative outlook of mind, of which I often felt that I alone in the circles in which I moved was aware, perhaps because I had grown up in and understood that milieu. I wrote an article in 1969 for some journal (I seemed to write endless articles on a wide variety of subjects in those days) pointing out that the easy times that youth was having, and the freedom of life styles enjoyed by so many, depended on the general high level of affluence then ruling, and that neither the affluence nor the freedoms it made possible could last much longer; I was right, as the future was to prove, but I was much derided for it at the time. People living in a golden age never see it as such, but quickly assume that every improvement in their life is now the norm and will continue forever. My basic pessimism, which never stopped me doing what I felt I should do, whatever the consequences, came more to the fore as the sixties ended. Perhaps I smelled Thatcherism on the horizon, as Kafka early in the century had smelled Naziism.

I had just about abandoned trying to make Ledlanet work as a commercially run estate, but found one way of bringing in regular and substantial income. It was by having shooting parties, five a year. This was organised by Jacques Chaix, who having been several times to Ledlanet and knowing of my problems, suggested that he could find French parties to come, about eight or nine individuals at a time, usually with wives or girlfriends to accompany them, paying a substantial amount for a long weekend to shoot grouse in August or September and pheasant between then and January. Not only did this pay for the upkeep of the house and estate, but it also made a contribution towards the loss of running a festival. By the end of the decade I was coming close to balancing both sets of books, and by 1973 we were in total profit, because our membership of over three thousand and annual increases in Arts Council and other subsidies, finally covered the artistic loss. By then we had year-round catering staff, and could make Ledlanet available for private functions and weddings in the quieter periods. Only in the early years did we have to use outside caterers. In the end, with Attewell running the house and staff during performance seasons and Jill Johnson, an Australian, running the kitchen for all the different activities, we found we could do it cheaper and better ourselves. Jill was resourceful and found occasions when she could occasionally do outside catering to the profit of Ledlanet.

In late February I went skiing again, this time taking Tanja, but instead of Val d'Isère, where I would normally meet Jacques and other French friends, went to Saint Anton. I would have found it embarrassing to return after two months where the hotel had seen me as a family man, in different colours. Before going there, I stopped in Zürich. I had been invited by the Duttweiler Institute to take part in a conference on 'the future of the novel' and had persuaded the Director who had invited me to also issue an invitation to Alan Burns, who I knew could talk well and enjoyed this sort of occasion. I also hoped, as a number of German publishers would be present, that one of them would be interested in taking him on as an author for his own country. We had been reasonably successful in finding European publishers for Ann Quin, but not for Alan or others of the group we were trying to turn into a new school of British fiction. For two days an interested group of writers, publishers and critics exchanged their views and their political stances: a left-right divide soon became evident, and I found myself duelling much of the time with Fred Praeger from New York, who I knew was financed by the CIA, and Luc Bondy from the Tribune de Genève and various U.S. publishing executives, while Alan Sillitoe, Adrian Mitchell, Alan Burns and others argued on my side. The conference was recorded and no doubt appeared somewhere in printed form, but to all appearances it was mounted for the benefit of a roomful of young German and Swiss university students and editors of publishing companies, all very earnest and making copious notes. Jim Haynes, whom I had known so well in Edinburgh, was there. He had been forced to leave that city when the Traverse Committee lost confidence in his ability to run the theatre on a budget or for that matter to co-operate with anyone other than with Jack Moore, who I considered to have ruined my play *The Voice*. Jack had become his guru and at the Traverse General meeting of members at which Jim finally was deposed, with Nicholas Fairbairn becoming the new chairman, Jim had said that he could not work without him. His subsequent history I shall relate later. He was now living in Amsterdam and editing a seriously pornographic sex-paper called Suck and presumably that was why the relatively mischievous Conference Director, a young Englishman, had invited him. Both Adrian Mitchell and Klaus Wagenback, a publishing friend from Berlin, made determined passes at Tanja, who managed to be very provocative and decolleté in spite of the cold Zürich winter weather. We left for Saint Anton by train, on which I started to look at the first issue of Suck, which Jim had given me, until the horrified eyes of the other passengers made me desist.

Aside from a few short stories and gossip, it consisted mainly of orgy photographs in which Jim Haynes and Germaine Greer were prominently recognisable among the tangle of bodies.

That first issue of Suck succeeded to a certain extent in its erotic intention to excite the reader's lust, but the subsequent issues, and there were not many, were increasingly the same, but duller, depending on rather bad photos of the editors and their friends disporting themselves self-consciously in various sexual positions. Germaine Greer soon resigned from Suck and claimed that she had no idea she was being photographed. Jim Haynes also started a Wet Dream Festival in Amsterdam, which was more of the same and consisted mainly of showing pornographic films on day-trips on a hired boat. His own account of these activities can be found in his rather unconventional volume of autobiography *Thanks for Coming*[26].

It was a short holiday in St. Anton, a very dull resort compared to my usual Val d'Isère. Tanja received many business calls at the hotel, so both our names were known to the desk and appeared on the final hotel bill. It was the first time that I had gone skiing with someone who was quite a good skier, and both sides of our relationship, bed and sport, went well. But she herself was nervous of that relationship becoming known to Rainer Heumann, an important literary agent in Zürich, who had also been an occasional lover and whose business provided a large part of her income. Heumann had a conventional marriage, but Tanja was something of an obsession with him: certainly he was in love with her. He was the principal agent of many best-selling authors, such as John Le Carré, and she was the British sub-agent for many of these; she also scouted for German and Scandinavian publishers, and many of these contacts had also come through Rainer Heumann. Whenever the telephone rang in our bedroom she would start suddenly: it had to be for her because I had told no one where I was.

On the way back to London I looked through all my pockets to find the hotel bill so that I could hide or destroy it, but it was not in my pocket. I arrived back at Wimpole Street, left my suitcase and went straight to the office. Two hours later the lawyer who had handled my divorce a decade earlier rang me. I was not to return home. The locks had been changed and I was locked out. Bettina had opened my suitcase and found my hotel bill on top of my skiing clothes with Tanja Howarth's name on it.

It had been an open marriage, not based on passion or deep love, and neither of us had been faithful, or even intended to. In the climate of the sixties and the ethics of our particular peer group, fidelity was not important. But in its way the marriage had worked well enough. Now it was over. I had been through much stress and many problems in ending my first marriage. All that was nothing compared with what was to come.

---

[26] Faber and Faber. London 1984.

Chapter 6

Politics

It was now March 1969. I spent a week staying in the Caledonian Club and then took a small room with bath in North Kensington, a once-middle class area that had a little shabby elegance left, but had gone to seed and offered short-term accommodation to migrants and the displaced like myself, at low weekly rents. I still had a discrete relationship with the German-born novelist I have called Vera, mentioned earlier, but I always had to be out before six in the morning, which was a bore. When I told her my situation she laughed and asked if I intended to commute daily from Ledlanet. Tanja had gone abroad again and when she returned there was always some problem at her place, where two or three other people were boarding, and where she received frequent nocturnal calls from John Wolff, a previous lover who was usually drunk by the evening but did not want to give her up. John was also a literary agent, and he had an attractive wife, Charlotte, who I could not help fancying myself. There was one night when the four of us had dinner, and we somehow ended up in my North Kensington room that had one double bed, where we all slept chastely, although John tried to get Tanja alone into the bathroom during the night and I woke up to find myself snuggled pleasantly against Charlotte. We were all partly undressed, but not totally. A funny night, made worse by the necessity every two hours to find a shilling for the gas meter. The situation seemed designed for us to sleep two and two with new partners, but the logistics of the situation made this impossible.

John became ever more alcoholic and then moved to Europe, while Charlotte, who I think was going through a period of acute depression, killed herself shortly afterwards. At about the same time I abandoned my uncomfortable and inconvenient room and moved in with Tanja at Overstrand Mansions, which faced the south side of Battersea Park. Her boarders gradually moved out, Anne Beckett being the last.

Tanja had another suitor, who she went out with occasionally and she did spend a night or two at his place. He was André Deutsch, who also had a long term relationship with a lady called Gwen who nobody I knew had ever met. I think that André was unaware of my presence on the scene. Rainer Heumann found out about me with time, but was not overtly hostile. When the three of us went out to dinner, I was a little uneasy about the many compliments he always threw at me, not about anything serious, but about my clever driving to pass another car or my taste in wine. He brought Tanja an air gun, a kind of pistol with which you could kill pigeons or small animals. At one point I threw it out of the window and after she had rescued it, removed it to my office where it sat in a drawer until I needed a gun for the dust jacket of a book by John Stonehouse, a political novel called *The*

Ultimate, which I published at the time of his disgrace. That story comes a little later.

Tanja's home was also her office. She would sit all day at her desk, telephoning publishers, and part of the ritual of her long telephone calls, which mingled trade gossip with flirtation and business, was having a cigarette in her hand. When I finally persuaded her to give up smoking, the hardest part of doing so was her habit of lighting up and exhaling smoke while talking and joking, which gave her a confidence which she associated with the ritual. I was quite often asked by her to look over manuscripts British publishers had sent her for others in Europe for whom she scouted and helped in various ways, but of course I was usually at my own office during the day. On weekends I was repeating the old routine of taking my daughter, Anastasia this time, to the zoo or elsewhere and she came to Ledlanet with me when possible. Jamie was with her mother in Monte Carlo, where Victor Churchill was now her second husband. I only saw Churchill once or twice more, the last time when he came to Brewer Street to my offices to try to blackmail me in some way, and with the help of Michael Hayes, who had succeeded George Allum after his death as our sales manager, I threw him down the stairs. Victor Churchill was a petty crook, a spiv in the parlance of those days, who together with Christya became involved in some scheme to import refined oil, declaring it as crude. They were caught and prosecuted and he, having gone to prison whereas Christya got off scot-free, came out, was arrested again on another charge and, while awaiting trial, killed himself in an Edinburgh hotel room. After that Christya went to America, calling herself Lady Spencer-Churchill. The complications that followed all that are part of her life the world will never know and is not in this book.

Tanja would sometimes come to Ledlanet, but she was not really comfortable there. Eddie Strachan was the surviving game-keeper and when his black labrador had puppies I decided to adopt one of them. I did this about the time of Tanja's visit, largely I think because she said she would like to have a dog. We then spent a weekend with Tom Craig, who had an engineering business in Edinburgh, at an island he owned with his family near Glencoe, called Shuna. Liking the name and having agreed that weekend to adopt the puppy, we named her Shuna. When the dog was about two months old I brought her to London and Battersea became her home for a while. The Park was handy for early morning and weekend walks, and at night I took her round the back gardens. I came to know Battersea park well, and quite liked an area where I could park my car in front of the door, most days driving into Soho to my office. One day Tanja took Shuna to the hairdresser in central London and she slipped out, being found two hours later, frightened and cowed, but not run over. She was a country dog who loved going back to Scotland and drove there with me frequently. She seemed to sense when Ledlanet was getting nearer, and when I changed gear for the steep climb up the drive, she squealed with delight, her tail thumping against the car doors. Sometimes I left her with Strachan, who lived in the lodge at the bottom of the drive.

I suggested going to Aix-en-Provence in the summer, but Tanja, with little French, was nervous of a town where I would be involved with French intellectuals, who frightened her, and listening to music, in which she had little interest. She rented instead a flat overlooking the sea in a villa at Cap d'Ail and went ahead with her son Peter. I was to follow when I was free, bringing Becky (Ann Beckett) with me, by car. I went there straight from my last Harrogate Conference, about which I wrote in the last chapter. What I did not relate there was that when I arrived in Harrogate a day before the others in my Sovereign (Daimler) car, which I had just bought second-hand in London, I had driven it down the steps at the station, steps I did not see. I had assumed they were the station entrance, and I damaged the undercarriage, which was only repaired on the day I had to leave. It gave trouble ever after. The previous evening with Jim Fraser, haranguing me not to employ Jenny, had led to my drinking too much, and I had a ferocious hangover as I drove south. I had to pick up Becky in London, and then drive on to Paris, arriving late that night. Fortunately she did much of the driving. The next day was the long drive to Cap d'Ail, where I spent about a week, Tanja staying on for the rest of the month. We spent several evenings with Jacques Chaix whose villa was only a short distance away. When everyone went swimming in the nude one night, Tanja and Becky declined, but not out of prudery: the returning party found the two of them sitting naked in comfortable chairs on the terrace of the villa.

The villa that Tanja had rented belonged to a white Russian lady, the widow of a Dutch gin distiller. Mrs. Bootz had two floors for herself and let out two top ones, the other that year to a one-legged British General, always challenging me to swim farther out to sea than I wanted. I was a reasonable, but not particularly strong swimmer and I quickly ran out of breath. We became friendly with Rosita Bootz, the daughter, a classical singer. She was trying to organise a local music festival in a small outdoor Roman arena, but it never took off.

In London my relations with Bettina became ever more poisonous. We had several meetings, but each time she exploded into a tantrum. Meeting her in restaurants was always embarrassing because she raised her voice, wanting everyone to hear her, and on the second such occasion I stood up and walked out. She went around London usually in the company of three other ladies, complaining about me, but not knowing that two of them had at one time had a fling with me. Others with whom she was constantly seen were Liz Kustow, recently estranged wife of Michael, one of Peter Brooks assistants, and Yvonne Ball. The latter needs some introduction.

Yvonne Ball had been Bettina's understudy in *Happy End* and I had come to know her husband Jimmy, as a private detective through that contact. Jimmy, who became a friend, quite brilliantly traced the whereabouts of a rogue printer who brought out pirate editions of best-selling books, and in my case of *Tropic of Cancer*. Jimmy had good police contacts and in Leeds they were able to tip him off that he might find it worth his while to visit a certain building on the moors, mentioning that there was a full moon that night. In the yard Jimmy found proofs and pages that had been thrown away, that enabled us to shut the printer down. Jimmy at this time was starting to study to become a lawyer, but he never took the time to become fully qualified. He had a flamboyant and romantic personality and took up activities that fitted his self-image. He only studied enough law to enable him to work from a solicitor's office, but took a course in criminology because it seemed more glamorous, which hardly advanced his career. He eventually took over the criminal law department of a large firm that represented trade unions and he defended their members who were prosecuted. He was good at this and was also a brilliant negotiator. I saw much of Jimmy over the next few years and he became my unconventional lawyer, often working as an individual and a friend, rather than as a member of a firm. He also represented me in some of my later court confrontations with Bettina. But in 1969 he and his wife were friends to us both who tried to bridge the growing gulf between Bettina and myself, now living apart. I saw my daughter Anastasia frequently, and she often came to Ledlanet, as did Tanja on occasion, but the latter, as I have mentioned, was never comfortable there, especially when performances were taking place. She could not understand why I would give up my own room to stars like Ian Wallace or to a conductor.

In Frankfurt, where she had to go for several days before the Book Fair every year to confer with her publishers, Tanja had a room permanently booked in a small hotel, but that year she spent many nights with me in mine, the Frankfurterhof. I became aware that in Frankfurt, where sex is often as much on the minds of the participants as books, that Tanja was a prime target, being always flamboyantly dressed to look as sexy as possible. She was invited to dinner by everyone and that year Tom Rosenthal, then Sales Director of Thames and Hudson, was making a big play for her. She finally had to tell him about me, but that did not put him off at all. That year a German television crew decided to make her their focus and they followed her around the fair as she called on different publishers' stands doing her business as a literary agent and scout. When we drove away together she was frustrated at not having seen the programme in which she was featured, tired by the fair and no doubt of me as well, because just then I stood in the way of her normal social life, and took her too often to performances in the theatre or at the opera that interested me, but not her.

That autumn season at Ledlanet was a brilliant one. When preparing it and putting the programme together I had asked Leonard Friedman to create a new Scottish-based orchestra for us. Working late at night with my secretary putting together the programme, I realised that it needed a name and created one on the spot, The Scottish Baroque Ensemble, because that was the season when we performed a baroque opera, Handel's *Alcina*, which I have described, and the name stuck: it eventually became the Scottish Baroque Orchestra. Not surprisingly, because Leonard loved women, there were many female members of the Ensemble, which varied in size from sixteen to about twenty-four. That was also the year when Jim Colclough became a permanent member of the team, replacing Rita Guenigault, who had been with us for a long time and had also stage-managed *Lorca* and *Happy End*. Rita had now moved to London and Jim Colclough involved himself in every side of Ledlanet's artistic life. He talked Jim Fraser into supplying raw material out of which he built sets for productions and did repairs around the house, and he also planned menus, sang some parts, understudied and in later seasons produced some of our operas. Rita was still sometimes around because she had a relationship with a local girl who also assisted her, the daughter of Adam Neilson, a local carpenter and small contractor. For a time they lived together at Kincardine, but never got involved socially with the singers, musicians, artists and helpers either at Ledlanet or in other theatrical ventures in which I was involved. As a pair they preferred each other's company. Jim on the other hand was anxious to know and be friendly with everyone and he was also a ladies' man whose conquests at Ledlanet could only be guessed at. I found him one night, during an interval, in the store room where we kept wine and alcohol stocks with the daughter of a prominent music critic while her father was being chatted up at the bar by Jim Fraser.

The Scottish Baroque from 1969 also played four concerts a year at Ledlanet and Leonard found them outside engagements as well. It became a well-drilled group that was consistently well-reviewed. When Lord Goodman paid us a surprise visit one afternoon – I had written to him asking him to use his influence to get the Scottish Arts Council to be more generous – he found Richard Demarco putting up an exhibition of paintings and the SBE rehearsing for a concert that night. He talked to Leonard, listened for half an hour, went away delighted, and, sure enough, our grant was considerably increased. The programmes were, however, eccentric, sometimes quite long and unexpected, because Leonard Friedman had a habit of introducing extra works not in the printed programme at the last minute, often with extra soloists who were not budgeted, leading to difficult negotiations after the event. Leonard always claimed to share Beethoven's birthday, and it was only after his death, when writing his obituary, that I discovered it was in fact two days away. But he would use this as an argument, once I had agreed to hold a Beethoven birthday concert every year on December 16th, to try my patience to its limit. The first of these was in 1969 and the programme that he played was twice as long as in the printed programme and contained no less than seven concerti, including the Mozart Bassoon concerto, played by his current girl-friend, (as wonderful a player as she was beautiful, who soon found him too eccentric and unreliable and left him), a cello concert for which Moray Walsh came up from Newcastle, a flute concerto with David Nicholson, our regular first flute and a first-class soloist, and four others. There were eleven works in the programme and it ended late. When I protested the cost, Leonard pleaded that it was his birthday and that even if I wanted to refuse him, I could not refuse Beethoven. There was not much Beethoven in the programme! It was the following year that James Loughlan came to conduct the SBE at Ledlanet, and having heard the appeal for funds that I would make nearly nightly to the audience, asking them to also become Members, which was two guineas for a single person, and being delighted with the performance of the players under his baton, refused a fee. As Leonard said afterwards, 'All he had to do was wave his arms. He knew we didn't really need him.' In fact the ensemble frequently played without a conductor, just following Leonard.

With four seasons a year there was a big mailing to be sent out, because the mailing list, many times the size of the membership which grew to be three thousand, would take a dozen people a full day to address, stuff into envelopes and stamp. We invented stuffing parties, initially at Ledlanet, later at Huntley Hall, which were in fact, enjoyable occasions, full of chat while we kept our hands busy. Members of our committee and other volunteers, which included any house guests at Ledlanet or at Huntley hall who could be dragooned to work, were gathered around long trestle tables. One lot wrote addresses, others stuffed the envelopes, others put on the stamps. In time the names and addresses were printed on sticky labels and the operation went faster. Jim Fraser kept us supplied with coffee until late in the morning, then wine, which went on all day and of course he organised a big buffet lunch. The stuffing parties always took place on Sundays and it was seldom we did not finish that day. The conversation was good, Jim often playing music on his hi-fi record player, and on occasion we had a pianist and sometimes even a singer to keep us entertained while we worked. Eva Figes was at one such stuffing party, complained at first, but then fell into the good humour of it all, laughing when Robin Richardson, the biggest theatrical agent in Scotland, a frequent attender, and supplier of many of our artists, called out, 'Alright, all out. Unless you agree an extra ten pounds an hour for unsocial hours and overtime.' Two very active members of our committee were a couple from Falkirk, William and Jessie Forman, generous with their time and money, who thought up many money-raising ideas, organised jumble sales and sometimes put up a clothes stall at Ledlanet, but these were not always appropriate to the atmosphere, and I eventually discouraged them. But they were wonderful people, tireless to help and perhaps the most efficient of all the stuffers.

The organising secretary of the Committee was a very personable lady called Joan Clark, whose husband was an affluent local gentleman farmer, who occasionally invited me to shoot and frequently to dinner parties; if ten people were staying at Ledlanet, he would invite us all. I first met Joan when she was in the audience at a talk I gave to a local woman's group, which was nearly very embarrassing, because I was totally unprepared. When the lady chairing the talk stood up to announce 'And now Mr. Calder will give us a talk on the Victorian novel,' my mind flashed back to the moment, many months earlier, when I had received the invitation to speak on a subject of my choice and had chosen that one because I rather wanted to catch up on the Victorian novel, of which there were many I had not read on the shelves at Ledlanet. I was prepared that day to talk about the arts in Scotland and bring in a pep talk for Ledlanet. I drew in my breath, crossed my fingers and started to talk. I was economical on dates and did not offer many details of novelists' lives, but I got through it and everyone seemed impressed. I finished by talking about Ledlanet, hoping that all the ladies present would bring their husbands to have an enjoyable night there. Joan and James Clark both came and she quickly volunteered to drive, fetch artists from airports and stations, help arrange flowers, and do any of the hundred little necessary jobs that do not need anything other than intelligence, leisure and willingness. She organised our various committees, which met to carry out different functions and was invaluable in every way. Unfortunately she had a number of fallings-out with Jim Fraser, who fancied her – she was a personable, self-confident woman with a formidable bosom – and Jim was never easy to handle, especially after a little too much to drink. His alcoholic tendencies grew worse over the years, and I had to call the major committee meetings ever earlier in the day, while he was still sober enough, as chairman, to make sense. The main purpose of our committee meetings was to explore ways of raising money, to assign volunteer tasks and to raise enthusiasm for my forthcoming programming. As the tastes of the committee were on the whole much more conservative than my own, I found that if I put the financial issues first on the agenda, we never reached the artistic programming, so that in practice, although Ledlanet was run by an organisation that depended on its members and was in theory democratic, I had a free hand to put on what I liked. But I took care to have something for everyone, and to cater to all tastes, while at the same time encouraging different members of our audience into enjoying new experiences and developing a willingness to try out the new, the modern, and the experimental. Ledlanet had become my laboratory to find ways of getting the arts to new audiences, and although there were some failures, they were far outweighed by the successes. In publishing I was doing the same.

* * * * * *

Two things happened late in 1969 that changed my life. One was my entry into book-selling. Better Books, once a wonderful outlet for my books, had become under Collins just another general bookshop, trying primarily to sell the Collins list, but not successfully. It had always been known as an avant-garde shop and its clientele were not right for a middle-brow publisher aiming at the more general reader. Suddenly they offered the shop to me and after some negotiation I agreed to buy it, the sale being concluded on the first week of January 1970. Within a few days I received a letter from the General London Council, telling me that the property was being requisitioned for demolition and redevelopment. Collins must have had some foreknowledge, although they denied it. This meant that for most of the year I was looking for new premises on Charing Cross Road. Also I discovered that Collins had let the considerable overseas library business, largely supplying Canadian public and university libraries, slump; in many cases they had simply written to their customers to say that they were discontinuing library supply. The following winter I made a trip across Canada, stopping in Saskatchewan, Alberta, British Columbia and elsewhere to try to recover what Collins had given away, but that essential bread and butter business had already been snapped up by other eager booksellers.

In the meantime I tried to restore Better Books to what it had been, a haven for the serious booklover, where he could find titles rarely stocked elsewhere. In the basement, run by a specialist, was the largest collection of books on films and everything to do with the cinema to be found in Britain. Alexander Walker, critic for The Evening Standard, was in almost daily to see what was new, as were London's other film buffs. Lee Harwood, a poet, was in charge of poetry and this was a real mistake. He refused to order and stock Mary Wilson's poems. They might not have been very good, but she was the Prime Minister's wife, and her poems were being asked for twenty times a day. Nor would he stock John Betjemen because he considered him a poor poet. Those easy sales of popular poetry in fashion would have helped pay for the hundreds of volumes that we seldom sold, including his own. People simply went to Foyle's across the street, and the next time did not come to us first when looking for a particular title. A series of managers were not satisfactory, allowing stealing on a scale that became ever bigger. This was in the wake of the student agitation of the late sixties, when one of their slogans was that books should be free, and as they weren't, they just stole them when they could. Unfortunately Better Books had exactly the books that students wanted just then, so we were the major losers. During the first half of 1970 Better Books took up far too much of my time, but I shall come back to that.

The other thing that happened that year was that I was asked to go into politics. Richard Beith and his wife Margaret had moved to Scotland from Hampshire, where they had been enthusiastic activists for the Liberal Party. They liked music and were soon Ledlanet regulars, coming to most of our productions, and I came to know them well. One day Richard approached me: they were looking for a Liberal candidate for the next election and they thought my qualifications were right. At that point I belonged to no party, but my sympathies were with Labour and I had always voted for them, although I was becoming very disillusioned with much Labour policy and the corruption that had infected Labour-controlled councils up and down the country. The arguments that I gave myself to accept the invitation were firstly that as a publisher I brought out many political books about causes in which I believed in order to influence public opinion, but I had never offered myself to put wrongs right and it was cowardly not to put my own head on the block, and secondly that the party for which I stood, as long as I was not positively opposed to it, was immaterial so long as I had a platform to say what I wanted. I knew many Labour politicians, but Labour had never asked me to stand. Perhaps my reasons were casuistry. The real motive was probably my sense of adventure, my liking for doing something new and having a new experience, or perhaps it was just vanity. At any rate, after a little reflection, I accepted. This must have been in late 1969.

1970 was the big Beethoven year, the bicentenary of his birth. We played much Beethoven that year, but I decided to also do something else and produce a documentary about his life in the collage style I had been developing ever since the *Happening with Robert Burns*. I produced a two-act text for two actors, one to play Beethoven and the other to narrate and to play a variety of other parts. The whole was to be interspersed with music, some of it taped, but with a live string quartet, led by Leonard Friedman, to play extracts from his three creative periods. I found a look-alike for Beethoven, the fine and then very popular actor Patrick Wymark, whom I had first met through his wife Olwen, whose plays I was publishing. I do not know what other lucrative acting jobs Patrick turned down, but he leapt at the chance to play Beethoven about whom he felt as I did. The narrator was Leonard Maguire, who now lived in what had once been the back lodge at Ardargie. I had put a considerable number of sound effects into the script, and with the help of John Rushby-Smith, a friend of mine who worked as a sound engineer at the BBC, who was also the husband of Tanja's best friend, I was able to get these made at the BBC in one of their studios for almost no cost. We needed the sound of an eighteenth century coach swaying and groaning on the roads of the period, recorded conversations, and piano and orchestral music. Having recorded piano music and a live string quartet not only reversed the normal logic, but would make the evening both musically and visually more memorable for the audience. John Rushby-Smith had the bright idea of having petards exploding in the dustbins outside the house as Napoleon's army advanced on Vienna, the noise driving Beethoven's ears to distraction, so that the first act could end with the crashing fortissimo bars of the Fifth Symphony as the composer shouts in agony and tears up his dedication of the *Eroica* to the French Emperor whom he had earlier admired. John Rushby-Smith later wrote a little poem about my *Beethoven* production.

> Exploding dustbins in the grounds
> (Such proto-Bonapartian sounds
> Were, like the lighting, less than more on cue)
> Made Beethoven rip up his page
> Of dedication, quit the stage,
> Rush up the stairs and in a rage
> Upbraid the switchboard guy (I wonder who?)
> That kilted laird, somewhat aghast,
> Fair reeled as the unscripted blast
> Drowned out the E-flat B-flat E-flat theme
> Of the Eroica. And all
> Who'd gathered in Ledlanet's hall
> Were stunned as from behind the wall
> 'It's all a fucking shambles!' came the scream.

The first night was certainly accident-prone, but the audience who had come to see in the flesh the star of the BBC's most popular television serial of that time, called *The Power Game*[27], where Wymark plays a tough international tycoon, rather like Richard Branson in a later age, did not mind at all. Patrick did not have much time to learn the part, so we had to rig up a lectern with a concealed light for him to read much of it, and there were other problems. When Beethoven, having pronounced his dramatic and famous last words, collapses and lies still in death on his bed, the quartet plays the Cavatina from the Opus 130, a slow, rather weird in its tonality, and very moving piece of music, during which Grillparzer's funeral oration is read by Leonard Maguire. Wymark could not control his emotion and tears visibly came from his closed eyes. Also, I did not realise how precarious his health was. A heavy drinker, he had to constantly soothe his stomach with something warm and mild, and during the interval he had imbibed several glasses of rum and milk. But the second performance was much better and with full houses we had a successful show and a good start to the Beethoven year.

On the last night we celebrated in the morning room which was used by the orchestra on the occasions when we had one. Everyone had left except Jim Fraser, Robin Richardson, Patrick, Leonard Friedman, Rushby-Smith and myself. Leonard wanted to play more music and started to play his violin, persuading John Rushby-Smith, who was also a composer, to accompany him. They then moved to the drawing-room, which during that evening had contained the buffet, where there was a better piano, and Patrick Wymark, who by that time believed the he *was* Beethoven went with them. Leaving Jim and Robin to their large brandies, I went too. John was an indifferent pianist, but inspired by Leonard, occasionally calling out

---

[27] In its first episodes, it was called *The Plane Makers*.

changes of key and other instruction, he played better, as he said afterwards, than he ever had before in his life. Poor Patrick's frustration at watching others make music which he so longed to do himself, was terrible to see. He turned the pages of the piano score, but not being able to read properly was no real help and he desisted and sat in frustration.

Back in London I had dinner one night with Tanja, John Rushby-Smith and his wife Uli, in Otello restaurant. John was looking very sheepish because he was in trouble, his wife having just discovered that he was having an affair. When the two ladies had left us alone for a few minutes, he leaned forward and said to me, 'She knows you by the way.' I had an intuition and was right: the other lady in question was Jenny Paull. It was not that long afterwards that their marriage finally broke up, but the real cause was, as I saw it, not a brief infidelity, but Uli's general discouragement of John's career as a composer. She wanted him to concentrate on advancement in the BBC, not on trying to be Beethoven as I overheard her say one day. In any case he soon met someone else, Elaine Padmore, also at the BBC, where she initiated music programmes and was an announcer on Radio Three. Once they were a couple I began to see them frequently, both in London and in Scotland. When they had a legal problem over the use of some land behind their house, I introduced them to Jimmy Ball who worked out a solution very cleverly. Elaine went on to become Head of Radio Opera and then took on the Wexford Festival, about which I shall have more to say.

I was now also in politics and had been adopted as the prospective candidate for parliament by the Scottish Liberal Party for Kinross and West Perthshire, where the MP was still Sir Alec Douglas-Home, no longer Prime Minister, but still a God to his party. I had done my bit against him by helping Willie Rushton in 1963 and now had been adopted myself. This officially took place at a meeting in Crieff in the autumn of 1969 and I then spent a number of weekends going around the many small towns and villages in the constituency, one of the largest and perhaps the most scenically beautiful in Britain. There had been no Liberal candidate since Duncan Millar had run seven years earlier, and with the help of a growing committee, which had been reorganised and given new life by the Beiths, I found where the clusters of previous Liberal supporters lived, people who had had no chance to vote for a Liberal in many years. There were a considerable number of them; the party had always come second in elections in the past, but now the Scottish National Party was firmly in second place, and the Labour vote was tiny. The Labour Party used the constituency purely as a training ground for raw political hopefuls to get some experience. The common wisdom was that if the Tories were to put up a black labrador with a blue collar it would get elected. In safe Labour constituencies the same was said of monkeys with red collars. Driving around the constituency took time. It was bordered by Fife and Stirlingshire in the south, and by the Trossachs in the West. It went north of Pitlochry to the borders of Inverness-shire, but did not include the city of Perth with its sizeable population. Before the constituency had accepted me I had been grilled by Jo Grimond and George Mackie in the Liberal offices in the House of Commons, who had asked me several questions about my more controversial books and my involvement in the Edinburgh Festivals that had led to press attacks, but they were short of candidates and found my general opinions on political and social issues acceptable. I attended meetings of the Scottish Liberal Party which took place fairly regularly in different Scottish towns, and I remember a big meeting in Peebles where David Steel was MP, together with Grimond and Russell Johnstone, one of the three sitting Scottish Liberals, in parliament. Grimond and Lord Mackie made a point, some time in 1970, of dropping in on me at Ledlanet, where they saw a conventional Scottish country house in its own estate, and they left with little comment. As for local people in Kinross, and even more so in Milnathort which was solidly Conservative, they knew I did not have a chance and saw the whole thing as a joke. Kinross with its council estates had a certain Labour following, which was polite to me, but they knew that their own candidate, a young man, had even less chance than me. The SNP had quite a formidable lady, Elizabeth Whitley, the wife of the minister of St. Giles Cathedral in Edinburgh, Harry Whitley, whom I had met at a dinner party once with Bill Watson. It was he who had once denounced *Salome* at the Edinburgh Festival, saying that the bad weather was the judgement of the Lord on the Dance of the Seven Veils, which of course he had not seen. If I remember rightly Sir Alec's majority was 34,000 and he was of course the darling of the local aristocracy, who vied with each other to entertain him and offer hospitality. But little by little people stopped me to promise their vote and I did quite well that way with farmers I stopped to talk to on the roads or called on in their fields or at home. I would drive to a village, call on two or three dozen houses, then go to the next and do the same. The point was to get my name known and my presence felt. Although those I spoke to were usually unwilling to tell you how they would vote, you could usually guess by their faces or by their saying, 'It won't be Tory' or more often 'It won't be Labour'. Many would tell you that they wanted Scotland to be free of England, so they had to vote SNP, but that once independence was achieved they would vote Liberal.

The election was called for early June 1970 and with the summer season of Ledlanet Nights still to come, I was formally confirmed as the official candidate; the requisite number of names in support was found to enable me to stand and Richard Beith organised all the paperwork. We rented a room in a building in Crieff as our headquarters and the committee room was soon full of ladies addressing envelopes under the direction of an enthusiastic local widow, Margaret Begg. My agent was a craftsman who had a shop in Pitlochry called Peter Roberts, a craftsman and stone-cutter who specialised in semi-precious stones, while Alan Clark became my shadow and companion, a kind of Sancho Panza. He was very short, not much above four feet tall, very broad and always kilted, somewhere in his forties. Wherever I went he went with me, map-reading through the roads that criss-crossed the mountains and glens, talking to the crowds in market towns, picking individuals out of groups to come to talk to me, knocking on alternate doors and keeping whoever opened them talking if it seemed likely I might win his or her vote, until I caught up. He knew the whole area well, watched out for lambs that might run in front of the car to join their mother, telling me where I could most usefully spend my time. We went into pubs together, shook hands and produced our arguments, handing out my campaign leaflet. On one side was my picture among a group of elected MPs, on the other I had summarised my policies in short sentences, that a few years later would have been called 'sound bites'.

I came across young men with families who told me that they did not bother to get a job because family benefits were such they would have little more spending money if they worked, and I heard exaggerated stories from others of such men who drank in the pubs until closing time at three o'clock, then called a cab, saying they would be back at five-thirty. But the resentment of taxpayers against the welfare state was evident, especially among older people and the childless. It was a time of full employment, especially for those with skills, and many tradesmen and technicians were buying their houses on mortgage, which put them into the middle classes. I sensed that here the men would vote Labour out of loyalty for the most part, but the wives, wanting lower taxes and more spending power, were leaning towards the Tories. Harold Wilson had lowered the voting age from twenty-one to eighteen which I felt was a great mistake. Few of those I met under twenty-one had any political knowledge or understanding of the issues before them, and I am sure that that applied as much to urban constituencies as to my rural one. Some evenings I had a group of six to ten helpers to knock on doors and we would cover a whole village. One day I found a whole group of mourners inside a house just after a funeral and was told that the lady who had died had been looking forward to having a Liberal to vote for again. It was a sunny summer, and I was offered meals in many corners of the constituency by supporters. I addressed meetings in town halls and in the back rooms of pubs and hotels, with occasional summonses to attend a party gathering in Edinburgh or Glasgow to be lectured on policies and photographed with the few Liberal MPs of which there were only seven then in the whole of Britain.

My sister, whose married name was Laptew, came up from London to help and, working from the Crieff committee rooms, was used largely as a courier to carry messages all over the constituency, the second largest in Britain. It was hard work, but I was enjoying every minute of it, most of the time out of doors in beautiful weather, addressing small crowds in village streets from the back of my Landrover, trudging up to farmhouses with Alan, often with my dog Shuna at my heels. By now she was ultra-obedient, would sit quietly outside a gate while I went in to knock on the door, or wait in the car while I addressed a meeting. There was hostility in some places, mainly in the Tory heartland around Crieff, where Home posters were everywhere and there were also many for the SNP, mainly on trees. The SNP supporters, who were nearly all very young, specialised in tearing down the few of mine we managed to get up.

I had quite a large meeting in Aberfeldy and noticed an unusually large number of young people at the back of the hall, which was surprising because it was usually the middle-aged and elderly who came to hear me speak. Right from the beginning I began to be heckled from them at the back, constantly interrupted in what I was saying, and it became obvious that these were young racialists who had probably done the same to all the other candidates. They were complaining about the number of black people coming into Britain, but if there was any part of the country where you very seldom saw a black face, it was there in central Perthshire. I pointed this out, but without in any way agreeing with them. Then suddenly, I had a spark of memory. 'Listen to me, you young thugs,' I said. 'I remember being in Pitlochry (which was only a few miles away) on the day that Italy came into the war. There was an Italian ice-cream shop where I bought my Beano and a penny cone. On that day I couldn't, because the shop had been smashed up. People just like you, with their stupid prejudices had ruined that man's livelihood. He had nothing to do with Mussolini or Italy coming into the war. He was a Scottish Italian who made good ice-cream.'

At that moment a girl, who had been vociferously barracking me like all the others, shouted out, 'That was ma faither' in a strong local accent. There was a silence. Then she began to hit her friends around her. 'You're wrong and he's right,' she yelled. Then I began to talk again with nothing prepared, but I was able to give a reasoned analysis of how and why some people had an instinctive and unreasoned – yes instinctive – prejudice against others who were in some way different. Any fascist group could inflame that prejudice that could quickly disappear once people came to know each other. We had fought a war against that fascism and what went with it. When I finished to much applause and a few questions, all of them friendly, I knew I had won every vote in that room. The older people had seen the young silenced and converted by a member of their own group, and I knew that it would win me votes from others as the word went round the next day.

About ten days before the election I had a telephone call from Patrick Wymark. 'What are you doing up there?' he asked. 'Why didn't you ask me to come and help?' He had been campaigning for the Labour candidate in Hampstead, but now he came back to Ledlanet to help me as a Liberal. We printed new posters to announce that 'Sir John Wilder from the popular TV series *The Power Game*, was to appear on all my platforms,' and from then on I spoke to full houses. I am not sure if it won me many votes, because it was

Pat they came to hear. With him he brought his girl friend, a young actress, Karen Fernald. She was poised and attractive, the daughter of John Fernald, Principal of the Royal Academy of Dramatic Art.

There was one evening when we were invited to dinner in Callender by Mrs. Tennant, the grand lady of the district, who happened to be a Liberal of the Jo Grimond stamp. My canvassing in the town had been ineffective as it was a public holiday and the whole town had gone off, either to a big city like Glasgow or into the hills to picnic. Not a door was locked. A fleet of furniture lorries could have invaded the town and emptied every home without hurrying. Rural communities in Scotland were still honest and the local policeman had nothing to do other than intervene in some minor quarrel. We had a meeting in the local church hall, and before that our hostess had invited Patrick, Karen and myself to an early dinner at her house. 'Tell me,' she asked Patrick, 'are you a real actor or a television thing?' He did not know how to reply. He was a top actor with a long stage career and a particular love of Shakespeare, but at that time it was his television series that made him a national celebrity. But his presence brought in some of the returning Callender residents that evening.

Many interesting things happened during the campaign. I had to attend a few platforms where all four candidates had a chance to express their policies before specialised groups of constituents. At one such, organised by the National Farmers Union, there was no doubt that the SNP candidate, Elizabeth Whitley, had done her homework best and had been prepared for the questions, giving detailed promises of what her party had to offer farmers. I had been remiss at reading the piles of paper that the party sent me almost daily, preferring, perhaps arrogantly, to make up my policy as I went along, which although broadly in line with official views and dogma, varied in some respects where I had strong personal views, and I felt confident enough to deal with any questions I was asked. So in front of the farmers I was shorter on detailed information than the others, and I know I did not do well that day.

One amusing incident was in Braco, near my Uncle Rupert Dawson's old house Orchil, where I had often stayed. Braco is a small village with a single long street, lined with houses on each side. As I drove up, so did another car plastered with Tory posters. I did some quick thinking. I had Alan with me and another helper, and there were three Tory ladies about to knock on the same doors. It was a hot afternoon and I guessed that most of those at home would be in their gardens at the back. 'Let's just go around the back doors,' I said, and we started at the end going down the same row of houses, where our opposition had started, entering the back gates while the Tories rang doorbells on the other side. Sure enough everyone was in their gardens, chatting to neighbours, hanging up washing, or gardening, or just relaxing in deck-chairs. The three of us leap-frogged around each other, handing out leaflets, talking to the residents, soliciting their votes. When we reached the end of the row and peeped round, we could see the three Tory canvassers, who had vainly been ringing all the doorbells, looking hot and bad-tempered coming to the end of the houses we had just done. We crossed the road without being noticed and repeated the same exercise on the other side, going back towards our car. When we reached the end, we found that the other car was gone. With no result the three ladies had given up and driven off. We had spoken to over a hundred voters.

All our envelopes were out in time as Margaret Begg and Margaret Ryder, another committee member, ran the operation smoothly and directed all the volunteer workers around the many small towns, many of which now had activists doing something to help. More than a hundred people were giving their time, and canvas cards were telling us where our strengths lay. Patrick Wymark met many of the local gentry at hotel bars and later regaled me with what they said about 'Alec' or 'Dear Alec'. It was interesting to hear an actor tell the same story many times, always a little differently, imitating the voices well, but with always a small variation in the phrasing. It was a good example of the freedoms that traditional actors often took with their lines, to which the most serious playwrights like Beckett and Pinter objected, wanting stage directions exactly followed and lines always delivered exactly as written, with no variation.

I do not think that the Labour candidate worked hard at garnering votes, because the party hardly existed in Kinross and West Perthshire. The SNP we saw all the time and they hated us because by splitting the non-Conservative vote we would reduce their future credibility. They tore down our posters, denigrated us as woolly and insufficiently committed to devolution. The Tories thought it 'cheek' to run against the previous Prime Minister and of course considered me a traitor to my class. There were some repercussions at future Ledlanet performances, but not many. Liberals were considered on the whole to be harmless idealists, and the Leader, Jo Grimond, was personally popular. I had hoped to have some support from Duncan Miller, the previous Liberal candidate, but he was Perth County Convenor now, stayed aloof and had probably been Toryfied. From Kincardine in the east to Loch Katrine in the west, from remote northern villages like Crianlarich and Rannoch where the great moor started, and the many beautiful lochs, the glory of the Highlands, I drove, wondering at the scenery. This area had once been heavily populated, but the clearances of nearly two centuries earlier, when landlords and lairds, many of them newly rich from the industrial revolution, had preferred to cover their land with sheep for profit and stags for sport than have surly tenants paying low rents, had emptied it out. Lochaber was almost a desert where the population was concerned. Crianlarich, which is sign-posted from hundreds of miles away, is a tiny village where many roads cross, with just a handful of houses, a hotel and a rail marshalling yard. But it is all beautiful country and I came to know it well and many of its people. It was an exhausting three-week campaign, but I revelled in it and discovered another side of myself, but also realised that selling is selling, whether it be timber, books, or yourself to represent voters in parliament.

Election day came and I was out early. I went first to Kinross to vote, naturally for myself, then I went all over the constituency to as many polling booths as possible, chatting to any of our supporters who were able to show the colours, which were not many, especially compared to the Tories who had covered them all, often with caravans offering refreshments. I was new to all this and did not realise that I was supposed to go into the polling booths, shake the hands of those handing out the voting cards and chat with them, so I didn't do it. There is a very low level of electoral expenditure allowed to each of the parties, and not being affluent and a new, reawakened political party with a small membership, we were well within our expenditure limit. The Tories on the other hand had printed their posters well before the election was announced and had many rich supporters who paid for what should have been accounted for in the election budget out of their own pockets: they were legally cheating. They also had hundreds of volunteers with cars, caravans, tents that could be erected anywhere, and other amenities available to them at no cost to the party. Early in the campaign I had gone to one of Sir Alec's election meetings and I sat in the front row with Alan Clark, while Richard Beith and other Liberals were at the back to ask questions. A burly farmer who was chairing the meeting came up to me warily. 'No tricks, Mr. Calder, I hope.'

'No, I just wanted to hear what Sir Alec has to say,' I replied, and sat quietly through it all, leaving my supporters present to ask questions we had prepared in advance. When Willie Rushton had run, I had asked the awkward questions.

On the eve of poll I persuaded Bettina – my committee had thought it very desirable – to join me on the platform and at the lunch the next day after the count in Perth. Right after that I took her to the airport in Edinburgh to fly back to London. Tanja was due to come up an hour later, but she caught an earlier flight and Bettina saw her walking on the balcony outside the airport restaurant. That did not help matters at all!

The Tories won with a reduced but still substantial majority, and I received nine percent of the vote, which was not bad considering that no Liberal had run there for seven years, but it was not enough to save my deposit. The final count was in Crieff, and the excitement of being one of those able to be present to check the count as the votes piled up and were put in piles of a hundred each, is one of the rewards given to those who worked for the candidate during the election. I found it very nerve-wracking as, starting at ten, it went on until the early hours as the ballot boxes came in from all the far-out polling stations. I made my little speech, promising to run again, and drove home. The next day was the lunch in Perth, one of the illustrations in this book. I had now become a political animal.

PURSUIT

* * * * * *

The election over I found that I was invited to many more local events. I opened the summer exhibition at the art gallery in Perth and the Milnathort flower show. I was still the candidate, and the last general election had been so close nationally that it seemed inevitable that the next one could not be far off. But the Tories had beaten Labour, caused largely in my opinion by the lowering of the voting age and the different self-perception of working-class men, who had bought their houses with mortgages, that they were now middle-class. Certainly many working-class women had moved to the right, and wives had tended to vote during the day when their husbands were still at work. I think it was then that large Tory posters on billboards had mocked the Labour leaders as 'Yesterday's Men', but it may have been later.

I had my usual lunch in Bianchi's with Peter Gellhorn where the popular manager, Elena, presided over the regular customers, all of whom she knew by their first name, writers, musicians and BBC men and women for the most part. This was in the same first floor room that had received the first ever television picture, sent by John Logie Baird from his bedroom on the top floor, because this building on Greek Street had once been his house. 'What's it to be this time?' asked Peter.

'*La Clemenza di Tito.*'

He drew in his breath. 'Lovely,' he said. And we started to prepare it.

Sometime towards the end of that year Tanja and I decided to split up, but remain friends. Through acquaintances of my sister, who by now had also been divorced from her Rumanian husband, Paul Laptew, whom she had married in Canada in 1955, I found an unusual place to live. It was an artist's studio in Pembroke Gardens, one of a circle of such studios, built in Victorian times. The owner, Vasco de Lazlo, was a fashionable portrait painter, and part of a social group that included Prince Philip, the Queen's consort, which used to meet once a week on the top floor of Wheeler's Restaurant on Old Compton Street. De Lazlo, an Italian, had spent so many years in England that he was to all appearances a prominent member of that section of the English upper classes that both creates and supports the arts, different only in its taste and pursuits from the aristocratic country cousins who came to London only for the races and Buckingham Palace Garden parties. De Lazlo belonged to a clique that had money, spent it lavishly in the most fashionable resorts of Europe, in Cannes, Saint Tropez, Athens and the Greek Islands, and in his case, Malta, which was a tax haven, because he had married a rich wife. He was now living there and had stopped painting and, although he would never have admitted it, was probably very bored and he had to keep returning to London to find some *joie de vivre* once again.

I rented his studio, but he kept squatting rights. All the furniture was his, including a glamorous white grand piano, but with a loose key action, more suitable to a night club than a concert hall. When he was there he played it rather well in the manner of Noel Coward. I took on the rental agreement of a certain Baron Frankenstein, who had rented it from de Lazlo; Frankenstein had obviously left it reluctantly for reasons I did not know, because he kept turning up again. His father had been Austrian Ambassador in London at the time of the Anschluss, who had remained in Britain. He was a pleasant and aimless young man about London, who I liked but with whom I soon lost touch.

The studio belonged to a trust which had been created to ensure that only practising artists lived there, but many had sublet to others who liked the eccentricity and calm of the place, set far enough back from passing traffic not to have to hear it, and closed to it during the night. My studio was large and cold, impossible to heat, except for the two small bedrooms which were behind a gallery which overlooked the studio itself, which was two stories high with a skylight overhead. On the ground floor there was a kitchen off the studio, above it a bathroom between the bedrooms.

I had only a few small gatherings there. At one a previous boyfriend of Bettina's turned up, Tony Hern, who had once engaged her to sing popular Viennese songs on his BBC Light Music Programme. He knew about our separation, so she must have talked to him recently. It may have been de Lazlo who invited the twenty or so people that evening. He himself came with a very beautiful dark girl he was painting. Hern went up to her, said, 'You are very beautiful' as if she were herself a painting, and walked out. I was later to meet his son who became the publisher Nick Hern.

I gave a fairly large party there to which Jo Grimond came, but he never talked to anyone in particular and he probably felt too remote from the mixture of literary people and others engaged in the arts. At one point I looked down from the balcony where I could see everyone: no one ever looked up and I could quite clearly hear each of the many conversations going on down below. Jo walked around for about an hour observing the scene, drank a glass and left. I think that for all his urbanity and sophistication he was not a mixer, and not particularly interested in the arts. In those years I always intended to go to the Orkney Festival which Peter Maxwell Davies had founded, but never did, but I discovered later that, although he was the Orkney MP, he gave it no support and was dismissive of it. Grimond was a strange man, admired by the left for his uprighteousness and obvious ability and intelligence, and considered by the right to be a traitor to his class. He was a God to his own party, that minority of about five percent spread thinly around the country. He was, I think, a deeply disappointed man, and he was soon to step down as Liberal leader.

I met a lady I had not seen for many years, now called Marcelle Arden. Her first husband had once tried to sell a mink coat, or it may have been sable, to Christya, probably in 1950, and on one occasion he brought along his bright-eyed little vivacious French wife, who I noticed was taking in everything round about her, my living style, books, records, furniture and expensive wife, living in Belgravia. Her husband and Christya were trying to cheat each other and nothing came of the negotiations, but I remembered her when I met her again, married to, but about to leave, her third husband, to whom I think she was not properly married, the best-selling novelist Alastair MacLean. Arden was her second and she seemed to alternate the two surnames, Arden and MacLean. If I remember rightly Arden had been a businessman living in Jersey and one reason I had not seen her around London for nearly two decades was that she had been living mainly there. I had a sort of flirtation with her, but it never came to much because she did not really attract me and her transparent phoniness was a big offput. I mistakenly took her with me to the BBC one day where I was on some kind of discussion programme and I could see from the eyes of the others present that they expected to see me in better company. She had spending money enough and was throwing it around to impress. She claimed to be a film producer, but as far as I could see she never made any films, but got involved with some producers interested in filming MacLean's novels. She had under some settlement acquired a considerable amount of his income, which was large as his adventure novels all sold well. On two occasions I met Alastair with her, perhaps more often, but he did not take to me. He was both vain and naive, very alcoholic, having a difficulty in maintaining his reputation, subject to writer's block for which I would think a permanent hangover was responsible. Since the success of *H.M.S. Ulysses*, his first novel, he had continued with a formula, all his novels having variations of the same plot. His heroines were nearly all called Mary, and he had changed Marcelle's name to Mary, which she accepted, but only in his presence. He disliked me instinctively because I was in his eyes a publisher of the kind of literature to which he could never aspire, and because he resented my coming from a different Scottish social class to himself. His publisher was Ian Chapman of Collins, who knew how to handle him and who probably thought that Marcelle was a scheming money-grubbing little vixen, which indeed she was. She needed a crutch however and saw me as being it, able to help her enter a more glamorous section of London society. She constantly invited me to her rented house in Notting Hill, which she soon changed for a large flat overlooking Hyde Park. She was having a drink at my studio quite late one evening when there came a knocking on the window, which was glazed. It was Tanja who had been dining with her new boyfriend, a tall man whose silhouette I could see against the glass. On impulse she had decided to call on me, probably to excite my jealousy, perhaps to excite his. I thought that for her to meet Marcelle was not a good idea. I was still obsessed with Tanja, and would in the future go on seeing her and even occasionally spend the night with her, but it had become apparent that our lifestyles were too different for us to live together. On that occasion I refused to open the door and they went away.

Tanja soon broke up with her new man and we saw each other more regularly for perhaps a few months. We were genuinely fond of each other and there was a certain mutual sexual need, but we knew that would diminish. She would have moved a fairly long way to meet me in doing the things I most enjoyed – it was there the main difference lay – but I could not do the same the other way. We telephoned each other quite frequently, but I knew she was seeing other men and I would quite frequently bring other ladies back to my studio. Once after a visit from one long-standing girlfriend on a night when I knew Tanja was having dinner with André Deutsch, I performed very badly sexually. The lady went back to her own place, and I drove round to Overstrand Mansions, not certain that she would be there. She was, woke up, and made passionate love with me several times, always wanting more. But gradually, because we knew we could not really share our lives we drifted apart and eventually became good friends and directed our passions elsewhere.

About this time I met another lady, an American working for the Guardian newspaper called Elizabeth Wyler, probably through a mutual friend, Bill Webb, the Literary Editor of the same newspaper, who was without any question the best Literary Editor of any newspaper in Britain at that time. She was a vivacious redhead, open to adventure, earning her own living, who had been and may still have been married to a British actor, Richard Wyler, best known for spaghetti westerns made in Italy. They were separated but good friends. I took Liz to the opera a few times, propositioned her and she accepted. I was putting some unusual advertisements on the literary page of The Guardian then, not the usual 'tombstones', but fairly long copy with small headlines, designed to be read as part of the literary page, and as I used fairly audacious and often non-politically-correct headings to catch attention, they were certainly noticed, but not very favourably, and I received several letters of complaint. Whether they sold books or not I could only surmise. Liz was good company, very sexy, and I quickly became fond of her in the best way, by which I mean that neither of us wanted a deep love relationship and were content with good companionship spiced with satisfactory sex. She knew I had other relationships and showed no jealousy, but she did want to have an interesting social life in my company. She knew all about Tanja, not from me, but from another journalist who had had an affair with each of them and who had told her that Tanja's large and well-shaped 'Bristols' in the terminology of the time, were 'the county and not the town'. There was one unfortunate incident when Liz was spending the night with me and I had a date with another lady for the next night. The other lady decided to leave her overnight bag with me early in the morning, saw us in bed together, and furiously walked out again. Liz, waking up, asked whose that voice was. I answered it was someone passing the front door.

My studio in Pembroke Gardens was used by me for editorial work and the longest session was twenty days that I spent there, not consecutively but spread over more than two months, with Aidan Higgins over his large third novel, *Balcony of Europe*, which was based on the time that he and his family had spent in Majorca, living on an Arts Council grant I had been able to obtain for him and royalties, largely money we had put up in advance against future sales, because I believed very firmly that he was a potentially important author whose reputation, already quite high, would continue to grow. We cut his manuscript down by about a third, reshaped sentences, pruned a book where the fine writing obscured and delayed the story to a more acceptable level, and ironed out the oddities. The manuscript was uneven, one brilliant passage being followed by a rather pedestrian one, and one had to read them together to bring lacklustre phrases up to the level of the best. Aidan's biggest indulgence was putting in words where he liked the sound but did not know the meaning, covering pages with the names of shrubs and flowers that he had found in the dictionary, although he had no idea what they looked like. I cut all that. He also liked giving his characters the names of authors he had found in my catalogue, Stuckenschmidt for instance. We would work every day from about ten-thirty, my having gone to collect him earlier from Muswell Hill where he lived, and we would work well until lunch at 1:00, which consisted of food I had ready, washed down with a gin and tonic and wine. The memory of Aidan, his sleeves rolled up, lovingly pulling the cork out of a bottle, is still with me, largely because of the look of pleasurable anticipation on his face. Then we would resume work, but he had a better head for wine than I, so by four o'clock I would begin to nod, and then become less severe, letting many things pass which I would not have in the morning. On one occasion, when Aidan had gone for a few minutes to the lavatory, I rewrote a sentence, adding a few words. When he returned he looked at the sentence. 'I didn't write that,' he said.

'No, I did,' I said. 'Don't you think it's better now?'

'I didn't write it. Take it out.' He was very possessive of his own words. I was allowed to improve by editing and suggestion, but not by rewriting.

We would work until about six and then either break up or sometimes have dinner alone or with friends. One night we dined at Liz Wyler's flat with the Webbs and it was a good evening because Bill Webb liked Aidan's work and *Balcony of Europe*, a year later, was the runner-up for the Guardian fiction prize, which Bill awarded. Those prize givings, which were at lunch time in the National Liberal Club were splendid affairs where all of literary London was present. The money, usually £300, was not very much, but the prestige was great and it was just as important as the Booker Prize in those days and usually given to a better novel.

There were occasions when Beckett was in London when Aidan spent an evening with us, probably a little earlier in the sixties. There was one evening when after dinner we all went to the flat of Bill Swainson, one of our editors, when he gave a party in South London. Sam had quite a bit to drink that night, and Aidan was cornering his attention, trying to get him to say something about his (Aidan's) work. Sam finally got irritated. 'Literary shit,' was his final pronouncement. It was only one of his occasional moments of savagery when pushed too far, but Aidan was deeply hurt and still remembered it years later. I met the artist Adam Cziernievski there that night, who had designed one of Aidan's book covers and was a good friend of his. Years later during the 1997 General Election campaign, when I was helping the Liberal candidate in the Suffolk Coastal Constituency, hoping to get Alexandra Jones into the seat occupied by John Gummer, (about which more in the last chapter), I ran into Adam's wife who remembered that night as one of the highlights of her life.

During the late sixties and early seventies, the drama list had expanded as much as the fiction list. We took on a theatre magazine which Robert Rietty, the actor, had started some time previously, largely as a vehicle to publish promising new plays at a time when few publishers were interested in them, and which he offered to us after half a dozen issues had appeared, for nothing if we would just continue it. We expanded it to carry articles about the theatre and theatrical issues, reviewed productions and books on drama, had regular columns and diaries, including one on opera, which I wrote myself. Gradually every issue began to have a theme. We continued publishing plays and the magazine grew in size as the subscriptions and sales rose. We had previously offered to take over Applause, which Charles Marovitz edited, and the compensation – because such magazines always lose money – would have been the chance to acquire a group of writers which the periodical had promoted, headed by Harold Pinter, not yet celebrated enough to have interested any of the few commercial play publishers, but Pinter was beginning to be known and I was interested. But the wily Marovitz was playing all sides and he used my interest to make a deal with Methuen instead, whereby they specifically took on Pinter with Marovitz getting something out of it, so a major author went on their list and not ours, while Applause died. Gambit, our magazine, appeared with regularity at first and with the later issues less so until 1986. But at the same time the drama list was growing. We had a part time drama editor and manuscripts flooded in. I went to see new plays with a double purpose now, not just for pleasure, but with possible publication in mind. We missed Tom Stoppard because in the year when his first play was premiered at the Edinburgh fringe I sent Arthur Boyars to see *Rosenkrantz and Guilderstern Are Dead* and he came back with no opinion at all, certainly no enthusiasm. That was when I realised that Arthur's mind was shaped to receive the knowledge of others and to regurgitate it, not to form his own original judgements. We lost Pinter because of Marovitz and Stoppard because of Arthur Boyars. My own oversight was Peter Nicholls. I went to the Glasgow Citizens Theatre to see *A Day in the Life of Joe Egg* and although I liked it and its production, I did not see how a play with such a subject, about an autistic child, could ever appeal to an audience. The play transferred to London and was a success.

We were however taking on many new playwrights and in some cases also representing them as theatrical agents, able to offer them to theatres for performance. One such was Vivienne Welburn, who caught the temper of the time with plays about youth, their frustrations, aspirations and lives, and the bittersweet quality of their romances and love affairs in a poetic language that was close to reality. We were able to get several of her plays performed in London and provincial theatres. The most successful was *Johnny, So Long*, which we sold to the Royal Court, where it had the usual three-week run and good reviews. *Johnny* first appeared in Gambit and then in a volume on its own in our Playscript series, and was followed by a few other plays of which *Clearway* was the most successful. As plays were bought by public libraries in towns with repertory theatres, some were found there by actors, producers and theatre managers and came to be performed.

A new school of playwrights influenced by the social and political drama of Ibsen and by Brecht was developing just then, following the two categories which had been labelled 'the theatre of the absurd' (in Martin Esslin's phrase) and 'the angry young men'. Just ahead of what I will call the 'seventies playwrights' came Edward Bond in whom the influence of Brecht, Ibsen and to a lesser extent absurdism could be easily detected. He was also angry. I came to know Edward well, largely through speaking frequently on the same platform, usually about censorship, often together with April Fox, a committed civil libertarian and feminist. Bond's play *Saved*, in which a baby is stoned to death by young hoodlums for no reason other than bravado, caused a scandal which made Methuen, his publishers, uncomfortable. When he followed it with *Early Morning*, which was basically an irreverent dream about Queen Victoria, Methuen refused to publish it and I did, which made Peggy Ramsay, the most powerful play agent in London and the most eccentric, very angry. I added another good name to my list, but had reluctantly to agree a couple of years later to let Methuen republish it in their first volume of *Collected Plays*, which was the same as losing it again. Bond would have continued with us, but our dozey drama editor, who proofcorrected it, changed John Brown to John Bull, which so infuriated Edward Bond, that he returned to Methuen with his next play.

It may have been a little earlier than this that I went to see Jean Genet's *The Balcony* at the Arts Theatre Club, where it was given as part of the Royal Shakespeare's London season because the play could not get a licence from the Lord Chamberlain for the Aldwych[28]. Before the opening, which was a matinee, I had lunch with Harold Hobson and the author. It was an amusing lunch, because Genet, whom I had already met a few times in Paris, was always impish and loved to shock. 'Are you a homosexual, Mr.

---

[28] Theatre Clubs, only open to members, were immune to censorship.

Hobson?' he asked the eminent, elderly and diminuitive critic. *Pédéraste* was the word he used in French.

'Non, pas encore,' responded Hobson. He could be just as impish, and they went on teasing each other. Then Genet turned to me, and asked if I was seriously interested in publishing his play. His regular publisher was Faber, who had an option but had offered no contract as yet. He said that if I committed myself then, at table and sight-unseen, I could have the play for publication, option or no option. I was very tempted, but I had my principles. 'No, Monsieur Genet,' I said. 'I would love to be your publisher, but I always read or see what I am going to publish first. As soon as the curtain comes down, I will make you an offer.' I was perhaps foolish, but Genet said 'then or never', so Faber published it. I would in any case have had terrible problems with Rosica Colin, the most difficult and possessive agent in London, who did not like her authors to even talk to a publisher or producer in case it weakened in some way her influence over them. She would have raised such a fuss that the contract would probably not have gone through anyway, and I certainly could not trust Genet to keep his word. Genet in those days was translated by an American, Bernard Frechtman, also represented by Rosica Colin. Frechtman used a colloquial American that was far too rough for the subtleties of Genet's writing, but no one else was allowed to translate him. Back in the days of Music Today, when I would put a literary spot into the middle of a concert of new music, I had once thought of Genet's prison poem about the convict who dreams that his manacles are turned to flowers, and I made my own translation of part of it, but Rosica would not allow it to be read, although no other translation existed, and I had to substitute something else. Later on, Lindsay Kemp, the mime and dancer, came to see me to ask what to do when his request to stage his own version of this work had been similarly refused. As there is no copyright in titles, I advised him to use the title and do his own non-verbal mime version 'inspired by Genet' and that is what he did, transforming the poem into a dance event that was very effective. This may seem to contradict my earlier strictures on changing an author's work, but what Kemp did would have had Genet's total approval. He was dead by then.

Gambit had a number of editors, the contents of each issue being planned by our drama editor, Robert Rietty, Marion and I without any disagreement that I can remember. The most eminent of the editors on the masthead was Irving Wardle, who consulted with us, but on the whole we gave him his head. Whenever we did not have an editor I took on an issue myself, so that most issues between Numbers 28 and 35 were usually mine. I did one on Beckett that included the first publication of *Breath*, Beckett's thirty-second play, one of two special Beckett issues that appeared, and particularly successful were No. 29 (New British Playwrights) with a taped disussion of a dozen younger playwrights and two issues (Nos. 31 and 36) on Political Theatre. For the first of these I again taped a round table discussion in my flat (I was then at Dalmeny House) with a large number of playwrights including Jeff Nuttall, Ken Campbell, Max Stafford-Clark, Roger Howard, Caryl Churchill and Anton Gill of the Arts Council, which worked very well and still reads well years later. Most of the leading British playwrights and some foreign ones like Simone Benmussa and the actor/director Jean-Louis Barrault also had special issues devoted to their work. The 'new playrights' discussion with Howard Barker, Caryl Churchill, Steve Gooch, David Halliwell, David Colgar, Roger Howard, Mustapha Matura, Alan Plater, Barry Reckord, Micheline Wandor, Tim Whitehead and Snoo Wilson was also successful.

At Ledlanet our production of Mozart's *Clemenza di Tito*, to which we gave the English title *Titus* as it was sung in English, as all our operas except one had been in the past, was a success. Even song cycles were sung in English wherever possible, because it struck me as counter productive with an audience, much of which was experiencing high culture for the first time, not to have everything understood by all who came. Every great composer has wanted to be performed in the language of the audience because the words matter, often as much as the score. Even Wagner insisted in his lifetime that he be performed in English in England, and I believe in New York as well. There are several extant early translations of Wagner, some by Ernest Newman, who was the greatest Wagnerian music critic in English. There were in existence excellent translations of Mozart's operas, the old Dent translations now being replaced by Andrew Porter's, and more and more translations were being made of the standard repertoire, whatever the language, many of them for Sadlers Wells Opera, which Lord Harewood, having become Managing Director after the death of Stephen Arlen, managed to get renamed The English National Opera in 1974 to the considerable annoyance of the Royal Opera House at Covent Garden. At Ledlanet we sometimes made our own translation, and I did one myself, Monteverdi's *Ballo del Ingrate*, which became *The Cruel Ladies*, which Adrian Sunshine, who conducted it, not trusting me, checked to be sure the musical notation values matched the text.

Our cast for *Titus* was a good one with Terry Jenkins in the title role, Janice Chapman as Vitellia, a part as difficult as Donna Anna, which she carried off brilliantly, and the wonderful and charming Japanese soprano Eiko Nakamura in the trouser role of Annius. Eiko became friendly with my daughter Jamie and returned from Japan in 1983 to be present at her wedding. Others were Lorna Brindley, Margaret Gale and Brian Kemp. The autumn season included concerts, folk songs and drama.

Once again, in an all-round excellent cast in *Titus*, the beautiful smooth mezzo voice of Lorna Brindley convinced us all that we had a big star in the making. But it was not to be. I programmed *Dido and Aeneas* for her the following year, and by then the glow was lost. The Glyndebourne chorus had made her sing with the sopranos that summer and the security of tone had gone. That story comes later.

I was having trouble with Better Books in London. Mindful of the need to find other premises, I rented what had been a shirt shop opposite Foyle's, so that whatever happened we would still have a presence on Charing Cross Road, and I moved poetry onto the ground floor and the important film section into the basement, giving each more space than previously. I also felt the need to expand the Better Books concept to other cities, because there was a lamentable shortage of good intellectual bookshops in English cities, and the London shop was now producing more than ten percent of my London sales. As my presence in Scotland was now so major, I decided to start a Better Books in Scotland, and to put into practice, disastrously, as it turned out, what I had learned from Professor Saitzev in Zürich about holding companies. I approached those Scottish friends who were affluent enough and interested enough in the arts to raise funds for an Edinburgh Better Books, the idea being that 51 percent would be owned by the London company and 49 percent would come from individuals, mostly friends, who I was sure would all be good customers as well. Those who came forward to help included Jim Fraser, Tom Craig, Patrick Prenter, Daphne Kennedy-Fraser, all important supporters of Ledlanet. I found ideal premises near the university at 11 Forrest Row, a short street that ran from the Chaplaincy Centre of the university down to McEwan Hall, where I had held my two Edinburgh Conferences. It was L-shaped on a single floor and I had little difficulty in persuading other publishers to give longer than normal credit on the initial order, as the shop would be stocking many titles that could not be found elsewhere in Edinburgh. Jim Haynes' old Paperback was long gone. Charles Street had already been demolished before he left the town to go to London and the bookshop had gone with it. Nothing new had replaced it. The new bookshop opened with a party and instantly began to do good business. I shall return to it later.

There were many problems at the London Better Books and the biggest was finding and keeping a manager who was both competent and honest. When I went there sometimes at lunchtime and took over the till for a while I would count the money that was in it and it would nearly always be more than the amount shown on the roll, money that had been taken that morning. If I went back later in the day I would find that the surplus was even greater. This meant that whoever was at the till had deliberately rung up less than he had taken in order to pocket the surplus at the end of the day. This enabled me to catch some culprits red-handed, but not all, because usually more than one person would ring up the money taken during the course of the day. I should have shut down and started with a whole new staff, but either from a feeling of justice, that I had to be sure who the culprits were, or simply from procrastination, because I had so many things to worry about just then, I only fired those I caught. In retrospect I am sure that they were all in it, nor were they particularly vigilant in watching out for customer theft, which went on all the time.

One of the big names in publishing just then was Robert Lusty, Chairman of Hutchinson. He was a large man who liked the sound of his own voice, pontificated in the trade press and the newspapers, and I always felt that he was particularly critical of me, intervening for instance in the *UGH* correspondence in a negative and quite irrelevant way. I had noticed during 1970 that he had published Hitler's *Mein Kampf*, because it was there in Better Books, but as it was of some historical interest, I had not felt that it should not be stocked. But then something else happened. I was invited to debate with him on the BBC Overseas Service on the subject of what a publisher's responsibility was or should be. I do not remember much about the discussion except that he inferred I would publish anything to make money (Henry Miller, William Burroughs and other authors of controversial subject matter), whereas he took his responsibility seriously and would do no such thing. Returning from Bush House to Better Books, the first thing that caught my eye was a pile of books next to the till, just arrived from Hutchinson. It was the Memoirs, or rather the proud justification by Lieutenant Calley of his Vietnam experiences, in particular of his massacres of all the inhabitants of My Lai, which had occurred not long before. So much for Robert Lusty who would not publish a nasty book to make money! I told them to take it off the counter, put it somewhere inconspicuous, and try to persuade the Hutchinson rep to take the copies back the next time he called.

The publishing list kept expanding and while Marion bought a number of books from American publishers, some of which I found interesting and some not, I concentrated more on developing series that supported the way I viewed literature, as a continuing chain, where each generation tried to build on or revolt against what had gone before, being at the same time interested in the ideas that came from contemporaries in other fields, painting, music, the performance arts and new philosophical thinking. I started a series that I called French Surrealism for which I took on the novels of Raymond Roussel, a surrealist father figure, whose method was very close to André Breton's, collaborated with Viking in New York to publish the *Collected French Writings* of Arp, contracted Magritte's *Collected Writings*, made a selection of Eluard's Poems, bought Penrose's translations of Picasso's plays and added Artaud, Vitrac and others to the list, seeing these authors as the immediate ancestors of the *nouveau roman*, which I had been publishing from the late fifties. J. M. Ritchie, teaching German studies in Hull, approached me to translate German Expressionists and that became another series of almost limitless scope. The literary works of that school were many and hardly any translations had ever been attempted. I published two volumes of the plays of Georg Kaiser, banned by Hitler and dying in Zürich at the time I was a student there (Why had I not found out who was currently writing there and met them instead of discovering the classics? I asked myself) and Ritchie put together two anthologies, *Seven Expressionist Plays* and a collection of expressionist war plays entitled *Vision and Aftermath*. At the Frankfurt Fair I spotted a book called *Expressionismus*, a detailed history of the whole movement with fascinating articles by people who had created it and a Who's Who of the creators in all the arts disciplines. This became *The Era of German Expressionism*. I had already published books on expressionist music and I found more. The Zürich publisher Atlantis Verlag became both my source for many such musical books, and they took some of mine. Dr. Hürlimann, the director, was connected with the Zürich Opera as well as the publishing firm and we met, discussed music and exchanged contracts. When he died his successor, Dr. Bodmer, continued the relationship. Our *Signature* series of smaller books featured the author's signature on the front cover on a white background, and it was intended to include writers already distinguished, together with others whose reputation was only locally established, but of the same quality, an 'elite' collection planned in the days when that word was not yet a football of denigration used by the popular press to sneer at the whole concept of quality. We started with Robert Nye's *Darker Ends*. Nye was an Edinburgh friend of Bill Watson's, a critic, novelist and playwright, and in this collection his poems were natural, lyrical, wise and sensitive with sometimes a haiku eastern feel about them. We were also to publish two works of fiction about this time by Nye, who we thought would stay with us, but when he had discovered a best-selling formula, he moved to a bigger publisher. We followed this volume of poetry with experimental work by new (although not necessarily in their own country) work by Kenneth Gangemi (American), Nicholas Rawson (English and recommended to us by Beckett), Reinhard Lettau (German), Mark Insingel (Flemish), Ted Joans (Black American jazz poet), Peter Bichsel (Swiss), Yuli Daniel (Israeli), Robert Creeley (American), Christian Enzensberger (German), Lyman Andrews (American), Chris Searle (English) and Eugenio Montale (Italian, later to win the Nobel Prize). Through this collection of lesser-known names, at least to the British reading public, we threaded shorter works by Beckett, Sartre, Higgins, Trocchi (his poems) and Artaud, whose *Theatre and Its Double* would turn out to be one of our most important best-sellers in future years: it started life as Number Four in the series. Number Twenty was an anthology of eight writers that included Beckett, Ionesco and Ann Quin, together with shorter work by other quality writers. Many who appeared in the *Signature* series also appeared in the main list with full length works. What I was doing of course, although it did not occur to me at the time, was producing books for the future rare book and first edition market: many of those volumes are now in treasured collections. I forget what we printed on average, probably only a thousand or so. The prices were modest, ten shillings (50 pence) for the first, and I do not think any went over two pounds.

In 1970 we brought out our own mass-market edition of *Last Exit to Brooklyn*, but as a co-edition, with Corgi, who distributed it world-wide. I wrote a Foreword explaining the history of the book and the trial, and Anthony Burgess wrote an Introduction in which he said: '*Last Exit* presents social horrors out of reformist zeal, not out of a desire to titillate or corrupt. Those who found the book capable of debauching its readers were evidently most debauchable and regrettably cut off from a desire to expand their charitable propensities.'

I thought of David Shepherd and Sir Basil Blackwell on whom the book had had such a 'debauchable' reaction, and also of Sir Cyril Black, bringer of the prosecution, and his bald round head and hairless pink face, lay preacher and slum property landlord who in Burgess' words was certainly one of those 'cut off from a desire to expand their charitable propensities.'

Marion Boyars had now bought a large flat in Chelsea and wanted to do most of the entertaining there. Burroughs was a frequent visitor at her parties and continued writing slightly more conventional novels, but now he was interested in them being filmed; Anthony Balch, who had made a short, rather playful film in Marion's previous Paddington flat called *Towers Open Fire*, now wanted to film *The Naked Lunch*. There were contracts and options discussed and perhaps signed, but nothing came of it. I was however very aware that many people were trying to cash in on Burroughs' current celebrity for their own benefit and that, not belonging to either his particular world of drug addition or of homosexuality, I was often seen as a hindrance, a non-hip 'square'. Burroughs was in most ways unpractical and naïve, willing to get involved in new and often quite crazy schemes to exploit his talents, and I could see that he would soon be robbed as Henry Miller had been robbed by hangers-on, so I tried to keep in touch to protect him. Burroughs got involved in a scheme to set up an archive of his work in Lichtenstein, a con trick that soon collapsed, and for a while he was in the hands of the Scientologists. Having gone through their induction in London, he then went to the advanced course in Edinburgh, which must have cost him a considerable amount of money, staying at the same hotel in Neuington that I had put him in once before. I saw him there and afterwards on his return to London, but he was very vague about what had happened to him in Edinburgh. In London I made the mistake of taking him to the Caledonian Club one summer evening after meeting him for a drink at his flat off Piccadilly. First he kept lighting up cigarettes, which was not allowed in the dining room, and after he had put each one out at the request of the steward he would without thinking immediately light another. When telling me about Edinburgh in response to my questioning, because I was interested in Scientology, having known several people who had nearly been ruined by it, he got wilder and wilder, accusing the CIA and others of being involved with the whole mind-control conspiracy of its organisation and using 'fucking' as an adjective in every sentence. As he had no sense of decorum his voice got louder and the consternation of the other diners in a very conventional club was evident. Having had our first course, I cancelled the rest and took him out to a quiet restaurant nearby where it didn't matter. If we had stayed longer my resignation would have been demanded. Not too long after that, Burroughs left for New York, where Ginsberg managed to get him a lecturing job.

I often saw Will Hamling, whose involvement in civil rights and with persecuted minorities sometimes went a little too far. The PIE (Paedophile Information Exchange) was one of the many groups that belonged to the NCCL and I doubt if Tony Smythe knew much about them or some of the other persecuted minorities who had joined his organisation, which was itself not popular with the authorities. Will was willing to defend everyone and he took up cudgels for scientology, which was under attack by investigating journalists and the police, rightly in my view. They had a very attractive and charming female parliamentary lobbyist, and Will began taking her with him everywhere, although I am fairly sure that their relationship did not go beyond the social. I met her several times with him, both in the Commons and elsewhere, and she did have a sense of humour. She would drive past Overstrand Mansions in the morning during the period when I was staying there, and later remark to me that she knew exactly how much I had drunk the night before by the angle at which my car was parked. She was too clever to try to convert me, and I made no secret of what I thought of the organisation that employed her, but we remained on civil terms with each other.

The Arts Council's Working Party on Obscenity drew up two reports, one for reform and one for abolition. At our final joint session, having read the two reports, the whole working party decided to ditch the first and unanimously adopt the second. This had been drafted by Benn Levy, the playwright. I offered to publish the report but Lord Goodman wanted André Deutsch to be the publisher, and as usual he got his way: it duly appeared as *The Obscenity Laws*[29]. I am sure André made no money out of it unless the Arts Council gave him a subsidy, which is possible as the copyright is in their name. But Goodman was not pleased by the report itself or by its conclusions. 'You're crying for the moon,' he said to us at our last meeting. 'No parliament will ever pass a bill such as the suggested one you have drawn up in this report.' He had wanted us to recommend the setting up of a panel of educated and liberal people to decide what could be published and what not, and he ignored the report's carefully argued case that showed why this would not work. Although published, the report was quietly dropped.

The published report itself had been heavily censored: it only paraphrases what the witnesses who gave evidence actually said, being careful to avoid anything that the press might jump on, such as Shepherd's

---

[29] London 1969.

early homosexuality. The working party that is listed has only nineteen names on it, whereas we started with many times that, and it only gives the names of those associated with an organisation, while there were many individuals on the committee, some of them well-known. John Montgomerie, who had fought our case, and was Goodman's partner, chaired the Working Party and he was perfectly convinced by the final conclusions, but this was not made clear. I am listed as representing the DLAS. Strangely, Benn Levy is not mentioned as the author of the Report itself, and his name is not in the book at all. It was the *Last Exit* case and my call on Arnold Goodman with Anthony Gray that led to the whole thing, but in practice censorship did decline from that point. John Mortimer, who had been on the working party, fought some more obscenity prosecutions for which the DLAS found much of the cash. His successes and those of other barristers, eventually discouraged the DPP from bringing more actions.

I did have another prosecution involving Better Books in Edinburgh. There was a complaint to the police about Richard Handyside's publication of *The Little Red School Book*, which was made to look like the *Red Book* of the writings of Mao: it was an anarchic book for schoolchildren, telling them how to be rebellious to get a better, more interesting and less authoritarian education. I was not particularly favourable towards it, but Better Books stocked it. Once again I approached Laurence Dowdell in Glasgow and once again he picked Nicholas Fairbairn to defend it in court, which he did and won. It was shortly afterwards that a group of us spent Hogmanay at the George Hotel's dining room in Edinburgh, and Nikky Fairbairn was in the party. At one point, probably about midnight, he produced two miniature silver pistols out of his waistcoat pocket and fired them in the air. I think they were only loaded with blanks, but possibly not. The noise was as loud as full-sized pistols and everyone was startled. 'I just like shocking people,' said Nikky. At about two in the morning I had to negotiate the long road to Ledlanet through snow and thick fog, and made it. The breathalyser had not yet arrived on the scene, but it was a foolishness that I would not repeat in later years.

I also became more involved in the literary life of Scotland and found several Scottish authors. The novelists I took on included Elspeth Davie, George Friel, Stuart MaGregor, and John Elliott. The first was a Glasgow schoolteacher, whose novels were cautionary tales about local people, their obsessions and the tragedies to which they usually lead. Elspeth Davie was a beautiful writer, with a fine style, but imprisoned in a kind of ivory tower from which she contemplated people and the things that make them tick with a gentle humour that showed her very accurate powers of observation. She was married to George Davie, who taught Philosophy at the University, and they both appeared on the surface to be shy and retiring, but this was, I think, a good example of still waters going deep. Once I had Elspeth and George Friel to dinner together at the Doric Tavern, and I was amazed at the ferocity of which she was capable when the two writers disagreed about something. She asked me once, 'How can I find out what people do in offices?' I am not sure if she ever did, but I suggested that she should try to work in one for a while. I had a large second collection of her short stories, which I had contracted to publish, but short stories always being slow sellers, I had applied to the Scottish Arts Council for a grant to reduce both the price of a large book – it would have been her fourth book with us – and our risk. It was only later I found out why there was such a long delay to the application, so that in the end she took the book away and sold it to Hamish Hamilton. The Chairman of the Literature Panel of the Scottish Arts Council was Alexander Scott, a poet and an academic, who had earlier compiled with Norman MacCaig a large anthology of *Contemporary Scottish Verse*, for my Scottish Library series. Scott was annoyed with us for having picked Tom Scott instead of himself, to edit and see through the press the *Collected Poems* of Sydney Goodsir Smith, which happened in 1975, and he wanted to stop us getting any more grants out of revenge. When Hamish Hamilton applied for a much larger subsidy than we had requested, they received it instantly.

I have not yet talked about Sydney Goodsir Smith. He had taken part in the Scottish day of my first Edinburgh Conference in 1962, and had on that occasion imbibed too much of the whisky that we had put in carafes on the table. I had called on him frequently after that at his hospitable flat in Drummond Place, where only too often I had myself imbibed rather too much, on one occasion sleeping through most of *Don Giovanni* after spending an afternoon with him. He was great company, with a wonderful sense of humour, a major Scottish poet, and together with Hugh MacDiarmid one of the two major figures on the Edinburgh literary scene. Sydney was Art Critic for The Scotsman, had written plays and much else beside poetry, and many volumes of his verse were in editions published by a variety of different Scottish publishers. For some time I thought about trying to collect his many poems, some of them out of print, into a single volume and finally through Robin Richardson made an offer, which was accepted. Robin somehow managed to get the agreement of many small Scottish imprints to let me publish a *Collected Poems* and this project went ahead; although it did not appear until 1975 after his premature death at only fifty-nine. I shall return to Sidney's poems shortly.

He was in every way a good and hospitable friend, loving everything old and comfortable. 'Old clothes, old furniture, old wine and old barleycorn' as he put it. He would come to Ledlanet to review our art exhibitions, stay for performances, and get back to Edinburgh driven by a friend or possibly by Hazel, his wife, who taught art at a school. I loved his poems, especially a new collection that was published in 1969 by Southside, an Edinburgh firm, as *Fifteen Poems and a Play*. The play was *Full Circle*, which became one of the new operas that Scottish opera were commissioning from Scottish composers just then; it had music by Robin Orr, Chairman at the time of Scottish Opera, having earlier been the Professor of Music at Cambridge of many of those who now worked for this burgeoning company, including Peter Hemmings, the General Manager. But the poems that appealed to me most in that volume were a short one *Said Heraclitus*, and a long one, to which I shall come. *Said Heraclitus* is about a problem that has largely ruled my life, the fatal attraction of a new lady that you meet when you are still fully involved with another, perhaps more than one other. Heraclitus said that everything is in flux, and as Smith so well describes it, it can apply to love as well, which I have experienced to my cost. Take the second stanza:

Aathin passes, aathing dees,
aathing an end maun hae:
This is the greit in the hairt o' things,
The *rerum lacrimae*.

The poem is bittersweet, pagan, regretful that things are the way they are. Other mortals suffer the pangs of desire and the pain of guilt, but poets understand very well that the tragedy we bring on ourselves is the very stuff of art, and the function of poetry is to express it. Erich Fried could not understand how his very English first wife could not understand his need for other women: 'A poet must always be in love,' he told her, 'and always with someone new.' Smith says:

But as we twyne, juist as we twyne
Anither trust draws near.

And so I have found it. Reader, you may by now intensely dislike the author of this book, but I hope it is an honest one. At any rate Sidney tells me that I am not alone in my long inability to resist temptation. His Scottish dialect, although difficult for some readers, adds, in my view, to the poignancy of the poem.

The long poem in the same volume is called *The Twa Brigs* and it was commissioned by the BBC for the opening of the Forth Road Bridge, and first read on the radio in 1964. It is a philosophical poem about the meaning of bridges, which join things, and in lyrical terms it is about the love of the Old Rail Bridge ('Auld Stumpy') for the new young and 'bonny, like a sprite' Road Bridge. It is to me the perfect poem: it has so much humour, and is colloquial in manner, bringing in history, associative thought and tenderness. I would reread it often at Ledlanet and finally I decided to find a composer to set it to music. I do not know or remember who suggested William Wordsworth, an English composer based in Scotland, but it was a good suggestion and when I brought Bill Wordsworth together with Sidney they got on like a house on fire. The Scottish Arts Council were persuaded to back the project and I programmed the work for performance in June 1973.

Sidney belonged to that group of Scottish literati who were strong nationalists, but with none of the hardness and nastiness I had come to associate with the SNP during my first election campaign. They were a colourful lot, and I particularly knew MacDiarmid, Smith, Douglas Young and some of the younger figures like Alan Bold and Stuart Conn. Douglas Young, an immensely tall bearded figure who looked like an old testament prophet, was Professor of Greek at Saint Andrews University. He had stood several times for parliament for the SNP and liked to tell jokes in Greek at election meetings. He was a good poet and also did some remarkable translations from Greek drama into Scots dialect. The grand old man was of course Hugh MacDiarmid (Chris Grieve) who had translated from many languages into English or Scots, but not without (as I later discovered) the help of earlier translations which he used as cribs. But his own output of poetry was enormous and his most famous poem *The Drunk Man Looks At the Thistle*, a long rumination by a thinking man who had fallen into a ditch, is a major classic now. I knew and liked Chris Grieve. In the Kinross by-election in 1963 where I had fielded Rushton, I had myself voted for Chris, who was running as a Communist at the time, purely because I knew him and he was a good poet, and because it was clear that Sir Alec would win in my case. After his death in 1978 I wrote a letter of sympathy to his widow in which I mentioned that I was one of the forty-three persons who had voted for Chris in Kinross. The editor of a woman' magazine (I think it was Anne Barr) wrote to various widows that year offering to print the most interesting letters of sympathy that they had received, and mine was one of those selected. When I went to New York some time later, I was stopped at Immigration by the official looking at my passport and checking it with his files. 'You're a Communist, Mr. Calder,' he said to me.

'No, I'm not,' I said, 'and I never have been.'

'But you've voted Communist.'

'Absolutely not.' Then I remembered the by-election and laughed, remembering too the letter to Valda, Chris' widow. I explained the situation to the Immigration officer who was plainly not amused and had never heard of MacDiarmid. But he did let me in, warning me I might be watched.

* * * * * *

After Sam Beckett won the Nobel Prize in 1969, he was pursued by the press, had difficulty in protecting his privacy and came under much greater pressure from his publishers to let them bring out those earlier works which he had been happy to see out of print. Eventually he became tired of saying no and agreed in most cases to allow his publishers to do what they wished. I had long wanted to reissue his early book of linked short stories *More Pricks Than Kicks*, first published in 1934 by Chatto and Windus, who now claimed that they had the right to reprint. Sam had allowed me to bring out 100 copies of a mimeographed typescript edition, only to be sold to scholars, in 1966, and another 100 in 1967. His weariness from the pressure – not much of it from me, because if Sam said 'No' I did not ask again – but from his other publishers and Barnet Rosset in particular, led to his agreeing to a commercial reprint of *More Pricks*. He wrote me that he had said 'Yes' to Barney, so I could proceed too. As Barney and I were not collaborating at this time, I put the book into production on my own. Before it was ready I went one day to Paris, and had a date to meet Sam for lunch at the Closerie des Lilas. When I arrived, straight from Orly, I could see that there was filming going on outside the restaurant, and going in I saw Sam sitting with Peter O'Toole, taking a break from his film to talk to an author whom he already knew and whom he had for some time been trying to persuade to let him appear in a filmed version of *Godot*. On my arrival O'Toole returned to the cameras and Sam turned to me with a worried look. 'I'd better get it out of the way now,' he said and opening his brief-case he pulled out the proofs of *More Pricks Than Kicks* that Barney had sent him. 'I can't let this old shit come out again,' he said. 'I'm sorry, but I've already written to Barney, and I'm afraid I have to stop you, too.' I took it with the best grace I could and we talked of other things. It was probably the threat from Chatto, to whom he had earlier written that he did not want it published again, but that if it was, it had to be by me, that led to his changing his mind a couple of weeks later and telling me to go ahead after all. It came out in 1970 and has had numerous reprints ever since. It was Barney's misjudgement in sending him proofs that had led to the hiccup. There was no need for the author to check a text again that was already fully proof-read. He also translated his post-war novella *First Love*, also suppressed until now, and that came out with us the same year. The only logical reason for the suppression, as with many of his other writings, was that the character of his protagonist was too close to the person that he really was. When writing he could not help putting himself into situations that paralleled his experience, but that retrospectively he found embarrassing.

At this time Beckett was being very productive, but moving towards ever greater economy of language. Many of the prose texts he produced were almost of novel length, but by cutting and pruning he reduced them to the length of a short novella. The same was true of his plays, ever shorter and more concentrated, although *Happy Days* still makes a whole evening. I may have been the first to read the typescript of this, because Beckett showed it to me when staying with Bettina and myself at Wimpole Street, and I cannot pretend that I really understood it at the time. But with Beckett instant appreciation of a text is rare: it yields up its secrets with rereading and one nearly always finds new felicities each time one returns to it. *Happy Days* was done by Madeleine Renaud in Paris, directed by Barrault her husband, who also played Willie. In London it was Brenda Bruce, a very conventional actress. Sam came for the rehearsals, went away unhappy, having with difficulty made the director and Brenda Bruce do things his way, but once he was gone, the production slipped into a less stylised format. Sam followed *First Love* with a translation of his immediate post-war novel, *Mercier and Camier* into English; after that he wrote short work only. One text, only a few pages long, *Imagination Dead Imagine*, we published on its own with a photograph of a Giacometti skull on the cover[30], and amazingly it sold well and had to be reprinted. The National Theatre approached me to perform it at their new Cottesloe performance space, and three actors delivered the text wearing black costumes on an empty stage with no decor. Beckett was now a well-known name and everyone wanted to perform him. He stayed with me again during the run of *Play* at the National. He was very struck during rehearsals by Billie Whitelaw who had been cast in it with Rosemary Harris and Robert Stephens and he remained devoted to her for the rest of his life, writing many parts for her in his later stage works. I sat through one rehearsal of *Not I* when Billie was overtired because she had been up all night with her sick son. Sam was making every effort to curb his natural impatience, because usually by the time he attended rehearsals all the actors were word-perfect, and Billie was certainly not. Several 'Fuck's proceeded from her mouth as she struggled to master her lines, her situation made more difficult because her face was hidden and only the mouth showed. A string of new Beckett publications, all short and very condensed, came out then and during the seventies, Faber doing the plays and Calder and Boyars the prose and poetry. The latter went through many editions and we continually added new work and Sam's untranslated poems as well. He was now selling much better than Miller and Burroughs, from whom we were getting more benefit from mass-market paperback royalties than from our own editions.

Publishing had changed considerably during the previous decade and would soon change again. Most novels had only a single hardback edition, which went increasingly to public libraries and which received reviews in the press with fairly small and diminishing bookshop sales; then a paperback contract was negotiated with a mass market imprint, which then achieved the major sales, so that trade publishers like myself of what would later be called 'consumer books' depended more and more for the bulk of their revenue on paperback royalties and not from their own sales. Increasingly authors became less happy about this and literary agents representing them began to demand the lion's share of money from the paperback for the author, whereas until then it was a fifty-fifty split. To keep their authors, publishers began to except 45 percent and then forty and sometimes less. And the next step was that paperback companies, being now in a position to approach authors and agents directly where a big sale was anticipated, would buy all the rights, sometimes bringing out their own hardcover or issuing a book directly in paperback without one. Our period of discovering and publishing best-selling authors was now over, not least because censorship had almost disappeared. Our most profitable days were over and soon we would have to

---

[30] *Head on a Stalk.*

rely almost entirely on the sales we could get from books that did not interest the mass market.

Publishing was getting more difficult and I also had Better Books on my hands where the sales were good but wiped out by both customer and staff theft that kept growing. During 1970 the theft came to about £40,000 and I could see major trouble ahead as I looked for new shareholders for the bookshop in London as well as in Edinburgh. I was also still the prospective candidate for my constituency, aware that an election was possible at any time. As a financial crisis was likely to come to a head at exactly the time I might have to go to the hustings, I resigned some time in 1972 in order not to embarrass my mentors and the party. A Glasgow school-teacher was found to replace me. He was pleasant, but did not have what I would have considered the right sort of personality for this particular constituency. At the next election, which was not until February 1974, he did however get an increased vote. But before my resignation I had done a considerable amount of what was called 'community politics', which meant looking into local parochial issues, ferreting out the various discontents that people gossiped about in their villages, and associating myself with a campaign to do something about them. I was particularly successful in this some time during the winter that came next, managing to speak up during a protest meeting at Rannoch where the representatives of all parties were present. At the point where the representative for Perth County said that it was too early to do anything, I said, 'Yes. Now you say it is too early and next we shall hear it is too late. I propose that at this meeting we set up an emergency committee to investigate and come up with a solution. Let's have a show of hands right now.' It was exactly what the Conservatives did not want. A considerable majority voted to set up a committee and I was on it. It was still in existence when I decided to resign.

It was on another occasion at Rannoch that we heard the news on the radio – a group of us including Margaret Begg and the Beiths had spent the night at the local hotel, after holding a meeting there – that there had been a riot among the students at Stirling University, and that the Queen, who had been opening a new building, had been insulted by a group of undergraduate drunks and all the tabloids were up in arms, demanding disciplinary measures, including even closing down this, the newest of Britain's universities. The Principal was a chemist called Cottrell, a charming, cultured and well-meaning man, who had, some time previously, been offered a large sum of money by a Mrs. MacRobert in her will. The lady had died a widow and left the money in memory of her husband and her three sons who were all killed in the war. The new building was put up, named after the family, and to the general surprise, Dr. Cottrell did not build a block of new laboratories or lecture halls, but instead, an arts centre. The MacRobert Centre was a full sized theatre with bars, restaurant, a bookshop and many other facilities, a venue for visiting theatre, opera and dance companies, for concerts and for university performances. It became a regular venue for Scottish Opera and for both Scottish and English theatres to bring their productions. Cottrell put together a board of advisors of about twenty distinguished people, which included such arts personalities as John Denison who having previously been Music Officer of the Arts Council in London, was now General Manager of the Royal Festival Hall, and others who had to come north for the meetings. I was on it and attended half a dozen sessions where the vision and ambitious plans of the University Principal for the MacRobert Centre amazed and delighted me. Now he was in serious trouble. The visit of the Queen was the climax of a new fund-raising drive to put up such new buildings as he might well have done in the past with the MacRobert money, and the behaviour of a few students, put on the front pages of the national press, effectively ensured that no one would donate, either individuals or institutions. I am told that it devastated Cottrell and not long afterwards he died. I cannot remember how or whether it was by his own hand.

I see from an old diary that I was busy all over the constituency in 1971, but do not have one for 1972, so it must have been somewhere late that year or early the next that I resigned as candidate for Kinross and West Perthshire. I was then well known all over the constituency and I still have the feeling that I would eventually have won it, if not at the next election then quite possibly at one of the two after that, because I knew a great deal about local issues, had started action groups in many places, and was trusted. My continual activity showed up the almost permanent absence of the sitting MP, who was then no longer Prime Minister, but now the Foreign Minister in the Heath government. But resign I did, and my successor reaped much benefit from my hard work.

I cannot say that my various crises blew over, but the urgency became less, and being by now a political animal who was attending both the national conferences at English seaside resorts and the Scottish ones in different northern venues, I had an itch to get another constituency, and I was given Dunfermline. Before that I offered myself to Hove, which I knew well, having canvassed there in a by-election for Des Wilson. I was on the short list of three, but did not get the nomination, and thereafter decided to stick to Scotland. For a year I repeated in Dumfermline what I had done earlier nearer home, found out the local issues, knocked on doors and my biggest success was in getting a housing group going in an urban area that had the most crime and worst vandalism. A rather eccentric local male nurse became involved and was soon Chairman of the group that organised a watch committee, created playgrounds to keep children out of mischief, and organised sports and social events. I felt I was getting somewhere. On one occasion the candidates for all parties (with no general election imminent) were challenged to swim two lengths of the local Olympic pool. The Labour man begged off, I agreed although I had a bad cold, which the swim might have cured because I felt better afterwards, but the Tory won, not surprisingly, as he once had been a navy diver. Had I stayed I would have eventually found myself running against Jim Fraser who was later to become the Tory candidate, but the constituency was normally Labour and it remained so. There was a worsening of my financial situation, the Better Books problem now being augmented by divorce proceedings with Bettina. I had made every effort to be helpful to her, even voluntarily paying the premium on her new duplex at Glengower Mansions in South Kensington, but she constantly brought me to court to demand more maintenance, and involved me in heavy legal expenditure, which made it necessary to resign once again as a candidate. Had I not I would have fought the General Election of February 1974. I helped the new candidate for Kinross instead.

Through all this I was keeping in touch with authors, reading manuscripts, signing contracts, correcting proofs, editing, answering letters and attending to as much as possible of the routine work of the publishing company. Marion did most of the commercial work and looked after her own authors, having taken over as well many who used to be mine because they stayed with her when in London, people like Robert Creeley whose early short stories and first novel *The Island* I had published before Marion came into the firm, as well as a considerable amount of his poetry. Michael Hayes was now our Sales Director. When his predecessor, George Allum, suddenly died, I had thought of Michael because he had previously been with Peter Owen who he did not personally like and had then gone to Trade Counter, our distributor. I had known Michael for some years, meeting him at Booksellers conventions and other trade events and going, on one invited visit to Lepizig, with Peter Owen and he. There were two hotel rooms at our disposal during the four day visit to the Leipzig Book Fair, a Fair that only East German publishers, party officials and foreigners were allowed to attend – local people and especially students, desperate to get in, were excluded – and it was hoped by those who invited us that we would buy rights to East German books and do some printing there. Michael wanted to share a room with me rather than with Peter, but I said No. Owen blotted his copybook on that occasion by taking too much advantage of our hosts. Our fares, hotel and meals were free, but Peter added a large drink bill to it, while I scrupulously paid all my extras, doing good business with them as a result, whereas Peter was frozen out. When Michael joined us he became an invaluable member of the team and took most of the sales headaches on himself. Unfortunately his need to increase his income sometimes led to his firing good reps, including one excellent one who covered London, Michael Ellison, in order to do his job himself and thereby acquire his commission, which reduced the time he was able to give to other work. The day came when Michael felt that by working for a literary publishing company rather than a larger commercial one he had spoiled his long-term prospects; and he left with rather bad grace to work for a firm of mass-market paperback distributors. I had liked him and was sorry that our relationship ended with a certain amount of hostility, although I knew he disliked Marion more than me.

One of my Scottish authors was the folk singer Matt McGinn. He wrote his own songs, delivered them in a raucous thick Clydeside accent, unnaccompanied, and he sometimes acted as well. He starred at the Glasgow Citizen's small theatre space, The Close, in a show called *Red Clydeside*, which gave the history of the city's revolutionary past, and he was in the second production of Edinburgh Festival Productions, a very Scottish *Macbeth*. This was performed at the Festival on the fringe the year after *Happy End*. The production was packaged by Robin Richardson, managed by his son, and had Leonard Maguire as a splendid Macbeth with Matt McGinn alternating with another actor as the Porter. Although he was a left-wing socialist, Matt came to campaign for me in the various election campaigns in which I was involved after that first baptism of fire in 1970, and he became a good friend in many ways. He wrote an autobiographical novel about his childhood experience, about when, during the war, he had been sent to a Catholic Reform school for stealing a bag of sweets from a stationer. The novel, full of gallows humour, rings true with its sadistic monks, harsh treatment of the small boys incarcerated and pen portraits of Glasgow characters. I published it and sold serial rights to a new evening newspaper that Robert Maxwell had just launched in Scotland, which gave it local publicity. Many Glasgow bookshops did not want to stock the book because they were politically biased against the author, but customers demanded it and they had to. Called *Fry the Little Fishes*, it did quite well and Matt started on another book, but never finished it. This was because he split up with his wife, got totally drunk in a room on his own on Hogmanay, knocked over an oil lamp, and burned himself to death. I hope he was too drunk to feel it. I went to his funeral one cold snowy day in early January. When the driver of the taxi I had picked up at the station, after getting off the sleeper from London, heard who was being cremated he parked his taxi and joined the queue with me to get in. Ahead of me on the snowy path was Billy Connolly, another popular Glasgow folk singer and character who had performed at Ledlanet, and we shook our heads together over Matt's tragic ending. There was no service, but a gathering that was more like a political rally, with Norman Buchan, an MP who was a friend and had supported me in my censorship battles, giving a fiery speech about Matt's career as a radical and a creator of hundreds of songs. At the end we all sang the *Internationale* and went out, feeling warmer, into the falling snow.

One day I was in Better Books in London when my daughter Jamie walked in. 'Hello, Daddy,' she said. 'I've left my mother and here I am. I've come back to live with you.' It was unexpected and a shock, but fortunately I had by then left the studio and was now in a flat in Dalmeny House in South

Kensington, opposite the Victoria and Albert Museum. I rearranged my life and Jamie, now a grown-up young lady, moved into my spare room.

It was quite a nice flat with two bedrooms, a big sitting room, a study that I hardly ever used, preferring a long oak table in the hall that also had several hundred of my books on the shelves, so that the study, which had a couch, became more of a place to put up the odd guest. One person who stayed there was Nikolai Bokov. April FitzLyon had told me about a Russian samizdat novel that had come to her, written by a Moscow dissident. The principal character in the story was a total drop-out whose brother was a journalist, and it was a hilarious satire on the whole bureaucracy of the Soviet regime, basically describing the life of a group of bohemians who would not conform to the system; it also showed evidence of a growing religious revival among the oppressed intellectual classes. April translated it and I published it as *Nobody*, giving the author's name as Nikto, which means the same in Russian. It did not do very well, but I sold it to an American religious publisher, and eventually had a visit from the author who had left Moscow with a visa for Israel, where he never went; nor was he Jewish. Nikolai Bokov stayed with me several days, gave me more manuscripts, which April translated, and they appeared in my New Writing series. He wanted to read every book on my shelves and was fascinated by my art books, poring over them for hours. Then he went to Paris and found a job with La Pensée Russe, a revanchist Russian newspaper where I visited him once. The office walls were hung with portraits of the late Czar and his family, and photographs of pre-Revolutionary Russia. Then I lost touch with him.

One of the authors I began to publish at this time was Naomi May. She came from a similar background to my own, a Scottish industrial family with large estates, and she was married to a Northern Irish accountant, whose father, Dermot May, had once been prime minister. I came to know Naomi and her husband Nigel quite well and was amused by their total loyalty to the Unionist cause and Nigel's to the Orange order. All their friends seemed very like themselves, especially after they moved to London with violence escalating in Ulster. I published *At Home* first, a picture of a man surrounded by three women, two sisters and his wife, set in Hampstead and with a surprise ending. Then came *The Adventuress*, a novel about her own Scottish background with the heroine a thinly disguised picture of herself, and thirdly I published a novel about the beginnings of the Civil Rights Movement and the beginnings of IRA activity. This was called *Troubles* and I went to Belfast to get her interviewed on the BBC, to push the book in local bookshops and give a party for the author. On the day I was there I could on two occasions hear bombs going off in the distance and the receptionist at the BBC, while Naomi was being interviewed by Sean Rafferty, said to me with resignation, 'You just have to learn to live with it.'

It was impossible to give a party inside Belfast, but Naomi had found a hotel outside the town. This was surrounded by three circles of barbed-wire, which one had to negotiate before one could get in. About a hundred people came, among them Sean Rafferty. I saw his cold blue eyes surveying the crowd of upper-class Ulster Protestants and knew instinctively that he was a Catholic. In a day I had developed that Belfast instinct that enabled people there to smell out on which side of the divide the person you are talking to belongs. It was very similar to what I had known from Montreal, but there it was the language that was the give-away. I was to see Sean more in the future. Naomi's books never did well for reasons that I could never fathom. They were all social novels in the British tradition, very readable, the characters well drawn and the plots full of surprises. Some of her short writing went into New Writers. But the reviews were not positive and I never had any success in selling them to mass-market paperback companies.

I was invited one night to a big European Community Dinner given for Willi Brandt, then I think Mayor of Berlin or possibly he had become Chancellor. Next to me sat Alastair Dunnett of The Scotsman whom I had known well since my cancelled talk at the Church of Scotland's General Assembly. I was catching a train that night to Edinburgh because I had been invited the next morning, a Sunday, to give the sermon in St. Mary's, a well-known Episcopal Church, that Sir Walter Scott had attended. When I told Alastair, he shook his head, 'Episcopal: No good will come of that.' But I went, intending to read the three short paragraphs that preface Bertrand Russell's autobiography, entitled *Why I Have Lived*, which I consider the most perfect and beautifully phrased *apologia pro vita sua* that I had ever come across. I then intended to expand on those words. I had prepared nothing else, being now so accustomed to public speaking that I had total confidence in myself to come up with something appropriate. But this time I couldn't. I read the Russell aloud with as much expression as I could, drew a deep breath and then found that I had nothing else to say. It was all in those three paragraphs. Haltingly, I explained my inability to follow such a beautiful text with anything that might demean it and stood down. Mr. Veitch, the minister, was very disappointed.

I had met a lady who I shall here call Alice, not her real name because I do not think that she would be happy if I gave it. She was the girlfriend of Charles Marovitz and I met her during Peter Brook's Theatre of Cruelty season at RADA, which was largely staged by Charles, and it gave Glenda Jackson her first major chance to star. Alice was selling tickets at the box office which had been set up for the occasion and I remember being very impressed by her at the time. Then one evening Marovitz and I were both on a large BBC programme as part of an invited group of people in the arts brought together to discuss where the arts were going or some similar subject. It was chaired by Huw Weldon and there were far too many of us for anyone to say very much, but I remember that the inspiration came from my Edinburgh Conferences, the atmosphere of which the BBC was trying to recreate. Afterwards Charles invited me back for a drink and I met Alice again, who was then living with him. At one point I looked down and saw a white rat with its front paws on my toecap looking up at me. Disbelieving, I said slowly, wondering if I could have drunk too much, 'I think there's a white rat standing on my shoe.'

'Usually we get a stronger reaction,' said Charles, and he explained that it was Alice's pet rat.

Charles and Alice split up, and running into her again, I began taking her out to dinner. I suppose my intentions were quite obvious, but I did not receive any particular encouragement and when I did propose a more intimate liaison she put me off. But it did finally happen and she became my regular girlfriend, keeping her flat in Regent's Park (she had by that time surreptitiously buried her dead rat in a nearby churchyard), where I sometimes spent the night, while she often stayed with me. But my lifestyle did not suit her: too many evenings were spent at the opera, at a restaurant afterwards and then home. She was also very suspicious of all the other ladies in my life, not without good reason, although at that time I was so fascinated by Alice that as far as I can remember I was seeing no one else, except perhaps socially. Alice came with me to Cap Ferrat, spent much time at Ledlanet, where she was very popular with everyone, and other than her natural female possessiveness I can think of nothing to say against her. She was extremely pretty, always smiling, had a quick wit, had acted in drama and at the time I knew her she was working for a film company, where making tarama for the office lunch seemed her main occupation, but decorative and witty girls with nice personalities are frequently to be found in film company offices. She was an important part of my life for perhaps two years or longer. She overheard a telephone call that she did not like one day and walked out. I kept putting off calling her to ask her to come back, thinking quite genuinely that she deserved better than me, but did not do so. After that we met infrequently. I will have to bring Alice back into this narrative a little later for events that were much earlier than our parting, but if she ever reads this, I hope she will realise that I missed her very much.

* * * * *

At Ledlanet, after a spring season consisting of concerts and miscellaneous events including the folk-singing duo of Robin Hall and Jimmie MacGregor, familiar to our audience from their nightly appearance on BBC television after the main news analysis programme, we started again in June with Haydn's *Creation* with three of our regular singers, Patricia Hay, John Robertson and John Graham, accompanied by the SBE and our own chorus. The chorus master was now Gordon Mabbot, and Roderick Brydon conducted. We had seven performances by Opera for All, giving us three popular works and then mounted our own production of two baroque operas, *Pimpinone* (Telemann) and Monteverdi's *The Cruel Ladies*, which I have mentioned earlier. This was conducted by an immensely tall American, Adrian Sunshine, who much favoured the first work, although I preferred the second, in which Patricia Purcell was a dominating Venus, Hazel Wood an effective Cupid and Richard Angas, also immensely tall, was Pluto. Sheila McGrow, a flexible and always pretty and vivacious soprano, sang in both works. The programmes must have been printed before we engaged Lindsay Kemp, because his name is not in it. He led the procession of cruel ladies back into Hades, where they are being tormented for having preferred to remain virgins than to say yes to men, after Cupid had brought them to the overworld to persuade the audience not to be like them. It was Monteverdi's clever operatic joke, written for a wedding in Mantua in 1608. The audience loved it, but not a distinguished diplomat who someone had brought to Ledlanet. He did not like Brian Mahoney's updating to contemporary Glasgow, where it was set in the wedding dress department of Goldberg's glitzy department store. The Goldbergs were corporate members of Ledlanet, but I am not sure that they saw it. The programme for that June-July season in 1971 had an advertisement announcing the opening of Better Books in Edinburgh during the forthcoming Edinburgh Festival.

I must go back to 1969 to tell of another experiment of mine. I had come to know the Church of Scotland Minister of Easterhouse, Peter Youngson. He was tall, red-headed and athletic, and had studied singing with Gottlob Frick while in the British army in Germany and had intended to enter opera as a career, being much encouraged by his teacher. But on leaving the army he had decided that he had a call from God and he entered the Church of Scotland. He had the worst parish in the country because Easterhouse, a dormitory suburb where many of the old Gorbals tenement-dwellers had been rehoused, then had the highest rate of violent crime in Britain. On the surface it contained neat little bungalows, each with its garden and television aerial, but there was absolutely nothing for children or teenagers to do, no playgrounds or sports fields, no entertainment at all except for watching television with parents at home. There were only one or two shops and a public house called the Ali Baba, which had a sign outside: NO GENTLEMEN ADMITTED WITHOUT A LADY, which said it all; males alone or in groups meant trouble. Easterhouse was notorious all over Glasgow, indeed all over Scotland for its gang violence. Having nothing else to do, the teenagers had gradually formed into street gangs that would then fight each other, their weapons becoming ever more deadly, and by the time Peter Youngson arrived to take over his church, there had already been several killings, mostly with knives. The younger children formed their own gangs in imitation of their elders, so while the parents stayed home in the evenings and looked at television, all around them was a culture of violence that affected all ages down to six or seven. And the girls, many of them, got involved in the street and gang loyalties as well as the boys.

Peter Youngson tried to do something about all that. He had dances in his church on Friday and Saturday nights, brought in bands to play dance music, started classes and organised games. This initiative was not popular with many of his elders who thought the church should be for religion and nothing else. He put on dramatic spectacles, often with music so that he could use his fine bass voice. One Easter he put on a passion play. In his congregation he found a genuine masochist who was suspended by ropes from a cross in delicious agony for half an hour during the performance. I am not sure how we met, but I used him to understudy my bass principal singers, and on Members' Nights gave him his own spot, when he loved to sing Mephistopheles' arias from Guonod or Boito or Berlioz. On one occasion I recommended him to speak on social deprivation and how it affected places like Easterhouse at the Scottish Liberal Conference, and he went down very well.

I conceived the idea of doing *Romeo and Juliet* in Easterhouse, which is a play about gang warfare as much as a love story. I knew that through his various activities Peter Youngson had brought many young people in their late teens out of the gang-war situation and he was always looking for new ways to keep them busy and interested, and so much the better if such ways could also be educational. We finally agreed to mount the play with professional actors, who I could easily get from the Glasgow Citizens Theatre, which is less active in the summer, and using about twenty of his young followers; their role would be to act out the crowd scenes, to dance, to fight, and to be the people of Verona. We would play for a week at Ledlanet, and a week in Easterhouse in his church, which could seat eight hundred. I approached the Arts Council for some extra funds and was turned down flat. They were entirely opposed to the idea. There was a fairly new director called Sandy Dunbar in the job at this time, who had previously been with Northern Arts in Newcastle on Tyne. He had his own circle of cronies, many of whom had followed him north, and he liked to support the arts in terms of what was most acceptable to the establishment and best for his own prestige. Mavericks and experimenters like myself did not appeal to him. I had no encouragement in Glasgow either. The councillors were much in the mould of Teddy Taylor, who was or would be the quintessential working class Tory MP (many Labour MPs were not dissimilar), always in favour of hanging, flogging, tougher prisons and the most restrictive family values. I was not even allowed to put up a poster at the Mitchell Library for a Shakespeare play because it did not have official civic blessings. But Peter and I went ahead anyway.

There were weeks of rehearsals, first in the church, later at Ledlanet. The actors had a little trouble accepting the Easterhousers at first, but they very soon began to get on well and the amateurs were very anxious to learn as much as possible from the professionals who they found glamorous. They learned to dance renaissance dances and how to fence and fight with swords without hurting each other: they learned how to swagger, how to gesture, how to express a whole range of emotions. The company began to bond together, and by the time we moved to Ledlanet for the last week of rehearsals on the stage, all Peter's teenagers knew the play by heart and were hoping that illness or an accident would give them opportunities to move into a speaking part. It was a good company with Maev Alexander as Juliet and Denis Lawson as Romeo and directed by Euan Smith. Edith Ruddick played the Nurse.

It was very hard work for me. We had a minibus at Ledlanet now, and every evening either I or Eddie Strachan would have to drive it to a pickup point to collect all the extras, many of whom had daytime jobs in Glasgow, and drive them to Ledlanet and back after rehearsals. Once we were performing, they had to be driven back late at night. But *Romeo and Juliet* was a great success with our audiences, and the teenagers from a Glasgow suburb were very impressed by the atmosphere of Ledlanet, to them a grand house, but functioning like a factory.

Then we had the week in Easterhouse. We brought what scenery we needed to the church, and I would spend the whole day putting leaflets through doorways, getting the ice-cream van to take them round, stopping people in the street, and doing a little flyposting. Just before the first night I had a fugue. Although I apparently functioned normally and did all the things I had to do, I suddenly realised, at about seven o'clock, when the crowd was arriving, that I had no recollection of anything that had happened since four in the afternoon. I had spoken to people and done things, but my mind for those three hours was blank. When I spoke to my doctor, he said it was a 'fugue' brought on no doubt by stress, but there was no explanation.

But the play worked in Easterhouse and I think a large part of the town must have gone to it, because there were few empty spaces on the pews. But Peter Youngson was having his own problems just then. He had played a major part in organising the early stages of the production, but after the first week had done less and less. After the first two nights in his church he disappeared and I was told that he had gone skin-diving up north, but that everyone had been told to co-operate with me and to let me use the church hall as well as the church, including for a final party. The reason, as I later discovered, was that he had fallen in love with one of his parishioners and did not know what to do after she had confessed a similar desire for him. He was a married man, probably with children. After his return when the play was over, he apparently had a break-down and was sent to a special home for Church of Scotland ministers with mental health problems, and after that to a very conventional church in a very middle-class town in Fife.

The play ran from Monday to Saturday and I gave a last-night party in the church hall for the cast and everyone who had worked on the production. I told all the youngsters that they could bring one person, boyfriend or girlfriend. But they were apprehensive and told me that there was a rumour that the worst of the local gangs intended to break into the party. I locked the door that led to the outside, and when everyone was in, locked the door to the church as well. There was wine, beer and soft drinks with bits of food and sandwiches. The party had not been going for long when there came a loud banging on the outer door. 'What do you want?' I called out. The room had gone deathly quiet. 'We're comin' in,' said a voice outside.

'No, you're not,' I replied. 'This is a private party.'

'There's drink in there and we're comin' in. Open the door or we'll break it down.'

'That's Rick,' said one of the youngsters. I knew all about Rick. He had knifed two people and killed one, but the police had never been able to pin anything on him because everyone was too frightened to give testimony against him. 'Stand right behind me and watch everything carefully,' I said to the crowd behind me. 'I'll try to talk him out of it.' I was as nervous as a cat, but felt that if I could not out-face a nineteen year old, I was not worth much. There was a spotlight in the hall, which I switched on and aimed at the door. Then I threw it open.

I was facing a young thug and he had a crowd of a dozen or so others behind him. 'You're Rick, aren't you?' I said.

He didn't like that. 'What if I am?'

'Well, I'd like to be friends. I've heard a lot about you.' I took a step outside and his hand flew to his pocket. I raised my hand. 'Let me explain. All these people have been working hard for weeks. It's only a small party to say thank you. Did you see the play?'

'Aye.'

'Did you like it?'

'It's aright.'

'Good. We wanted you to like it. We'll do another next year. Would you like to be part if it?'

'I dunno. But we're comin' in.' He took a knife out of his pocket and put the point against my stomach. 'So get oot 'o the way.'

The crowd standing behind me could see all this quite clearly. I raised my voice. 'Now Rick, don't do anything foolish. There are too many witnesses. And I want to be friends. Let's take a step outside.' He stepped back but kept the knife pointed at me. I moved a little forward. 'Now look, Rick. Let's meet tomorrow and talk about things then. And about what we can do together next year.' I lowered my voice. 'I don't want to make things difficult for you, so put that knife away and shake hands. Show everyone that we're friendly.' He slowly closed up the flick-knife and put it away. I put my arm around his shoulder; we were the same height. 'O.K., Rick, so that's settled. We'll meet tomorrow right here. And thank you for understanding me. We'll be good friends.' Stepping back I waved at his gang and closed the door. I have seldom been so frightened as when that knife point touched me, and it took me a few minutes before I could breathe properly again.

I did go there the next morning; I had to in any case to clear up, remove lighting equipment and props and do other end-of-play chores. Rick never came.

That is not quite the end of the story. Several of the actors, one in particular tried to organise an ongoing drama group with the youngsters they had come to know so well and with others who joined in, and later on Frankie Vaughan, inspired by our example did the same for a while, and received much press coverage for it. We had very little press ourselves. But it proved what can be done. What the world lacks are enough people with the time, energy and backing to do social work by introducing deprived youngsters to the arts and by involving them in it. Properly done it will work every time and give those for whom unimaginative authority has no use, interesting lives. Even the Ricks of this world can be changed into good citizens.

* * * * * *

As Ledlanet continued through the early seventies, I tried to give my audience not only as much variety as possible, but a chance to hear as many of the greatest works of the concert repertoire as I could. We did Bach's *Art of Fugue* and *Musical Offering*, the Mozart *Requiem* in a programme that included his *Masonic Funeral Music* and a Bach Cantata, many of the great chamber works of Haydn, Mozart, Beethoven, Schubert, Brahms and so on, down to the moderns, who if not so well-liked, were tolerated better than elsewhere, because they were sandwiched in with better-known classics and our atmosphere, with its long interval copied from Glyndebourne, made each evening so memorable that complaints were very rare. I could not understand why, when one booking brochure full of attractive events went out, that it was the Mozart *Requiem* that sold out first, until the arriving public, more men than women that night, all began to give me the masonic handshake. It was the *Masonic Funeral Music* that was the draw. *Dido and Aeneas*, in spite of Lorna Brindley's vocal problems – she was adequate and no more – went well enough, and was coupled with *La Serva Padrona*, sung of course in English, with Sheila McGrow at her most delightful as the soubrette. Many theatrical troupes did their performances for two or three nights, and Edward Beckett, Sam's musician nephew, came with the Irish Chamber Orchestra in a programme that went from the light to the operatic with Veronica Dunne, Ireland's most prominent opera singer, whom I had known for some years, and others. We paired a very clever production by George Mully of Walton's *Facade* with the Thorpe-Davie version of Burns' *Jolly Beggars* and gave the Beethoven arrangements of Scottish Songs that George Thomson, that great figure of Edinburgh's golden age, had commissioned from him. I had much resistance over this, both from Julian Dawson, who played the piano in the trio that accompanies the songs, and from the singers, who said the music did not fit the words. But I had bought the recording with Fisher Dieskau and others that Deutsche Gramaphon had issued in the bicentennial year, and I knew that properly done they were irresistible. Pat Hay and John Graham, who had been a couple for some years now, sang them with John Robertson, three of our regulars, and the latter asked if he could extend the programme with Beethoven's Song Cycle *An die Ferner Geliebte,* which he sang very beautifully. The concert was a triumph, the applause bringing the singers and musicians back over and over. As he passed me going up the stairs to the back corridor for the last time, John Graham said to me, 'You were right again, you bastard.'

Gluck's *Alceste* was our main offering in the autumn season in 1972 and the main role was sung by Anne Connolly, an Irish singer who indulged a little too much on the Members' Night the day before the opening, and was a bit off-form at the first performance, but fine after that. Richard Angas, then at the start of his long career, looked just right as Hercules with his great height and enormous frame. In 1973 our summer season ran for three months, during which the *Twa Briggs*, the setting of Sydney Goodsir Smith's poems which we had commissioned from William Wordsworth, was performed by Sheila McGrow (the new bridge) and Paschal Allen ('Auld stumpie', the old bridge) at the beginning of a triple bill. The two were later to marry. It was followed by Lindsay Kemp's production of *Pierrot Lunaire* (the third time we had done it) it which he mimed and Josephine Nendick sang. The evening ended with John Dankworth's setting of T.S. Eliot's *Sweeney Agonistes*, which I had seen and liked in London when it was given a single performance some years earlier at a memorial evening for the poet after his death. We cast it with local singers, John Graham singing Sweeney and Linda Brown and Phyllis Cannan doing wonderful cockney accents as the two good-time girls, amidst an all-round good cast. Jim Colclough sang Wauchope, produced it with great imagination, and designed an effective and sinister set, and Julian Dawson conducted the whole evening. Brian Mahoney produced the *Twa Briggs* and had intended to do the speaking part of Father Time in *Sweeney Agonistes* from behind a curtain. He had a sudden heart attack and was unable to perform, so I went up the hillside to be alone and memorised it. When the audience heard my voice, there was loud laughter from all over the hall.

Johnny Dankworth came up to Glasgow during the late rehearsals for a day. We rented a rehearsal space, ran through the score with the orchestra in the morning, and gave him a dress rehearsal in the afternoon. He was immensely impressed, made one or two corrections to the score and returned happily to London.

I had had the idea for some time of performing on alternate nights *Hamlet* and Tom Stoppard's clever play based on it, *Rosenkrantz and*

Guildenstern Are Dead. Now we ran through the whole of July and early August in a production of the two where the repertory company at Edinburgh's Lyceum gave us great assistance. Stephanie Beacham played the Queen, John McEnery Hamlet. The beauty of doing the plays in alternance is that the big roles in one are the small ones in the other. We had trouble filling enough seats for so many performances, especially early in the week, but the season was undoubtedly successful. On one night Richard Demarco, who was running some kind of summer school, brought a bus load of American girls, many of whom refused to leave in his bus. 'We're staying with the actors,' they said.

The autumn season followed hard on the summer one, only the Edinburgh Festival intervening. That year our big production was Mozart's *Idomeneo*, which Ande Anderson returned to produce. We had a splendid black singer in Sandra Browne, I think from Jamaica, in the role of Idamante. Her Afro haircut may have looked a little out of place, but the audience loved her. Although her's was not the most important role, Ande instructed that she take her curtain call last, because that was the way the public would want it. John Kingsley-Smith was our *Idomoneo*, Gwenneth Annear, Laureen Livingstone, Dennis O'Neill and John Graham completed the cast, which was conducted by Jonathan Hinden in Jim Colclough's production decor. Dennis O'Neill in a short time would be one of the most important tenors in Britain. Sandy Dunbar of the Arts Council was contemptuous of our mounting such an opera, not having digested that we had years of experience behind us of similar productions of major works by Handel, Mozart, Gluck and other composers, where an orchestra under twenty produced a very acceptable sound, and of contriving exciting productions in our small playing space. But by now we were working hard on getting a new building, and had architects' plans for a theatre able to seat about six hundred to be built behind the house. It would be entered through Ledlanet's first floor level, and would have an adequate orchestra pit and all amenities. The house would still provide the dressing rooms and the catering. Jim Fraser was prepared to put in money and I knew he could raise more from his friends. We had made an approach to the Gulbenkian Foundation for a sum equal to forty percent of the cost and expected the Arts Council to come in with the same. The balance we would have to raise from our supporters. During that autumn of 1973 our plans were advanced and we were talking about a new building within a year and a half.

The previous Christmas I had had another idea, which was turned down by the Arts Council, which felt it had done enough for us with the summer drama season, but I felt it could pay its way without subsidy. This was to mount a Christmas production of *Hansel and Gretel* with piano. The six principals would all stay in the house, they would be paid only a modest fee, but everything would be found, all meals included. Jim Colclough would build the set, produce the show and sing the Witch. We would rehearse in the house for two weeks and open on Boxing Day, running into the New Year. That rehearsal period was more like a house party than anything else. Jill Johnson turned out wonderful meals. Both my daughters were there and the younger, Anastasia (Stas for short), sat through all the rehearsals, a dog on each side of her, and knew the opera by heart. Sheila McGrow was a delightful Gretel, Linda Brown played her brother, Paschal Allen and Isobel Mann were the parents, while the Sandman and Dew Fairy were sung by Rhona Cowen. Gordon Mabbott, our chorus master, was musical director and conducted from the piano. We decided to give each of the children who came a gingerbread man on the way out, and during the performance week we were busy making gingerbread men in the morning, some of them in rather bizarre and suggestive shapes that the public never saw.

With so many children and bench seating, we were able to get nearly a hundred extra bodies into each performance, but so great was the demand for tickets that we could have sold out each performance twice over. It was an enormous success, loved by the audience of all ages. We had a children's choir from a Fife school, dressed as angels, to sing the lovely lullaby chorus that ended the first act, and many eyes in the audience were wet. I decided that we must revive *Hansel and Gretel* for Christmas the next year to accommodate those who had been unable to get a seat, and for the many who would want to come back. Colclough's set, made out of materials obtained from Jim Fraser, was a marvel of imaginative creation and I do not think it cost even ten pounds. There were many grumbles coming from the Arts Council in Edinburgh. We had ignored their directive not to have a Christmas production and had made it work at a profit to ourselves, with the additional benefit of excellent press reviews. Our ingenuity in doing things on a shoe-string did not make us popular because it showed up other organisations who were more conventional and bureaucratic. I was lucky in having Jim Fraser to contribute so much, materials as well as cash, and in my active committee that did so many things in their own time and with their own money and were happy to be part of a success story that was much talked about and that now hardly ever had an empty seat. I was lucky too in the team we had brought together, Jim Colclough able to do so much creatively, and Attewell who ran the catering, house-cleaning and upkeep, not just of our four festival seasons, but as well for the shooting parties, conferences that were held there, and the lettings for weddings and other activities that kept Ledlanet going all year round. I realised too the enormous advantage of owning your own premises, where if you wanted you could rehearse all night, as Ande Anderson in particular liked to do, and being so remote that there were no neighbours to complain. We were looking forward to the next step, a new building in which we could do so much more. Then we would be in reality what we were often called, a Scottish Glyndebourne. I was determined however that Ledlanet would never have the snobbery of Glyndebourne. We did encourage our audiences to dress up, and I always did myself, usually in a kilt, but that was because I knew people enjoyed doing so: it made the evening more festive. But no-one ever felt uncomfortable because they were not in a dinner jacket.

I did have one awkward moment. David Nicholson, our first flute, was also Father of the Chapel, the spokesman for the Musician's Union. One day just before a performance – I think it was *Alceste* – he said that the orchestra wanted to talk to me and I joined them in the dining room, which was their Green Room. Then David said that they were entitled, aside from their normal union rates of pay, to full expenses calculated as from where they lived to the nearest station, which then was Perth, considerably to the north of Ledlanet, and from there the taxi fare. As they usually piled five into a mini with their instruments and shared the petrol for the thirty miles from Edinburgh and forty-four from Glasgow, and one of them lived only two miles away, I thought this was very unfair and said so. David, speaking for the eighteen people in the room told me that they had to insist on the union expenses and they would not play that night for the audience, already sitting in their seats a few yards away, unless I agreed. Sweating, I said, 'I have to agree, but this may well be the last straw that closes us down, and that won't help you either.'

'You agree then,' said David.

'Well, yes. I said so.'

'Good. Now we're going to give the money back to you as a donation.'

The point of the whole exercise was to satisfy the union, but even more to use us against other organisations whose circumstances were much better than ours, but who constantly complained that we were getting away with what they couldn't. They had put me through the wringer first, and then made their gesture. Our programmes always listed our donors, so I put their individual names in our programmes from then on, which was appreciated as it was not expected.

The various theatrical bodies in Scotland would meet about three times a year and during the sixties it formed itself into a Federation of Scottish Theatres. We would meet in the towns where the theatres, mostly repertories, were located. The various musical organisations would also meet, but always in Edinburgh, and I belonged to both. Joint problems were discussed, co-operations investigated and friendships made. We all visited each other's performances when we could find the time. Scotland is not a big country culturally in spite of its big land area, and those who did something in the arts found it very useful to keep in touch and support each other, because there was still a deeply ingrained Calvinist puritanism that was suspicious of them, and a section of the population that considered the arts a waste of money that should go on other things. I had long admired the German theatrical organisations that had trade union support, which encouraged people who work together to go in groups to the theatre and the opera, and I suggested that we might invite a representative of the Freie

Volksbühne to come from Berlin to tell us how they functioned. A representative duly came to our meeting in the Byres Theatre in Saint Andrews, and at his own expense. The chairman was Alex Patterson, who managed the Byre, a worthy man, but with a rather unbending Scottish dourness and not much imagination. I had expected that we would listen to our guest, question him and that our two hour meeting would be devoted to nothing else. But Alex had prepared an agenda where the Freie Volksbühne was the third or fourth item, and after only a few minutes he wanted to move on to whatever came next. I protested that the man had come all the way from Berlin and deserved at least an hour of our time, but got nowhere and felt very embarrassed. During 1973 I was elected Chairman and a meeting was held at Ledlanet where I made sure everyone had a good lunch and invited those who could to stay for the performance that evening. Giles Havergal, Director of the Glasgow Citizens Theatre, was very funny, because Joan Knight from Perth Theatre, the retiring Chair, had been very insistent he attend. 'One can miss a few things in the theatre, but meetings never!' he intoned, pulling his eyelids. It was that day that I proposed that we produce a monthly calendar of all arts events going on in Scotland to be scattered around public places, hotels and wherever people could see them. Some time later this actually happened.

The musical meetings were chaired for some years by John Noble, who never missed an opportunity of voicing his dislike of Wagner. As Peter Hemmings, General Manager of Scottish opera, programmed as much Wagner as possible, and put on the first *Ring* cycle to be seen in Scotland, there was always some contention at the meetings, which never really did anything, but became a sounding board for the thirty or so persons who attended. When Noble died, John Rankin, a retired Director of the Bank of Scotland, replaced him, and things went on in exactly the same way. Peter Diamond only attended on one occasion.

One person who gave me much support at Ledlanet was Kenneth Ireland. He was the Director of the Pitlochry Festival Theatre, a martinet with a heart of gold whose main defect was an ego and a vanity of which I am sure he was unaware, although it was obvious enough to everyone who met him. Pitlochry put on five plays every year during a two-month summer season in what was at first a canvas-covered building which later moved into a permanent one. The seasons eventually became longer to cover the whole tourist season. Plays were added one by one as the summer progressed until during the last month it was possible to stay for five days and see a different play each night. The repertory would vary from Victorian melodramas and the London hits of a few years earlier to an occasional play by a contemporary English, Scottish or European playwright and I did manage to sell Kenneth a few of the plays I was publishing. With time the repertory given became more ambitious and usually there was one play in a season that offered the audience, which was not a high-brow one in any sense, some challenge. Kenneth Ireland gave me much good practical advice, always insisted on paying for his ticket at Ledlanet and for whatever he consumed, because he knew we needed every penny. He was originally an accountant and he ran his theatre with competence and efficiency, working both staff and actors very hard. But he made some enemies and was eventually deposed by a new Chairman he had brought in, who wanted to exercise power himself and afterwards everything soon became slacker. Ireland could not believe what was happening to him, had a stroke and thereafter retired to Edinburgh, becoming very reclusive. His contribution to Scottish culture is much underrated.

After *Idomoneo* I had planned to revive *Handsel and Gretel* and had planned a number of concerts for the Christmas season, starting with Monteverdi's 1610 *Vespers*. Then came the big shock. Bettina had asked if a friend of her's could visit Ledlanet. I saw no objection and she looked all over the house. She was an American lawyer who Bettina had sent to make trouble. She subsequently wrote a report, for which she was in no way qualified, but that did not matter, on the fire hazards of the house. We knew there were certain things that needed doing, but the regulations in question were designed for much larger theatrical spaces, not for a country house with several exits and large windows giving onto the ground outside from the room surrounding the hall where the audience sat. As we expected work to start on a new building the following year, we did not want to spend money on innovations that would be out of date in a short time. The report was sent to the Scottish Arts Council, the fire authorities, to the County Clerk, to the local M.P. and several other bodies. One day a man came with a summons that revoked our licence to give performances, and all attempts to do something to reverse it were useless. I cancelled the Christmas season except for the Monteverdi *Vespers* and a Carol Concert, which were given in Kinross Town Hall, and arranged on those two nights for the Green Hotel nearby to cater for our audience after the concerts. This was at the time of the big coal miners' strike, which was crippling the country and electricity could only be used three days a week for heating. The hall was heated for the *Vespers* in the evening, but not for the rehearsals during the day, which made it difficult for the orchestra to play or the singers to sing in a freezing cold room. I myself had a bad cold, and went several times to the pub to dose it with whisky. After the performance, which was a particularly good one in spite of all the problems, I circulated around the tables at the Green Hotel, then ate and drank myself, and started to drive back to Ledlanet, five miles away. Some malicious person had told the police to follow me. As I drove off a police car came round the bend behind me, followed me onto the main road, stopped me and I was breathalysed, then taken to the police station for a blood test. Because of my cold and the whisky, I was over the limit.

Although we could not give performances at Ledlanet, we could hold a ball, and we had one on Hogmonay. At five minutes to midnight a police car pulled up at the front door and a policeman handed me a summons to appear in court for drunken driving. 'I didn't want to spoil the new year for you, so I'm giving you this during the old year,' said the police officer. I have never understood the logic of that.

* * * * * *

Certain years stand out in my memory with particular pain and 1974 was one of them. The closure of Ledlanet was a severe blow, but I was certain that I would find a way of getting it open again and of course our plans were well advanced for the new building. But Bettina did not stop there. She had been to Portugal and I believe had given one or more concerts there, but she had been to see the Gulbenkian Trust with whom we had been negotiating, and suddenly I heard from them that they were withdrawing the offer on which the whole plan for the new building had been based. This gave the Scottish Arts Council an excuse to withdraw as well. The architects who had done the work and who had been verbally promised by Jim Fraser that they would be paid began to ask for money on account and Jim having become moody, put them off. He had in the meantime become the Conservative candidate for Dunfermline, where I had for a time been the prospective Liberal candidate. Both Better Books were now in real trouble. I had employed Paule Thevenin, previously manager of Hachette's International shop in London, to open a big department in Edinburgh of French books, but it had developed too slowly. We were selling at French prices, much lower than any other British shop, but I was unsuccessful in breaking down the ingrained buying habits of those British institutions that bought French books. Daphne Kennedy-Fraser, a very well-meaning but unpushy spinster – there is no other word to describe her – who was on the Ledlanet board and had developed an infatuation for Leonard Friedman, which was much joked about, had worked at the Edinburgh University Library who bought their books from France with long delays and paying heavy carriage, whereas they could get them at French prices only a few yards away. The Librarian would not come to look, and Daphne was unable to persuade him to order from us. Paule was a lovely person, but I could not hurry her. I asked her to make up a list of the most essential titles of French literature so that I could do a mailing, but months passed and she never finished it. Every French-speaker in Edinburgh came into the bookshop to chat and gossip with Paule, but few bought anything, and they took up time when she should have been doing other things and completing the list. I had found through Victor Herbert a backer for the London shop who put some money in. He was Russ MacLain, an Irish American who had made money out of IOS during its boom days as an investment manager, and unlike Victor had not lost it all again. But Russ wanted some control and constantly changed my policies to make it less of an intellectual and more of a general bookshop, cutting down on stock buying and many of our regular customers began to go elsewhere on Charing Cross Road.

In the February election Jim Fraser ran for parliament. He gave some parties in his suite in the King Malcolm Hotel in the town, but received not very many votes. At the end of the month I went skiing again at Val d'Isère, this time taking Alice with me. I skied down a hollow at full speed in order to have the momentum to get up a steep incline on the other side, and just then a lady cut across my path. I either had to go straight into her at speed or throw myself sideways. I did the latter and badly smashed up my leg, having to be taken down in an ambulance sled. It was the first time I had ever had a serious skiing accident. The two ligaments of my left leg were seriously stretched. I could have had an operation in Val d'Isère to tighten them, a risky business, but the local doctor had a bad reputation and I decided to wait until I was back in London and by then it was too late. I did have an operation to remove the cartilage some months later, but that did little good and I now had a permanent bad leg that would frequently go stiff on me so that I could not walk.

Back in Britain, now on crutches, I tackled my problems, but found my lack of mobility a big handicap. I was still trying to keep the membership of Ledlanet together and one day I was in Glasgow where I was trying to meet one of our more generous supporters to get a cheque from him, but it was rush hour and every time a taxi came near someone else rushed ahead of me to catch it. When I finally caught one it was too late: the man had left his office.

During the time I was skiing the Edinburgh directors of Better Books had held a meeting and decided to close the French section. Knowing little of my negotiations with French publishers from whom we had our large stock on consignment, they had a sale, selling the French books at give-away prices and dismissing Paule. All the books could have been sent back for full credit, but we had to pay for books we had remaindered. My morale was now very low. The situation was bad in London as well. I had found a new shop, right up at the top of Charing Cross Road, next door to Centrepoint, and we closed the original shop and the smaller one that had held poetry and film books. A Ledlanet patron, an architect, who had occasionally been generous and for whom we had mounted a few chamber concerts in his house in the Cleish Hills across the valley, volunteered to design the new shop without charging us, but the firm of which he had been a partner sued us for the work done. Eventually I had to put the London Better Books into the hands of the receivers, while I looked for new capital. I never found it, and the receivers sold the fifty-one percent stake in the Scottish company to a remainder dealer called Kevin Connolly. So much for 'holding companies' and what I had learned from Professor Saitzev!

PURSUIT

I had also lost my right to drive for a year. On the ninth of January I was fined in the Kinross Sheriff's Court and had to surrender my driving licence, which meant that I was now dependent on being driven to and from Ledlanet. This also meant that I spent less time there and more in the London office. I see from my opera record that I went much more to the opera in London that year than I had been able to do in the years when Ledlanet Nights was taking up so much of my time. The shooting parties continued, both that January and in August when the grouse season started, but by the autumn my leg was constantly letting me down, because one false step and it would seize up most painfully. I learned, once I could abandon the crutches, to walk with great care, but I had to have frequent physiotherapy and heat treatment. Having lunch with Ande Anderson one day, he told me that he had seen Bettina and she had said to him, 'Aren't I clever. I've shut down Ledlanet.' She was crowing all over London. To annoy me further she had taken Anastasia away from the French Lycée, where she had been getting on well, and sent her to Dartington Hall in the west country, a school that had a bad scholastic reputation and very little discipline, where she became a boarder. This gave Bettina more free time, cost me much more money, and did no good to Anastasia's educational prospects. She never went to a university. Jamie in the meantime was studying accountancy and working at Peat Marwick and Mitchell as an apprentice. The long Calvary of being constantly summoned to court by Bettina on one pretext or another was continuing and my solicitors were not representing me very well. On occasion I represented myself to save money.

That summer, to escape again, I went to the Bregenz Festival with Alice to hear some music and relax from my woes. The first people I ran into were Charles Osborne, my old friend from the Arts Council in London, and Ken Thompson, who had been his boyfriend since their schooldays in Australia. It was around this time, probably a year or so later, that Bettina, who was singing in Australia, introduced Charles to another man, a Festival Director, who started a relationship with him, thus ousting Ken. This was quite deliberate on her part. Charles and Ken eventually got together again, but Ken has never forgiven Bettina.

One of my problems where court proceedings were concerned, was that Bettina declared no income, so that all the costs fell on me. I heard that she always wanted to be paid in cash wherever she sang, which was mainly in Europe, so she paid no tax and was able to get legal aid. She had published a little collection of poems in 1972 called *Briefs* and had sent me a copy in which she inscribed 'Shattered glasses leave splintered pictures'. It is bitter, fragmented poetry, with lines such as 'Fill the cunt/don't think'. She did not seem to get on well or for long with the other men in her life. She told one mutual acquaintance 'I only fuck rich,' and indeed an early lover was the rich Eddie Kulakundis from a Greek ship-owning family, who returning from abroad one day rang her from the airport to tell her that he had just married the actress Susan Hampshire. She later persuaded my friend John Rushby-Smith to set some of her poems to music, but once he had done it, she froze him out. She broke up with her entourage of women, her ferocity being too much for them. The Balls stopped seeing her. Yvonne began working for Calder and Boyars, keeping our books part-time when she was not working as an actress on television and Jimmy eventually represented me in court against Bettina. Both the Balls came fairly frequently to Ledlanet.

In 1968 I had gone for the first time to the Wexford Festival. This delightful event had been started by Tom Walsh, a local doctor and anaesthetist in 1951 and took place in what had once been a cinema, the Theatre Royal, not as small as Ledlanet, but having much in common with it. We had done some of the same operas, especially two of Mozart's and my first visit was with Sheila Colvin, who only stayed two days. On the first, after hearing *La Clemenza di Tito*, we were eating at the Talbot Hotel, where we joined another couple we had just met, Tony Quigley and his wife. Tony was a civil servant, born in Ulster but working in Dublin. We were enjoying ourselves, when Tony said, 'Here's a man you must meet' and caught the arm of a man leaving the room. It was Ulick O'Connor, well-known writer, but with a reputation for impulsive behaviour. Surely enough, O'Connor refused to be stopped, and when Tony protested he said, 'I don't give a fuck.'

'No man uses that word in front of my wife,' said Tony, whereupon O'Connor knocked him down, upsetting the table at the same time. The head waiter put things right, found more food and I gather Ulick O'Connor was finally presented with the bill. It was an enjoyable weekend and on my last night, when Sheila had gone, I sat up late talking to Marie Keene, the wonderful Irish actress who not long before I had seen perform Beckett's *Happy Days* in Joan Littlewood's Stratford East theatre, probably the best performance of the play I have ever seen, with Alan Simpson as Willie. Wexford was the last time I ever saw her.

During the summer of 1974 I was invited to Ireland to open a literary festival at Listowel. Liam Miller of Dolmen Press, who published a quality list of Irish authors in fine collectors' editions had arranged the visit, and we lunched together in Dublin with the poet Thomas Kinsella, and then caught a train to our destination. I had prepared a little speech, but we were in the public library and everyone present was standing, all eyeing the tables at the side, filled with plates of canapés and bottles of wine. Nobody would want to listen to me for long, so I ditched what I had prepared, said how pleased I was to be there and let the party begin. The first person I talked to was Tom Walsh, founder and director of the Wexford Festival and we soon became great friends. From then on, every time I went to the Festival, and after Ledlanet had closed I did not miss many, I would go to his lunchtime parties and spend time with him, eventually publishing his big book about opera under Napoleon III, *Second Empire Opera*[31]. He was a genial man who shared my love of books and music, had an impressive library and a wonderful collection of records, and I would often meet him outside Ireland.

We gave three balls at Ledlanet that year (1974), which helped to keep our membership together. I went to Wexford in October, but before that, in September, I was suddenly brought back into politics. I was asked at short notice if I would be willing to stand in Hamilton, where there had not been a Liberal candidate for some years. Hamilton was not a safe seat for anyone, Winnie Ewing having won it for the Scottish Nationalists in 1967, and it had see-sawed ever since between the SNP and Labour. I agreed and took the night train to Glasgow because the election had already been called. I telephoned my office from the station and was told that Roy and Lucy Jones had committed a joint suicide during the night. Marion had obviously been told about it in advance. Lucy had been diagnosed with terminal cancer with only a few weeks to live and Roy had felt that to struggle on with all his disabilities was not worth the effort. They had taken powerful pills, listened to their favourite music on the record player and drifted off. With a sombre heart I took the train to Hamilton to meet the committee, be adopted and start my campaign. I had to do nearly everything on foot, because I was still not allowed to drive.

I took a room in a local hotel for the duration. There were certain difficulties, the most immediate being a disgruntled member of the committee who had a list of the membership of the Liberal Party in the constituency and the electoral rolls. He did not want to do anything, nor to hand over what he had. I telephoned him to be told that he had no time to be bothered and as the election was more than two weeks away, there was no hurry. When I told him that envelopes had to be addressed by hand to all the voters, and there were not many volunteers to do this work, which was why we had to have everything that day, he answered 'Next week is soon enough.'

'I am going from here to the court to get an injunction,' I said, 'and you will have to pay the cost of it.' That did it, and I had the whole file that evening. By now I knew what I was doing. I went to the public library, to see the County Clerk and other officials to get the important statistics that covered health, education and employment. Armed with these I prepared a manifesto and my election leaflet, which was a two-sided printed page, in pads of a hundred, which could be torn off, put through letter-boxes or handed to people, small enough to go into a side-pocket. On one side was my picture and a brief biography. The other side was a series of one-liners, my policies. It was economical, easy to digest, cheap and convenient. Then I went to Labour headquarters and asked to see Mr. Alex Wilson, the Labour MP. He received me with surprise.

---

[31] London 1981.

'I thought I would call on you, Mr. Wilson,' I said, to tell you that I intend to run an honest and honourable campaign purely on the issues. There will be no personal attack or abuse from me. There is no reason not to be friendly and I am sure we will be on good terms when it comes to the count.' I thought that this might reduce any temptation to try dirty attacks or rake up any scandals in my past.

The next day I had a letter back from him, thanking me for my visit and wishing me good luck in taking as many votes as I could away from the Scottish Nationalists, who he knew were his biggest threat. My intervention would reduce that threat enormously.

We found a butchers shop that was to let for a short rental, which still smelled of raw meat, and I went canvassing. Hamilton was a strange place, not far from Glasgow, a county town with a number of factories and a mixed middle-class and working-class population. There was no culture of any kind, no theatre, concert hall or museum. The only public entertainment available during the whole year was the Salvation Army's Christmas carol concert. The usual two issues came up frequently, capital punishment and abortion, and I gave my stock answers. Almost the entire population lived in Hamilton itself or the smaller town of Larkhill, only a few minutes away. The campaign was a dull one. I found volunteers to drive my car, which I fitted up with public address equipment, from which I would deliver slogans and play tapes, either the triumphal march from *Aïda* or *The Blue Bonnets* played by a military band. This brought people out on the street from the housing estates that I drove through. Joan Clark came over at times to help and keep me company, so did my daughter Jamie, who canvassed with me, Sheila Colvin came over once or twice, and I frequently had my dog Shuna. A local couple were the backbone of the organisation, the Woodwards. It was they who had asked the Party to find them a candidate. Gradually more and more people came forward to help. I found myself often trudging along wet streets with my bad leg wondering why I was doing this. There were a few public meetings, but not many people came to them. I stayed in a small hotel.

The count on election day went on until the early hours of the morning and Alex Wilson won. The SNP had a much smaller vote because of my intervention and I was much taunted by their young supporters for speaking proper English. No outside prominent Liberals came to help, because it was far from being a target seat. As always I met some interesting people and became involved in a few issues, some of which I followed up after the election, mainly to do with individuals who had been badly treated by the social services. My main impression was that the local Labour Party was extremely corrupt. As soon as a man became a councillor he registered himself as a contractor. I brought Jim Fraser down one day to give me an idea of what the new housing, and repairs on the old ones, should be costing, and it was clear that everyone was overcharging massively for very shoddy work. This was the period when corruption had become very widespread in Labour Councils and scandals would soon be emerging in which as a publisher I would be involved in the exposure.

My diary for 1974 had the contemplated dates for the Ledlanet autumn season. The two operatic productions were to be Handel's *Hercules* and Carl Orff's *The Moon* on which latter I had already started work on a translation into Scottish dialect. The previous year, after Frankfurt, I had gone to see Orff, then an old man, and had received his permission to perform it as a chamber opera with a reduced scoring, which I would find someone to make for the SBE. I had spoken to Ian Wallace who I wanted to sing Saint Peter, a part made for him, and had cast the whole work in my head. The story of *The Moon* is that it is first seen as a giant balloon in a village tree, lighting up a village, from which it is stolen by a group of peasants on a binge from another village, who when they die, each take a quarter of it to the vault where they are buried, put it together and use it to light the vault while they celebrate. Saint Peter comes down to stop the party, takes the moon away and hangs it in the sky. It was a perfect work for Ledlanet and I could give it local references for my two local towns, Milnathort and Kinross. But it was not to be.

I did go as usual to the Frankfurt Book Fair and found to my surprise that many people thought that I had retired from publishing and that Marion was now running the publishing company. Going to New York in January, I heard the same thing, but much more specifically. Marion was making frequent visits there and had told everyone she saw that I was now a sleeping partner doing other things. I returned to have matters out. On my first morning in the office I received a telephone call from Marion, saying that she would not be coming in that day, but wanted to invite me to dinner that night, on my own, and she named the restaurant where we had first met. She knew of course what I must have heard in New York. I arrived first and when Marion came in, she sat down and her first words were: 'I want to break up the partnership.'

I was too dazed to say anything while the consequences flashed through my mind. This was her way of cutting short any recriminations and avoiding explaining herself. When I did open my mouth, I was as direct as she. 'Alright,' I said.

It took several months to work out how to divide the company and pour the assets into two new ones without incurring a tax liability. We took legal advice and then asked the Publishers Association to recommend someone who could act as adjudicator for the split up. Marion started a new company in her own name, and I went back to the original one, registered in 1950, John Calder (publishers) Ltd. We found a dealer in archives and antiquarian books, who looked around in America and finally found the Lillie Library in Bloomington, at the University of Indiana, who were willing to buy the company's correspondence, documents and everything not needed for day-to-day business. Breon Mitchell, who was Chairman of the

Library and Professor of German at the university, came over and spent days looking through cupboards, climbing up to top shelves where piles of musty old correspondence, invoices and miscellaneous papers were stored, everything that had accumulated since we had moved to Brewer Street from Sackville Street. When we had made that last move we had to leave our old papers behind and Alex Trocchi and friends had spent a day sifting through them, finding much interesting material that he then sold to the University of Texas, just before the building was demolished. Now we were able to negotiate £100,000 for the archive, less a commission to the broker. That should be enough to finance the split.

Now that the break-up was imminent, Marion was in a much better temper. No announcement had yet been made to our staff, to the press or to the trade. Her motives were transparent enough. She resented it every time an article appeared in either the trade or the public press that singled out someone like Nora Smallwood as a prominent woman in publishing, and she would write in to say that she was also a woman in publishing with authority. She hated the greater attention given to me by other publishers, particularly at the Frankfurt Book Fair where reputations rose and fell and gossip was almost as important as business. She wanted to be famous and admired. Now she had a stable of authors of her own, who looked to her and not to me; it was headed by Ivan Illich, the guru for radical chic dissent from the traditional common wisdom, and now she also commissioned books from prominent political figures whom we knew largely through our involvement in censorship issues and the DLAS, rather in decline just then, but of which we were still the joint secretaries. William Hamling, Chairman of the society, who had done so much to make it a success, died in March 1975. He had had one heart attack and was just recovering from it when, laughing at a television programme at home one night, he had another, which carried him off. We chose Stuart Hood to be his successor, and the DLAS continued its work, but there were very few censorship prosecutions now, and meetings became infrequent. We had tried to start Scottish and Irish branches, but the Irish quickly decided that they wanted to be totally independent and soon disappeared through inactivity; the same thing happened in Scotland where Nicholas Fairbairn was very happy to be named as Chairman, but never called any meetings. The Scottish DLAS remained just one item in the list of Fairbairn's various titles and activities in his overlong *Who's Who* entry. Tony Smythe left the NCCL to go to Mencap, where he was involved in mental health issues and I lost touch with him. I am not sure how I met a young barrister called Ron Rosen, probably through my divorce problems, but he eventually became involved in the DLAS and then its Chairman, but doing little that I can think of after Stuart, Marion and I resigned, which was about the time of the break-up of the publishing company.

Marion took over two political series, *Open Forum* and its sub-series *Ideas in Progress*, and I started a new one, very similar, *Platform Books*. Among the titles which were to appear in Marion's new list were books by Hugh Jenkins, Labour Minister for the Arts from 1974 to 1976, Enid Wistrich, prominent as a labour member of the General London Council, who was involved in particular with Film Censorship, Julia Kristeva's book on Chinese women and a wide variety of titles on social, technological and sociological issues. *Platform Books*, to which I shall return, tended to be more directly political, and certainly more controversial.

The Adjudicator, or Arbitrator, who the Publishers Association finally chose for us, was Peter du Sautoy, who had recently retired as Chairman of Faber and Faber. His was not an easy task, as he soon found out, and he must have regretted taking it on. First he had to find a balance. Living authors with whom we had personal contacts were asked to choose their publisher. Beckett, Robbe-Grillet and virtually all the French authors chose me. The German ones had mainly been contracted by me, but knew us both and were not much concerned who it was. Where there was no preference or an indecision, Peter could decide and as things had to be weighted and past, present and probable future sales were the easiest factor to quantify, it meant that having Beckett, with many titles selling well, and the incoming royalties from Henry Miller and William Burroughs continuing, I had to cede many authors I would have liked to have kept. Although neither of us had met Hubert Selby, whose *Last Exit* had caused the most important national prosecution after *Lady Chatterley*, Marion went to see him to get him and his future novels into her stable. I did the same with Henry Miller, making a special trip to California to explain what was happening, and get his assent to staying with me.

I had only seen him infrequently since the Edinburgh Writers' Conference and the publication of *Tropic of Cancer* had been negotiated solely with Dr. Hoffmann. He had paid one visit to London in the early 1970s and we had given a lunch and reception for him at the Savoy hotel in a private dining room, which started with a press conference, and enabled him to meet old friends like Lawrence Durrell and others in the literary world who admired him. Afterwards he had asked if I would drive him around London to look at places he remembered and we did a tour. The most interesting part of it was the five minutes we spent on the northbound carriageway of Hyde Park, opposite the Dorchester Hotel.

It might have been a month before that when he had written to me that his young wife, the jazz pianist Hoki Tokuda, who he had recently married in his old age, was coming to London, and would I look after her? Marion and I took her to lunch in Soho – she was staying at the Dorchester – and it was obvious to us both that she had not the slightest interest in seeing or being entertained by her husband's publishers. She had a very obvious beard-burn, so she obviously had not been lonely the night before. Now Henry wanted to look at the Dorchester hotel, not to go in, but just to look at the building from the street. It is not difficult to imagine what voyeuristic fantasies were going through his head as he gazed at the Dorchester, and then we went on to look at other old haunts.

When I went to see him at Pacific Palisades in 1975 it was my first visit to Los Angeles and I had no idea of the geography of the city. I had booked into a hotel in Century City, took a taxi from the airport, and on the evening of my arrival tried to take a walk around the neighbourhood, but desisted after twice being stopped by suspicious police cars. I overheard a conversation from some film people at the next table, who were looking for properties and on my way out of the hotel restaurant left a note with them saying I was a British publisher visiting and had a book that might be of interest to them. It may have been George Foa's *The Blood Rushed to my Pockets*, which I thought of as a vehicle for Danny Kaye or it may have been another book, perhaps Stonehouse's *The Ultimate*, which I had just published. I left my room number on the note and sure enough Garcin Kanin (or was it his brother, also a screenwriter?) telephoned me an hour later, so that for some months there was correspondence over the book in question, but the initial interest fizzled out eventually. The next day I drove in a hired car to see Henry Miller, who was expecting me. But when I arrived at about twelve o'clock I was told that he was still in bed and could I come back later at three? I drove along the sea to pass the time, saw a museum advertised, and drove in. It was the Getty Museum for which one normally had to have a reservation because it would only take the same number of visitors for which there were parking spaces, but I was lucky. I did a quick tour of the antiquities and paintings, at one point getting close to a very small Leonardo to see it better. A voice behind me said, 'Put your hands slowly in the air and take two steps back.' I could feel something hard in the middle of my back: it was a gun. The security guards do not let you get too close to pictures. I lunched in the snack bar and went to see Henry.

He had recently had a hip operation, was very uncomfortable because of it, and could not use his swimming pool behind the house. He was in a dressing gown, and opened letters while we spoke, one from Durrell. We spoke of many things, and he said much good about Maurice Girodias who he had finally decided was a good man after all and on the side of the angels. He also told me he was in love again (Hoki was gone by now), but he did not tell me with whom. As he had a very beautiful secretary, who had admitted me, and passed occasionally through the room, I made the obvious guess. When I asked to go to the lavatory, I found myself in a luxurious bathroom where the sponge-rubber mat underfoot was shaped like dozens of female breasts and nipples. Old age had not changed Henry's preoccupation with sex. He signed the agreement I had brought with me and I left, driving back to my hotel down Sunset Boulevard. I enjoyed a bottle of local Burgundy that night at dinner, and went back to New York, and then a few days later, to London. I had kept Miller as an author

Burroughs also agreed when I saw him in New York on the way back that I was his publisher. He was living in a loft in what seemed a dangerous part of town, in or near Little Italy. He had a kind of sword-stick with a coiled metal wire inside it, for protection, and told me he could still run fast enough to escape muggers. I met one or two rather dubious looking people during the evening I spent with him, one of them a strange character called Hubert Huncke, who has since become celebrated as a kind of American Genet. I did not take to him much.

Peter du Sautoy had many meetings with us, including two or three lunches. We had agreed to accept his arbitration – he was known to be fair – but Marion constantly appealed against his judgements. Once the authors themselves had decided on which side they wanted to go, I still had too much weight on my side, so writers like Peter Weiss, who was selling well and whom I knew far better than Marion, and had recently died, were given to her. In fact, Marion being originally German, Peter du Sautoy took the easy course of giving nearly everyone from Germany eastward to Marion, which meant all the Russian authors like Yevtushenko, and the Dutch and Scandinavians, and such North Americans as Robert Creeley. Peter du Sautoy often became exasperated, to the point on one occasion of walking out in the middle of lunch at La Braganza, a fish restaurant in Soho. A few out-of-print books were forgotten in the division, such as *Jules and Jim*, made famous by the film with Jeanne Moreau, and *One Flew Over the Cuckoo's Nest*, which Marion hastily reprinted without consulting du Sautoy once the final settlement had been made.

My relations with Bettina were particularly poisonous at this time. The two women, she and Marion, had never liked each other, but now that I was a common target, they became friendly on the surface. Bettina suggested that she might be able to talk Beckett into leaving me and moving to Marion, but she was soon disabused. Sam, whenever I saw him, would tell me that Bettina was out to hurt me in every possible way 'to put it mildly' as he said more than once. He met Tanja with me on one occasion in Paris, and got on well with her, and once I drove to see him in Ussy with Alice, coming back from the south of France, which was a mistake, because my philandering as he saw it, with different women, did not appeal to him. Later on there were other ladies who begged to meet him, but I always refused.

Marion and I continued to share the same offices, each having a floor to ourselves and a joint general office. As the summer advanced we had a new problem. A young American, Tim O'Grady, who Marion had employed, became Father of the Chapel for the Journalists Union, which had persuaded some of our staff to join their new publishing division. I had never liked him and suspected that he was a mole put in to make trouble. He was an editor who always suggested impracticable and uncommercial projects that did not even fit our literary image, and he began demanding editorial control of our programme for the editorial staff. Naturally this was refused, whereupon he called a strike and our office in Brewer Street was picketed by about thirty members of the union, sent every day to stop anyone going in or out. One of the pickets was the man who had been the first manager of the Edinburgh Better Books, Michael Radford, whom I had quickly come to mistrust. There was also a demand for higher salaries. Certainly we did not pay large ones: no publisher with a list like our's, aimed at long-term sales from authors who only gradually became known to their potential readers, ever could. Maureen Cleeve was apparently earning £7 a week from us at one point and left to go into journalism because we would not pay one pound more, or so she told another author of mine many years later. At the time she was going out with Kenneth Alsopp, who had so strongly supported us. But Ken was dead by now. He had had a wooden leg, the result I think of the war, and was in constant pain; he finally took his own life.

The postman would not cross the picket line, so we had to go to the post-office to collect our letters and parcels every day, and many who came to see us would also not cross it. I had strong presentiments that Tim O'Grady was not what he seemed. I had caught him going through our correspondence files months earlier. It may well have been he who cut the signatures out of the letters from well-known authors, but certainly he was collecting names and addresses, because he wrote to all our authors to support the strike. I may have been paranoiac, but I suspected that the CIA, who had reason not to like us, might have been involved, and certainly the union – the book publishing branch was a new venture for the Union of Journalists – were using us, small and defenceless, to threaten the bigger publishers and to recruit more members in firms such as Collins. But I had one victory. Collets on Charing Cross Road, a Communist and famous left-wing bookshop, when I went to speak to them, believed me that the strike was a sinister manoeuvre by a common enemy, and went on buying and stocking our books.

The strike was one factor that led us to publicly announce the split of Calder and Boyars. There was no-one among the strikers who was the slightest use to me – the union members with one exception had all been taken on by Marion – and the exception was Chris Davidson, our production manager, who had joined the union, but not the strike. It as also a very hot summer, and standing outside in the blazing sun was no pleasure for the pickets. They finally disappeared and the union left us alone. Tim O'Grady went, I know not where. This left us with one editor, Agnes Rook, who was the only one who was any good anyway, and she eventually worked just for me. After a while she preferred to work from home.

My own financial troubles were getting worse. I had used Ledlanet as collateral to raise the money to pay the ever-increasing court costs and maintenance for Bettina and Anastasia, and Ledlanet was now used hardly at all. I would go there on my own and spend two or three days alone in the house, receiving visits from the Formans, Joan Clark, Jim Fraser and others. I would occasionally see Nicholas Fairbairn, but he had changed in character. From being a radical and liberal personality, he was now a High Tory, and not a pleasant one. Having failed to get elected in an Edinburgh constituency, he was very surprisingly adopted for my own constituency of Kinross and West Perthshire at a meeting of the local Conservative Committee that was held during the summer holiday period, and very badly attended. The local conservatives, and Joan Clark was one, were appalled. They saw him as eccentric, too clever and effeminate. He had ceased to be friendly to me because he wanted to replace Jim Fraser as Chairman of Ledlanet, and I could not allow this. Jim had many failings, the biggest his increasing alcoholism, but he had been extremely generous over the years, and in any case he was my nearest neighbour at Huntley Hall. I soon realised that the eccentric Fairbairn saw everyone as either willing to feed his ego and prospects or as an enemy. He did us damage at the Arts Council, where it was important to stay on their books, because I could not then face any possibility that Ledlanet would not overcome its difficulties. We had been through many crises and had always come through them. In 1973 we had finally managed, from all our different sources of revenue, varying from ticket sales, catering and fund-raising events, to subsidies from various sources, including our French shooting-parties, which Jacques Chaix organised with great efficiency, to show a small surplus. Because the house was so little used now, and especially because it was not heated during most of the long cold and damp winters, the next blow to come to me was dry rot. It spread rapidly. I brought in Rentokill to get rid of it. They removed timbers, tore down walls, treated many parts of the house, but under the lead tiles, and there were many acres of tiling on the roofs, and in invisible places, the rot grew, not only dry rot, but rising damp as well. More money had to be borrowed from the bank and the overdraft grew with unpaid interest inflating it further.

Better Books Scotland, under Kevin Connolly, was quickly run into the ground, the shelves becoming emptier, and it was finally sold off. The same happened in London. From my Soho office, where I continued to bring out what books I could, and from Ledlanet where I only used my bedroom and the morning-room now, I watched my little world collapse. Bila, the poodle, had died, Shuna, the labrador, was my constant companion. In London I walked her across Hyde Park in the morning and back again in the evening. At lunchtime I took her to St. Anne's churchyard on Wardour Street and she did her business near the tombs of William Hazlitt and Jonathan Williams, founder of the Royal Literary Fund, and of the one-time King of Corsica, who had died in London after mortgaging his Kingdom to some gullible speculators, a spot frequented by Soho's down-and-outs because it had benches.

415

Through this difficult time two things kept me going, good friends, both male and female, and my love of music and theatre. In 1971 I had made a musical tour in Europe with Jim Fraser and there were to be others. The shadow had not yet fallen on Ledlanet and after that year's successful summer season I went south, saw Cavalli's *La Calisto* at Glyndebourne with Janet Baker, caught up with office work, and then drove to Frankfurt where Jim Fraser flew to join me. His doctor had put a real fright into him and he was determined to give up drink, and that meant that I must do nothing to encourage him. From the airport we drove as far as Würtsburg, because we were on our way to hear some Wagner in Bayreuth. There I introduced Jim at dinner to German apple juice, which can be quite delicious and with a little imagination you could think you are drinking a kind of wine. After he had gone to bed in his own room, I sneaked down from mine to have a brandy, but the next day stuck to apple juice. It was the beginning of August and we went to *Die Walküre* and *Siegfried*, two days apart, seeing the sights and staying at an old Schloss that was now a very atmospheric hotel. The *Lohengrin* on the day after was reserved for trade unions, not Jim Fraser's favourite people, but I managed with some string-pulling to get in. Jim enjoyed Bayreuth and always felt comfortable anywhere where stout men were seen everywhere and many were stouter than he. But on our second night in Bayreuth, when there was no opera, the strain of not drinking was getting to be too much. We had visited the swimming pool, which I had used, but not he, and he was sweating on a very hot day. We went into another hotel in the town and 'I just have to have a beer,' he said, and had one. Then Harold Rosenthal walked by, editor of Opera magazine and an author of mine, and we invited him to dinner. Jim drank much wine at the meal and the good resolutions were gone for good.

From Bayreuth we drove south through Austria to Vienna, where Jim had never been, found a hotel on the Kärntnerstrasse and then had a strange experience. I had wanted to stop in Salzburg to go to Mozart's *Mitridate*, but Jim's mind was set on Vienna, so we drove on. He led me into a bar, where, before we could order a drink, two girls came and sat next to us. I wanted to tell them we preferred to be alone, but Jim immediately invited them to a drink and insisted on ordering more. Each time they ordered a 'cocktail' which I knew to be just fruit juice. Jim was very innocent in many ways and I could not make him understand that we were lending ourselves to being cheated. The girls then wanted us to move to a private room, but I said no, although I could see Jim was tempted. Finally I called for the bill and it was massive. Jim had drunk half a dozen large brandies, I had probably had wine, but the 'cocktails', and I knew they were only watered fruit juice, because I had tasted one, were the price of champagne, only much more. I refused to pay and worked out a sum that was excessive enough, but much less than was demanded. The proprietor came dancing out. 'Lock the doors. Call the police,' he shouted to the barman.

Jim Fraser was now very nervous. 'Let me pay and we'll get out of here,' he pleaded, but I saw no reason why we should. I told the man that I was very happy to see the police called, and I hoped that they would make trouble for him. The police duly arrived and it was clear that they were all in league together. 'Give me your names and addresses,' said a policeman, and then added, 'Are you married?' The implication was clear.

'My friend and I are here to see the Minister for Culture,' I said. 'He has never been in Vienna, speaks no German, and he is Chairman of an opera company in Scotland. We came in to have a drink and these girls joined us. Out of politeness my friend offered them a drink. Nothing more than that. I want to make a formal complaint against this place and I shall speak to the Minister.'

My bluff worked. The police looked uncomfortable and went away. The proprietor said, 'Alright. You're very clever. But in Germany, they'll do worse to you. Now get out.' Jim was sweating, and not having been able to follow the conversation in German was not sure how I had managed to get the doors unlocked and the police sent away. He was very quiet that evening. We ate in our hotel, had a night-cap and went to bed. We went to Paesiello's *Barber of Seville* (not Rossini's) at the little court theatre at Schönbrunn and a very bad *Merry Widow* at the Theater an der Wien before driving on to Verona, where we bought tickets to Verdi's *Macbeth* for that night. We were sitting in the restaurant next to the arena where the opera was playing when I said, 'That's funny, the radio is playing the overture to the opera we're about to hear.' Then I realised that it was not the radio: the opera had started. We had not adjusted our watches on coming into Italy and it was an hour later than I had thought. We hastily finished, paid, and climbed the stairs to our seats on the stones at the top of the giant arena. They were not the most comfortable, but they gave a magnificent view of the giant spectacle below and at the same time of the moon and stars. At the interval I could see Charles Osborne and Ken Thompson in white dinner jackets in the expensive seats down below, but we never met them. Then we drove to Monte Carlo, where my mother had a spare flat with two bedrooms, where my brother had recently been staying. We went to *Carmen* in the outdoor theatre in Nice, the Arènes des Cimiez, had dinner with Jacques Chaix at Cap Ferrat and lunch on the beach with my mother and John Barnard, and some American friend of their's, fatter than Jim, very ignorant about everything cultural and dismissive of English music. 'There are no English composers,' he said, 'only Handel, a Joyman.' I let it pass. Jim was happy there. We also called on Rosita Bootz at Cap d'Ail. I had had a little fling with her in Amsterdam some time previously and after Jim went to bed went out with her to continue it. It was a working holiday, because Jim was a heavy companion in more ways than one.

I went to Bayreuth with Jim again, but this time as part of a party of friends who had signed up for a package visit for the famous (or infamous)

Boulez-Chereau *Ring* in 1976. In the party were Sheila Colvin, Eleanor Kay, Jim's then new girlfriend, Joan Clark's sister, recently divorced from a local small factory owner, (a Ledlanet regular whose father had once been the blacksmith who had shoed the Ledlanet horses some decades earlier), an architect friend, Jack Notman, who had also been involved in another enterprise of mine that I have not yet related, Duncan Black, a senior civil servant from Edinburgh, and Jim's two elder sons. I ran into a French author of mine, Yves Navarre, about whom I shall have more to say, and Tom Walsh from Wexford, so we ended up as quite a big party.

That Bayreuth visit was very memorable. There were about forty people in the whole group and we flew to Heidelberg from which a bus took us to the same Schloss hotel where Jim and I had stayed in 1971. Our first performance was a remarkable *Parsifal*, only my sixth performance of this great work, in Wolfgang Wagner's production (his more admired brother Wieland was now dead), with Horst Stein conducting and René Kollo singing Parsifal. We particularly admired the smooth transformation scenes; the orchestra was wonderful and all the singers good. The next night was the controversial *Rheingold*. One member of the tour party was Lord Halsbury, a judge, to whom our tour guide had given the best seat for every performance, whereas many of us had very inferior seats; the tickets, all part of the package, were unevenly distributed depending on how our guide and tour leader rated his tour members. Halsbury hated the production of *Das Rheingold* so much that he sold his tickets for all his other performances at double the price to someone outside our group. My brief discussions with him made it clear he was not someone I would get on with anyway, and we hardly saw him after that. The modern staging of Chereau's *Ring* was a harbinger of horrors to come as produceritis gradually invaded the opera world, productions and decors that had little to do with the composer's intentions, but much with the desire of the Producer to make his mark. So much has been written about this version of the *Ring* that I will not weary the reader with more, but it was much hated by the bulk of the audience who booed for up to half an hour after each of the four operas, while the sizeable French minority who had come to support Boulez and Chereau cheered as loudly as they could. It was like the Franco-Prussian war back again.

Yves Navarre, a French author of mine, managed to get into performances for which there were no tickets through Chereau, and he attached himself to us. On non-performance days we went out to look at nearby Bavarian towns, most of them very picturesque. Tom Walsh found only one good thing about *Rheingold*, the moment when Wotan cuts of Alberich's finger to get the ring, rather than pulling it off, and that has been copied since. In a recent production, I saw the whole hand cut off. But otherwise a *Ring* in which everything clashed with tradition was not liked, except for the French element in the audience on purely chauvinistic grounds. Local German Bayreuthians to whom I spoke told us that the orchestra had decided to play as sloppily for the Boulez as they could, and the critical comments of many of the singers about what they had been told to wear and do was the common gossip of the town. Ian Judge, an English producer who was all in favour of the innovations, boiled over in rage at the criticisms that came from some of our group, and especially from me. It made the week, that included a conventional *Tristan and Isolde*, more than memorable. Jim, who was now a little heavier every year, had great trouble walking up the incline from the town to the 'green hill' on which the famous Festspielhaus is built, and I think he was pleased when the Wagner week was over.

During our week there I called on the executive offices, introduced myself as Director of Ledlanet Nights, a Scottish Opera Festival, and as a result we were given a tour of the building and of the technical facilities, with Jack Notman being considered our 'Techniker'. We were shown how the stage functioned and the various electronic gadgets. I found it fascinating, but I think Jim was a little bored. Four days later we were seeing more opera at the Edinburgh Festival, Verdi, Mozart, Schönberg and another *Parsifal*, this time from the Deutsche Oper an der Rhein.

The other big operatic experience that year came a month earlier in July. Edward Bond and Hans Werner Henze had collaborated on a pacifist opera and it caused a minor scandal when performed at Covent Garden. The Guards Band, which marched and played on the stage while the orchestra played in the pit, had apparently not been told that they were being borrowed to play in an anti-war opera and the press made much of that. There was an enormous cast and the production was lavish, but highly effective, and in many ways provocative, conducted by David Atherton, who was now making a reputation for modern works, and it was produced by the composer himself with more than eighty individual parts for the singers. The press was generally negative on purely political grounds, and Hans Keller in Opera magazine was almost hysterical in his condemnation of this overtly 'Communist' work. Norman Lebrecht, in a later reference book[32], called it 'an agitprop disaster'. I could in no way agree. I thought it incredibly exciting and relevant, agitprop perhaps, but so is most of Brecht who was by then acceptable enough in Britain and throughout Europe. I went to see it again, and liked it even more, and was bowled over by the music. Shortly afterwards I was in Berlin and had lunch with my friend, H. H. Stuckenschmidt, author of the most important Schönberg biography (I had published a short early version of it and some years later the complete extension). He was just as opposed to the opera, which I had seen the night before in the Staatsoper in a very insipid and watered-down version, as was Hans Keller. I am an admirer of Henze, have seen many of his operas and know his music fairly well, but still think that *We Come to the River* may well be his masterpiece. I live in hope that I shall see it again, but it is unlikely.

---

[32] Norman Lebrecht. The Companion to 20th Century Music. London 1992.

I think it was on another occasion in Berlin that I met Luigi Nono at a lunch given by Stuckenschmidt, who was Professor of Composition at the university. It was a very convivial lunch and I enjoyed the distinguished company that our host had brought together during a Berlin Festival, particularly Nono's and that of his wife Nuria, who was also Schönberg's daughter, born late in the composer's life. Afterwards Nono and I walked through the streets of Berlin talking. 'What are you doing tonight?' asked Nono.

'I'm going to hear Karajan and the Philharmonic,' I replied, 'Beethoven and Brahms, I think.'

'Can you still listen to all that?' asked Nono. 'I'd rather stand here in the street and listen to the traffic. It's much more interesting.'

* * * * * *

My new list under my old and now my new imprint came out during the autumn of 1975. It was too late for some books already in production not to bear the Calder and Boyars imprint, but I published Ian Wallace's autobiography, a novel by John Stonehouse under the pseudonym James Lund (*The Ultimate*), Sidney Goodsir Smith's *Collected Poems* and many other titles, under my own name. During the late seventies I produced about twenty-five titles a year, including reprints. Calder and Boyars had been doing about twice that, but it was some years since we had on occasion put out two to three hundred titles a year, including our American imports.

The Wallace autobiography went well and was reprinted. The reason that Stonehouse's novel, which was a political thriller in which the IRA, largely under the direction of a dissident CIA man of Irish origin, succeeds in blowing up the entire British Cabinet, had to appear under a pen-name, was that he was about to be sent to prison. Here a little digression is necessary.

Stonehouse and I had collaborated over *Gangrene* and he had found me a not very successful barrister for the first *Last Exit* trial, but we had since kept in touch. I attended a large and very politically glamorous party at his house in Potter's Bar in North London, where his wife Barbara, a very attractive woman and an accomplished hostess, entertained the entire Labour hierarchy of the sixties, or so it seemed, including Harold Wilson, then Prime Minister, with whom I traded memories of Bordeaux back in the early fifties. Then Wilson suddenly dropped him from the cabinet and the always hyperactive Stonehouse got more involved in the London Co-operative Society to which he was elected Chairman. When the 'stamp wars' started between different retailing chains to try to get more customers to buy always from them by collecting stamps issued with purchases, Stonehouse fought against the stamps and he also succeeded in fighting off a Communist challenge to his Chairmanship.

One night, when I was still with Bettina at Wimpole Street, I gave a dinner party at which John Stonehouse and Alan Sainsbury were both guests. Alan was a Labour peer and Chairman of Sainsbury's Stores. I had first met him in 1951 when I was a very new publisher at a dinner party given by Mark Marvin, a not very successful theatre impresario, and at that first encounter Alan Sainsbury had described himself as a grocer, which he was, but perhaps the biggest in Britain. I had known him through my two marriages: he certainly had an attraction towards Christya, much resented by his wife, who however I discovered would have her own lunchtime trysts with other gentlemen at the Royal Festival Hall, not a place at which she was likely to run into anyone who knew her at that time of day. But I certainly kept my mouth shut. I never saw her again after that, and usually Alan came on his own when I was married to Bettina.

Both Stonehouse and Sainsbury were prominent members of the Labour party, but it had not occurred to me that they were also both involved in big stores until I brought them together at that dinner. They were inseparable and spoke to each other all evening, both being involved then in combating the new craze for green or blue stamps to encourage customer loyalty, whereas they relied on competitive price. I was rather surprised to be invited to the annual dinner of the London Co-Op, but not when I saw that the guest of honour was Lord Sainsbury. But from that time, it was all downhill for poor John Stonehouse. He became involved in setting up a Bangladeshi Bank and also in import-export deals with Nigeria, counting on his old contacts from the days when he knew these countries and their rulers as Colonial Secretary in Labour governments, or Shadow Secretary in opposition. He saw himself as a new tycoon with a social conscience, bringing benefits to black minorities and at the same time making himself a fortune, but John was naive in commercial dealings, too trustful of others, and he put his money and credit into schemes where he could easily be cheated and was. At the same time he was a ladies' man. His wife knew of his affairs, but tolerated them as they never lasted long, but then he became involved with his secretary Sheila Buckley, who was also a part of his business dealings. When he saw that everything was collapsing around him, he tried to rescue as much of his money as possible, while at the same time disappearing to make a new life with Sheila.

The way he did this was to remove money from the Bangladeshi Bank in which he was involved, which was quite illegal, even if it had originally been his own money, and he sent it to Australia through his secretary. He then faked his suicide in Florida: his clothes were found on the shore and it was assumed he had drowned. He flew to Australia under an assumed name with a faked passport, receiving communications and money there from Sheila Buckley, who intended to join him when the time was ripe. But this tall Englishman, paying regular visits to a bank and post-office, attracted attention, and he was arrested on suspicion of being Lord Lucan, who having killed his children's nanny in mistake for his wife had also disappeared. Stonehouse was soon identified and returned to England, where he was formally charged. While he awaited trial I saw him frequently for lunch, and agreed to publish his novel *The Ultimate*, but under the name James Lund (echoes of James Bond), which he was convinced would become a best-seller. I hoped the same, but saw it at least as an interesting political thriller. John could write factually quite well, but he was not a fiction writer, his style being too close to the boy's adventure stories he had read as a child. As he was now a pariah in the Labour Party, he started a new one, the English National Party in order to have a label as he was still an MP. He was tried and convicted a few days after our last lunch and was then evicted from parliament. He wanted his royalties to be saved and passed to Sheila. The counts against him were many, ranging from trying to obtain £125,000 life insurance to help his family, to illegally withdrawing money from the businesses in which he was involved, thereby insuring their earlier insolvency. Some of the charges were very minor, such as using an American Express card under the name J.A. Markham and the name he adopted in Australia, D.C. Mildoon, to obtain credit. But he was sentenced to six years imprisonment and Sheila Buckley to two years, the latter suspended because the judge remarked that she had no doubt been overwhelmed by Stonehouse's strong personality. In the short time before he was sentenced, he finished two other books, *Death of an Idealist*[33], an account of his career and disgrace, and *My Trial*[34], which he wrote day by day while the trial was going on, and which appeared only days after the sentence. He was our second MP author to go to prison, the first having been Peter Baker.

Sidney Goodsir Smith died while his *Collected Poems* were still in proof. He had made many changes, above all simplifying his Scots dialect poems to make many of them easier to read by non-Scottish readers. I asked Hazel, his widow to recommend someone who could finish the proof-reading who was sufficiently familiar with his work, and she named Tom Scott. This made Alexander Scott, who felt that it should have been him, a bitter enemy. He attacked the edition when it was published as corrupt, blamed me for changing the spelling and anglicising many of the poems, and would not accept that this had been done by Sidney himself or in some cases indicated by him to me or to Hazel or others. One result was losing Scottish Arts Council support, especially in the case of Elspeth Davie, as has been told. Alex Scott continued sniping at me up to his death.

I was taking on other French authors, as I had always done, outside the *nouveau roman* group, and Yves Navarre, mentioned above in connection with Bayreuth, was one. He was a friend of Jean-Pierre Rémy, and they were quite similar except in their sexual orientation, Navarre being gay, as were his novels, while Angrémy was always seen with very attractive girls. I could

---

[33] London 1975.
[34] London 1976.

not take on both, and instead of Angrémy (who under that, his real name, was also French cultural attaché in London) chose Navarre, partly because he was warmly recommended by Donald Watson, who had translated Ionesco and Obaldia for me, and now wanted to translate Yves as well. I came to know Yves well because he was often in London and I gave a party for him at Dalmeny House, introducing him, perhaps rashly, as possibly the new Proust. He was to be the first author I came to publish under a new imprint I was about to start in New York.

I had been approached at the Frankfurt Book Fair, probably in 1976, but it may have been a year later, by a man called Bob Speer who wanted to set up a distribution service in the U.S. and was looking for British publishers who had books to sell there which were not committed to American publishing houses. I showed enough interest to receive a call a month or two later in London from a colleague of his called Hank Coleman. They were both Texans, based in Dallas. Hank however had some knowledge of Britain, having been for a time at Durham University, and if he did not quite have the charisma of Bob, who had been the fast-talking star salesman for Viking Press in New York, he was a lot brainier. I was impressed enough to pay a visit to Dallas on my next American trip and meet the group that had just started South-West Book Services. They put me up in a hotel, which they paid for, entertained me royally and showed me their offices and warehouse, where not much was happening yet, but the potential seemed good. It was only later that I learned how the company had started, and it was like this: a local lady, who had made a considerable amount of money in nuclear medicine, had approached Bob Speer, asking if he could help her to get her father's memoirs published; he had been a local country lawyer who had recently died and she felt a duty to carry out this last wish of his. Bob published it with her money, asking her at the same time to capitalise a distribution company to sell it. Then they had taken on small local publishers and they were looking for more. Bob Speer saw a big potential for British books if publishers had American rights. Several people in London had been approached other than myself, but they were all holding back. I was the first to go to Dallas.

Back in London I spoke to others who had been approached, including Clive Alison of Alison and Busby, a fairly new publisher, and Colin Haywood of Duckworth. I said that there was no doubt that they had exaggerated what they were, but I liked the people and felt that the potential was there. Several of us then decided to try out South-West and sent them books to distribute. The first results were promising and we sent more.

I was making several trips to New York around this time, had started to see Sigmund and Phyllis Miller again, and I was invited to stay with them. Phyllis was an inveterate match-maker and she introduced me to a number of ladies, and I did have a few brief relationships, but never let her know about them. I also met an old flame from London, who had worked for the

BBC for some years and came from a well-known British Jewish family. She was now doing publicity work in New York and was happy to see me, finding many of her American clients distasteful. Because of family connections – her brother had for some years been a prominent personality in Israeli politics and was well-known in the U.S. – she was asked to promote many Jewish causes, but found the pushing-for-recognition side of many New York Jews not to her taste. She took me to some big fund-raising banquets and apologised for the vulgarity that characterised them, but it gave her a good income even while she was dismissive of her employers. I shall call her Miriam for the purpose of this book. When I introduced her to the Millers, she was lionised by them too, but found them at least amusing and intelligent. Sigi at this time was trying to write popular crime novels, with limited success, and Phyllis was working for the Village Voice in their book advertising department. I did meet one lady through the Millers called Martha Gelhorn. She was cultured, interesting and open to interesting experiences, and took to me, so we started an affair, where the intellectual side was more important than the physical. The Millers suspected something was up, but could not be sure and we never told them. I introduced her to opera, which like many Americans of her background she thought of as the preserve of a social elite and of no particular intellectual interest. A *Tannhäuser* at the Metropolitan Opera, produced and sung with great conviction, convinced her that she should think again. After a while I was staying with her rather than with the Millers.

I decided to go to the American Booksellers Convention in Atlanta, and to create some effect there to get my imprint better known, I brought over Jeff Nuttall, who planned a 'happening' at the convention. I took him around New York, introduced him to my favourite booksellers, in particular to Arthur and Roseanne Seelen, friends from years back, who ran a specialised Drama Bookstore, and we planned the happening. I had started a new imprint as an American trading name. If things went wrong, I did not want the odium or smell of failure to follow me back across the Atlantic. The name was Riverrun Press. Riverrun is the first word and the unprinted last one of Joyce's *Finnegans Wake*. I assumed that it would strike a chord among those I most wanted to reach, the teachers of literature, who would with luck soon be setting some of my books for their students to read. I printed a handsome four-page brochure, explaining the name and my policy for introducing my catalogue into the American market. Jeff then wrote letters to some fifty booksellers whose names we found in the standard reference book, promising events and surprises at the Atlanta convention. The idea was that a certain lady would be there who had to be recognised and found, or there would be trouble. We both stayed with Martha Gelhorn who decided to come to the convention with us. She took a big shine to Jeff, one of the world's great characters, open, bluff and unconventional, a good writer and a good artist with a passion to educate the world and help it to discover the force and the meaning of art as a life-enhancer. In New York he would sit for hours in subway stations watching the graffiti on passing trains, elaborate designs that New Yorkers hated and he loved. We had pleasant dinners in Greenwich Village where Martha Gelhorn lived, discussing art, literature, the world and the forthcoming conference.

Jeff went a day ahead of me to prepare. At the airport he asked a policeman the way to the Booksellers Conference. The man looked at him. 'Bookmaker, bookseller, whatever the hell y'are,' he said in a voice that Jeff loved to imitate. 'If ya go down them stairs, I guess yo'll find what you'se lookin' for.' By the time I arrived he knew the town quite well and was dismayed by the way whole living districts had been torn down to make way for big shiny hotels and department stores. He loved the southern accent, very pronounced in Atlanta, laughed at the waitress called 'Pame' (Pam) who brought us drinks, and he prepared his happening, which went wrong because a lot of our letters had not arrived. Jeff had thought the zip-codes were telephone numbers. So half-way through the convention, a large fat man came walking among the publisher's booths, naked except for briefs, his face and body twisted out of recognition by cellotape wound tightly like ropes around him, wearing a poster saying 'This is what Mary Thompson does to a man.' It was Jeff himself and certainly he attracted attention. In fact the police were called, so we rushed him out of sight and did not associate the event with our books, which were exposed on a joint stand with the other books being offered by South-West Book Services. Bob Speer was in his element, no longer an employee of a big company, but President of his own new one. Hank Coleman was Vice-President.

In Britain I had published Yves Navarre's *Sweet Tooth*, a macabre novel about the raunchy and very rough New York gay scene of the sixties, which Yves had witnessed and no doubt been part of. I printed a new cover, using a drawing of the author by David Hockney, and issued it in New York under the new imprint and with the Dallas address. Yves came over and I employed Miriam to promote it, but she was not keen on gay books, so found a friend, also English, to take it on, who managed to get it reviewed. I offered it to Hollywood, who were interested, but they were still nervous of gay subjects and this book was a very strong one. However Yves enjoyed New York, looked up old friends, took me to some gay restaurants and we went together to the Metropolitan Opera to hear *Carmen* with Régine Crespin. This was in November 1978. When Yves heard that I finally was going to pay his hotel bill – we were both staying at the Algonquin – a big smile came over his face. 'Now I really will enjoy the opera,' he said.

I brought another gay author to New York a year later and had the same problem with Miriam. This time it was David Galloway, who had been a witness for me in the *Last Exit* case. I had published his very effective novella, *Melody Jones*, about an affair between a gay night-club entertainer and a married man who falls in love with him. The affair goes wrong and ends in tragedy because of their class difference; what spells glamour to one is seen as tacky by the other, but it is a little gem, and in my opinion the best thing David Galloway, whose several novels tend to depend on a clever idea or a gimmick, has written. It appeared in *New Writer Twelve* in 1976 and on its own in a new series, Riverrun Writers, that I issued some time later. I think however that the publicity we were looking for may have been for a later novel, a take-off on Raymond Chandler, where the tough detective is a blonde lesbian with a gay black assistant.

A conference of publishers was organised in Dallas. There were ten British publishers, all staying in the hotel where the conference took place, and about seven or eight Americans. The first session, all sitting around a long table, was amusing. We each made a statement about who we were and what our books were like. The left-wing British publisher Pluto Press, represented by Michael Kidron, was followed a few minutes later by a right-wing American fundamentalist religious and political one. Each wanted to change the world. But it was civilised enough and went on for several days. We had all had our books there with South-West for some months, and although sales were reasonably satisfactory, doubts had risen about the financial stability of the company, especially when we realised that one lady had provided all the money and was not going to provide any more. South-West was run by a group of sales people who had little business sense, however good they were at selling, and they had no idea of budgets: they spent money whether it was there or not, and much of the expenditure was wasteful or too inappropriate for their size and means. They had brought out a large printing of a catalogue describing everyone's book: it was handsome, heavily illustrated, looked rather like a literary magazine of the Village Voice variety, and it ran to over six hundred pages. It was a considerable feat to produce it, but the cost was high, and they never thought of asking the publishers to contribute to the cost of what was an effective selling tool. There was a resident salaried artist on the staff who spent much of his time drawing cartoons of Bob Speer and others around the office, but no management system was visible. At our last session we wanted to hold a private meeting first, which was chaired by Colin Hayward, with Kidron taking notes of what we wanted to know, and then we confronted Speer and the senior half-dozen of his selling people. He had much rhetoric, but little in the way of satisfactory assurances, and we all left unhappier than we had arrived. I am not sure what caused the good feeling and confidence of our first meeting to deteriorate during the next three days, but we gradually sniffed out the real situation, and in fact the company was not far from collapse.

I had one pleasant experience. A lady journalist who came from the local Dallas paper to report on our presence, picked me out to interview personally, probably at the instigation of Hank Coleman, and we became good friends. Some time later she came to join me at Albuquerque because I wanted to go to the Opera Festival at Santa Fé as I relate in the next chapter. Her name was Julia. I had to pay several visits to Dallas in the late seventies and paid for most of them with a deal I made with PanAm, whereby they gave me free transatlantic travel in return for an advertisement in a number of our books. I also had an affair with Jill, one of the barmaids at the same hotel, but on two other occasions. She was English, had been pulled out of some trouble by the Mormons, who found her jobs, took ten percent of her earnings and tried to brainwash her in various ways. She had escaped from them, which is why she was working in a hotel and not in an office, but the Mormons were always looking for her to get her back, and apparently they could be very nasty to defectors. I am not sure what happened to her in the end. She probably returned to England.

During this time I was crossing the Atlantic frequently and spending time in New York, calling on booksellers to help the reps of South-West Book Services. They finally collapsed early in 1979, just after Harold Hobson's *French Theatre Since 1830*, which had had few British reviews, received a long and very positive one in the American Library Journal. The warehouse in Dallas had just closed after a last ditch attempt to sell the company had failed, and I was unable to get my books out. None of the orders could be serviced and that review which would have sold probably two thousand copies to American libraries, as well as other reviews that appeared at about that time, were wasted. Sigi Miller then introduced me to a man who was interested in investing. Jack Berger talked to a lot of people including Bob Speer before the collapse happened and was impressed by him, more than by me. He was willing to invest but made it clear he would be tough if things went wrong. He wanted me to put Ledlanet up as security, and I had a number of meetings with him to work out details of an investment in Riverrun Press. On occasion he let me use his office. I did so when David Galloway and his German boyfriend came there to meet Miriam, but she did not take to them, so it fell through and we found someone else. In retrospect, with the problems that would come later, I was very pleased that no deal ever went through. I cannot remember why it went wrong.

I found a New York firm of distributors that was basically a partnership between a local Italian-American called Lorenzo de Grazie and an English entrepreneur who were trying to do exactly what Bob Speer had done. They did not have their own warehouse, but used one called Mercedes in Brooklyn, run by a young man called Joel Goldstein, who I found very difficult to deal with. Lorenzo had an office in the Flatiron Building at the junction of Broadway and Fifth Avenue, two main streets that sweep north and south at an angle and are bisected by this famous triangular-shaped building where they cross. I had already been taken there once by Alger Hiss, who I still saw occasionally, to meet Edith Tiger, who ran the Emergency Civil Liberties Committee, located in the building just underneath Lorenzo's office. Edith Tiger at the time was trying to help Alger in his, ultimately unsuccessful, battle to get his case reopened and his name cleared. Finally, after many months I managed to get my books out of Dallas and into the Mercedes warehouse. I realised however that I would have to put together a new sales force myself. Lorenzo was quite useless.

One thing leads to another and one person to another. Staying on occasion at the Algonquin Hotel in New York, I encountered at its Blue Bar, a famous meeting place, a man called Charles Avery who was there every evening, chatting to whoever came to sit beside or near him at the bar. He had done various things in his life, almost certainly had some private money, enough to cover his drinking bill if nothing else, and he worked at Grand Central Station as a booking clerk, although he certainly had had a better job earlier in life and a better social position. He was an amateur actor who acted when he could at the Comedy Club, a rather up-market establishment on the east side of midtown. This was frequented mainly by yuppie young men, Wall Street brokers and the like, who enjoyed acting as a hobby, or being part of a theatrical set-up. The club had short runs of popular plays, a bar and restaurant. I found myself frequently chatting to Charles, who introduced me to his lady friend, an eccentric actress in her late forties called Elaine Swann who did mainly television advertisements, and acted on stage when she could, but who was, like Charles, one of the pillars of the Comedy Club. They took me there, made a fuss of me, introduced me around and I met some interesting people. Anyone with an English accent was very welcome in their circles. Charles at that point, interested in talking, drinking and acting, in about that order, was a platonic boyfriend. Elaine had another boyfriend that she confided to me she shared with another lady in London, Sue Telch. She suggested that I should look her up when I was back. Elaine had an apartment on Bleecker Street in Greenwich Village, just off Seventh Avenue, the centre of the most interesting bohemian area of New York, with hundreds of restaurants, bars, theatres, and every kind of boutique, including the most interesting bookshops. My friend Martha had lived nearby, but now had moved to Cooperstown in Upper New York State, where on two occasions I went to visit her. She had had two cancer operations not long before I met her. Somewhere around 1980 the cancer came back and she died in Cooperstown. Elaine Swann played tennis every day, not well, but with determination, and having the opportunity to move into a block of apartments further uptown, where there were tennis courts for residents on the flat roofs, she moved there, and I sub-let her apartment. It was quite large, but more than half the space could not be used as three rooms were filled with old theatrical costumes and clothes she was unlikely ever to wear again. I had in practice a bed-sitting room with kitchen equipment, and a bathroom. But I was very happy there because I was in New York's equivalent of London's Soho, right on a main subway line, and Lorenzo's office was easy to get to. I already knew the area well from many evenings spent there with Barnet Rosset in the past, and he did not live far away. I saw him occasionally, mainly in two local literary bars, the '55' and the Lion's Head. The old row had been made up.

It was in the '55' that I met Jeannie Adams and began talking to her on a bar stool. It was the night I had arrived from London I remember, but we got on well and almost every time I went there in the evening, I saw Jeannie. She worked for a travel agency and soon I was using her to get cheap travel around the States, which became my main activity during the next decade and the subject of the next chapter. We were never more than friends, but we became very good friends.

In London I rang Sue Telch as Elaine Swann had asked me to do, and she was free to go out to dinner that night. She was a very personable lady, an interior designer with a very open and sophisticated manner, in her thirties. Her tastes were popular in that she went to musicals rather than opera, and light comedies rather than heavy dramas, and read best-sellers rather than serious literature, but she was a wonderful mixer who got on well with everyone. During the war she had developed an Australian accent because her father had sent her out there for the duration, but he had quickly made her take elocution lessons on her return to get rid of it. Her step-father was Dutch and she spoke the language. She was already divorced from Mr. Telch, a car-dealer. She came back to Dalmeny House with me for a drink after dinner and although I thought it unlikely that she would accept my pass, she did. 'I will sooner or later, so I might as well say yes now,' she said, as if in resignation. We were an unlikely match. Most of my women have been about my own height and either slight or plumpish, but Sue was much taller and was rather like the more sophisticated type of west-end actress. Our relationship went on until she married again, and was more a friendship where sex was always available and taken for granted, but with no emotion involved. She felt free to accept any man, even several in a day, and her approach was that of a highly sexed man rather than of a woman. Professionally she was successful and specialised in creating rooms like men's clubs, liking leather furniture and designing decors for country hotels, golf clubs and old castles. One of her main sources of revenue at the time I met her was redecorating suites in London's large hotels, especially on Park Lane. Rich and often Royal Arabs would stay there, turning a luxurious environment into a pig-sty during their stay, even reputedly roasting whole animals on spits in their suites. We became good friends, not having to hide anything from each other, and she was always able to look after my dog when I was away.

Shuna became a major problem once I started to spend more time in the United Sates and I had to leave her then with one of the ladies in my life. I mated her with the dog of a local landowner in Kinross when she was about four and when she was heavily pregnant at the beginning of 1972, I took her to a pet shop in Edinburgh to find a large basket. On the floor was a large red high-topped imitation leather receptacle and she climbed right into it and made herself comfortable. She had chosen her maternity bed, so I took it back with me. I had Alice with me at the time and she stayed at Ledlanet for the following week with a dog of her own, Muffin, a Yorkshire terrier, who apparently watched and wagged her tail as the puppies emerged one by one in the red basket. I was in London in my office and every few minutes Margaret Jaquess, who sat at our switch-board at reception, came in to tell me that another puppy had been born. The first was almost albino white but became golden as he grew up, the next nine were all black like the parents. I went up before the weekend to host the last French shooting party of the season, and Shuna was very resentful at having to stay with her litter and not go out with the guns.

It was not long after that, perhaps a fortnight later that I had to take the whole basket with its ten puppies down south because nothing was happening at Ledlanet until the spring. Alice was with me and we stopped in Newcastle-on-Tyne for lunch, parking the car on the quayside in front of a restaurant. When we emerged the Tyne had risen and the quay was submerged up to three feet while a desperate Shuna was frantically barking to get attention. The water was up to the back seat and the dogs were already getting wet. I threw off my overcoat and jacket, climbed through the water to the lower level of the quay where the car was, unlocked the car door, opened it, told Shuna to swim, and she was pulled up by Alice. Then I handed the puppies out one by one, then the basket, and returning to the restaurant borrowed a blanket. Apparently this flooding was quite usual in winter, but there was no sign to warn anyone. I called a taxi, told the driver to find a comfortable hotel and we went to one in Gosport, where all the dogs were bathed, dried and fell asleep. The next day a local garage, that I suspected had removed a warning sign, because they were quite accustomed to drying out cars and it was good for business, got the car going again, but it gave me trouble from there on. It was the same car I had once driven down the station steps at Harrogate.

The dogs were at Ledlanet until early summer, then I found good homes for them all. My sister took the golden labrador, which became her family pet, Sandy, and another one, Daisy, was intended for my daughter Stas, but the problems with her mother were such that she ended up with Chris Davidson, my production manager. One went to my friend Brian Mahoney, the television producer who had done many things at Ledlanet, and who lived on an island on Loch Lomond: he called his dog Barra, after another island.

There are two Ledlanet Christmases worth-while relating. The first must have been somewhere towards the end of Ledlanet Nights, when performances were over for the year. I had my two daughters present, Brian Mahoney and his wife Jean, their two boys and also Barbara Wright, a friend who translated many of our French authors, including some Robbe-Grillet and Duras, and most of Raymond Queneau and Nathalie Sarraute. She had also translated an Italian libretto for Ledlanet. We were looking after ourselves, Attewell having his own Christmas at home, and we were cooking a large turkey for lunch. Jean said 'Why don't you all go for a walk? Leave the kitchen to me.' It was a lovely morning and we all went through the wood and up to the hill with its wonderful panoramic view, returning after twelve. Smoke emerged from the kitchen as we came near. The turkey was burned to a crisp, various pots and pans had boiled over, and there was no sign of Jean. But Brian instantly realised what had happened. I had had no idea that Jean was an arrested alcoholic: the sight of a full brandy bottle had been too much for her, and she had wanted us out of the way to drink it. She was now in her bedroom, barely conscious. All afternoon we could hear Brian shouting at her in fury and trying to wake her up, while the rest of us opened tins and had a most unchristmassy picnic.

The other Christmas must have been my last there, much later. I had the Balls, Ron Rosen, the barrister who was defending for me, and Ron's German girlfriend who had brought an infant daughter. We were again looking after ourselves, although Attewell looked in occasionally. The house was a sad place now, Rentokill having pulled much of it apart to get at the dry rot, and Attewell's role was more of a caretaker. It was a Christmas of legal talk, chess, eating and drinking and not much else. Even Jim Fraser preferred to invite us to Huntley Hall than to come to a house only partially heated, redolent of memories and visibly deteriorating. My financial situation was desperate and I tried to deal with my crises day by day, and get through the next one. The banks would lend me no more, and a judge, who had ordered me to pay even more to Bettina, had no sympathy with my desire to keep Ledlanet and no interest in what it had been culturally or could be again. 'He should sell it,' he said. And of course I had no alternative then. Land prices were depressed at the time, the house was in bad shape and the London Estate agent who put out a brochure and charged me for it, came up with no offer at all. I put my library and some of the furniture into storage in Dunfermline, sold the contents of the house for a fixed sum to an unpleasant couple that thought my private clothes were included and took things like my silver sporran without my realising it. Many things of historical importance kept in drawers, which I forgot about in my extreme depression, where thrown away. They included the albums of photographs of the whole Kennedy family, including dozens of Jack as a teenager (all the Kennedys had stayed at Ledlanet), my grandfather's unpublished memoirs, which I had intended to keep, and the marvellous modern paintings of Pulsford and other artists who were friends of mine. I should have put them into storage, and I think I did put one or two, but they never came out again. Everything the purchasers did not see as immediately saleable they burnt. They made a fuss over the Velasquez copy, and some newspapers created a story out of this great 'discovery' that could have saved my bacon, but that was soon discredited.

An Edinburgh couple bought the house itself. When they divorced they sold it to a local farmer who had already bought the home farm. Jimmy Provan who had once rented it from me, had now gone to work for his father-in-law who owned a chain of newspapers including the Glasgow Herald. Later he would become the Tory European Member of Parliament for Teeside. That was the end of Ledlanet, but I will come back to it again at the end of this chapter.

* * * * * *

Two publishing companies now shared a building in Soho: Marion had the top floor, and still kept the same office in the middle of the three rooms for herself, while I occupied the middle room of the three on the second floor, with Chris Davidson in a larger room next to me overlooking the street. I think Agnes Rook, and for a time Bill Swainson, were in the outer room by the stairs, editing manuscripts, but later it was Martin Hoyle. I had taken Swainson with me to Dallas for the big meeting of publishers, and his quiet sensible manner and obvious competence must have appealed to Clive Alison, because he soon left to work for Clive as Production Manager. John Quilliam, a friend of Chris', did our audit and came in occasionally to write up the books. Yvonne Ball did some bookkeeping for both Marion and myself. On the first floor, just above Lina Stores, was the general office that the two publishing companies shared, a reception desk where Margaret Jaquess answered the 'phone, sold books from the general stock we kept in the outer office to the general public and to booksellers needing a book in a hurry for a customer. She also looked after Shuna at times who kept her feet warm in winter, and when Daisy became Chris's dog, she was there too. There was a constant stream of authors, translators, printers' reps, and others coming in and out. Berry Bloomfield had retired by now to live in a boat with her husband and I had a series of short-term secretaries, some of them earlier doubling with work for Ledlanet and going there during the performance seasons. We had Irene, a Rhodesian girl, at the time of the strike, who felt quite at home that hot summer when the grass in all of London's parks turned yellow: to her it was normal. One secretary married an Indian accountant from Kenya. She had become friendly with Ian Wallace, who sang at her wedding; we both noted the disapproval of their very middle-English family to the dark-skinned bridegroom, who was taking her to Nairobi with him, where, as Ian remarked 'his skin would be more acceptable than her's.' Another of my secretaries, Claire, married Tom Craig after he had obtained a divorce from Penny. They all remained friends and I continued to see them, but less frequently after Ledlanet was sold. Michael Hayes continued to sell books for Marion and myself, until he decided his income was insufficient and left to work for a wholesaler.

My office problems began to centre around Chris Davidson. He was in charge of the office when I was overseas, and he took too much advantage of it. He decided to join me rather than Marion, when we divided, but I began to realise that the real reason was probably that I was more tolerant, easy-going and trustful. His expenses, all taken out of petty cash, mounted ever higher, and Yvonne pointed out to me that they were getting to be a serious drain on the company. It came to the point where I had to have a confrontation with him. He had in many ways become more eccentric, dressing weirdly, sometimes in punk clothes, was always friendlier to gays than others, and I realised that although he was firmly in the closet, he had a double life. We had previously published an *Opera Directory*, a large reference book that first came out in 1961, listing everyone working in opera, giving valuable information about opera houses, contents of opera publications and addresses of opera publishers, availability of scores and much else. Ann Gardiner, who also worked for the Dossé Arts magazines in the fifties, selling advertising, had brought in thousands of pounds of advertising for the Directory, and had made a heroic trip to New York the year before publication to get advertising from artists' agents on behalf of their clients. Ann Ross, who had been Rafael Kubelik's secretary at Covent Garden, had been in charge of the editorial part. The publication had taken an enormous effort and was profitable, but Marion had not wanted to go through so much sweat and toil again, and it was only after we had divided the company that I was able to start on a new edition of what had been intended to be a bi-annual reference book, especially invaluable to casting directors, rather like *Spotlight*. I had employed Martin Hoyle to start with the compilation. He was a friend of Sheila Colvin's and she knew he liked compiling lists. But sitting in my office the compilation was going very slowly, and the main reason was that both he and Chris were spending more time talking to each other than working. There came the day when my dissatisfaction with Chris came to a head. When I said that he was not giving enough time to his work, he responded why should he when my whole life was a holiday, which annoyed me enough to fire him. Part of the beginning of the row had been over money for which he would not account satisfactorily, and afterwards, in court, he said that my secretary had overheard me saying that he had been caught with his hand in the till. I do not remember ever saying it, but I was certainly thinking it. He sued me for compensation other than the redundancy money I gave him, and was awarded a little more by the Unfair Dismissal Tribunal, but it did him no good because, by telephoning his lawyer several times a day, he spent many times the amount he received on unnecessary legal fees. Martin left with him out of solidarity, so a new *Opera Directory* never appeared. I had the wrong person working on it in any case, so its non-publication was inevitable.

At just this time Reginald Davis-Poynter, who had once been the head of the publishing empire that Granada had put together under Sidney

Bernstein, and had later started his own firm, decided to give up and retire. He had an assistant, Sue Herbert, who had also been at Granada and had left with him, and I recruited her to join me. Sue had worked her way up to a position of authority in Granada, and was now working with smaller publishers of lesser means and with a less prestigious position for herself, and she really did not like it, but publishing was changing, and security of tenure, which was important to her, no longer existed. She came to me on condition I would meet her pension demands, which were greater than I had ever had to consider in the past, but I needed someone competent and agreed. She was to stay with me as office manager until 1997.

In America I had kept up with the many reps who had worked for South-West Book Services, especially Dan Wedge in New England, Stuart Abrahams in Chicago and Dosier Hammond and Steve Mandel in California. The New York rep for Lorenzo was quite useless, so I did New York myself, getting good orders in particular from the string of bookshops along Madison Avenue, from the university shops, those in Greenwich Village, and such famous literary havens as Gotham Book Mart. But the Mercedes service was slow, largely because Lorenzo was not a good customer and also because he was a bad payer. I was doing some of my printing in Toronto at this time with Hunter-Rose, whose salesman James Bruce, an Englishman, became a friend. He designed a catalogue for Lorenzo and did many things of that kind. I spent one New Year's Eve with him, starting with a drink with Bill Colleran who was in New York, then we had a late dinner and went to a jazz club in the Village, drinking whisky in a bar, and parting in the cold morning at five. I think I was in Bleecker Street then and the year was probably 1979.

Long before that, in Paris, I had had dinner with Sam Beckett at the PLM Hotel, across the street from his apartment, a week or so before his seventieth birthday, which was on the 13th of April 1976. I asked him what he was writing. 'I'm just finishing a text,' he said. 'Seventy is old age and when you're old work has to be your company.' He went on to say that this time it was written in English, so I would have the rights to sell to publishers in other languages. This was very important to me, because the company would keep a quarter of that revenue, the exceptions being Rosset in the States and Lindon in France, with whom Sam dealt directly. I pondered his words about work becoming his company. 'Is that what you're going to call it?' I asked, 'Company?'

'Perhaps,' he answered, 'I'm still thinking about it.' But *Company* it was, and it became the most successful of all his later prose works.

Beckett's reputation was now about as great as Joyce's and he was a collectible author. His first editions were treasured, and we took advantage of this to bring out de luxe limited editions of his main new works in special bindings, numbered and signed by the author. Beckett was always amenable to do this boring chore of signing copies. Art publishers were constantly approaching him to let his texts be illustrated by artists who wanted to associate their names with his. Signing hundreds of such volumes took up much of Beckett's time. He of course received copies for himself, but usually he gave them away to friends. In *Endgame*, the main character Hamm, once he realises that the end has finally come, throws away his few possessions, the props that give him some mobility or ability to sleep. 'Discard,' he says and this became Beckett's motto as he dispossessed himself of the things around him that others wanted. I was only seeing him about four times a year at this time as I was so much in America, but found there was a market there for Beckett limited editions.

In Paris I had a regular round of calls to make on publishers, authors, friends and others whose company I enjoyed and wanted to keep up with. One such was Maria Jolas, whose name has not yet appeared in this narrative. She was a survivor not just from pre-war Paris, but from the war before that. She and her husband Eugène Jolas had founded the magazine Transition in 1927, the most influential, and in my opinion the best, of all the English language literary periodicals that were published in Paris during the twentieth century. Before that she had studied singing in Paris, and had met her husband in the States when he was a penniless refugee from Alsace, which previously a German province, was once again a French one after 1918. Maria was able to finance his career from her own family money after they married. The patron of Joyce, whose *Finnegans Wake* appeared in serial form in Transition, and the friend of countless writers and artists, she had been living quietly on the Rue de Rennes ever since her husband died in 1952, translating French writers, and most especially Nathalie Sarraute into English. A left-wing political activist, she also supported radical causes and translated manifestos, even for students, without ever asking for payment. Sarraute was a close friend and each had a holiday cottage in a little village not far from Paris. She started translating Sarraute for George Braziller in New York, then for me as well. Whenever I called on her I heard fascinating anecdotes about Paris between the wars and all the people she and her husband had known. She would launch into a story about Joyce and break off to remark, 'I never told Ellmann about that.' Richard Ellmann, Joyce's biographer, had spent months interviewing her. She remembered Beckett as a young man about Paris in the early thirties, commenting, 'No one had ever heard of him then and he didn't like it much.' I learned much from her, brought her contracts for translations and begged her to write an autobiography. She started it and I still have about seventy pages about her childhood in Kentucky, her slave-owning grandfather, a Scottish immigrant called McDonald (her maiden name), and her early years in Paris. She put it aside to translate a manifesto, then had a new Sarraute novel to do, and she never returned to it. Once, she told me, her mother had taken her whole family, which was numerous, on a tour of Europe. The children were all in their mother's room on a fine sunny morning at the Villa d'Este near Como, one of the grandest hotels of Europe, when her mother having glanced into the gardens, suddenly said 'Call the manager. We're not staying in the same hotel that lets in niggers.' She had just seen the Aga Khan, surrounded by his servants and secretaries, who were opening the letters and parcels that brought him tributary money and jewels from his followers world-wide. That told me something about the right-wing family from which she had come. She was now over eighty, full of laughter and conversation, and always welcoming to every visitor interested in the Paris literary scene. She questioned me about changing tastes, who was in literary fashion, and current literary gossip.

I frequently saw Nathalie Sarraute, who lived in grand-bourgeois comfort in the smart eighth arrondissement of Paris with her husband Raymond, a retired judge, a courteous and gentle man who pandered to her every whim and protected her from annoyance, just as during the war he had protected her from the Nazis, because she was Jewish. Nathalie had come to Paris as a little girl when her parents' marriage had broken up, had studied law at the Sorbonne and at Oxford, and spoke four languages fluently. She was jealous of her reputation and highly critical both of her contemporary rivals and of such figures as Beckett about whom she had little good to say. She and her husband had hidden Sam for a while when he was on the run in 1940, and their different accounts of that time each showed more irritation towards the thoughtlessness or bad grace of the other than gratitude. Now that Beckett had won the Nobel Prize and was acclaimed everywhere, she was jealous and dismissive. But not Maria Jolas who had followed his rise with pleasure. After all Transition had published some of his early work and he had done translations for it as he had for many other periodicals in Paris during the thirties. The famous manifesto that appeared in its first issue is highly provocative and for once I can allow the word 'elitist' to be applied to it. Its twelve points end with: THE PLAIN READER BE DAMNED.

I still went to the various Liberal Party conventions and meetings, both in Scotland and in England, and was now willing to be a candidate again. The party had been doing better for some years now, had more MPs and more candidates were coming forward, but then came the Jeremy Thorpe scandal. Several senior members of the party had known that Thorpe was bisexual, but not me. I had approached him once and been surprised when he told me he was not interested in having an authorised biography written about him. Now I knew why. He was given a difficult grilling by Emlyn Hooson, who had been defeated by him for the party leadership some years earlier, in a private meeting of Liberal MPs, and by the end of it they knew he had to resign. He was tried for attempted murder and acquitted because the jury obviously believed that he might have attempted to frighten his blackmailer, but not to kill him, but his career was over. I attended the big meeting that was held in Birmingham in 1976 where the Liberal Party, now temporarily headed by Jo Grimond again, voted to make David Steel the new leader. I had voted for John Pardoe who I felt had a Churchillian streak in him more likely to turn the tide in our favour than the cautious Steel. I had also been a member of Pardoe's policy think-tank that had only had half a dozen meetings, two of them in my Dalmeny Street flat, and I admired him greatly; he was my kind of left-leaning Liberal. But the dirty tricks of the Tories got him out of his marginal seat in the 1979 General Election, and thereafter he disappeared from politics.

1979 had two elections, a parliamentary one and a European one. Given my many European connections and my knowledge of European politics, because I kept up with more than just literature and the arts, I suggested to the Party that I would be interested in fighting the European election. But I had a serious rival in Menzies Campbell, an Edinburgh barrister, who had once stood against Russell Johnstone for the leadership of the Scottish Liberal Party. I knew I stood no chance in such a contest. But I was lucky because a General Election was called for May and Meng Campbell decided that he would fight the possibly winnable seat of East-Fife. He did eventually take it, but not just then.

His withdrawal meant that I could contest the very large area of Central Scotland, which comprised five Westminster constituencies. The European election came just after the British one, a month later. While preparing for my own campaign; I decided that this time I would go to help an independent candidate in the first election, Eddie Milne.

Eddie Milne had been the Labour MP for Blyth, who at a time when corruption was rife all over the Labour constituencies of North-East England, had not only refused to join others at the trough, but had refused to keep his mouth shut about what was going on. Having replaced Alf Robens, a prominent trade union leader, before becoming first an MP and then a Labour peer, Eddie was quickly approached by the developers who were using public money to build new town centres, housing estates and commercial complexes at great profit to themselves, while filling the pockets of local councillors with bribes and kickbacks. The most notorious figures in the scandals that eventually erupted were T. Dan Smith, Leader of the Newcastle City Council and John Poulson, the Pontefract architect, but there were hundreds of others, including the Deputy Leader of the Labour Party, Ted Short, who was under heavy suspicion.

I knew about Eddie from political friends, went to see him and commissioned a book, which was one of the first titles to appear in my new *Platform* series, which had a distinctive look: the blurb started on the front cover and ran over to the back. Entitled *No Shining Armour*, which I took from a speech that a colleague had made to attack him, this publication soon caused me the greatest trouble since *Last Exit*, a decade earlier.

Edward Milne went straight to work on his book and when it was finished I went up to Blyth for four days to edit it with him, staying in his house. Eddie and his wife looked after me well, even bringing in some wine, not part of their normal life style. I had brought a flask of whisky with me in order to have a late night-cap and I was a little embarrassed one morning when coming back from the bathroom I found that Em (Emily) had made my bed and must have seen the flask in my open suitcase. The book is Eddie's story, his life in the Labour movement, his fourteen years as MP for Blyth, which ended in the second election of 1974. He had been expelled before the first, February election of that year, from the Labour Party after publicly denouncing the corruption he had uncovered, all of which was later proved to be true. Once expelled, he had gone on to fight the October election as an Independent Labour candidate and had won against Ivor Richards, who had been put up against him as the official Labour candidate, by a majority of over 6,000. Then Labour had really set out to destroy him, and blacken his name and they won the next election by a tiny majority of 74, except that everyone believed he had really won, because several hundred postal votes mysteriously disappeared. I published his book to enable him to have his say, and it was selling well all over the Northeast until the Labour Party through their solicitors threatened W.H. Smith, who then stopped selling it, and local bookshops, who did the same. I had spoken to many of Eddie's supporters who had promised to testify if there was any court action, but now they were intimidated, threatened with the loss of their jobs, of their trade union membership, party cards and of any future prospects. People wanted to buy the book but it became difficult to obtain. And the writs began against my firm.

They all came from Lewis Silkin and Partners, Labour solicitors. One by one, starting with Ted Short, and then the MPs, the councillors and others named in the book, they brought actions against me. I took legal advice and I should not have. I settled with Ted Short and agreed to rip some pages out of the book. Then the next writ came and then another, thirty-six in all. Had I been willing to fight I think most of them would not have proceeded, and I would have won against those that did. On top of all my other financial problems I now had this one. But I knew I had been right to publish the book and that Eddie was telling the truth. That was why, when the next election came, I went to try to help get him back into parliament.

I had previously seen civic corruption in Hamilton and had been involved in fighting it on Tyneside through this book. When I was approached by two journalists, Martin Tomkinson and Michael Gillard, to publish another book on the activities of John Poulson, who by then had been convicted and was in prison, I had it carefully read by lawyers and published. When two or three writs from minor persons mentioned came in, I told them to go ahead. We would defend. No one proceeded with their threat. I am now convinced I should have done the same with Eddie Milne's book.

Many more titles came out as *Platform Books*, all with relevance to the modern world. An excellent symposium on *Inflation* covered the history of a problem that was serious in the seventies and suggested what the options were. Peter Hain, who I had known as the Leader of the Young Liberals, wrote books for me, on *Community Politics* and *Policing the Police*, the latter in two volumes. Feminism, new approaches to education, ways of dealing with industrial problems, terrorism, and even a right-wing book anticipating Thatcherism, were all represented in the series. I took on the right-wing book because the author had argued his points so lucidly that I felt I should adopt a Voltairian approach and publish views with which I personally disagreed. My letter accepting the book was not answered for three months and then by the widow. Her husband had died five minutes after opening my letter, presumably with joy. I published it anyway, but it did badly in spite of the later success of the views expressed. Charles Osborne now came to my help. The Arts Council had been giving us grants on some individual literary titles where I had applied and given a business assessment, showing the probable loss on each book and I was seldom far out. Now it was suggested, as I was the best-known publisher of avant-garde literature that lost money but eventually justified itself, that it might be possible to give me an annual block grant to cover my whole publishing programme.

Meetings took place with the senior officials and the literature officers who agreed that a plan for regular annual subsidy could be worked out providing I turned the company into a non-profit trust. As we had never paid out a dividend even in our best years, and were unlikely to ever do so, I agreed this and the Calder Educational Trust was set up. Bill Webb, Stuart Hood and Barbara Wright agreed to be trustees with myself. Our first year's grant was set at £25,000 and this went gradually up to £35,000 in 1981.

Before that, probably shortly after the division of Calder and Boyars, I had made an attempt to set up a new company with outside capital, and talked to a few individuals who were interested in coming in. There is not much on paper about those negotiations as they were all verbal, but one central figure was an American lawyer, closely associated with the Democratic party called Martin Ackerman. He was already financing a publishing company that did small art books about contemporary American artists. I gave a party at Dalmeny House where several of my long-term authors were present, for him to meet them and to get some new ideas. Not much came out of that directly, but it seemed settled that he would find some substantial money providing it suited his tax write-off plans. He told me how he bought paintings at one price, and had experts value them for him at many times that figure. He would then donate them to his old university and write a large amount off his taxes. Something like that was in his mind for me.

It was the summer and he was going to Cap Ferrat where he had rented an apartment near the Hotel du Cap, and it was just when I also intended to spend a week with Jacques. My friend agreed to invite Ackerman and his wife to lunch to help me impress them. They turned up in a taxi and were surprised to see, not a household of English-speakers as they had assumed, but a French cross-section of actors, people in public relations or business, a doctor and a dentist, Jacques Chaix's friends. Martin Ackerman spoke not a word of French, his wife did a little and everyone tried to make them welcome, but the American had only one subject of conversation and that was the value of everything in dollars. He kept trying to tell Jacques what he could sell his property for, and could not realise that his host did not give a damn what it was worth, nor did he care to talk about money and business on a lovely July day when about sixteen relaxed people were sitting out of doors on the terrace slowly eating and drinking while idly looking at the yachts sailing by. Jacques told the wife that she should fine her husband a dollar every time he used the word.

Ackerman invited the whole household to come to have a drink at his apartment a day or two later, and a few went out of politeness, but it was not a success: he only had kir to drink and did not know the right proportions of the syrup to use. I forget now whether I decided then that he was not a suitable investor for my company or whether it was he who backed out, but nothing further happened. It was probably the following year that I tried to interest a rich young American, who had written a novel, to invest in Riverrun Press. There were many meetings in New York with his family's lawyers, because the money was his father's, and it was a lawyer I had to convince that the money would not be lost, but that too came to nothing in the end. The investment would in any case have had to go to a separate imprint to publish new books, working together with the trust, because the Calder Educational Trust could not offer any return on investment. There was no problem about a separate American imprint, my Riverrun Press Inc. I had however learned a lesson by now, that any outside investment brings with it individuals whose aims, interests and agendas might be very different from my own, especially where foreign literature was concerned. Being able to read several languages I did not differentiate between the nationality of the author and what he had to say: only the content and style of the book itself interested me. A translation was of course more expensive to bring out than an English manuscript, but that was the reason the Arts Council were willing to help; very few other publishers were translating good literature at the time because it simply did not pay.

I took on a new London rep, Darryl Richards, whose wife also travelled part time. I was not his only publisher and although he was a good salesman, I always felt that not enough of the time he spent with a bookseller customer was going on my list, especially time examining the shelves to see what had been sold and what was left. I myself spent more time now making sales trips out of London, calling on provincial towns as I had in early days on leaving

Calders Ltd, going down all the south coast towns or through the west country and South Wales, Mr. Camp's old territory.

I had known Molly Parkin for some years. She had been fashion editor of the Sunday Times and I had tried to persuade her to write a book on the politics of fashion, either for *Open Forum* or perhaps it was for *Platform Books*, probably the latter. But she wanted to write novels and I did not see her as a novelist. We had several meetings, pleasant and enjoyable as she was a very attractive and lovely person, but she knew what she wanted to do and went ahead to write a number of light-hearted and sexy fictions that were obviously based on her own life and her various boyfriends. They were very funny, quite wicked in the way they portrayed some current politicians, and although they were not the kind of fiction for which I was known, I would certainly have contracted them if I had had the chance to read them in manuscript. She was snapped up instead by W.H. Allen, who sold them well. Then she married the painter Patrick Hughes, left the Sunday Times and moved to New York, living in the Chelsea Hotel, which is residential for many writers, musicians and artists, famed for having been the place where Dylan Thomas and many others had died under usually unfortunate circumstances. I saw Molly and Patrick frequently when I was in New York. They had obtained free rent for six months by giving the hotel a large canvas to hang in the entrance hall, one of Hughes's rainbow paintings. They were an interesting couple, sex, art, food and white wine being their staples of conversation; they enjoyed New York, but did not feel entirely comfortable there. Molly came to see me at Lorenzo's office when he was still alive, and he never quite got her name right, confusing her with Dolly Parton, the buxom folk singer, then much in the movies or on television. She finished a novel about her New York experiences and I agreed to publish it in the U.S. under the Riverrun imprint. It documented the break-up of her marriage to Patrick with whom she still lived, and her affair with an American rock singer, who also attracted Patrick. It is a funny novel like all her work, but also sad: Molly's talent was to find the underlying truth behind the facades we build and the impulses that make us behave as we do. For reasons that were still not clear to me, I never in fact published the book. I was warned by a mutual friend, an English girl who did publicity in the States for Laura Ashley, that Molly's type of brash humour and provocative sexuality would never go down in the States and that it was too alien to what was acceptable to Americans. That was certainly not the reason why the book did not appear; it was probably because of my involvement in so many different things that her novel never rose to the top of my priorities. But I did not lose touch with her.

I broke off my financial discussions with Jack Berger, with whom I was negotiating for an investment in order to fight the European elections of 1979, promising Jack that this was my political swan song. In New York at a party on my last night I met a man called Hume. When he heard that I was returning to London the next day he asked me as a matter of urgency to telephone his daughter about whom he was very worried. She was very wild, he said. She had been brought up conventionally in a comfortable home that he had created for his family in the middle-class part of the Bronx, but she had revolted against his lifestyle and become a total hippie, travelling to many countries and marrying an Englishman, whom she had already left. I rang up Lesley, his daughter, on arrival and she came to have dinner with me. I found her to be very unlike her father's description. She was Lesley Cunliffe, and had been married to Marcus Cunliffe, Professor of American Literature at the University of Sussex, whom I had met on occasion. I found her charming, attractive, intelligent, a free spirit perhaps, but hardly the wild woman her father had described. When I told her I was about to start my campaign for the European parliament, she volunteered to be my political secretary, and I engaged her. I forget if she was paid or not, but she was to do the job extremely well.

But before the European election there came the General Election. Edward Heath had been deposed by Margaret Thatcher as Leader of the Conservative Party. Callaghan was the Prime Minister and everyone knew the election would be close. I had decided to help Eddie Milne and I went up for the last week of the General Election, taking Sheila Colvin to help. We stayed in Whitley where at breakfast the first morning another guest, returning from some other part of the country complained about all the 'commonwealth citizens' as Ugandans and others from the black commonwealth had come to be called in the political correctness of the day, 'ruining the country'. What he liked about Yorkshire he said was that 'people were English' not 'commonwealth citizens'. With this bit of English prejudice ringing uncomfortably in our ears, we went to help Eddie. My previous soundings in the area, when I was preparing, and then publishing *No Shining Armour*, had seemed to indicate that Eddie had a good chance of winning his old seat back. Metro Radio, the local independent radio station in Newcastle, had backed him and his anti-corruption campaign. They had been helpful to me and my book, and they had an active investigative reporter who had dug up much of the dirt on the official Labour candidate, a fox-hunting, high-living barrister, who looked more like a Tory than a Labour MP. But when I began going around the council houses I realised that Eddie had a difficult fight. Everyone loved him, but the constituency had been flooded by big names in the Labour party, even cabinet ministers, and the message they were giving out was that this election was crucial for Labour, the alternative being a Tory government led by Margaret Thatcher, whose hard-line right-wing views on unions and social issues were well known.

On doorway after doorway people who liked Eddie and had voted for him in the past, told me that they had to follow the official line this time, even if they disliked the official candidate, who as an MP had hardly been visible since 1974. There was not a door in the constituency that had not been canvassed. I knew that Eddie would pick up votes from some Liberal and even soft Conservative tactical voters, who admired his courage and honesty, but there were not many of those in a constituency that had always been a safe Labour seat in the past. Ron Rosen had been up to help Eddie the week before, but I think that his London manner and obvious Jewishness in that heartland of Englishness, would hardly have helped. I left just before the last day and went to Scotland to start my own battle. Eddie lost. When I rang early the next morning to hear the result, Eddie's wife Em, said to me: 'Oh John, he lost! It's terrible, and by a big majority. This is the end.' It was. Eddie died not long after of despair and a broken heart. Em left Blyth and went to live with her daughter in Edinburgh.

Lesley Cunliffe moved up to Ledlanet. There was a big anti-nuclear demonstration going on at Torness where they were building a nuclear station. The protest involved local people who were afraid of living close to such a dangerous installation, and even Edinburgh residents, not that far away, were nervous about it. The anti-nuclear movement was strong then, and I had a book near publication, Robert Jungk's *The Nuclear State*, translated from German, which had already had a large influence on the anti-nuclear movement in Germany and Austria. The argument of the book was that no nuclear station could ever be totally safe, that a contamination of the environment always followed, and that the security necessary to guard against sabotage, terrorism or incompetent management, justified the imposition of secrecy and authoritarian measures. A nuclear state could never be open, democratic or liberal. Naturally I joined the protest, but principally as an observer and a political candidate in order to show my solidarity. Duncan Campbell of the New Statesman, who had contributed to one of my *Platform Books* symposiums, came up to ask what I was doing there. 'I'm the Scottish Liberal candidate for Central Scotland,' I answered.

'Are you bedad,' he commented, and moved away. We saw a whole hillside with camping-out couples, hundreds of them. 'Idealism and free love,' commented Lesley, approvingly. The next day a sympathetic farmer dumped large bales of hay early in the morning against the perimeter barbed-wire fence which made it easy for hundreds of protestors to scramble over the wire, eventually being evicted by large numbers of police. Torness went ahead, but at least the protest made more people aware of the issue.

I attended a meeting where all the trade union leaders present were in favour of nuclear power because it created jobs; they sat together with the directors and promoters of British Nuclear Fuels. I asked one of them if he would send people to a certain death just to create jobs or prosperity, but he did not understand the relevance of my question. Campaigning in an area as large as Central Scotland was near impossible. I went to the big malls and marketplaces, to the centre of High Streets and wherever I saw people gathered. Everyone was fed up with politics with the General Election only a month behind. There were no meetings because people did not come to them anymore. They got their politics from television, but most simply turned off political broadcasts and debates. It was obvious there would be a low poll.

I added up the General Election vote of the five constituencies. If everyone voted the same way, Labour would win, but the Labour candidate, a woman, was unenthusiastic about Europe and as usual the Tories had the money, organisation and determination to make their presence felt. I stood with my loud-hailer shouting out the same messages over and over. No-one stopped to listen, but most would hear the short messages to the end before they were out of earshot. It was unsatisfactory, but I found no better way of making my presence known and getting some kind of message across. I met my SNP opponent, Dr. McKintyre, a previous Provost of Stirling, and got on well with him, agreeing in particular in our opposition to nuclear power. The Tory candidate was seldom seen, but his workers managed to be everywhere with their posters and banners on every High Street.

Lesley Cunliffe brought her boyfriend up, one of two she had in tow at the time. He was Stanley Gebler-Davis, a journalist, who at the time worked mainly for the Londoner's Diary of the Evening Standard and frequently contributed light frothy articles to Punch. He settled in to become my press secretary and wanted to write all my speeches, but I did not have the opportunity of making many and those only to specialised groups like farmers and others with a special interest in Europe and the Common Market. 'Just give me some jokes,' I told him. He gave me one, about how well the Irish were doing out of the common market compared to the English who on the whole pretended it didn't exist. As there was a plethora of Irish jokes about at the time, the idea was to show that everyone joked about the Irish, but they should be joking about us. I told it to a large group of farmers. One burly man got up and said, 'I'm Irish and I didn't like that.' Thereafter I told my own jokes or none.

These were the last days of Ledlanet, a ghost-house now, but our bedrooms were still there and the morning room was the only room that was still used. I advertised my telephone number on my election leaflet, saying that I could be rung by any constituent between eleven at night and one in the morning. I had two open lines for the election and after I had returned every evening the three of us would sit in the morning room, eating what Attewell had left out for us, drinking wine, and then malt whisky while the telephone calls came in. Stan or Lesley would keep one caller on the line talking, while I spoke to the previous one. In between we managed to eat. Lesley would go off to bed around midnight, leaving the two of us to answer late calls and listen to records. This life suited me well enough for the weeks of the campaign. I would sleep until seven or seven-thirty and be up preparing for the day with Lesley. Stan did not come down until after nine usually, and as Lesley put it, 'Stan in the morning is not a very appetising sight.'

He was really only there because of Lesley, but he managed to get a few items about me into the newspapers and went around with me for part of the day, often visiting the pubs in the larger towns like Perth or Stirling, talking to the locals and picking up the gossip. But by nature he was an anarchist of the right, much more in sympathy with the Conservative Party than the one for which I was running. He was very Irish, rather slovenly, witty and generally unconventional, but he got on well with those he met, not necessarily asking people to vote for me, but at least telling them I was running. We shared a love of music and of certain writers like Joyce and Beckett. Fife was part of the European constituency and I trod my old ground in Dunfermline, where I went down a coal mine, an interesting experience but not one I was anxious to repeat. During my visit one man was caught smoking behind a buttress, a serious offence that endangered the lives of everyone down the mine, and he was reprimanded. If fired he could never have worked in a mine again. It was very hot and the mine extended several miles under the sea. The men would only be working for less than an hour every day. The rest of the eight-hour day was spent travelling on small railway cars to the coal face and back, with forty-five minutes allowed for washing up. There can have been few worse jobs, however well paid.

In Saint Andrews I saw fishermen throwing lobsters back into the sea, and wanted to buy a few, but they refused. The price was too low, and as they could not get enough for them in the market, they would not sell to me either. While I was talking to them the landlord of the Cross Keys Inn, who knew me, came up. 'What are you wasting your time for here,' he shouted at me. 'Get back to your books.' I could not help but feel he was right.

Two Dutch young Liberals came to help me and spent a few days travelling around with me. We were all given lunch by a retired colonial office civil servant up in the north of the constituency. He was interested in the old Dutch colonial empire and asked questions, finding the links between those who had worked in the army of the dominating power in Indonesia, and had had to return to the mother-country when independence arrived, and the presence in Britain of Ugandan Indians and Gurkhas.

On election day I cast my vote early in the morning at the school in Milnathort and toured the constituency, driving down the Forth along the Fife Coast, saying Hello to a few old friends, coming to the border of Glasgow and then heading north. I must have called on about a hundred polling stations. Then, dead tired, I drove to Ledlanet. For three weeks I had lived on fish and chips and the odd Chinese take-away, a few meals with Liberal supporters, and Attewell's cold collations. Stan had enjoyed it all and told me that the Conservative candidate's election agent had told him that I deserved to win as I had worked hardest and would have been the best representative for the constituency in Europe. Lesley went to many teas given by Liberals that I could not attend. She was well-liked by the ladies who invited her; they saw her as a girl with good manners and a Scottish name who happened to have an American accent. Her father would have been pleased. She thought of moving to Scotland, but never did.

There was one big local issue and that was the closure of a major fruit processing and tinning factory near Pitlochry. I had meetings with the representatives of the workers, but the Tories muscled in with promises to try to save the factory. It was the recently elected MP for Perth who made the promises and said that Margaret Thatcher, who had just become Prime Minister, would personally intervene. It was all hogwash of course, and the poor bewildered workers who were hoping to save their jobs did not know which way to turn, but listened to us all, hoping some other concern would buy the factory or that some money could be found for the management to take over and start producing potato crisps or some other product to supplement the poor sales of tinned fruit. No fan of tinned fruit myself, I wrote letters, promised to do what I could to find a European buyer or some European money after the election. I even went to Brussels when the election was over, but there was nothing to be done. The factory closed for good the following month.

There were two days to wait before the count in Perth Town Hall. I had a respectable vote, but the Tory won, Labour doing especially badly. Although I dabbled in politics many times after that, I never ran again.

Chapter 7

Odyssey

I returned to New York, trying to pressure Lorenzo de Grazie to give more effort to my books, and then went on a selling trip to California where I met the reps who, up to their collapse, had been selling for Southwestern. One of them, Steve Mandel, made an appointment to meet me at a restaurant on the bay near Berkeley. When I arrived there at twelve noon the restaurant was shut and I waited in the boiling sun inside my car – there was no shade anywhere else – until he turned up an hour and a half late. 'Did you have a break-down?' I asked.

'No. I went for a swim,' he answered without concern or apology. I was learning something about California. I had done some selling myself in the past, going around with the reps, and I must have had a reputation, because Dosier Hammond, who had been selling our books in Los Angeles, refused to spend a day with me in the bookshops, which was the best way for him to learn my list and how to sell it. 'I've heard about you,' he said. 'You drive everyone into the ground.' A normal day calling on seven or eight bookshops was apparently too much like work for most Californians. There was one very personable man, Jon Levine, very personable, tall, dark and handsome, who had not minded a full day with me in Los Angeles. He was a good salesman who did particularly well with lady buyers, many of whom were exceptionally attractive, and with the men as well. He taught me where the bookshops were. Gradually I came to know my customers and found that properly presented, and I would in those days carry a bag full of samples as well as order forms and catalogues, my books usually had a ready market. There were many literary bookshops on the west coast then and many of the university shops were also open to take those titles that might appeal to students and lecturers. Some of my European authors were taught at the universities and did better than in British towns. I was often selling upward of five hundred books in a day and sending the orders to Brooklyn to be sent out.

In July I went to Santa Fé, both to attend the Festival and to sell books, also doing so in the state capital Albuquerque, which lies on the flat plane under the mountains, where Santa Fé, a picturesque Spanish-looking town, crowns the top. I had stayed in touch with Julia Sweeney after our meetings in Dallas and she decided to come to meet me. We spent one night in a hotel in Albuquerque in their only free room, which turned out to be the bridal suite. It was a chaste night however, not because of any unwillingness on her part, but because she had some infection, or it may just have been a euphemism for her period. She remarked with a smile the next morning that it was a terrible waste of the bridal suite. We saw two operas at the Festival, *The Magic Flute* and Berg's *Lulu* in Arthur Jacob's first English translation, and enjoyed our exploration of the town; once the reason for her chastity had disappeared, we enjoyed each other as well. I was to see her periodically in the next few years, staying with her on subsequent visits to Dallas, and she also met me in New York and London. She soon left journalism and started her own public relations business, which was thriving when I last heard from her.

I had known a French lady in London who had a small art gallery and entertained very lavishly, mainly in her flat near Oxford Street, ostensibly because it was good for selling paintings, but really because she enjoyed entertaining. She seemed to drink only champagne and it flowed freely at her parties, where the guests were a mixture of artists, diplomats and the current glitterati. We became very friendly, but only that, and she seemed to think me a literary lion. Frequently on Sundays I would go with her to the afternoon parties given by Jean Gimpel, of the art gallery of that name, although by then he was retired. They were pleasant occasions, held in his large garden in Chelsea and I met many interesting people. Gimpel was the author of *The Cathedral Builders*, which had appeared in the series of little books published by Editions du Seuil in France that Barney Rosset and I had once published as Profile Books together, and on that account he treated me as his publisher. He was a generous and witty host, no longer an art dealer, but very knowledgeable, and he obviously loved women. He had a way of asking an artist's wife if her husband was a good artist. If she replied in the affirmative, he would tell her that good artists all treat their women abominably and therefore she should rush into his arms. If she was not sure of his merits, he would ask, 'Why do you want to stay with a bad artist? Come to my arms.' His wife would keep a watchful, slightly amused eye on him through all this.

The French lady in question was Suzel de la Maisonneuve, and she was as grand as her name. She was large, effusive, blonde with flowing long hair, had a steady flow of conversation and easy laughter that was infectious if a little artificial, mixing English and French. She had been married to an American General and had two teen-age sons, but they lived with their father.

She came to the Frankfurt Book Fair one year, bringing a Swiss banker friend with her, and I introduced her around. Then she moved to Washington D.C. where she rented a house in a central section off Pennsylvania Avenue and near the Holiday Inn where Ronald Reagan was later nearly assassinated, and she invited me to stay with her when in the capital. When I did, I visited all the bookshops and discovered the Book Annex in Georgetown to be the best outlet for my list. It was part of the Olsson chain, and I became friendly with Jim Tenny and Robin Dina, two booklovers on the staff. Suzel's house had numerous visitors coming and going, many of them prominent politicians. Her walls were covered by the work of painters she was trying to sell and there were more champagne parties. She was very into Republican Party politics, probably because of her former husband, but I met authors there too, and her artistic friends must have been mainly on the left, which the politicians were certainly not. It was the early days of the new Ronald Reagan presidency, January 1980. I stayed with her on three occasions, and on each there was a party to sell paintings, although I doubt if she ever sold many, other than those she bought for herself. Her background was aristocratic and she lived like a rich woman, but I detected that all was not quite what it seemed, and felt an underlying financial anxiety, but above all a need to be in the swim of things, as if hanging onto a past celebrity. On one occasion she had another house guest, Eleanor Riger, a sports producer for ABC television. She was without question a Democrat and her views being not dissimilar from my own, we got on well. After one of her six o'clock parties, Suzel had to go to a fund-raising Republican dinner and said that we could both come if we behaved ourselves, did not air our political views and avoided political argument. The guest of honour and principal speaker was William Casey, head of the CIA, who, on our arrival, was all over Suzel, kissing her hand and using his few words of French as gallantly as he could. At the dinner we were all at tables of six or seven and most people were only drinking water. I caught the waiter's eye and managed to order a bottle of wine for Eleanor and myself to help make a dull evening less so, but we could not help giggling at some of the speeches. After dinner Suzel said she had to go to some meeting in one of the upstairs bedrooms of the hotel and we waited for her for an hour, speculating abut what she could be doing. 'We were just about to get a room ourselves,' said Eleanor when Suzel returned; she laughed but gave us no explanation, and took us home. Eleanor and I met again in New York, where she lived, and an affair inevitably started. I introduced her to Barney Rosset, whose interest in sport was as great as her's, whereas mine was nil. I spent a weekend with her at her house at Martha's Vineyard, playground for the cultured rich and even sold books there in the local shop.

It must have been that summer, in 1980, that I made a sales trip, certainly not my first, to the American west coast, but this time I explored the two states north of California. Eleanor came out to join me and we travelled from San Francisco up through the Napa Valley. I had taken some good orders in the Bay area, where my best customer was Lawrence Ferlinghetti's City Lights Bookshop, famed for having championed and published the beat poets, and having the best range of poetry and books on surrealism in the U.S. This was were Barney Rosset had done much of his prospecting for new authors such as Jack Kerouac twenty-five years earlier.

Our first stop was in Eugene, where I found two bookshops. One of them recommended that when I got to Portland, my next stop, I should go to Powell's. It was not listed in the directory of the American Booksellers Association that I was carrying with me, an immensely heavy volume, weighing over ten pounds. In Portland I found most of the bookshops conventional and not very interested in books other than best-sellers, but I was well received by Blackwells, which wholesaled books from Britain in the U.S. and supplied libraries. They gave me lunch and promised to promote my books. But the most interesting shop turned out to be the one recommended to me, Powell's. It was to become even more interesting in the years to come. To quote what the Guide Michelin says about three-star restaurants, it was 'worth the journey'.

What I learned from Mr. Powell on that occasion was supplemented by the things he told me on later visits. His shop was on Burnside, not the most salubrious street in Portland, but as it ran east and west through the centre of the town from the main interstate highway to the wealthier suburbs in the hills, it was a main thoroughfare. Powell had owned a small shop that sold general goods and one day he was offered what he called 'a mountain of used books' for $500. He knew nothing about books, but having viewed them, the mountain seemed immense and he bought them. He then put up some shelves and filled them with his new purchases, in no particular order, the bulk still sitting in the warehouse. Many were pre-war and they all had the original prices and that is what he demanded from customers; refusing to sell for any less. Soon he had taken thousands of dollars, and was constantly refilling his shelves from the mountain that never seemed to diminish. Then he rented the shop next door and then the one next to that. He had to employ someone who knew something about books, who organised them by author, increasing the sales but not lowering the prices. Soon Mr. Powell was selling only books, now arranged into categories. Then he rented a large warehouse behind his shops, filled it with bookshelves ten or twelve high from the ground, built of the cheapest pine, which can be found everywhere in Oregon, and the 'mountain' went into it. By then, not long before my first visit, the fame of Powell's had spread: 'phone calls were coming in from near and far looking for particular books, and new-book salesmen had begun to call. His manager began buying new books, but also second-hand from those who queued to see him, carrying boxes filled with them. Although he now had a large and growing turnover, Mr. Powell much resented receiving invoices from publishers, and he complained to me about it, but he was already a prisoner of his own success and the momentum could not be stopped. On each return visit to Portland I found that more building had taken place and by the end of the century Powell's occupied several city blocks, had one whole building for customer parking and was without any doubt the largest bookshop in the world, still without any money having been spent on prettifying the space, but its completeness was astonishing, covering every category of book and as far as I know in almost every language. Much of the firm's business is to other bookshops: phones were ringing all day long with customers and dealers looking for particular titles. When old Mr. Powell died, his son Michael took over; but by then there were Powell bookshops in other cities and in Portland's suburbs.

The secret was simple and it has seldom been copied. Mr. Powell knew nothing about the book-trade, but he put all editions, new, old, hardback, paperback, large, small, onto the same shelves side by side, and in the early years translations as well. People had the choice and they bought what they wanted. It was a long time before there were any computers at Powell's. When people 'phoned from New York or Tokyo, whoever took the call went to the shelf and looked. There were probably a million books on my first visit: today there must be several thousand times that. Mr. Powell would sit at the cash register, taking thousands of dollars and complaining about publishers' invoices coming in, but with no intention of decorating his premises, and he never gave discounts. There were no carpets on the concrete floors and no amenities, just books, every kind of book in every kind of condition. Money went on electric light and staff wages, and his overheard must have almost stopped there. In my view he was right. He had stumbled on the secret of success in a trade where so many fail because they give more attention to systems and decor than to the product that they deal in. On one of my subsequent visits when Sheila Colvin was with me, he told her: 'My mother was an ignorant Austrian woman who could not even write her name, and here I am with the biggest bookshop in the world.'

I took my biggest order of the whole trip from Powell's on that first visit, and Eleanor Riger and I then drove to Seattle, staying in a hotel in mid-town. I discovered many more bookstores there, but since that first visit all but a handful have disappeared. But I did sell many thousands of books in the North-West area and we visited a local winery, Saint-Michelle, and saw some of the sights as well, including the turning restaurant in the middle of the Seattle Centre. Then we went on to Vancouver, and I visited the shops there and we took the ferry, on which we could not get a drink, to Victoria, on Vancouver Island, where I looked up the poet Robin Skelton, who had emigrated to Canada some time earlier and was living there. He filled me in on the local literary scene and the politics of British Columbia, in which at that time both culture and civil liberties were under threat, as well as academic freedom, because of the stance of the ruling Social Credit Party. All my Canadian orders I sent to Brian Donat in Toronto, who was selling my books in Canada. I shall describe him later.

Back in New York I plodded around the bookshops, all of which knew me well by now. I ran into Allen Ginsberg in one of them, New Morning, which had the distinction of having sold over a hundred copies of my edition of Tzara's *Seven Dada Manifestos* within a week, after it had received a favourable review in The Village Voice. It was a book that did well in many American cities because it had eye-catching pages with large eccentric typography, was easy to read with short articles and playful exaggerations, and because Dada always has a fashion. I remember walking all over the West Village with wet feet in melting snow with Ginsberg, talking and avoiding other pedestrians on narrow footpaths, and I got to know him well for the first time. We discussed world politics, literature, mutual friends, authors we knew in common, like William Burroughs, and civil rights, his great interest at the time. He was on the committee of PEN and was active trying to get imprisoned writers free. Ginsberg was a lovely man, unconventional, natural, easy to get on with where there were common causes and mutual interests to discuss. He belonged to the less clannish type of gay person, with whom I have never had difficulty in making friends. We met infrequently after that, but always with warmth and much to say.

There were about fifty New York bookshops that took my books, and I made field trips that took me for one or two nights away to upper New York state, New Jersey and New England, so that my list was selling in many places. I sold books in the early days from Lorenzo's office, but his company slumped and he died soon after. Most of my American selling came later.

* * * * * *

In August 1979, which is before many of the events I have recorded above, I was driving north from London to Ledlanet during the late evening and early night. The Edinburgh Festival was just starting and now Sheila Colvin had realised her ambition and was one of the two deputy directors under John Drummond, who had succeeded Peter Diamond. She shared a birthday with her boss which may have been one of the reasons he did not accept her when she first applied. She was in despair then, because she felt it was the one job for which she was uniquely qualified, but Drummond soon changed his mind and took her on. Her co-deputy was Richard Jarman, whose background was mainly in ballet management. On the car radio I listened to news about the festival, and then heard an announcement that David Mercer was dead. He had been visiting Israel, either because a play was being performed or for some film project, and had died of a heart attack. His had been a strange career and a difficult life. His later reputation gradually faded, but may be revived one day.

John Drummond's first festival was not too much of a signal of what was to come in later years. Diamond had put on glamorous productions of popular operas like *Carmen* with starry casts as part of a deal with recording companies, whereas Drummond at first used smaller British companies to put on a less popular repertoire, and spent the major money on concert artists and orchestras. But he brought enthusiasm and thought to the festival, wanted to lead taste rather than follow it, and he was more in the Harewood mould, wanting both to interest himself and educate the public. Because of Sheila, I was invited to several of Drummond's late-night parties. Then came the Frankfurt Book Fair, where Marion and I now had separate stands, having shared one for the previous four years, but that had not worked out too well. I remember David Galloway, teaching in Germany, but writing novels for me in English, being much on my stand during the previous year and helping me to translate press releases about my new series of opera guides, (which I shall come to later), while the curious Marion was eavesdropping with annoyance at what she though was a *coup* I had pulled off in planning a series with the English National opera as partners. In 1979 I had Alice Watson, our new sales manager, with me. We had driven from London and stopped at Brussels overnight, where I had an appointment to meet the Dutch writer Harry Mulisch. Unfortunately we went to the wrong station and missed Harry. I telephoned his wife in Amsterdam, who told me he was much annoyed, had gone off to eat a lobster, and would then take the last train back. I asked the hotel concierge where he might be found eating lobster and was guided to a restaurant street off the Grand Place. I described Harry to Alice and we went down all the restaurants on the street, taking different sides. At about the eighth I found Harry, just finishing his meal.

We joined him and he was so amused at the way we had found him that he got over his upset and stayed the night. The next morning we settled the contract for his novel *Two Women* and for a number of his short stories to appear in our *New Writing and Writers* series (as it had been renamed from Number 13 to enable us to publish short work by established writers together with our new discoveries). Then we drove on to Frankfurt, where for the first time we had the display stand to ourselves. Sheila Colvin came for the last two days, not having been there before. There were some pleasant dinner parties that year, one with Alex Stefanovic, now working for an Italian publishing company, having left Yugoslavia, and Bill Webb, reporting the fair for the Guardian. Bill was by now a good friend. But the fair was changing and literary publishers were few now and not very visible; a best-seller culture had taken over and money had become more important than talent and quality. Old friends still met and shared views, reminiscences and gossip. There was one nice evening when a group of us that included Helmut Kossodo, Robert Jungk and his wife, Sheila and Jim Haynes, all having met more or less by accident, had dinner and played such literary games as each describing the best book they had read during the past year, which in such company becomes a kind of competitive sport. Literary publishers went to Frankfurt now as much to amuse themselves and see friends as to do business. These days I sold few rights and bought only what would anyway have been sent to me in London, because by now I had little competition where European authors were concerned.

The great age of translation that had characterised the sixties was over. Then publishers would snap up young hopefuls from Eastern Europe or those who had created some noise in the literary press of Italy or Sweden. Too much money had been lost on books that were hardly reviewed, if at all, when published in translation, and they had had very small sales. This applied more to Britain than elsewhere, but it was true generally. Now the well-heeled commercial publishers had taken over from the Feltrinellis, Barrals and Einaudis, individualists who wanted the prestige of literary giants in their catalogues, even if the sales were mainly to university professors and a few intellectual readers. Literary agents now held auctions at the fair to get the highest bids and any publisher was appropriate for any book if the money was enough.

Girodias was of course no longer around. The last book he had sold successfully was *Candy*, first issued in Paris in 1958 and he had sold it to all the publishers who had published *Lolita* at a dinner given for him at the fair that year. Then had come the years of penury and now he was bankrupt, brought down by his biggest folly, La Grande Severine. In fact the second volume of his memoirs only goes up to that time, and he never wrote a third. The volume ends with Rosemary Ridgewell making a return visit to Paris and cornering him at an awkward moment in his restaurant; she had come back to move in with him. I shall quote (my own translation) the last lines of the book.[35]

> Her problem seemed to be insoluble. This woman, young, beautiful, and, it must be said, strangely intelligent, seemed to be condemned to the sad destiny of all the women who have to bare their bodies for the public gaze: why, how, and by what perverse logic had she come to this? And how and why had she come to intervene in my life in such an intense manner?
>
> I ordered another bottle of champagne.
>
> 'Listen, Rosemary, I want to be your friend...'
>
> 'Who cares! You can keep your friendship, I want you to fuck me, you understand? Fuck and fuck and fuck.'

La Grande Severine was a running sore for Girodias from the beginning, and it lost him all the fortunes that came his way from rights sales of his most successful books, all of which had erotic content, but many were also of great literary interest. Girodias went to the receiver's sale of his company's assets with enough money to make a modest bid, not expecting that anyone else would be interested in a few unsold books and contracts for copyrights that always expire in a bankruptcy, but J.P. Donleavy, who had cheated him over *The Ginger Man*, sent his wife to the sale, and she outbid him. Now Donleavy owned even the name of Olympia Press.

Girodias had earlier started an English Olympia Press with the finance of New English Library, then still run by Christopher Shaw, but it had not lasted long. I had helped it at the beginning, mainly with advice, but it was seldom taken. The most amusing episode was a Foyle's literary lunch, which Christina Foyle was persuaded to give for the 'Traveller's Companion' series, under which label Olympia U.K. issued its list. Most of the people who had paid to attend the lunch thought that it was given for travel books, not for an erotic series taking advantage of the cessation of prosecutions after our successful appeal, in the *Last Exit to Brooklyn* case. One of the guests at the top table was the Attorney General, Griffiths Jones, who left immediately

---

[35] Le Jardin d'Eros, Paris, 1989.

after Maurice Girodias, the guest of honour, had made his speech, which left those present in no doubt about the subject matter of the series. It had fallen on me, also at the top table, to give a little address introducing him, which I was later told by the lady who was his secretary at the time I did gracefully, but I never gave away much about the books themselves. There were many mutterings among the staid regular attenders of Foyle's literary lunches as they left. Edna O'Brien, one of the celebrity authors who had been invited to give glamour to the proceedings, had much enjoyed the atmosphere of scandal that had grown throughout the room after Maurice's speech, and having drunk rather a lot, said on the way out, to no one in particular: 'Won't someone take me somewhere and fuck me?' Having an appointment, I couldn't take her up on it. Somewhere around that time Harold Pinter did, because I kept seeing them together.

During the publicity visit, organised by NEL's P.R. firm, which gave me an excellent lunch at the Mirabelle before it all started, Maurice debated against censorship at the Oxford Union. He had been overconfident and took too much advantage of the students' hospitality before the debate started, which made him slightly drunk when his turn came to speak, so the whole evening was a shambles. He had not understood that Union debates are very formal affairs and that he was up against skilled debaters. It is at university debates that the politicians of the future get their early training, and any guest should carefully prepare his argument, but leave room for improvisation depending on what points are advanced by both sides on the floor. In those days I was frequently asked to debate myself at Oxford, Cambridge and other universities, for some reason frequently at Durham, and I knew the rules and always prepared carefully. Maurice had by now become largely out of touch with reality. He had lost his Paris company and the new British partnership did not last long. He went to America hoping to recover his fortunes there.

Going back five years, I had once agreed to house his daughter at Ledlanet for the summer. Valerie was about seventeen at the time, wanted to improve her English and see something of Britain. Before she was to fly with me, initially to London, her father took me to lunch and was unusually reticent. Finally he came out with, 'I think she's a virgin. Please look after her.'

'If she loses it, it won't be with me,' I replied laughing. 'But I'm not going to be a policeman either. She's old enough to look after herself.' We flew to London and, after a day or two, drove to Scotland. She met another French girl of her own age and for part of her stay they hiked through the Highlands for a fortnight. My only concern was that she was epileptic with 'grand mal', which I only learned about after her mother telephoned Bettina the day after her arrival. But there was no mishap.

* * * * * *

One day I received a telephone call from Howard Aster of Mosaic Press in Toronto. Howard was an academic with links to CBC (Canadian Broadcasting Corporation) who ran a cultural publishing company with a mixed list of novels, poetry and cultural books with political resonances, largely centred around Eastern Europe. His books were distributed by Kampmann, who for a time distributed me as well, but there were other publishing connections as well. He and a group of six other Canadians had been invited to visit China as guests of the government, and the only condition was that they would be expected to give a few lectures and talk to Chinese writers. One of their members had dropped out: would I like to replace him? Of course I would and I cancelled all my engagements for several weeks to join the party. We flew from Toronto, stopping in Alaska for a few hours, my second visit to Anchorage airport, then to Tokyo where we also spent a few hours, and eventually, on a different Chinese flight, arrived in Beijing as Peking had now been renamed. There we met a group of English-speaking writers, most notably a famous translator, Gladys Waugh, an Englishwoman who had married her Chinese husband at Cambridge and returned with him to China. They both had a hard time during the Cultural Revolution, had been badly treated in gaol and were lucky not to have been killed as so many intellectuals and teachers were. Everyone in that first writers' group was very traditional intellectually and while respecting the Chinese classics, many of which Gladys had translated, the current emphasis was on social realism. Baudelaire was a dirty name and the very idea of decadence or *art pour l'art* was anathema to them, but they admitted that there were younger writers who might be influenced by moderns like James Joyce if they had the chance to read him, writers who put the individual, his dreams and private desires at the centre of their writing, whereas what the state wanted were novels that showed everyone striving harder to make a better economic future for all.

My most memorable moments were both concerned with a lady who translated for me on two occasions. The first was a lecture I gave in English at the University, which was meant to last an hour, but in fact lasted nearly four. My translator, half-English, half-Chinese and brought up in England with an English father, spent some time with me before my lecture to make sure that the terms I would use were clear to her, and apart from admiring her great beauty and charm, I was much impressed with her competence and determination to get things just right. The lecture was given in a large class-room where a large kettle of hot water was always on the boil. The students would periodically go over to it and fill their jam jars which contained tea leaves, so that tea was being drunk right through the session. I gathered that the tea leaves often had to last for weeks, so that the tea must have been very weak.

My lecture was on Western Civilisation, and I did not know how much the students already knew. I soon discovered that the answer was nothing at all; they had never heard of what the Greeks had done, or the Romans, and they had only vaguest idea of anything that had happened since. I was not too surprised when, looking through the public library the following week, I found very few books in any non-Chinese language, and those were mostly over fifty years old. I threw away my notes and improvised from scratch, going through the basics. When I said that western culture was based on tension, they could not understand me. Life was based on tension, but art should be the opposite, peace and calm, beauty and tranquillity, relaxation against a background of benevolent nature. That of course is just what Chinese painting is, and as far as I knew, most literature as well. I went through the mechanics of explaining that western art is like an acrobat on a tightrope: when the rope, or rather the wire, breaks, that is the moment when art happens. For four hours we discussed such concepts, fuelled in their case by numerous refills of hot water on their bleached-out tea leaves. My interpreter was exhausted at the end, but loved it. She then, on her own, arranged for me to spend a day with the Chinese Youth Theatre, which in spite of its name is a well-equipped theatre company of actors, all of whom have to play instruments and perform acrobatics, and they were the only company performing western plays. I told them about modern British and American plays, European ones as well, recounting the plots, the number of characters, scenes and other relevant details. They did the same for me with Chinese plays and showed me videos; what most impressed me was the make-up and the gestures. Western characters were made up to look like what they should be: there was no political correctness in ignoring the colour of the actor or other characteristics. The actors moved as was right for the period, style and fashion of the play and the gestures were perfect.

At one point I related a Howard Barker play, one in which the Roundheads invade a church where a sculptor is just finishing the statue of a dead Cavalier, which the widow had commissioned. In spite of his protests that it was his masterpiece, they started to smash it, exclaiming 'There is no pity in history,' which is (the last three words) the title of the play. They liked that phrase so much they promised to perform the play the following year, and did.

We visited the Summer Palace, a day's train journey away and the town of Xian, where we saw the underground terracotta army, still being excavated and cleaned with small brushes, and we went to a restaurant where the food consisted of dumplings fashioned into dozens of different animal shapes. Howard had brought his small son, Mischa, who soon got very tired of looking at temples, but we did all the sights, the Great Wall, which is apparently visible from the moon, Tianamen Square and the mummified body of Mao, the great Emperors' Palace with its gardens, the tombs of the Mings and other Emperors and much else beside. I also visited a print works. This had modern Japanese machinery and I was surprised when I saw women folding sheets of paper by hand, where machines to do this work at hundreds of times the speed were sitting unused just behind them. It was explained that there was a shortage of work and they preferred to keep the women busy the old way than send them home while the machines did the work. I asked if they could give me some prices to print books and I was given astonishing low estimates: but then came outside intervention. They did not want to print for export, because they did not want the responsibility if anything went wrong; in any case if they did decide to print for me the prices would be different from those suggested by the manager of the works.

We had a young Canadian poet in the party and he was ill at ease from the first day. He had never been abroad, was afraid of the food and the alien culture around him. When he came down with some small ailment, an upset stomach I think, he was terrified to take the Chinese medicine prescribed for him. We had several interpreters, one an attractive young wife, who had a child she was seldom allowed the time to see, and another a man, who was principally with me. The young wife told us of her life: the state took precedence over everything: couples were split when they were given jobs, often far away from each other, and only if you knew someone influential could you appeal. You could not change your job, have a second child or behave in any way unconventionally. The male interpreter was inquisitive about the morality of the west and kept on cross-questioning me. I made a deal with him that I would help him to improve his English if he helped me learn some Chinese, and every day I made progress. The hieroglyphics on old tombs were good practice to start reading and phonetically I picked up quite a lot, enough to be able, at the final banquet given for us, to make a little thank-you speech in Chinese which I had learned by rote. My interpreter was especially interested in homosexual practices in the west. 'But of course they don't really do anything,' he suggested tentatively and when I assured him that there was plenty of homosexual physical sex he looked pensive, then decided he had better not ask any more, but a few hours later he would be back with more questions. I assumed that he was a closet gay who would have the chance to come out and practice the following year when he expected to be sent to the United States to study at a university. We met a personable Scottish communist girl who had been teaching in Beijing and some others who had been imported to teach from English-speaking countries. We met several high-up officials, some of whom gave us an interesting overview of what was happening economically in the country. Draconian methods were sometimes necessary we were told to produce enough food for everyone, to build enough shelter, and to gradually raise the standard of living which was less than $100 a year for the average person. Building was going on all over Beijing and everywhere else we looked. At least there were no wars or famines just then, but the slow liberalisation that was taking place was already enabling those with an acquisitive or entrepreneurial instinct to make money by selling imported clothes and goods from the west to those with a little money, which was usually obtained from dealing with westerners. The good hotels with western standards were only for people like us: even the most important Chinese visitors and officials had to stay in hotels designed for Chinese.

The events of Tianaman Square occurred the following year. From what I had seen of the students I was not too surprised: knowing nothing of history and with the government's need to maintain 'face' in an era of change where the students did not really understand what they were doing and the inevitable consequences of it, it was not surprising that they allowed themselves to be caught in a trap where it became only too easy to recognise and isolate the leaders and the most obdurate, and to victimise them. This does not make the tragic events less so, but it is easy to understand what happened. The reason that a group of Canadians were given such favourable treatment was first of all a sense of gratitude to Canada for being the first nation to recognise the new China after the revolution in 1947, and secondly the special influence Howard Aster wielded there. He had been often before and he was trusted by high-up officials.

One bit of business came from the Panda series of English language paperbacks, looking rather like Penguins which we imported after the visit and which I sold for Mosaic Press in Britain. The series contained a mixture of classics and new writing, but I soon found that Chinese importers in London were doing the same thing, so it was not a success. We also developed a plan to produce a big *History of China* as an international project, but there were too many not very serious people involved and it never got off the ground.

Sean Connery, perhaps the most successful of all the actors who have played James Bond, had never lost his attachment to his native Scotland and he has occasionally been willing to fund the arts in Scotland out of his substantial income. In the late sixties he set up a foundation, the Scottish International Educational Trust, to support them, and he put Richard Demarco in charge, not a very wise move, because, while Rikky certainly did a great deal to further the arts, he always wanted his name to be strongly linked to whatever activity currently engaged him, and spent the money at his disposal in any way that was important to him. He was never someone who could be trusted to be responsible with the money of others. In addition to making Rikky Director of his Foundation, Connery also put a tough lady into the office to do the main administration and secretarial work. She was Anne Tautee, who very soon was fighting Demarco's attempts to use Connery's money for his own ends and activities. Demarco was eventually pushed out, but the Foundation continued under new management, and Anne Tautee came to work for me.

Having been brought up to look at the world in commercial terms, she had some trouble in adjusting to the peculiar atmosphere of my office, trying to promote literary authors and values, with considerations of profit being very secondary, but she was an enthusiastic person and no doubt found my lack of deviousness refreshing. Several things happened, all at about the same time after my European electoral campaign, but I cannot put a strict sequence to them. Ledlanet was sold: I am not quite sure when, but it must have been in 1980 or soon after as I was still there in June 1979 during the election, and there was probably another shooting season to bring in some money later in the year. I do have my diary, parts of it, and in a very tattered condition, for 1980, and it shows many transatlantic trips, visits to Paris, dinners with Sam Beckett – at that time we were meeting at La Palette on the Boulevard Montparnasse, where he always had grilled sole and pommes frites, and had abandoned his old haunts on the Rue de la Gaité, as well as the Coupole, the Closerie and the Falstaff, preferring a place that was always quiet, where he could walk to and from home or take a direct metro – and other activities. Times were difficult for me and the loss of Ledlanet was traumatic, so much so that I made no real attempt to think about what I should be keeping from the house or to find other solutions: I was undergoing a string of misfortunes, and could no longer trust in luck to find some way out; I had lost most of the self-confidence that had brought me through two decades of a changing society, where I was always on the outside of establishment views, and too individualistic and classically-orientated in my tastes to be a hippie. Lorenzo de Grazie had died in New York and the office was closed; that now seemed the main priority: we had stocks of books sitting in the Mercedes warehouse in Brooklyn and no one was doing anything to sell them. One day in September 1980, Anne Tautee and I took the 'plane to New York to see what could be done. Anne had trouble at Immigration, because the official did not understand the purpose of our mission and she had no money on her, but I sorted it out and got her through. A friend of her's had lent us a flat on the East Side and we arrived there one Sunday evening. The next morning we went early to the Flatiron Building and up to the office. I had remembered that Lorenzo had sub-let it from a man in the office next door and we knocked on it. We could hear him talking on the telephone and after a while he came to the door. He name was Berny Rosten and he did indeed have the main lease on Lorenzo's office that I had been using during the previous year when in town. He had in fact, just as we knocked, been talking to someone who wanted to rent it. He let us in to the locked-up office, which consisted of one medium-size room and a small outer office. Piles of letters and parcels made it difficult to push open the door; they had been accumulating for two months. Anne and I got down to work, opening up everything: there were letters, bills, orders and cheques. There were enough of the latter two to enable me to make up my mind. I went to see Berny next door and asked if he would be willing to let me the office. I explained the whole history, he was sympathetic and finally agreed. We opened a new bank account and banked the cheques, taking careful note of which books had been paid for. We wrote to all the other British publishers who had been involved with Lorenzo, who, as it soon became clear, had been for some time on the point of bankruptcy and had not been particularly honest in his dealings with either booksellers or publishers. There had been a young black girl called Arlene working there. We managed to contact her and got her to come back to work for us for two weeks to help us understand just what had been going on. In the end we gave her a proper job because she was very good at all the work that had to be done. I went to Brooklyn to see Mercedes and managed to get the books moving out again.

After a week, with Anne running the office with Arlene's help, I went out to sell books, first around all the New York bookshops, and then I made trips to Boston, Washington and Chicago. The other publishers wrote in gratefully and soon we were able to give them the money that had come in for their books. After a while we had nine British publishers willing to let us distribute them. Some were in the group that had previously been with South-West Book Services in Dallas, others had been recruited by Lorenzo's English partner, who after one more meeting in New York, disappeared from the scene. I established a new company, Flatiron Book Distributors, named after the building. One by one, other British publishers came in to visit us. One of the first was Glen Thompson, a director of Writers and Readers Co-operative, a company run by a group of enthusiastic young people in London, with money largely put up by John Berger, the art critic and novelist, and Peter Fuller, another art critic, and their friends. Thompson had originally come from New York. He was a restless, energetic black man who had found his niche in London, but now came back frequently to New York to help me promote the co-operative's books and to develop new publishing ideas. He had acquired enough of an English accent to impress those New Yorkers he met in our circles and Anne was quickly attracted to him, so that her loyalties became divided. Writers and Readers were, like my own company, left-wing publishers and to some extent literary, but they were more interested in fashionable trendiness than I was, and our list was much more serious. The three of us became something of a trio around places like Joe Allen's and El Quixote, the Spanish restaurant underneath the Chelsea Hotel, where I still ran into Molly Parkin, although by now both she and Patrick, no longer living together, were about to return to England.

We had nine British publishers in our distribution group, but I decided that we should broaden our image and we took on two American houses as well. One was Fiction Collective, which had been started by Michael Braziller, George's son, as a co-operative where the writers paid to produce their own books, but Michael handled the management and distribution: it gave new writers who were outside commercial norms a chance to get reviewed and to sell. Michael backed out after his father declined to continue selling the series, and the writers themselves kept the co-operative going, but they were looking for effective distribution, which I offered them. The other was a rather esoteric company called Station Hill Press. They had some good books and some indifferent ones, and we did what we could for them for two or three years, but found them so unreasonably demanding, difficult to deal with, and ungrateful for the considerable effort that went into offering their books around the country, that I eventually dropped them.

Fiction Collective were quite good at promoting themselves, but were not very systematic in following up their successful public readings in taking the names of attenders and building a mailing list. We collaborated well with them, but their books were hard to sell and we had many returns. Many of the novelists in the group were also academics. They were literary in a very American way and I came to know several of them personally, such as Mark Mirsky, who taught at Columbia, Ron Sukenik, a Professor at Boulder in Colorado who edited The American Book Review from his university, and Mark Leyner, who was *de facto* running the co-operative at the time they came to me, together with a young lady who did all the administration.

I was involved in several promotions about this time. I had published a volume of plays by Simone Benmussa. She had been assistant to Jean-Louis Barrault for a number of years, and when, having given tacit support to the student protests of 1968, he was persecuted by De Gaulle who took the Odéon Theatre away from him, which then obliged him to dismantle most of his team, she took a job with Gallimard, handling their performing rights, while giving all her spare time to Barrault for nothing. She also started to write plays, which were mainly adaptations of works with a feminist bias, taken from stories by George Moore, Henry James, Virginia Woolf, Nathalie Sarraute, Edith Wharton and the like. They were successful in France, then in the U.K., sometimes in New York, always directed by herself. She soon had a group of admiring actresses and actors performing her work, which was translated into English by Barbara Wright. Her English groupies included Stephanie Beecham, Julia Foster, Susanna York and Susan Hampshire. I devoted an issue of Gambit to her work (No. 35), which included the text of *Appearances*, her Henry James play, in which Daniel Massey played Henry James. This was performed in the Mayfair Theatre, where an American lawyer, who had a small theatre of his own in New York, Alexander Racolin, backed it, before bringing it to Manhattan. When the Manhattan Theatre Club bought the rights from me to perform *The Singular Life of Albert Nobbs*, which had done very well in London with Foster and York in the cast at the New End Theatre, I decided to give a party to enhance her reputation.

Susan Teltch had by now married a New York stockbroker called John Marvin. He was wealthy, a fairly cultured WASP (to use American parlance), and she was just the wife he needed, because she had English upper-class charm, entertained well and was able to redecorate his New York apartment with such good taste that he was able to sell it at a very high price and move to another, which she also redecorated; she did the same for his country home. John Marvin had just divorced his rather neurotic earlier wife, with whom, quite coincidentally, I had myself had a fling at about that time, having met her at a party. When Sue found out she went into peals of laughter, and talked about it all over New York, especially as the wife had been suicidal, and she credited me with saving her life. But the Marvins, who invited me around quite frequently now that I was so often in New York, wanted to help me in any way they could and entertaining was both easy for them and would increase their circle of interesting acquaintances. They were very happy to give a party for Simone Benmussa and the cast of the play, including the theatre management and whoever else I wanted to invite: these were the critics and other writers who would enjoy meeting my author. But I reckoned without the lady, Lynne Meadows, who ran the theatre and her rather snotty committee members, who knocked all the names off the list except their own group, so none of the people I really wanted were there. In addition Simone felt cheated in that the contract they signed, very late and after rehearsals had started, was not what I had negotiated.

The Marvins also agreed to give a party for Fiction Collective. This followed a reading by a group of three or four writers of the group in the auditorium of the Huntingdon Hartford Building. The profile of a certain lady caught my eye during the reading and I saw her again at the party afterwards, which was given at the Marvins' Fifth Avenue apartment from which they were soon to move. Sue had a date for me, someone they thought a suitable match, but I never even met her, because, playing the barman, the lady I had noticed came to get a drink and I talked to her all evening, while pouring drinks. She was the mother of Mark Leyner, who had been reading earlier, and with whom I had had frequent meetings. Her husband was there as well, a lawyer who was not very keen on having a literary son and was rather bemused by the whole party. He had just told his wife that he was tired of the marriage and needed to be alone. Talking to me was both a way of stifling her anger and getting back at him. One of us 'phoned the other the next day and we met for lunch the day after that.

I was by then living in Elaine Swann's Bleecker Street apartment, and after a preliminary weekend when we tried to drive out of Manhattan, but my confusion with the freeway system wasted so much time that we ended up coming back and booking into a mid-town hotel, we began to meet there. Her husband, who was having an affair with a Texan lady, was already suspicious about me, having seen his wife talking to me for two hours or so at the party, and he had in a few days become unsure of what he really wanted to do; he now would have liked the best of both worlds, but it was too late. Muriel Leyner cut the knot and he moved out of their house in Maplewood, in a smart part of New Jersey, which soon after was sold. Muriel moved to

Hoboken across the Hudson River from Manhattan and began to see different men, but mainly me.

Anne Tautee and I were invited for Thanksgiving by Charles Johnson, manager of the Mercedes warehouse in Brooklyn. He was a very nice man, much more so than his boss, who I found shifty and unreliable. Charles and his wife gave us a pleasant day in their New Jersey suburban house, which we reached by train. It was a lovely clear day, crisp with snow on the ground, and we made two new friends who were also invited: they were an Irish painter, Liam Roberts, and his very pretty English girlfriend, who was a secretary to the Secretary-General of the United Nations. Roberts was a very interesting artist who painted his pictures on the floor of his tiny one-room apartment in central Manhattan, but made his living mainly by designing commercial covers for different magazines. I was to see more of him and would accidentally meet him elsewhere, once on a boat returning from Ireland, once in Paris. His girlfriend obviously loved him, but could not live with him, because as Jean Gimpel had observed, good artists are not good for women. Charles Johnson soon left Mercedes and I only saw him once after that. He and his wife liked musicals, so I took them both to see *Eva* with Eleanor Riger as my companion.

We were selling many books, but the problem was getting paid and I found that paying the eleven other publishers as regularly as I could was leaving nothing over to pay for my own list, because booksellers were slow payers and some never paid. We were all working very hard and Anne constantly complained that I left her no time to see New York; she had not even been able to go to Bloomingdale's, which had been high on her list of priorities. Much time was spent on the 'phone trying to extract cheques from booksellers and I was far from pleased with the sloppy Mercedes service. Anne went back to Britain for Christmas 1980, returned after three weeks, but did not stay too long after that. I was flying frequently across the Atlantic, spending about equal time on each side, and most of it selling. I left London to my commission man, Darryl Richards and his wife, who did the smaller accounts and the feminist shops, and went myself around the provinces.

I was in New York for Christmas that year, spending both Christmas Day and New Year's with the Marvins, going to the Met on New Year's Day to see *Hansel and Gretel*. I also gave an office party just before Christmas to which authors, booksellers, other publishers and friends all came. On Christmas Eve I went to have a drink with Bill Colleran who was in New York and took James Bruce, who was there to see publishers on behalf of his Canadian printing company, Hunter Rose, along with me. Then James and I had dinner and I ended up in Arthur's, a jazz bar on Sheridan Square, where we parted at about five in the morning. A few days later Sheila Colvin came to New York, where she met a friend of her's called Deirdre Robinson. I had always been a little suspicious of Dierdre, who had been in Holloway on some smuggling conviction, and who was now a nurse-companion to an old woman in Florida. She and Sheila did the town together while I worked, going to a matinee of *Forty-Second Street* on New Year's Eve, after which they met me and we went to a string of New Year's Eve parties with Phyllis and Sigi Miller, the first one being rather staid and the others less so. Somewhere around midnight as we trudged through falling snow from one party to the next, the two girls began singing and dancing the theme song from the musical they had just seen in the middle of the street, which amused, but also alarmed the Millers. Aside from the madness of it all, there was traffic about. Sheila and I had dinner with Bill Colleran and his American girlfriend two days later at her Sutton Place apartment and I think the composer Morton Feldman was also present. I had met him several times, but I think that it was on that night that he first tried to sell me his new *Treatise on Orchestration*, that in more affluent times I might have seriously considered. Then Sheila returned to London and I did the same a week later, which must have been when Anne Tautee returned to New York to relieve me.

Among the people I kept up with were Alger Hiss, who was living very simply with his wife in Massachusetts and still trying to get his case reopened. I saw many of the people involved with Civil Liberties and having Edith Tiger, who ran Emergency Civil Liberties, so close in the office directly under mine, brought me into contact with several others. I met Victor Nevasky, a good friend of Hiss, Corliss Lamont, whose book I had published back in the fifties, and many of the old intellectuals whom I had known in the McCarthy witch-hunt days again. There was an annual Civil Rights dinner in New York and I attended several of them, all in the autumn. The chairman of these dinners was Rabbi Bob Goldberg whom I had first met in London with Tondi Barr. He was the liberal Rabbi who had married Arthur Miller and Marilyn Monroe, had given her sufficient instruction for her to be admitted into Judaism, and he was now the Jewish chaplain at Yale University, where his synagogue had portraits of six liberal Jewish prophets down one side and such secular Jews as Spinoza, Freud and Einstein down the other. We met several times and had dinner together. He was very concerned about Tondi's bad financial position and wanted to help her if he could. He had even proposed to her once, but she had never even considered it. She was fond of him, but knew, as everyone other than he himself knew, that he was gay, but could not face it. Bob often chaired these Civil Rights dinners and he was a witty and good speaker. Of the few who had led the civil rights marches through the Deep South with Martin Luther King he was the only prominent Jew and he had been arrested many times and come near to being lynched. He was a fine man and a courageous one.

I had come to know Victor Nevasky quite well, mainly by attending Emergency Civil Rights dinners in New York. When he published with Viking a book about the Hollywood witch-hunt, in which I had been indirectly concerned in my early publishing days, I acquired British rights and published it as a large-format paperback in 1982. Victor was the editor of The Nation, an equivalent to the New Statesman in Britain, and there were many liaisons between the two opinion journals, sharing many writers. This was the time when the Falklands War broke out and I was also trying to commission a book from Alexander Cockburn on that. Unfortunately getting Victor over to Britain to publicise his book was rather abortive as the newspapers and other media were only interested in the war and not about what he had to say about the witch-hunt. I gave a party for him at Green's Court in my house next to the office and Vanessa Redgrave came, but only because she wanted to ask Victor to appear in court for her in America where she had a libel case to do with her political views, which were under media attack. In New York, Cockburn, although he had signed a contract, suddenly became impossible to reach. I found myself talking to a real or supposed brother who sounded just like Cockburn on the telephone; he never wrote the book, so a great deal of work in getting together material for it was wasted. At this point I was crossing the Atlantic sometimes two or three times in a month, trying to lighten the financial problems of London with more time travelling in the States, and increasing my sales there.

In October 1980, before some of the events related above, I had been at the Wexford Festival, where I saw three operas, two of which, Puccini's *Edgar* and Carlisle Floyd's *Of Mice and Men* were new to me, bringing my opera score to 493 operas and 1789 performances. Jim Fraser had decided to come that year and he brought Eleanor Kay with him. They were not getting on well, but she had burnt her boats, and with two small children by the husband who had divorced her, was now totally dependent on him. We went to the first two operas, but then on the Sunday, our last day in Wexford, he started off in a very bad mood and was at first shouting at Eleanor – I could hear it in the hotel through the wall in the next room – and then was telephoning his lawyer to cut her out of his will. She came into my room where I was not yet dressed to complain to me. 'Please, Eleanor,' I said to her, 'Don't stay here. If Jim comes in he will make assumptions and think we are having an affair. If you want to talk go down to the dining room and I'll meet you there for breakfast in a few minutes. But go *now* before Jim comes in.' She did and I met her downstairs and waited for Jim to arrive.

That morning the three of us went to Tom Walsh's annual pre-lunch drinks party in his house. Jim Fraser, playing the big man, and he had recently been put on Scottish Opera's finance committee as he was a regular donor, began to criticise Peter Ebert, saying that Scottish opera would not employ him again. This was a terrible thing to do in Wexford where Peter Ebert, son of Karl, who with Fritz Busch had been artistic founders of Glyndebourne, was very popular, having directed several operas there. I whispered to Jim that this would only make him look a fool and pulled him out, taking him to lunch at Carne on the coast, some miles away, to a seafood restaurant I knew. He was quite unpleasant over lunch and this went on through the afternoon and evening when we saw our last opera. Afterwards, back at the hotel, he wanted to make it up and called for champagne. I had to get up very early to drive to Dublin to catch a 'plane to London, did not want to drink any more, accepted his apology, said that there were no hard feelings, although I wished he could control his drinking and his words with others, because it hurt him and embarrassed me. Then I went to bed. I never saw him again.

I was in my New York office early in 1981 when I was told he was dead. I would have liked to have been at his funeral, but it was impossible. Sheila went for me. Eleanor was not allowed to sit anywhere except at the back of the church, was frozen out by Jim's wife and sons, and a week later told to leave Huntley Hall. She found a small cottage in the hills and began to drink herself. Jim had left some money with a publican in Milnathort for a wake. About a dozen locals and Sheila Colvin went to it. Huntley Hall, which I had given to Jim and on which he spent a fortune, with its music room, swimming pool, sauna and gold taps, was quickly sold off. His business soon folded as well and his three sons all developed their own different careers. Jim was a difficult man, his mind a maelstrom of resentment, ambition, lust, kindness and generosity. Looking back among those I genuinely miss, I often think of Jim Fraser.

I have briefly mentioned my series of Opera Guides, about which I was organising advance publicity at the Frankfurt Book Fair in 1979. They were the brainchild of Nicholas John, an enthusiastic young man who worked for the English National Opera, putting together their programme material and he made his programmes, that people bought on going to the opera, full of fascinating articles and pictures about sources, related subjects and background material to do with the opera in question. He was the first employee of a British opera company to be given the title Dramaturg, which means in effect literary manager. His original idea was to put out a series of booklets about individual operas, selling at about a pound, but I thought they would be much more valuable if they also included the libretto, and in discussion we added other features. The first four came out in 1980 and were *La Cenerentola*, *Aïda*, *The Magic Flute* and *Fidelio*. The were priced at £2.00 and $4.95, the thought being that they might be sold by programme girls in Britain who would not want to have to fiddle with a few pennies in change, but that in America, where bigger discounts were the rule, one had to raise the price and always make the book five cents less than the dollar price, because things were done that way. The ENO, as part of the deal, would buy 2,000 copies of each at half price for sale in the theatre and to their mailing list, which helped us to pay the printer promptly. In addition they were designed by the ENO who also provided all the editorial matter, which was especially commissioned by Nicholas John. We would give a royalty to the opera company for this material, which they paid for directly, another royalty to the translator (we printed the original libretto facing the English translation) and a third to the music publisher if the opera was still in copyright. I also agreed a one percent royalty to John himself as editor. This was later questioned by the ENO accountants who felt that as John was getting an adequate salary from them and was doing this work in their time, that any additional royalty should be going to them and not him.

The series was a success and we continued to issue them four at a time until we had more than thirty, when it became necessary to reprint the more popular ones, so that by then we often published two new ones with two reprints or some other combination. The prices gradually went up with inflation until they reached a price of £6.00 each, with some oversized ones at more. Sometimes more than one opera was put into a volume, especially if the libretto was English, so *Peter Grimes* and *Gloriana* went together, four Tippett operas were published as *The Operas of Michael Tippett* (he was later to write one more), three Monteverdis were published together and there were double volumes of operas by Richard Strauss, Janacek, and Stravinsky. We also did a Bartok volume where *Bluebeard's Castle*, his only opera, was paired with a detailed description of his two ballets.

We sold them in bookshops and music shops, and to opera companies performing operas that were in our series, and they soon became our most profitable publishing activity. I took them all over the U.S., put them into the San Francisco opera company, into smaller companies that I visited on my travels and into the Metropolitan Opera shop where they sold in thousands. We had two mishaps there: one was when the ENO did an American tour and visited the Met with *Rigoletto*, which in Jonathan Miller's production was set in Little Italy with many references to the New York Mafia; a local Italian congressman raised an objection so that our Guide, but not the performance, was banned; the other problem came much later, in the nineties, when Schirmer, whose libretti were sold in the lobby, complained that we were cutting into their sales, and we were then banned altogether. The Schirmer librettos had mainly very old and out-of-date translations, so it was Gresham's Law at work, the bad driving out the good. No appeal worked: they were a big company with contracts and connections that were probably profitable to some individuals inside the system and I was an outsider.

I went to operatic conventions to push them, especially Opera America, which was attended by all the main officers of American and Canadian opera companies. I met such old friends as Peter Hemmings and Thomson Smillie there, whom I knew from their earlier days with Scottish Opera, and in the latter case from Wexford, where Thomson had become the third director of the Festival, following Brian Dickie, who had taken over when Tom Walsh retired. I was occasionally put onto a panel on these occasions when the organisers realised that I had seen more operas than anyone else who attended these conventions and knew a great deal about the subject.

I met a girl in the elevator of the Flatiron Building one day, chatted her up enough to meet her later, and then took her out a few times. She was an ex-alcoholic and had been going to a meeting of Alcoholics Anonymous in our building when I met her. AA was like a religion and I found it difficult to have a glass or two of wine at meals in her company, and besides, she was very temperamental. She had worked in a bank, but was now looking for a job and I thought she might be able to sell for me. She had never been to an opera and telling her that to sell my list she had to know something about it, I took her to one. She was totally alienated, had no idea of what music or even drama was all about, and walked out. That ended that.

We had a rather pretty and sexy red-headed girl among Anne Tautee's successors, who was intelligent and competent, but she eventually left because she wanted to earn more than I could pay her. I inadvertently found a CV she had typed out, where she had so exaggerated her function and importance when working for me that I found it very funny. We also had a young man who wanted to come as an intern. He could never arrive on time in the morning, was always ill, presumably because he had too-much night life, and when alone in the office he did not even bother to answer the telephone. He did not last long. I found an out-of-work actor, John White, who for about a year sold books for me in New York and New England and I bought a car for him. Unfortunately he was a terrible driver, did not look after the car, had constant accidents, and eventually left to teach at a Catholic College.

Then came Gary Pulsover, an American who had been a member of the Writers and Readers Cooperative, who was brought back from London by Glenn Thompson. At first he filled in when Anne was with us, only temporarily back in England, and he took over all publicity and promotion at which he was good, writing catalogue copy and press releases and answering our two telephones which rang constantly. Then he became office manager. Arlene was still with us, transferring orders to the warehouse by modem and doing other jobs, including much of the typing. Gary found a street Arab (his own word, but it was very apt), called Jason, who had been selling gadgets on the street and we experimented giving him a job selling our books. I took him round, showed him how, and he was not bad, but very greedy, calculating his commission on each order that he brought in and wanting to be instantly paid. He had no sense of responsibility, even less of loyalty to a company that depended on everybody pulling together, always saying behind my back that 'he wasn't going to break his ass for me' and eventually I got rid of him, but not before he had told Muriel Leyner that she would be better off with a virile young guy like himself than with an old man like me. I was then fifty-three.

I had to make another west coast trip and suggested to Muriel that she might like to accompany me. She was nervous about it and asked advice from friends who told her that I might well be a serial killer and she could disappear without trace, but she really wanted to go and assented. She flew to meet me in Vancouver and having done my business there she drove down the coast with me as I sold the books of our group in Seattle, Portland, and the Californian towns. The reason I had picked that particular time, in July and August 1982, was that the Seattle Opera House were giving a Pacific North-West Festival, that included two *Ring* cycles, the first in German, the second in English. We saw the German *Götterdämmerung* and then the whole series in English, spending two days in Portland in the middle. When I drove into the latter town I found a hotel by instinct, never took much notice of its name, had dinner there, and went first thing the next morning to Powell's where I spent the whole day, selling my entire list successfully and even buying books that caught my eye to be sent back to me in New York. But then I could not remember where the hotel was or its name. I drove around looking, and then the car broke down. I found a garage to fix it – it was now early evening – and hunted through the list of hotels in the 'phone book. My fifth call was lucky. Muriel was frantic by then, not sure if I had decided to vanish or had had an accident. We went for a good dinner at Jake's, a famous fish restaurant near Powell's, recovered our equanimity with lobster and a good local wine, and the next morning I went around the other bookshops. But when I called for Muriel she was unwell, but drove northward with me nevertheless, back to Seattle. On the way we stopped at a small shack that did hamburgers and hot dogs with a wonderful view of Mount Saint Helen, a snow-capped volcanic mountain, but all she could swallow was tea and dry toast, while I amiably chatted to a large cowboy type of man for a few minutes, I forget what about. Muriel was amazed that such dissimilar men could find anything to say to each other. That night I went to the opera on my own because she still had a stomach upset.

It was a successful sales trip down to San Diego and then across the Painted Desert inland towards Phoenix. At one point I was very worried when fuel ran low, and as far as I knew there was no habitation for many miles ahead. But with my alarm light showing a shack appeared in the distance and as I drew near I saw a fuel pump and it worked!

From Phoenix, we flew to Armadillo in Texas, where we found a motel that was infested with lice and washing those off was no easy matter. It was a horrible town, kept alive by defence contractors and the armaments industry, and not good for selling my books. I never returned there. I did fairly well in the other towns of Texas, in Austin, San Antonio, Dallas and Houston, and then flew once again to Albuquerque, where I visited the shops I knew and then drove into the hills to Santa Fé. The rather simple cheap hotel that had not worried Julia Sweeney did worry Muriel, so we went to a better one in the centre. We stayed long enough to see five operas, *The*

Marriage of Figaro, Mignon, Die Fledermaus, Die Liebe der Danae (which I was seeing for only the second time) and a new one, *The Confidence Man* by American composer George Rochberg, which brought my total to 509 (1884 performances). Only a few months earlier I had seen an opera with a very similar theme, Krenek's *What Price Confidence?* in Nottingham.

My experience of Santa Fé seldom varied. The days were beautiful and hot, the evenings coolish, and a rain storm usually started within an hour of the opera beginning, which meant that those in uncovered seats had to dash to the back and stand; the orchestra received some of the rain if the wind was in a certain direction. The rain never lasted long, but it was a nuisance. The back of the stage was usually open, so the audience could see the lights of Los Alamos, home of the first atom bomb, in the far distance when the weather cleared. It was a fantastical setting for an opera festival, but short on amenities, especially for ladies for whom there were insufficient lavatories. On one night we gave a lift back to town to a man who said he was 'in the music business', but turned out to be a part-time reviewer. I had often noticed how Americans studiously try to give a commercial aspect to activities that elsewhere were considered professional and intellectual ones: to be a musician or critic is somehow wrong; to be in the music 'business' is O.K. In the same way university professors have 'offices' whereas in Britain they have 'studies'.

During the eighties I travelled all over the U.S., on each trip starting from a central point such as Cleveland or Denver or Austin, where I would arrive by air, hire a car, and then either call on all the bookshops within a two hundred mile radius, returning at the end to the airport where I had arrived, or else drive more or less in a line and leave the car at the last town on the tour. In this way (and I then had Marcus Colleran with me, about whom more later) I drove from Des Moines through Iowa to the main towns of Wisconsin, taking in Chicago and ending in Milwaukee, and on another occasion southward from Chicago through Kansas, Tennessee and Louisville, where I contacted Thomson Smillie, now running the opera there, happy with his standard of living, but not with the philistinism of local audiences. In Louisville I came for the first time across the Borders chain of bookshops, that were soon to spread across the United States. Then back to New York and then Britain. One regular call was Minneapolis, where the important B. Dalton chain had their headquarters. One spent a day going from one buyer to another, each with his special subject, and presented new titles, which were then ordered to be sent in varying quantities to the B. Dalton shops all over the country. One got to know the buyers well, usually having lunch with two or three of them in the middle of the day. Minneapolis also had a cultural life, but other than the Guthrie Theatre, where I saw a few theatrical performances, I had no time to get involved in it. I did particularly well at the university there, but there were several university shops and they all took time. At one of them, Savron's, which is now gone, I had great difficulty making a second appointment: the man finally agreed to see me, but for only a few minutes. When I came in, he said: 'Oh, Mr. Calder. The last time you described every book. It took a long time and frankly I couldn't sit through all that again.'

'How did they sell?' I asked.

'Oh, very well. But please, not all that again.'

'Why not let me take the stock, see what you need and give you just what you would order anyway?'

'Oh, would you do that? And not make me listen to you?' I had not realised that I could be such a bore, but to relieve him of it was good for my sales and saved time: from then on, he was friendly and gave me *carte blanche* of which I never took too much advantage.

In neighbouring St. Paul's there were also good bookshops. One called The Hungry Horse had a big selection of poetry and was good for literature in general. It was a centre for local writers and had many public readings. There was a Lutheran seminary there with its own bookshop, a most unlikely customer for what I had to offer, but the manager was extremely interested in serious literature and bought surprising quantities. I suspect that he did not sell much, but wanted to support publishers like me and either kept many of the books for himself or found some way to dispose of what he couldn't sell. Others who called on him seemed to have the same experience. On each call we had a long talk about politics and the state of the world.

One sales rep whom I had first met in Dallas, who continued with me over the years was Stuart Abraham. He had a girlfriend, Patsy, who was an extremely good painter and had studied in Paris: she divided her time between selling books and her own work, and she also illustrated books for publishers. Sue Marvin had seen her work and she bought several paintings. I eventually would stay with them when in Chicago. They had many lists to carry and their sales for me were uneven, but fairly regular, but it was still necessary for me to supplement them with my own efforts. They knew everyone in the book-trade in the Mid-West and I made a few sales trips with Stuart to other towns. One good stop was a suburban shop in Birmingham, a northern suburb of Detroit, which was otherwise a disappointing town for serious books. It was run by a couple, the Lichters with whom I became friendly enough to be always invited to stay with them, when there. They arranged for me to give talks both at the local library and in their shop, always about authors I published and about literary movements, such as Bloomsbury, impressionism, expressionism and the *nouveau roman*. They organised many activities in their shop, Maximus, and as Birmingham was an affluent neighbourhood, it became a centre where they could sell expensive art books as well as my literary paperbacks and opera guides, which were deliberately low-priced, because I knew that many of the readers of my books, especially students and university staff, were not affluent. One day the wife told me that her husband had taken up golf and was much less in the shop. He would meet new customers that way, he had told her. This struck me as unlikely, and I was right. He was having an affair which eventually broke up the marriage and the bookshop as well, which in any case was encountering difficulties because a Crown Bookshop had opened nearby, offering heavily discounted best-sellers. It finally closed; another good customer gone! It was a lament I was to repeat often in the next few years.

What made my travels easy and as cheap as was possible was the splendid lady called Jeannie Adams. I had met her in the '55', one of the bars on Sheridan Square in New York that attracted the local bohemians, the kind of people you might expect to find in an O'Neill play like *The Iceman Cometh*. She was there most evenings after working all day in a travel agency where she specialised, much against the will of her German boss, in finding the cheapest way for her customers to travel, hire cars and get favourable hotel rates. Most of my American travel arrangements I entrusted to her, and she was also a friend, although I seldom saw her outside the confines of the '55', where I would meet her for a drink and to collect my tickets.

I had my favourite bookshops all over the country and by the middle eighties had visited every state except Oklahoma, Alabama, Montana and Alaska as far as bookselling was concerned. But the trade was changing rapidly and my best independent customers tended to disappear as the chains became ever more ruthless and Crown Books was the worst of them. I made many friends by saying I would not sell to Crown. Their policy was to pick an area where a local bookshop had built up a regular clientele and find nearby premises which they would open just before Thanksgiving, offering a range of books, especially those most in demand, at heavy discounts, which even the most loyal customers of the established shops could not resist. They might still go there for their more esoteric purchases, but the bread-and-butter best-seller sales, which enabled bookshops to carry slower-selling titles, simply disappeared and, sooner or later, they would have to close. Then Crown would probably take over their shop, especially if the premises were attractive. Crown's other tactic was to buy the lease from the landlord and force them out that way. Other chains would soon start imitating them. If some of the independents had followed the example of Powell's in Portland, they might have been able to evade that fate.

Although in 1980 I had commission reps who were supposed to sell my books in most parts of the U.S., they really did very little, but demanded a ten percent commission on the territory they were meant to be covering, which in many cases came to more than the sales they actually took, as books ordered from bookshops by customers, and others ordered for academic courses, were included in the regional sales and could not be separately identified except at great cost. I still had Dan Wedge in New England and various groups elsewhere, but after a time I usually dropped them for non-results. On one occasion I called on the university shop in Albuquerque on the day after my commission rep had been there. He had sold only one copy each of two still unpublished books. I came out with an order for over two hundred, nearly all of them titles I had in stock. The other shops in the town had not seen him, except one where my catalogue had not even been shown. I ended the relationship.

I went to two annual conferences in America every year, that of the Booksellers, held in May, and of the academics, the Modern Language Association, which was between Christmas and New Year. At each I had a stand to display my books, as in Frankfurt, and I had to be on it all day, sometimes with help, sometimes on my own. There was a Samuel Beckett Society at the MLA and I would go to their sessions, and was sometimes asked myself to give a twenty minute talk, but more often I was making points after the talks of others. Barney Rosset often went, but he stood outside the door, afraid to be bored, and most of them were indeed boring. But I came to know the academics who taught Beckett that way. It also became obvious that many had little interest in the subject except where it might advance their careers.

I was in Chicago at the ABA[36] when the news came through that Henry Miller had died. Grove Press draped their stand with photographs of the author and with slogans proclaiming their championship of Miller, whom Barney Rosset had first read and admired as a schoolboy. He had fought many court cases to defend his novels at great legal cost to himself. But Henry Miller, along with D.H. Lawrence, had brought him his greatest fame, and no-one had ever doubted his courage. Barney still had money, but was losing it fast, unable to put any brake on his expenditure, and publishing books was probably the least of them.

After Chicago I went to Boston and spent a day with Maurice Girodias. Some time previously I had seen him in New York, where, after his French bankruptcy, he had started an American Olympia. He had found a novel way of raising new capital: he had booked several round trips from Paris to New York, hoping to meet someone on the 'plane who would back him to start again, and on the third flight he was lucky enough to meet a printer who he was able to convince to give him sufficient credit to start a new list. This became a mixture of books he had first commissioned in Paris and new authors he found in the States. On my previous meeting with him there, he had had a small office off Union Square, very untidy and chaotic. He must have had a secretary or assistant, but I never saw anyone other than himself, and he was sleeping on a mattress on the floor. He was then still enthusiastic about the States and his future prospects there, enjoying walking around New York and looking at the architecture, which he claimed no American ever noticed, but he did not like American wines, which I was beginning to enjoy; he lost no opportunity to denigrate them. In addition to publishing new erotic authors – Clarence Major was his biggest discovery at the time –

---

[36] American Booksellers Association Conference.

he had taken on a number of controversial political titles, as he had always done to his cost in France. He now had similar and catastrophic experiences in New York. Maurice had published a scatological novel in which Henry Kissinger, then Secretary of State, was the principal character and he was sued for libel. But his downfall came through an exposé of scientology: the scientologists had always been quite ruthless to anyone who set out to attack them, and Maurice, who had lost none of his naïvety, was an easy target. They sent him a girl who applied to be his secretary, and he engaged her. She became his companion and probably his mistress, and then one day the two of them went to New Jersey on some mysterious jaunt, where she suddenly disappeared and he found himself arrested by the FBI, who were in waiting on some information they had been fed, obviously by the scientologists; they found drugs on him, which he always claimed had been planted, although I know some, including his brother who thought otherwise. Personally I had never in any way associated Maurice with drugs. The various charges that were then brought against him, some obviously concocted by the scientologists, were many, including libelling Kissinger, and he was ordered to be deported. He managed to get a stay by marrying an American, Leila Lyon, a member of the well-known Boston Cabot family, who was studying medicine. The publishing company went into bankruptcy, and soon after Maurice moved to Boston where Leila was now an intern in the local hospital.

This was his situation when I met him in Boston. He had spent several months writing his book, the same one that he had contracted in Frankfurt several years earlier. The French version, *J'Arrive*,[37] which only goes up to the beginning of the war, had come out in Paris in 1977, and he had now translated it into English. When I saw him he was just finishing it and it would eventually appear as *The Frog Prince*[38]. He intended to take the bus to New York (the cheapest means of travel in America) the following week to see publishers. He already had a tentative offer from Farrar Strauss and Giroux, which he intended to use as a bargaining counter to get a higher offer from someone else. I told him not to be a fool: Farrar Strauss were good and serious publishers of literature and he could not do better, but as usual he ignored me. He eventually went to Crown Publishers who sold it badly and quickly remaindered it.

We had a long and boozy lunch. I picked him up at Leila's apartment, but never saw her. She was working very hard at the hospital and had to spend most of her nights as well as her days there. Although for Maurice it was a marriage of convenience that enabled him to stay longer in the U.S., there was real love between them, and they remained very attached to each other through all his coming vicissitudes. We talked in French for four hours in a little restaurant in the port, scandalising the waitress by drinking three

[37] Paris 1977.
[38] New York 1983.

bottles of wine and following it with brandy. He was tired of America by now, bored by his poverty in Boston, and his total reliance on Leila, but hopeful that his book, the manuscript of which he had left to be photocopied on our way to the restaurant, would restore his fortunes. I have never known a more panglossian optimist than Maurice Girodias, always living in a golden tomorrow, about to be brought into being by his latest plan, idea or project. 'C'est sûr,' he would say. 'Cette fois il y a aucune possibilité d'un échec.' He never took my advice, nor did he take the counsel of his very competent American lawyer, Leon Friedman, who liked him and did everything possible to help him, but to no avail. 'I have never had any client,' Friedman told me later, 'who always, quite deliberately, did the exact opposite of what I told him to do, except Maurice Girodias.' I found a hotel in Boston and went to bed at seven o'clock. I was in any case tired after the ABA in Chicago, and the liquid drunk at lunch made an early and long night imperative.

Maurice did go to New York, eventually sold the book to Crown Publishers, where it achieved the results related above. Not long after that, needing an eye operation that he could not afford in America, he returned to France, where I was to see him again throughout the eighties.

In New York, Anne Tautee, having become interested in investing in one of Glenn Thompson's ideas, which was to publish Shakespeare's plays in a comic book format, but with the complete text emerging from the characters' mouths in bubbles, went back to England to develop the series on her own. At first I engaged a young girl who lived in the apartment over my head on Bleecker Street to replace her, but she had no competence and I had to fire her. She soon had her revenge. My nephew, Constantine Laptew, who had settled in Toronto, asked if he could use my place when in New York one weekend. I told him to make no noise as my sub-tenancy was not legal, and the landlord, who had a shop on the street level, must not know about it. My nephew Cotty gave some kind of a party and the girl overhead registered a formal complaint with the landlord, which revealed my occupancy, and I had to leave. I eventually found another place on Sixteenth Street that belonged to an actor called Elliott Swift. The arrangement was unusual: I could occupy it during the week while he was away teaching outside New York; he had it for the weekends. We sometimes got mixed up with the dates, but became fairly friendly.

Some of my sales trips were to Canada. In the days of Calder and Boyars, we had had a series of different Canadian distributors who stocked and sold our books there, varying from the largest Canadian publishing companies to the smallest, but we had always found Canada a poor market. Now I moved my books to Brian Donat, son of the actor Robert Donat, and we became friends. I stayed with him and his family when in Toronto – he lived outside the town – and he often slept on a couch in my Sixteenth Street apartment during his frequent visits to New York. In Canada he represented mainly university presses, both British and American. At first he had Marion Boyars' list as well as mine to sell, but in the early eighties he dropped her. I made several sales trips with him, travelling in his car around the bookshops of Southern Ontario. He found it very boring listening to me doing my sales pitch to booksellers, and would go away to drink coffee while I talked, coming back later to sell his other books. I travelled with him once to the East Coast, stopping in Montreal and Sherbrooke, even passing my old school, but without seeing it, and on to Halifax and other towns in the Maritime Provinces, and then to Prince Edward Island and Newfoundland. In Halifax there was a local book fair. The reps of different publishers set up displays of their books in their hotel rooms, and booksellers went from one to the other giving orders for what was on offer. These trips with Brian were instructive, but I cannot pretend I enjoyed them: I liked Brian but he was rather heavy-going, and he really did not trust my books to sell in his market. I took good orders, but he cut them down, fearful that the returns would be too high. What he really liked were orders from public and university libraries, because those were always paid for and never returned.

I had one unusual experience when, at the beginning of a trip from London, when I had several destinations on my itinerary, the plane that should have gone to Montreal was diverted to Toronto. The man sitting next to me persuaded me to spend the night in Waterloo, his home town, because it was near to the airport, and he told me I could do good business there. He left me in a motel, picked me up the next morning, showed me around the town and took me to a sandwich lunch at the university restaurant. I have long forgotten his name, but he was a real character, a mythomaniac living an imaginary life. It was only in the afternoon, as things slipped out that I realised what he really was. He had been an undertaker and was now trying to get some new enterprise off the ground; what it was I cannot remember, but it was soon obvious enough that he had some impossible dream in which he had involved others, but they all knew it was a dream. I met a man with him who joined us for lunch who had worked at some point in the same undertaking business, from which my new friend had apparently been fired, as well as a girl, currently a primary school teacher, who was to be his assistant in his new dream-business, on whom he was obviously very sweet. His wife, he told me, thought he was crazy and gave him no encouragement. He constantly produced one-page printed leaflets for me to read, which at first I thought had been written by him, but they were passages that had caught his eye out of self-help or inspirational books he had read, all very heavily clichéd. I had originally intended to go to Toronto after Montreal, but I settled my Montreal business by telephone and then noticed that some short plays by Beckett were opening that night at the University Theatre in Toronto, directed by Alan Schneider. My new friend drove me in and was willing to go to the plays if seats were available. They weren't, but I found Alan Schneider backstage and he gave us two house seats.

It was a strange evening with three very short Beckett plays, followed by three very long ones by Francis Warner, an Oxford Don, of whom I had heard, as he was one of the many academics who were taking an interest in Beckett's work at the time. He had a project to build a theatre with Beckett's name under the quandrangle of Saint Peter's College in Oxford, and he had involved Buckminster Fuller as the architect. I learned from Alan that part of the motivation behind the present production of six plays was to publicise the scheme and raise money for it; the other part was obviously to promote the career of Francis Warner as a playwright. It turned out to be a long evening with the three Beckett plays over in half an hour and the three by Warner running to something like two and a half. Afterwards I met him and his very pretty girlfriend, who was also at St. Peter's and writing a thesis on Artaud. We were then taken to a party given by Al Lattner, and this was a very strange experience altogether.

Al Lattner was a Toronto property dealer, obviously very successful, and I was told much about him by Alan Schneider and the London art critic John Russell, who was also at the party. Toronto was undergoing a boom and Lattner was spreading his wings, not just in business, but in cultural matters as well, much in imitation of his mentor, who had recently died, a much-admired builder and philanthropist called Emmanuel Zacks. Lattner's house was very luxurious and had a large indoor swimming pool, which was well-heated and basically an extension of the drawing-room. Steam was constantly rising from the water. Around the walls of the pool, as around the walls of all the other rooms, valuable paintings were hanging, some modern, some old masters. One did not have to be an expert to see that there were impressionists like Manet and Renoir, a Rubens, several Picassos, a Graham Sutherland, and other famous names. John Russell confirmed to me that they were genuine and also echoed my first impression that they would not last very long in the steam of the swimming pool. 'He doesn't care,' he told me. 'He says he'll buy more when he has to.' I met Sorel Etrog at that party, I think for the first time. Sorel was a Rumanian-born artist, mainly a sculptor, living in Toronto and just then much in vogue because of the building boom. Many of the new edifices going up, banks, office blocks and civic structures, had large sculptures by Etrog standing outside them to catch the eye or to decorate the lobbies. He knew Beckett, admired him enormously, and he attached himself to me for the rest of the party, urging me to be less modest and to blow my horn a little louder. 'You have to be seen to be part of what is going on right now,' he said. Just how I was supposed to do this was not clear, except perhaps to be conspicuously seen at every fashionable gathering and to put a price on my presence.

My much over-awed friend drove back to Waterloo and I found a hotel in Toronto. On television the following evening I saw Francis Warner being interviewed: he was being very donnish and English and was trying to explain to a naïve and obviously out-of-her-depth girl who Samuel Beckett was, who he was himself, where Oxford was, and what was taking place in the University Theatre. Then, the next morning, I continued my trip, selling books, if I remember right, through the towns of Ohio and in Chicago.

At one of Suzel de la Maisonneuve's parties in London I had met an obviously affluent American lady from Chicago – it was of course on another occasion – and told her I would be in her city in a few days. She asked me to telephone when I arrived. That was my first visit to an MLA Conference, so it must have been in the very early eighties or even earlier. I was to meet Jim Knowlson and John Pilling there, because there was some special Beckett meeting taking place among the academics. Knowlson was then editing a Journal of Beckett Studies that I had agreed to publish some time earlier, and which was appearing about two or three times a year, and he and Pilling, both teaching at Reading University, had collaborated on a book about Beckett's later writings entitled *Frescoes of the Skull*. On my second day in Chicago I was invited to a party by the lady I had met in London, and that familiarised me with the grander section of the city's lake-shore, which her apartment overlooked. Later I was to get to know many of the other, to me more interesting, sections of the city.

I had known Jim Knowlson for some time, and had been a speaker at the first of several Beckett Conferences that he organised at the university that later was to house a large collection of Beckettiana, because Sam had decided to be especially generous to Reading. It was there that I first related in public my experience at meeting a worried looking Sam, who had been welcomed on board by a 'Commandant Godot'. I had once later spent an evening with Jim and Girodias in Paris in Chez Vodka, the Russian night-club to which Girodias' old friends from La Grande Severine had moved, and as we brought Maurice with us we were made especially welcome and Jim had one of the best nights of his life, ending in the celebratory early morning, with half the clientele singing Russian songs, seeing a side of Paris that few academics ever did. Now, in Chicago, not knowing the dangerous reputation of the city to people walking around it alone at night, he went out on his first night to explore the night life and lived through it uneventfully enough to be told the next morning of all the terrible things that might have happened to him. There was a large meeting in a conference room of about thirty Beckett-minded scholars, mainly American, some British, a very disparate group of men: I do not remember any women. It was chaired by Calvin Israel, who I have heard claim an intimacy with Beckett that was highly unlikely as it included having dinner with him and Suzanne, the latter having made the meal. The meeting was partly called to hear a young man, who started by admitted his fury at never having met the master, or had the opportunity, as he assumed others had had, of being told things about his work by him (Beckett hated discussing his work, saying he was not a critic, and usually refused to answer any but the most obvious questions put to him). He wanted the approval of the others to his project, which was to computerise Beckett's work to find the preponderance of key words or some such. This would help his academic standing, he obviously thought, but amused glances were exchanged. 'You can have the happy part,' he pleased, 'let me do the unhappy side of it.' The naïve nakedness of motivation and ambition, so different from the careful discretion of the British reticence and that of the more senior Americans present has never struck me more forcefully than that evening. But I was certainly aware of the growing Beckett industry among university teachers. Hundreds of academics had by now latched onto Sam, were writing books about him, teaching him, building their reputations on him, and already they were splitting into factions, wildly jealous of each other, counting up the number of times they had seen him or that he had answered their letters: they all wanted to be seen to be more intimate with him than the others, and they exaggerated wildly. Poor Sam, having already to give much of his time to translating himself from French to English or vice-versa, and to work with his German translator, also found himself obliged to answer hundreds of letters and to constantly meet visitors to Paris, often people who simply wanted to be able to say that they knew him. He did this with courtesy and a military schedule, always punctual and allowing exactly as much time as he had planned, usually half an hour.

He was also unwittingly roped into impressing or at least meeting people in order to further the careers of others. Francis Warner, he of the long plays which had followed Beckett's short ones in Toronto, was always on the look-out for people with money to finance his proposed theatre under Saint Peter's College, which Buckminster Fuller had been persuaded to design and which was to be called the Samuel Beckett Theatre. Some of the potential backers were brought to Paris to meet Beckett, who had no interest at all in the project of having a theatre named after him, but would agree to meet Warner and the backers for a drink, to be polite and look appreciative. Warner never got very far: I never heard if any money was ever put up, and if so what happened to it, nor if Buckminster Fuller was ever paid for his design.

One American academic who came to Paris to meet Beckett was Stanley Gorlinski, probably in 1980. Beckett made an appointment to meet him and his wife Marsha in a café. Gorlinski was so nervous about meeting the great man that he hardly closed his eyes all night, and when Beckett arrived, promptly on time as usual, Gorlinski found he had lost his voice and was unable to get a word out. When Sam asked him if he would like a beer, saying he would have one himself, all the poor man could do was nod his head, and three beers were ordered. When they had drunk them, Gorlinski was still speechless. Beckett stood up and said, 'Well, I'm sorry you're not feeling well, Professor Gorlinski. Perhaps we'll talk more another time,' paid for the drinks and left.

Once back at his university, which was the State University in Columbus, Ohio, Gorlinski wrote Beckett to apologise and to say that he had no idea what had come over him. He went on to say that he was organising a Beckett conference at his university and asked if there might possibly be some small unpublished text that could be read at it. Sam then did something quite extraordinary: he sent Stanley Gorlinski a brand-new play entitled *Ohio Impromptu*. It was the only time he had ever given a place name to a play and the 'impromptu' had nothing to do with Ohio, nor was anything about it impromptu except probably the impulse to send it to Gorlinski for its world première. The conference went ahead and I was one of the large number of people who were invited to attend, taking advantage of the opportunity to call on all the local bookshops in Columbus. We were housed in a large hotel overlooking the campus of one of the largest universities in the United States. Many academics were there to give talks, but the centre of the whole event was the play, which was performed by David Warrilow and Rand Mitchell; Alan Schneider was there to direct it. In my three days in Columbus I took some good sales from the two university bookshops and some shops in the town, sat through the conference, gave a little lunchtime talk myself where, on an impulse and from memory, I gave a rendering of Vladimir's speech as dramatically and as well as I could in direct imitation of Nicol Williamson's delivery. It went down extremely well.

The première of *Ohio Impromptu*, given only one performance, was a special occasion and everyone felt privileged to be there: it belonged to what I call Sam's 'ghost period', where remembered loves and friends come back to haunt the memory. Suggested or imagined ghosts played a large part in Beckett's writings of the period, both in his stage plays and those he wrote for television and there is a ghost of a sort in *Ill Seen Ill Said*, which I was publishing. It was a way of symbolically extending the brief span of human life: memories that live on become ghosts of the persons remembered, one more in the chain of theatrical and literary conceits that Beckett had invented during the course of his career.

It was a fascinating play, soon to join the repertoire of short Beckett works that were filling Garfein's Clurman Theatre in New York. For Gorlinski to have been handed such a jewel was to put his name into theatrical history, and Sam, of course, knew that. What a recompense for an embarrassing incident! I reviewed the play for the Guardian in London, told the story about the Paris meeting, which I knew about from the accounts of the two protagonists, which differed hardly at all, except that twenty years later, Stanley told me that he had in the event been able to get out a few words.

A new charter airline had just started to operate that week and a large group of attendees to the conference had booked to be on the first ever flight of People's Express. It flew from Columbus to Newark, one of New York's airports, although it is in New Jersey. Critics and other theatrical notables had travelled to Columbus for the performance and on the 'plane back someone joked that the New York theatre would be immeasurably poorer if we crashed. I think that I first met Warrilow on that occasion, an English actor who had started Maboo Mines as an experimental New York theatre company, but having also worked in France in several capacities, was bilingual and also performed in French. He was less known in England, and later more in Paris, where he would be prominent in performing Beckett and Pinget for the next decade. I shared a taxi with the actors into New York. It was good to renew my friendship with Schneider, and I saw him fairly frequently in New York through the early eighties.

Jack Garfein, who had been to my 1963 Drama Conference, was now running two adjoining theatres off Broadway, where he had found a growing audience for Beckett's short late plays, all of which Alan Schneider negotiated with the author and directed for Garfein, who could never quite decide what he wanted to be, a producer of intellectual theatre or part of the commercial rat-race; he had obviously not been very successful in Hollywood. He was now divorced from Carroll Baker, who had written a biographical book that was far from complimentary about him. Garfein was very much on the make, but rather crudely so, and I met no-one who really liked him, but he was doing good theatre, thanks to Schneider, who often voiced his doubts to me privately, but persevered. Beckett was sympathetic, because he knew that Jack Garfein was an Auschwitz survivor, but when at one point Beckett refused some contract and Garfein threatened to sue him, he too broke off direct contact. Alan told me that on several occasions he had come close to breaking with Garfein and was always on the point of writing to Beckett to explain his feelings, but he never did, because, after all, there was no one else who would allow him to mount one series of Beckett plays after another as he was then doing. The runs of the plays became longer as the public wanting to see them grew. Garfein had little to do but take the profit. I went to the Clurman theatre frequently, had lunches and dinners with Garfein who obviously thought me a bigger fish than I was, always in fashionable restaurants and I sometimes brought Muriel Leyner with me. She was annoyed every time, because he was so self-absorbed that he never recognised her, however often he met her. He liked to meet intellectuals who could reassure him that he was doing the right thing, and there were occasional public discussions in the theatre when Tom Bishop, Martin Esslin, Ruby Cohn and others associated in some way with Beckett would take part, including myself. I came to know people involved in various projects, Everett Frost, for instance, who was re-recording some of the radio plays and another strange character called John Reilly, who was making a documentary about Beckett with money from the National Foundation for the Arts in Washington. Every year he requested and received more money but the documentary never seemed to make much progress. I was interviewed for it, but Reilly's questions were not very apt, and I had to evade them and talk on to say something that might interest the potential viewer. Barney was much in Reilly's pocket as he was now very broke and borrowing money where he could: Reilly was able to get valuable introductions through Barney to people who could help him.

Two other people I saw much of at this time were Dougald McMillan and Martha Fehsenfeld. They both lived in Chapel Hill, where Dougald was a rather eccentric Professor of Literature, having once been a star pupil of Richard Ellmann when the latter was teaching at Northwestern University in Chicago. As an academic he was very like Ellmann, infatuated with the world of James Joyce and of Beckett, his natural follower. Once, when I called on Maria Jolas in Paris she had given me a manuscript, a history of Transition, that she and her husband had edited. I read it and instantly gave the author, who was Dougald McMillan, a contract, and sold it fairly well. I saw Dougald, who I liked immensely, a genuinely enthusiastic scholar, quite frequently both in Paris and London. He loved the theatre and at one performance of Barrault's superbly imaginative production of *Christophe Colomb*, had gone back to see it repeatedly, saying it was the best performance he had ever attended in his life. Martha was a minor academic, who wanted to be an actress, and was like Dougald besotted with Beckett. I eventually commissioned the two of them to write an analysis of Beckett's plays for me, based on historical productions. While this was being written by Dougald, with Martha doing most of the research, I went frequently to Chapel Hill, both to sell books and see the joint authors. I discovered that Dougald Macmillan's eccentricities consisted chiefly in not allowing anything to divert him from any new enterprise that caught his imagination. He started a restaurant in an old railway wagon that could never have made him a penny and he started a local publishing company that never published anything in line with his real interests which were in literature. He published some mediocre books about local history, some right-wing diatribes by southern American crackpots, not because he was personally right-wing, but because he believed that the country was full of right-wing fanatics who would buy them and yield him a big profit. All he ever got back was a series of law suits for publishing books that he was paid to bring out incompetently. His gifts as a teacher were legendary in Chapel Hill and as an academic he knew how to research a subject or an author and write interestingly, but he frittered away his talents with silly schemes all of which lost him money. I discovered that he had inherited a large amount of forest land and that he was always having great swathes of it cut down to pay for his latest folly. He had a house on the shores of Lake Michigan where I paid him a visit one summer. Dougald was much overweight, a compulsive fast-food eater, and watching him being pulled through the air by a motorboat attached to a kite-like device was an unforgettably comic sight. I declined to do more than swim myself.

One afternoon I was working on the manuscript of *Beckett in the Theatre* with Dougald in his house in Chapel Hill when there was an electric storm that put all the lights out. We had just finished the chapter on *Krapp's Last*

Tape, about half-way through a very large manuscript. It was about six o'clock and I did not feel like continuing by candlelight. Also it was his co-author Martha's birthday and we were invited to her house for dinner. 'That's it, I declared, 'We'll make it two volumes and the first ends here.' We went to dinner at Martha's, where inevitably the conversation was all about Beckett. 'If you don't change the subject, I shall leave,' said Dougald's wife. 'I've had enough of Beckett and I'll scream if you don't stop.' She was right of course.

But the marriage was soon to break up and Dougald had all his written material, except what I had taken away with me on that last visit, removed and kept by his wife. The first volume was published in 1988. His wife had all the software and not only the second half of *Beckett in the Theatre*, but of another book I had commissioned from him, a biography of Hugh MacDiarmid. For the latter he had spent a year in Scotland doing research, sending his daughter to school in Edinburgh (which she liked so much that she returned there as an adult), and completing most of the book in that time. His co-author, who provided much of the material, was Michael Grieve, MacDiarmid's journalist son, who I also knew well. There were problems in publishing the book, because MacDiarmid had led a fairly wild life at one point, giving syphilis to many women, as Dougald discovered. He also unearthed much plagiarism: MacDiarmid did not know all the languages that he claimed to read, and made much use of existing translations. There were also other unsavoury facts that would have made trouble both where his widow, Valda, was concerned, and that his son would wish to suppress. For this reason I had been in no hurry to publish and the entire manuscript was in Dougald's computer. At time of writing I have still not been able to locate it.

Martha Fehsenfeld was engaged to do Beckett's *Happy Days* at La Mama in New York. I had had a long relationship with this theatre, run by and subsidised by a successful dress designer called Ellen Stewart, and she was 'La Mama', so named by the company. I had know them in the sixties in Britain, when I represented her company and sold them to Michael White to perform Paul Foster's play *Tom Paine*, at the Edinburgh Festival and the Gaity Theatre in London[39]. Now La Mama, just off the Bowery, was mainly rented out to others. I do not know who produced Fehsenfeld's *Happy Days*. I have seen the play with different actresses and Martha's was strange, not quite professional and with some odd line deliveries, which she claimed was the way Sam wanted them delivered, but I could not believe this: they sounded too odd. After the first night there was a pleasant gathering of

---

[39] I have not related this incident yet, which happened during the sixties. It was a big responsiblity for which I was never paid because it did not succeed financially (the theatre was too big to fill and the company a large one). I spent much time bailing the company, by British standards a largely amateur one, out of gaol on various small charges, from drug offences to creating a nuisance to others.

Beckett fans in Pheobe's, a bar and restaurant that catered to local artists and performers. Martin Esslin, who was present, was trying to separate himself from the different and rival Beckett factions who were more vociferous and antagonistic to each other in the U.S. than in Britain. Martin was now teaching at American universities, mainly at Berkeley, just south of San Francisco, where I occasionally was invited to speak to his theatrical seminar when in California. He often when I met him in New York or elsewhere had one of his students with him: on this occasion it was an Australian girl who asked me to look her up when next in Sydney which was, I think, later that year. Martin remained rather aloof from the quibbling rivalries of Beckett academics and maintained a balance. The only subject on which we disagreed was politics: he had swallowed the whole American ideology of success and money, was comfortable in a world where his status meant receiving free computers and other perks from educational suppliers, and listening to ignorant diatribes from colleagues against the evils of socialism and welfare governments, while in no way compromising the intellectual history he taught, which meant explaining the theories of Marx and Freud, Lenin and Lucac, as well as the great writers of the last two centuries. He was an advisor to the Magic Theatre in San Francisco, whose Director often came to his seminars to learn, and to other theatres in the Bay area as well. I would meet him frequently at the ABA conferences held in different cities and on my travels around America.

Jack Garfein also treated him as a guru and to check up on the information he received from others including Schneider and myself. I came to know all the actors associated with the Clurman Theatre, such as Alvin Epstein, who played several Beckett parts and who performed an evening with a German actress-singer, which was much like the Brecht-Weill show that Bettina had been performing ever since *Happy End*. I suggested to Garfein an evening of *Molloy*, broken up between two actors, and prepared a script which I gave to him. He then showed it to Epstein, and I never saw it again; the matter was just dropped without any decision being made. Warrilow was much around the theatre, playing some Beckett parts. He was, like many actors, an alcoholic who could control his drinking when he was acting, but when I first knew him, I had no inkling of his weakness. When, on one occasion, Garfein gave a late night party in his penthouse apartment, all alcohol had to be out of sight before Warrilow arrived after his performance, a totally misconceived gesture given his self-control. Once in Paris I went with Tom Bishop to see him perform in *The Marat/Sade*, where he played Marat. Afterwards we all went to the Café Lipp, where, questioned by Sheila Colvin as to how he had mastered French well enough to perform in the language, he simply replied, 'I just worked very hard.' He drank a glass or two of wine on that occasion, but never took too much, and in the next few years when I often saw him on stage, sometimes in parts that involved great feats of memory, he was always in perfect control. In all the time I knew him, nothing was allowed to get in the way of his determination to be 'the best'.

The changes in the New York office had been far too frequent after the departure of Anne Tautee and later Gary Pulsifer, and finally I had an idea which turned out well. I had known Claudia Menza for many years. She had worked for fourteen of them for Barney Rosset at Grove Press, and that alone was a unique qualification. I have said much about Barney's eccentricities, but not about his vagaries as an employer. He changed his mind from day to day, forgot what he had said previously, or what instructions he had given even hours earlier, and nothing was ever his fault. His employees had to change direction whichever way the wind blew, and he would shout at them in a fury if they gave him any argument. Barney really did no work himself: he would sit in a chair with the television-set on, reading a pornographic magazine and drinking either wine, beer or rum and coke; this would start when he got to the office, which was usually in the same building and sometimes in the next room, by which time he had already had a beer or two to start the day. For Claudia to have survived fourteen years of being shouted at and always in the wrong, even when carrying out Barney's exact instructions, was a real feat. Claudia had left Grove to start her own literary agency, which she ran from home. At some chance meeting I asked her if she would be willing to run my office and her agency from there at the same time. I would pay her for two-thirds of her time, give her free rent and use of telephone for her agency, which was not doing well just then, and which would then take up the other third of her time. She agreed to the arrangement and it worked well for a number of years. She was efficient and gave me the necessary backing, leaving me free to go out and sell. I did all the selling now, all the publicity, editorial work and accounts, with Claudia backing me up, also doing some of it and keeping a record of all the banking.

I went to an ABA conference in a Southern town, I think in Texas, but it may have been Atlanta, where I ran into John Pizey, Grove Press's one time sales manager. I had various memories of Pizey: he was English, had worked for the British Book Centre, which Peter Baker had started, but after Peter's bankruptcy it was taken over by Robert Maxwell. He then became a nation-wide salesman for Penguin Books, was successful in the job, and poached by Barney Rosset. Pizey knew what Barney liked, which among other things was spending money, and he treated himself to the best hotels and restaurants on expense account. My previous meeting with him had been at the Pump Room of the best hotel in Chicago, perhaps the most expensive restaurant in town, where he had treated me to a sumptuous meal. Now he was out of a job and looking for a new opportunity. He was living in New Hampshire, had married a second time, and had two families, three teenagers by the first marriage, and a toddler by his new wife. He attached himself to me at the ABA conference and came to see me again in New York.

I remember that our British accents had greatly impressed the southern ladies sitting with us at table at the final ABA dinner. 'Just like Masterpiece Theatre,' they chorused.

I had sold a few books, especially opera guides, to MacMillan's Music Book Club, and was dismayed to hear that it was to be discontinued along with two of their other book clubs. This interested Pizey who suggested that we might buy the three, the other two being a History Book Club and a 'Birding' one, that is a book club devoted to bird lovers. We looked into it and decided to make an offer if we could raise the money. Riverrun Press was banking with the European American Bank and I had become friendly with one of the officers, Ian Aitken, a Scot like me. We also spoke to Jack Berger who was interested in investing, but as the bank was willing to give us all we needed we decided to proceed without him. John Pizey then found a warehouse near his home, in Dover, New Hampshire, where we could hold the stocks of the bookclubs and where, with considerable relief, I also moved my own stock of books from the Mercedes warehouse that had become increasingly expensive and unco-operative now that Charles Johnson had left.

At first everything went well, but John Pizey was in charge, and increasingly I found that his last priority was getting my books out; his only interest was in the book clubs and he revelled in his new self-importance as the boss. Whenever I showed up, nobody knew who I was. Every book I had on music went into the club, but getting paid for them was another matter. I negotiated a good deal with the Metropolitan Opera Guild, whereby membership in the Music Book Club was advertised in their big annual gift brochure in exchange for books supplied to them and some services, and I contributed several ideas, but John seemed to me to be not working very hard and taking too much money out of the enterprise in his salary and expenses; he might still have been working for Rosset. Expenses rose faster than sales and the word began to go round the staff that 'we were not going to make it.'

Little by little things began to go wrong. Once we had reached the point of no return, I was getting no service for my own books and Pizey's main energy was going into arranging that when collapse came, the banks would turn to me and not to him. All his property, his house and bit of land, was put into his wife's name so that it could not be seized. To make matters worse his wife developed a crush on me. I did everything possible to discourage it, but Pizey quickly realised the situation – she had probably told him – and I witnessed the marriage breaking up, which made my relationship with Pizey even more precarious, and in no way did it make things easier for me where the EAB bank was concerned. I had to reach an accommodation with them for long-term payment, while realising that they were unlikely to get anywhere with Pizey, who could simply declare bankruptcy, so they left him alone. As far as I was concerned bankruptcy was not an option I was willing to contemplate.

Jimmy Ball, bringing Yvonne with him, came to New York to help the negotiation with the EAB, a bank that had suddenly turned nasty on me. I had a New York Civil Rights lawyer called Len Wineglass who had started the negotiation, but Jimmy was a chess player and he put up a façade that impressed the other lawyers. He took quick offence in a way that made the other side apologise, which instantly put them at a disadvantage. Once having cooked a deal, Jimmy got Len to telephone to say it was all off, which eventually led to more negotiation and a better deal, which earned me a long delay in payment. As I had a Canadian expectation when my mother's generation were to be all gone, that became the long-term security. As part of the tying-up Jimmy and I had to go to Montreal for a day; this greatly worried Yvonne, who was sure he would get into some mischief with me out of her sight. I had not realised before that Jimmy lost few opportunities to make a pass at any attentive female and Yvonne was well aware of it.

I moved my books away from Dover to Merrimac, a distributor in Massachusetts that was selling the books of Marion Boyars, but mine went there only as a temporary measure. I went to see Michael Bessie, a prestigious figure in New York publishing, who had sold Athenaeum Press, which he had founded in the fifties, to Harper and Row, and was at the time, together with his wife, publishing a specialised literary list under their umbrella. Mike was unable to persuade his company to take me on, but he sent me to Eric Kampmann, a former salesman of their's, who had set up a distribution company to sell for a number of different smaller publishers. Then our series of warehouse disasters began to fall into a pattern.

Kampmann was no good at selling my kind of book and I had to continue my own selling trips. He himself was personable, very proud of his wife, an attractive fashion model, who on one occasion entertained his publisher clients in his New York apartment, looking very self-conscious as if she were on a cat-walk, but Kampmann himself was always full of overconfident hype. Like most salesmen he did not know how to run an office, much less a warehouse, and he thought in terms of best-sellers and major book accounts, the B. Daltons and Barnes and Nobles, who were big but had not yet reached the near total dominance of the American book trade that was to come. He was simply not interested in the literary and independent bookshops who were my major customers, and as I had to sell to them myself, I increasingly asked myself what I was doing with him. In the meantime Merrimac collapsed and Marion Boyars also joined Kampmann. He had a New York office on Fortieth Street, but was constantly changing warehouses, and I could smell failure in the air; the whole set-up was just too much like South-Western. With Kampmann's office processing all the orders we no longer needed Arlene, but I persuaded Kampmann to take her on.

Unfortunately about the time she left us she became addicted to crack. She retained her key to our office, came in on weekends, took cheques out of the chequebook, made out cash cheques, forging my signature on them. The bank had been accustomed to seeing her come in for years, so she had no difficulty until Claudia and I realised that there was always less money than we thought in the account (we had now moved to Citibank). When we examined the cheques we quickly realised what had happened. Claudia and I went to Kampmann's office with the forged cheques and confronted Arlene, who broke down immediately. She was of course sacked. Her mother promised to repay in instalments and did so for a short while, but the payments soon stopped. Arlene apparently went to Florida and took a cure.

Bill Colleran had a son, Marcus, whose mother was Dutch, Bill's first wife. He was interested in working in the U.S., so I imported him to go around the whole country and sell my books. Marcus was very tall, very good-looking and personable, and I was sure that he would be an impressive salesman for me. For two weeks we stayed in New York and he occupied Muriel Leyner's couch. It was originally intended for him to stay with an old girl-friend of Bill's, but she asked a large rent which I could not afford. After taking him around New York bookshops we set off together for Des Moines. It was a Sunday and we had lunch in New York before flying. Unfortunately Marcus opened the car window and never closed it, so everything he had in the car was stolen, as was a large manuscript I was editing. This was the collected writings of René Magritte, translated from French by Jo Levy, and I had spent many months editing the translation of about fifteen hundred pages. It was never found by the police. It would have taken me well over a year, given the pressures on my time just then, to go over all that work again, but the French publishers soon withdrew rights altogether because of the delay, which was then already two years overdue. It would have been a steady backlist seller and I still remember my despair at the loss occasioned by the open window. I was to have other such losses in the future.

With some replacement clothes, but without the Walkman and tapes that Marcus had brought to lighten his travels, we sold our way from Des Moines, through Iowa City and other towns on our way to Chicago. In New York I had asked Marcus to produce his driving licence when we were hiring a car, but he said he did not have it on him. In Des Moines he admitted that he did not have one and had driven for years in the Netherlands without one. As there was no way he could rent a car without a driving licence he took a test in Des Moines, but failed the theory. In Chicago the bureaucratic regulations for a non-resident made it impossible for him to get one, so I had to send him back to New York and then Amsterdam, telling him not to come back until he had a valid driving licence, while I finished the trip on my own.

After that Marcus Colleran got on quite well, becoming friendly with Stuart Abraham in Chicago, where he eventually made his base, travelling from there all over the country. It was expensive to have a full-time salesman selling only my own list, but by now we had left Kampmann and there were only the two of us to cover the entire United States, while I, of course, also had to spend time in both offices, travel round British towns and keep all my European contacts going as well. Then Marcus fell in love with an American girl called Jackie and they married. She too was selling books, but she did not want Marcus with his astonishing good looks to be constantly meeting new people: and to take him out of the path of temptation she made him give up his job and stay in her home town, Atlanta, where he found a job at the Oxford Book Company, the biggest bookshop there. On my various travels I met him occasionally in Atlanta.

There was, while he was there, a little Beckett Festival in Atlanta, where several of the plays were performed, and I went to it, took part as lecturer and panellist, meeting a man, who I was to come across frequently at Beckett Conferences who had memorised the longest work in the Oxford English Dictionary and could trot it out on any occasion. It is 'floccipaucinihilipilification' (the action of estimating something as worthless). I also met a lady from Washington there quite by accident, and in our few minutes conversation took her telephone number. When next in D.C. I looked her up and she became a friend, but the relationship remained platonic. She was an attractive and obviously comfortably-off divorcee with a house in Washington's elegant Georgetown. One evening a street beggar asked us for money and having no change I passed on. But returning from a restaurant on the river we brought some left-over food back to him. He flung it at us with an obscenity and thereafter I avoided such gestures. Begging was everywhere in America and was just then also becoming rife, under Margaret Thatcher's withdrawal of welfare, in Britain. In the New York subway clever beggars asked for food which led to people giving them money, which they would otherwise not have done, thinking the money was going on drugs. Once they had the money, the beggars made no bones of their ploy, even boasting of it, which surely I would have thought would stop the impulse to give next time.

Once in London, going home to Green's Court on my own, I was stopped by a man covered in blood. He told me he had been mugged and robbed, that he had asked the police to give him overnight shelter and they had refused. He was not so badly hurt that a hospital would take him in. On an impulse I took him back, let him sleep on my sofa and lent him enough money to take a train to Newcastle. Later I found that he had helped himself to a number of silver objects in the house which I had kept from Ledlanet. Other occasions when I have tried to help someone after falling for a hard-luck story have been similar and now I am more careful.

Many amusing incidents occurred during my many odysseys around the U.S. I would encounter many attitudes, the worst often from feminist bookshops. There was one in Los Angeles, which I visited at least once a year, which would take nothing by a man, but ordered most books by female authors. I had a very sensitive novel by Harry Mulisch, *Two Women*, about a female relationship, which was always turned down because 'No man can understand women well enough to write about them.' Tired of hearing this, I chanced my luck one day and told them, in utmost secrecy that Harry was really Harriet. It was very difficult for a woman to get published in Holland, so she had to take a man's name, I told them, which could not have been further from the truth, but it was believed and the book was ordered. Within a week of arrival they had ordered more copies and in the end the shop sold hundreds. The 'secret' which they had solemnly promised to keep was of course all over Los Angeles and I hope they never discovered the truth.

My relations with Harry became strained. I was asked to go to Amsterdam to sign a contract for his new novel *The Attack*, spent a pleasant day there with him and the Dutch Literary Agency, whose director was a good friend, and ate a Rijstafel with Harry, who had just had his stomach removed and was growing a new one; he could only eat a very little several times a day. An American publisher, Pantheon, run by André Schiffren, was also interested, but not committed. Schiffren was a man with whom I had several quarrels, because, running a subsidiary of Random House, he had the benefit of their unlimited cheque book to make the highest offer for a book, but did not have to take the personal responsibility for its success. His speciality was to go after authors who smaller publishers had established, which meant he was buying an established reputation, not making his own discoveries. Harry did not want to lose the chance of having a big American publisher, but I told him that these days, with a shrinking British market and copyright restrictions being largely ignored by the Americans, I had to have the world English market or nothing. Harry finally agreed and the contract was meant to follow. It never did and eventually he signed with Schiffren so I backed out. He had asked me why the book could not appear under a joint imprint in both countries. I told him that publishers did not work that way. I had published *Two Women* and three of Harry's novellas in my *New Writing and Writers* series, wonderful stories, which I had intended to put together later in a single volume, but I never did after that. *The Attack*, a wartime novel, was badly translated by Pantheon: The Social Democrats became the S.S. in their version. I should mention that in the fifties I had known the founder of Pantheon, Kurt Wolff, one of the original German expressionist publishers and a contemporary of the original Rowohlt, Heinrich Ledig-Rowohlt's father. Wolff was a gentle man, who had encouraged me as a young publisher on my early visits to New York, where as a refugee from the Nazis he was much frustrated by American unwillingness to publish quality authors just for their own sake. His article in a book I published in English, translated from German, Paul Raabe's anthology of *The Era of German Expressionism*, is a little masterpiece. Entitled *How Do Publishers and Authors Meet*, it is a practical guide to what a publisher has to do to get started, told with insight and much humour. He was a man I always wished I could have known better. He had a horrible death in Frankfurt, squeezed by a train against the railing of a bridge he was crossing.

At the Frankfurt Book Fair, talking to Russian publishers, I heard about an author who was then having a great success in their country. He had written a John Le Carré-type spy novel called *Tass Is Authorised to Announce...*, where the hero is a KGB man in constant conflict with the CIA. It had been made into a television series that was so successful that on the nights it went out the streets of Moscow and Leningrad, and no doubt other towns as well, were empty as people were glued to their television sets. I made enquiries, traced the author, contracted English-language rights to the novel through the official Soviet literary agency, and found a young man, an Englishman who had lived in Moscow called Charles Buxton to translate it for me. The author was Julian Semyonov and I invited him to come to London and New York to help promote the English translation which appeared in late 1987, first in England and a month later in the States.

Julian arrived in London and I put him up at the Imperial Hotel in Russell Square where in earlier years I would go to sweat in their Turkish steam and sauna baths, a magnificent series of tiled caverns, now gone. There was a signing party in Collet's bookshop on Charing Cross Road that was well attended and where Julian constantly referred to me as his 'owner'. I gave a press conference at the Caledonian Club, followed immediately by a lunch. At the first event, Semyonov, Charles Buxton and I fielded many questions about the cold war, which was ending, the situation of spy fiction and the current politics of the Soviet Union. This was the period of *Glasnost* and Gorbachev was carrying out major liberal reforms without trying to break up the Soviet system, but encountering much opposition from old-line Communist officials and party members, who were afraid of losing their privileges. Semyonov was a good friend of Gorbachev and had appeared on platforms with him. Once when Gorbachev was talking of economic co-operation with the west and Semyonov had asked 'What about cultural co-operation,' the Soviet premier had told him publicly that that was his job. Certainly Julian Semyonov was the most popular and biggest-selling author in the Soviet Union at the time he came to me.

Andropov, Gorbachov's predecessor, only a short time in office before he died of cancer, was the man behind *Tass Is Authorised*. He had telephoned Julian one day and asked him to come to his office. At the time he was head of the KGB, not yet of the government, and the author had gone with considerable nervousness to the meeting, wondering what he had done wrong. He was at the time a successful crime writer who had been on many journalistic assignments for the official news agency Tass. These had included polar expeditions, journeys to Cuba and South America and interviews with Che Guevara and he had also covered the Vietnam War from the Vietcong side, having walked the whole Ho Chi Minh trail. He was told by Andropov that what was needed was a Russian fictional hero, an equivalent of James Bond or Le Carré's George Smillie, to interest the Russian reading public which was becoming familiar with western political thrillers, which always depicted MI5 and MI6, and CIA operatives, in a favourable light and the KGB as villains. Could he write such pro-Soviet political equivalents? He was willing to give Semyonov access to KGB files to help him.

Julian said 'Yes,' he would do it, but he did not want to know anything too secret in case something that might get him into trouble leaked out. The result was *Tass Is Authorised*. It had become a monumental success and the TV serial of it, which is meant to take place in an African republic where a popular socialist regime is being undermined by the CIA, which is organising a coup, was filmed in Cuba. Semyonov's face was recognisable at home from many television appearances and his name was a household one. Politically he was loyal to his country, but like Gorbachov he was a liberal and a reformer. I was to spend the next month with him and we became good friends.

The lunch at the Caledonian Club was a great success. At the last minute I invited the Observer reporter who had been at the press conference to stay on and he gave us a main article on the back page of the Arts section. The twenty people present included Orlov, a cultural attaché from the Russian Embassy, Bill Webb from the Guardian, at that time especially interested in the politics of Eastern Europe, various literary editors, political leader-writers and potential reviewers. There was much discussion of the Gorbachov reforms and speculations as to which of Stalin's victims might have their reputations rehabilitated under the current thaw. In particular there was discussion about Nikolai Bukharin. Julian had a personal interest here. His father had been Bukharin's secretary, and this had made him suspect, even as a child, so much so that the only university course that he had been allowed to take was at the School of Oriental Studies. As a result he had a working knowledge of Japanese, Chinese and Vietnamese. He also spoke Spanish, German and French, and his English was extremely fluent.

Personal appearances on radio and television took us to Glasgow, where he was on BBC radio and there were press interviews in many London newspapers. We visited a number of bookshops, where he signed copies. The North American tour included a visit to Canada, and for this he needed a separate visa, but my friend at the Canadian High Commission, Diana Jervis-Read, then cultural attaché at Ontario House, helped to speed this up. The consular official did in a day what would normally take a week, and gratefully accepted a signed copy of the book. Jane Bown, asked to photograph Julian for the Observer article, met us at the Canadian passport and visa office and took him into Grosvenor Square. She eyed him carefully: he nearly always wore a form of combat fatigues when travelling. 'Outdoor man,' she commented.

'I like her,' he said to me afterward. 'Did you see her eyes? She's an artist.'

Then we set off for America together. I lent Julian my copy of *Darkness at Noon*, which he read on the way over. We were not sitting together because he was a chain-smoker. Su Herbert came over with us to help man the New York office during our American tour. Claudia and I had spent a considerable time on the telephone in the previous months getting Julian press, radio and television interviews. Kampmann had a man whose job was to sell by telephone and organise such promotions, but he did nothing at all. Claudia delighted in ringing to tell him each time she completed another engagement. By the time we arrived she had set up interviews with newspaper journalists, and TV and radio stations all over the US, enough to keep us busy every moment for the next fortnight and a half.

We arrived at Newark and went in Muriel's car and a taxi into Manhattan, losing the taxi at one point, where I had a sudden fear that the CIA might have kidnapped Julian, but we found him eventually and installed him in the Chelsea Hotel. Then we all had dinner in a group that included Claudia Menza and Barney Rosset, because Rosset had agreed to let us hold a party in his large loft the following night. We were in El Quixote, a favourite restaurant of mine, just underneath the Chelsea Hotel. Then Su went off to stay with Claudia in her Greenwich Village apartment and I to stay with Muriel. The next morning Julian was interviewed in our office by the New York Times for the first of two long articles that appeared, one later that week and another the week after. Su took over one of the office desks and she and Claudia did the office work while monitoring the tour and feeding out additional information to the press.

The party at Barney's loft was a big success with many important American authors, critics and journalists present, in addition to some booksellers and many friends. Sue Marvin, as she now was, came with John, her husband who commented, 'Not one token black, but five.' One of them, Jerry Williams, now with Time magazine had once edited Maurice Girodias' short-lived Olympia Review in Paris. Barney at the time had a Korean girlfriend called Kim, who worked as a chemist: she was very beautiful, but very perverse. I had seen her scandalise restaurants more than once with her antics, such as pulling other women's breasts out of their decolletées to fondle and admire them. Now she set out to seduce Julian, who rather naïvely went into a large cupboard with her. As soon as he had lowered his trousers she left him there and returned to the party. 'But she promised me,' he complained as I went to rescue him.

During his week in Britain, Julian Semyonov had refused all alcoholic drinks, but at Barney's he started to drink wine. When we left he was quite drunk, but had no intention of going to bed. We had the greatest difficulty in getting him into his hotel room because he wanted to go out on the town and drink more. This was when I realised that he was an arrested alcoholic.

He was back to normal the next day fortunately, because he had several more interviews just booked; the New York Times article in particular greatly increased the interest. Orders now began to flow in from bookshops: Kampmann had not done a good job of selling him, but now his book was being asked for. The first reviews were all good, as had been the pre-publication notices that had appeared in book trade and library journals. Comparisons were made with British and American spy writers, usually to Semyonov's advantage.

Now several mass-market paperback companies who had read the reviews got into touch and I was able to get them bargaining against each other. I said that I wanted an advance of $100,000 and would accept the first offer for that amount, but no less. From New York we went to Boston, where Julian made a television appearance and had a long interview over lunch with the Christian Science Monitor, an influential paper, as well as a shorter one with the Boston Globe. The reporter from the first was convinced that Julian was a KGB operative and said so in his piece, a long one which started on the front page and spilled over two internal ones. When Julian read that he was accused of being a KGB Colonel he laughed. 'If I were in the KGB I would be at least a General,' he exploded. From Boston I put him on a 'plane to Toronto.

I had arranged for Howard Aster, who had invited me to join his group on the China trip, to get him some Canadian interviews, and had sent him a small part of the edition to sell in Canada. Julian made a television interview and was featured in the local press, meeting the Russian parents of Howard and his wife, who ran an antique shop, so part of the time he was talking his own language. I was to pick him up again in Chicago, where I went around the bookshops for two days, receiving the night before he arrived an offer from Avon Books, agreeing to my $100,000 advance, so the promotion had been worth-while. Half was to come immediately on signature of the agreement, the balance on paperback publication. It could not have arrived at a better moment. Kampmann was not selling our list very well and we badly needed a cash injection.

I met Julian off his 'plane. He was interviewed by the Chicago Herald Tribune, who printed a big piece on him. and he appeared on television. Then we went on to the west coast, first to San Francisco. Would I pay for a haircut and beard-trim? Of course I would. Then the press interviews started, but the most interesting broadcast was on a left-wing independent radio station, Radio Pacifica, funded by supporters, that was run on a shoe-string (but nevertheless had a network of channels in several American cities). My friend Victor Herbert, who I knew from Paris days (Beckett's *Endgame*) and who on one of my earlier California sales trips had bailed me out when my principal British credit card was cut up by a bank in Los Angeles because I had apparently just exceeded the limit (American banks do this with pleasure because apparently they get $50 each time they do it), had volunteered on his own initiative to give a party for Julian in the hills above Berkeley, where he now lived with his girlfriend Susan Goldstein, who taught women's studies at the university. Muriel had flown in the day before and we drove up to his house, bringing Paul from City Lights Bookshop with us, purely as a friend because political thrillers was not what the shop sold. There was a surprise: a prominent member of the Hollywood Crime Writers' Guild, a friend of Julian, who himself ranked as a kind of honorary member, had came up from Los Angeles for the party. There were warm embraces and we were to see him again in a few days.

From San Francisco we flew to L.A., but as Jeannie Adams had arranged the tour to take advantage of the best travel deals on offer, our flight was not a direct one and involved a stop-over in Las Vegas, where for an hour, late at night, we watched other passengers feeding the one-armed bandits, gambling slot-machines placed all around the waiting room, until we could fly on. When we arrived our luggage was still in Las Vegas and would not arrive until later. We booked into an airport hotel, Julian grumbling that he had to take medicines that were in his bag, and I promised to collect it in the early hours. I slept for three hours and returned to the terminal, where the floors were being swabbed down. I slipped and fell backward. At first I thought I might have fractured my skull, but was able to get up, collect the bags and return to the hotel, where I woke Julian who had an early television appearance on the Sonia Friedman show. My head was hurting and so was my wrist. Julian had become accustomed to starting every day with a bacon sandwich and demanded one, but I told him that such was Los Angeles traffic in the morning, he would have to wait until we were through it and near to the studio in down-town L.A. By now I could not bend my wrist and had trouble in driving, but managed it somehow. Julian got his bacon sandwich and then noticed there was something wrong with me: both my head and wrist were throbbing. I tried to hide the pain and we arrived at the studio, with me sitting in the waiting-room while he was interviewed. It went badly because Sonia Friedman had been driven by a Russian taxi-driver that morning, who had told her not to trust anyone from Russia who was acceptable there, and who was in the US on any kind of a mission. She had given him a very hard time. But now he was concerned with me and insisted on driving us back to the hotel, where he went to get more sleep while I went to the airport clinic. This was very interesting. While waiting to be seen I observed the airline staff who were there, obviously with many symptoms of tiredness, stress and ailments stemming from their jobs. There were more pilots, stewards and stewardesses than members of the public. It made me think seriously about the hazards of air travel. My wrist was X-rayed and they told me it was broken. They could bind it up, but I should have it properly seen to as soon as possible, otherwise it would probably set badly and need to be broken again so that it could set properly.

We had dinner that night in Hollywood with Julian's crime-writer friend, who was working on a film. Julian now doing all the driving. He had a good interview with the Los Angeles Times Herald that afternoon, and the next morning we flew on to Washington D.C. There Muriel rejoined us from New York. By now I was having great trouble in dressing, shaving, doing even the simplest everyday things because I am right-handed and it was my right wrist that was broken. But the schedule was tight and every day Julian had many engagements, so there was no stopping. In Washington he made a recording for the PBS main evening news programme, called I think, *All Things Considered*; it went out nationally and in the afternoon. Then he was meant to talk to the Voice of America. This involved us finding an address in the suburbs, where a Russian lady let us in, not being very pleased to see me with Julian, who she had thought was coming alone. There was no evidence of any broadcasting equipment in her house, but she certainly wanted to talk to Julian, but alone. When she went out of the room to get a drink, I think some tea for us, Julian whispered, 'Don't leave me alone with her,' and I didn't, although she suggested several times that I might be less bored reading the newspaper in the next room as they were talking in Russian. At one point she produced a microphone, but soon gave up the pretence. She had a copy of the book, did not like the translation which, she said, was 'not American'. 'Why should it be?' I replied. 'It's in good English.' I suggested at length that we had to be going. We were expected at the Russian Embassy that was giving a reception that night for Julian. 'Oh,' she said, 'They didn't invite me.'

Once we had made our escape, Julian smiled. 'She must be at least a Colonel,' he said. If her mission was to get Julian to defect, she had failed, and as she had never been alone with him, she could not spin a story to her controller about Julian that might get him into trouble.

We picked up Muriel and went to the Russian Embassy. This was a period when relations between Moscow and Washington were at a low ebb. The Americans had built a new embassy in Moscow only to find that the KGB had installed bugging equipment all over it. In retaliation they had refused to allow the Russians to move into their new Washington Embassy. They were still in the old one, a mansion that had previously belonged to the Pullman family who built and owned the overnight sleeper carriages for American railroads. We were admitted to what on the outside seemed a gloomy building, passed armed and uniformed Russian soldiers in the entrance hall, and were ushered into a cheerful large room with vodka, caviar, canapés and wine on offer. The ambassador and his wife were very welcoming, made much of my author who enjoyed the occasion much more than the Voice of America lady's attempt to corrupt him, and we later learned that while the reception was going on the Russian Foreign Minister Edouard Shevhardnadzne had arrived at Dulles airport to be met by the First Secretary, not the ambassador. Julian was honoured indeed.

The next stop was Miami, where we arrived in hot, sticky heat. 'Singapoor,' said Julian, fanning himself as we emerged from the 'plane. We had a meeting with some of the press at our motel, but Julian, after talking on the telephone in Spanish to the radio station where we were expected that evening, suddenly became very nervous and did not want to go. I realised a little later that he was afraid of being assassinated by the Miami Cubans, who probably knew his name well as *Tass* had been filmed in the country under the Castro regime. He seemed very relieved when we left Miami for Philadelphia the next morning.

Our main arrangement there was for Julian to appear at a phone-in radio station. Our interviewer (I say 'our' because on this occasion I also sat in the studio and took part) was a black man who told us that the station's signal could be heard as far away as Chicago, perhaps a thousand miles distant.

He and Julian got on well, although Julian was dismayed when told that the programme would be on the air for over two hours. But once he got going he lost count of time and it was nearly three hours when we wound down at two in the morning, and he could easily have gone on much longer. One listener asked Julian his views on race and colour prejudice. He said that his daughter's boyfriend was an African, he liked him and had no objection to the relationship. He gave much credit to his country for the recent reforms, praised Gorbachov and condemned American racism. He ended up by invited his interviewer to visit him in Moscow. This had, however, been an invitation that he had extended to many others who had interviewed him. In Britain one of his engagements had been at a school, a visit organised by Laurence Staig, then still Literature Officer of Eastern Arts, and on that occasion he had invited the whole school, saying that he would organise a Russian one to pay a return visit.

Back in New York we were contacted by a young Russian who was working on Wall Street for a New York financial house, who obviously saw him as a way to open doors into the new Russia. He wanted Julian to lengthen his visit and arranged a lecture for him at Yale, but this was after my own departure. He did stay longer, but the lecture went somehow wrong, and the man became a general nuisance because he had no real power to organise anything in particular, did everything badly, and it was obvious that his employers, whom he was trying to impress, did not trust him very far. Muriel Leyner gave a dinner party in Hoboken and invited him to it, but he was not a success. He wanted to know who was Jewish (about half of those present), asked everyone personal questions in a tactless way, and I might have thought him a CIA operative had he been brighter. He had no interest in Semyonov as a writer. Several other Russians got in touch in New York, some knowing him slightly, but they all wanted favours. I realised that the city had a large number of Russian immigrants who were not doing well, some of them in touch with and trying to make money from the Russian black market, always trying to pull off shady deals.

Some months later Muriel and I went to Moscow to visit Julian. He was in Yalta, but made arrangements for us to get there from Moscow. We went there by train, which under pressure from Julian in Yalta, was reluctantly booked by Intourist; they resented the pressure on their bureaucratic slowness of procedure from a well-known personality. The train took more than a day and a half to reach its destination and all I had brought with me were liqueur chocolates and a bottle of whisky. One had to jump over a dangerous gap between wagons to get to the restaurant car: there was little there to eat and nothing I liked. I asked for bread and cheese, but that was reserved for breakfast, not a time I felt like eating cheese. An old woman constantly came by the compartment with tea, but nothing else. There was neither wine nor vodka available, perhaps because Gorbachov was putting severe restrictions on alcoholic drinks and drinking hours. In Moscow people were going to lunch at three o'clock to evade the alcoholic ban which he had imposed on lunchtimes, which lasted until that hour.

At some stations there were peasants selling fruit, but I did not dare get off the train in case it moved off. The countryside was obviously not prospering and we had occasional views of the roads that had to carry goods between towns: they were broken, narrow, often just a mud-track, and I had no difficulty in understanding why there were shortages in a country that could produce so much; the inefficient superstructure and the deadening bureaucracy could not distribute in any way efficiently. Food arrived in the warehouses of Moscow, already stale, and mouldered away after sitting there for weeks. I was no admirer of capitalism, which works through fear, coercion and greed, but at least with more motivation there was less waste of the essentials of life.

In Yalta Julian put us up in the best hotel which was quite comfortable, but with no visible service and crawling with cockroaches. Nobody cared. I went to see Julian on my own in his little house. A large Alsatian dog obviously wanted to kill me. Julian held him back, swearing at him, and let me in. He was in a bad mood. He had brought a word-processor back from America, bought with the paperback advance, and he had just pressed the wrong buttons and wiped out a weekend's work. The dog sensed the anger and eyed me as the cause of it.

I then got down to work with Julian. I had brought with me the translation of the second novel we were to publish, *Seventeen Moments of Spring*. 'Go by the French edition,' he said. 'That translation is perfect.'

I had it with me, far from perfect, but it was not mistakes in translation that worried me, but the logistics of the plot, which involved cars racing around Berlin during an air-raid in the last month of the war in 1945. Some of the simultaneous events he described were just not possible, given the geography and the clock-timing. When I pointed this out in specific detail he became angry and growled. So did the dog, jumping to its feet and looking at me with bared teeth. 'Please, Julian. Put the dog in another room until we've finished,' I pleaded nervously, and then we began to rewrite what was necessary.

The two days in Yalta included a visit to Chekhov's house, which was closed, but Julian arranged for us to be shown around by the caretaker, and we also went to the historic spot where the wartime meeting of Churchill, Roosevelt and Stalin had taken place and where in 1944 the future of Europe was decided. Then we were on an overcrowded Aeroflot 'plane back to Moscow with overbooked passengers standing in the aisles, everyone bringing flowers back with them, and of course there were no seat belts. I went to the TV station, which at that moment was getting ready for the arrival of the Reagans coming in from Washington. The lobby was full of the familiar faces of BBC presenters sitting around the hallways, Peter Snow on the staircase, waiting to see the officials who could give them facilities. The purpose of my visit was to get the western rights to Semyonov's television series to sell and to arrange for the cassettes to be sent to me. There were also visits to the opera and to a concert of new music. I saw Rimsky-Korsakow's *The Czar's Bride* for the first time. I had by now learned to go to the box-office and pay in roubles and not to book at five times the price through Intourist. And the waiters at the National Hotel's restaurant were so unpleasant that most of the time I went to the small hard-currency snack-bar, which had reasonable snacks and fast service.

Before going to Russia I had met with him a Russian crime-writer in Paris called Georgi Weiner, who now entertained us at his flat in Moscow, where I met three generations of his family, including two very street-smart boys, speaking good American English, his father-in-law, a retired Professor, and various friends, my only evening spent with a Russian family in intimate surroundings. I had earlier helped Weiner in Paris to buy some computer equipment, having met him there with Julian. In Moscow Weiner used his celebrity to enable us to jump the queue to visit Lenin's tomb. A long line stretched back for miles because it was an anniversary of the end of the war, and tens of thousands of ex-soldiers were in Moscow to seek out old comrades. Weiner had a word with those at the head of the queue and they graciously let the foreign visitors pass ahead of them. The tomb was closed to the public four months later.

I was to see Julian frequently during the next year, once at a crime-writers' party at a Russian restaurant in New York and several times in Paris, where on occasion he had one of his daughters with him. We published *Seventeen Moments of Spring* and were preparing to publish a third novel when I heard that he had been taken ill. I was having difficulties selling him in Britain just then, because the end of the cold war, and more cordial relations between the Soviet Union and the West, had made it much more difficult to sell spy fiction that depended on the readers being able to bask in an atmosphere of tension built on hostility. Loss of contact with the author, combined with other problems that were about to overwhelm me, together conspired to prevent further publications going ahead, and we only produced the two Semyonov novels.

Julian had gone to a party and had given in to his weakness and drunk too much. In a taxi, being taken home, he had a heart attack and this was followed shortly after by a massive stroke that totally incapacitated him at the age of fifty-nine. He was moved a little while later to a clinic in Switzerland, then he was back at his dacha outside Moscow in the care of his estranged wife who no doubt hated him as much as he disliked her; at that point he could still neither move nor talk. Then I heard that he had died. My obituary appeared in The Independent in London.

* * * * * *

I had for some years been organising theatrical readings to promote the books that would most benefit from such efforts, especially where the author's name was well-enough known for there to be an interest, and where there was a nervousness that he might be too difficult to read on one's own. I had a group of half a dozen actors whom I knew well and I recruited them to read programmes of extracts, usually with introductory and explanatory material which I wrote for them. I called this activity The Theatre of Literature and under that name we appeared in many places, especially at Festival and Arts events. I offered these programmes to the organisers at a flat fee, which depended on the number of actors involved, so it was up to the hosting body to do well or badly out of them according to the numbers they attracted. We had several engagements at the Edinburgh Festival, even more at the Cheltenham Literature Festival and we appeared at major events all over Britain. This helped to sell books and we featured several authors, but pre-eminently Beckett, who was ideal for public presentation as so much of his work is in monologue form. After *Company*, Beckett produced another short work, *Ill Seen Ill Said*. Both works were successfully read on the BBC's Radio 3, and I found them ideal for my own group at art centres, lasting just an hour. The second text was written in French and subsequently translated by the author, so I did not have the foreign and other rights to exploit as I had with *Company*, but I loved the language and the cadence, one of the author's most enigmatic novellas, and over a period of time I finally puzzled out the meaning. It was very effective when read aloud, three actors, Angela Pleasance, Leonard Fenton and Sean Barratt, usually sharing the text between them. The Theatre of Literature functioned in an irregular fashion, doing between two and three, and twenty or thirty, performances a year. Laurence Staig was the Literature Officer of Eastern Arts, one of the regional arts boards that had been functioning for some time to supplement the work of the Arts Council on a more local basis, and he regularly found us engagements to perform in the Eastern counties of England in the neighbourhood of Cambridge. One day he also invited me to mount a two-week promotion of my writers, appearing on platforms together in threes or fours in about a dozen venues. I put together a small group of my authors, mainly in threes, remembering my earlier successes with the three French novelists. Two of them were willing to come again, but not together, Robbe-Grillet and Sarraute. Our venues went from Bedford to Cromer in the north-eastern corner of Norfolk, where Trevor Hoyle, a novelist, Howard Barker, an English playwright, and Simone Benmussa, a French one, appeared together and to an audience unaccustomed to such talk; they gave the audience a fascinating glimpse into what it means to be a writer exploring new ways of looking at life and finding the language to put over their ideas. The size of audience for our various engagements on this tour, which consisted principally of discussions between authors, varied enormously, some of the best attendances being at the smaller venues, while the lowest of all was for Nathalie Sarraute in Cambridge. The most successful, in terms of interest as well as size, was in my view the one in Colchester. I drove there with Alain Robbe-Grillet, whom I had picked up at the airport in London together with Brian Gysin from Paris, who was only marginally my author (*The Third Mind*, written jointly with William Burroughs). William Burroughs had agreed to come, and had cancelled, but Brian was, as it turned out, a more than adequate substitute. He is well enough known in the history of modern art and literature for it to be unnecessary for me to say much about him here, but he was a large, affable man, nearing seventy, one of the early surrealists, who had once exhibited his work on the street when it was refused by a *salon*. He had been expelled from the surrealist group by André Breton because he was homosexual, and had had a mixed career as painter, writer, restaurateur, theorist and latterly as a rock musician, singing with a group of younger people. He was in fact extremely ill at the time he came to Britain with emphysema, but he spoke well and interestingly and explained Burroughs' work much better than Burroughs would have done. Alain Robbe-Grillet was, as always, clear, fluent and precise: once again I translated for him, but it hardly seemed necessary at the university, where our session was held. He did however take umbrage at being put, as we all were, in university accommodation. He had insisted before coming that he would only stay in the best hotels and travel first class. His air ticket was not first-class and for some months afterwards he was still trying to get me to pay him the difference on what the other would have cost. In Ipswich, his other venue, he put up with the old-fashioned hotel we were in because Dickens had stayed there. Also on the platform in Colchester was Alan Burns, back from his years in America, teaching in Minneapolis. He was now being published by Marion Boyars, who had been given him in the split, but he had a new contract with me for a book on accident in art. The whole tour, the authors changing as those who had come and left were replaced by others, was a considerable success and Staig had organised a travelling bookshop to follow us around, selling the books of the featured authors wherever they appeared. The only sour moment was caused by Marghanita Laski, who had been put on the Arts Council panel as Chairperson of the Literature Committee by William Rees-Mogg, and would soon do as much damage to the previously liberal policy of the Arts Council as was possible. Our last session was in the public library in Bedford, where Christopher Small, author of *Music Society Education,* a radical revaluation of the purpose of music in the community, spoke, together with others. He had a Jamaican boyfriend called Neville with him, a dancer then working for Lambeth Borough Council. They were both offered a lift back to London by Marghanita Laski, which gave her an opportunity to quiz him. Whatever he told her, and he apparently expressed much gratitude to me for understanding his ideas, which were far from conventional, and publishing him, did not impress her. She later told Staig that she had found him rather silly. And she certainly had no sympathy with the flavour of my list. Not long after that I had official notification that my Arts Council grant was to be discontinued.

The whole East Anglian promotion was a success from everyone's point of view in spite of the poor turnout to hear Nathalie Sarraute, and everyone had enjoyed it. Simone Benmussa, a great animal lover, was much taken by Laurence's old English sheep-dog, Nana, which, knowing me, was always all over me. 'Elle t'adore,' she said enviously. Laurence tried to repeat the experiment the following year with Jonathan Cape, but Tom Maschler messed that up just as he had the events more than a decade earlier in Better Books by giving the job of thinking about it and organising it to someone fairly junior, who did it so incompetently that the Jonathan Cape tour was a total flop and Staig never attempted another such promotion.

The Arts Council was now becoming a very different body. Jenny Lee had made it a fairy godmother for all the arts, not questioning the viability of arts activities in commercial terms or the validity of what artists of all kinds wanted to do. There were a few charlatans who took advantage of the open-handedness of that golden age, but not that many, and statistically they were insignificant. The arts all flourished under Wilson, Callaghan and even Heath, because the Tories were not necessarily philistines, and did not want to appear as such, until Margaret Thatcher arrived in power in 1979. Then the previous 'milk-snatcher' as she had been known when Minister of Education, became the scourge of the trade unions and a subsidy-snatcher from the arts. Sir William Rees-Mogg, ex-editor of The Times, who had editorialised against me for years, had become chairman of the Arts Council and he set about firing such civilised officers as Charles Osborne, who could be criticised for the time off that went into writing his many books and visiting Australia and the United States on journeys that had nothing to do with the Arts Council, but nevertheless did his job with efficiency and competence. In a short time the Arts Council's officers were nearly all political appointees, and culture had to wear Tory clothes to be helped. Michael Schmidt, who was to receive the subsidy for his Carcanet Press that had previously gone to my company which I had on the Arts Council's request turned into a trust, was always on view at Tory conferences.

I asked for a meeting with the Literature panel and brought Barbara Wright with me. She was not allowed to open her mouth. Marghanita Laski cut me off very quickly as I put my case and it was obvious that this panel, then consisting largely of popular thriller and children's book writers would not have much sympathy with the kind of serious literature in which I specialised. They would not know the names of the authors where a sprinkling of academics could have informed them, probably had no knowledge of non-British contemporaries, and in any case would have considered serious literature as unwelcome competition. My £35,000 a year was reduced to a one-year cut-off grant of £10,000 and after that there was nothing.

* * * * * *

I had met Bogdan Drozdhovski on a number of occasions during the seventies when he was the Polish cultural attaché in London. He was amiable, voluble and enthusiastic, a big, bearded shambling man, who over lunches would tell me about current Polish writers, especially playwrights, and he was one himself. We already had some Polish writers on the list, most notably Gombrowicw and Rozewicw, and I knew that the Polish theatre in particular was very lively and full of talent just then. I invited Bogdan to guest-edit a Polish issue of Gambit, and he enthusiastically agreed. I found Cathy Itzin, who was Polish-speaking, and living in London as a free-lance editor, to help him from the British side. It became a double issue, Gambit No. 32-33, but I also published it as a book under the title *Twentieth Century Polish Theatre* in hardcover. It was a comprehensive survey and included three modern plays. Just then I received a telephone call from Peter Hemmings. Scottish Opera was to give a few performances in Poznan, Wodz and Warsaw and there were a few extra seats on the chartered 'plane. Would I like to go with them? I would of course and did. At the airport in Warsaw I was offered a guide, who thought I might be interested in strip-tease, a new innovation on the Polish scene. I said No, it was culture that interested me and I was soon able to lose him after he had tried to sell me some black-market Polish currency. I went to the two operas, *The Rape of Lucretia* and another that Scottish Opera gave in the theatre attached to the Palace of Culture, a Stalinist monstrosity which the Poles liked to joke had the best view in Warsaw because it was the only building from which you could not see the Palace of Culture. I was horrified that all the seats, and very many were empty, were reserved for senior party members and the official guests of the government. Hundreds of young people were desperate to see the Britten opera in particular, but were unable to get tickets. I went to the Warsaw Opera House, the Theatr Wielki, a magnificent building where I saw a ballet by Minkus, which particularly impressed me because of its junior *corps de ballet*, eight or nine year old girls, who danced in and out at intervals as perfectly as their seniors. A few days later I saw Penderecki's *Devils of Loudun* and then a double bill of *Master Peter's Puppet Show* with Salieri's *Prima la musica e poi lo parole* which had first been given at Schönbrunn together with Mozart's *Impresario* in 1786, which I was especially happy to catch. I had been considering doing a Salieri at Ledlanet some years earlier and had looked through all the scores in the National Library at Vienna. There were only fifteen people in the audience in the little studio theatre under the roof of the Teatr Wielki, and I estimated that at least two hundred people must have been involved in the production as singers, orchestra, stage staff and administration: the auditorium was small, but the stage quite big: heavy subsidy keeps such rare operas on the boards for collectors such as me. I visited the museums, saw one of my authors, spent half a day in the offices of Dialog, the theatre magazine, and an evening with Bogdan Drozdhovski. He picked me up at my hotel and took me to see a Polish production of *King Lear*. He was himself a Shakespeare translator, but this was not his translation. At the interval he said, 'John. You know *King Lear*. I know *King Lear*. This translation is not worth it. Let's go and eat.' We left with his wife who did the standard thing as we passed the street where they lived: she pleaded a headache so that the men could go off on their own.

'John,' said Bogdan, 'last night I went out with my son and we drank too much wine. Do you mind if we drink vodka?' I didn't mind, and he took me to the Writers' Club where, rejecting the white vodka we know in the west, he ordered a bottle of brown Starka, which we drank with our meal. This was followed by a different vodka, quite unsuitable for decadent western stomachs, and we ended up back at my hotel, where in the back room late-night bar, only open to hotel residents and government officials, all of whom would be Communist Party members, we continued drinking. Bogdan insisted I try one vodka after another: we ended up with a slivovitz called Passover vodka, which he told me was sold to Israel where Rabbis drank it. It was so alcoholic that a match applied to it burnt away more than half the contents of my glass. I lifted the burning rim to my lips, which it scorched, drank it when it cooled and put it down. 'Thank you, Bogdan,' I said. 'I'm about to pass out. I hope to just make it to my room before I do.' I only just made it, rushing past the old lady who sits all night in the corridor guarding the morality of the hotel and just managed to get into my room. I fell on the bed and woke up to broad sunlight.

It was a beautiful May morning. I felt fine, walked all over central Warsaw, called in on the Union of Polish Writers and spent an hour with the secretary of the Union with whom I later kept in correspondence, and in the evening went to a reception at the British Embassy following a string quartet concert. The reception consisted of a single glass of wine because the press had recently criticised the excessive hospitality of British Embassies, especially in Washington, and they were being very careful. I met two Edinburgh friends there, Duncan Black and Bert Davies, and I had dinner with them, finding myself in bed by eleven o'clock. I woke up at about five with the most blinding headache of my life. The amount of vodka I had drunk with Bogdan had carried me through all the previous day, still in a state of inebriation, although I had not realised it, had felt quite normal and nobody had noticed anything strange about me. It only hit me after twenty-seven hours. I spent that next morning wandering about Warsaw in a daze, looked at bookshops, bought a recording of Rimsky-Korsakov's *Invisible City of Kitezh* and a few second-hand books, and at noon went to Bogdan's office. He was the editor of a large-circulation magazine, *Poezia*, and I had been invited to attend an editorial meeting. 'How you feel, John?' he asked.

'Terrible,' I answered.

'Me, too,' he said. 'Have a beer.'

Before leaving I had another meeting with the editors of Dialog, meeting more of their very intelligent and well-informed editorial staff and writers, and thought about acquiring more Polish playwrights for my list. On my final night I dined in another hotel and the floor show turned out to include a strip-tease. I returned on the charter flight with Scottish Opera. Some months later Drozdhovsky was in London. I took him to a Sri Lankan restaurant in Earl's Court and ordered him their hottest curry in revenge for the vodka experience. 'I am in hell,' he screamed, clutching his throat.

* * * * * *

I had left Dalmeny House and for a time moved into Sheila Colvin's flat on Allan Street in West Kensington. Then an opportunity came up. I would sometimes spend the four days of the Easter holiday alone in the office, catching up on work that needed a sustained period of concentration, and one Easter, it was probably 1981, I was doing all the royalty statements, of which there were hundreds. On the Monday, the last day of the holiday, as I was arriving I saw our aged landlord Hyman Fine, carrying furniture down the stairs of 1 Green's Court, the door of which was immediately adjacent to 18 Brewer Street, our office, and out into the street. 'Mr. Fine, what are you doing?' I asked.

'Don't you worry, Mr. Calder,' he said. 'I have a court order to expel these terrible prostitutes, and I'm just taking away their furniture.' I could hardly leave a heavy-set portly old man to do this on his own – although as one of the richest men in Soho I could not imagine why he would want to – and I spent two hours helping him, for which he was very grateful.

That gave me an idea and the next morning I rang him up. 'Mr. Fine,' I asked him, 'would you be willing to let me that building? I'm looking for a place to live.' He immediately agreed and Sheila and I moved in. There were three floors as in my office next door, a room in each. A metal bar inside the door from which the stairs led upward indicated that it had once been a Jewish home. I shelved the large first floor room to take my books, organising them by author and subject, although most of the Ledlanet library, including all the books I had published over the years, were still in storage in Dunfermline. This room took a big dining table on which I did much of my work and it had a sitting area that included a sofa-bed for occasional visitors. The movers were quite shocked as they were carrying bedroom furniture right up to the third floor and they thought that the top was all I had. They could not understand anyone moving from a comfortable basement flat in fashionable Kensington to one room in sordid Soho, until I told them I had the rest of the building, which had to be furnished from what I had put into storage. The middle floor was a sitting room and kitchen. I installed a bathroom, kitchen, cupboards and all that was necessary and spent the eighties there. Underneath was a café, but I seldom used it. It was very convenient to have the office next door, saving much travelling time, and I could easily walk to most of London's theatres, opera houses and concert halls from there.

Sheila became active in the Soho Society which was run by local residents to protect their interests and combat the vice and sleaze industries. I was away a great deal, making trips to America and Europe, to provincial bookshops and sometimes to Australia and elsewhere. Sheila was also away a great deal, mainly in Edinburgh. One night we went to the opera and on return found most of Green's Court on fire. The firemen did not want to let me pass, but I insisted I had to save precious documents and managed to get in. The fire was stopped before it did any real damage to my house, but the walls were singed, the windows cracked, and the whole might have gone up in another few minutes. The fire had started across the alleyway in a house that had several Indian families squatting, several to a room. Much of the night was spent giving tea and comfort to other residents who had been burned out or whose homes or workshops were partly destroyed. The next morning the police put Mr. Fine, the landlord who had allowed the terrible overcrowding to take place in his properties, under a considerable grilling in our offices and nearly arrested him. I had to redecorate my own place, but fortunately the library and the manuscripts, of which there were many, did not suffer.

One Saturday night near the end of the eighties we heard noise and banging in the office next door. On Sunday morning we discovered that Marion Boyars had done an overnight flit, taking all her things, many of mine, all the contracts and even the light bulbs. Many of my files were missing. I managed to get some of them back, little by little, but much time was spent in the next few months trying to retrieve contracts, manuscripts waiting to go into production and important correspondence. Even in the next millennium much is still missing.

When still at Dalmeny House I had been startled one day to hear on the radio that Peter Hain had been arrested, and I hastened to contact him. I had known him in my days as a Liberal Party candidate when he was President of the Young Liberals. South African, he was a very cocky self-confident young man, but still not much at ease in British society, and I can remember him at a ball at some Liberal conference at a southern seaside town, where he told me he was wearing a suit for the first time in his life. I had commissioned two books from him, *Community Politics*, which was a manual of how to become known in the area where your are standing for election by investigating and exploiting local grievances in order to win votes at the next election, and two volumes entitled *Policing the Police*, which did not make him popular with the constabulary. It was not surprising then that they took great pleasure in arresting him when they had the chance to do so.

What happened was this: he had been at home working on a book and needed a new typewriter ribbon. Having waited to listen to the one o'clock news, a regular habit, he jumped into his car, parked it on a single yellow line and ran into a W.H. Smith. Just then there was a bank robbery on the same street and he was seen running to get into his car before it was ticketed, and the licence number was recorded by a member of the public. Found at home, he was arrested. He was of course cleared at his trial, but my friend Jimmy Ball, who had close police contacts, told me that they still believed he had robbed a bank and had been able to get away with it. Soon after he switched to the Labour Party, and eventually was elected to parliament for South Wales. At the time of writing he is a Minister in the New Labour government of Tony Blair.

I made a visit to Berlin in the early eighties but forget the purpose of the visit. Sam Beckett was there rehearsing a play, and I went to see him at the Akademie der Kunste. We had drinks in the lobby with Theodor Adorno who was also staying there; the Akademie is a conference centre financed by the city, which offers accommodation to distinguished visitors in the arts who are spending time in Berlin. Then we had a pleasant dinner, but a short one, because Sam was rehearsing a play and was very preoccupied with it. I was sitting there again the next day when William Burroughs and Allen Ginsberg walked by and I agreed to see them for lunch. When we all met the following day Fred Jordan from Grove Press and Susan Sontag were in the party. Susan was very preoccupied with her cancer, which later was cured, but that was the main topic of her conversation, and it became the subject of her next book. When I mentioned that I had been seeing Beckett they wanted to see him too and asked me to arrange it. Knowing that Sam was very busy and this being a Sunday that he would be memorising his text and making notes for the next day, I was reluctant to disturb him, but under pressure from my lunch companions I went to the telephone. He agreed to meet the party right away, but asked if we could make the visit short. The others insisted on bringing along a bottle of whisky, and we had a rather stilted conversation because Sam's mind was obviously on his work. He always memorised his texts so that he did not have to consult the book or script with his bad eyes in the dim light of the stage. Berlin had been the first to invite him to direct his own plays, and he would read each part to the actors with exact timing as if he were conducting a score, but in Berlin it was the German text he was directing in Elmar Tophoven's translation and with German actors. Those he was working with now, probably Held, Wigger and other actors who knew him well, gave him few of the difficulties he often had in Britain with old-style traditional actors who felt they could do things their own way, changing the words and improvising their movements. The precision of Beckett's direction had brought a new kind of actor into being just as Wagner's demands had created a new kind of singer. He was always happy in Berlin where he could take his time and rehearse as long as he liked.

This was the second and last time that Burroughs met Beckett, and no doubt, the previous meeting in Girodias' restaurant was still in both their minds. Burroughs later complained of Beckett's remoteness, and no doubt the others, hoping for a relaxed gossipy session about literature and people they knew were also disappointed, but Sam when working did not like diversions. When meeting people in cafés he could time his own exit, but this was not possible when people call on you. I was sorry I had made the 'phone call'.

When travelling through the mid-west in the States I had paid several visits to Burroughs. Before moving to Lawrence in Kansas he had lived for a while in New York in a kind of warehouse space that seemed to operate like a commune. I can only imagine what went on in 'the bunker' as they called it. There seemed to be about a dozen people living on one floor in this strange building on the Bowery with its warren of bare rooms and communal central space with a long table where the inmates ate, talked, drank and no doubt indulged their various habits. James Grauerholz, who having started as Burroughs' amanuensis, now seemed to control him utterly, appeared to be in charge, a sinister figure whom I disliked more every time I saw him, and it was clear that the feeling was mutual. Here I met Burroughs a few times, but forget what we had to say to each other: he had become a guru to the rock and roll fans of the day, although I doubt if they knew much about his work. Grauerholz took him off to Kansas where Burroughs had his own little house where he shot at dogs, animals he disliked and was afraid of, with a BB gun, kept about nine cats, and worked. Occasionally he would be picked up by Grauerholz for some gathering at his own apartment or to go to friends of his. It was obvious that Grauerholz and his entourage were doing very nicely out of William Burroughs Communications, the company that he had set up, which received all the royalties. All Burroughs himself needed were a few crusted doughnuts every day, a bottle of vodka, Coca-Cola to mix with it, and cat food. He worked in his bedroom that looked to me exactly the same as his little room in the Beat Hotel on the Rue Git-le-Coeur in Paris where I had first met him. The other rooms were for cats, files and visitors. I put together a *William Burroughs Reader* for Picador, in 1983, rather like the *Samuel Beckett Reader* that had appeared the previous year (very different from my previous *Beckett Reader* for N.E.L.), Burroughs was very pleased with it, but I sensed that Grauerholz wasn't. He wanted everything to do with Burroughs to go through him. But I had several talks with Burroughs on my visits to Lawrence, and although ageing he had not changed much, the same obsessive subjects, mind-control, guns, rabid dogs, the CIA, world conspiracies, coming up again and again. There were gun collectors' manuals and magazines about military warfare, the kind of thing hard-line young American fascists like to read, scattered all around his house. He was not allowed to keep guns there, except for the BB, but played with a variety of weapons every time he was at Grauerholz's place, taking pleasure in eviscerating a dog's stomach with one of his collection of field knives in his fantasies which he would act out in mime. The writing had not improved but was purely narrative now, free of experiment, but not of fantasy. He probably could have been certified as mad.

I had edited a collection of his articles, as had Dick Seaver, now publishing him at Viking, and Grauerholz began putting every kind of obstacle in the way of publication, wanting to make changes, not liking my title and insisting on seeing more proofs. I could see exactly what he was up to and went ahead, not letting anyone else see my final editing, but accepting Burroughs' title *The Adding Machine*. This came out in 1985 by which time Grauerholz had managed to ensure that relations were bad and getting worse.

The most avaricious of all American agents, James Wylie, came into the act to make things worse still. He offered three future novels, still unwritten, to the highest bidder, and it seemed unlikely that any of Burroughs' old publishers could contemplate continuing with him. I kept negotiations open but knew that sooner or later I would lose an author on whom I had taken great risks.

Con Leventhal was perhaps Beckett's oldest friend. He had taken his post at Trinity when Sam decided that he was not going to be an academic, and stayed there until he retired, then moved to Paris to live with Marion Leigh as his companion. He developed cancer, was in hospital, had an operation, and had to return for check-ups in London. I met him and Marion Leigh on the day when he had just been told that the cancer was gone and he was greatly relieved. I took them both to lunch at Wheeler's and Con was very happy with his new lease on life. But then the bad news came: the cancer had returned. Con's morale collapsed and he died in terror. Sam told me about it in Paris in deep depression. I think he had expected more stoicism from his old friend. But Con's last years had been happy ones. He was a constant companion to Sam for whom he was meant to be doing some secretarial work for which Sam paid him, but this never consisted of doing more than forwarding Sam's post when he was out of town. Con received a legacy late in life and spent it with Marion going around the world. He had many friends and some of them put together a Festschrift for him after his death in 1979. Some time in the late sixties I had asked him to make a collection for me of Beckett's surrealist translations from before the war. This had been one of Sam's sources of revenue, a meagre one, mainly translating for little magazines such as Alan Titus's This Quarter and Jolas' Transition. Con had done a good job, but then Sam decided that he didn't want this work, translations done in a hurry to earn some money, to appear again in print: it simply wasn't good enough. I disagreed with this modest denigration of what was quite unique work, but bowed to his decision and sent the material back to Con. I never saw it again.

My all-night sessions, sitting up, drinking and talking with Sam Beckett were now a thing of the past. During the late seventies and early eighties I usually tended to meet him in the bar of the Coupole for a drink or at La Palette to have dinner, rather than at the Closerie des Lilas, the Falstaff or in the Rue de la Gaîté as in the past. La Palette was never full, had good fish, and the waiters knew him.

On one occasion in 1982 we had arranged to meet there and Sheila was with me. I asked her if she could leave us alone for half an hour as I had a delicate subject to discuss and left her in a bar across the street. The delicate subject was money. We had produced some expensive first editions of the more recent novels and prose texts using special paper and de luxe bindings to sell to collectors and the royalties on these were high. And Beckett's other books were all doing better, especially the novels and poems. On the other hand we no longer had best-sellers coming along to cover most of the overheads, while the avant-garde fiction list of mainly European writers who had previously been studied in the universities was selling much less well. Margaret Thatcher was already throwing a blanket of philistine xenophobia over university studies, and the old school of literary editors no longer existed as the new newspaper proprietors, interested only in circulation and not at all in culture, appointed ever less-well informed journalists to these jobs. Rupert Murdoch in particular had instructed his staff to get well-known people to review books about well-known people, while anything considered high-brow, off-beat or foreign had great difficulty in getting reviewed. And of course we had lost our main crutch, our Arts Council subsidy. We owed Sam a great deal and could not pay it. He was extremely sympathetic and told me not to worry; I could pay when things were better or when I could. He also agreed, although that may have been on a different occasion, that should anything happen to him, I could have five years to pay up the arrears and he later confirmed this in a letter.

Sheila then joined us and we had a pleasant dinner. Towards the end of it I asked if there was anything new in the pipeline. Sam reached under the table and took a plastic-covered manuscript out of his brief-case. 'I have this for you,' he said, 'but you might not like it and you certainly don't have to publish it.'

He left us right after dinner and began walking home along the Boulevard Montparnasse. Sheila and I went to have another drink at the Falstaff where we met Marion Leigh and Josette Hayden, two widows consoling each other, and like us having a final drink. We chatted with them until they left, stayed a little longer and then returned to our hotel, my habitual Michelet-Odéon. Once in bed I suddenly remembered: Sam's manuscript, where was it? I telephoned the Falstaff but nothing had been found. Sheila and I dressed and rushed there in a taxi: the restaurant was closing and chairs were being put on tables. Where we had been sitting there was nothing to be seen. I went to the garbage cans at the back of the restaurant and began to look through the egg-shells, broken glasses and what had been left on plates, and finally found, to my intense relief, the blue plastic folder that I had carried in there four hours earlier. I took it back to the hotel, by now fully awake, and began to read it. It was *Worstward Ho*, a text of incredible compression, even for an author as economical with words as Samuel Beckett. It begins:

'On. Say on. Be said on. Somehow on. Till nohow on. Said nohow on.'

I came to the fourth paragraph. One of the most significant messages that I had found in Beckett's writing was the comfort he gave those who for one reason or another were not successful in life – at least as the world sees success in terms of money made, tribute earned or fame acquired – because for many people just living in the way they wish and doing satisfactory work is success enough. But for many others, like most of Beckett's characters, the Molloys, Malones, Vladimirs and Estragons, success is not possible in any sense except in so far as just surviving a little longer can be called success. Beckett says it makes no difference because we all come to the same end, and in his *Duthuit Dialogues* he makes it clear that no real artist ever considers himself a success because he pursues perfection but never believes he finds it.

'To be an artist is to fail as no other dare fail,' he says there, and goes on: 'that failure is his world and the shrink from it desertion, art and craft, good housekeeping, living,' Now, reading *Worstward Ho* I came across the following:

'All of old. Nothing else ever. Ever tried. Ever failed. No matter. Try again. Fail again. Fail better.'

I mightn't like it, Beckett had said. I did not have to publish it. Oh yes I did! It came out in 1983. Beckett was not to write much more after that, a few short works for stage and television, *Stirrings Still*, and one last poem.

* * * * * *

John Drummond had been the director of the Edinburgh Festival since 1979 and his programming became better year by year, culminating in his homage to 'Vienna 1900', the hothouse out of which so much modern art developed at the turn of the century, which was in 1983, his last year. His festivals had much in common with those of Harewood, who had devoted much of his first year to the music of Schönberg, starting with the *Gurrelieder*, and Schönberg again played an important part in Drummond's Vienna year. Schönberg's daughter, married to Luigi Nono, was invited to come and Dr. Leonard Stein, who ran the Schönberg Institute in Los Angeles, gave some fascinating lectures, as did Martin Esslin, whose years at Berkeley – after leaving the BBC he had become an academic in America – now induced him to give American pronunciations to such words as 'baroque', which sounded oddly to those like myself who had known him for many years in London. But the crowning glory of Drummond's last year at the Edinburgh Festival was a superb exhibition of Viennese secession and expressionist art from the late eighteen-nineties to the beginning of the first world war, which was put together by Peter Vergo.

It was that summer that Drummond came to Paris to meet Beckett to discuss some matter in connection with setting up a European Art Foundation, and I was along, partly to effect the introduction, but also because I was trying to persuade John Drummond to have a large Beckett element in the following year's festival. We were to meet at seven o'clock in the Coupole bar and left the question of dinner open, depending on how Sam was feeling. But he was in an affable mood, arrived precisely on time as usual, chatted for half an hour and agreed to dinner. We all walked (Sheila Colvin was with us) down the Boulevard Montparnasse to the Closerie des Lilas. But it was no longer the meeting place for writers and artists that it had been previously. The old habitués might still use the bar, but not the restaurant, which was now an expensive tourist trap. Once seated and having looked around, Sam was obviously extremely uncomfortable. Drummond was sensitive enough to pick up the atmosphere and folding his napkin as the waiter approached, said 'One of us is not feeling well' and led us out. We went into a nearby Chinese restaurant. Once seated again Sam beamed. 'That's better,' he said, and we enjoyed the evening.

Anecdotes about Sam and especially his one-liners are now legion. It must have been about that time that I was walking with him down the Boulevard Saint-Jacques on a very fine morning. 'What a beautiful day,' I commented.

'So far,' said Sam.

* * * * * *

Early after my setting up an office in New York I had contacted Alan Schneider. He had come to my Drama Conference in 1963, had directed

Barney Rosset's *Film* with Buster Keaton using Beckett's script and having the author present, and I had often met him in London where he had mounted productions of plays by Ionesco and Albee. In New York Beckett was having a boom now, mainly because of the plays that Schneider directed in the Harold Clurman Theatre on 42nd Street for Jack Garfein. Experience had made Schneider suspicious of Garfein and his motivations, but, as he said on several occasions, at least he was willing to keep the plays running as long as the audience came, and Alan had *carte blanche* to do them the way Sam wanted.

I had many lunches and dinners with Garfein and even sold him an Obaldia play that he never produced. He was unsure of himself, always asking for second and third opinions of the merits of plays he had been persuaded to contract. On several occasions I had Muriel Leyner with me when I met him, and she was always annoyed that he never remembered having ever seen her before. He changed the name of one of the theatres (he had two side-by-side in the same building) to the Samuel Beckett Theatre. This involved a gala dedication ceremony with a large price charged to be present, so I did not go. On one occasion I was asked to take part in a reading that had several people involved, and at the last moment my time was cut to five minutes as mine was not a name known to the public. Nicol Williamson was to read before me and was also told to keep his contribution to only a few minutes. At the run-through I met Nick and we went to have a drink together where he regaled Muriel, who was with me, with the story of our trip to Ussy to see Sam. When his turn came to go on stage he spent twenty minutes telling the same story and another twenty on a Beckett recitation that totally destroyed Garfein's plan for the evening and considerably extended it, but the audience was much entertained as a result.

My last meeting with Alan Schneider was when he came to have a chat at my 16th Street apartment. Elliott Swift came in, recognised Schneider, and insisted we listen to him singing Elizabethan songs to his own guitar accompaniment, so that we had no time to talk. It was his way of imposing an audition on Alan. Then Schneider went to London to direct a new play at the Hampstead Theatre Club. I was on the telephone to Sheila in London when she told me that the radio had just announced that Alan Schneider had had an accident and was in a hospital on life-support. I rang his wife Jean who was just about to catch the Concorde to London, having already been informed. I rang Garfein's office, which telephoned the hospital for confirmation. Coming out of the theatre early in the morning to post a letter to Beckett just before rehearsals started, Alan had tried to cross the street as the lights were changing. A motorcyclist accelerated too early and knocked him down. After two days on life-support, being irrevocably brain-dead, his wife agreed to shut off the machines. On that evening I went to a Pinter triple-bill that Alan Schneider had directed. At the end the leading actor came on stage to announce Alan's death that day. 'Alan never stopped, never rested,' he said. 'Rest well now.' I spent a few hours with Jean at her house north of New York on a Sunday to comfort her. She was drinking heavily, but coming to terms with her loss. 'For years he promised me a holiday together,' she said, 'but he was always too busy. Now it's too late.'

Two weeks later I met Sam at the PLM bar in Paris and we discussed Alan. The letter posted to him in Hampstead had arrived the next day. 'I hope it wasn't the only letter he was posting,' he commented, but it was. Eerily, the doctor who had received Alan's body in the hospital was also called Beckett.

During the following year Garfein built a mythology around Schneider. Alan's book *Entrances* came out posthumously and at later dates Jean published other writings, and she also sold his correspondence with Sam for a large amount of money. I sometimes asked myself why Alan's book had not been offered to me, but I knew the answer. It had been sold through a literary agent and agents very seldom came to me with a book they considered saleable: I was the last resort, a publisher who paid small advances and kept a book going for many years however small the sales. What literary agents like is a large advance, from which they get a slice, usually ten percent, but increasingly over the years it became more than that, and they prefer the book to be remaindered when the main sales are over, thereby giving them the opportunity of perhaps selling it again to another publisher. They do not like to receive annual small cheques with royalty statements where their commission is not worth the time and expense of recording it and paying the author. This is what happens with most of the books I publish. Manuscripts most of the time come to me directly from the author, often against the will of a literary agent who has failed to sell it elsewhere, or else I found books on a foreign publisher's list in another language, or else I would approach an author to commission a book from him, usually in this latter case a non-fiction title.

Although his contract would have enabled him to continue for some years longer, Drummond resigned after his Vienna year from the Edinburgh Festival, tired of the back-biting and criticism. It is impossible to please all tastes in Edinburgh and the town counsellors, philistines most of them, had become too much for him. He was followed by Frank Dunlop, his complete opposite in personality. Drummond was Olympian, elitist, self-assured, knowledgeable and volatile. He was quick-witted and could talk on any subject at the drop of a hat. But he made many people feel uncomfortable and he was undoubtedly arrogant. Edinburgh, and not only the philistines, found him hard to take in spite of his competence and talent. Dunlop was down to earth, also knowledgeable and a professional theatre director, especially of popular musicals, but he was interested in giving the public what it wanted rather than what he wanted. He had had wide experience – his previous job was running the Young Vic, a basically experimental theatre near the Old Vic – and he could talk to people on their own level whatever it was, unlike Drummond. And that is why he got the job.

During Drummond's last festival I had persuaded him to let me set up a bookstall in the booking office of the Festival at the foot of the Mound. It worked extremely well, not least because the new computers made ticket-buyers wait up to half an hour until they could order their tickets, so my bookstall and the food caterers always had captive buyers hovering about. I employed the son of Stephanie Wolfe-Murray, whose publishing company Canongate Press was just around the corner, and local students to man it. On the last day of the festival I wrote a letter to The Scotsman praising Drummond for having made the festival less official and stuffy. His own farewell letter, thanking Edinburgh prior to his departure as Festival Director, followed mine, and he was not pleased. 'Good morning, Mr. Letter-Writer,' he said waspishly as he walked past my stall and went upstairs to his office. But Allen Wright, features editor of The Scotsman, for whom I had done some reviewing that year, agreed with me. Drummond, in spite of his Augustine presence and character, had really taken the stuffiness out of the Festival, and those words had been used as a headline over my letter.

Earlier in his tenure, in 1980, I had suggested to Drummond that he let me revive the Writers' Conferences. He had liked the idea, but instead asked Frank Delaney, a BBC colleague, to organise a literary event and this took the shape of readings and lectures in the Assembly Rooms, 'not the same animal' as Sean Hignett, attending one of them, said to me. They received little press attention and attracted no controversy. But I became friendly with Frank and his girlfriend Bridget Roden, and we dined together frequently during the following year, met in Frankfurt and elsewhere and kept in touch.

Then it was Frank Dunlop with whom I was dealing in Edinburgh and he was open to suggestion. I had been lobbying for a long time for a big Beckett element in the Edinburgh Festival, and what had been the seed I tried to put into Drummond's mind finally took hold with Dunlop's in 1984. He agreed to take several Beckett plays and it was the Schneider productions from New York that were imported, while I put together a Theatre of Literature production of excerpts taken from different works in order to demonstrate how Beckett saw life from pre-birth to death. This was entitled *To Its Beginning To Its End*, a line taken from one of the poems. Dunlop accepted the idea, but engaged Peter James to produce it. The cast had Angela Pleasance and my old friend Leonard Fenton in the cast, together with Sylvester McCoy, basically a comic actor who had been playing Dr. Who in the science fiction television series, but who soon became a Beckett addict. Dunlop also agreed to have a Beckett Conference as part of the proceedings and James Knowlson agreed to organise this, a series of lectures and discussions with about a dozen specialists, including Tom Bishop, Martin

Esslin, Enoch Blater and a number of academics from Britain, Europe and America.

I acted as an assistant director for my own production, although I would have preferred to do the whole thing on my own, but Peter James was easy to work with. He put me in charge of the line readings, while he organised the movement. We were in the Church Hill Theatre in Morningside which had about five hundred seats and we had a good audience if not a capacity one. The plays that had come from New York occupied the same theatre, my show running for ten performances and two Beckett programmes of short plays filling the theatre for the other festival dates. Many people who I had not seen since Ledlanet days emerged during the season, such as Ian Fraser from Dunblane, who had been behind my cancelled Church of Scotland General Assembly talk, and I renewed old acquaintance. My own show was too long, going on for nearly two and a half hours, and when I did it again, I knew I must cut it to half that length. Beckett requires great concentration on the part of audiences and ninety minutes is about as long as such a programme, taken from plays, novels, poetry and other writings, should last.

It was good to see David Warrilow again, but he arrived in Edinburgh having not quite recovered from a painful attack of shingles. I found a sympathetic chemist who was able to help him, but his ailment in no way diminished his performance of *Piece of Monologue*, which superbly ended one of the two Beckett evenings from New York. He was not very happy when, just after the curtain dropped, and having intended there to be a period of silence to allow the atmosphere of the piece to weigh with the audience, Knowlson stepped blithely onto the stage to make an announcement, and David complained bitterly to me about it. I had a complaint myself, but never voiced it: *Piece of Monologue* is really one of Beckett's late prose pieces that normally would have come to me for publication. When Warrilow went to see Sam to ask if there was a new play he could première, Sam looked in the drawer and handed him the just-finished text, which had not been written especially for him as he later claimed. But because it was then treated as a play Faber claimed the right to publish it.

There has been much controversy in recent years about which of Beckett's plays belong on the stage and which are for reading only. All his work is so inherently dramatic that every first-person work comes over very well when read or presented dramatically, but even those, mainly early, works, which were written in the third-person, are effective if adapted. The problem is the appropriateness of the adaptation. Sam Beckett had a superb sense of how to make things work for an audience. Instinctively he knew that plays like *Waiting For Godot* would never have the same impact to a television audience as in the theatre, and works he wrote for television were written with a proper sense of the possibilities and restrictions of the medium. The later prose works written in the first-person come over well when delivered by actors who understand the work, but the problems usually lie with producers (or directors in the American sense) who either do not understand the work itself and think whatever they dream up doesn't matter, or those who want to put some perverse interpretation of their own on the text. One of the worst examples of the latter, and perhaps of the former as well, was Deborah Warner's nineties production of *Footfalls*, which the Beckett estate had to stop in mid-run. I shall return to this subject in the next chapter.

The whole Beckett element in the 1984 Edinburgh Festival was a considerable success, and to encourage audiences in advance I wrote a long explanatory piece for the souvenir programme and another for The Scotsman. I was in a taxi with Garfein when I saw Avital Mossinsohn, who was staying with Iain Crawford, the previous Publicity Officer of the Festival, about to enter his flat late at night and I stopped the taxi to say Hello. Avital was the Director of the Jerusalem Festival and he invited us both in for a drink. Being tired I declined, but Jack Garfein accepted, and as a result his company was invited to perform at the next Jerusalem Festival. Avital also used a television version of my own programme. He took me to lunch at the next Festival in Edinburgh, commenting at the end that that was the only payment I could expect to receive as he had exceeded his budget. The Garfein company also performed in London at the Donmar Theatre a fortnight later.

* * * * * *

At the beginning of 1984 I decided to go to Australia to try to pick up my Australian sales which were far from good, and to see what was wrong, although I knew it had to be the growing American infiltration of what was traditionally, in the case of copyright works, a British market. I went first to San Francisco from New York, spent a week selling books there and in the middle of January flew to Sydney with a short stop-over in Hawaii. I booked the trip through Jeannie Adams as part of a round-the-world trip that would eventually get me back to my starting point, in this case New York. I had a distributor in Sydney who stocked my books, amusingly called Wild and Wooley, named after the two founders Michael Wilding, a local writer and academic, and Pat Wooley, an American who had moved there, who I knew to be a radical feminist from California. I was organised to pile up many bonus miles, something I never normally had the time to think about, and had a supply of stickers to put on each ticket as I used it. Somewhere along the way I lost the stickers and was told to write the code number on the tickets, but the computers never picked it up, so in the end I received no bonuses. As my habit was always to travel by the cheapest method, bonus miles were normally minimal anyway, but there is a flaw in my character that makes me forget to do what I should when travelling, so that I have never had a single benefit from all the millions of miles I have travelled. I cannot explain it. Somewhere underneath lies the conviction that everything should have one price for everybody and one should not have to waste precious hours of one's life in finding the cheapest way to travel or at least to pile up bonus points. The situation is the same with compiling points when filling up my car.

I arrived in Sydney early in the morning, rented a mini and drove to the hotel in King's Cross into which Pat Wooley had booked me: it was called the Texas Tavern and I slept until the afternoon. Going into the nearby car park where I had left the rented red car I quickly saw that it was not there. I reported it to the attendant, but just then someone else who worked there came up. He remembered me entering in a blue car. Then I remembered myself: I had been driving a red car in San Francisco, now I had a blue one. When travelling one often makes the same mistake with hotel numbers.

I had dinner with Pat that night, who was as friendly as a radical feminist could allow herself to be with a male, even one like me who always supported sexual equality. The next morning I went to the warehouse where I was flabbergasted to see American editions of very many of my book titles in large quantities and very few copies of my own, which contractually were the only ones allowed to be sold in Australia. Of course this had been going on for years and she made no apology or attempt to cover up. She represented a number of publishers including New Directions and what annoyed me in the first place was seeing several skids of Céline's *Journey to the End of the Night* in a defective New Directions edition, whereas mine, having been slowly edited by myself over a two-year period was only just coming out in hardcover. What I was looking at was the American paperback, several hundred of them. Fortunately they did not distribute for Grove Press, so they only had my Beckett editions but not many of them. I was soon to see the Grove editions of Beckett all over Australia, brought in by another distributor. I remembered that once, many years previously, when I had complained to Grove about their market violations, they had denied selling into my markets and had even shown me their export files which contained none of my titles. But I saw many violations of the books of other British publishers, so they had obviously cleaned up their file just for my visit, but not thought that I would notice that they had been violating other publishers' titles. Pat just shrugged her shoulders. She was American, favoured the American book, and was fairly certain that I would not go to law, and in any case I needed to sell my books in her market somehow.

I have not yet related my problems over publishing Céline and this is perhaps a suitable place to do so. His masterpiece *The Journey to the End of the Night*, which had won the Prix Goncourt, very controversially, in 1934, had been for many years available in Penguin Books, but in an inadequate translation. It was Elizabeth Wyler who suggested to me that such an important book, which Penguin had recently allowed to go out of print, should be made available again and I decided to commission a new translation and acquire the rights, which I did from Gallimard. Another Céline, a sequel to the *Journey*, had been translated by Ralph Mannheim, an American living in Paris, and I approached him. He was interested, but only for a considerable fee. He had started his career as a German refugee in America by translating *Mein Kampf*, not a pleasant task, but had developed a considerable reputation for his English renderings of both German and French writers, his previous Céline being *Mort à Crédit*, published in America as *Death on the Instalment Plan*, which I anglicised, when I published it in 1989, to *Death on Credit*. For *The Journey* I did get an Arts Council grant for the translation: it must have been during the interim period when they had reduced my subsidy but not yet cut me off. They gave me $7,000 towards the $10,000 that Mannheim had demanded. New Directions were just going out of print. Their old edition had the same lacklustre translation by John Marks as the Penguin and they agreed to take the new Mannheim one. This promised to enable me to save on production costs and I too generously agreed to give them half the benefit of the subsidy, so that the translation ended by costing us $1,500 each.

Ralph Mannheim was fairly old and not very well and he needed the money. He did the work quickly, but when the translation arrived, and it came in instalments, what worried me about it most were the American vulgarisms and colloquialisms, many of which did not exist in 1932 when the book first appeared in France. *Salaud* was translated by 'mother-fucker', *curé* (used abusively) as 'sky-pilot'. The first would bar the book from being read on school or university courses, the second would be simply incomprehensible. But the problems did not end there. With the Gallimard edition in front of me I quickly noticed a missing sentence, then a whole paragraph that was not there, as well as mistranslations and some condensations as if the book was being revised for digest. On more than one occasion I found places where Mannheim had turned two pages without noticing and had simply joined up sentences rather than going back to put in what he had missed. I edited the book carefully, translated what had been left out, and kept up a considerable and ever more angry correspondence with Mannheim, who I also visited occasionally. He did not like my objections to certain words and terms ('Céline would have wanted them'), nor did he like his lacunae being discovered.

New Directions had received a copy at the same time as myself. They had not bothered to check it but had gone straight into print. The result, because my editorial time was limited by all my other activities, was that they came out with the book two years before me, following their hardback very quickly with a cheaper paperback edition which is what I saw in Pat Wooley's warehouse. The problem was not limited to Australia: the American paperback established itself everywhere, including Britain, and it took years to oust it with my own complete edition.

The other big problem with Pat Wooley was her feminist view that any book by a woman had to be better than any book by a man, and as a result her whole sales effort went on such authors as Marguerite Duras and Nathalie Sarraute, of which I did not complain, while totally neglecting Beckett, Ionesco, and Robbe-Grillet. Miller and Burroughs were out in mass-market paperbacks, which Australian censorship having been dropped about five years after its *de facto* disappearance in Britain, made it impossible to sell my editions except to libraries. Pat really was just out of sympathy with most of my list.

I set out to show her what could be done. I spent two weeks in Sydney and its environs, calling on every possible bookshop, large and small, including the chains where I managed to get in more titles than they had ever stocked before. Of course I saw American editions everywhere and tried to use persuasion rather than threats to persuade them not to discontinue. I was everywhere well received, met many old friends that I had known in London, and I also called on the Features and Literary editors of newspapers to try to get some publicity. Some shops wanted to receive my books directly from Britain and I saw no reason not to agree. I met a number of authors, literary agents and publishers, went to the theatre and the opera, and often, after a hard day in the January heat that was often over 100 degrees Fahrenheit, went in the evening to one of the beaches to cool off in the ocean. One of the original partners in Writers and Readers Co-operative had gone to Sydney to set up a distribution for their books, but I did not feel that he would last long and did not consider going with him, although I knew I would eventually have to find an alternative to Wild and Wooley.

Sydney Opera House is an amazing building which now symbolises the city as Big Ben does London and the Eiffel Tower Paris. But inside, it is a mess. I saw two operas, *The Magic Flute* and *Otello*, one in the opera house so-called and the other in the concert hall. Basically they are two cinema shapes parallel to each other, the acoustics in the second being marginally better than in the Opera House. The performances were adequate, and I heard some singers who never came to Britain, most notably Joan Carden who sang opposite Alberto Remedios in *Otello*. Yvonne Kenny, later to make her mark in Britain, was Pamina in *Magic Flute* which Bonyinge conducted. One of my most memorable Paminas had been Joan Sutherland before she moved into the bel canto canary repertoire in the early fifties. Now Bonyinge would not let her sing it any more. I managed to get my opera guides into the opera house to be sold there, but foresaw trouble because there was no-one to really take responsibility for them and it would have been easy to steal them.

I discovered a charming restaurant just a little north of Bondi Beach after swimming there one night, where I could sit and watch the towers and lights of Sydney in the distance and eat seafood with a good dry white wine.

521

Although my hotel was a dump, it was very central and I stayed there throughout. I never used the restaurant and the bar had as many cockroaches as customers. The barman simply ignored them. King's Cross is the vice-district, so I was accosted by prostitutes several times a day. 'Why not?' they always said when I excused myself. Some were quite attractive, but I could think of several reasons why not.

I made many friends in Sydney and was invited to some pleasant dinners, but much as I intended to keep in touch with people who had been kind to me, I inevitably lost touch. It is just not possible, being as itinerant as I was after losing Ledlanet, to keep up with people other than those I was encountering at the time. I went to Melbourne next, which had an Irish look and feel to it, staying in the Italian quarter. I found several good outlets for my books which had never been properly presented there, many of them near the university and looked up the Wild and Wooley rep, who was unaware that they existed. I was taken to the Melbourne Club by Colin Duckworth, a Beckettian who was Professor of French at the university and was invited to his house. He was also much involved in the Australian theatre. I was later to publish his novel *Steps to the High Garden*. I met several authors, most notably Peter Craven and Gerald Murname and a young poet who slept out of doors because he said that in that climate it was quite unnecessary to pay rent just to have a roof over your head. Gerald Murname, who I liked very much and for a while considered publishing, was a real Melbourne eccentric: he had never been on a train or aeroplane in his life, and had never been out of Melbourne, but wrote novels about places he had never seen such as the Australian outback, that were realistic and convincing. 'I shall spend my life in the Melbourne suburbs,' he told me, 'and never see anywhere else.' He sounded wistful rather than sad. I also spent a day with Barrett Reid, who had once taught, and seduced Charles Osborne at his school in Brisbane. I went to a Saturday lunch party at his house and afterwards toured a local wood while he pointed out the local varieties of trees.

The I moved on to Adelaide, a very rectangular city, built of white stone, that somehow reminded me of parts of Cannes and Monte Carlo. Everywhere there were statues of royalty and long-dead generals. There were not many bookshops there for my kind of literature, but I made a useful contact with the Festival Theatre that sold some books. One evening I drove down to the sea and went onto an old sailing ship that was now a restaurant. A large group were celebrating at a nearby table. 'What are ye, a snob or something?' a large red-faced man shouted at me in his strong Aussie accent. 'Why don't you come and sit here?'

So I joined them. I sat next to a lively lady whose husband had won the golf tournament that afternoon, the reason for the celebration, but the man was so tired that most of the time his head was on the table. His wife told me how dull he was and how much she disliked golf. At one point the bawdy conversation got round to where a man should kiss a woman first and the waiter was asked his opinion. 'I wouldn't kiss her anywhere,' he said. 'I'm gay.'

'Oh, you're not are ye?' said my red-faced friend. 'Ye cahnt be. That's not Austrilian.' This set the table off on a new theme and the waiter was no doubt pleased when we left. I was invited round to the red-faced man's house where the party continued until it was getting light, at which point I left to drive back to my motel in Adelaide.

The next morning I was flying to Perth. First I drove back to the shore and left – it was early still on a Sunday morning – a half bottle of whisky, a bottle of wine and other things I had not consumed in my room, on the man's doorstep with a thank-you note, and drove on to the airport. That evening I drove around Perth to work out the next day's itinerary, because I had only two days to make all my calls. On Monday morning I went first to the university, then to Fremantle, the artistic suburb of Perth, and the next day called on the shops in town, none of which I found interesting. Then I had a night-flight to Singapore.

Singapore is a strange city. Then it was still under the iron rule of Lee Kuan Yew, an English-educated Chinese lawyer, who strictly enforced the law to such an extent that you were arrested if you dropped a piece of paper on the street, while such messy substances as chewing-gum were strictly banned. Tailors chased me down the street, fingering my suit and offering to make me a new one in a single day. My local agent was the Singapore Times that had its own bookshops and they ordered from my new book catalogue, after which I went to the university to find that in a country with no copyright their practice was to buy one copy of a book, which was then available to be photocopied cheaply on the spot by students and staff, in part or in full. A long line of photocopiers were in constant use. There was not much else to do there. In the evening I wanted to have a Malaysian meal and asked a taxi to find me a restaurant that was Malaysian. He took me a considerable distance to a cinema and told me there was a restaurant on the first floor. But it turned out to be Chinese, so I left. There were no taxis in that part of town and I started to walk back towards the centre. And then the monsoon hit the streets.

Within a minute I was drenched through, and as the air was very warm, steam rose from my body. For an hour I tramped along the street in the downpour until I reached some lighted shops and managed to buy an umbrella, not that it now made any difference. I eventually came to a long market-place where there was a double row of little kitchens under canvas. Each had a different dish to offer and alongside, also under canvas, were table and chairs. The idea was to go down the line of kitchens, fill a plate with what attracted your eye and eat at one of the tables, which I did, washing the food down with beer. I was having a Malaysian dinner at last, drenched through, but not cold. Then I walked back to my hotel, took off my clothes and walked gratefully into a hot shower.

The next day I flew to Bombay. This was all part of the round-the-world ticket. I did not enjoy my two days in Bombay. The taxi that took me to my hotel nearly bumped into a cow and if it had touched her I am sure the driver would have been lynched. A crowd gathered round and threatened him with sticks. The hotel was perfectly decent with separate European and Indian restaurants, but I only ate in the Indian one, except for breakfast. Every time I went out of the hotel I was surrounded by children with outstretched palms, many of them being guided by seated women on the roadside, and any change I had was quickly dispensed. I took a taxi to see my agent who had never sold my books well. He was in an office overlooking a dirty and cluttered courtyard in a dilapidated building that might once have been white. He looked through my catalogue. 'Why don't you publish some books on cricket?' was the only comment I remember.

My room overlooked the docks and the sea which was a few hundred yards away and I was on the top floor so I had a good view. The wide street in front of the hotel had hundreds of bodies sitting or lying on them, some of the millions of homeless who are born, live out their existence and die in the open. Periodically I would see a line of mourners following a dead body being taken to be burned at a large incinerating open space that was just visible in the distance. Long columns of black smoke constantly rose from it. Twice I saw lorries passing slowly while the municipal employees searched among the homeless poor for those who had died in the street. Their bodies were unceremoniously thrown into the open lorries which were making their way to the funeral pyres in the distance.

I am told that there is much to enjoy in Bombay, but the poverty and misery distressed me so much that after the visit to my agent and one or two brief sorties into the open I stayed in the hotel, either in my room or talking to other Europeans in the hotel bar, which would not serve anything alcoholic to Indians. The bureaucracy at the airport to leave the country was frustrating: I had to pay for an exit visa, have my luggage searched and fill out more forms before I could get on my flight. From there I went to Frankfurt, where I spent a night at the airport hotel and then on to London.

* * * * * *

In 1985 driving towards Paris after the Frankfurt Book Fair I heard on the car radio that Claude Simon had just been awarded the Nobel Prize, another in the long list of my authors who had won major literary awards. It was a brief announcement at the end of a BBC news bulletin and it was not repeated an hour later. Back in London where I was constantly appealing against the loss of my Arts Council subsidy, I spoke to Luke Rittner, then Secretary General of the Arts Council. He was unaware of who had won the

Nobel Prize and supremely uninterested. In reply to my letter written at about this time he replied that the Council had decided that my list was no longer considered to be of any interest or importance. As I was publishing the same writers who had been considered worthy of subsidy earlier, this made no sense, but it was ideology, not sense that mattered now. Two other prizes came our way at the same time, the Italia for Howard Barker's radio play *Scenes from an Execution* and the Scott-Moncreiff awarded to Barbara Wright for her translations of Nathalie Sarraute. I pointed out in my reply to Luke Rittner that the juries who decided major prizes obviously had a higher opinion of our authors than the Arts Council Literature Committee, but he never answered.

I had never been to Stockholm, although I could have gone on any of the previous occasions when an author of mine had won the Nobel Prize, but now I decided that this was an experience I should undergo at least once in my life. I went at the beginning of December and it was already dark when the 'plane landed at 14.30. I went to the hotel, rested and was picked up for dinner by Claude Simon's Swedish publisher to be taken to a restaurant where about twenty of us, including Simon's various publishers from many countries, all had a pleasant evening. Jerôme Lindon was among them and as few of the others spoke French I mostly conversed with him. He was an old hand in Stockholm, having been there to collect Beckett's Nobel Prize in 1969, because Sam would never go to any such public occasion. The next day I visited some bookshops in the morning and in the early afternoon put on my dinner jacket and joined a special bus that took us to the National Theatre for the Prize-giving ceremony. A citation was read out for each laureate, which took about two hours as there were many winners in different disciplines; the prizes were awarded by the King of Sweden who officiated in his uniform, saying a few words to each before handing over the citation and a cheque. In between, the Stockholm Symphony Orchestra played short pieces of music. Then we were taken in buses to the Town Hall where a large banquet was waiting for about two thousand people, perhaps more. I sat next to a university bookseller from Uppsala who wanted my catalogue and filled me in about the proceedings. We had a long drinkless wait until the royal party arrived, the King, his family and the court officials parading along a gallery above the hall, followed by all the Nobel Prize winners. The band accompanied the arriving top tables by playing *Land of Hope and Glory*, much to my surprise. The dinner was a long one and our wine glasses were not even filled more than twice.

At the end of the banquet some of the Nobel Prize winners consented to say a few words and the atmosphere was by now much more relaxed. The most amusing came from an American who had won a physics or chemistry prize. 'You know,' he began, 'I come from California where Nobel Prize winners are thick on the ground in the universities. One day, recently, I was driving with my wife through the desert and we had to stop for gas at a little isolated shack with a single pump. The man put the nozzle in the gas tank and then started to kiss my wife and she kissed him back, a long embrace. "Well," I said as we drove away, "what was that all about?"

"Oh. He used to be my boyfriend."

"Well, just think. Now you're married to a Nobel Prize winner."

"But if I'd married him, he would be a Nobel Prize winner."'

After the banquet we were moved to the adjoining hall where the party went on until dawn. I managed to talk to Claude Simon, who was constantly being pulled away to be interviewed by press and television and photographed. He was unhappy that he had had to bring his wife and not his girlfriend, Eva, who was the sister of his Finnish publisher, Eerki Reempaa, a man I liked very much. It was Eerki who on one occasion at the Frankfurt Book Fair was approached by Swifty Lazare, a Hollywood literary agent. He interrupted our conversation to say, 'I understand that you are the biggest publisher in Finland, so I am going to offer you Richard Nixon's biography, and he mentioned the two million dollar advance that was being paid in America.

'Excuse me,' said Eerki, 'I am talking to my friend Mr. Calder. If you paid me a million dollars I would not publish Richard Nixon. Please go away.'

Claude Simon was always complaining of the slowness with which I brought out his novels in English compared to the speed with which they appeared in Finnish. It was only about this time that I realised that it was Eva Reempaa who was behind the Finnish interest. It was Jerôme Lindon who on this occasion had told Claude that he had to bring his wife and this was no occasion to flaunt his mistress.

There was a lunch the next day in the offices of the Swedish publisher with Claude Simon present. 'You have made us very happy,' said the publisher in a little speech in English. I then went to a reception to open an exhibition at the French Institute with photographs and memorabilia to do with Simon's life, especially his involvement in the Spanish Civil War and Second World War, and stayed another day to visit more booksellers, resisting with difficulty the blandishments of Swedish friends to stay longer ('You haven't even been to the Stockholm Opera! How can you resist that?') and returned to London.

During the following year I saw Claude Simon with Eva twice in New York, went with them to see a sculpture by a friend of his which had been erected on Wall Street, took them to El Quixote, which he much enjoyed ('Je suis chez moi') and on his advice went to see an exhibition of African sculpture at the Metropolitan Museum, which however I failed to find interesting. I also visited him several times at his flat in Paris. But little by little I saw how the Nobel Prize with all the razzmatazz that went with it had changed him. The simple man who had the eye, the style, and the questing mind of a great writer was now taking his celebrity seriously and he became aloof and unaccommodating. His two greatest novels, *The Flanders Road*, published in 1960 and *The Georgics*, which appeared in 1981, had convinced the Nobel jury. Thereafter the literary impulse seems weaker. He wrote a short book about winning the Nobel Prize and what had happened in Stockholm, which has some interest, but I saw no reason to translate a book that could have no English language sale. He had always been difficult to put over to the reading public, even in France. The problem in my opinion lay in the padding, the quite unnecessary long-winded pages of description that had little to do with his main theme, because in essence he describes actions and the motivations behind them, drawing general conclusions from the events of history. One has to wade through much extraneous matter to get to what is important, and this shows a lack of self-discipline in the writer that increasingly in the late work becomes self-indulgence. An intelligent and sensitive editor could help him to prune his work, but by the time he had won the Nobel Prize it was too late. This is a great pity because the best of Simon is superb, his images of war and battle are unforgettable, and he can make the reader feel the futility and the horror of human conflict, the corruption that surrounds it and the hunger for profit that so often causes it. His elderly and incompetent Generals, his panic-stricken staff clerks, and miserable mistreated cannon-fodder soldiers are beautifully drawn and totally believable, but one has to wade through much drudge to get there. This is not the case with the earlier novels, masterpieces of a more economically written style, and they still wait rediscovery by a new generation of intelligent readers. The day may come when judicious editing will find him a new readership because he deserves the sales that go to Bellow, Vidal, Grass and the best South American writers who have achieved both literary recognition and best-seller status. Two years after the Nobel Prize his sales with me had slumped to a trickle and he was not doing well in France either. It was a constant effort to keep any of his novels on the shelves of the better bookshops.

* * * * * *

I was driving through the Scottish Highlands in April 1987 on one of my bookselling trips when I saw a telephone box by the side of Loch Ness and stopped to telephone my office. They asked me to ring Jim Knowlson immediately and when I did he told me that Sam Beckett had collapsed in the street in Paris and was in hospital. This had happened before and was to happen again during the next two years. Sam hated having people help him stand up again and he took to going out less, and as his sorties were largely to get food, he was soon undernourished, and in addition he had contracted emphysema. He was trying to give up smoking and found it difficult to overcome the habit of a lifetime. I was very worried, but he recovered enough to be allowed home.

The previous year had seen his eightieth birthday. For this occasion I put together a second *Festschrift*. The one I had produced twenty years earlier for his sixtieth birthday, *Beckett at 60*, was long out of print. It had contained a long list of contributors from Arikha and Arrabal to Alan Schneider and Alan Simpson, taking in writers like Pinter, performers like Madeleine Renaud and many old friends and colleagues, a collection of reminiscences and tributes. The new one I called *As No Other Dare Fail*, a quotation from the last of the *Duthuit Dialogues*, which I have recorded above in connection with my first reading of *Worstward Ho*. It contained longer articles about the writings from critics, as well as personal memories, and by now there were new people to contribute. I confined my contribution to an introductory article entitled *Embarrassing Mr. Beckett*, because I knew that he really did not want this *Festschrift* and would be unavoidably embarrassed by it, but we all wanted to do it. Tom Bishop at NYU in New York did much more for the birthday. In Paris and New York he put together a series of events to celebrate the anniversary, again against the author's wish, but Sam, hating publicity of a personal kind, nevertheless submitted to the inevitable.

In Paris most of it took place at the Pompidou Centre. There was an exhibition of John Minihan's Beckett photographs in the downstairs lobby where the theatre held a number of lectures and discussions. I met Ruby Cohn in the street on the morning of the day when we would both be speaking, but she would not stop to talk as she had to practice her French. My own talk, on a platform I shared with Colin Duckworth, there from Australia, was entitled *Beckett et St. Francis d'Assise* and in it I compared Sam's generosity to that of the saint who gave a beggar his cloak, finding in their mutual love of animals another link between them. The conference went on for a week and was supplemented by David Warrilow giving a recitation of *The Lost Ones*, accompanied by his moving a collection of miniature marionettes, rather like toy soldiers, around inside a cylinder shown in section with the audience sitting around him in what was a small arena in Barrault's Theatre du Rond-Point. In the same programme was an interesting version of *Come and Go* where the three women were all shown in mirrors placed above their invisible sitting bodies. There were more events at the American Centre and elsewhere. Minihan's photographs were a great success and in a generous gesture he allowed the Pompidou Centre to keep them, which he would later regret. Minihan had managed to get entry to Beckett after he had left his very fine series of photographs of an Irish wake in Athy for Sam to look at, and thereafter he had been allowed, with some reluctance, to take photographs, some of them in 1980 in rehearsal at Riverside Studios in London when Beckett had been there to overlook Rick Cluchy's productions before they went to Australia.

Barney Rosset came from New York. He had now sold Grove Press to George Weidenfeld, who had persuaded Ann Getty to put up the money so that they could run it together, but Grove was really only a stalking-horse to enable George to get Getty money into his own company Weidenfeld and Nicolson in England. Barney now thought that his money worries were over and that he could go on running the company as he always had. He had brought with him, all travelling by Concorde, his wife Lissa, his son Peter by an earlier marriage, Ann Getty's son, then a student at Yale, and a friend of his, another student. The young Getty and his friend were staying at the Ritz and Barney with the film director Joe Strick, an old friend, on the Rue de Seine. One morning Barney and Lissa were in a taxi with Minihan and myself when Barney began to abuse his wife who had taken a letter for him to Getty at the Ritz. He accused her of wanting to sleep with the young man because of his wealth, quite illogically and in a sudden flare-up, which was quite common with him. That night a large group of us were at the Coupole and the only one who never contributed to the bill was Getty, who apparently took it as his seigniorial right to be entertained by others. I certainly paid much more than my fair share and Minihan was commenting on it years later.

Although he would take no part in the proceedings, Sam was persuaded by Tom Bishop to meet a small group of friends at the bar of the Coupole late one afternoon. Barney was invited with strict instructions to come on his own. Tom's annoyance when Barney walked in leading Lissa, Peter, Getty and Getty's friend, a black student, was intense, but all he could do was fume. Sam only stayed a few minutes then left.

Throughout the conference Barney had been staying at Joe Strick's just around the corner from my Michelet-Odeon. On the morning that he had to leave with his entourage to fly back by Concorde he came round to my hotel at nine o'clock. 'Can I get a beer here?' he asked and sounded desperate. The hotel did not cater, but managed on this occasion to find two bottles of beer which he drank thirstily. Barney could never start the day without some alcohol.

Ruby Cohn lectured me on not seeing Sam often enough, and as this was the period when I was doing much travelling in North America, she was probably right. He had given her permission to put together a collection of his unpublished writings, mostly early critical work, but including a number of letters and the fragments of an early unfinished play about Dr. Johnson, *Human Wishes*, which I had published earlier in 1983.

Less than a month after Paris Tom Bishop did the same thing in New York, and I took part in one of two symposiums and chaired an evening of Beckett's poetry. There was another exhibition of Minihan's photographs, and again, flattered by the attention and praise, John said that NYU could keep the large prints: again he was to regret it. The main reason was that in both cases magazines and the authors of books about Beckett made use of these photographs without any payment to the photographer in whom copyright still resided. It was suspected that in some cases fees were paid, but not to John Minihan.

Tom Bishop had lined up a long list of American and Irish poets, to read Beckett's poems and some prose in a large hall at NYU, and among others were his wife Helen, Susan Sontag and the Vice-Chancellor of the University, Jay Oliva. I was worried by the number of readers because it is a mistake to make a Beckett evening too long. Helen Bishop wanted to read *Rockaby*, which was twenty minutes on its own. I told Tom we would have to have a rehearsal, but he said that it was impossible to ask well-known poets and celebrities to rehearse. The only person who wanted to go over what he had to read was the Vice Chancellor, who had been given *Whorescope*. I spent two hours with him going over it, and in the event he was the best of them all.

Just before the reading there came disturbing news, but not surprising to me. Barney Rossett had just been fired from Grove. In spite of all my past problems with him I felt sorry and had the idea of making an announcement at the poetry reading if Barney could manage to sit through it, because it could only be made at the end of the evening.

I started the proceedings by reading, or rather reciting because I had gone to the trouble of memorising it, the opening page of *Worstward Ho* and was followed by the poets. In spite of my fears, Helen Bishop got through *Rockaby* in very fast time without spoiling the rhythms. Unfortunately some of the best-known poets were poor readers – I forget whether it was John Ashbury or Richard Howard who was the biggest disappointment – but the biggest problem came near the end of the evening when Susan Sontag, to whom I had given the last three pages of *Ill Seen Ill Said* to read, decided on her own to read much more, and she went back in the text to give us a quarter of the book. In the meantime Barney, getting ever more impatient, was sitting in the front row waiting for the announcement, and we were considerably over-time with people, including the press, starting to leave. As soon as Susan had finished I made the announcement, which caused an exclamation of disbelief and shock and did not please Susan Sontag one bit, because I had cut short her applause. Then I finished with the last paragraphs of *Worstward Ho* and ended the evening.

Tom Bishop had invited all the readers and a few others back to his house in Washington Mews. 'You made up for a few sins tonight,' said Barney, 'and you had many sins to make up for!'

Barney was now in a difficult situation. He was well-known and admired in New York because Grove had the biggest reputation there for introducing avant-garde literature. He had published many of the beat writers, taken on my European list except where Seaver had done this directly, while Fred Jordan, a German who had spent some time in England as a refugee before moving to New York, had been responsible for German-language literature. I had my quarrels with Fred. He had tried to make trouble for me with Robert Jungk and I had always found him shifty and devious. Now with Barney gone he managed to increase his role at Grove as an editor and missed no opportunity to bad-mouth Barney, who whatever his many faults, had always been good to him and had overlooked his many incompetencies, because Fred was willing to crawl, flatter and accept abuse to keep Barney's favour. Claudia and I had a name for him: Uriah Heep. Barney did not quite know what to do next, but he was not going to give up. About this time Lissa, his fourth wife, left him and he developed a relationship with Astrid Myers, a lady who had not only charm and good looks, but was able to understand Barney well enough to put up with his tantrums, infidelities and many eccentricities. She was the best thing that had happened to him in years, perhaps ever, and she helped him to reorganise himself.

My mind could not help going back to a lunch with George Weidenfeld at the Caledonian Club at the time of his negotiations with Barney. George was then very afraid of Barney renegeing on the deal before it was signed, but the purchase was the key to getting some Getty money into his own concern. He knew exactly what the Getty income was per second and was savouring it as if it were his own. He was feeling me out to see if I would also be willing to sell, because then he would have the world market on many important authors, but I was in no way tempted. Then a short time later, the deal finally sealed, there was a party in San Francisco to celebrate it in the Getty mansion during the ABA. Martin Esslin, with whom I had lunched at Stanford a few days before, was a frequent guest there now as a prestigious intellectual and had told me of the set-up. Weidenfeld was much around the Getty mansion, acting as host and very much at home there, flattering the local dowagers at lunches and paying great attention to his hostess. Getty himself was never seen. He was a composer who spent his time in his sound-proof music room writing music of a very traditional stamp and by contributing funds to orchestras and occasionally opera houses he managed to get some of it played. I often ran into Ernest Fleichman, whom I had known in London, and who was now Manager of the Los Angeles Philharmonic. He was a frequent target for Getty, and another was Peter Hemmings, who after Scottish Opera and Australian Opera had been brought by Fleishman to Los Angeles to start the opera company there. Peter had half-heartedly agreed to give Getty's short opera *Fat Jack* on the theme of Falstaff, but I do not believe he ever did it. Ann Getty was obviously a grass widow and Weidenfeld had become her *cavalière gallante*. The ABA party was a lavish one, and they gave another for academics in City Lights. One night I saw Ann, George and a group of their friends, looking extremely uncomfortable in a North Beach bar called Tosca which had become iconic because the beats had used it during the fifties. Barney was being made much of then and was naïve enough to think that his troubles were over. By the spring of 1986 he knew the truth.

The newspapers carried many stories about Ann Getty and George Weidenfeld, who were seen together in New York, in Frankfurt and many other places, and there was much speculation and innuendo about what their real relationship was. Barney cut all those out of newspapers and magazines and sent them to the husband. George set up a translation prize with a conference in Leeds Castle, but it was obvious that only his own translators could win it. He organised another conference in Israel, one purpose of which was to promote Getty's music, so the composer went. John Rusby-Smith brought his new girlfriend, Margaret, whom he later married, a singer. Getty was all over her, wanting her to sing his songs. 'But they're not right for my voice,' she complained. 'That's alright, my Dear,' he insisted. 'I'll arrange them any way you like.'

George Weidenfeld had made it his business to know as many important figures in world politics and big business as possible. He took Ann Getty around to introduce her to crowned heads, prime ministers, influential ambassadors and others who might impress her, but the indications were that although flattered, she was extremely bored. George hired some very expensive New York publishing executives, and, knowing the Getty income per second, he thought that expenditure would never matter. But he reckoned without the Getty business managers, who when they saw the first accounts of Grove-Weidenfeld, stepped in to stop it. Many millions had been lost and there seemed little likelihood of improvement. I do not know the mechanics of Weidenfeld's dismissal, but Getty must have been persuaded that he and his wife had been made fools of, and George retreated to Britain. Some time later he met a very rich American lady, who saved him once again, but thereafter he sold Weidenfeld and Nicolson, while remaining titular chairman. Ann Getty had paid a single visit to the Grove office during all that time, and had been two hours on the telephone ordering clothes for the weekend. As far as I know she has never given her own account of the whole affair.

* * * * * *

During the time I had known Maurice Girodias in New York, some years earlier, he had taken me one day to a strange congress in a large New York hotel where Armando Verdiglione had organised a conference lasting several days on sexuality, and he introduced me to the presiding genius, an Italian psychiatrist who published a journal called Spirale which appeared in separate French and Italian editions. The congress was partly to promote the journal, more to promote himself, a man who seemed to have unlimited private means. When he heard I was publisher with offices in London and New York, he became interested, and the following year I was invited to Rome to a similar congress and a year after that to one in Tokyo.

I arrived in Rome directly from New York in the morning and went straight to bed in my hotel, only to be woken an hour later and told that I was expected right away on the platform to speak. Dressing hurriedly and feeling very tired I took a taxi to the hotel where the conference, again on sexuality, but in connection with literature, was being held, and found myself on a platform with three other speakers, one of whom was the French intellectual novelist and theoretician Vivienne Forrestier, who was talking about Nathalie Sarraute as I arrived. I had intended to prepare something for the next day, but had not a thought in my mind until I got up to speak, which I did for about twenty minutes, I think in French, but I cannot even be sure of that and have no memory at all of what I spoke about. I seem to remember answering some questions in Italian. No doubt I mixed my languages. Nobody seemed concerned and I received the usual splattering of polite applause. For the next two days I listened to others, enjoyed Verdiglione's hospitality, went to a literary party where I met some publishers I knew and flirted mildly with an attractive woman journalist. Nobody seemed to know exactly what Verdiglione was up to or where the money came from. We were all present for his own talk, *Playing My Own Guitar*, which I found rather incomprehensible.

I was surprised to be reinvited to Tokyo, but I was. The flight left from Paris and on the 'plane were many people I knew, my authors Arrabal and the very elderly Borges, several journalists and a scattering of mostly French intellectual figures. I spent much of the time – not on the 'plane, because he was too fat to sit anywhere except first class – with François Erval from Gallimard, who edited their *Idées* series and was responsible for books from Germany and Eastern Europe; he was also co-editor of La Quinzième Littéraire, a small circulation but influential literary periodical. It was a long flight with a short stop-over at Anchorage, but this time, on arrival in the evening I was able to go to bed.

Verdiglione's conferences always inspired many rumours. People like François Erval went because they wanted to see interesting foreign cities and only a few actually spoke, although everybody, except a few big names who were there mainly to be interviewed, photographed and to lend weight by their presence, expected to speak. There were a few erudite and several not so erudite short lectures from professors, authors, journalists and scientists. It was obvious that Verdiglione saw me as a potential English-language publisher and he could obviously afford to subsidise such publication, but I was unsure of what he was trying to say and why. The purpose of the conferences was a mystery to everyone. The first laugh in Tokyo came from a Japanese speaker – about a third of those present were Japanese – who spoke in English and said that it was not really acceptable in Japan to speak about sex in public and especially not in the morning. Erval was anxious to take a day to see Kyoto and we agreed to go together. But Verdiglione, every time I tried to leave the room even for a pee, would stop me at the door, saying that I was expected to speak in a minute. Finally we took a whole day off and an early train to Kyoto. At the station some business executive was leaving on a trip and his whole office was there to see him off, all the women with handkerchiefs in their hands simulating tears. We passed Mount Fuji, not very high and surrounded by factory chimneys pushing out smoke, very unlike the postcard images. We visited Kyoto's temples and palaces and took the train back. Erval, a compulsive eater not only had a big lunch, but insisting on stopping all the girls going through the train ringing little bells with different dishes on offer, to have each one. Not only did he eat everything on offer throughout the conference, but he would buy hamburgers at night to take to his room. We found it almost impossible to find anything actually made in Japan: everything in the shops was made in Europe or America. The final straw was seeing 'Benihana of New York' on a sign.

I was only called on to speak on the day we were in Kyoto, so to my relief I never did. I really had nothing to say to people who had no idea why they were there, except as cultural tourists and to see interesting people. That was the last time I saw Borges who died not long after. I had seen him frequently on his London visits in the sixties. He was still lucid, but very frail, and I have no idea why he braved such an arduous journey at his age.

My trips to Paris now tended to be brief, at most three days. They usually included a lunch or dinner with Sam Beckett, more often than not these days at the PLM across the street from his apartment, where I seldom visited him now. Among the coach parties of Japanese and American tourists at the PLM he could be anonymous and to cross the road was only a small risk. He was very distressed about Barney who had written to ask if there could be some text he could publish on his own. He had already started a new imprint called Blue Moon and was soon to start another, North Star, for specialised short work and poetry. Obviously Astrid's name had some bearing on this.

Sam was reluctant to let Barney publish old works that he had held back. He considered allowing him to do the untranslated *Eleutheria*, written before *Godot*, a rather Pirandelloian play which Blin might well have performed had it not had a larger cast and more complicated stage decor than the latter which had launched Beckett's career into world-wide fame. But he decided against it. Then he thought of the unpublished first novel, *Dream of Fair to Middling Women*, but hated this early work, so he started on a new text, a short one, to which he gave the title *Stirrings Still*. He dedicated it to Barney and sent it to him and to me at the same time. It was a description of an old man, alone in his room, dreaming of getting out into the open air, only a few pages. But then new inspiration came and he wrote a second section and then a third. But it was still only a few pages. I could publish it on its own or else hold it until I was able to reprint the *Collected Shorter Prose*, which I had put together and first published in 1984, at the same time as a complete edition of all the poems that I was allowed to publish in both languages. On its own *Stirrings Still* would only make twenty pages. Many artists had been illustrating special editions of the shorter works and it occurred to me that that was the best way to go, to do a limited edition with illustrations by an acceptable and well-known artist. Barney and I could then share the edition. He immediately liked the idea when I suggested it to him, but insisted that his first wife Joan Mitchell should be the artist. She was now living alone with two Alsatian dogs in a village outside Paris, where she had a house and a studio at the bottom of her garden. I went to see her there to discuss it. We had lunch in a restaurant, then I read her the whole text, commenting on it, and with some reluctance she agreed to try to come up with some visual element for a limited edition. She had tremendous admiration for Sam, who had always been attracted to her. Physically she was very much his type, solidly built, of slightly less than medium height, outspoken and uninhibited. Since her relationship with the Canadian artist Jean-Paul Riopelle had ended, she had lived alone and been drinking heavily. During our day together we got through several bottles of wine. I looked at her recent work, mainly abstract and not far from that of her mentor Willem de Kooning, and as it got dark I left her. She always worked at night and was ready to start.

We corresponded about the illustrations and then, apparently because she had read something derogatory about me from one of my old girlfriends in a newspaper, she wrote that she had decided not to proceed. There may have been another reason, such as the not being able to come up to the challenge of the text. I asked Sam for another suggestion and he told me to come to his apartment. When I entered I saw that he had a row of books lined up on the desk between us. They were all illustrated by Louis de Brocquy. 'What about Louis?' he suggested.

'Sam, you know perfectly well that I'll accept any artist you want,' I said. 'I'm perfectly happy with Le Brocquy.' I only knew rather vaguely about him, and I already owned several of the books displayed on Sam's writing table, but I had to convince Barney who finally, somewhat reluctantly, accepted that it could not be Joan. I went down to Nice to see Louis, who lived and had his studio in the hills behind the town. I spent a pleasant day with him and his wife, Anne Madden. He had recently attended a wine auction where he had rather overextended himself by buying a large quantity of very good wine and he was rather rueful about it, but I at least had some of the benefit. He agreed with enthusiasm, but wanted me to print with a local art printer who had worked with Picasso, Matisse and others. We went to visit him and I liked the work he was doing. Terms were agreed all around and I took the address of Peter Wilbur who Louis wanted to design the book. I found a suitable binder in Paris on the Rue du Four and selected orange soft calf for the binding; unfortunately it was never used as Wilbur had other ideas and picked an oatmeal linen instead. I had many meetings with Peter Wilbur in London, an experienced designer who organised the type-setting and lay-out of the book in London, and eventually the sheets were printed in Provence and the book bound in Paris. I always intended to collect the expensive orange calf-skin, but with all the problems of the following months, never did. It was all much trouble and expense, but we ended up with a handsome book, quarter-bound in parchment, with natural linen and cotton cloth, printed by Pierre Chave in Vence on French deckle-edged Velin de Rives, and signed by Samuel Beckett and Louis de Brocquy. The two hundred and twenty-six copies were numbered one to two hundred, and twenty-six copies were lettered. It had a slip-case of the same material as the binding. The Le Brocquy illustrations included an impression of Beckett's face for the front cover embossed in gold, a complex portrait as a frontispiece in colour from which, after a few minutes study, one could make out Beckett's face leaning forward as if to sign the book and eight very effective black and white lithographs. The plate was broken after printing and Le Brocquy was promised we would not try to reproduce the illustrations. Not long after that Barney would break the promise without telling anyone and he used miniature reproductions of the lithographs in a small paperback edition.

That however was not the worst of his misdeeds. As the binding was very expensive I only bound initially forty copies, twenty for each of us, plus the lettered copies which were to go largely to Sam's list of special friends. I spent much time going around London, Paris and New York, delivering these by hand. One went to the doctor who at that point was calling on him every day (I had trouble finding his address), and of course Jerôme Lindon got one, Arikha the artist, Tom Bishop and I forget who else from the long list that Sam gave me. We sold our twenty bound copies at £2,000 each to collectors and I told the Paris binder to bind twenty more. Then I discovered they were gone. I had paid the binder on account, but not yet his whole bill, and Barney having gone secretly to Paris, paid off the binder, only for the binding of course, bound up the rest of the edition and took them all to the States. I insisted that he send back immediately the eighty that were mine, but he replied that I would have to pay the remaining binding costs first. As I had not wanted them bound yet, I said No. The wrangling went on, and then as he owed money to Lyall Stewart he gave him all the copies as security. I did at a later date manage to extract one for a special purpose, but that is another story.

In the summer of 1988 Beckett had another fall, this time at home, and after recovering in hospital, Edward, his nephew, found a place for him where he could be looked after. It was a retirement home called Le Tiers Temps and he was the only man there: the other residents were all old women who spent the day in the lounge looking at television and dozing. Beckett preferred to stay in his room and had all his meals brought to him there. The food was, like all hospital food, uninteresting and watery, and I tried to find a way of having good restaurant meals with things Sam liked brought in occasionally, but he would not hear of it. He would sit there picking the vegetables out of his plate and leaving the meat. I visited him more often now and it was in Le Tiers Temps that he signed all the copies of *Stirrings Still*, completing them in a day. He would read a little, but not much, spending some time doing crossword puzzles, only occasionally trying to write. On one visit he asked me how to spell 'hedgehog', then went on to say it didn't matter. He had changed it to 'porcupine'. I was less worried by his memory going than by realising that he did not have a dictionary: he had brought nothing from home. The next day I bought him the Collins-Robert English-French dictionary so that he would have the two languages and dropped it round. One day he had a visit from Tom Bishop and said, 'I'm sorry about this and I know perfectly well who you are, but I cannot at this moment think of your name.' Tom was very upset and kept referring to it every time I saw him.

He was very accessible to anyone walking in on him now. There was no concierge that I ever saw, and if you knew where the room was you simply went and knocked. He must have had several unwelcome visits, but he was always happy to see old friends. Most visitors would bring him a bottle of whisky, and he never lacked either wine or spirits to drink, but after the 'hedgehog' incident I would bring books. I brought him Ellmann's Yeats biography, a new book on Norah Joyce and other volumes in line with his interests, occasionally a novel by a new Irish writer such as John Banville. Several regulars went to see him there including Peter Lennon, and John Montague brought in a group of visiting Irish writers one day. Once when I went to see him I had Sheila Colvin with me. She did not at all mind being left in the lounge because she understood that he only wanted to see old friends now, but Sam asked after her and I admitted she was outside. He immediately brightened up. 'Oh, bring her in,' he said and I did. There were only two glasses, so she used his tooth-mug and told me afterwards the whisky tasted of toothpaste. On one occasion I was there when Suzanne telephoned and for some time he was on the line, humouring her, but obviously some kind of quarrel was going on, and he eventually put the instrument down with a sigh, saying he would call the next day.

In January 1988 I made my second trip to Australia and this time brought Muriel Leyner with me. We left on New Year's Eve from Los Angeles, asked for champagne at midnight, which they reluctantly brought because they were saving it for the Australian New Year a couple of hours later. In Fuji we had a stop-over of several hours and then took a different 'plane because we were going first of all to New Zealand. There was a coup just then in Fuji and the situation was tense, but rather than having to wait eight hours at the airport, I took a taxi to a holiday hotel, where we could sleep, eat and bathe in the pool until departure time, trying not to look directly at the young soldiers – they all seemed to be about fourteen – who were carrying machine guns and seemed prepared to use them. The other problem, which we only discovered later, was that all our luggage had gone to Australia, instead of being transferred to our New Zealand flight. We bought bathing suits and beach clothes at the hotel, which was our only change of clothing when we finally arrived in Auckland. We were met by my New Zealand agents, the Kranses, an American couple who had gone to live there during the McCarthy period in the US to escape the poisonous political atmosphere. They had worked for Oxford University Press for years and now represented a number of publishers, having converted a shed at the bottom of their garden into a small warehouse. They took us to a hotel that was really a service flat with a wonderful view and left us there. The next day, a Sunday, I spent with them in their house going carefully over my list and the day after went selling books in Auckland with Krans. His excited face when the two of us returned in the evening was a picture. 'Look at this,' he said to his wife, 'some of these orders are three pages'. We had taken orders for several hundred books that day, more than he had ever sold in a year.

My author Christopher Small, who had grown up in Hamilton North in New Zealand was in Auckland, and we saw him briefly. He had been giving some lectures and was about to return to London. We went next to his home town, as dull a little place as one could imagine and I easily understood why he had left it. Arriving in the evening it took a while to find our hotel and then there seemed to be nowhere to eat. Seeing some girls getting cash at a machine we followed them and sure enough they led us to a Chinese restaurant, which seemed to be the only place still open. The next day I did the bookshops, took some orders and continued driving south. Wellington was the next stop, a town that has several mini-earthquakes every day, where I again sold books and then drove back to Auckland, from which, after a week on North Island we went to Melbourne. I had been advised that South Island was so depopulated that it was not worth the trip, but I probably made a mistake.

New Zealand seemed to be caught in a time warp, and was very like the Scotland of the thirties. The cars were mostly from that decade, were constantly repaired and kept on the road, because the tax on imports was so heavy. I met a few local poets and liked the people, all very British, but they seemed to be living half a century earlier. Attitudes were provincial and as the country is a long strip of land between two coasts everyone seemed to have a boat, the main leisure activity. The big discovery were the excellent white wines, then unknown in Europe. And the people, with little to worry them, were all exceptionally nice.

In Melbourne I made contact with Detlef Thema, a young German who was selling our books there and I was at least able to evoke some enthusiasm for them. I knew where the bookshops were from my previous visit and sold the list well, leaving it to Detlef to keep on after I had left. We were well entertained by Mary and Colin Duckworth, saw *My Fair Lady* at the Opera House where June Bronhill, who had delighted London in the fifties at Sadlers Wells in Mozart soubrette roles and many other parts, was still able to sing a small part. She was obviously a local heroine: born June

Gough, she had taken the name of the town that had raised the money to train her voice and send her to Britain, and she still had charm and some voice left at fifty-eight. Seeing her brought back memories of her high soprano, perfect diction and tone, and bouncy vivacity in so many lighter roles I had seen at the Wells, and of her *Lucia* at Covent Garden, where she had replaced Joan Sutherland. She had more applause than the stars that evening.

Then we went to Sydney, gripped by Centennial fever. The tall ships were there from all over the world, the Prince of Wales had come to represent the Queen and was nearly assassinated, and a few days of public holiday meant enforced leisure for me. But we went to *The Magic Flute*, the same production as on my earlier visit, but with singers all unknown to me, and to *Carmen*, but for some reason I did not record the cast in my opera record book, probably because I lost the programme. Sydney was very busy, the town full of sailors and tourists who had come for the Centennial. I looked up a few people I had known from my previous visit, saw some theatre, found a few new customers, and some new restaurants, but my books were now in a Melbourne warehouse, and the situation had changed little since my previous visit. The years when I went to Australia were years of reasonable sales; in other years they were invariably poor.

Muriel returned to America and I continued westward, spending time again in Adelaide and Perth, much as on the previous visit. Then I flew to Munich, with a change of 'plane in Bangkok. I was particularly miserable during the second flight because there were no non-smoking seats available in spite of my reservation and I was surrounded by heavy smokers. In Munich I saw my old doctor, Tibor Csato, now living with a German sculptress whose work I much admired. A good age now, he had written a book, which was a collection of memoirs, observations on his reading and philosophical speculation, and I promised to edit it and publish it when I could. That day has not yet arrived. Jutta Rothenberger was looking after him well and he was happy. I managed to get to the opera to hear Thomas Allen sing *Don Giovanni*. Then I was back in London.

* * * * * *

Ledlanet was gone, the shooting parties were over, and I could no longer ski. Some months after the accident I had had the cartilage removed from my left knee, so it no longer seized up on me, but I had difficulty in walking any distance without discomfort and attempted no other exercise. Then Jacques Chaix fell ill. He had a form of leukaemia where the white cells constantly ate up the red, and he had to have ever more frequent flood transfusions. He made every effort to continue normally, once swimming out to sea at Cap Ferrat and forbidding anyone to follow him, coming back totally exhausted an hour later. Every time I saw him he looked worse, was short of breath and moving with difficulty, but still trying to lead the life to which he was accustomed. I had lunch with him one day in his flat in the Boulevard Maillot, after which he had to go to the American Hospital, where he was being treated, to receive his blood transfusions, and to see the doctor. I stayed on in his flat because I wanted to see Alain Robbe-Grillet who lived on the Boulevard only a hundred yards away, and was returning from the country but had not yet arrived. I was still there when Jacques returned. He could hardly stand, his face was the colour of old oak, and he collapsed onto a chair.

'Merde,' he said, 'now I have jaundice as well.' Ulla Wagner, a German girl in Paris who for years had been one of Jacques' many girlfriends but was now living with another man, was also there, and they had waited for Jacques to return so that they could take him off to the country for the weekend. I suspected their motives for several reasons. Jacques had used Ulla to handle many of his business affairs and she had access to his Swiss bank account. Jacques should be in bed, not making a supreme effort to go to the country, but I could not dissuade him and he left with them. I never saw him alive again. I gave Lucienne, his housekeeper, my whereabouts for the next fortnight with telephone numbers in case anything happened and urged her not to forget to telephone me. But she never did.

I had to go to New York the following week and during this visit Muriel Leyner's father died after many days of fighting for life. He had emigrated from Russia as a young man, first to Britain which had made him an Anglophile, dressing very correctly and very careful and even pedantic in his use of English, and then he had moved on to the States, where as a lawyer he had fought many civil rights cases and been a thorn in the side of Boss Hague, the Tammany Hall-type corrupt Irish political head of Hudson County in New Jersey, who had run his Democratic Party machine like a personal kingdom. I attended the funeral, a Jewish one, and then heard from my office in London that Jacques Chaix had died. It was not Lucienne who had passed me the news but Germaine Fougier, whom I had first met with Jacques in 1948, then a young singer, now a Professor of Singing at the Conservatoire. I flew back to Paris, met Germaine and had dinner with her that night.

The next morning was Jacques' funeral. I went first to the hospital and saw my old friend's body before the coffin was closed, meeting his sister there whom I had known for years, but who now hardly recognised me. A church service had been arranged by Germaine in a Catholic Church, although Jacques, brought up like me as a Catholic was totally lapsed, while Germaine herself was a practising Protestant. These things do not matter after death, when only formalities count. On one side of the church was Jacques' sister with her family and the employees of the factory who had been given the day off to attend. On the other were Jacques' many friends, many of them past girlfriends. I saw people I knew from Cap Ferrat and Val d'Isère or at dinners that Jacques had given in Paris. The priest circled the coffin in what was certainly not an orthodox service, spraying it with holy water and saying that now Jacques understood the mind of God. Then we were in the open air, remembering faces and names. None of Jacques' friends were invited back to the wake which his sister had organised in his apartment.

Instead a small group of us, including a sweet little girl who had always been very fond of him, Germaine and I, and Ulla and her boyfriend all went to Les Grandes Cascades in the Bois de Boulogne, an expensive restaurant. The latter two looked very pleased with themselves and it was obvious that Ulla had been to Switzerland to empty out the bank account. They had the good grace to pay for lunch.

The next day I had another funeral. This time it was John Stonehouse and a Church of England ceremony in Southampton, where he had moved with Sheila, his second wife, whom he had married after his release from prison and with whom he had had a small son. Barbara had divorced him while he was inside and married again and she did not come to the funeral. Bruce Douglas-Mann was there and he gave the address which was affectionate and honest, pointing out John's many abilities and his early promise, but admitting that as a man he had become flawed. Bruce was no longer an MP, having lost his seat when he switched to the Social Democrats in the post-Falklands election, losing it, not to the official Labour candidate (he had until then been the Labour MP), but to the Tories in the wake of Thatcher's triumphal military victory.

There was another funeral that year. Erich Fried had had a long battle with cancer. On one occasion I wanted to go to visit him in hospital, but was told that he would be out in a few days. When I telephoned again the following week he had just left to do some readings in Germany. However weak he was he kept on, translating Shakespeare into German, turning out a constant stream of new poems, and doing readings and lectures wherever and whenever possible. His funeral was in a graveyard in West London that had just been sold to private developers by Lady Porter's Tory regime at the GLC for a token sum for which the buyers had to pay to keep up the cemetery, but could otherwise do what they wanted with the land, one subject of discussion at one of the largest funerals I have ever attended. A 'plane load of young Germans had come for the occasion and I saw many friends, most of them old lefties like Bill Webb and Stuart Hood, whose ex-wife Jill – I had brought them together at Bojava in days long past – told me that one day she might forgive me for introducing her to Stuart. She was a solicitor now.

The ceremony was secular, although presided over by the Reverend Paul Oestreicher, who had followed Erich at the German department of the BBC. 'If Erich is wrong and there really is a heaven,' he said at the end of his fluent address, 'I know what he is trying to do now. Get us all in.' At the graveside all the mourners picked up a clod of earth to throw it onto the coffin. There were so many of us that there was nothing left for the gravediggers to do; the hole was completely filled. I had translated a few of his last poems the night before, very moving but in no way self-pitying or sentimental farewells to the world, and I gave them to Katherine, his widow, at the wake. Three years later I published a second volume of Fried's poetry, *Love Poems*. Both collections were to have several reprints and more volumes were planned a decade later.

* * * * * *

The late eighties were full of problems, the largest being the difficulty of achieving sales that would cover the overhead and our obligations to printers and authors. We now had to pay the rent on the whole building from which Marion Boyars had moved out, quite illegally, but I had no time to think of that; it was too big for us and certainly too expensive. Our American sales were quite good due to the time I had spent selling there, but the overhead ate up all the incoming revenue, while collecting money from slow payers was agonising. The London office was more economically run since Su Herbert had replaced Chris Davidson, but Thatcherism was taking its toll in a xenophobic dumbing down of international culture, while review space was going to the big advertisers, so it was much harder to create awareness of what we were publishing. In America we no longer sold other publishers' books, and this helped with American sales, because I knew by now that a buyer will always buy approximately the same number of books whether he is offered a hundred or a thousand. And I was still paying for the inefficient Kampmann sales and fulfilment, even though they were responsible for few of the sales. I spent much of my time in warehouses – Kampmann changed them fairly frequently – usually going from bad to worse. I made many trips to their one in Bridgeport, where I knew the first names of all the packers, none of whom had ever seen anyone from Kampmann. They would refer to 'suits' who were sometimes seen on the top floor. At one point in Bridgeport I saw all the returns, even in the original binders' parcels, being dumped into skips to be thrown away. I stopped it, but it must have been going on for at least a month. Nobody cared because no-one from Kampmann knew what was happening and it was easier to throw books away than to return them to stock. I spent two days rescuing books and re-shelving them.

Then Kampmann went bankrupt and I found another warehouse in New York State, more than an hour's drive from New York City. I checked it out carefully, and it seemed solid as it belonged to a public company. What I did not know, was that just as I joined it, it was being sold to an individual, who was soon himself in trouble.

In Paris I saw Maurice Girodias when I could. He was in a bad way, living off charity, mainly from his brother Eric Kahane and his sister, and writing the second volume of his memoirs. We would lunch, usually in a cheap Chinese restaurant, because he was a vegetarian now. He was living in an almost empty bare apartment near Alésia, not far from where Jim Haynes had his studio. He had picked up new enthusiasms, Breton nationalism, the persecution of the Cathars (he was convinced he was reincarnated from one), support for one of the socialist leaders, Michel Rocard, who was trying to change his party's policies, and other matters. On his return to France he had undergone an operation to save his sight and some time after that had developed intestinal cancer which had led to another major operation which had much weakened him. But he still had his ironic sense of humour and had kept his looks and his charm. Maurice was much hurt by the things that were being said and written about him in articles and books that were appearing about his years in publishing, mainly by writers whose literary careers he had started. They described him as a bandit who had cheated them, but as I knew well he had in those days been totally unprofessional, never expecting a book to last beyond one printing and paying a fair price for that in cash, keeping no records. He had simply bought manuscripts on which he hoped to make a profit with no thought of continuing copyright going through his mind. It took him by surprise when interest in his titles was shown in other countries and he was never at ease in the world of contracts and royalty agreements.

I introduced him to Odile Helier, whose Village Voice bookshop was now the best outlet for English language books in Paris, and he gave a talk there about the Paris of the fifties and sixties. His old Olympia editions were continuing to sell there, although I have no idea where they came from. On one occasion he heard that I had been in Paris and had not contacted him and he was very annoyed. I offered to read his manuscript to help make corrections and find errors, and he promised I could, but never let me see it until it was published in 1990.

He had developed a bitter grudge against Barney Rosset and a strong hatred for Dick Seaver, considering them, and especially the latter, as being responsible for estranging authors from him, such as William Burroughs. He had certainly been cheated in America over *Candy*, but by Walter Zacharius of Lancer Books who used one of his employees, an attractive black girl called Sarah Uman to bamboozle him when he went to America to try to find out what had happened. That story, very funnily told, is in the second autobiography[40]. Sarah Uman, then or later, accused Barney Rosset of being the father of her child, but he disproved it with a blood test.

Maurice wrote an open letter to Samuel Beckett, which was published in some newspapers, attacking Seaver and Rosset for his woes, and other articles on various subjects appeared in Le Monde and elsewhere. His book was finally published by Editions de la Différence and had good reviews. I found it a delightful read, very funny, but his sequence of events was chaotic,

---

[40] Le Jardin d'Eros, Paris, 1990.

and he never failed to exaggerate situations to make a better story. A little before publication I was in Paris with John Minihan and I took him along to lunch with Maurice at Zeyer on Place Alésia, where we sat outside in lovely early summer weather and John was able to get some good photographs. It was to be our last meeting.

* * * * * *

Our office lease was coming to an end and we were told we would have to leave the building in which we had been working since 1963, while I was living in the next door house where I had been since 1982 and still had some years to go. I was given a schedule of dilapidations and began to realise what was in the small print that no one had ever read. We were obliged to repoint the building on the outside, totally repair the roof and redecorate the inside. Negotiations fell on deaf ears and we were taken to court, where we appeared but got nowhere. I had to stop production of all books, stop paying royalties and I found an Indian contractor called Sabu who undertook to do the work as cheaply as possible. He found an old deer rifle in my flat which had come from Ledlanet, so antiquated that a bullet could no longer be found for it. He wanted it so much that he gave me a considerable discount on his work. But the final bill was still £84,000 which we had to somehow pay and then leave the building. The overdraft went right up and I was asked by a new bank manager to repay it. Then it became clear that Mr. Fine also wanted my flat. I suspected that Marion had something to do with Mr. Fine's new animosity. She was also seeing Bettina which could only mean that there was some plot between them, because they had always disliked each other. I was becoming paranoiac as everything increasingly went wrong and I realised that old enemies encircling me were apparently in touch with each other. During Beckett's last visits to London Bettina had always tried to contact him, and out of old friendship he would see her when possible, always telling me about it; her bitter animosity towards me had in no way diminished. Now I began to suspect that she was trying to help Marion to get Beckett's books for her list if I were to go under, because my difficulties were certainly no secret.

I had kept in touch with Lesley Cunliffe and Stan Gabler-Davis after my last electoral campaign. Lesley became involved with Hugh Massingberd, a journalist who had succeeded Stan as her regular boyfriend, but she later died in 1997. Stan developed cancer, which he was told was inoperable. There was a series of farewell dinners to say goodbye to old friends, one of them at my flat in Green's Court. His current girlfriend Doreen Mahon would anxiously sit by him on all these occasions. Then he did have an operation and I went to see him in hospital afterwards. He was sitting up in bed with Doreen on one side of the bed and a priest on the other. On the hospital tray between them was a bottle of vodka which they were getting through quite rapidly. 'I'm taking my pain-killer by the fastest route,' said Stan. When he emerged from hospital there was a series of celebration dinners for 'the miracle'. Doreen, having lived through the many farewells, now found the celebration of the miracle too much to bear, and she left him. Not long afterwards, the morning after a party in Cork he was found dead on the floor.

Suzanne Beckett died in June 1989 and Sam was able to attend the burial in the Montparnasse cemetery. I was not there, but I heard that looking at the grave he had commented 'Enough room there for two.' Then in early December he collapsed in his bath and on being told I went immediately to Paris. So did Barney Rosset, bringing with him a Time-Life photographer. For several days we waited for news, but all we knew was that he was in hospital in a coma and that the end must be near. I spoke to Lindon, but he would tell me nothing further. Barney wanted to see the retirement home and I reluctantly drove him there with the photographer, making a further mistake of going in with them and indicating where Sam's room was, but I would not go in it. A minute later a nurse shooed them out and I felt ashamed at being with them because the photographer wanted to take pictures and somehow it had not occurred to me that Barney would be so insensitive as to encourage him.

It was now only a few days before Christmas and I had to move offices, so I returned to London were we moved into a small suite of rooms on Neal Street in Covent Garden. We gave a small office party there as we always did for authors and staff on the 20th, and the conversation was all about Sam. The newspapers had reported that he was in a coma. One reporter, from the Irish Times apparently, found out that he was in the Hôpital Sainte-Anne and managed to get into his room for a minute where he caught his eye, but then was chased out. I kept in touch with Edward Beckett in Paris because this was one funeral I wanted to attend at all costs and asked him to keep in touch.

We arranged our new offices which seemed very cramped compared to Soho. IMEC in Paris, which collects publishers' archives, helpfully agreed to take everything not current for which we had no room. Several large filing cases went by lorry. Su Herbert had the best room in the new offices with the library of our past publications around her, while I took a small office that communicated with the corridor as well as the central general office, where we were now reduced to three people, the other being Margaret Jacquess, who had been with us since our early days in Brewer Street as receptionist. We all missed Soho. The restaurants had neither the same quality nor the variety, but we did find some reasonable places nearby. But it was handy for the two opera houses and for quite a few theatres including the National, about twenty minutes walk away. During that week I had a 'phone call from John Minihan to tell me that his framed photograph of Beckett had just fallen off the wall. Could this be an omen? I tried to telephone Edward

Beckett, but did not reach him until after ten on Christmas eve. He told me that Sam had died the previous night. Why had he not 'phoned me? There was so much to do and he had simply forgotten. The funeral was to be a simple burial at eight o'clock on the 26th, Boxing Day, and no announcement would be made until it was over, because they did not want a large crowd of Parisians to descend on the cemetery. There was no transport to Paris on Christmas Day and no ferries were crossing the channel. It would be impossible to get there, even if I could swim twenty-two miles in winter and walk two hundred. I was devastated.

My obituary appeared in The Independent on the 27th and The Scotsman tailored a piece I had written about Beckett for them earlier into another. James Knowlson wrote a few paragraphs more to follow my London one. Then I had to go to Washington D.C. to the MLA and there was a wake for Sam in a pub there, suitably called Murphy's. I particularly remember talking to Mary Foliet, a New York academic who was to become a close friend, who thinks we first met there, but I think it was earlier. I had telephoned Barney on Christmas Day to tell him and I asked him to keep it to himself until the next day. But he immediately 'phoned around New York, managed to reach Mel Gussow of the New York Times, who tried to get his obituary in for the following day, but the news was not believed by the duty editor in charge, who probably thought that Beckett was unimportant anyway, so that it appeared on the 27th when it was largely overshadowed by the death of Ceascescu who had been executed in Bucharest following the popular rising there.

I was kept busy which fortunately gave me no time to think about the loss of one of my oldest friends at the end of a year in which I had lost so many others. It was the end of an era and I told my doctor, Martin Scurr, in a year that had been bad in every way, of my depression at seeing nearly all my oldest friends, mostly older than myself, dying one after another. 'You must make new friendships,' he said. So 1989 came to an end and I reflected on the significance of '9' in my life. 1939, 1949, 1959, 1969, 1979 had all been significant years, bringing change into my life. What was to befall me next would not be pleasant.

Chapter 8

Abyss

1990 and 1991 were two of the worst years I can recall, getting progressively worse. I returned from the U.S. and started to deal with my mountain of problems. As Shakespeare so well put it, 'when troubles come, they come not single spies, but in battalions'. We were still paying for the decoration of the old offices, which had included putting on a new roof, and for the move to the new one, and we owed a mountain of debt to our normal suppliers and to authors. And this was just the time when the banks, with whom I had always enjoyed a good relationship were radically changing their policies. All my adult life I had been accustomed to knowing my bank managers personally, and I had always as a matter of caution kept two accounts, for both my business and personal affairs, and with different banks. Since 1949 I had banked principally with the Midland Bank in London and since 1962 with the Clydesdale in Scotland, and I also had accounts with the National Westminster. I had started Ledlanet Enterprises to run the Scottish estate and Ledlanet Nights banked with the same village bank in Milnathort, where I had a private account as well. I would regularly lunch with the London bank managers, who knew how the publishing company was developing and details of my future plans. Most of the time there was an overdraft, which waxed and waned with need, but I could normally count on having the same manager for six or seven years at least, who would introduce me to his successor on retirement. Now all this had changed. Managers were being retired in their forties to make way for a new tougher breed of young men who had no desire to know you or to know anything about your business. If there was an overdraft they only wanted to know what immediately negotiable security lay behind it. These young men were only around for a few months, and our account then suddenly became the responsibility of a woman manager, who wanted the overdraft paid off instantly, just when we were in our greatest difficulties. This came at the end of 1990. In the meantime I carried on as best I could.

The National Theatre decided to put on a memorial evening for Samuel Beckett and I helped them with the arrangements, producing the record that Pat Magee, now dead, had made to promote *How It Is*. Others wanted to get in on the act and there was talk of a competing memorial evening at the Royal Court. I was caught up in the crossfire with Michael Kustow, now at Channel 4 Television trying to get the rights to televise the evening and being especially anxious to obtain my co-operation for what seemed to me to be a distorted and popularised view of Sam's work. I increasingly passed the problems over to Edward Beckett, Sam's nephew and heir, who put together a string quartet of his musician friends to play some Schubert at the beginning of the evening in the Olivier auditorium of the National. The event took place on the first of April where a packed house heard a number of leading actors reading extracts from the work and there were some appreciative speeches as well. Just before the performance I had a serious talk with Edward who agreed to be patient over the royalties that were due.

Throughout the seventies, eighties and nineties the Theatre of Literature continued to function on an irregular basis. We put on programmes with our usual teams of actors, all of them highly experienced and able to take over from each other at short notice if a theatre, film or television engagement should suddenly come up. Beckett was the author around who most of the programmes were built – both in the U.S. and Britain - but we did a Claude Simon, an Eluard, a noveau roman reading among many others, including the series of short one man shows I had devised for a single actor, mainly in the Waterstone shops, where they had good reception when the management did some preparation and publicity. We were invited to put on a European Evening for the Stockport Festival and I rehearsed it carefully in London with Ariana Bishop and Stephen Thorne, experienced actors but new to our group. The programme was designed to bring European writers of significance, Simone Benmussa, Nathalie Sarraute, Alain Robbe-Grillet and others to the attention of a probably not very intellectual local public. It was a disaster: one person turned up. It was the night of a cup-final, but the total lack of any effort to publicise the event was obviously the main cause. The actors were given a good dinner, put up in a good hotel and sent back to London the next day, having done nothing.

It was years later when reading John Drummond's autobiography[41] that I realised that the Stockport fiasco was part of the European Arts Festival that he had been asked to organise at short notice to celebrate the British Presidency of the European Community and small amounts of money had been offered all over the country to promote some local event with a European dimension to it. The money had been taken by Stockport and my event, with readings from four European writers in translation exactly filled the bill. But they had nothing else to promote it and no doubt had most of the money over after paying us. I learned from him that other events I had attended, such as the Mnouchkine *Atrides* in Bradford (which Drummond wrongly says happened in Halifax) and Roberto Gerhard's *The Duenna*, which enabled me to add one more to my opera tally and went to Leeds to see with Opera North, were all part of the same European Festival, which the Tory government, having given some subsidy, then did nothing to encourage, promote or taken any interest in. No-one knew there was such a Festival taking place.

I was doing more travelling around Britain now because that was where money was most needed. In America, however well the sales went, the overheads kept mounting, so there was never money that could be sent back,

---

[41] Sir John Drummond. *Tainted By Experience*, London 2000.

and there was endless trouble with the warehouse that was simply incompetently run. The Theatre of Literature did many readings and I scripted my forty years of publishing into a dramatic show, which I delivered with two actors, first at Riverside Studios in London, then at the Ubu Theatre in New York, and we also took it to the Demarco performance space in Edinburgh and to other venues. I told the story of those publishing years and with the actors played out key moments such as my early days with Eric Turrell, the Alger Hiss Fiasco (various actresses much enjoyed playing Blanche Knopf), the American disaster with my Opera, Theatre and other Annuals, through to the partnership with and separation from Marion Boyars, who was portrayed as she was, and with as much kindness as I could muster. She came to one Riverside Studios performance, which was designed to also be a fortieth birthday party: first came the show, lasting about two hours with an interval, then drinks with the audience in the bar, with the drinks being paid for by those who drank them. Marion obviously did not enjoy seeing herself presented in this way and with her own words, which I remembered very well being used, because I have always had a good aural memory both for music and conversations. She heard them coming back at her from the lips of an actress. Different performances had different casts: Leonard Fenton played most of the men, Karen Fernald and Elaine Padmore most of the women. Elaine, whom I had first met with John Rushby-Smith, was now the most often-heard voice on Radio 3 in the mornings, reading the news and announcing the musical choices, and she also sang with a small opera company that at one point asked me to be a director, but as there was nothing I could really do for them, I soon resigned. I changed *Damned Publishing*, as I entitled my publishing documentary, to allow her on some occasions to sing some songs during the evening. She also took part in other Theatre of Literature presentations, including a show at the Stamford Literary Festival which Laurence Staig subsidised from Eastern Arts, but it was so badly organised and publicised by the locals that it was a fiasco. Only two people turned up to hear Howard Barker, who would have been furious had he not been put up in a hotel that he had always wanted to visit, and my own show, whatever it was on that occasion, probably *To Its Beginning to its End* with Elaine Padmore, Sean Barratt and Leonard Fenton, and myself as narrator, was only saved by my running into an artist I knew, who telephoned around to get an audience, and by a conference of little magazines which happened to be there at the same time and decided to come from their event to mine. I remember at the end of their meeting, which I went to, launching into a bitter attack on 'the evils of Thatcherism' which apparently astonished Alastair Niven, who had recently become Literature Director of the Arts Council and was present in that capacity.

Leonard Friedman had kept the Scottish Baroque Ensemble going after Ledlanet Nights ended and the Scottish Chamber Orchestra developed out of that with largely the same players. Now Leonard found some money to launch a kind of festival on the Island of Mull and he invited me to take part by giving a lecture on Beckett. I had spent the early months of 1990 selling my books in America, Ireland and Britain and in the year following Beckett's death I had also been frequently lecturing about him. I ended a trip around Scottish bookshops by going to Oban by train, Muriel joining me in Glasgow to take the West Highland line there, and from Oban we took the ferry to Mull, arriving by bus in Tobermory and having to climb a steep hill with our bags to the Western Isles Hotel, where most of the artists taking part in the Festival were staying. Leonard himself was invisible. Different musical events had been announced at different venues on the island at different times and nearly all of them had been changed at the last moment, forcing the audiences to go from place to place, usually arriving after a concert had started and often finding there was not one at all. It was a typical Leonard Friedman muddle. My own lecture also had a change of venue and time, but no-one knew quite where. At the hotel I dined with Robin Orr and his new second wife, a Swiss lady, who made every possible difficulty for the hotel staff with her questions of what went into sauces and dishes and her many complaints about the service. Somewhere in the middle of dinner the manager came to Robin, distinguished Scottish composer, ex-Professor of Music at Cambridge and first Chairman of Scottish Opera, to say: 'You've been upsetting my staff. I would like you to move to another hotel first thing tomorrow morning.' Poor Robin! He could not have been more gentle or easy-going, but Doris, his new wife was another story, and he was putty in her hands.

The next day as we came downstairs Leonard was in the hall, fiddle in hand, and playing a musical greeting to all who descended the staircase. We attended a rehearsal of part of the Bach Double Violin Concerto where Richard Friedman, Leonard's son, played together with Marion, a young professional who had also recently formed her own gypsy orchestra. This was followed by a movement of the Mendelsohn Octet. Both works were under the direction of Emmanuel Hurwitz, distinguished leader of many London orchestras, now in semi-retirement, who guided the young musicians – because this festival was really a short music school – for a performance that was to take place part on the Easter Sunday on the nearby Island of Iona, an icon for Celtic Christianity and the spiritual home of the Church of Scotland. The fact that so many of the musicians taking part were Jewish seemed irrelevant: it was just another place and another opportunity to play. Mendelsohn after all was Jewish and Friedman jokingly said that he intended to introduce some Max Bruch into the church ceremony.

In the afternoon there was a concert in Tobermory given by local children who had been coached by Kay Horowitz, Manny's wife, for about a week. It was an eye-opening occasion, showing how much could be accomplished by experienced teachers in just a few days. Children from about seven up to twenty had been organised into an orchestra able to play a variety of music ranging from *Pop Goes the Weasel* with the younger ones to Mozart and Haydn and sophisticated Highland fiddling with the elder. The local music teacher, who admitted he had to teach instruments he could not play himself, was given a new energy and enthusiasm. The hall was filled with parents, relatives and friends of those taking part, and all the children expressed their preference for classical music over pop.

I gave my lecture between two rehearsals in one of the halls to those who happened to be present and fell into the ad hoc mood of the whole occasion. We all had dinner on the Saturday in a restaurant some miles from anywhere and afterwards heard the final rehearsal of the Bach, Mendelsohn and some other music played with assurance and love – there is no other word for it – by musicians old and young, old-timers like Manny Hurwitz and Leonard Friedman giving the principal parts to the youngsters. The sight of the semi-circle of totally engrossed musicians playing the Mendelsohn Octet has indelibly etched itself on my memory. On the Sunday morning we all took a very damp open ferry to Iona in the rain, our feet getting wetter as the water sloshed over them in the heavy rolling sea. The service was not too long with some music in the middle and then the congregation heard the pieces that had been rehearsed. The players were invited to a lunch given by the Church itself (the Iona Community as the cloistered group calls itself), while the rest of us found a place where we could get snacks, but no drinks other than tea and coffee. After a wait the others joined us and we took another wet ferry back to Mull.

It was my first and only visit to the island that I knew only from literature. It is crime-free and nobody ever locks their doors. Fishing, agriculture and tourism keep the place alive but unfortunately I had no time to visit the Mull Little Theatre, where a husband and wife team put on simple productions of small cast plays. I knew the couple from the theatre conferences of my Ledlanet days; they provide such culture on Mull as is not home-produced. With the festival over, the last survivors, waiting for the train in Oban, did a post-mortem with the usual gossip and much criticism of the eccentricities of Leonard Friedman. He had a new girlfriend with him who had on one night made him sleep in the corridor outside their room, and the criticism went from the way he held his violin to his messy private life and failings as an organiser. But everyone had enjoyed themselves nonetheless, although we all knew we would have difficulty collecting the expenses and fees that had been promised. I saw some old friends like Penny Craig and Conrad Wilson and had made some new ones like the Hurwitzes and the young musicians.

A week later I was at the first of the Theatre Conferences which the playwright David Edgar, who was also now Professor of Creative Writing and Drama at Birmingham University, was starting to hold there at the Manor house, once the home of the Cadbury chocolate family, one of their conference centres. About a hundred people involved in the theatre, actors, theatre managers, directors and one or two theatre publishers like myself, spent a weekend discussing our problems, the overriding one at the time being the serious cuts to the subsidised theatres and repertory companies imposed by a Thatcher government with no interest in culture. The atmosphere of fear that pervaded the conference could be clearly felt. Only one or two courageous individuals such as Philip Hadley, who now ran Joan Littlewood's old theatre at Stratford East, dared to say what everyone was thinking, and he also attacked the creeping censorship that was dissuading theatres from doing political plays or anything controversial, such as gay drama. The conference was in fact the culmination of David Edgar's play-writing course and the students attending had a wonderful chance to mix with theatre professionals and make contacts for the future. Up to 1999 I continued to go every year, except one, to these Birmingham conferences, held annually in April or May, always learning much from them and increasing my theatrical network of acquaintances. The Arts Council would send an officer, usually Ian Brown, whose smooth platitudes were well put-over, but convinced no-one.

I was then travelling again, both around Britain and in the States, covering towns on the American East and West coasts and others in-between. Gregory Mosher, who was now running the theatres at Lincoln Centre, decided to put on a Beckett evening and I made suggestions of what should be read and some, but only a few, of my suggestions were accepted. I read myself, choosing a very powerful section of Arsene's speech in *Watt* which Ronald Pickup had read at the National Theatre evening, and I asked if I could start the performance as the extract made such a good introduction to Beckett's attitude to the world and to life in general. Barney Rosset was also asked to take part and wanted to read from his correspondence with Beckett, but in the event it was read, rather boringly, by an actor instead. Mosher then tried to dissuade me, but I had carefully worked on the piece and wanted to deliver it. In the event it went down extremely well and John Simon, reviewing the evening in New York Magazine said that the two best performances came from me and Barry McGovern, who very funnily delivered the 'stones' episode from *Molloy*, which he knew well as part of his one-man show, *I'll Go On*, taken from the Beckett trilogy. Billie Whitelaw also took part, but she was rehearsing for a film, had come straight from the studio and was tired and off-form. Simon panned her, very unfairly.

Sometime in the late eighties I had met a young man in New York called Ben Schiff. He and his father ran a specialised publishing company where they picked literary texts and commissioned artists to create illustrations for them, subcontracting from the publisher who held the copyright, if there was one, in order to produce small de-luxe editions to sell at a high price to art collectors. The level of artist employed and production standards had gone down, but Ben, a trendy young man who had done all the things that the New York *jeunesse dorée* usually does, from drugs to getting himself into other trouble, had decided to reform himself and give the publishing company a new lease on life. He bought many books from us for his own library, both in London and in New York, but only paid in instalments, and as I write there is still a fair sum outstanding.

However I liked him because he was intelligent and knowledgeable, and he approached me to let him do a Beckett, having already contracted an Ionesco from Rosset. We agreed on *Ill Seen Ill Said* and he produced a small edition in a slip case where the illustrations were only just barely visible. I also wanted to do a new edition of this, a favourite text, and Schiff had designed a special typography, which I could also use. It turned out not to be very suitable for a trade edition, because the spidery letters did not always show up when offset, but at the time it seemed it would save me the setting cost. I was asked to read the proofs and did so very carefully. Sam was now in Le Tiers Temps and I did not want to impose on him to check them, although he did agree Ben Schiff's request that he sign the hundred copies of the special edition.

I already knew the text of *Ill Seen Ill Said* very well. I had arranged readings, mainly done by Sean Barratt and Leonard Fenton at numerous arts centres, usually preceded by my introductory talk and had read it often for my own enjoyment, lingering over the cadences and the images it evoked. But now, suddenly, three words jumped out of the text at me. They were 'full of Grace', the words that follow 'Hail Mary' in the prayer that every Catholic child has to memorise. There they were embedded in the text along with all the other partial quotations from Shakespeare and the Bible, and as I was later to discover, from Milton as well. The text is about an old woman, living alone in a house from which she goes out to tend a grave and be observed by twelve ghostly sentinels. Of course she was the Virgin Mary. Everything else in the novella suddenly fell into place.

The next time I saw Sam, it must have been only a few months before he died, I waited until we were both half-way through our glasses of whisky, when I said: 'Sam, I know you don't like answering questions about your work and I've very seldom asked you one, although you've often volunteered information. But there's one question I have to ask you. It's about *Ill Seen Ill Said.*'

'I know you particularly like that text,' he answered. 'What's the question?'

'The old woman. She is the BVM, isn't she?'

Sam had been sitting on a straight-backed chair next to his little round table, looking into his glass. Suddenly he shot up as if he had received an electric shock. His hand went up and the whisky splashed into the air. He looked at me with the most panic-stricken expression I had ever seen on his face, and then looked down, put his glass on the table and his head in his hands. 'I don't remember, John, 'he said. 'I don't remember.' He could not tell a lie but this was the nearest to one I had encountered.

* * * * * *

On the third of July in 1990 Maurice Girodias died. He had received good reviews for his book and he was talking about it on a Jewish radio station in Paris when he collapsed in the middle of a sentence and was dead within minutes. Surely it was the perfect way to go! His life had been a roller-coaster ride, up and down, and after years of failure to which he had resigned himself with ironic humour, but never without some hope, he had finally died on a high. A month later he would have been down again. I went to Paris for the funeral and a group of us, Jim Haynes, Michael Lehberger and Karl Orend, whom I had originally known as a buyer at Waterstones in Nottingham, sat for two hours in the Père Lachaise crematorium while his body was slowly burnt. Eric Kahane had organised the funeral but had arranged for no speakers or tributes. The Mozart Clarinet Concerto came over the loudspeakers once we were sitting down. 'I won't be able to hear this again for a long time,' I said to myself. It was followed by one of his flute concertos, then another one, then the bassoon concerto. We all sat there in silence except for the occasional whisper while recordings of all Mozart's wind concerti were played on tape and then we were out in the sunshine. There were dozens of women, mostly his old girlfriends, Maurice's two wives, his two daughters and a few old employees and publishing colleagues. Pauvert's absence caused comment. Christian Bourgois had apparently arrived late, looked inside and gone away. The four of us who had arrived together found a bistro outside the gates and toasted his memory. I felt the loss most. Fraser, Chaix, Beckett, Girodias, all close friends for so many years, all now gone! Eric, on the steps on the way out, had nervously ventured: 'If anyone would like to say something...' But it was too late. There is a shelf at Père Lachaise with Girodias' ashes and on the plate is 'Une Journée sur la terre.' It was intended to be the title of his three-volume autobiography, but no trace was ever found of the third volume, which he had told me was well-advanced.

By now I was an experienced obituarist, sometimes doing three or four a week, to be held on file, of writers, publishers, politicians, musicians and others where I had the necessary knowledge or was able to find out what I needed. It became a useful supplement to my income, because I could take very little out of the company and my entire inherited income now went to Bettina. At our last encounter in court the judge, a Mrs. Butler-Schloss, had ruled that my family income must go to the wife, that I could keep what I earned, and that after more than two hundred days in court she must now leave me alone. She was to sue again, but that will come later. My obituary of Girodias appeared in The Independent for which I was now writing many such final tributes, and I took copies of it to New York with me a fortnight later where I organised a gathering of Maurice's old friends at El Quixote. About twenty of us had dinner in the semi-private back section of the restaurant and among those present were Iris Owens, Norman Rubington, Leila Lyons (the second wife), Leon Friedman, and one of his American secretaries. Everybody got fairly drunk, no-one more than Iris Owens who set about abusing most of the women present and especially Leila. I could only take so much of the slanging matches between old rivals and left early, as did Leon Friedman, Maurice's long-suffering American lawyer whose advice was never taken, but who still retained an affection for him. But one of the people at the dinner was Ann Patty, an editor at Simon and Schuster, and in charge of their Poseidon imprint, a quality list. 'Why don't you translate Maurice's book?' she asked me. I was of course the only person present who had read it. It was very long, very inaccurate, but also very funny, 540 pages that ended with Rosemary Ridgewell's return to Paris to seduce him. First of all I had no time, but whoever translated it would have to do massive research to get the facts right, put the sequences in order and curb the exaggerations, an almost impossible task, and the result would not be nearly as amusing to read as the original. But I had an idea. I might, I told her, be willing to write another book about the whole crowd of expatriates that made up Maurice's milieu, centred on him, and using his book as a guide. And that was what I was persuaded to do shortly afterwards, to write a completely different book about Maurice Girodias' life and what it represented, bringing in all the colourful characters who had written books for him and trying to catch the atmosphere of post-war Paris. I eventually signed a contract with Simon and Schuster for normal royalties and an advance of $40,000 of which I received a quarter at the time. I, of course, was much in need of money just then and it went straight into the publishing company. I had meetings with Leon Friedman and Leila Lyons and a pleasant evening where several people who had known Maurice all had dinner at Leila's flat to discuss the book. Leila was now a doctor working for the New York City Health department, where her function needed as many social science skills as medical, dealing with teenage pregnancies and ventilation systems that spread contagious diseases in buildings that had no fresh air. Then I started to write the book for which I borrowed Maurice's title *The Gardens of Eros*, but made the gardens singular.

One of my acquaintances in London at this time was Colin Tweedie, a Scottish lawyer who was now running the Association for Business Sponsorship of the Arts in succession to Luke Rittner, previously mentioned and now the particularly inept Secretary General of the Arts Council. I liked Colin who had made some efforts to find a sponsor to help me to publish more books after the Arts Council debacle, but nothing ever came of it. He did invite me to several ABSA functions for a while, and then dropped me. I ran into him on the train to Glyndebourne that summer when we were both on our way to a new Michael Tippett opera, *New Year*. Tweedie had just talked to Rittner, mentioned what he was going to see and been told 'The more fool you.' There is no reason why the Secretary General of the Arts Council should particularly like modern music, but he should certainly not be so publicly dismissive of the work of a musician who by general agreement was the outstanding living English composer at the time, Benjamin Britten having died fourteen years earlier. My mind went back to the first night of Tippett's earlier *The Ice Break*. The Arts Council had their own box at Covent Garden and on that occasion it was occupied by Luke Rittner and his party, who were quaffing champagne and eating smoked salmon sandwiches both before the curtain and during the first interval. But when I looked up at the box just before the second act started I saw that they had all left. They were not paying for their box and presumably not for the champagne either, while their general behaviour was calculated to attract as much attention as possible from the audience taking their seats. For a man in his public position to then ostentatiously steal away was a disgrace that should have cost him his job, but this was the period of Thatcherite philistinism and contempt for good manners and Luke Rittner typified it. No. 29 in my Opera Guide series, which Nick John was still editing for me, was *The Complete Operas of Michael Tippett*, containing the opera texts and several articles about the four he had written up to 1979, when he had declared that he would write no more. Now the volume could no longer be called 'complete'. It had, rather to my surprise, sold very well and it went quite quickly out of print. When I reprint it I shall have to add *New Year*.

I was an admirer of David Freeman, the Australian who had started Opera Factory, which had presented extremely imaginative productions, mainly of early and modern operas. The company had started in Zürich as a mini-opera company performing in small spaces and Freeman had started a second Opera Factory in London. Now he was doing plays as well. The previous year I had much enjoyed his complete *Faust* at the Lyric Theatre in Hammersmith with Simon Callow in the title role, the best production I have ever seen of Goethe's play which is done only too rarely, and that summer of 1990 I took Ruby Cohn, the drama professor from San Francisco to see Part I of *Morte d'Arthur*, also produced by Freeman, of which I had high hopes. Unfortunately, except for a few brilliant moments, it was a failure and Ruby did not thank me for taking her. I went to Part II on another night with my old friend Judith Radstone. Freeman was by now established enough to have done some major productions at the big opera houses in London, New York and elsewhere, but everyone has his failures. I was still going to odd places to see rare operas: *New Year* had been number 651 (2388 performances) and I saw two other new operas the following week, both on Red Indian subjects: one was Grétry's *Le Huron* at the Buxton Festival and the other Stephen Storace's *The Cherokee* given in a school in Hadleigh, Suffolk, where our old editor Agnes Rook had now retired with a dog and a canary called Caruso.

At the Edinburgh Festival in August I presented the much shorter version of *To Its Beginning to its End* in the Saint Cecilia's Hall, devising new movement with a much shorter text and it was extremely successful. The cast was Angela Pleasance, Sean Barratt and Leonard Fenton, and I spoke the narration. I also recreated *Damned Publishing*, but not in the official festival, which was still run by Frank Dunlop. It was during that Festival that I went to see Kenneth Ireland for the last time. After he had been removed from Pitlochry which led to his stroke, he had lived quietly in Edinburgh and become reclusive, now largely and undeservedly forgotten. He was to die soon afterward.

I was still spending more than half of my time selling books in bookshops, and concentrating largely on the back-list because we could afford to publish few new titles and author pressure forced me to reprint certain books as a first priority. In September I was calling on booksellers in New York and towns in New England, especially the seats of such universities as Yale and Harvard. Then I was doing the same in British Northern towns, and on occasion organising readings by my actors in art centres and – a new activity – readings by a single actor in Waterstone's bookshops, the result of persuading John Mitchinson, the marketing director, to promote these. They worked very well where the staff did the appropriate publicity and preparation, very badly where they didn't. In some places, and in York in particular, this activity which had been foisted onto the branch bookshops by their head-office, created some resentment. On my next visit to Waterstone's in York, I was uncivilly treated and on a later visit told not to check the stock – they would not let me do so even though there was an obvious mutual advantage in my knowing what they had and did not have – and on my next visit after that I was told I was banned and not to come again, with no explanation given. It must have gone back to the original reading of work by Beckett done by Leonard Fenton, with on that occasion both John Mitchinson and myself present. Leonard read to an audience of only about twenty and there was probably resentment from the staff at having to stay late for the event. I ended the year at the MLA in Chicago where I had to give an early-morning lecture on Beckett to the Samuel Beckett Society of America with a streaming cold. I also made contact there with Bogdan Drozdhovski's son Piotr, who was now teaching in America, and then went on to San Francisco to do more bookselling, returning to New York late in January and then to London. After that I was still travelling to sell books in Britain.

All this time my money problems were getting worse. Pressure from the banks, the difficulty in collecting what was owed by American booksellers, who had to be constantly telephoned and coerced or threatened, the cancellation of contracts by authors' agents because royalties were overdue and difficulty in paying our monthly accounts because overdraft facilities were constantly being reduced, were taking their toll. Su Herbert, running the London office could not help herself expressing her dissatisfaction to others, including to authors on the telephone, and the Beckett royalties were now my major anxiety because the estate wanted to be paid and it became obvious that Faber was approaching the Beckett heirs, Edward and his sister Caroline Murphy, to offer inducements to come over to them. They had the plays and wanted the novels that they had originally rejected. Robert McCrum had had meetings with me to discuss ways of making a Beckett complete edition, but that was just a method of opening negotiations and feeling me out. There was over £40,000 due in Beckett royalties and I could see no way out except by an injection from a new investor. I had a meeting in Paris with Jerôme Lindon and Edward Beckett, but the latter cancelled for lunch at the last moment, and although he was sympathetic, Lindon made it clear that the royalties had to be paid and quickly. Sam had given me a letter saying that I had five years to meet arrears, but the five years were now up. In addition to the company's difficulties I was being sued by Hyman Fine to do more to the old building and it was obvious that he also wanted to recover the house at 1 Green's Court where I was still living, having made a comfortable bijou residence out of a sordid run-down brothel. I contacted Ron Rosen, the solicitor who had previously been a barrister, and had now set up his office on Piccadilly, assuming that he might be the best man to deal with Fine, who was now over a hundred years old, but still in sole control of his property empire with no visible assistance. There were meetings in solicitors' offices, but the situation was hopeless and I agreed to leave Green's Court. Once again everything had to go into storage, this time near Aldeburgh because Sheila, having left the Edinburgh Festival, had now become the manager and chief executive of the Aldeburgh Festival. She was able to house my Bechstein piano and some other things. I still had much of the Ledlanet furniture and library in storage in Dunfermline. Storage charges were also a considerable drain on me. My sister had some of my belongings in Sussex, but now she had sold her house to look after our mother in Greece.

I have not said much in this book about my younger brother. Having divorced his first wife, a German, and then spent some years living in Greece, he then had a Greek wife, but had divorced her too, and was dividing his time between Greece and Thailand, where he bought a property, then a teenage girl from her parents, who eventually, some considerable time later, he married. We were totally different in every way and while I disliked him in no specific manner he positively hated me. He had done nothing with his life, but had been careful to save and increase his income. He was making pornographic films for a while and these attracted some attention from the English tabloid press, but by some oversight on their part they never connected the man selling his wares to the porn merchants of Soho with myself, who had worked and lived in Soho for many years. My mother was now old, in the care of two born-again Christian

American nurses, most of the time in Monte Carlo, but part of the time in America, mainly Palm Beach because it suited the nurses. Now my brother hatched a plan to get my mother and her considerable income under his control. My sister and I could have prevented it, but my brother had the connivance of the nurses, while I was too overwhelmed by my difficulties to give my mother's situation any thought. She considered me improvident and, under the influence of the nurses and pushed by my brother, she excluded me from any direct benefit under her will. I had once made one derogatory remark about Billy Graham, which certainly played a part in their attitude to me. What my brother did was transport our mother to Greece where she spent the rest of her life with nobody to talk to except the nurses and my brother when he was there, in a remote suburb of Athens. He then had the benefit of her entire income, and he soon got rid of the nurses, so that she was in the care of a local one under his control. My sister then had to spend most of the nineties until my mother died in Athens to try to counteract my brother and to keep her company. It was clear to me what was going on, but I had missed the only opportunity to prevent it, and it was by no means certain that any action on my part would have made a difference.

Every year now I would make an Irish tour and although this varied both in duration and in the direction taken, it was nearly always in the autumn and included a weekend at the Wexford Festival, where my old friend Elaine Padmore had now taken over as artistic director. In Wexford there were always pleasant lunches and late night dinners and over the years those I would see there would include Stan Gebler-Davis until his death, Maráse Murphy, who was later to become my landlady, who reviewed opera for the Irish Times, Tony Quigley who had married Margaret Prandy, previously in charge of the Irish Chamber Orchestra, Tom Walsh until he too died, and there were always singers like Felicity Lott, whom I had first met when she was married, many years earlier, to someone I knew in publishing. Usually I would start and end in Dublin, going either clock-wise or counter-clockwise around the island, taking in the west-coast towns of Cork, Limerick, Galway and Sligo and going on to Belfast and sometimes Derry. If trouble in the north seemed likely, which would mean road-blocks and a very real danger of having the car stolen or vandalised, I would leave the car in Dublin and take the day-train up for my Belfast visits. I always enjoyed the Irish tour because the Irish love and respect books, and having a number of Irish authors helped. I would see writers and friends, usually lunching with John Banville in Dublin who in addition to having become a best-selling novelist was now literary editor of The Irish Times. When I asked him how he could find the time to write and also be a full-time literary editor, he told me that he mainly wanted to get his hands on all the books that came in. He had a greed for them and there was no better way. When the Irish photographer John Minihan was made redundant by London's Evening Standard he spent the money buying a house in Ballydehob in West

Cork and I would often visit him there. I never failed to sell many books in Ireland.

On my American bookselling trips I often lectured where I knew professors at the universities and usually stayed with them. I gave lectures in Boulder organised by Ron Sukenik who also edited the American Book Review and whose novels I had once sold for Fiction Collective, in Tallahassee where Stanley Gontarski now taught, in Bloomington where my archives now were and Breon Mitchell was President of the Library, in Chicago, Detroit, at New England universities and on the west coast. They helped towards my expenses but above all assisted me to get my authors known and to make new contacts in the universities. My British lecturing had been more for causes than about literature. In early 1991 there was a big Beckett Conference in the Hague and I was there three times in six months, first to talk about Beckett in preparation, then to attend an operatic evening that included Morton Feldman's *Neither* on a Beckett text, which Pierre Audi staged, and the third time to take part in the conference itself. This was just after helping my daughter Jamie to run for parliament on the Liberal Democratic ticket in Stafford, which I shall mention later. Barney Rosset was at the conference and very worried because he had contracted prostate cancer and was seeking advice about treatment. I went to Amsterdam with him after the Hague so that he could consult a specialist. He had heard of a place to stay, apparently from an American dominatrix: advancing years had in no way diminished Barney's interest in the kinky. I found the place with considerable difficulty, just off a canal where I could not park. It was a kind of boarding house. We were admitted by a man who looked half spider and half circus clown, a sort of Quasimodo, who showed us dirty rooms and a single bathroom where the water ran out through a hole in the floor. I left hastily, and Barney, seeing no signs of any erotic activity, was also pleased to leave and find a more conventional hotel.

In Amsterdam I visited the bookshops and went to my old haunt, the Kring, where in the past I had met writers, publishers and musicians. Although it is a private club, all I ever had to do to be admitted was to drop the name of some well-known Amsterdam figure in the arts, Karel Appel or Harry Mulisch or Peter Schat. Membership of the Scottish Arts Club in Edinburgh also gave one admittance and this time I used that. I was amazed to find that a club that on every previous visit had been full of gesticulating, talking, eating and drinking arts personalities and their mates was now empty, and it was a Friday night. I asked the barman for an explanation and he asked me who I knew. I mentioned a few names, all of my generation, and he laughed. 'They are all out in the country with their fourth or fifth wives,' he said, 'trying to make a new baby.' Young people apparently no longer packed into the Kring at weekends if at all. I also took a tram to the suburb where Marcus Colleran had his bookshop. His marriage had broken up but he seemed happy enough. It was not an intellectual neighbourhood, so he did not think he could sell my books there. Barney Rosset's Dutch advice did not help him to make a decision about his prostate, so he returned to the States where eventually he had the seeding treatment, then still quite new, which had been developed in Seattle. He had it done there successfully, thus avoiding surgery. His biggest anxiety had been that he might become impotent.

The blow finally fell. The Midland Bank closed the account and so did the National Westminster. Pressure was coming from Minuit and Edward Beckett. Through my auditors, Ramsay Brown, I managed to open a new account with Barclay's in Whetstone, near their office; they gave the right reassurances because the bank was not particularly keen to have a publisher. One week I had to pay the salaries of Su Herbert and Margaret Jacquess in cash because we did not yet have a cheque-book. I had left Green's Court and found a room in a nearby building on Meard Street, which was furnished. But money was still being claimed by Fine and he was in a position to bankrupt the company. I had no option but to put it into liquidation. I had to appear in front of a firm that wound up companies called Valentine's, where I swore on oath that my statement of affairs was accurate and John Calder (Publishers) Ltd., the name that I had registered in 1950 after having started in business the previous year, which had been changed for fourteen years to Calder and Boyars, and then changed back in 1975, was no more. The new company Calder Publications Ltd. was set up in Baltimore through our American auditor, Hal Feldman, but it was trading mainly in England. As our debts other than royalties to authors, to Fine and to the banks, were minimal at that point, we were able to pay all trade debts, and eventually we caught up with most of the royalties, but I felt no compunction in not paying whatever Fine was still claiming, having given him a totally refurbished office building and the house next to it as well. As for the banks, they had earned a fortune from me over the years and were directly and stupidly responsible for the closure. Bettina got wind of the situation and began contacting everyone she could think of, telling them to stop trading with me, to break contracts for publication and dreaming up every other nastiness possible. But things settled down and I was still publishing.

Robert McCrum had come to see me from time to time to discuss putting all of Beckett's work into a joint edition, but it was soon clear that what Faber was really after was to try to get the Beckett novels away from me. It was then suggested, shortly after I had moved the offices from Soho to Covent Garden, that Faber would be interested in a take-over that would put new money into the company and let me continue to run it. I asked them to put in their proposition into a letter and I would consider it. Then I had to make a quick trip to America and on my return found the letter waiting for me. 'You won't like it,' Su Herbert had warned me on the telephone and on reading it I certainly didn't. But it never hurts to talk and I went to a meeting at Faber's offices with Matthew Evans, the Chairman, Robert McCrum, who by then I thought of as the Faber hatchet-man, and their financial director. The offer came down to just this: they would pay a small lump sum to take over all my Beckett copyrights, would buy all stocks of Beckett's titles we had in print at our balance-sheet written-down price, about five pence a copy, and they would put me on an advisory board to recommend how Beckett should be edited and published in future, and for which I would receive a small stipend. I listened in silence and looked at them. 'What I don't understand,' I said, 'is why you're saying all this. Can it be that you really thought I could be interested in such an insulting offer? Can you really think I'm all that stupid?'

The meeting soon broke up and that was that. From then on Matthew Evans, who by the end of the nineties was making a fool of himself in other ways as one of Tony Blair's puppets, preaching a philistine populist message from the House of Lords where Blair would put him, passed out of my life. He had once published Jim Haynes' very eccentric autobiography, made up largely of newspaper cuttings of his various exploits, and I had come to the party, where he had commented on meeting me, 'Ah, the man who invented Jim Haynes?' and passed on. Once I had unwisely allowed Kathleen Tynan, then writing her biography of Ken, to borrow two thick cuttings books about the two Edinburgh conferences and they were never returned. But one of them was eventually sent to Jim from Faber's because they found his name in them. How did it get to Faber? I have never been able to trace the other, but was happy at the return of one.

The biggest current problem was the money owed to Minuit and the Beckett estate, especially the latter. I had to find an angel of some sort and all I had to offer was a stake in the Beckett copyrights, which I would retain if royalties were paid. I was given a month to find the money. I telephoned Harold Evans in New York, then the head of Random House and suggested lunch, and without hesitation he gave me an appointment at the Four Seasons Restaurant, fashionable but new to me. I flew to New York at the beginning of January 1993 to meet him. The restaurant needs describing: it was the setting for power lunches, as the phrase was then, and the point was to be seen to be there by as many celebrities as possible in order to establish that you are one yourself. I arrived first and was shown to the table reserved for Harold Evans. The room was square with all the tables against the four walls and nothing in between except serving tables and bustling waiters. This meant that everyone was staring at each other across the room because everybody sat side by side and not opposite each other. I was reminded of the boxes in nineteenth century theatres which are so arranged that their occupants can see each other much better than the stage. Evans arrived and I started to explain a proposition whereby I would transfer half of the benefit of Beckett copyrights in consideration for a lump sum to cover what was owed. He never really listened except to the polite preliminaries about mutual acquaintances and when we had met last. His eyes forever travelled around the room to see who was there and he would constantly wave to other tables. Every time another publisher passed our table he would stop him. 'Have you seen the month's figures for paperback sales?' he asked each one. 'Random House came first.' At one point during our lunch Henry Kissinger crossed the room to speak to him. I was trying to think of a way to avoid shaking his hand, but I need not have worried. Kissinger was only interested in talking to Evans and had no desire to meet me. By the end of lunch, and I noticed that everybody in the room seemed to be drinking nothing but mineral water, he had taken in nothing of my proposition, and was much less friendly. He had though he was just entertaining a publisher from England who might have a big best-seller to offer him. He told me to ring his young assistant and explain what I wanted to him. And that was that. The young assistant was not helpful.

I received a 'phone call from Ken Bullock in California. I had known him as a man with theatrical links, who had worked for a while at Limelight, a film and drama bookshop in San Francisco and I had met him in places as diverse as Portland, Oregon (Powell's) and Venice in Italy. It was hard to pin down exactly what he did in life, but he had many connections. Now, when, he rang me, I asked, but without any hope, if he happened to know anyone who could help me in a financial jam. He said he knew somebody who might be interested and gave me the name of Edgar Aronson, who sometimes financed things that appealed to him. It was the day before my last in New York. I telephoned Edgar Aronson, and he invited me to lunch. We got on well and I explained my dilemma, but said that I had to return to Europe – I was flying to Paris – and that much as I had enjoyed meeting him, it was obvious that he could not help me in the time available, which was in fact at that point two hours. He heard me out, said that he felt he could trust me, and if I would return to his office after lunch he would be willing to give me a cheque. He paid for lunch, saying that the British always tipped too little and he wanted to return to that restaurant, and we went to his office. It was a small and neat suite of rooms, decorated with testimonials to his service in the Marine Corps and he had made it obvious that he was a patriotic American who had done well in finance and whose current hobby was his yacht. We roughed out an agreement, signed it, and he thereby acquired a residual interest in most of the Beckett works that were mine. He then gave me a cheque for $60,000. As a result I was able to pay £40,000 in royalties just before my month expired. That last minute reprieve is something that I still have difficulty in believing.

There was a Beckett Conference at Monte Carlo in May 1991, given in the Princess Grace Library, which organised an Irish literary event each year in memory of Grace Kelly, the wife of the ruling Prince Rainier; the princess had died in a car crash a few years earlier, the circumstances of which are still mysterious. There were about fifty persons present, largely academics whom I knew from previous Beckett conferences and we were all housed in a luxurious hotel overlooking the sea, while the Library itself was in the old town very near to the palace, so that we lunched in an open-air café on the main square and dined where we liked in the main part of town. I knew Monte Carlo well of course from the many years my mother had spent there; she was now in Greece. I met George Belmont for the first time, Beckett's one-time close friend in the late twenties when they had been exchange lecturers in Paris and Dublin, but they had become estranged due to Belmont's membership of the Vichy Government during the war as a junior minister for Education and his general right-wing stance in the period before the war started. His real name was Pelorson, but he had changed it after the liberation of Paris because of his disgrace. He and I shared a platform to give personal reminiscences about Sam. The conference went on for several days. Both Edward Beckett and his sister Caroline Murphy were there, the second with her husband, Paddy, who looked a bit mystified by all the proceedings, but could enjoy a holiday at a pleasant time of the year. There was a Beckett theatrical performance in the opera house, Garnier's little heavily ormulu-decorated adjunct to the Casino, where Princess Caroline made a nice little welcoming speech. What I particularly remember was the opening address at the conference by the Irish Ambassador to France, who told an anecdote about Beckett, who had gone to the Embassy in Paris to renew his passport. While waiting he fell into conversation with an Irish tourist who had been mugged, lost his wallet and had eaten nothing since the previous day. Sam emptied his pockets to give the man some money to get some food and then found that he could not pay for his new passport, and he even had to walk home as he had not a penny on him. A typical Sam story!

Beckett events continued to proliferate and I was involved in many of them. One I organised myself, and it must have been before I realised the full extent of Barney Rosset's perfidy in moving my *Stirrings Still* special edition from Paris to New York. I arranged a reading of the text at the Irish-American Centre on Fifth Avenue, of which I had met the President, Dr. Kevin Cahill some time earlier. It was a special occasion with Barry McGovern, who had already had a great success in New York with his one-man show *I'll Go On*. Edward Beckett had come for the reading as well and I had a long wait for him at the airport because he arrived without a visa. But the occasion was a triumph and very good for Barney's ego and his post-Grove Press reputation. I went on the club's invitation list as a result and went to several of their receptions until a new turn of events made me avoid the place.

This had to do with a man called Eoin O'Brien. He had written a book about Beckett's early life in Ireland, *The Beckett Country*, illustrated with evocative period photographs. Dolmen Press had originally intended to publish this, but Liam Miller's too heavy indulgence in drink and his ill-health had frustrated our plans – I originally intended to publish the British edition in unison with him – and in the end it was published by the author and distributed by Faber, but apparently with little enthusiasm because they sold it so badly that at one point I was asked to take it over. O'Brien had formed his own imprint, Black Cat, to publish it. It was a good book, showing a detailed knowledge of Beckett's work and its sources in his early experiences in Ireland. The many autobiographical and family references had been put into the context of actual places and people and O'Brien had been industrious in finding photographs of the postman of Beckett's boyhood, the schools he had attended, the teachers who had taught him, and the like. I came to know O'Brien, saw him in London and Dublin, attended splendid dinners in his house which seemed to go on all night, which did not prevent him, a practising surgeon, from getting off early in the morning to his hospital.

I was in the New York office one day when I received a telephone call from Jerôme Lindon to tell me that he had decided that Beckett's first unpublished novel, *Dream of Fair to Middling Women* could now be published. This astonished me because I knew of Sam's aversion to this early work, basically the first novel of a clever student experimenting with words and imaginatively writing of his amours in a high-flown manner that showed off his considerable erudition and knowledge of languages. It was undergraduate stuff and Sam had resisted the clamour after winning the Nobel Prize to get all his unpublished work into print with more determination where *Dream* was concerned than any of his other work. It was Eoin O'Brien who had brought about Lindon's decision. He had told him that Sam had said, during an unrequested visited after one of the falls that had brought him to hospital, that he was willing to see the work published some little time after his death. He had never said anything like that to me or to Lindon or to Edward or anyone else. It was O'Brien's word alone: it seemed to me unlikely then and has continue to seem unlikely ever since to everyone who had known Sam, but Lindon chose to believe it. Did I want to publish it? No, I didn't really, but I knew perfectly well that if I didn't Faber and Faber would. What I did not realise at the time was that Eoin O'Brien wanted to be the publisher himself through his own Black Cat Press, and as Lindon had said that as the publisher of all the other Beckett novels it had to be me, O'Brien went about it by guile. He declared his willingness to edit a manuscript that existed in two versions, one in the archives of Dartmouth College in New Hampshire where it had been deposited along with other Beckett unpublished manuscripts by Lawrence E. Harvey, an American scholar and author of a book on Beckett's early poetry, almost certainly without Beckett's knowledge at the time, and the other a typed copy which was owned by the Beckett Archive at Reading University, to which Sam had been particularly generous. I could see no objection to this offer and O'Brien edited it with Edith Fournier's name added as co-editor. I shall have more to say about that lady later.

Then the difficulties began, delays in finalising the manuscript being only one of them, and I was asked to allow O'Brien to publish a small limited edition at the same time as my trade edition. There were meetings in Dublin and Paris, constant changes of publication dates and difficulty in seeing the final editing. I had a contract to publish and Eoin O'Brien tried to negotiate himself into the contract, not just as editor, but as publisher as well. He knew of my financial difficulties and while overtly sympathetic he saw his way to using these to his advantage, expecting me to collapse at any moment. I had already had some flak thrown at me for the many errors in the first posthumous Beckett publication of unpublished work that I had brought out, *As the Story Was Told*. This contained his final text, *What Is the Word* and other writings, some of which had appeared in other collections, but I had not proof-read it myself and there were some ghastly mistakes which had been overlooked by the person who did. This was of course just at the time when I was undergoing the most difficult trials of my entire publishing career and giving all my attention to survival. I had been most heavily criticised in Ireland, quite justifiably, and O'Brien who had treated me as a close friend now became the opposite, and used every ploy possible, including that unfortunate last publication, to undermine my credibility. What I did not realise until later was that Edith Fournier had a part in that undermining and having Jerôme Lindon's ear, she was making him increasingly suspicious of me.

Edith Fournier was a strange lady. She had obviously had a crush for years, like so many others, on Sam Beckett, and had made it her business to know what he was up to by befriending Suzanne and spending time with her when she was unable to go out, which meant that she knew what was in the Beckett correspondence of the final year. Somewhere along the line she transferred her crush or at least her allegiance to Eoin O'Brien and she worked on Lindon to get him what he wanted. When that failed she became generally obstructive to me, advising Lindon to block publication of the *Complete Poems* (nearly a hundred pages more than the last edition I had published, which was many editorial hours made useless until there is a change of heart). Beckett had not wanted his *Proust* to be translated into French and had declared that *Worstward Ho* was untranslatable. She did both after his death. She had once wanted me to publish her translations of his untranslated French poems and we had some meetings about this, but her antagonism, with undoubtedly O'Brien behind it, made any further discussion impossible. Unfortunately Lindon continued to take her advice concerning Beckett up to his own death, which was after this book ends.

There was a meeting in Dublin just before Christmas at the end of 1992. O'Brien had already jumped the gun and brought out his own Black Cat edition of *Dream of Fair to Middling Women*, and it had been reviewed in the whole British and Irish press. The meeting, in a solicitor's office, was to try to make a deal of some kind. O'Brien had signed no contract to publish, only one with me to edit the manuscript. The meeting broke up without any agreement. He continued to sell his edition in all my markets and he never paid a penny in royalties to anyone. Although Lindon knew he was a pirate he would take no action himself – Edith Fournier no doubt had a hand in that – but urged me to sue. I knew only too well that there could be no greater folly than for a British publisher to sue an Irish one in Ireland. Centuries of old resentments would be almost visible ghosts in the court room. So I let it pass and brought out my own edition the following year, trying to displace, little by little, the Irish edition with my own in the bookshops.

In New York Richard Seaver had been keen to publish *Dream* under his own imprint Arcade Books, and he pursued me to obtain American rights, even coming to Applause Bookshop where Claudia Menza, Glenn Young and I were doing a reading of Erich Fried's poetry, to catch me when I was likely to be in a receptive mood. But money was still a major concern and as his distribution through Little Brown would certainly be superior to my own, at least where a hardback was concerned, I finally made a deal whereby he acquired hardback rights from me, but I retained the paperback. This turned out to be a wise move. The hardcover sold quickly in America and was reprinted, but the returns, large ones, came back from the chains just as the new printing arrived. Seaver paid for the hardcover edition, the cost to be set off against royalties, while I was left with the continuing paperback sale, which does not dry up with an author such as Beckett as hardcovers usually do. In the end I did fairly well out of the publication, but my reservations about publishing it at all were still there. O'Brien remaindered his edition soon after mine appeared. I had a stock of *The Beckett Country* at my British warehouse, which I should have retained against my considerable claim against O'Brien. Unfortunately, when he asked for them to be returned, Su Herbert, without a thought and without consulting me, sent them back to him. O'Brien was on close terms with Cahill in New York, which is why I stopped going to the Irish-American Center.

Edgar Aronson, who I saw fairly frequently during the next year, both in New York and in London, had prevented me losing Beckett. But I was losing many of my other better known authors. Michel Hoffman, son of the agent with whom I had concluded the Henry Miller contracts, cancelled them all because of late royalties. James Grauerholz was anxious to take Burroughs away from me, and Burroughs was by now putty in his hands, increasingly senile and just wanting to be left alone with his cats, his lethal toys and his typewriter. Working though a London agent he cancelled all contracts. I was soon to lose more books, partly because I could not afford to reprint them, partly because the authors were persuaded by their publishers in their own countries to leave me. But there was still a considerable back list and I continued to give the majority of my time to selling it. I had left the London representation to Darryl Richards, but now I began to sell in London as well.

After a few month in Meard Street, I made an arrangement with Marèse Murphy, who was now married to a retired banker and living most of the time in Dorset, to occupy a room in her flat in Bloomsbury with the use of the rest of it. When she was there she would sleep on the sofa or in the bedroom if I was away. I still did not have my own furniture, which was in storage, but I was now planning to find a place in France, possibly in Paris. I liked Marèse, whom I had known for a long time, but I found it difficult to get used to the smoke that went everywhere with her, because it was only in an opera performance that she did not have a cigarette in her hand. Her views were far to the right and she was intolerant, but we both liked the same kind of music and books, and enjoyed good food and drink. And she was good company. At one of her parties I met Penelope Turing, also a critic, who had written a book about Hans Hotter. He was obviously her hero, and her admiration for him made her book, which I agreed to publish, go much over the top, but Hotter helped her with it and the most interesting chapters were his comments on interpreting roles and how to act in opera. I sold the book to a German publisher with Hotter's help. He was an amazing man and even after his official retirement he went on doing speaking parts and giving master classes.

I had known David Applefield for some years. He had approached me years earlier in Paris to contribute to his magazine, Frank, which was published in English, and I had also given him short works by Beckett and others. He was an American who had gone first to Canada then to France to avoid the Vietnam War and he had a family in Montreuil on the east of Paris, where he suggested I might look for a place to live. I had found something that seemed just right in Clamart, south of Paris, a house that had just been built and was being sold by the children of the couple who had built it before they were killed in a car accident. Jim Haynes had introduced me to a lawyer, Emile Gourian, half-American, half-French who could set up various things I needed, such as a new company in America, and I asked him to negotiate the lease of the house, but he messed up the deal, so I lost it. I was soon to learn much more about M. Gourian. He turned out to be a crooked lawyer who was to get Jim Haynes into years of trouble as a result of a generous gesture, which Gourian turned against him.

One day when I was selling books in Boston I received a message from David Applefield. There was a house going just across the street from him, and he thought it would suit my needs. So, on the telephone from Boston, between the Grolier and the Harvard Bookshops, I told him to take it. When I saw it a month later I was not impressed: two tiny rooms, a kitchen and bathroom, all in bad repair over a garage, that I thought I could possibly later turn into a library. But when the lorry arrived from Dunfermline with all the Ledlanet furniture that I had retained and several large cases full of books, it occupied the whole of the garage and also the basement underneath it, where I later tried to put up some book shelves, but desisted after the old wiring started a fire down there.

There was an old foundry that consisted of a number of useable spaces around a courtyard on the Rue Edouard Vaillant in Montreuil, and here, together with others looking for space for their professional activities we started an office. David Applefield was by now doing some publishing of his own and producing reference books, mainly about Paris for tourists, and we shared a large open space on the first floor of our building, having a hangar next door and more space underneath. Gradually I conceived the idea of creating a theatre. Montreuil was no farther away from Paris than other theatrical complexes such as La Cartoucherie in the Bois de Vincennes. David introduced me to the Director of Culture for Montreuil, Jean-Marie Morel, an enthusiast whose eyes glowed a little when I said that Montparnasse was finished and the next centre of Parisian culture might well be Montreuil. Obviously all these years after the demise of Ledlanet Nights I was still suffering from withdrawal symptoms and looking for an opportunity to get back into the swing of theatrical and musical productions. I also knew it was my last chance because the years were now beginning to drain my energies. What happened then belongs to the next chapter.

New calamities hit me in New York. The warehouse to which I had moved after Kampmann turned out to be not only inefficient in getting out my books, but to be undergoing its own financial troubles. It had been bought by an individual without the manager giving me any inkling of this: he was a gambler who had run up a big tax debt, which he was unable to pay. The staff were so reduced that there were no packers, so that I was unable to get books out in December, and in the new year I was given short notice that the warehouse had been seized by the Revenue and if I did not remove all my books in three days I would lose them. Claudia recruited a friend of her's, Richard Derus, to help and for three days we packed up books for about ten hours a day and managed to get them removed by several trucks, altogether about three hundred thousand volumes. I had little time to find somewhere else, and chose the American Book Centre in Brooklyn, owned by Manny Gomez, with whom I had one brief meeting. My negotiation was mainly with his son-in-law, who seemed pleasant enough, and it was he who ran the day-to-day operation. But I soon discovered that all the past problems I had had with warehouses were nothing compared with what was to come. There was a proviso in the contract for extra charges if the monthly turnover fell below a certain figure. It did every month because books were simply not invoiced and sent out when they approached that figure. Then massive extra charges were added for storage, which had not been stipulated in advance and it was clear that I was in the hands of the worst exploiters I had yet known. The warehouse was on a high storey near the Brooklyn docks, reachable only by an industrial elevator to which only ABC had access. They had me by the short hairs. Things went from bad to worse. I was desperate to get my books away, but it soon became clear that I was in the hands of clever manipulators who by having possession of my books had all the cards in their hands. I went to Leon Friedman, who was not encouraging. 'Give me $30,000 and I'll sue,' he said, 'but I advise you to save your money and write it all off. You would have to sue in Brooklyn where the attorney general is a relative and Brooklyn courts are notoriously corrupt. It would probably take years anyway.' I was able to find another warehouse in New Jersey, not the first I had known there, (this chronicle has not tried to name all the warehouses into which and out of which I moved my books during the quarter century that I was publishing in the U.S.) but they seemed decent people and were able to tell me many horror stories about Manny Gomez, who threatened to sue them every time a client managed to escape from ABC and go to them. I sent more books out from Britain, including new titles, to Whitehurst and Clark, the warehouse in Edison, but was unable to negotiate with Gomez and his son-in-law. They then sent out a list of all my titles they were holding and claimed that they had seized them against unpaid charges. And they announced an auction. I decided it would be wiser not to go to it myself and sent a lawyer who had been found for me by Edward de Grazia who had fought some of Grove Press's past obscenity cases and was a friend. Claudia went with him and we fixed an amount which he would bid for my books. I waited in a nearby café until they came back with long faces: Manny Gomez was in Florida on the telephone the whole time and he had raised every bid. I rang Leon Friedman. 'That means he now owns the books,' he told me. All the cream of the list, books by our best authors; the opera guides which had been doing well in America, and of course all the slower-selling titles as well, all were lost. I could sue, but I had already been told what the probable result of that would be. A month later the whole stock of books was sold; probably at a few cents each to Dedalus, remainder dealers in Washington.

And that was only the beginning of my problems. Dedalus sold the books, not only all over the U.S. but all over the world. For the next two years I found my books at a fraction of the proper price turning up, not just in remainder shops, but in new bookshops as well. The big American chains bought thousands and those they did not sell quickly they tried to return to my new distributor for full credit. When I discovered this I instructed Whitehurst and Clark to accept back the books, which after all were stolen property, but to give no credit except where books had been obtained from them, and to say why. This meant in essence that they could return as much as they had bought, over and above the remaindered copies, since Whitehurst and Clark now had some of the same books, even though they (the chains) had probably sold most of them. And as they claimed I now owed them money, they would pay no bills. This argument was to go on for years, so that in effect I was selling only to the remaining independents and the academic shops of Barnes and Noble, the biggest American chain, about which unsavoury rumours explaining their rapid growth were in any case very current throughout the book-trade. Borders, the other big chain, also tried to return for full credit books that they could only have obtained, directly or indirectly, from Dedalus. The remaindered books were soon turning up in Canada, Australia, Europe and in Britain as well. I was fighting a constant war against American wholesalers who were bringing in books that undercut my own full-priced editions, and of course I had to reprint many of the same titles as they went out of print.

Claudia had married her long-term boy-friend some time earlier. Charles Frye was a university teacher of black history and philosophy, black himself, whose university appointments were always in the southern states, Washington D.C., then Texas, then Louisiana, so Claudia was much away to visit him, while he only occasionally turned up in New York. I liked him immensely with his quiet wit and unusual fields of knowledge. One year the MLA conference was held in New Orleans at Mardi Gras time and it was fun to discover the city of so much history and the home of traditional jazz, which was really the only jazz that appealed to me. I also discovered a very addicting local drink, the Cajun Dry Martini. From the time that Charles Frye began to teach at the University of New Orleans Claudia never missed a Mardi Gras and she went to New Orleans for many weekends during the year. Charles was also a writer, of poetry and fiction as well as of books and articles connected with his academic studies, and Claudia, as a literary agent, was tireless in her efforts to find him the right outlets for his writing. She was also full of stories about their experiences, some of them very threatening whenever they had travelled as a mixed-race couple in America, especially in the south.

This gave me an idea. Claudia was herself a poet and I knew from attending her readings in New York that she was a good performer. She was also very worried about her husband who had been diagnosed with cancer, and she wanted to keep him as occupied as much as possible to take his mind off his health. I had for years been devising performance scripts to promote the authors I published. Why not a Claudia and Charles Show? It did not take me long to put the script together. It took the form of a light-hearted dialogue between them, bringing in anecdotes from their life together, including the menacing ones, and sprinkled with readings from his work and her's. I then organised a British tour for them. If space allowed I would reprint here Claudia's very funny account of that tour. It appears in a *Festschrift* that was published in 1998 by Mosaic Press to celebrate my fifty years of publishing[42], which came in fact a year later. They both came to Britain, rehearsed in my office under my direction, changing and improving the script as we went along, and we then drove to the Cheltenham Literature

---

[42] In Defence of Literature, ed. Howard Aster. Toronto 1998.

Festival where they gave a brilliant performance. Unfortunately the audience was not as big as it would have been had General de La Billière, the British commander of the Gulf war campaign not been simultaneously giving a talk in the next room. Charles, a seasoned lecturer, but with no acting experience, who had worried me a little with his low-keyed delivery in rehearsal, suddenly expanded in front of an audience, discovering a deep resonant voice that perfectly matched Claudia's quick delivery and floating soprano tones which could produce a wide variety of inflections and a laugh-producing gift for comedy. They were a good team.

From Cheltenham we made a little tour before their next engagement. Claudia was anxious to show Stonehenge to Charles and we went there, to Bristol and elsewhere before the next Claudia and Charles Show, which was at Kingston University just outside London. Then I sent them off to Newcastle-on-Tyne where I had been able to get them invited to a conference on inter-racial relations, where their show turned out to be the highlight except for one mishap: Claudia passed out in the middle of it, but then recovered and went on to the end. Not long afterwards Charles Frye died, but that trip certainly did much to raise his morale at the time.

The death of her husband was very painful to Claudia, although she hid her grief well and carried on normally. But now Richard Derus who had helped us to pack up books to go to ABC, had joined Claudia in the office as her assistant in her literary agency, and although I could afford no extra overhead, she constantly passed over to him part of her work, for which she then said he must be paid. There were other problems in the office just then. Claudia had many black writers on her books and a constant stream visited the office, often using our photocopier to make copies of their manuscripts and other documents, and no payment was ever made for this. The overused photocopier needed constant repair. With all our problems, trying to sell a much smaller range of titles because we had lost all our old stock, the overhead had to go down, but the opposite was happening. The appearance of the office did not help: Richard was a very open homosexual who had plastered the walls around his desk with eye-catching photographs of gay marches, showing himself and others in weird costumes. His section of wall was well-calculated to shock any conventional visitor. One morning we were being visited by two young women from Citibank from whom we were trying to get an overdraft. They came in, both looking like the conventional bank employees they were, a few minutes after one of Claudia's Rastifarian writers had walked in and was starting to photocopy a manuscript, all the time gesticulating wildly and keeping up a stream of comment about his activities which was not likely to impress my invited visitors, who did not look as if they liked Richard Derus' wall decorations either. They left rather hastily and there was no point in following up the visit. They had seen what our office looked like and we knew how they would report it.

In fact Claudia, whose grief was affecting her judgement in many ways, was now using Richard Derus as a crutch and he became more dominating and self-important, so that on my visits to New York, where in any case I spent most of my time out selling books, doing my office work early in the morning or at night, I felt and was treated more and more as an intruder. I was paying the rent, all the bills and two-thirds of Claudia's salary, but had no space that was my own. The final straw was when, on my first morning in New York, having arrived from London the night before, I received a telephone call from a man who sounded like a raving lunatic, threatening me with writs and summonses and not letting me get a word in until I managed to elicit that he was a lawyer representing a printer who had recently reprinted two opera guides for us. The money had been sent from London to pay the bill and Claudia had cheque-signing powers. Claudia looked up from her desk. 'Oh John,' she said, 'there's something I haven't told you yet.' I got rid of the man on the telephone, telling him to ring again an hour later, and by then I knew that the money sent to pay the printer had gone instead on a variety of other bills, not least of which was a demand for payment from Richard for work that I did not want him to do, much of which Claudia was being paid to do herself. The threatening lawyer was just too much. I wrote a letter to our principal trade creditors, office suppliers and the like, sending them ten percent of what was owed and promising to send the balance in monthly instalments over three years. I told Claudia that I had to close the office and she would have to work from home. She was not willing to do that, so I let her have the office on her own and closed up, still selling my books from the warehouse, but now doing everything from London. Without an American address, the creditors had little option, other than suing me in England, but to accept my offer. It took the three years to clear the debts, but the printer in question, the Rose Corporation of Orlando, Florida, never stopped sending me threatening letters and faxes, even though I never missed a month, and they went on making demands after the final cheque had been cashed.

I was always on the lookout for ways of getting a substantial sum into the company in London. Attempts to find a buyer for the archives that had accumulated since 1975 got nowhere. I had talks with Sotheby's who were interested in Beckett manuscripts and I put together a collection of letters from him, first editions and rare books I had collected over the years, including the signed copies of Beckett novels and other work in special editions. I also put in what I valued most, Sam's own original prompt copy of *Waiting for Godot*. This was the first French edition which he had used during the rehearsals of Blin's first production at the Théâtre de Babylone. It included all his cuts, much new material that he had added in his own handwriting, and in the little volume there were changes and notes on every page. It also had the author's appointments written into the back pages and other personal notes. Sam had given it to me and I treasured it.

Unfortunately at the time he had made this wonderful gift he had written on the flyleaf 'for John and Bettina', because he was staying with us in Wimpole Street at the time. Bettina, during the eighties, sued me to get it for herself because of the signature. When I asked Sam what to do, he evoked the judgement of Solomon. 'Burn it and give her half the ashes,' he suggested. But I could not do this, and the courts eventually ruled that it was mine. Now I had to part with it to save the firm. The Sotheby auction took place during the Gulf War of 1990. The entire collection was valued at £80,000 and the negotiation was partly engineered by Sasha, the son of Millie Gervase, at the time Bill Colleran's girlfriend. As my need was great they agreed to advance £40,000 out of which Sasha took a substantial commission. Because of the war the auction, held just before Christmas, was badly attended and the main interest was in the *Godot* prompt copy, which had a reserve of £30,000. Trinity College in Dublin offered £29,000, discovered the next day what the reserve was and paid the extra thousand pounds. So I received no more and owed money to Sotheby, who obviously embarrassed by the unsuccessful auction, which, given the national obsession with the war, should have realised much more, or else the auction should have been postponed, did not press me. They later suggested that I might work it off by writing copy for Sotheby catalogues, but never followed this up although I agreed a willingness to do so.

As the nineties advanced it was obvious that more economies had to be made in London as well as in New York. We joined a consortium of small publishers to rent space in a building near King's Cross, where we only had one small room and two desks, so I could never sit down there on the days when Margaret Jaquess, now nearly eighty came in. We also had only one telephone line. In the room next door was Peter Day who had bought Alison and Busby, another publisher not too unlike ourselves, that had been unable to continue. They had been with us in Dallas and had filched our editor Bill Swainson to be their production manager twenty years earlier. Now Peter Day ran it on its own with some help from a publicity company who had taken over the main lease and divided up the building. There we stayed, operating on a shoe-string, uncomfortable but still publishing until, at the end of 1997, we moved once again. Su Herbert, who had been worried for years, especially about what would happen to her pension if we had to close down, and was unsatisfied with her salary, left us, but then went to work for Peter Day.

By now I was living in France, working in London, but most of the time travelling to keep the list alive and supporting myself personally by writing for newspapers, articles, obituaries and reviews. I had been through an extraordinary series of disasters, but I always had Sam Beckett's key injunction before me: ON.

Chapter 9

Montreuil

I was asked in an interview on a French radio station why I had decided to move to France. The answer that I gave was only partly true, it was 'Margaret Thatcher'. It had been painful to me to watch from 1979 onwards, a country that had developed a successful welfare state, an egalitarian educational system that had given opportunities to many young people from unprivileged backgrounds to develop their talents, a National Health Service from which on many occasions I had personally benefited, disintegrate so quickly as Thatcher relentlessly put the clock back and destroyed all that had been best in Britain. The BBC had once been the best broadcasting system in the world, but the Tories hated it, referring to it at one of their conferences as The Bolshevik Broadcasting Service. A series of destructive ideological wreckers were put in to destroy it, including Marmaduke Hussey, and William Rees-Mogg, who has already appeared in this book, whose reward was to be knighted and then made a peer by the Iron Lady. There is no clearer account of how this destruction was brought about than by John Drummond in his excellent autobiography[43], which appeared in 2000. Dolts and incompetents with no idea of what public service should mean, no values and no ideals, were brought in to replace the creative and dedicated men and women who had made the BBC the wonder of the world, and as the quality faded out bureaucracy reigned supreme, so that what had been set up as an independent corporation increasingly became an instrument of government, as broadcasting so sadly is in most other countries. The British had proved since 1945 that they had a talent for the arts, especially drama, painting, sculpture, dance and music, the latter a fairly recent development, to add to Britain's established reputation in literature. Now under Thatcher that too was coming apart. Yes, Margaret Thatcher was indeed one prime cause of my decision to move to France.

But there were other reasons. I wanted to get as far away as possible from Bettina and her constant summonses to bring me back to court, all paid for by Legal Aid and then reclaimed from me. She was of course hiding her earnings in order not to pay tax. I was told by those who met her abroad that she always insisted on being paid in cash and she certainly never declared her income from sources other than the considerable amount she was getting from me, where tax was deducted at source by the lawyers in Newcastle who administered the income from the trusts set up by my late grandfather. Perhaps she did not declare that either because it was enough to make her ineligible for legal aid. The less I was living in London, even though I mainly worked from there, the better. Most of my most important publishing contracts were now with French publishers and it seemed

---

[43] Tainted by Experience. A Life in the Arts. Sir John Drummond. London 2000.

reasonable to be able to see them more frequently as well as those authors who were still alive. Strangely enough the opposite happened. When I visited Paris usually staying at the Michelet-Odéon, I would go the rounds of Minuit, Gallimard, Grasset and Seuil, see authors and visit bookshops. Now it was only the bookshops I did regularly. Having a place in Montreuil, however dingy and uncomfortable, but some way out of the centre, I now went to Paris less frequently and when I did it was to see the bank, meet visitors and carry out a few necessary functions. I went fairly frequently to Jim Haynes' Sunday nights: he gave buffet dinners every week, open to the first seventy or eighty people to book, which were polyglot meetings of a wide variety of people from all over the world. A couple of articles about his Sunday evenings in airline magazines increased the numbers who came, so that you could meet actors and film producers, writers and publishers, journalists and painters, and now, because of the airline publicity, business people from California or Iowa, looking rather puzzled at the bohemian collection of artists, tourists and people Jim had picked up on the street in Paris or on his various travels. He had been teaching ever since he arrived there, exactly what was always unclear, but Media Studies was the title of his course, which was given to young Parisians who mainly wanted to learn English and from Jim received a general background discourse about his life and career, sexual politics, diverse opinions and whatever else crossed his mind while he gave lectures that had the minimum amount of preparation, if any. He got away with this for thirty years until he was reluctantly retired at sixty-five. Even Christian Bourgois, who had for years referred to me as his best friend in England, I hardly ever saw. I had however become very friendly with Olivier Corpet, the director of IMEC, who when I had to move in London to even smaller offices, volunteered to take over all my archives, other than what was necessary for the day-to-day business and to keep them in good order. They were transferred to a hollow mountain near Melun, which was now an enormous warehouse, housing the books of many publishers, where IMEC, a branch of the Ministry of Culture, occupied about a quarter of the space. The warehouse was invisible from the air. It was under a wooded hill alongside one of the tributaries of the Seine, next to some very grand palatial houses, and could only be entered by two large doors a few yards apart. Before the war it had been an enormous mushroom factory and during it the Germans had kept munitions there because bombers could not see it. Now it housed my papers, whatever had been accumulated since 1975, along with those of many French writers, archives of other publishers, some of them extinct, and old literary reviews. A small team worked there, cataloguing, searching out material needed by researchers, and bringing in new collections of literary material. IMEC (Institut des Memoires des Editions Contemporains) was the brainchild of Olivier Corpet, who now often invited me to lunch and tried to make me at home among his staff and friends. I gave a lecture in the reading-room of their Paris headquarters, went to their frequent receptions, and through their recommendations was asked to write articles for French newspapers and to take part in radio broadcasts. I also had hopes that they might help me to replace my lost British subsidy with a French one. Corpet was also the publisher and editor of the Revue des Revues.

In Montreuil I pursued my hope of starting up a new Ledlanet in La Fonderie. The loss of Ledlanet was still painful and there were few nights when I was not back there in my dreams, always with a sense that I was somehow a trespasser, putting on performances under huge handicaps and never sure when I might be told to leave. Old friends like Jacques Chaix and others now dead peopled these dreams. I still met Sam Beckett quite frequently in them and as in the later plays of Ionesco, the living and the dead mingled together in a landscape that was familiar but no longer part of my waking life. My new neighbours, those who had taken the complex of buildings together with David Applefield and I, occupied one-half of the courtyard, and we took over the rest. Friends from the Parisian theatre would come to visit me, bringing with them theatre architects and administrators to inspect the buildings. It was agreed that we could have two performing spaces, one of about four hundred seats and the other a studio with a hundred and fifty, together with a bar and restaurant. The nearby market-place was empty in the evening and could be used for parking. The mayor, who was also a deputé, came to inspect and we had a long talk about the 'cousinship' of Bretons and Scots, both Celts. Morel was a frequent visitor who approved the scheme and started the machinery moving to get us the necessary funds.

But then things began to go wrong. First our neighbours, one a man who constructed stage sets, one a photographer, and others who occupied part of the complex, decided that they did not really want to be part of a new theatrical centre. The work that had to be done to make the whole place functional for more humdrum activities was turning out to be more costly than I had thought and the bills were mounting. David had an accountant who came in the evenings to write up his books and she started a fire, almost certainly caused by a cigarette that she had not put out properly, late one night. This burned a hole in the floor through which many things dropped, and the smoke did considerable damage to my library from London, consisting both of my publications and other books I could not house elsewhere. We took on a man who had been administering a ballet company to help us to put together a dossier for the cultural department of Montreuil. The town was willing to back us, but neither of us were good at the paperwork requirements of French bureaucracy. He spent months on it, but he never let us see the final shape it was taking. Then he sprang a surprise. He had redesigned the principal theatrical space so that it would suit a ballet company, but not a multi-use theatre that could do drama, opera, concerts and other functions as we had instructed. He also proposed putting on the board of management various friends of his. And David, who had a family, was now being nagged not to get involved in something that would never make money and would involve him in more difficulties.

In the meantime we had organised a number of events. There were concerts of different kinds, all of which attracted a public. One was given by Jenny Paull, who brought her accompanist from Lausanne and presented an oboe lecture-recital. She was now living in Switzerland, had married and divorced a Swiss diplomat and had a daughter. Morel was impressed that I published Claude Simon in English and was very keen to have him come to Montreuil. I already had a programme that I had devised around Simon's novels, which had been given a few times in England. Now I put together the same programme in French and Pierre Chabert, the veteran actor of Beckett and Pinget, whom I had known for years, agreed to do it, recruiting two other actors, Raymond Segré and Jean-Marc Magella to join him. We rigged up a stage, hired the necessary lights and industrial heaters, because it was now winter, to heat the hall we were using. I had to get permission from Lindon and Simon to perform the extracts in French and this was given, but Claude Simon wanted the rehearsals to take place in his apartment. Although he was very difficult at the beginning, he warmed as the days passed to what we were doing, urging more expression where at the beginning he wanted the readings to be as flat as possible. But when, the day before the performance, he came to Montreuil where the premises were still far from ready and open spaces in the walls had still not been filled, he took fright and wanted to cancel the whole thing, which was impossible at that late date. He then said that he had developed a cold and could not come, so the expectation of M. Braard, the mayor, and Morel of having him there was disappointed. But the event itself was successful. The Mairie provided the seating and other conveniences, we had a packed house, and the actors, who had rehearsed with an intensity that paid attention to every small inflection in a way that no British actors would ever allow themselves to do, were more than impressive. Beforehand we opened a bar in our offices and afterwards held a reception there, where Chabert was surrounded by admiring ladies from the cultural department and the library of the town. I had asked the local bookseller to make available Simon's publications and he sold more copies of Simon on that night than he had ever done in all the past years. The evening gave a considerable spurt to my whole theatrical project.

I was approached by Fanchon Fröhlich, whom I had first met at the Theatre du Soleil's four-part production of the *Oresteia* when it came to an old mill in Bradford, and whom I occasionally saw when I went to Liverpool. She was a kind of action painter who belonged to a woman's group that painted large canvasses jointly and as an experiment I turned one of our proposed performing spaces over to them for a week: half a dozen women painted all day on large canvasses laid on the ground in front of a public that came and went, inspired by a pianist who improvised a background music to accompany their work. I also put on an exhibition of John Minihan's Beckett photographs, borrowed from the Centre Pompidou at the same time. The painters were British, French and Italian and they brought considerable life to La Fonderie, but I was not able to do anything for them after that one week.

But that was before we had taken on our administrator. He passed the dossier onto the Mairie before David and I had it. The Mairie had reserved 800,000 francs for our project, expecting to get a similar amount from the DRAC, the main government subsidising body for the arts. Now we had a detailed budget for the wrong plan and we were in effect being blackmailed. Either we agreed with a project that was a complete distortion of what we had commissioned or it would fall flat. We knew that at the slightest hint of conflict or trouble the town would back out. In addition, David under family pressure had cooled.

'If you don't agree to do things my way,' said our snake-in-the grass, 'you'll lose everything and have wasted your time.'

'So will you,' I said. 'I'm not going to be blackmailed.' And that was that. I knew I would never have the will to start all over again with a new theatrical project. I could feel my energy decreasing as I approached seventy. David Applefield and I withdrew from La Fonderie and turned our shares over to the others with the best grace we could muster.

David had become a director of my publishing company together with others who had agreed to give their names when I had to reorganise. I had hoped that he would take an interest in the list and learn to become a publisher in the same mould. But that was not his character. He switched from one project to another of his own and took no interest in the list that I was struggling to hold together. He had good relations with the town, but after a number of projects had gone wrong these had obviously become weaker. He was writing novels, but did not take enough time to revise them and his literary magazine Frank appeared at ever greater intervals. He also had a compulsion to always be late, which is not a good way of making friends. If I had thought of him as a possible successor I had been wrong. I liked him immensely, but he was not a businessman and I wished he would give all his time to being a literary editor, which was his real talent.

Marèse Murphy had sent a young Irish girl to see me in London and when she moved to Paris I took her on to help me with my office work, much of which I had transferred to Montreuil. Among other things she typed a book I had written on the *Philosophy of Samuel Beckett*, which I then offered to Oxford University Press. At La Fonderie she had worked for David as well, and as she had had commercial experience in the past he asked her to try to sell advertising for the guide books he was compiling and for his commercial work in connection with computers and websites, not a subject on which I personally had knowledge or experience. Something in David's manner put Sheila off him and I noticed this later with other people he employed. But

Sheila and I got on well. We had similar cultural interests, music and opera being among them, and somehow David with his very different background and values set him apart from us. She was in any case living with a man whom she was about to marry, and not liking the atmosphere, she left. But I still saw her and Mark Dillon quite often, sometimes going to dinner at their flat where Mark, who had trained to be a Chef in Burgundy, would turn out gourmet dinners in a tiny cooking space with little apparent effort. And sometimes I would take them out to restaurants and go to musical events with them.

Now David Applefield involved me in something totally new. Among his different activities he was teaching at the American University in Paris and at a school called the École Active Bilingue, which taught pupils from a variety of different backgrounds and nationalities in English and prepared them for university entrance. He was probably undertaking too much, but he felt that he could not continue with the two English courses that he was teaching for British A level and asked if I could possibly do them for him. Given that I was crossing the Atlantic every few weeks, selling books to booksellers all over North America and in all the towns of Britain, that I was running my London office, small as it now was, and had recently finished writing, not only the *Garden of Eros*, which had run into trouble with Simon and Schuster, to which I shall return a little later, and was regularly churning out copy for newspapers, it seemed impossible. I had other commitments besides, and the suggestion was ridiculous, but still I thought about it. I did need to earn some money in France and shortage of time had never deterred me in the past. It would be interesting and I certainly had enough knowledge to teach any syllabus dealing with literature, English or otherwise. I went to see Mme. Conchant who ran the school. She was desperate and would rearrange anything to accommodate me. So on the understanding that all the courses could be squeezed into the first three days of the week I agreed to teach there. I would have to return to London every Wednesday night and be back in Paris late on Sunday, but it was just possible, and the holidays would give me just enough time to keep up with the U.S. where I still had sales, but no longer an office. I gave my agreement on the nineteenth of September in the autumn of 1994 and taught my first two classes later that day.

I had to take a medical examination, arrange social insurance and get myself a working permit, all of which took me up to Christmas and the salary, welcome as it was, did not cover as many of my Paris expenses as I had hoped, but I was enjoying teaching, found it very easy and I only had small classes. In one of them were two girls and two very different boys, one from an obviously troubled home with many complexes but with a natural acting talent which emerged as we read Shakespeare and other dramatists together. I reread all the set books, Jane Austen, Thackeray, the Brontë sisters and several modern authors, much poetry and drama and revelled in rediscovering Milton and introducing my friend Robin Skelton's anthology of thirties poets, peppering readings of Dylan Thomas, T.S. Eliot and other poets and writers I had known with stories about them. I had two very bright girls, one Irish and the daughter of a librarian, the other a Cecil, whose father was then Tory Leader of the Lords. I was always trying to find new ways to make my classes interesting, but the administrative functions that went with the job were irksome, and I did not enjoy correcting examination papers, which of course was essential, because it was the best indication of how my students would do when they had to sit their A levels. Then the following January I was having a drink with David Applefield one night when he told me that he had agreed to teach two history courses that started the next day at the University of Nanterre, notorious because that was where the student revolution of 1968 had started. He felt that he could not do it. Was there any chance that I could take the two courses for him. They were both on Tuesday mornings, one on American history, one on British, two hours each. Tuesday mornings were my free ones: I had two classes at the École Active Bilingue that day, but in the afternoon. Being in a receptive mood at that instant I agreed and the next morning took the RER express train all the way across Paris to Nanterre to teach the two classes, probably not in exactly the way someone else might have done, because my knowledge of early American history was largely based on books that cover the history that Americans try to avoid – for instance, the massacre of American Indians up to the middle of the nineteenth century was massive and altogether about 55 million native Indians were wiped out by shooting, deliberately-spread disease and other genocidal methods. I taught a class of about a hundred, largely Arab and North African students, who were interested above all in the American holocaust and the slave trade. The other course was on British history from the civil war to Victorian times and that too I knew well. So for three months I taught those two courses on Tuesday mornings as well as my two literature courses later on in Paris on the Avenue Victor Hugo where the school was. Occasionally I brought visitors to Paris to my classes, Leonard Fenton, for instance, so that students could get a feel about the way an actor approaches a play, and he was closely questioned by them.

For a year I taught the two classes at the École and for three months two history courses at Nanterre. One Saturday I was asked if I would help make up an audience at the university for a guest lecturer who was talking on Scottish literature. The man was Keith Dixon who covered a lot of ground to a French academic audience of about forty who had no idea that there was a Scottish literature and who had never thought of Sir Walter Scott or Stevenson, let alone modern Scottish writers, as being anything other than English. When Dixon, who taught at Grenoble and was the only lecturer in France on the subject, moved into the moderns I asked him why he had left out certain names and a dialogue began between us that went on for some minutes. 'I know who you are,' he suddenly exclaimed. 'You must be John

Calder.' From that point on it was all cross-talk between us, with the others asking questions. Keith had persuaded his university to subsidise some translations of modern Scottish writers and when we met next to dine near the Bastille he gave me the three volumes that had so far appeared and hoped that I might continue the series, which so far had not sold well. A little later I brought up the subject with the Scottish Arts Council who had already been approached, but I was in no position to do anything myself and although I had thought of doing some French publishing in France the difficulty of setting up a distribution network was a task I could not face just then. The idea fizzled out.

I was receiving my salary regularly from the school, but not from Nanterre. My various attempts to see the secretariat between or after classes was not getting me very far, and of course I was an outside lecturer doing only four hours on Tuesday mornings. 'What's the trouble,' I asked a junior assistant in the office. 'Is it because I haven't enough hours?'

'No, it's because you have too many years,' she blurted out. I realised then that I was sixty-eight and already three years past the obligatory academic retiring age in France. It took me three months after I had finished the course to get paid, and that took many letters and telephone calls. It did not stop them from giving me other tasks to do, such as correcting the examination papers of students for courses other than mine, while my students' papers were corrected by another lecturer.

I had no trouble over my age at the school, which was very anxious to have me back for the following academic year. My calendar was so full that it seemed madness, but either the interest of teaching or vanity at being so much wanted, made me accept and at the end of 1995 there I was back again, teaching the same students for their second A level year in English, plus a new group for their first year, and in addition I agreed to take on the philosophy course. Then for good measure, and because I wanted to experiment with raising the level of general knowledge, I suggested another course on the History of Civilisation. This became a two-hour weekly course which, although voluntary, was packed out in the biggest assembly room in the school at 3.55 every Wednesday afternoon, after which I had to catch the metro to Orly airport to get back to London and return to publishing the next morning. My philosophy course was innovative. I had the notes of the previous year's philosophy 'Prof', but found them turgid. Also I had my own ideas and my own favourite philosophers. On top of that it seemed to me that with young people it was necessary for them to think of philosophy not so much as an academic discipline as of a practical help to getting through life, to making decisions and solving personal problems. On the first day I asked how many smoked and most of them did. I then asked them to read the warning on their cigarette packets and having digested that to tell me why they smoked. Smoking was a subject which came up many times and by the end of the course most of them had ceased.

I had one problematical student that year. In fact I had many and tried to help those whose problems had a possible solution, but I shall only talk of this one. She was extremely intelligent, came from one of the Baltic states and was staying with relatives in Vincennes. She was in my English Literature course and was having trouble with some of the set books, both classics and such modern novels as Golding's *Rites of Passage*, which she had difficulty in understanding because of unfamiliar expressions. So I gave her extra time, reading with her, and she learned very quickly to understand the archaic words and customs which we came across. But one day I gave the class a text without naming the author or the source in order to exercise their analytical and critical talents. It was a passage where Karl Marx describes the working conditions of seamstresses in a London sweat-shop, making dresses and gowns for the debutantes of Victorian times during the high season when everything had to be done quickly and there was no time to sleep or eat other than at the work bench. The girl in question recognised the passage and the next thing I knew was that Mme. Conchant, the Principal of the school, had a letter of complaint about me from the relatives of the girl. Why was I teaching Marxist literature? What were my qualifications to teach anyhow? They understood that in spite of my age I had no background of teaching. I also went to meet the couple with whom the girl was staying at a café in Vincennes and the meeting did not go well. Like so many East Europeans they were extremely reactionary and wanted capitalist and anti-socialist principles taught. Fortunately the girl was not in my philosophy class where I went into all the political systems, pointing out pros and cons of different theories, analysing the opinions of opposing philosophers and making the students think out for themselves what they thought was best. Most of them ended up as Platonists: it was better to have wise men specially educated to rule with authority than to leave affairs of state to the whims of democratic voters who most of the time did not have the knowledge or education to know what was best for them: their conclusions, not mine. I also countered much of the received wisdom of the textbooks. I have never been able to grasp the genius of Kant in spite of my respect for so many other philosophers who revere him, and Descartes has always struck me as a hypocrite pulling the wool over the eyes of the University of Paris theologians of his time. His proof of God struck me as extremely refutable, but I was never dogmatic. I taught what the textbooks said but pointed out my disagreements, which may have created some difficulties for my students at examination time, although it cannot have hurt their reasoning powers.

Every week I turned out several pages of text for the Civilisation course, and saw where this might eventually become a textbook. I summarised the early civilisations, explained all the religions, and went through the history of art and how it intertwines with political and social history. There was no examination, but everyone was required to pick a topic and write a paper on it. Unfortunately too many of them were plagiarised straight out of the internet, mainly encyclopaedia articles. I grew weary of finding the same wording repeated time after time.

I still travelled around British bookshops and around American ones, I still wrote articles and obituaries, I still managed to get to the opera and the theatre, but not as often of course. I did organise some outings to the theatre for my class but the logistical problems of block-booking and the uncertainty of the quality of what we were going to see (Britten's *Turn of the Screw* for instance at the time we were reading the Henry James novella, badly done at the Opéra Comique) soon discouraged me from doing this often. I kept the school photocopier busy and it was assumed that I was now a fixture and would continue teaching the same course the following year, but alas, I had to get back to my real work after two years of what had really been an indulgence. What I did realise at this time was that nearly everything I had been doing all my life was a form of teaching: this applied to publishing, politics, the lecturing I had done to every kind of audience and on the media, my Ledlanet performances and my Edinburgh Conferences. I was always trying to raise the level of culture, awareness and the quality of life through whatever activity in which I was engaged.

There were some lighter moments. When teaching *Henry V* I realise that the following week was the anniversary of the Battle of Agincourt. I had my class memorise some key speeches, wrote some more lines and on the weekend bought some toy swords, helmets and a crown at Hamleys in London. Then at lunchtime on the day my class swooped on the common room and the Principal's office, arrested everyone in the name of the king, quoting Harry's love of France, which was so great that he would not give up a single village of it. It caused a small turmoil and much amusement. There was an English janitor, but the word does not describe his functions, which extended from issuing textbooks to dealing with the personal problems of the students and generally keeping order. His name was Brian Hewitt and he had been a shorthand typist to Field Marshall Montgomery during the war, chosen because he was at the time a teetotaller, known to be discreet and a very rapid shorthand-typist. He had many anecdotes about Montgomery who had obviously trusted him, been fond of him, and had accorded him special leaves and privileges. I tried to sell the newspapers a personality article about him, but perhaps not seriously enough. A year later I was asked to be the principal speaker on the graduation day in 1998 and I tried to make my address as inspiring as possible, as I was talking to young people going out to make their careers in the world, who would have the task and the responsibility of making a better world than the one they had come into. I was afterwards much congratulated by parents and staff.

I was a little worried on that day because I was having trouble with my prostate. Barney Rosset's prostate cancer had been treated with the seeding procedure, as far as I could see successfully, and I knew another American, Jerry Kaplan, who had also had it done. When I was diagnosed with the same complaint I was sent by Dr. Scurr for tests and then to a London surgeon who wanted to operate. When I mentioned the seeding procedure he bristled. Neither my own doctor nor he had mentioned it, and Scurr knew nothing about it. I took other advice in Paris and discovered that while no one was doing it in France, there was one doctor in England, Dr. Daniel Ash, who had learned the procedure in Seattle and was treating some patients in Leeds. I went to see him, was accepted and in the summer of 1997 underwent a four-hour operation whereby hundreds of tiny radioactive seeds were implanted into my prostate to wear away the cancer. I was in the hospital on the night before and the night after and all went well. But Trevor Cunningham, in the same ward, who had the same operation immediately after me, was less lucky. In the middle of the night he was in agony, unable to urinate and full of liquid, so that nurses had to insert a catheter. Thereafter we telephoned each other at intervals to check our progress which was satisfactory. He was a retired salesman with a young Indian wife, who being himself still comparatively young was enjoying his early retirement and leisure, living near Coventry, but often travelling abroad. The night after the operation I was able to go to the opera in London. Surgery or chemiotherapy would have disabled me for at least a month. There is a conspiracy of secrecy about this procedure for prostate cancer. Doctors seem to know little about it and never to recommend it. Patients have to find out from each other. It is understandable that surgeons are unhappy about a competitive treatment, but I fail to understand why GPs are not better informed so that they can give those who need treatment the choice.

I was given another decoration by the French Embassy and for the first time was able to attend the ceremony, which was held in the library of the French Institute in South Kensington. I was allowed to invite about a dozen people to watch me being handed the medal and rosette of the Order of National Merit. This was in fact a promotion to Officier as I was already a Chevalier of the same order and also of the order of Arts and Letters. David Applefield came over from France with me and we stayed at the Caledonian Club. His mobile telephone disconcertingly went off in the middle of the ceremony, but he managed to get the ambassador, M. Guéguenod, to give him a copy of the over-flattering address, which later appeared in the previously mentioned *Festschrift*. Afterwards some of those I had invited, including my daughter Jamie and her husband who had arrived after the ceremony was over, were all looking for a place to eat, and I brought them all back to the Caledonian Club, where we had a pleasant dinner. One of those present was Sir Harold Atcherley and his wife Elke with whom I was now becoming increasingly friendly. He had been Chairman of the Aldeburgh Festival and had included me in some of their festive occasions. On one occasion he and his brother-in-law, Julian Grenfell, a Labour peer, and their wives invited me to join them in a visit to go to a special dinner in

Chagny, a village that held romantic memories for them. On another I was invited to his house in East Anglia on his eightieth birthday and later to a weekend where the group of friends that were involved, nearly all in various arts, included John Drummond, now knighted, and Sheila Colvin, who was herself picking up honours that included honorary doctorates, the OBE and a French Chevaliership. We formed rather a large group that began to meet regularly. One of us was the delightful Diana Jervis-Read, who having been at Ontario House was now the Canadian Cultural Attaché. Diana was exceptionally attractive, full of energy and good humour and did her job extremely well at a time when Canada was cutting back drastically on arts expenditure. She radiated an enjoyment that was very contagious.

I still went regularly to Wexford to see rare operas every autumn, but Elaine Padmore had now left to take over as Intendant in Copenhagen, where I visited her twice, once to see some opera, another time for an IMEC Conference of Little Magazines. She had learned Danish, was getting on well there, had become chummy with the opera-loving queen and was a central figure in the cultural life of the city. Seats were very cheap because heavily subsidised and I was particularly impressed with the words written over the theatre's proscenium: NOT FOR PLEASURE ALONE. Elaine's next move was to be to the Royal Opera House, Covent Garden.

I have mentioned David Edgar's annual theatre conferences, most of which I had attended over the previous several years. The last one was held in 1998 and at it Howard Brenton made a furious denunciation of what New Labour was not doing for the arts. A new philistinism was doing more damage than even the deliberate cuts that the Tories had instigated since 1979 to reduce them, depoliticise them and remove their availability from those who lived outside big cities or were not affluent. Now Tony Blair's New Labour was dividing the arts that they called 'elitist', which were only for a small educated minority of 'snobs' and those they considered 'popular', i.e. without intellectual content or need of special concentration on the part of audiences. It was a time when a countryside march, uniting different interest groups had been very successful and had attracted much press attention. I suggested that we should organise a similar march or rally, perhaps trying to get a million people into Hyde Park in support of the real arts. Tariq Ali thought that this would take a million pounds to organise, but it seemed to me that at a time when arts lovers and those professionally involved with them all over the country were thinking the same way that such a rally was possible and would attract mass support. At a vote there was unanimous agreement from the hundred or so people present to support such an initiative, and I went away with my mind busy with thoughts of how to do it.

A week later I went to a birthday party given to celebrate John Carewe's seventieth birthday. I had seen little of Carewe since we had worked together for Music Today, but knew that he had been Simon Rattle's teacher. He was now also a gifted photographer. The room, in the crypt of a church, was filled with well-known musicians, many of whom I knew, and I circulated among them with my new plan for showing the government that the arts mattered by organising a massive rally the following year in London. Nearly everyone I spoke to, including Simon Rattle, Carewe himself, players, singers, conductors, composers and agents, were willing to give their names as sponsors. After that I lobbied everyone I met who was involved in the arts, made telephone calls and wrote letters. I talked Lord Harewood, who I invited to lunch at the next Edinburgh Festival, into becoming Chairman of what was now named the National Arts Rally, and a little later John Tusa, the veteran BBC broadcaster, previous Head of the World Service, and now Managing Director of the Barbican Arts Centre, and Norman Rosenthal, Exhibition Secretary of the Royal Academy of Art, to become Vice-Chairmen. Our first meeting of about fifty people from among those whom I had recruited was held in a Committee Room of the Royal Academy and we had a few meetings there until it became clear that some of Rosenthal's Royal Academy colleagues were not really with us, and had not done simple tasks they had been asked to do, such as opening a bank account. My office suddenly had much extra correspondence to deal with, as well as photocopies of leaflets, and the updating of the growing list of sponsors. Although we now had opened a bank account for the NAR and we had many donations, I used none of this and paid for the additional expenses out of our general publishing income.

Harewood then decided that he was now too old to be an active Chairman and became President instead. We decided to replace him with Peter Hall, who had attended our meetings and I took him to lunch to get him to agree. He suggested that we change our name to the Shadow Arts Council, because the rally had run into logistical difficulties to do with hiring Hyde Park. Increasingly our meetings became bogged down with disagreements. We moved away from the Royal Academy, held a large meeting at the National Liberal Club which John Elsom, one of our active sponsors, organised and then had a meeting in the Cabinet War Rooms, now a museum, but with a meeting room that could be rented. It was here that Sir Peter Hall was formally elected chairman. He immediately said, 'Thank you. I now propose that we change our name to the Shadow Arts Council.' No one demurred and it went through on the nod. Present at the meeting was Amanda Todd of the National Campaign for the Arts that had been started at about the time that I lost my Arts Council grant, who complained that we were 'reinventing the wheel'. Why were we competing with them? They had never helped me when I approached them fifteen years earlier and in my opinion they had done very little for anyone in all that time, but she had her say and was extremely hostile to our new and more radical lobby coming into being. But it was a good meeting and a number of persons present, including Clive Bradley, ex-Director of the Publishers Association, volunteered to give time to further our activities.

Immediately afterwards on the same day, Peter Hall went to another public event where he received an award for his theatrical achievements and announced that he had just been elected Chairman of the Shadow Arts Council. The press knew something of us under our previous name, but this was a surprise and they immediately began ringing sponsors who had not been at the meeting to ask them about their allegiance. These included Tom Stoppard, contacted in California, Harold Pinter, Sir Simon Rattle and others, who of course knew nothing of the change of name and were not pleased.

This led to a weekend of telephone calls on my part to these same personages whom I had lobbied so hard during the previous year in order to explain what had happened at the meeting. The change of name was not very popular and we lost some of our sponsors. Clive Bradley and Michael Kennedy, the latter working at the Richmond Theatre, gradually took the executive functions of the Shadow Arts Council over from me, and I was able to concentrate on those many other activities for which I could find the time.

I had paid a visit to my mother in Greece in the spring of 1994. She was very bored, constantly complaining, being looked after by a Greek nurse and my sister, who had even more reason to be bored. I stayed three days and returned to Paris. The following February she died. Apparently my brother had gone to visit her with a bad cold, had given it to her, and having a weak heart it was too much. She died in the night. I was still teaching in Paris then, but her body was flown to Montreal for cremation and the funeral was during the following week when there was a school holiday. I went over for it.

Bettina knew about the death as quickly as I did and wasted no time. There was an old court order that I had to give her a lump sum on my mother's death. The death would not in the circumstances give me any new capital because my mother had been the recipient of an income from her father's trust, and this would not be broken up until the last of the six Wilson sisters died. The judge had either been unaware of this or had assumed that my mother would be the last to go. In the event her elder sister, Gertrude Raymond, was still alive in Montreal. Shortly after my return to London a tipstaff came to arrest me in my London office and I was told that I would not be released until I had paid the entire amount. I spent a day in custody until I found a barrister who brought me in front of a judge just before the courts closed. There was no time to explain there that I could not pay now an amount that I might receive at some future date when my aunt departed, but I was given a temporary release on handing over my passport, which I had to get back to return to France to teach. Lawyers finally settled the matter, but in the meantime Bettina attacked me legally in Montreal and I had to get another lawyer there to defend me. Fortunately I had a better one than she did. I had to go to Montreal twice in the next few months and finally the matter was settled with a final payment, while she reluctantly signed an agreement to sue no more.

Bettina had been in New York and had seen Barney Rosset just before the funeral, and I suspected that she must have been in Montreal at the time of the funeral itself. My brother had behaved in a very secretive way and would not tell anyone where he was staying, so I later drew some conclusions from that. He came to the service, which was the day after the cremation, but not to the cremation itself, after which a box with the ashes was put in the same mausoleum where her parents were buried. I have made no secret in this book that I had little liking for my brother and I knew that his feelings towards me were even stronger. It soon emerged, when the accounts from Greece became known, that he had helped himself very handsomely from my mother's income while she was in Greece. He continued to intrigue against me during the following year to try to prevent me getting a small lump sum that I should receive under the will. It was my sister and Jacques Brillant, a Canadian living in Monte Carlo who was also a trustee of the will, who outmanoeuvred him on that, because otherwise I would not have been able to move to my next address in Montreuil, a ground floor and basement flat near the Mairie where at least I had space for all my books and what I had kept in furniture from Ledlanet. It had previously been an office, had been on the market for five years, and although far from luxurious, it had what I needed most, wall-space for books. Here for the next year I built shelves, alphabetised the library and settled in. The small lump sum was enough with a loan from my Paris bank to give me a new home at last.

I had finished my book about the Girodias circle of expatriates some time earlier and had delivered the large manuscript to Simon and Schuster. Ann Patty gave it to her husband to edit and he was critical because what I had written was partly literary history and partly sketches of all the personalities who had started literary magazines and publishing activities in post-war Paris, especially the Girodias authors, and what had later become of them. He thought it should be a much smaller book about only a few people, the best-known names. While we were arguing Simon and Schuster was bought up by Paramount Pictures and many employees were made redundant including Ann Patty, while the Poseidon imprint under which my book was to appear was shut down. Several months later a new team of editors found the manuscript and called me in. They liked the book, but it was too long, too full of names they did not recognise and big books did not sell, they told me. They had just published a big book on Dreiser and it had sold badly. 'A small book on Dreiser would probably sell no better,' I commented, but they did not see the point. I set about cutting it, but just then another book on Olympia Press appeared, although not with first-hand material like mine and full of errors. They felt there would no longer be any interest. So I took the manuscript away and Glenn Young said that he wanted to publish it. This was after I had closed the office on Broadway, and

I was having another negotiation with Glenn at the time, who ran the Applause Theatre Bookshop and Applause Publishing Company, to rent a little space in his office so that I could work from there when in New York? Finances were still bad and I had to keep my overhead to a minimum while trying to bring the most necessary books back into print after the ABC warehouse disaster and the difficulties I had had in Britain. Glenn agreed to give me a small room and during the one week I was in New York I moved in, installed a telephone line, went around my bookselling visits and saw those I had to see. Glenn had the manuscript of *The Garden of Eros*. He had asked me for names of people who might give quotable comment and I suggested Frank Kermode, then teaching at Columbia. Now he told me that he had the quote and it was good. But he had sent out several large chunks of the manuscript without keeping a copy, assuming I had one. I did not have any complete copy, as it had been altered so much. Realising that he had made a careless mistake he became angry, although I did not realise it until returning to the office on the Friday to pick up my suitcase before leaving for the airport. I found a letter addressed to me by Glenn. It said that he had changed his mind and did not want me in his office. While I was reading this Glenn walked in and was discomfited to see that I had not already left. He did not want to publish the book either now and obviously had such a bad conscience about losing a quarter of the manuscript that he did not want to face me again either. I then decided that it would be easier in the end to just publish it myself.

In early 1996 I received a letter from the Office of Fair Trading to tell me that it intended to take action to bring the Net Book Agreement to an end. The book trade was undergoing a transformation, one that had started many years earlier. I had once tried to make Better Books the centre of a chain of good literary bookshops, and having started the Edinburgh shop after buying the London one from Collins, I had intended to make Newcastle on Tyne the next target. I have already told how the plan went wrong. But shortly after I left bookselling, Tim Waterstone, who had previously been with W.H. Smith, succeeded where I had failed. The growth of the Waterstone chain had been the best thing that had happened to the book trade throughout my career. Tim had created a number of large bookshops throughout the main cities of Great Britain, all run by enthusiastic young graduates who knew about and liked books, and with an emphasis on literature, they also managed to cover all subjects. They were usually located on main streets and brought people into bookshops who had never visited one before. Increasingly my books were being bought from Waterstones, whose secret formula was good staff and wide stock-holding. Once at a Cheltenham Literature Festival I had found myself on a platform beside Tim Waterstone and was able to pay a quite sincere tribute to the transformation that he had brought about, and he was very pleased and became a friend. But another chain had grown, not so much in imitation, but as commercial competition anxious to find ways of increasing their market share by cornering the best-seller market, and they were little interested in the quality of what they stocked. Terry Maher, an accountant who had managed to get into a position of authority in a group that had originally been an academic chain, was anxious to discount books to increase sales and his petitions against the Net Book Agreement were placed next to the tills in Dillons shops for customers to sign, while he lobbied members of parliament and the press.

The Net Book Agreement had been the crutch of the trade since early in the century. A hundred years ago the growth of department stores had depended on finding loss-leaders, objects on which the stores were willing to lose money in order to bring in customers to buy furniture, clothes and other expensive items. Books proved to be perfect for this: customers would come in to get whatever book was popular at the time for half what a bookseller had to charge, and this put many of them out of business because it was the best-sellers that enabled them to carry stocks of good books that sold more slowly to discriminating customers. The Net Book Agreement had taken years of negotiation before booksellers and publishers agreed to bring discipline and order into their trade rather than a cut-throat competition that could only lead to great cultural damage. Over the years the Publishers Association had been many times to court to defend price regulation, the last time in 1962. Now the OFT was attacking again, one of the last acts of vandalism of an out-going and discredited Tory government that would be heavily defeated the following year.

I took up the challenge hoping that most publishers would do the same. But no, British publishing had now become so Americanised that the big publishers in particular seemed happy to go along with a destruction that they hoped would damage others more than themselves. Some of the independent publishers felt as I did, as well as Clive Bradley, the Director of the Publishers Association who had been a rigorous defender of the NBA for years. He agreed when I contacted him to give me what help he could, but warned that his current chairman of the P.A. was on the other side and so were most of the big guns of the trade, who in any case were mostly in the employ of their masters in New York or Boston. Clive provided me with copies of the most important book on the subject, *Books are Different*[44], which not only gave a full report of the last time in the sixties that the Publisher Association had gone to court to defend the Net Book Agreement, but a history of the circumstances that had brought the NBA into being. Although a number of other publishers came to meetings and were willing to appear as witnesses, I found that it was up to me alone to go to court and to make the necessary preparation. To employ lawyers would have incurred costs we could not possible afford, so I had to do it on my own. Not entirely on my own however, because John de Falbe, one of the owners of John Sandoe, a

---

[44] Barker and Davies, *Books are Different*, London 1966.

lively and adventurous bookshop in Chelsea from which Sandoe, the founder, had now retired, joined me in the fight and so did two librarians Jenny Glayzier and Sherry Jesperson. We all appeared together as objectors to the demand of the OFT to make the Net Book Agreement illegal because it limited free competition. Whereas in 1962 publishers and booksellers had been solid in their determination to defend the NBA, and there were then many more publishers and independent booksellers, now the power lay with the big groups, mainly American-controlled and very few people realised what the issues really were.

Our hearing began on the 20th of January 1997. From the start it was obvious that the judge, Sir Francis Ferris, who was always addressed as 'My Lord' was against us. This was hardly surprising as he had previously been the leading counsel to the OFT. Against us we had nearly a dozen lawyers and lawyers' clerks and they needed several wheeled trolleys to bring into the court all the dozens of files that they had collected to support their case. This consisted of evidence they had acquired from all over the world, not just about the book trades of every country from Argentina to Zululand, but much quite irrelevant material from other trades that had nothing in common with books. The cost of sending out all their queries and employing people to compile, analyse and draw the conclusions they wanted must have been staggering, especially as many of them were highly paid lawyers. Against all that were four individuals with no legal representation who nevertheless knew more about the issues involved and the consequences that would follow than those who wanted to thoughtlessly destroy the NBA.

Against us we had one publisher, Richard Charkin, who had recently been fired from the Reed Group of companies that had by then acquired nearly all the British literary imprints which had been my rivals over the years, they having earlier been bought up by Paul Hamlyn and sold on, first to Elsevier in Holland, then to Random House in America and then to Bertelsmann in Germany when they bought Random House. He was at that point engaged in computer publishing, a buccaneer who had not a good word to say for literary culture, which he claimed could always find money to survive from old ladies in Hampstead. One witness who would not commit himself because of a lack of evidence of the possible effects of abandoning the NBA was a Dr. Fishwicke, who compiled statistics for the book trade: he sat solidly on the fence although we had expected him to be on our side, as he had been in private conversation. There were the usual right-wing economists preaching the virtues of free competition, who obviously had no interest in literary culture at all and probably did not know that such a thing existed. The OFT put up many words, but no real argument: they simply did not understand the whole concept of literary and intellectual culture and of how a best-seller-dominated book-trade, out of which everybody did badly by cutting each others' throats, also made it impossible for a wide range of important but slow-selling titles that mattered to an educated minority to, first of all be published at all, and then to have a long-enough life on booksellers' shelves.

Of course, by the time of the court case, the NBA had already been abandoned by a considerable number of publishers, including most of the big ones. What I was fighting for was the right to put a price on my books and ask booksellers to sell at that price, always with the hope that those who had abandoned the NBA would come to their senses and want to return to it. The French example was the shining one that I wanted to bring up in court and I had approached major figures in the French book trade to come to Britain to give evidence, but the judge although he had accepted written evidence against us from abroad, none of which I am sure either he or the two lay assessors, retired business men who sat with him, had even glanced at, he would not allow any live evidence from Europe to be put before the court. Jack Lang, when Minister of Culture in France, after the great wave of bankruptcies of good booksellers that had followed the abandonment of price maintenance in the 1970s, had passed a law in 1981 to prevent discounting at more than five percent and the benefits to the French book trade had been enormous. The supermarkets who had used books as loss-leaders decided to continue selling books after the law was passed and they found that the public were just as willing to pay full price if it saw a book it wanted. That supermarket public seldom went into bookshops anyhow, but those who normally did returned to buy their books where they had previously. The result was that the number of books sold increased overall. None of this could be explained in court except as hearsay evidence by me.

One of my key witnesses was George Liebmann from Baltimore. He was a lawyer who was also attached part-time to a Cambridge College. His father had been an independent bookseller in New York who was forced out of business by ruthless price competition. A quiet, well-organised rather dry man, he had a fire in his belly on this particular issue, and he was only too willing to give evidence. He came from the States two days before he was to appear and I produced him in the witness-box on the sixth day of the case. The judge did not want to hear him and kept cutting him short, but Liebmann talked right through Ferris, making his points until he was told to shut up. None of the witnesses on the other side had been limited in what they had to say or been so discourteously treated. Clive Bradley who was in court – and he was a qualified barrister himself -- was shocked at the partisan prejudice of the judge and also at the way he treated me, stopping me in questioning witnesses and constantly telling me to shut up and sit down. Against us we had a woman barrister, whose wheedling and insinuating manner seemed to please Ferris; he let her go on as long as she liked, whereas I was usually stopped after a question or two.

Among my other witnesses were a Scottish publisher, Bill Campbell, brought there by the librarians, John de Falbe, Tim Waterstone, founder of the chain, from which at that point he had sold out to W.H. Smith, although he was to re-emerge on the scene later, the retired publisher Rayner Unwin, John Mitchinson, formerly with Waterstone's, then with Harvill, the politician Sir David Steel, and some others. Ainslie Thin of Thin's, the Edinburgh University booksellers (not the Ainslee Thin previously mentioned, his uncle) had agreed to come, but now I found I could not reach him by telephone or in any other way: he had obviously become nervous of sticking his neck out. André Deutsch came to court and sat right in front of the witness-box, giving the proceedings his full attention. That was the day I had two literary witnesses, Tom Stoppard and Auberon Waugh, who in addition to being a novelist was now also editor of The Literary Review. They were good value in the box and were much photographed at the entrance to the High Court in the Strand where the case was heard, being newsworthy. It was a building for which I had much dislike having had so many painful experiences there in the past. This was one occasion on which I needed publicity, but the press took little interest: there was rarely a reporter taking notes other than The Bookseller and other trade journals, and only Steel and the two writers were thought worth photographing. After all, the big newspaper proprietors of the time were not interested in cultural matters and neither were their editors.

Liebmann went back to the States, the case ended and we were given a judgement on March 13th. As I expected we lost and the NBA was declared illegal. In my final speech, which I had been warned by the judge must not be too long, I reminded him that the previous counsel for the OFT in 1962 had said afterwards that it was one case he had not much minded losing because the publisher's' arguments had been so persuasive. Clive Bradley had been very helpful in finding the obituary in which this was quoted. But the judge had made up his mind in advance and that was that. At the next annual general meeting of the Publishers Association, the chairman said some kind but totally insincere words about my defence of the NBA, and I took the occasion to make a strong attack on the cowardice and folly of those who had done nothing, contributed nothing, and obviously did not care. Bradley, because of his disagreement with the Chairman, was forced to take early retirement, which later enabled him to become involved with the Shadow Arts Council.

* * * * * *

Between the hearing and the result I moved houses in Montreuil. I now had an old office, not in too bad repair, but it had been empty for five years and was much in need of decoration. The night before the move Jim Haynes came over to help me and we spent half the night putting books into cases and everything else into tea boxes or suitcases. The next morning Muriel Leyner and a friend, Ruth Bonipace, arrived from New York and they helped once in the new place. Jim and I were both exhausted and waiting for the movers. It took the whole day to get everything out and into my new home on the Boulevard Henri Barbusse. Two Jacobean chairs and a matching double seat built to contain rugs or other objects, I put into the outer hall. An antiquarian dealer came by as they were arriving and offered to buy them. I moved in bookcases and all the tea chests and other packages, most of them ending up in the middle of the large underground conference room, soon to be a library. A wonderful handyman, M. Michebu, who had done some plumbing and small jobs for me at the old address, now got to work to paint some of the rooms, install a bath and create a kitchen out of one of the offices. I told him it would all take years, but 'peu à peu' I would get it right. Over the next year, M. Michebu put up shelves and I acquired more from IKEA near the airport as I gradually settled in. The Channel Tunnel was now finished and I was able to start travelling to London by train. On one of the first occasions I learned from a taxi on the way to the Gare du Nord that there had been a fire in the tunnel early that morning. In the general confusion at the station I decided to follow the train stewardesses and do what they did, which enabled me to get a train to Charles de Gaulle airport and a plane from there to London while other passengers were still at the station.

The next General Election was now imminent. I had been active in all the previous ones, either taking part in a tactical voting campaign or helping my daughter when she had stood for parliament in Stafford and on that occasion I had given her two weeks, helping her to fight the Thatcherite Bill Cash. This time I decided to help in a marginal seat, and as I could always stay with Sheila Colvin at the Red Cottage in Aldeburgh (She was still running the Britten-Pears Festival there) I decided on Suffolk Coastal, John Gummer's constituency. I had always found Gummer one of the least appealing of the Tory Ministers. He had been involved during the earliest BSE crisis in a stupid gesture: forcing his small daughter to eat a hamburger in front of television cameras to reassure the public that beef was safe (he was Minister for Agriculture then) and he was also a lay member of the Church of England Synod, where he exhuded the kind of nauseating piety that Dickens or Burns could so well describe. It was a pleasure to try to get him out and Alexandra Jones, the Liberal-Democrat candidate, in second place, seemed to have a good chance of winning in an election where the long Conservative hegemony seemed certain to end at last. The Tories were beset by corruption scandals, the badly-hidden sexual peccadilloes of so many of them had humiliated them, and tactical voting would obviously play a large part in this election. I volunteered my services and was asked to drive the candidate around the constituency, take part in canvasses and do all the usual things I had done so often before. The constituency borders had however been changed since the last election and it was now not so clear who was really in second place. In the end it turned out to be the Labour candidate. Alexandra Jones tried hard, but the press were largely favouring her Labour competition. Gummer was returned, but with a much reduced majority.

The election was on the first of May. I did not go to the count, preferring to sit in Aldeburgh, watching the results come in until the early hours, sometimes falling asleep. When it was clear that the Tories would lose by a landslide I opened a bottle of champagne. Then came the exciting results. Portillo was out. Then Martin Bell was elected as an independent member for the safe Tory seat of Tatton in place of the disgraced Neil Hamilton who had taken many brown envelopes of cash from Mohammed Al Fayed, owner of Harrods. I recorded the events in a poem that I shall quote later.

It was on the 15th of July that year that I received the French decoration and the Ambassador's commendation then went into the *Festschrift* that some of my friends had been preparing, with my knowledge but without my knowing the detail. I had suggested some of the people who might contribute and many of the suggestions were taken up, which resulted in contributions from Lord Harewood, from Richard Beith, who had first lured me into politics in 1970, also writing about the Ledlanet Nights he had enjoyed, from Bill Webb, Barbara Wright and others. The whole was edited by Howard Aster, whose Mosaic Press published it, while Jim Haynes and David Applefield did most of the field work. The cover photograph was a very unflattering one of me in Leipzig on my way to give a lecture, looking very old and bowed and there were other photos taken by David, John Minihan, Jane Bown, Richard Beith and others. The volume also reproduced book jackets and the like. Many friends wrote short tributes.

There were some embarrassing things in the book too. A Serbian artist whom I had met with Haynes at a New Year's party and had taken home because she lived a minute away from me in Montreuil, and whom I had met again a few weeks later and invited to dinner, wrote a piece about our quite chaste evening together. We had talked, and as she was interested enough to ask me many questions about my life, I had told her quite a lot over a bottle or two of wine. Jim got her to put it on paper and of course it was exaggerated enough to make amusing reading, but still very much out-of-kilter with the rest of the volume. George Liebmann wrote a contribution but this was lost by Howard Aster when sent to him in Ontario. The rest of the volume consisted of old articles of mine or articles about me from the press, and it ended with a near-complete bibliography of the books I had published over the years. To do this Howard Aster and his assistant Amy Land came and spent about two weeks in Montreuil when I was away, taking down the titles from my shelves and listing them. Tributes and letters from Sam Beckett and other authors made up the rest of the volume. I was embarrassed at the amount of work that had gone into a project I would never have encouraged, but of course I appreciated the generous impulse behind it. It was called *In Defence of Literature*, the same title I had chosen for a collection of my writings on other writers which had not been published because of lack of funds during those late eighties and early nineties.

Howard Aster did more than that. Jim Haynes had a little publishing company that had mostly published his own life-style books, such as *Hello, I Love You!* which was his greeting to any girl that took his fancy. I had been having a poetic revival and for two years had produced a number of poems that varied in style and content, some of which had appeared in such periodicals as David Applefield's *Frank* magazine. Jim made a deal with Aster and they appeared under the Mosaic Press imprint. The last poems were written at the end of 1998, one on New Year's Eve. They came out the following year. Howard Aster then asked if I could sell them in Britain and I began to do so with reasonable success although it was embarrassing to go into a shop and propose my own writing and the *Festschrift*, which must have appeared to the buyers as an act of narcissism. Jim took the title of the poems from two of them: *What's Wrong? What's Right?*

I had been invited annually for some time to the conferences of little magazines organised by Olivier Corpet of IMEC, who it must be remembered himself edited the *Revue des Revues*. IMEC also housed my archives which were very capably kept in order by André Derval, who like his Director had become a real friend. I no longer published any magazine, but as Corpet said on one occasion, 'There is always the magazine of the imagination.' I had come to know and like the participants from many countries at these conferences, Claus Clausen, from Denmark (really a general publisher), Irena Prokhorova from Russia, Gaby Zipfel from Germany, Jani Virk from Slovenia, Walter Famler from Austria, who had once written a long interview with me for his journal Westpennest (The Wasp) and so many others. The conference at Vienna had been sponsored there by the Austrian Ministry of Culture, Claus Clausen had found funds from the City of Copenhagen to pay for our meeting there, and in 1997 we went to Moscow because it was the fiftieth anniversary of the Russian Revolution and also eight hundred and fifty years since the establishment of the city. A few days before I had heard on the BBC news one Sunday morning in Montreuil that Princess Diana had been killed only a few miles away in a car crash with her lover while trying to evade the press. My sister's comment on the telephone had been 'Oh, the Queen will be pleased.' Now in Moscow on the day of the funeral an enormous screen had been set up on the Arbatt near Red Square because there was as much interest in the royal funeral among Muscovites as in Western Europe. In the building where our meetings took place the security guards were all glued to a television screen.

Olivier Corpet's Little Magazine Conferences were about co-operation, problem-sharing and making new friends. But in Moscow where at least half the people in the room were Russian or from the Baltic states the Russian presence dominated the conference and we were given, first in Russian, then in English, a history of Russian literary publishing and of the 'thick magazines' in which much of the new work first appears. This was slow, ponderous and of limited interest amongst those who wanted to discuss their own personal problems to do with government subsidies, censorship and better ways of finding subscribers and selling their publications. We listened to the deep Russian voices, heard about the poverty of Russian poets, about how much Gorbachov, loved in Europe, was hated in Russia and the matters that most interested the visitors hardly came up at all.

At the end of one afternoon's session Olivier handed me a book he wanted me to read and I took it back to the guest house of the Lithuanian Embassy where we were staying and left it there. Later on, as we were finishing dinner in the conference building, I was told that the time had come for me to give a reading. I had not realised that I was expected to read in public from the volume that had been handed to me. It was the work of one of the Russian poets present who was about to read in Russian after which I was expected to read the translations. I had something of a reputation as an actor in that group, which is why I had been chosen. I had to go back to collect the book and follow each poem after it was read with the translation. Then I was asked to quote some Beckett poems which somehow my memory allowed me to do, then some Shakespeare. I had become Olivier Corpet's court jester!

The Moscow visit had been the idea of the Swedish cultural attaché in Moscow who had attended our Copenhagen conference the previous year and he gave us a lavish reception on the last night after which many of the others went out on the town, while I went to my room and felt inspired enough to write a poem, *Moscow Night*, which appeared the following year in my collection. On this occasion IMEC paid my fare to Moscow as well as my keep, a generous gesture. There was another meeting of editors a year later, but this time we met at the Abbaye d'Ardenne near Caen in Normandy, where IMEC were establishing their archives and conference centre. There, a smaller group, with little to distract them, held more practical sessions, only once leaving the building (it was almost a fortress) and we ate excellent food, drank the good Sancerre that Olivier always provided when he entertained and we got to know each other much better. I had been asked to find a Scottish literary magazine editor and suggested Joy Hendry, and having inspected her magazine Chapman, Corpet invited her. On the last night she organised a Ceilidh in which everyone was persuaded to do a party act. But this was the last of these conferences. There was pressure to go to Algeria, to Slovenia, to Latvia, and Corpet felt that the various nationalistic demands were getting out of hand. There was a meeting the following year, but it was organised from Eastern Europe where the agenda had more to do with internal politics than the promotion of literature and the cost now fell on the individuals who had to pay fares, accommodation and maintenance. Olivier Corpet, David Applefield and I all backed out.

I still made my American journeys and had little difficulty in selling my books among the few remaining independent booksellers, all of whom knew me well, but the catalogue was much depleted, although I found one big plus. It was difficult working in New York without an office from which to make telephone calls and to receive messages, but at least I had no overhead. Any money that came in could go to pay printing bills as well as reduce the old debts from the time of the close-down. Little by little I was reprinting the most important books until all of Beckett was back in print and I kept our best-known authors, such as Borges, Céline, Robbe-Grillet, and Trocchi in stock and on the shelves of my customers, while bringing out new volumes of plays by Howard Barker and others who were still producing new work and whose reputations were growing. We had moved to offices near Waterloo on a floor just above the National Theatre's training premises, where all day long the noises of rehearsals came up to us. I had let one of our rooms to Black Sparrow Press, which meant that my small staff, which was now Elena Goodinson, who had replaced Su Herbert, and Margaret Jacquess, now in her eighties, had some company, especially as I was away most of the time selling books. I now had a new idea, which was to produce a series of smaller texts, as I had once produced the series of Signature Books. I brought out twelve small volumes of the shorter works of Samuel Beckett, which were available both in individual paperback volumes and as a boxed set, and although the sales were smaller than I had expected, at least they were steady. On reflection, as these were the lesser known works, I realised that I was probably not doing too badly. They appeared in 1999. I was doing much of my printing in Canada now, mainly with Webcom in Toronto. That company had a jovial Sales Manager called Ron Hearnden. On one occasion when he visited me in Paris I met him at the airport and took him to a hotel where David Applefield had booked him in, and while getting his luggage out of my car he brought the door down on my head. Although I was gushing blood I managed to get through the evening with the help of a bandage and wine as a pain-killer, and as a result I think I received favourable printing terms and longer credit. He was probably relieved not to have been sued.

In the summer of 1999 I again mounted *Damned Publishing* to celebrate my fifty years in the trade, and this time made a deal to perform for a whole week at Riverside Studios. I updated the script and five of us performed it. Once again I started with my own narration and then the actors and I played out all the memorable incidents, so many of them having been the subject of this book. Claudia Menza came over from New York to take part, was in turn Blanche Knopf and many American ladies, finally playing herself, first working for Barney Rosset, then for me, then telling the story of that last trip with her husband Charles, and finally reading some of her own poetry in a special spot I put in for her. The others were Karen Fernald, Leonard Fenton and Sean Barratt. It was a good week and drew reasonable audiences.

Among those who turned up were Jack Garfein who had read about it coming from Paris on Eurostar and Tim Waterstone. Marion had died not long before, so that this time she could not see herself portrayed. In its review The Bookseller said that I would not have dared to portray her were she still alive, but, except for one sentence, the script concerning her was the same. I did not repeat the exercise in New York this time.

I was also realising that in my seventies there were now many things I could no longer do, and that my appearance, except to surviving old friends, was not conducive to persuading others much younger when I had an idea to promote or to sell books. When I took Claire Armistad to lunch in June that year in order to try to persuade her to review more of my books in the *Guardian*, I could tell from her face that she had been expecting to meet someone much younger and more interesting to someone of her generation, and the ever younger buyers of the Waterstone branches were obviously wondering what I was doing outside an old people's home.

One night Leonard Fenton came to have a drink with me near my office. It was the birthday of his ex-wife and he asked me to join their family party in a restaurant. I had to get up early the next morning, but went for an hour. Among the group of Fentons and their partners was Toby, Len's son who had recently come back from South America and was looking for a job. It was some time later that he came to see me and I decided that he was just right to be trained to carry on my firm one day. He joined me in early 2000, doing mainly selling and he was quick to learn the list and had plenty of energy. Then one day Toby came in rather shame-faced. 'There's something I haven't told you,' he said. 'I applied some time ago for a special journalism course run by the British School of Printing. Only a few are taken and they've just accepted me.' There is no way you can persuade somebody not to do whatever they really want to do, especially if there is a challenge involved, so with many misgivings I told him to go ahead, but hoped he would come back. Months passed and it was obvious that a journalistic career attracted him, and he was offered entry positions onto newspapers, but as an unpaid apprentice, which he could hardly afford and so late in the year 2000 he returned with the position of Sales Manager.

In 1999 Mosaic published my collection of poems, the last of which had been written on the last day of the previous year. Most of them had come to me on my own when travelling, usually in restaurants and were the fruits of reflection, but often they came directly from my observation of people around me and overheard conversations. Some, I hope, were funny, and while Beckett in no way influenced their form, as he had once influenced some plays I wrote in the sixties, his view of the world, which had also become mine, was very present in the sentiments expressed. One in particular was political and based on the disillusionment that I and most people I knew now felt with a Labour government that did not want to reverse any of the destructive changes that had been brought about by

Margaret Thatcher and John Major in British society. It harked back to that election night of 1997 and is called *Euphoria Lost*.

> Those of us who hated Thatcherism
> the low Toryism of an upward-thrusting
> unpleasant lower middle class,
> philistine readers of the tabloid press
> which has no time for culture
> had our brief wonderful euphoric moment
> as tactical voting put Portillo out
> and Martin Bell, white knight and voice of decency,
> humbled the grease-palmed Hamiltons
> and strident Major became a simple private,
> and we welcomed Tony Blair.
>
> That euphoria's gone into the middle way
> which is no way at all:
> clean Toryism, or so it seems,
> but the poor are poorer
> and the rich richer
> and the ill iller
> and education worse. As for culture...
> That's too depressing!
>
> I write these lines in France.
> Thank God for France.

As the twentieth century, which had known as many horrors as most of the other centuries where we have historical knowledge, came to an end, I was finishing this account of a life, not yet finished, but peopled with much event, many memories, a variety of very different activities, and above all encounters with many remarkable men and women. Causes are still being fought and I am still involved in them, but the Shadow Arts Council, which I suspect will again change its name, is now in the capable hands of Clive Bradley, who having been forced into early retirement, now has time to give it, although he has many other activities too. The abyss of the late eighties and early nineties has largely passed, although many storm clouds are still on the horizon, and I will have to deal with these. Many old friends are gone, a few remain, but I have made many new ones, and whereas my friends in the past were usually older than I, now they are younger. I keep up friendly relations with old girl-friends who are now real friends and companions; the fires have cooled, and I have no regrets about that. My follies are, I hope, ended. I still publish books and intend to write more myself. There is a considerable well of my unpublished recent poetry: it comes naturally now and I know that those who have read what has already appeared have for the most part enjoyed these *péchés de vieillesse*. As far as I know I am now the doyen of active publishers, at least in Britain. The Calder Educational Trust, set up at the instigation of the Arts Council in the days when they favoured our activities, still owns everything we do, and the trustees, at the time of writing are Bill Webb, Barbara Wright and Stuart Hood, who are charged to keep it going from its existing resources and to monitor its future progress.

Beckett said to me before his seventieth birthday that in old age work has to be your company. Like him then, I am an old man now, mostly alone outside of the office, but not really lonely: I have some good friends, many books to read, plays I want to see, music I want to hear, but above all much more work to do, and I am always behind with it. In Montreuil I have numerous small reasonable restaurants where I can go to escape solitude, reflect, sometimes write a poem. In London, Beoty's on Saint Martin's Lane has become my favourite watering hole, near two opera houses and many theatres where Michael Frangos, Mr Kikes and John Kashimeris look after me well and amuse me with political gossip and culinary party tricks. I am as much their friend as their customer. Tiredness and worry are inevitable in a world getting harder where my energy is less, especially my ability to cope with unpleasantness and pressure. I work long hours and only take off the odd day in a year, but what are my depressions and problems compared to the lot of others in a world dominated by cruelty, revenge, poverty and ignorance.

I mentioned storm clouds. Aside from the state of the world, which in an era that now has George W. Bush and Vladimir Putin confronting each other in a revival of the cold war across the globe, there have been three problems that have caused some worry. We have lost many authors, and they were not only some of the best-known names, although not necessarily the best writers, but the ones that sold best and helped us to continue making new discoveries that inevitably lose money at first and sometimes always will. But during the abyss years much went out of print and could only be brought back slowly. This has not been helped by authors who would not wait if they saw an alternative, and by foreign publishers from whom I had sub-contracted rights. The biggest problem was with a lady who had gone from Flammarion to Gallimard, which had become less a literary house than a commercial one run by non-literary businessmen. She tried to cancel contracts where I could not reprint the books in question in three months, and when I put some books into production to keep those rights I was notified that this would not be accepted. But the excellent Maître Emmanuel Pierrat, who Olivier Corpet persuaded to intervene on my behalf, did so, and the lady in question stopped persecuting me. There was no particular interest among other English-language publishers in reprinting my authors from France, especially as they would have to commission new translations in most cases, so it is probable, as increased royalties would be coming into

Gallimard, that she was simply told to accept the situation. I also had various problems with the publisher whose courageous activities and superb list had made me admire him above all others, Jerôme Lindon. His one-time friendliness had cooled ever since the death of Sam Beckett, and he was adamantly opposed to readings of Beckett's work in public, except where a precedent had been established in the author's life-time, and often I discovered that he had given rights to publishers in countries that were only just discovering Beckett, where the translation rights really lay with me. Increasingly I had to tread on eggs. I had known him for nearly half a century, yet we still called each other 'vous'. He was to die in the week of Beckett's ninety-fifth birthday, in April 2001.

The changes in bookselling became ever a bigger worry. In America the chains had proved to be unreliable customers and where they had bought my books cheaply from Daedalus and tried to return them to me for full credit they had been downright dishonest. In Britain the growth of Waterstones was a disaster once the management fell into the hands of administrators who knew nothing about books or about the needs of the book trade itself. The need to be the biggest and to have the largest slice of the cake led them into policies that could only lose money, and the biggest cause of falling profits was a catastrophic discounting policy. Without making a reasonable profit on best-sellers and whatever books are in greatest demand, booksellers cannot afford to sell the slower-selling quality books aimed at the most educated of their customers. And this was happening at a time of general dumbing down, an unadmitted conspiracy between politicians, newspaper proprietors and commerce. People increasingly know less, read less, learn less of import from the media, and trust to a growing general prosperity (which cannot possibly last) to cushion their lives. And all this at a time when the need to be aware, to be able to think independently, to understand what the politicians are doing, rather than just hearing what they are saying, has never been more important. Brave new world indeed!

In Shakespeare's *Tempest*, where that much used term is first used, the Brave New World has an ironic ring, and it still has to me. Unless mankind (and womankind of course) can find a way to end all wars, abolish tyranny and to nip those with evil ambitions in the bud, there will be no future world, at least not on this planet, which has already been so despoiled and emptied of its resources. Perhaps genetic development will make a safer world possible, but it seems more likely that science will spiral out of control and become another tool of globalising power-seekers and either condemn mankind to continuing tyranny of one kind or another, or to its final destruction. I see not much hope but desperately want to be wrong. I feel much as Bertrand Russell, once my guru, did about the future of the world which he spent his whole life trying to save from its own destructive impulses, and the hope, not a very strong one, expressed in what to me is the most inspiring and beautiful single page of prose of the last century, namely the preface to his *Autobiography*[45]. Like him I hope, but do not really believe that creative man can overcome destructive, greedy and power-hungry man. Evil has a strong motor that drives ambition outward to take power over others. Art, which to civilised beings gives life such meaning as there is, has a different motor that is focused inward towards power over oneself. Because art satisfies it has no need to be greedy. Beckett, my other guru, believed that man is imperfectible and to quote *Godot* 'There is nothing to be done.' But he too went on trying: his key word is always 'On.'

And now I must bring this chronicle to an end. It is the tale of a life not yet ended, and I have tried to make it an honest one. I have attempted to do good, to increase awareness, to put into the world works of art, mainly but not entirely in the field of literature, and I had hoped to educate as many as possible, where I could, through both conventional and unconventional activities, into becoming better than they would otherwise be. I have done much harm to some and it is admitted and much regretted. One cannot always know the consequences of our passage through the world. I have been both lucky and unlucky at different times, and sometimes good luck has led to disaster and vice-versa. In my middle seventies I find that there is no religious belief that I can sustain, but never stop thinking about the question and the whys and wherefores of human existence. Meaning is our own creation: we must make it come to life out of our sense of responsibility, out of our thought-processes, out of our guilt, sometimes out of our despair. No large group of people can ever agree as to what is important or meaningful or true. That is why tolerance is essential and doubt is good. These are human concepts and they do not concern other forms of life that live just for survival or comfort or pleasure. And is that not also true of most of humanity? Only a few, among them most of my friends and acquaintances, and certainly most of those I have published, and I myself, are condemned to search, to probe, and to puzzle out answers to the conundrum of existence. In my brain I think there can be no meaning; in my bowels I would like there to be. And I know that both brain and bowels can be wrong.

January 16th 2001

[45] Bertrand Russell, *Autobiography*, London, 1967.

INDEX

605

611

619